Public Schools USA

A COMPARATIVE GUIDE TO SCHOOL DISTRICTS

WITH DISTRICT APPRAISALS & RATINGS

BY CHARLES HARRISON

WILLIAMSON PUBLISHING
CHARLOTTE, VERMONT 05445

Library of Congress Cataloging-in-Publication Data

Harrison, Charles Hampton, 1932–
   Public Schools USA: Comparative Guide to School Districts
  /by Charles H. Harrison.
     p. cm.
  Includes indexes.
  ISBN 0-913589-36-5
  1. Public schools—United States—Statistics. 2. Public
schools—United States—Evaluation. 3. School
districts—United States—Evaluation. I. Title.
LA217.H375   1988   87-34313
371'.01'0973—dc19   CIP

Cover and interior design: Trezzo-Braren Studio
Typography: Villanti & Sons Printers, Inc.
Printing: Capital City Press

Williamson Publishing Co.
Charlotte, Vermont 05445

Manufactured in the United States of America

First Printing April 1988

Notice: The information contained in this book is true,
complete and accurate to the best of our knowledge.
All recommendations and suggestions are made
without any guarantees on the part of the author or
Williamson Publishing. The author and publisher
disclaim all liability incurred in connection with the use
of this information.

ACKNOWLEDGMENTS

The following persons gave invaluable assistance in the collection and processing of information: June Alexander, Cynthia Harrison, Mildred Messinger and Cynthia Roberts.

TABLE OF CONTENTS

Introduction

"How are the schools?" is the first question parents ask whether they are moving their family across the state line or across the country (nearly a million families do so every year). It's not easy to get answers. People ask a real estate agent, or perhaps a friend of a friend of a friend. Some parents talk to a store clerk, the editor of the local weekly newspaper, or the town librarian. One man we heard about spent days going from one district to another just to dig out average scores on the Scholastic Aptitude Test (SAT).

At last, parents can find reliable, well-researched answers in *Public Schools USA*.

Real estate salespeople wonder what they should tell clients with families about the schools in the cities and towns where they are showing homes. Not wanting to rely on hearsay or misinformation, they often avoid questions about the schools. Now they can get help in this book.

Company executives need to advise employees and their families who are being relocated about the school systems in the new area. Now they can give specific information so families can choose the district most compatible with their unique needs. It's all in *Public Schools USA*.

Teachers and school administrators looking for their first position or planning on a career move seek very detailed information about districts—information usually unavailable through other sources. They can get more information in this book and make better

decisions about the systems to which they apply.

In fact, this book is for anyone in search of comprehensive and reliable information about public school systems in the United States today.

It is the *first* book to examine hundreds of districts in the nation's largest metropolitan areas and growth centers, and then offer the results of that examination to people on the move.

For each district, you can now read more than 20 important statistics that will help *you* make decisions based on information *you* deem important. We will provide guidance by telling you how a district's data compare to state or national statistics, as well as other yardsticks.

In addition, we have asked knowledgeable persons in each district to give their fair appraisals of the schools. These careful *observers* include responsible members of parent groups, the League of Women Voters, and the American Association of University Women. Experienced editors and reporters of daily and weekly newspapers as well as other active citizens also have helped in this fair appraisal.

Armed with statistics and observations, you can make informed decisions about what is best for your family, your employees, your career, or your clients. Parents no longer will be on the outside looking in when it comes to making crucial educational decisions that affect their children's futures.

TAKING A HARD LOOK AT OUR SCHOOLS

Public Schools USA includes approximately 500 school districts with enrollments of 2,500 or more students. That is nearly 14 percent of all school districts of that size in the country.

What this means is that *we have probed to a greater depth inside more of America's schools than most studies that purport to describe the quality of public education in the United States.*

We have examined the school systems using many of the same statistics that state and federal education agencies use to hold districts accountable. In addition, we have compiled data that many other researchers overlook.

These include such telling statistics as the following:

- Number of students per music and art specialist in the elementary grades. This is a means for gauging a district's commitment to developing students' ability to express themselves, and to be creative. It is a good indicator of a district's attitude toward developing the "whole" child, while exposing all children to opportunities too often reserved for a select few (e.g. learning to play a musical instrument).

- Number of Advanced Placement courses offered in the high school. This is a way to measure how challenging the academic curriculum is for the ablest students. There's no question but that America loses some of its brightest students to academic boredom. Advanced Placement courses are a sign that a district is committed to academic growth for all students who need to be stimulated to go beyond the limitations of the typical high school curriculum. These courses also demonstrate the district's resolve that their brightest students should compete fairly with the brightest students from other districts for the nation's top colleges.

- Number of students suspended and expelled. This statistic is indicative of how tough the district's disciplinary code is, reflecting how serious the school board, administration, faculty and students are about quality education.

In addition to the twenty-plus statistics in the Statistical Profile, we asked knowledgeable observers in each district a series of questions for a Fair Appraisal. These questions are based on the conclusions reached by a number of scholarly papers that have considered the attributes of effective schools.

We took our lead from the nationally-renowned Educational Research Service, which sifted through two decades worth of research on effective schools and concluded that the following factors were critically important if children were to receive a quality education:

1. **Leadership.** "A school's effectiveness in the promotion of student learning was found to be the product of a . . . unified effort which depended upon the exercise of leadership. Most often the research depicted the building principal as the key person providing leadership to the school."

2. **Instruction.** "Teachers in higher-achieving schools understood the special learning characteristics of the students they taught. They more frequently adapted instruction to students' levels of ability and promoted more opportunities for learner success."

3. **Environment.** "Environment was another element that affected school effectiveness. The effective schools researchers found that high-achieving public schools had climates that were purposeful and orderly. Maintaining adequate facilities . . . was found to be important to effective school programs."

These three criteria became the basis for our Fair Appraisal of each district.

LISTING IS NOT SELECTIVE

We have not tried to pick the so-called *best* districts in an area. In the first place, what is best according to one set of standards may not be best in light of other standards. Certainly, what is best for one student's needs or priorities, may not be best for another's special needs. We believe we offer enough information about each district to allow readers to judge what schools might best serve their needs.

Not every district in each metropolitan area or growth center is included in the book. We began with these criteria:

- Districts located within approximately 25 miles of the core city.
- Districts organized from kindergarten through grade 12. (The only exception is in the Chicago area where most districts offer kindergarten through grade 8 only or grades 9–12 only.)
- Districts with an enrollment of at least 2,500 students.

We have reasons for choosing these criteria.

Twenty-five miles is a reasonable commuting distance to the core city (obviously a primary concern to those who work in the city), although many persons travel greater distances to their job.

It was more effective and efficient to collect data from districts that offer all grades (K–12). Also, readers might find it difficult to make comparisons between K–12 districts and those that are only K–8 or 9–12. However, we know many K–8 and 9–12 districts offer an excellent educational program, and we urge readers not to overlook them.

Most school districts in the United States have an enrollment of under 2,500; indeed, there are a number with fewer than 100 students. We had to draw the line somewhere. One of our considerations was that a K–12 district with an enrollment of 2,500 or greater is likely to have enough students in its high school(s) to ensure a broad and varied curriculum. Also, larger school districts are by their very nature less accessible to families trying to get answers and, therefore,

our research in the larger districts is more valuable. We appreciate, of course, that many smaller districts are first-rate. We suggest, therefore, that you not discount them, and that you even try getting statistics similar to those we use to help you make your informed choices.

SOME DISTRICTS DID NOT RESPOND

Every attempt was made to send a Statistical Profile to all districts that met our criteria in the selected metropolitan areas and growth centers. Indeed, if a district did not respond to our first mailing, we sent another letter and Profile. With an undertaking of this size, it is certain that some districts were overlooked, and we apologize to them.

We did not hear from every district to which we mailed a Statistical Profile. In cases where a district did not return a completed Profile but we did obtain a Fair Appraisal, we included the Appraisal comments alone.

Some persons might argue that our information does not provide a *complete* picture of a district. Frankly, we have never heard two educators agree on what data *would* constitute a complete picture.

What we have done is to enable every American to fairly evaluate hundreds of school districts in the United States using a great many yardsticks that educators themselves, government statisticians, and scientific researchers consider important and valid.

PART ONE

Public Schools USA

Districts listed in *Public Schools USA* can be evaluated and compared with other districts using the *Statistical Profile, Fair Appraisal,* and *Effective Schools Index (ESI).*™ To assist readers who are moving into a major metropolitan area from a rural area or small suburb, we have suggested a comparable metropolitan area in size and, perhaps, therefore in attributes and weaknesses for each area listed. We believe this provides a helpful method of assessing reasonable expectations in city public schools, thereby opening the reader up to the wealth of possibilities and innovations, while being wary of potential pitfalls. A healthy comparative view between similar areas can only improve our judgement about how we are handling educational issues and priorities.

STATISTICAL PROFILE

We asked districts to supply 22 statistics that educators consider to be important indicators of a system's commitment to supporting and offering a comprehensive, quality instructional program to all students in a setting conducive to learning. Approximately a third of the statistics are annually made public by the U.S. Department of Education for each of the 50 states. Most of the remaining data are collected for reports to state education departments, various accreditation agencies, and other education organizations and agencies. Of course, districts use many of the statistics to guide their own planning and performance. We point this out because it is important that you know that we were not asking for obscure information that would have involved a lot of additional work to compile.

The *Statistical Profile* enables readers to answer such critical questions about the public schools as the following:

- Is the financial support adequate?
- How well does the curriculum prepare students not only in basic skills but also in the higher academic skills needed for college and for many jobs?
- Does class size (teacher-student ratios) permit some individual instruction and enable teachers to exercise effective classroom management?
- How concerned is the district that students be able to express themselves through art and music and learn the importance of the arts to their daily life.
- How well does the district cope with students who are turned off by schooling and those whose behavior may adversely affect other students?
- Does the district offer salaries that are likely to attract and keep capable, industrious teachers?

Beyond this, individual statistics can be used to help you fill your needs. If you have a child who needs a lot of individual attention, you'll focus on teacher-student ratios. If your secondary student is aiming for a top competitive college, then several college statistics will be especially important.

STATISTICS EXPLAINED

Grade organization

A school district can organize in a variety of ways. A fairly standard pattern is elementary schools composed of kindergarten through grade 5, middle schools that include grades 6–8, and high schools composed of grades 9–12. Many parents and educators believe grade organization is important. For example, some persons do not like a middle school that includes grade 9 because, they claim, ninth-graders are too sophisticated for the younger children. Others prefer a 7–9 middle school and a 10–12 high school (similar to the junior-senior high school arrangement of decades past) because it allows for a smaller high school student body. Also, some districts have noted that their organizational pattern includes elementary schools that range from pre-kindergarten through grade 5. It may be the only clue to a pre-school program offered by the district.

Percentage of schools built before 1955

If a majority of school buildings are more than 30 years old, even if they have been renovated, it *may* indicate an inability to provide adequate, up-to-date facilities in good condition. Science labs, vocational classrooms, physical education facilities, and theatre arts spaces may be especially limited. Buildings also may be overcrowded. A close inspection of buildings is advised.

Total enrollment

This figure includes all students registered for the school year ending June 1986.

Average daily attendance (ADA)

Almost all students miss a day of school occasionally because of illness or other good reasons. But students also may be absent frequently without good cause. This statistic shows the percentage of students enrolled by a district who actually attend school on an average daily basis. For the United States, the figure is approximately 95 percent. A district whose ADA is 90 percent or less may have a serious truancy problem and/or an exceptionally high number of suspensions and expulsions. These problems, of course, may warn of such other problems as ineffective teaching, poorly targeted curriculum perhaps missing either the low-achievers or the high-achievers, or poor administration.

Current expense per student in ADA

This statistic shows what a district is spending for instruction and other services that directly support students. Not included are expenses for new construction and payments on existing debt.

The figure is influenced by these factors:

1. Increase in revenue from federal, state or local sources.
2. Decrease in revenue. It would be important to learn the cause of a decrease in revenue, particularly in the case of a district whose current expenditures per student are markedly below other districts in the area. This could mean the problem is in the district itself. For example, taxpayers may be unwilling to vote an increase in the tax levy or millage rate. A local governing body that controls the purse strings may have placed its top priority elsewhere. Perhaps the district is simply poorer in taxable wealth than its neighbors. Behind these problems could be others, such as a local or regional recession caused by the death of old industries and the transfer of others.
3. Enrollment increase. If enrollment goes up while revenue remains about the same in real dollars (adjusted for inflation), the current expense per student figure will decline.
4. Enrollment decrease. The current expense figure can go up if enrollment declines but revenue remains about the same or increases.

If possible, you should compare figures for the past five or six years. A pattern of decline in a district is far more significant—and worrisome—than a one-year change. See Appendix A for state-by-state statistics on current expense per student in ADA.

High school dropout rate

A 1986 study conducted for the Council of Chief State School Officers reported 16 basic variations in the collection of dropout statistics. We asked districts to tell us the percentage of freshmen enrolled in 1982–83 who graduated four years later in 1985–86. High school dropouts are students who leave school before graduation. The reasons for leaving (other than moving) may be dissatisfaction with school, frequent suspensions, permanent expulsion, employment, and pregnancy. The statistic supplied by districts also may represent some students whose families move out of the district. However, these students are roughly balanced by students moving into the district. Nationally, the median dropout rate in 1985 was 23 percent. (See state-by-state statistics in Appendix B.) This is high. The 1986–87 rate is even higher.

Percentage of eligible students who took either the Scholastic Aptitude Test (SAT) or the American College Testing Program's Assessment (ACT)

This statistic is important for better understanding the significance of a district's average combined score on either test. For example, if only a small number of students took the test—perhaps just those most likely to be accepted into college—the average score would be higher than if nearly all students, including many not even on a college track, took the test. Obviously, if most students in a district take the test and the average test score is still higher than in other districts, that district has a very strong college preparatory curriculum. The College Board, which administers the SAT, calls on districts to encourage as many students as possible to take the SAT. According to College Board officials, many students, particularly from minorities, who might not otherwise consider going to college, are prompted to consider that option simply by preparing for and taking the test.

Average combined score on SAT or ACT

Both tests measure a student's breadth and depth of academic preparation and the student's ability to handle college-level work. The tests do not measure achievement in specific courses or subjects. However, they do show how knowledgeable students are in such academic disciplines as English, science and mathematics, and how able students are in comprehending what they read. SAT scores range from 200 to 800 on each part of the test (verbal and math), so a combined score can range from 400 to 1,600. *Nationwide, the combined average SAT score in 1986 was 906.* The ACT score can range from 1 to 36. *The ACT national average in 1986 was 18.8.* (See state-by-state statistics in Appendix C.)

Percentage of 1986 graduates who enrolled in 2-year or 4-year colleges

This statistic can be important for two very different reasons. A high percentage would indicate a strong academic program and affluence in the district. Most persons would consider this a plus. However, in some instances, a district that has an excellent college preparatory curriculum does not do as well for students who intend to go directly into the job market or the armed services after graduation. Persons who are especially concerned about vocational preparation might want to take a close look at that curriculum, especially in a district that emphasizes college preparation.

Subjects in which Advanced Placement courses are offered

The Advanced Placement Program sponsored by The College Board offers 25 college-level courses for high-ability students (e.g. art history, chemistry, computer science, English literature and composition, physics, and Spanish language). High school students who do well in AP exams usually bypass entry-level courses when they go to college. Oftentimes, students can receive college credit for AP courses, saving hundreds of dollars in college credit hours. The more AP courses a district offers, the more likely it is that the curriculum lays a solid academic foundation and challenges its top students right through the senior year in high school.

Percentage of students who passed the state reading test

Nearly 75 percent of the states now give all students a test that measures their competence in reading. In some states, students must pass the test in order to be promoted to the next grade or to be graduated from high school. Most state tests measure the most basic skills. Therefore, we consider a passing rate of less than 85 percent to be very low.

Percentage of students who passed the state math test

The same states administer a test of competence in mathematics. With this test, we view a passing rate of less than 80 percent to be very low.

Teacher-student ratio in elementary grades

Although research has never clearly shown that achievement is higher in classes of 20 students than in classes with, say, 25 students, most educators accept the following assumptions about small classes (as reflected by the teacher-student ratio):

1. Teachers have better control; the result may be less classroom disruption.
2. Teachers are more able to pay attention to individual needs.
3. Students have more opportunity to take part in classroom discussions and projects.
4. It is harder for a lazy or unprepared student to hide.

The teacher-student ratio for elementary schools in the nation ranges between 1:20 and 1:30.

A district that maintains a low class size is one that is able and willing to spend the extra money necessary to hire enough teachers and provide the space to maintain a low ratio. It also is a district that may strive harder to actually fulfill the promise all educators subscribe to in principle: to educate each student to the limits of his/her potential.

We asked districts to supply statistics that reflect the ratio between classroom teachers and students. Some districts also compile data that reflect the ratio between instructional staff and students. Instructional staff may include specialists in art and music, school nurses, librarians and other support personnel. The ratio of instructional staff to students normally would be lower than the teacher-student ratio, but, of course, it would not be indicative of class size.

Teacher-student ratio in secondary grades

More variation in class size exists in the secondary grades (middle and high school). A typing or physical education class, for example, normally would have more students than an honors class in literature or chemistry. The teacher-student ratio for secondary schools varies between 1:18 and 1:28.

Counselor-student ratio in secondary grades

School districts employ counselors, primarily in their middle and high schools, to help students select courses and to guide them in their choice of college or career. It is generally agreed that in most school districts the counselor-student ratio is too high. The ratios recommended by the American School Counselor Association are as follows: Middle school, 1:250–350; high school, 1:200–300. In many districts, the ratio is so high that students are apt to see a counselor for an hour or less during the entire school year.

The more time a student spends with a counselor the more likely he or she is to be guided carefully and correctly. Some parents complain that their children are improperly placed in the educational program because counselors have not given the children enough time to thoroughly examine their academic performance, potential, and interests. The results can be that some students who should be directed into a college-preparatory track are not, and other students who are better suited to a vocational/technical curriculum leading to a job skill are set on a course that will leave them generally unprepared for either college or the world of work.

Number of students per music specialist in elementary grades

Some persons believe instruction in music and art is a frill. Indeed, expenditures for these subjects often are the first to go under the knife when budgets are cut. However, many persons believe students need a balanced education that includes exposure to music and art. The Music Educators National Conference recommends that elementary schools have at least one music specialist for every 400 students to conduct a "basic" program. A "quality" program would require one specialist for every 265 students.

Number of students per art specialist in elementary grades

The National Art Education Association recommends these standards: for a "basic" program, 1:400; for a "superior" program, 1:300.

Number of volumes in senior high school library

Today's students may not consider themselves a reading generation, but the fact is that most of the knowledge and much of the pleasure of the centuries remain between the covers of books. It is important, therefore, that students, particularly in the higher grades, have access to a large number and wide variety of books (as well as other audio and visual media). In 1975, the Association of School Libraries, a division of the American Library Association, set a standard of 8,000 to 12,000 books (hard cover and paperback) for a school library. A revised standard is due in 1988.

Beginning teacher's salary

Some critics of teacher education complain that a number of college graduates attracted into teaching are from the lower half of their college class and cannot find better jobs. Therefore, they will accept low-paying positions in public schools. Conversely, top students who would like to teach do not enter this profession because the salaries are noncompetitive with business and industry. Specifically, women, who still account for more than two-thirds of the teaching force, are now able to move into well-paying careers previously closed to them. For these and other reasons it has become increasingly important that a district offer salaries that will lure and keep teachers who are well-qualified and dedicated.

The beginning teacher's salary is important because, when compared to other districts, it shows the district's desire or ability to compete for new teachers. Many of today's teachers were hired 30 to 40 years ago to cope with the baby boom after World War II. A number of them will be retiring soon. The beginning teacher's salary, then, is one indicator of how well the district is preparing itself to replace these teachers.

Maximum teacher's salary

Of course, a school district not only must attract good, new teachers, but it also must hold on to its good, experienced teachers. While it is helpful to examine a district's complete salary scale (covering teachers at all levels of experience and preparation), the maximum teacher's salary is an indicator of a district's holding power. Incidentally, the maximum salary usually is paid to a teacher with a doctorate and 15 years of experience or more.

It should be noted that some districts deliberately set salaries high at the bottom of the scale and offer minimal increases for experience and preparation. The small yearly raises at the top of the scale could cause many teachers to leave early.

Average years of experience among teachers

Some persons are most interested in school systems where a majority of teachers are young, the average years of experience ranging from eight to twelve years. Others feel more comfortable with an experienced, older faculty, where the average years of experience range between 15 to 20. Nationwide, the typical district faculty today is more experienced than it has been in a number of years, but it also is older. Many districts in all states report the average age of teachers is in the forties. Since it is difficult for a teacher with a lot of experience to move to a new district (too expensive), the average years experience statistic may well be indicative of faculty morale. Teachers who feel good about the administration as well as the resources and support available, tend to make their decision to stay in a district longterm early on.

Number of students suspended and expelled

This statistic includes those students who are given what is called today *in-school suspension*. These are students who are being punished for minor infractions and pose no threat to other students. They are suspended from their regular class schedule, but continue to take instruction at school in special classes. The Gallup Poll for more than a decade has found that discipline is one of the chief concerns of parents of school-age children and other citizens. This statistic is one indicator of a district's level of student misbehavior and how it copes with such disruption.

Readers might be suspicious about an exceedingly low figure for a fairly large district (e.g. 10 suspensions for the entire year in a district of 10,000 students). It *could* mean that students in that district are exceptionally well behaved and controlled, but it also could mean poor record-keeping by the district, or students who misbehave simply go undisciplined.

An unusually high figure may indicate that a district is reporting number of suspensions rather than number of students suspended. For example, instead of 100 students being suspended, 25 students each have been suspended four times. (We asked for number of students suspended.) Also, look at ADA in relation to suspensions. If you have a high degree of absenteeism and a low suspension rate, you may have a school that is lax about truancy.

STATISTICS SOMETIMES QUESTIONED

Naturally, we assume districts reporting statistics that are a matter of public record are truthful. Therefore, we have not doubted the credibility of data supplied or of persons supplying the data. If a district omitted a statistic, we sometimes contacted the district to determine if the omission was an oversight and if a figure might be available. If the statistic is not known by the district, the letters *NK* have been printed. This notation is to show the difference between a district not knowing a statistic and a statistic not being applicable to a district (*NA*). In many cases, statistics were provided that were inappropriate either through misunderstanding or because of a unique data collection method used by the district. We have noted these aberrations.

FAIR APPRAISAL

The Statistical Profile supplied by each district is, we believe, a very valuable tool for taking the measure of a school district. But we thought readers also would find it helpful to hear from knowledgeable lay persons who live in the district, or, in the case of some newspaper reporters and editors, "cover" the district regularly.

Consequently, we personally interviewed hundreds of lay persons who might have firsthand knowledge of a district and who might be relied upon to be fair and responsible in their comments. We previously have listed the kinds of persons queried.

The questions asked these persons include the following examples:

1. Does the district have an effective means for screening principal candidates?
2. How much say do teachers and parents have in the selection of their principal?
3. How would you characterize the quality of additional learning opportunities available to bright or gifted students?
4. How would you characterize the educational program for students not planning to attend college?
5. How would you characterize the level of classroom disruption and student vandalism?
6. How would you characterize the quality of building maintenance and repair?

These and other questions were grouped under three headings: *Quality of School Leadership*, *Quality of Instruction*, and *Quality of School Environment*. As previously noted, the national research on what makes schools effective points to excellence in these three areas as being critical to effective education.

We stress that information supplied and views expressed by these responsible observers are theirs alone. Other equally knowledgeable lay persons might respond somewhat differently to the questions. However, we believe the responses from most other persons would not be in total contradiction to what is presented here.

Readers should regard and weigh these Fair Appraisals of school districts as they would responses given by persons whom they respect

and to whom they might put questions if given the opportunity.

Through the Fair Appraisal, readers can gain valuable insights about a school system. Consider these examples:

- The district's program for gifted and talented children looks great on paper, but parents who know better warn that the program mostly consists of extra homework.
- The district is very proud that 75 percent of its high school graduates go on to college, but the editor of a local newspaper knows how bad the curriculum is for the remaining 25 percent.
- A district's Statistical Profile doesn't look very good. However, the education chairperson of the local League of Women Voters reminds readers that the system has some very good magnet schools and the new superintendent is making the kind of waves that eventually will wash away a lot of deadwood in high places.
- A member of the local chapter of the American Association of University Women, a former teacher, says that, despite what one might expect, the level of classroom disruption and vandalism in a particular district is not very high. One reason is a new, tough disciplinary code.
- Observers in a district may warn readers that if they choose to settle there, they should make sure they buy a house on the north side of town because the school leadership and, therefore, resource allocation are better there.

There are hundreds of such pieces of advice included in the Fair Appraisals. Some comments are spicy, some witty, but none of them beat around the bush.

And the comments are *in addition* to the observers' ratings of leadership, instruction, and environment. We consider the Fair Appraisals so helpful that we have included observers' reports even in cases where a district did not return a Statistical Profile.

EFFECTIVE SCHOOLS INDEX™

An Effective Schools Index (ESI)™ has been computed for each district with a Statistical Profile. Each district can earn up to 10 points for each of the 10 key indicators selected from the Statistical Profile. *The median ESI score for the country is 58. A perfect ESI score is 100.*

The ESI is a place for readers to begin. It provides a manageable tool for comparison. It is a way to get a handle on the raw data in the Statistical Profile without having to memorize national averages or state averages. The ESI gives you a yardstick that crosses state and regional lines. You can compare current expense per pupil for a district in New York to school districts in Minnesota or California without comparing state averages. The ESI, in effect, does the computing for you.

There are many ways to use the ESI. A person might decide to look first at those districts in a metropolitan area that have an ESI score of 60 or better. Or, based on experience or other knowledge, a reader might be confident that District X in a particular metropolitan area offers a fine, comprehensive educational program. The ESI for District X is 68. The reader, then, might search the listings of another metropolitan area to see if there are any districts with an ESI score of 68 or better. Or on closer inspection, the reader may look at where other districts vary from District X. The variations may or may not be statistics important to the reader. Thus, it is a starting point.

A reader also initially might compare ESI scores for individual categories. For example, a person particularly concerned about financial support for the educational program might consider comparing ESI scores for the key indicator *current expense per pupil*. Someone else, who believes the Scholastic Aptitude Test (SAT) statistic is a good yardstick by which to measure overall effectiveness of the academic curriculum, could choose to first look only at scores for that category. Again, the ESI has ranked scores nationwide, so the reader only has to compare the ESI, not the raw data.

Readers are cautioned not to rely solely on the ESI. Some districts, particularly city systems, do not always show up well in the statistics, but their Fair Appraisal might reveal attributes worthy of consideration. And some very fine districts simply did not provide adequate data necessary for a high ESI. (Omissions received an ESI equivalent of zero.)

ESI KEY INDICATORS

Average daily attendance (ADA), current expense per pupil, dropout rate, combined score on SAT or ACT, percentage of eligible students who took the SAT or ACT, subjects in which Advanced Placement courses are offered, teacher-student ratio in elementary grades, teacher-student ratio in secondary grades, counselor-student ratio in secondary grades, and number of students per music specialist in elementary grades are the 10 statistics used in the ESI.

The significance of these categories was explained earlier, but an obvious question is why these 10 statistics and not others. We believe these 10 statistics provide a good overview of a district's financial backing, ability to keep students of all ability-levels interested in schooling, class size, quality of academic curriculum, and commitment to the creative arts.

Zero to 10 points were awarded in each of the 10 categories according to how well a district fared when compared to national or state standards for the year ending June 1986. In cases where a district misinterpreted a statistic, an ESI of 0* was given for that statistic, indicating that an attempt was made to provide the information requested. Similarly a 0* was given where information simply was not applicable (NA). However, a 0 without qualification (asterisk) was given for information not known (NK). Therefore, any ESI score with an asterisk should be viewed as possibly 1 to 10 points higher, had appropriate information been available.

Here are the standards for each key indicator.
(A more comprehensive ESI gauge is available in
Appendix D.)

Average daily attendance
—national average is 95%

Current expense per pupil
—see Appendix A for state-by-state averages

Dropout rate
—national median is 23%

Combined score on SAT
—national average is 906

Score on ACT
—national average is 18.8

Percentage of eligible students who took the SAT or ACT
—10 points equal more than 60%

Subjects in which Advanced Placement courses are offered
—10 points equal 10 or more courses

Teacher-student ratio in elementary grades
—10 points equal 1:20 or below

Teacher-student ratio in secondary grades
—10 points equal 1:18 or below

Counselor-student ratio
—10 points equal 1:200 or below

Number of students per music specialist
—10 points equal 250–299

All ESI scores are based on a sliding scale. For example, the national median dropout rate is 23 percent. A district whose dropout rate is 13 percent or lower earned 10 points; 14 percent, 9 points; 15 percent, 8 points; and so on to a figure above the national median, 0 points. Thus a school's score in the ESI is not on a type of pass-fail system, but rather we have chosen to award ESI points relative to the school's degree of commitment and performance within a reasonable range of the ideal for each statistic.

IMPLICATIONS OF THE DATA

This book never intended a scholarly research of American public education. However, the data collected from some 500 districts and the informed opinion of approximately 1,000 observers from those districts point to at least three significant findings that are illuminating and, we think, to a great extent reflective of conditions in most of the nation's public schools.

These three conclusions based on our survey of districts are as follows:

1. Districts find it increasingly difficult to meet the mounting costs necessary to keep aging physical plants in good repair.

2. Vocational/technical education is not gaining favor with students, their parents, and school counselors *despite the fact* that many regional vocational/technical schools are updating their curricula and the U.S. Department of Labor advises that most skilled jobs in the future will not require a college education.

3. Many districts offer more and better learning opportunities for their gifted and talented students, but low-achieving students are not faring as well, although large sums of money continue to be earmarked for them.

VICIOUS CYCLE GRINDS ON

School districts have trouble keeping up with routine repairs and maintenance primarily because when school boards are forced to trim their overall budget, due to action taken either by legislative bodies or voters, building maintenance and repair are often the first categories decimated. The cruel irony, of course, is that inadequate repair and maintenance today inevitably lead to major repairs and renovations or even new construction tomorrow, which costs far more money.

The situation perhaps is best appreciated by examining districts in a few metropolitan areas across the country.

Over half of the schools in the Buffalo area are more than 30 years old. One district reported that 100 percent of its schools are that old, and three other districts said that at least three-fourths of their schools are over age 30.

Said one observer in the Buffalo area: "The buildings were let go for 15 years." Now, the School Board has embarked on an ambitious (and expensive) renovation project.

In the Cincinnati area, an average of 49 percent of school buildings are at least thirty years old. Nearly half the districts in our Cincinnati listing have had to resort to special tax levies within the last three years in order to make major improvements to school buildings.

Observers in two districts in the Detroit area reported buildings deteriorating rapidly because tax levies have failed to pass. Said one person, "Some of the buildings are falling apart." An average of 30 percent of the schools in the area are at least 30 years old. Another observer, who reported the condition of buildings as good, said this achievement "was very recent." A major bond issue enabled this particular district to make up for "years of neglect."

Even in the Houston area, where some school districts have built most of their schools within the last 10 years to accommodate a temporary population boom, an average of 32 percent of the schools are over 30 years old. An observer in one of the largest districts reported the quality of maintenance and repair is excellent, but voiced the fear that "this could change quickly and drastically because 80 percent of the buildings are at least 30 years old and because budget cuts in the near future seem likely."

California is one of a number of states where a cap has been placed on how much local districts can spend. A consequence has been a decline in the quality of building maintenance and repair. A typical comment from observers in the Los Angeles area is this one: "Most of the schools are over 30 years old, and the district has not had the money to regularly repair them." Said another observer: "There is a huge backlog of deferred maintenance throughout the district."

In the summer of 1986, the National Governors Association, in its comprehensive report *Time for Results*, found school facilities to be a neglected area. "Local school boards have little control over some of the reasons for the decline in the quality of building maintenance and repair," said Jean McDonald, NGA research associate. Cuts in state funding and inflation, for example, are major factors affecting school upkeep.

It is also true, however, that "education officials have not paid much attention to facilities over the years. And scant information exists anywhere about the condition of school buildings," Ms. McDonald said, "mainly because state education departments don't collect much data about them."

The only national statistic she could come up with for the background papers on which the NGA report on facilities was based is that 20 percent of the school buildings in older cities were built before 1920 — almost 70 years ago!

One of the governors' recommendations to the states was that they should "restore buildings where maintenance needs and safety improvements have been deferred." But the governors shied away from suggesting a price tag, Ms. McDonald said, because, "it would be so high." Presumably, state legislators might be scared away by the cost before they could carefully consider the needs.

A QUESTION OF DOLLARS & SENSE

On the one hand, districts (or county and regional agencies) in many states have spent heavily to update vocational/technical facilities and equipment. On the other hand, some educators, parents and students in those same districts are deciding against vocational education for reasons that don't show very good common sense.

Those are at least two ways to describe what is happening in vocational/technical education, according to our survey and also the American Vocational Association in Arlington, VA. Another important factor affecting vocational/technical education today is the raising of standards for high school graduation. "When 37 states added academic requirements for graduation," said Gladys Bashkin, editor of the AVA's *Vocational Education Journal*, "it made it difficult for many high school juniors and seniors to remain in their vocational/technical program." The reason is that the additional required academic courses often make it impossible for vocational/technical students to spend half their school days in the vocational/technical program as is generally required for completion of course requirements. Clearly, we have a case of good intentions gone awry.

Still another problem revealed in our survey and mentioned by the AVA and other educators is that some high school counselors apparently influence a number of students and their parents to turn away from a vocational/technical education program *even though the students might benefit more from it than from a track aimed toward college.*

Officials in a district outside Pittsburgh, for example, reported that less than half of the district's high school graduates went on to college. Yet, observers were critical of counselors for mostly ignoring a good vocational/technical curriculum.

According to Ms. Bashkin at AVA, "counselors routinely deny they steer into a college preparatory program students who might be better qualified for and more successful in a curriculum offering them marketable skills." One criticism of counselors often heard, said Ms. Bashkin, is that "they are products of the college track and they know very little about the vocational/technical track."

Counselors come in for harsher criticism from Tom Hebert and John Coyne in their book *Getting Skilled.* "Whatever counselors may wish to do," they write, "their days are filled with clerical business and the never-ending tide of students with schedules to be changed. With paperwork and college counseling taking up the hours, only one high school student in five—20 percent, nationwide—receives *any* vocational counseling."

An observer in a district in the Portland, OR area gave a fair rating to the district's curriculum for students not planning on college. The program would be a lot better, the observer said, "if more students who aren't really interested in college were instead counseled into a program that would prepare them for a good job."

"Many parents and students and some educators have little knowledge of the kinds of opportunities available at a vocational/technical school and the quality of the training," said Ms. Bashkin. When state legislators, whose decisions often affect the quality of vocational/technical education, are taken through a good vocational/technical school, they "go bananas," she said. They are pleasantly surprised at how good the job preparation really is.

An observer in a district outside Chicago told an interviewer for *Public Schools USA* that the vocational/technical education program "doesn't get the attention it deserves because the majority of parents and other citizens think every high school graduate *is going* or *should go* to college." They seem to forget, said the observer, that "at least a quarter of the graduates in the district do not attend college." The irony is that the vocational/technical school for this district is a regional one, which is typical around the country, and its curriculum is considered quite good.

WHAT SHOULD WE EXPECT?

In 62 percent of the districts in the Dallas metropolitan area, observers rate the program for low-achieving students (not handicapped) a notch or two below the program for gifted and talented children. A similar picture emerges in most other metropolitan areas from the information collected by the *Public Schools USA* survey.

Readers may wonder why this is so, especially since federal and state governments have been spending a lot more money for a longer period of time on low-achieving students than on gifted and talented students. Indeed, the 1987 federal appropriation for low-achieving students through Chapter I of the Elementary and Secondary Education Act is approximately $4 billion, while the appropriation for gifted and talented programs is approximately zero.

The answers are several.

In the first place, many educators and most laypersons—including our observers—may expect more results more quickly from programs aimed at low-achieving students than the schools can possibly deliver.

Consider two fictional characters: John is in a program for low-achievers, or slower learners; Joe is in a program for gifted and talented. Both are fourth-graders. John, when he entered the program, already was two grade levels behind in reading and most other basic academic subjects. Joe, on the other hand, was well beyond the fourth grade level in nearly all areas when he was enrolled in the program for gifted and talented.

John has a lot of catching up to do before he can move forward, not an easy task for any child—or his teachers and parents. Joe, however, can move even farther ahead because of enrichment opportunities, and he can react quickly to each challenge.

Also, John's painfully slow progress will be measured, to a large extent, by achievement tests. And the test results will show just how small John's measurable gains are. On the other hand, Joe, in the enrichment program for gifted and talented, may be sharpening both his ability to think critically and his creativity—skills which are, for the most part, not subject to simple evaluation by test.

The above scenario is based on the comments and observations of two knowledgeable persons. One is Chrissy Bamber, a program associate with the National Committee for Citizens in Education, a group that, among other things, keeps track of what the federal and state governments are doing for low-achieving and/or disadvantaged children. The other person is Kathy Balsamo, former director of the National Center for Gifted Children.

But the difference between remedial and gifted programs goes far beyond realistic goals and accurate measurement of results. Ms. Bamber also points out that while the federal and state governments have appropriated large sums for remediation of slow learners, "as many as half the children who are considered eligible for such aid never get helped."

"Another factor," said Ms. Bamber, "is that teachers and parents have greater expectations generally for high-achievers than for low-achievers." If a child is labeled gifted or talented, people automatically expect the child to *want* to do well and, in fact, to do well. But low-achievers are perceived to be the kind of children who don't really care about learning and probably can't learn much regardless of the attention given. So you can see the seed of what gets played out in these children's lives over and over.

A number of observers reporting to *Public Schools USA* also pointed out that parents of gifted and talented children usually are more vocal and more aggressive in behalf of their children. If they are not satisfied with their child's program, they call or visit school officials, including school board members. Many parents of low-achieving students are more reluctant to take on district administrators and teachers.

Typical were the comments from an observer in a district outside Chicago. The observer rated the quality of additional learning opportunities for gifted students as good to excellent and stated: "Better than most; strong parents group." The same observer found the quality of additional instruction for low-achieving students to be fair to good. The comment here was: "Parents don't provide the pressure."

We also discovered from our observers that programs for gifted students are typically strong in the secondary grades, particularly in the senior high school. However, observers often reported that additional instruction for low-achieving students is more likely to be better in the elementary grades than in the upper grades. An observer in the Minneapolis-St. Paul area complained that the remediation program did not intervene early enough and also was weak at the secondary level.

Another finding from our survey is that programs for gifted students are generally of more recent vintage and are expanding, often with "new" money from state governments. Ms. Balsamo said, "More than 25 states have mandated programs for the gifted, and much of this legislation has been passed within the last six years." Such programs tend to be more dynamic and gain more publicity. Special programs for low-achieving students have been around in some form for almost 25 years (the Elementary and Secondary Education Act goes back to the mid-1960s). One observer described the two programs in a district outside Minneapolis this way: Additional learning opportunities for gifted students have "grown tremendously" while additional instruction for low-achieving students is "limited in scope."

The good news out of the survey is that those remediation programs whose quality is rated highly are very often ones that are located in recently opened learning resource centers. These centers, which sometimes serve gifted students as well, provide individual tutoring for low-achievers and offer independent learning on personal computers.

PART TWO

MAJOR METROPOLITAN AREAS WITH DISTRICTS

Public Schools USA

METROPOLITAN AREA

Albany, NY

Five districts in the Albany metropolitan area completed the Statistical Profile. Fair appraisals alone were received for three additional districts. Districts in this area may be compared to districts in the Rochester, NY metropolitan area.

AREA AT A GLANCE

SCHOOL DISTRICT	ENROLLMENT	ESI
Albany	7,700	
Burnt-Hills/Ballston Lake	3,432	80
East Greenbush	4,205	
Guilderland	4,015	
Niskayuna	3,309	75
Schenectady City	8,019	60
Scotia–Glenville	2,705	63
South Colonie	5,329	80

ALBANY

ADDRESS OF CENTRAL OFFICE:
School Administration Building
Academy Park, Elk Street, Albany, NY 12207
ESI:None†

STATISTICAL PROFILE	DATA	ESI
Grade organization:		
Percentage of schools built before 1955		
Total enrollment		
Average Daily Attendance (ADA)		
Current expense per pupil in ADA		
Dropout rate		
Percentage of eligible students who took the SAT		
Average combined score on SAT		
Percentage of graduates who enrolled in 2- or 4-year colleges		
Percentage of students who passed the state reading test		
Percentage of students who passed the state math test		
Teacher–student ratio in elementary grades		
Teacher–student ratio in secondary grades		
Counselor–student ratio in secondary grades		
Number of students per music specialist in elementary grades		
Number of students per art specialist in elementary grades		
Number of volumes in senior high school library		
Beginning teacher's salary		
Maximum teacher's salary		
Average years of experience among teachers		
Number of students suspended and expelled		
Subjects in which Advanced Placement courses are offered:		

†A Statistical Profile was not received from this district.

FAIR APPRAISAL

Quality of School Leadership
The youngest and newest principals are, for the most part, the best qualified; many older principals seem to have been hired because of inside politics. The quality of leadership can vary greatly throughout the city, and it is often hard to replace ineffectual administrators. Parents and teachers have very little say in the selection of principals, but principals have some say in the quantity and quality of resources assigned their school by the central office.

Quality of Instruction
The brightest students may choose from a wide variety of Advanced Placement courses. Some of these courses are given at nearby colleges for credit. On the other hand, observers gave a poor rating to additional instruction for low-achieving students. The good news is that the district is conscious of this failing and is making slow progress toward improvement. Students looking forward to college generally are better served than those going directly into the job market.

Quality of School Environment
Classroom disruption and student vandalism are not as much of a problem as they are in some other cities of the same size. Also, the district does a good job of maintaining and repairing its buildings.

BURNT-HILLS/BALLSTON LAKE

ADDRESS OF CENTRAL OFFICE:
50 Cypress Drive, Scotia, NY 12302
ESI:80*

STATISTICAL PROFILE	DATA	ESI
Grade organization: K–5/6–8/9–12	20%	
Total enrollment	3,432	
Average Daily Attendance (ADA)	95%	8
Current expense per pupil in ADA	5,294	4
Dropout rate	1%	10
Percentage of eligible students who took the SAT	71%	10
Average combined score on SAT	981	8
Percentage of graduates who enrolled in 2- or 4-year colleges	75%	
Percentage of students who passed the state reading test	100%	
Percentage of students who passed the state math test	93%	
Teacher–student ratio in elementary grades	1:17	10
Teacher–student ratio in secondary grades	1:16	10
Counselor–student ratio in secondary grades	1:278	6
Number of students per music specialist in elementary grades	324	9
Number of students per art specialist in elementary grades	688	
Number of volumes in senior high school library	19,159	
Beginning teacher's salary	$19,805	
Maximum teacher's salary	$36,335	
Average years of experience among teachers	19	
Number of students suspended and expelled	44	
Subjects in which Advanced Placement courses are offered: American History, Calculus, Chemistry, English Composition, English Literature	5	5

*1986–87 statistic

FAIR APPRAISAL

Quality of School Leadership

Generally, principals are hired from within or outside the district on the basis of leadership ability, although one principal, who parents and students were not too pleased with, was hired because of seniority. Once hired, principals tend to stay in their positions indefinitely. Teachers and parents do not have much say in principal selection, but parents may be otherwise involved in decision-making. For example, parents and other citizens were asked to research data regarding a proposed school closing. Because the district covers a large area, students may be moved from one elementary school to another to even out class size and to make best use of resources. Students can be moved once without parents' approval; thereafter, parents must consent.

Quality of Instruction

The observers believe the additional learning opportunities both for gifted and low-achieving students are good. Bright students can move on to more advanced instruction at every level. "An effort is made to tailor instruction to the individual," said one observer, regardless of whether the student is bright or low-achieving. The college-preparatory curriculum is rated good to excellent, although one observer thinks it is not quite as challenging as it was six to eight years ago. Although vocational education is provided, guidance counseling for students not planning on college probably is not as thorough as it should be.

Quality of School Environment

The level of classroom disruption and vandalism is low. The School Board, which was praised as "one of the most hard-working and knowledgeable in the area," has a good plan for keeping buildings in good repair.

SCHOOL DISTRICT

EAST GREENBUSH

ADDRESS OF CENTRAL OFFICE:
School Administration Center
East Greenbush, NY 12061
ESI:None†

STATISTICAL PROFILE	DATA	ESI
Grade organization:		
Percentage of schools built before 1955		
Total enrollment		
Average Daily Attendance (ADA)		
Current expense per pupil in ADA		
Dropout rate		
Percentage of eligible students who took the SAT		
Average combined score on SAT		
Percentage of graduates who enrolled in 2- or 4-year colleges		
Percentage of students who passed the state reading test		
Percentage of students who passed the state math test		
Teacher–student ratio in elementary grades		
Teacher–student ratio in secondary grades		
Counselor–student ratio in secondary grades		
Number of students per music specialist in elementary grades		
Number of students per art specialist in elementary grades		
Number of volumes in senior high school library		
Beginning teacher's salary		
Maximum teacher's salary		
Average years of experience among teachers		
Number of students suspended and expelled		
Subjects in which Advanced Placement courses are offered:		

†A Statistical Profile was not received from this district.

FAIR APPRAISAL

Quality of School Leadership
The superintendent has been in office for more than 25 years, and observers believe he too often selects principals from among male teachers who also have been in the system a long time. While a committee of teachers may be consulted about a candidate for principal in their school, their advice is not considered crucial. The quality of leadership seems to vary from school to school; low teacher morale frequently is a symptom of weak leadership.

Parent organizations are not very effective, due to leadership turnover and lack of support from principals.

Quality of Instruction
The district offers excellent preparation for college, but the curriculum for students going directly into the job market is weak. "The occupational education program seems to prepare students for traditional employment," said one observer, jobs that may be short-lived. The emphasis on instruction for the college-bound may be due in part to changing population in the district. East Greenbush was mostly "country" until a few years ago when more persons whose careers were in business, state government, and the professions began moving in.

Quality of School Environment
Classroom disruption and vandalism are not problems. Buildings are in excellent condition thanks to policies set by the School Board and administration and a recent bond issue for building improvements.

SCHOOL DISTRICT

GUILDERLAND

ADDRESS OF CENTRAL OFFICE:
State Farm Road, Guilderland, NY 12084
ESI:None†

STATISTICAL PROFILE	DATA	ESI
Grade organization:		
Percentage of schools built before 1955		
Total enrollment		
Average Daily Attendance (ADA)		
Current expense per pupil in ADA		
Dropout rate		
Percentage of eligible students who took the SAT		
Average combined score on SAT		
Percentage of graduates who enrolled in 2- or 4-year college		
Percentage of students who passed the state reading test		
Percentage of students who passed the state math test		
Teacher–student ratio in elementary grades		
Teacher–student ratio in secondary grades		
Counselor–student ratio in secondary grades		
Number of students per music specialist in elementary grades		
Number of students per art specialist in elementary grades		
Number of volumes in senior high school library		
Beginning teacher's salary		
Maximum teacher's salary		
Average years of experience among teachers		
Number of students suspended and expelled		
Subjects in which Advanced Placement courses are offered:		

†A Statistical Profile was not received from this district.

FAIR APPRAISAL

Quality of School Leadership
Leadership is rated highly; qualified principals are found throughout the district. Teachers have some say in the selection of principals, parents to a lesser extent. Principals can influence the quality and quantity of resources allotted their school by the central office.

The School Board is open to ideas from parents and other residents; therefore, parent–citizen groups are effective. Indeed, a member of the School Board is also a member of the PTA Council.

Quality of Instruction
Bright students have a number of special projects to choose from, including writing workshops and art classes for the gifted. The district offers low-achieving students the kinds of remedial programs common to most districts; in addition, it also supplies tutors in every subject. The curriculum for students going to college and the one preparing students for the job market are rated good.

Quality of School Environment
The incidence of classroom disruption and violence is low. School building maintenance and repair are rated excellent.

NISKAYUNA

ADDRESS OF CENTRAL OFFICE:
Van Antwerp Road and Dexter Street
Schenectady, NY 12309
ESI:75

STATISTICAL PROFILE	DATA	ESI
Grade organization: K–5/6–8/9–12		
Percentage of schools built before 1955	17%	
Total enrollment	3,309	
Average Daily Attendance (ADA)	96%	9
Current expense per pupil in ADA	$4,500	0
Dropout rate	1%	10
Percentage of eligible students who took the SAT	89%	10
Average combined score on SAT	1,050	10
Percentage of graduates who enrolled in 2- or 4-year colleges	84%	
Percentage of students who passed the state reading test	100%	
Percentage of students who passed the state math test	100%	
Teacher–student ratio in elementary grades	1:23	7
Teacher–student ratio in secondary grades	1:24	4
Counselor–student ratio in secondary grades	1:270	7
Number of students per music specialist in elementary grades	200	10
Number of students per art specialist in elementary grades	500	
Number of volumes in senior high school library	36,000	
Beginning teacher's salary	$19,758	
Maximum teacher's salary	$36,537	
Average years of experience among teachers	16	
Number of students suspended and expelled	25	
Subjects in which Advanced Placement courses are offered: Biology, Calculus, Chemistry, Computer Science, English, Foreign Languages, History, Physics	8	8

Quality of School Leadership
School leadership is rated highly, although some qualified female candidates for a recent opening were unexpectedly passed over. Both parents and teachers have some say in principal selection, and parents and other citizens are called upon periodically to advise the administration and board.

Quality of Instruction
The high school received an award of excellence from the U.S. Department of Education in 1983. The middle school and two elementary schools now have been nominated for awards. The district has a large number of high-ability students (the district is home to many researchers at a local General Electric lab and to many state employees working in Albany). In fact, a committee of teachers and parents recently called attention to the need for teachers to be more "sensitive" to the needs of "average" students. Excellent programs exist for gifted and low-achieving students; a pre-first grade helps children who need extra preparation for first grade, including those with a language problem (a number of Indian and oriental families live in the area).

Quality of School Environment
Classroom disruption and student vandalism are negligible. The condition of school buildings is generally good, but voters early in 1987 rejected a bond referendum that would have financed major repairs.

SCHENECTADY CITY

ADDRESS OF CENTRAL OFFICE:
108 Brandywine Avenue, Schenectady, NY 12307
ESI:60

STATISTICAL PROFILE	DATA	ESI
Grade organization: K–5/6–8/9–12		
Percentage of schools built before 1955	76%	
Total enrollment	8,019	
Average Daily Attendance (ADA)	93%	6
Current expense per pupil in ADA	$3,580	0
Dropout rate	16%	7
Percentage of eligible students who took the SAT	35%	4
Average combined score on SAT	936	6
Percentage of graduates who enrolled in 2- or 4-year colleges	58%	
Percentage of students who passed the state reading test	99%	
Percentage of students who passed the state math test	99%	
Teacher–student ratio in elementary grades	1:23	7
Teacher–student ratio in secondary grades	1:20	8
Counselor–student ratio in secondary grades	1:300	6
Number of students per music specialist in elementary grades	312	9
Number of students per art specialist in elementary grades	784	
Number of volumes in senior high school library	13,647	
Beginning teacher's salary	$17,901	
Maximum teacher's salary	$33,857	
Average years of experience among teachers	17	
Number of students suspended and expelled	NK	
Subjects in which Advanced Placement courses are offered:	7	7
Biology, Chemistry, Computer Science, English,		
Math, Physics, Sociology		

Quality of School Leadership

In recent years, the district has made a greater effort to find and hire the best candidates as principals. The search extends outside the district. Also, the district now grooms qualified female teachers in the system for future positions. Principals are rotated among the schools on a regular basis, a system that seems acceptable to most parents and teachers.

Teachers and parents have some say in principal selection, but not much. However, parents are frequently involved in making other important decisions. For example, parents were given extraordinary authority to create an open-classroom school in an abandoned building, and they even helped design curriculum and hire teachers.

Quality of Instruction

"Like most city school districts," said one observer, "Schenectady has its problems, but they really seem to care about kids and about addressing problems." The observers rate as good the additional learning opportunities both for exceptionally bright students and low-achieving students. The district recently won six first place awards in a regional Odyssey of the Mind program for gifted students. A new program offers remedial instruction to children who have left kindergarten but are not quite up to the demands of first grade. The district serves learning-disabled children aged three and four.

The observers believe the district's college-preparatory curriculum is good, even though only 58 percent of 1986 graduates went on to higher education. The vocational education program also is rated good.

Quality of School Environment

Most school buildings are old. Also, the city is hurting financially (the largest industry, General Electric, has been shutting down some operations and laying off workers), and maintenance and repair have not received high priority.

The district did not provide a figure for suspensions and expulsions (see Profile), but the observers believe student disruption and vandalism are serious problems in some schools.

SCOTIA–GLENVILLE

ADDRESS OF CENTRAL OFFICE:
1 Business Boulevard, Scotia, NY 12302
ESI:63

STATISTICAL PROFILE	DATA	ESI
Grade organization: K–6/7–8/9–12		
Percentage of schools built before 1955	66%	
Total enrollment	2,705	
Average Daily Attendance (ADA)	95%	8
Current expense per pupil in ADA	$4,919	2
Dropout rate	1%	10
Percentage of eligible students who took the SAT	72%	10
Average combined score on SAT	956	7
Percentage of graduates who enrolled in 2- or 4-year colleges	37%	
Percentage of students who passed the state reading test	92%	
Percentage of students who passed the state math test	98%	
Teacher–student ratio in elementary grades	1:24	6
Teacher–student ratio in secondary grades	1:26	2
Counselor–student ratio in secondary grades	1:330	4
Number of students per music specialist in elementary grades	326	9
Number of students per art specialist in elementary grades	704	
Number of volumes in senior high school library	14,793	
Beginning teacher's salary	$16,660	
Maximum teacher's salary	$26,400	
Average years of experience among teachers	14	
Number of students suspended and expelled	528	
Subjects in which Advanced Placement courses are offered: Biology, Calculus, Chemistry, Computer Science, English	5	5

Quality of School Leadership

Capable principals have been selected from both within and outside the district. Screening of principal candidates is by the central administration and School Board. Parents and other residents play an important role in school decision-making. For example, a number of citizens served on a district enrichment committee, and a parents' committee early in 1987 recommended the partial reopening of a closed school to accommodate an additional kindergarten (enrollment is climbing again). It had not been an option considered by the School Board. "You sometimes hear that there are too many committees," said one observer.

Quality of Instruction

The curricula for gifted and low-achieving students are rated excellent. A Pyramid program challenges bright students; elementary students, for example, recently submitted their own musical compositions and paintings to a regional competition. "Teachers are receptive to the needs of low-achieving children," said one observer, and a pre-first grade was scheduled to begin in the fall of 1987. The observers think well of programs for college-bound students and those heading into the job market. However, one observer said counseling for college-bound students and their parents is better than that afforded other students.

Quality of School Environment

"You don't get away with anything," said one observer, speaking of the district's strict disciplinary code, which parents, students and teachers helped devise. The unusually high number of suspensions and expulsions (mostly in-school suspensions) reported by the district (528) attests to the strictness. A group of students was suspended, for example, when their parents took them out of school for a day of skiing. The school buildings are kept in good repair and are well-maintained.

SOUTH COLONIE

ADDRESS OF CENTRAL OFFICE:
102 Loralee Drive, Albany, NY 12205
ESI:80

STATISTICAL PROFILE	DATA	ESI
Grade organization: K–3/4–8/9–12		
Percentage of schools built before 1955	0%	
Total enrollment	5,329	
Average Daily Attendance (ADA)	94%	7
Current expense per pupil in ADA	$5,418	5
Dropout rate	3%	10
Percentage of eligible students who took the SAT	65%	10
Average combined score on SAT	950	7
Average combined score on ACT	19.8	
Percentage of graduates who enrolled in 2- or 4-year colleges	65%	
Percentage of students who passed the state reading test	98%	
Percentage of students who passed the state math test	88%	
Teacher–student ratio in elementary grades	1:17	10
Teacher–student ratio in secondary grades	1:16	10
Counselor–student ratio in secondary grades	1:307	5
Number of students per music specialist in elementary grades	268	10
Number of students per art specialist in elementary grades	708	
Number of volumes in senior high school library	37,023	
Beginning teacher's salary	$18,800	
Maximum teacher's salary	$36,365	
Average years of experience among teachers	18	
Number of students suspended and expelled	183	
Subjects in which Advanced Placement courses are offered:	6	6
Biology, Chemistry, Computer Science, English		
Foreign Languages, Math		

Quality of School Leadership

The school board goes outside the district to look for the best candidates for principal, and candidates are screened by top administrators (*sometimes* with an assist from school parents and other citizens). Principals have some say in the quantity and quality of resources allotted by the central office. Parents are occasionally involved in making decisions.

Quality of Instruction

A recent reorganization plan did away with K–6 elementary schools and created K–3 and 4–8 schools. The observers believe the plan helped to reduce class size and make better use of resources. Efforts to provide additional learning opportunities both for gifted and low-achieving students get high marks. Exceptionally bright students may take part in special projects and field trips. "The School Board is particularly sensitive to the needs of low-achieving students," said one observer. It helps that a branch of the state's Board of Cooperative Educational Services (BOCES) is located within the district.

The observers rate as good the curriculum for students going on to college and fair to good the curriculum for those going into the workplace or armed services.

Quality of School Environment

The district once had a reputation for rowdy students, but the administration and teachers have "worked hard" to improve discipline. The district reported no school building older than 1955; the reason is that older buildings have been closed, primarily because of declining enrollment. Two years ago, maintenance and repair were fair to poor, but the district budgeted more money for maintenance and repair in 1986–87 and also placed buildings on a regular cycle for major repairs and renovations.

Atlanta, GA

Six districts in the Atlanta metropolitan area responded to our inquiries,
including the core city. Georgia is one of those states (most of them in the South)
that has mostly county school districts, although some of the larger cities
are separate districts. Districts in this area may be compared to those
in the Greensboro–Winston Salem, NC metropolitan area.

AREA AT A GLANCE

SCHOOL DISTRICT	ENROLLMENT	ESI
Atlanta	71,826	53
Clayton County	34,235	28
Douglas County	13,450	39
Fayette County	10,581	65
Gwinnett County	52,449	49
Marietta	4,600	62

ATLANTA

ADDRESS OF CENTRAL OFFICE:
210 Pryor Street, SW, Atlanta, GA 30335
ESI:53

STATISTICAL PROFILE	DATA	ESI
Grade organization (two systems): K–5/6–8/9–12 & K–7/8–12		
Percentage of schools built before 1955	51%	
Total enrollment	71,826	
Average Daily Attendance (ADA)	93%	6
Current expense per pupil in ADA	$3,572	10
Dropout rate	33%	0
Percentage of eligible students who took the SAT	46%	7
Average combined score on SAT	691	0
Percentage of graduates who enrolled in 2- or 4-year colleges	46%	
Percentage of students who passed the state reading test	88%	
Percentage of students who passed the state math test	78%	
Teacher–student ratio in elementary grades	1:24	6
Teacher–student ratio in secondary grades	1:22	6
Counselor–student ratio in secondary grades	1:361	3
Number of students per music specialist in elementary grades	422	7
Number of students per art specialist in elementary grades	903	
Number of volumes in senior high school library	18,579	
Beginning teacher's salary	$18,504	
Maximum teacher's salary	$35,628	
Average years of experience among teachers	14	
Number of students suspended and expelled	1,686	
Subjects in which Advanced Placement courses are offered: American History, Biology, Chemistry, Computer Science, English, Foreign Languages, Latin, Mathematics	8	8

Quality of School Leadership

The quality of school leadership varies greatly from school to school and from one section of the city to another. Some principals have been appointed more on the basis of *who* they know rather than *what* they know. Parent groups have pressured the central office to get some "bad" principals fired. Poorer areas of the city (often low-income black neighborhoods) tend to get the least able principals. "Sometimes they [poorer areas] manage to get a really good principal," said one observer, "but he/she usually moves on before long."

Keeping watch on principals and other school business are an active PTA and at least three other parent–citizen groups. These three are the Northside Atlanta Organization, the Council of In-Town Neighborhoods and Schools, and a citywide group called APPLE Corps. "Parents are listened to," said one observer.

Quality of Instruction

Programs for bright students are rated as fair to good. The city is justly proud of its magnet schools (14 of them) that cater both to the college-bound student, with special curricula that include the law and the arts, and to students going directly into careers, with schools specializing in such fields as food service. Also, Atlanta is one of the few major cities in the nation with a districtwide program of volunteer service for high school students. Students must spend at least 75 hours working without pay in schools or in community organizations and institutions before the end of their junior year.

The parent–citizen groups criticized the district for not giving enough remedial help to students who fail the state tests in reading and math. In addition, parents complain that some special education classes provide only "baby-sitting" and do not prepare mentally and physically impaired students for jobs and independent lives.

Quality of School Environment

As in most cities of its size, Atlanta has a problem with classroom disruption and vandalism. However, parents and school officials are developing new guidelines for student behavior and school discipline. The condition of school buildings is rated fair to good. The district is closing the oldest buildings and renovating others.

CLAYTON COUNTY

ADDRESS OF CENTRAL OFFICE:
120 Smith Street, Jonesboro, GA 30236
ESI:28

STATISTICAL PROFILE	DATA	ESI
Grade organization: K–6/7–9/10–12		
Percentage of schools built before 1955	15%	
Total enrollment	34,235	
Average Daily Attendance (ADA)	94%	7
Current expense per pupil in ADA	$2,524	3
Dropout rate	25%	0
Percentage of eligible students who took the SAT	45%	5
Average combined score on SAT	847	2
Percentage of graduates who enrolled in 2- or 4-year colleges	45%	
Percentage of students who passed the state reading test	98%	
Percentage of students who passed the state math test	94%	
Teacher–student ratio in elementary grades	1:23	7
Teacher–student ratio in secondary grades	1:27	1
Counselor–student ratio in secondary grades	1:423	1
Number of students per music specialist in elementary grades	1,000	0
Number of students per art specialist in elementary grades	1,777	
Number of volumes in senior high school library	19,443	
Beginning teacher's salary	$18,400	
Maximum teacher's salary	$34,182	
Average years of experience among teachers	9	
Number of students suspended and expelled	2,884	
Subjects in which Advanced Placement courses are offered: Mathematics, English	2	2

Quality of School Leadership

Clayton County is one of the few county districts in Georgia where the superintendent is elected. The year 1986–87 was the first time in 16 years that a nonincumbent was elected and the first time ever that a Republican was elected. Years ago, it helped a principal candidate to be a political supporter of the superintendent, but that is not a factor now. Because the district has expanded rapidly, most principals are new. Parents and teachers have hardly any say in their selection.

However, the PTA is otherwise a very effective voice in decision-making. "We have one of the most active PTAs in the state," said an observer. It was the Clayton County PTA, for example, that played a major role in getting the state legislature to pass a child protection law. And five of eleven School Board members are former PTA activists.

Quality of Instruction

The program for bright students is rated excellent, with special opportunities at all grade levels. When the Governor's Honors Program chooses the best school musicians, between one-third and one-half of those selected come from Clayton County. Even the junior high schools have an orchestra. These achievements occur despite a high number of students per music specialist in the elementary grades (see Statistical Profile). The opportunities for low-achieving students are rated "not as good."

The curricula for college-bound students and those heading for the job market are both rated highly. The district boasts that each school (including elementary schools) has at least one counselor.

Quality of School Environment

The incidence of classroom disruption and vandalism is low. However, students can face suspension for violating a school's dress code (and in-school suspension was not an option in 1986–87). The district has no uniform code; each principal can draft his/her own. The condition of school buildings is very good. Many of the buildings have been built within the last 10 years.

DOUGLAS COUNTY

ADDRESS OF CENTRAL OFFICE:
P.O. Box 1077, Douglasville, GA 30133
ESI:39

STATISTICAL PROFILE	DATA	ESI
Grade organization: K–5/6–8/9–12		
(In some areas) K–2/3–5/6–8/9–12		
Percentage of schools built before 1955	25%	
Total enrollment	13,450	
Average Daily Attendance (ADA)	94%	7
Current expense per pupil in ADA	$2,825	5
Dropout rate	34%	0
Percentage of eligible students who took the SAT	25%	2
Average combined score on SAT	850	2
Percentage of graduates who enrolled in 2- or 4-year colleges	25%	
Percentage of students who passed the state reading test	91%	
Percentage of students who passed the state math test	84%	
Teacher–student ratio in elementary grades	1:22	8
Teacher–student ratio in secondary grades	1:21	7
Counselor–student ratio in secondary grades	1:450	0
Number of students per music specialist in elementary grades	900	0
Number of students per art specialist in elementary grades	900	
Number of volumes in senior high school library	13,287	
Beginning teacher's salary	$18,450	
Maximum teacher's salary	$35,413	
Average years of experience among teachers	9	
Number of students suspended and expelled	709	
Subjects in which Advanced Placement courses are offered:	8	8
American History, Art, Biology, Calculus, Chemistry, English, European History, Spanish		

FAIR APPRAISAL

Quality of School Leadership

The superintendent is elected in Douglas County, and some principals may have been appointed because they supported the winning candidate. The quality of leadership varies with some low-income areas sometimes getting the least qualified administrators. Principals are screened and hired by the superintendent and School Board. Principals have some say in the quantity and quality of resources assigned to their school.

Neither the PTA, which is connected to the national organization, nor the strictly local PTOs are very effective in decision-making. They often lack support from key administrators. Another group, however, Supporters for the Gifted, convinced state officials to reinstate some funds for teaching bright students. The result was that the district lost only one teacher for the gifted instead of five.

Quality of Instruction

The opportunities for bright students are rated from good to excellent; accelerated learning (including early promotions) is available in most schools. Additional learning opportunities for low-achieving students also are deemed good to excellent. The district provides a good college-preparatory program and strong vocational education. The observers feel the needs of minority students are well met; one observer called the schools where most black children go among the best in the county.

Quality of School Environment

The incidence of classroom disruption and student vandalism is low. In recent years, the district has made a "massive" effort to repair and renovate school buildings.

FAYETTE COUNTY

ADDRESS OF CENTRAL OFFICE:
210 Stonewall Avenue, Fayetteville, GA 30214
ESI:65

STATISTICAL PROFILE	DATA	ESI
Grade organization: K–6/7–8/9–12		
Percentage of schools built before 1955	5%	
Total enrollment	10,581	
Average Daily Attendance (ADA)	94%	7
Current expense per pupil in ADA	$3,383	8
Dropout rate	8%†	10
Percentage of eligible students who took the SAT	70%	10
Average combined score on SAT	847	2
Percentage of graduates who enrolled in 2- or 4-year colleges	75%	
Percentage of students who passed the state reading test	96%	
Percentage of students who passed the state math test	96%	
Teacher–student ratio in elementary grades	1:24	6
Teacher–student ratio in secondary grades	1:23	5
Counselor–student ratio in secondary grades	1:350	4
Number of students per music specialist in elementary grades	400	7
Number of students per art specialist in elementary grades	400	
Number of volumes in senior high school library	20,000	
Beginning teacher's salary	$18,816	
Maximum teacher's salary	$35,995	
Average years of experience among teachers	10	
Number of students suspended and expelled	275	
Subjects in which Advanced Placement courses are offered:	6	6
American History, Biology, Chemistry, English, Physics, World History		

†When questioned about the low dropout rate, a district administrator said it was "approximate"; the actual figure is probably somewhat higher.

FAIR APPRAISAL

Quality of School Leadership

Principals generally are selected because of their ability to provide educational leadership, and they are uniformly capable throughout the district. No special screening procedures for principal candidates exist; parents and teachers have some say in principal selection, but not much. The central office tends to listen to valid, special requests for human and material resources coming from principals.

Parent organizations in the district sometimes take on important research projects, gathering data on specific school problems and issues. Such studies command the attention of the central administration and School Board.

Quality of Instruction

Additional learning opportunities for gifted and low-achieving students are rated good. Bright students may attend special classes and receive individual attention. Observers also rate highly the curricula for college-bound students and students moving into the job market.

Quality of School Environment

The incidence of disruptive behavior and vandalism is considered very low. The condition of the schools is very good.

GWINNETT COUNTY

ADDRESS OF CENTRAL OFFICE:
52 Gwinnett Drive, Lawrenceville, GA 30245
ESI:49

STATISTICAL PROFILE†	DATA	ESI
Grade organization: K–5/6–8/9–12		
Percentage of schools built before 1955	9%	
Total enrollment	52,449	
Average Daily Attendance (ADA)	95%	8
Current expense per pupil in ADA	$2,600	4
Dropout rate	19%	4
Percentage of eligible students who took the SAT	72%	10
Average combined score on SAT	885	3
Percentage of graduates who enrolled in 2- or 4-year colleges	66%	
Percentage of students who passed the state reading test	95%	
Percentage of students who passed the state math test	92%	
Teacher–student ratio in elementary grades	1:25	5
Teacher–student ratio in secondary grades	1:25	3
Counselor–student ratio in secondary grades	1:500	0
Number of students per music specialist in elementary grades	345	5
Number of students per art specialist in elementary grades	345	
Number of volumes in senior high school library	17,000	
Beginning teacher's salary	$19,527	
Maximum teacher's salary	$38,068	
Average years of experience among teachers	10	
Number of students suspended and expelled	122	
Subjects in which Advanced Placement courses are offered: American History, Biology, Calculus, Chemistry, English, Physics, World History	7	7

†Most figures are for the 1986–87 school year.

FAIR APPRAISAL

Quality of School Leadership
Principals are rated highly throughout the district, but teachers and parents have little say in their selection. Principals have some voice in deciding how human and material resources are assigned by the central office. The district superintendent was named by a national organization as one of the top 100 superintendents in the country.

Local School Advisory Councils meet regularly with their principal, and their views are listened to and frequently acted upon. A major issue in the district has been book censorship. The School Board listens to opposing groups: Citizens for Excellence in Education, which argues for the removal of some books, and Georgia Coalition Against Censorship. So far, it is a "standoff," said one observer.

Quality of Instruction
The observers are high on programs for bright students and low-achievers. Gifted students often engage in independent study, and small groups may take part in high-powered discussion and creative thinking. The curricula for college-bound students and those planning to work following graduation are considered good to excellent. The district has a fairly new vocational–technical center.

Quality of School Environment
Very little class disruption and vandalism are reported. New in 1986–87 was a policy requiring parents of disruptive students to attend their child's classes. Gwinnett County is one of the fastest growing in the country, and the district is having trouble keeping up. New schools often have trailers alongside to take care of the student overflow.

MARIETTA

ADDRESS OF CENTRAL OFFICE:
P.O. Box 1205, Marietta, GA 30061
ESI:62

STATISTICAL PROFILE	DATA	ESI
Grade organization: K–5/6–8/9–12		
Percentage of schools built before 1955	10%	
Total enrollment	4,600	
Average Daily Attendance (ADA)	95%	8
Current expense per pupil in ADA	$3,049	6
Dropout rate	NK	0
Percentage of eligible students who took the SAT	65%	10
Average combined score on SAT	874	3
Percentage of graduates who enrolled in 2- or 4-year colleges	66%	
Percentage of students who passed the state reading test	99%	
Percentage of students who passed the state math test	94%	
Teacher–student ratio in elementary grades	1:16†	10
Teacher–student ratio in secondary grades	1:16†	10
Counselor–student ratio in secondary grades	1:350	4
Number of students per music specialist in elementary grades	475	6
Number of students per art specialist in elementary grades	2,500	
Number of volumes in senior high school library	14,328	
Beginning teacher's salary	$20,159	
Maximum teacher's salary	$38,976	
Average years of experience among teachers	13	
Number of students suspended and expelled	222	
Subjects in which Advanced Placement courses are offered: Calculus, Chemistry, English, History, Music, Theory	5	5

†These ratios have been lowered by including teacher aides in the computation. Each regular classroom (as well as classes in special education and remedial education) contains an aide.

FAIR APPRAISAL

Quality of School Leadership
Principals generally are selected on the basis of leadership ability, and all schools and sections of town are treated equally. Because of the size of the district, principals usually get the resources they need.

Parents and other community residents are very active through a local organization called Marietta Area School Supports (MASS). Several years ago, MASS helped rid the schools of a drug and alcohol problem. More recently, the group has studied and suggested action on a variety of issues, including instruction about AIDS. The central administration and School Board generally support the group's work.

Quality of Instruction
The learning opportunities for bright students are rated fair. Although a gifted program exists, it lacks consistency; also, no effort is made to evaluate its effectiveness. Additional instruction for low-achieving students gets higher marks. Each classroom has a computer used to assist students with reading or math difficulties. Another program teams low-achievers with high-achievers to stimulate a greater desire for learning.

The curricula for college-bound students and job-bound students are called good. Available vocational courses include ones that prepare students to be assistant chefs and to work in the growing Atlanta tourism industry. The district adequately meets the needs of minority students.

Quality of School Environment
Very little classroom disruption and vandalism exist in the schools. District employees do a good job of keeping school buildings in good repair and clean.

METROPOLITAN AREA

Baltimore, MD

Maryland school districts are county districts, with the exception of Baltimore City.
We received Statistical Profiles from two districts and Fair Appraisals alone from two others.
Districts in this area may be compared to districts in the Washington, DC metropolitan area.

AREA AT A GLANCE

SCHOOL DISTRICT	ENROLLMENT	ESI
Anne Arundel County	63,865	
Baltimore City	111,897	20*
Baltimore County	80,854	
Howard County	24,993	58

Indicates district misinterpretation of one or more statistics in the ESI. For each misinterpreted statistic, a score of 0 was given instead of a possible score of 0 to 10 points.

SCHOOL DISTRICT

ANNE ARUNDEL COUNTY

ADDRESS OF CENTRAL OFFICE:
2644 Riva Road, Annapolis, MD 21401
ESI:None†

STATISTICAL PROFILE	DATA	ESI
Grade organization:		
Percentage of schools built before 1955		
Total enrollment		
Average Daily Attendance (ADA)		
Current expense per pupil in ADA		
Dropout rate		
Percentage of eligible students who took the SAT		
Average combined score on SAT		
Percentage of graduates who enrolled in 2- or 4-year colleges		
Percentage of students who passed the state reading test		
Percentage of students who passed the state math test		
Teacher–student ratio in elementary grades		
Teacher–student ratio in secondary grades		
Counselor–student ratio in secondary grades		
Number of students per music specialist in elementary grades		
Number of students per art specialist in elementary grades		
Number of volumes in senior high school library		
Beginning teacher's salary		
Maximum teacher's salary		
Average years of experience among teachers		
Number of students suspended and expelled		
Subjects in which Advanced Placement courses are offered:		

†A Statistical Profile was not received from this district.

FAIR APPRAISAL

Quality of School Leadership
Principals usually are selected for their leadership ability, but the quality of leadership varies in this large district. The district begins at the Baltimore City line and extends south through suburbs and rural country to Chesapeake Bay. The process of selecting principals is "in transition," according to one observer. Neither teachers nor parents have much say in which candidates are picked.

Parent and community groups are sometines effective. One observer indicated that citizens perhaps organize too often into small splinter groups that lobby for a narrow cause.

Quality of Instruction
The additional learning opportunities for bright students are rated good. Many accelerated courses are offered (including five or more Advanced Placement courses), and some gifted students take courses at nearby colleges. Instruction for low-achieving students, on the other hand, is rated only fair. Also, the observers said the district was not doing all it could to meet the learning needs of minority students.

The curriculum for students going to college is rated fair to good, although the majority of graduates enroll in two- or four-year colleges. The preparation offered students moving into the job market also is rated fair to good.

Quality of School Environment
Overall, classroom disruption and vandalism are not serious. Although most school buildings are not old, their condition is described as only fair. A lack of funding for maintenance and repair and bureaucratic red tape are blamed.

BALTIMORE CITY

ADDRESS OF CENTRAL OFFICE:
3 East 25th Street, Baltimore, MD 21218
ESI:20*

STATISTICAL PROFILE	DATA	ESI
Grade organization: K–5/6–8/9–12		
Percentage of schools built before 1955	20%	
Total enrollment	111,897	
Average Daily Attendance (ADA)	87%	0
Current expense per pupil in ADA	$4,315	5
Dropout rate	13%†	10
Percentage of eligible students who took the SAT	36%	5
Average combined score on SAT	736	0
Percentage of graduates who enrolled in 2- or 4-year colleges	30%	
Percentage of students who passed the state reading test	99%	
Percentage of students who passed the state math test	82%	
Teacher–student ratio in elementary grades	1:35	0
Teacher–student ratio in secondary grades	1:37	0
Counselor–student ratio in secondary grades	1:1400	0
Number of students per music specialist in elementary grades	††	0*
Number of students per art specialist in elementary grades	††	
Number of volumes in senior high school library	NK	
Beginning teacher's salary	$17,000	
Maximum teacher's salary	$33,147	
Average years of experience among teachers	15	
Number of students suspended and expelled	2,026	
Subjects in which Advanced Placement courses are offered	None	0

† This figure may be higher; the average dropout rate for Maryland in the fall of 1985 was 19%, and urban areas around the country average over 20%.

††The district misinterpreted these statistics.

FAIR APPRAISAL

Quality of School Leadership

It is more common today for principals to be selected on the basis of their ability to provide educational leadership; candidates from within the district must take part in an internship program that stresses management skills. However, some principals still are chosen mostly because they have been teachers or assistant principals in the district a long time. Not surprisingly, the quality of leadership varies greatly from school to school. "A few principals exert innovative leadership," said one observer, "often 'thumbing their noses' at school regulations. Most do what they're supposed to [and they] are generally weaker." Teachers and parents have hardly any say in the selection of principals.

Quality of Instruction

Instruction for bright students is rated good, with the Central GATE School offering a tailor-made curriculum for the gifted. Satellite programs vary in quality. Additional instruction for low-achieving students is rated poor. An observer said the problems are "not providing enough instruction, not providing it soon enough, and not evaluating the way low-achieving students are taught."

In an effort to attract high-achieving students, 15 or more magnet schools offer an excellent curriculum to college-bound students. Those going directly into the job market do not fare as well; preparation is spotty.

Quality of School Environment

For a city of its size, classroom disruption and vandalism are relatively low. Building maintenance and repair are described as fair. Not enough money is budgeted for school building improvement.

BALTIMORE COUNTY

ADDRESS OF CENTRAL OFFICE:
6901 N. Charles Street, Towson, MD 21204
ESI:None†

STATISTICAL PROFILE	DATA	ESI
Grade organization:		
Percentage of schools built before 1955		
Total enrollment		
Average Daily Attendance (ADA)		
Current expense per pupil in ADA		
Dropout rate		
Percentage of eligible students who took the SAT		
Average combined score on SAT		
Percentage of graduates who enrolled in 2- or 4-year colleges		
Percentage of students who passed the state reading test		
Percentage of students who passed the state math test		
Teacher–student ratio in elementary grades		
Teacher–student ratio in secondary grades		
Counselor–student ratio in secondary grades		
Number of students per music specialist in elementary grades		
Number of students per art specialist in elementary grades		
Number of volumes in senior high school library		
Beginning teacher's salary		
Maximum teacher's salary		
Average years of experience among teachers		
Number of students suspended and expelled		
Subjects in which Advanced Placement courses are offered:		

†A Statistical Profile was not received from this district.

FAIR APPRAISAL

Quality of School Leadership

Most principals are chosen for their leadership ability; however, the quality of leadership varies throughout the district. "Some schools and some programs are favored, financially and educationally, over others," said one observer. Another observer said, "Good, forceful principals attract and hold good faculty. Bad principals are difficult to remove." A principal "track" exists in the system, which is designed to prepare future administrators. Principals' say about resources allotted them varies, depending on their clout.

Parent and other citizen groups are sometimes effective. The problem, according to observers, is many PTAs are more concerned with school projects than in representing parents on issues.

Quality of Instruction

The additional learning opportunities for bright students are rated good to excellent. A gifted and talented "track" exists through all grade levels and at *most* schools, which means *some* schools may be left out. The curriculum for low-achievers receives much lower marks, although one observer, a former teacher, thinks the district has made great strides in general with low-achievers in particular.

Observers rate the college preparation program good to excellent; they think job preparation is fair to good.

Quality of School Environment

Classroom disruption and vandalism are not major problems. Disruptive students may be removed from their regular schedule and placed in special classes. The condition of buildings is good to excellent.

HOWARD COUNTY

ADDRESS OF CENTRAL OFFICE:
10910 Route 108, Ellicott City, MD 21043
ESI:58

STATISTICAL PROFILE	DATA	ESI
Grade organization: K–5/6–8/9–12		
Percentage of schools built before 1955	11%	
Total enrollment	24,993	
Average Daily Attendance (ADA)	99%	10
Current expense per pupil in ADA	$3,981	4
Dropout rate	2%	10
Percentage of eligible students who took the SAT	75%	10
Average combined score on SAT	963	7
Percentage of graduates who enrolled in 2- or 4-year colleges	78%	
Percentage of students who passed the state reading test	96%	
Percentage of students who passed the state math test	73%	
Teacher–student ratio in elementary grades	1:27	3
Teacher–student ratio in secondary grades	1:24	4
Counselor–student ratio in secondary grades	1:415	1
Number of students per music specialist in elementary grades	600	3
Number of students per art specialist in elementary grades	600	
Number of volumes in senior high school library	15,488	
Beginning teacher's salary	$16,235	
Maximum teacher's salary	$33,565	
Average years of experience among teachers	12	
Number of students suspended and expelled	806	
Subjects in which Advanced Placement courses are offered:	6	6
Calculus, Computer Science, English, Foreign		
Languages, History, Physical Sciences		

Quality of School Leadership

Most principals are selected for their ability as educational leaders, but the current selection process has existed for only four years. Consequently, some principals were hired when standards were not as high and training was not as thorough. Unfortunately, the most ineffectual principals are either moved from one school to another or "kicked upstairs." Principals have some say in resource allotments.

Parent–citizen groups have been especially helpful in asking the School Board to improve school maintenance and pushing for better programs for gifted students.

Quality of Instruction

An excellent program for gifted students exists at all schools for all grade levels; the program has a director. The additional instruction for low-achieving students is not as good. Observers rate the preparation of students going to college as good, and they also are high on the curriculum for students planning to enter the job market. A pilot effort to raise the achievement of minority students began recently.

Quality of School Environment

Many of the schools were built in the '60s and '70s when open spaces for flexible grouping of students were popular. Many teachers and parents prefer the traditional classroom grouping, but the School Board and central administration remain committed to open space grouping.

Generally, the incidence of classroom disruption and vandalism is low, but a rash of suspicious fires plagued the district in 1986–87. Buildings are well-maintained and kept in good repair.

Birmingham, AL

Four districts, two city and two county, responded. Districts in this area may be compared to districts in the Atlanta metropolitan area.

AREA AT A GLANCE

SCHOOL DISTRICT	ENROLLMENT	ESI
Bessemer City	5,464	39
St. Clair County	5,630	39
Shelby County	13,506	67
Vestavia Hills City	3,399	65

BESSEMER CITY

ADDRESS OF CENTRAL OFFICE:
P.O. Box 868, Bessemer, AL 35021
ESI:39

STATISTICAL PROFILE	DATA	ESI
Grade organization: K–4/5–8/9–12		
Percentage of schools built before 1955	75%	
Total enrollment	5,464	
Average Daily Attendance (ADA)	95%	8
Current expense per pupil in ADA	$2,380	6
Dropout rate	27%	0
Percentage of eligible students who took the ACT	38%	5
Average combined score on ACT	15	0
Percentage of graduates who enrolled in 2- or 4-year colleges	43%	
Percentage of students who passed the state reading test	95%	
Percentage of students who passed the state math test	96%	
Teacher–student ratio in elementary grades	1:28	2
Teacher–student ratio in secondary grades	1:22	6
Counselor–student ratio in secondary grades	1:440	0
Number of students per music specialist in elementary grades	None	0
Number of students per art specialist in elementary grades	None	
Number of volumes in senior high school library	14,138	
Beginning teacher's salary	$15,886	
Maximum teacher's salary	$27,784	
Average years of experience among teachers	13	
Number of students suspended and expelled	378	
Subjects in which Advanced Placement courses are offered:	6	6
American History, Art, Biology, Calculus, Chemistry, English		

FAIR APPRAISAL

Quality of School Leadership

Principals generally are hired for their ability to provide educational leadership, but quality varies somewhat from school to school. Most principals are hired from the ranks of teachers in the district, and screening of candidates is in the hands of the superintendent and School Board. Parent involvement in decision-making is effective in a few schools, but in others parents play a minor role.

Quality of Instruction

Teachers' abilities are tested in Alabama, although the testing system has been challenged in court. The special learning opportunities for bright students are limited. "With the focus on trying to improve achievement of below-average students," said one observer, "gifted children are on the losing end." The additional instruction for low-achieving students does not go much beyond remedial teaching provided through federal funds. The district supplies some teacher aides, but not enough to go around.

The program for students going on to college is rated fair to good; six Advanced Placement courses are above-average for a small high school. However, one observer complained that counselors are more concerned about students with problems than about students interested in college. A separate vocational school is considered fair to good.

Quality of School Environment

Classroom disruption and vandalism are not major problems, but the condition of buildings is. Most buildings are old and simply breaking down. Bessemer is an old steel center that is trying to make a comeback with new industries, and funding for school construction is scarce. In the fall of 1987, however, the district was scheduled to close one existing high school and add a wing to the other, newer high school. Some other older schools will be closed or renovated.

ST. CLAIR COUNTY

ADDRESS OF CENTRAL OFFICE:
P.O. Box 248, Ashville, AL 35953
ESI:39

STATISTICAL PROFILE	DATA	ESI
Grade organization:	†	
Percentage of schools built before 1955	40%	
Total enrollment	5,630	
Average Daily Attendance (ADA)	97%	10
Current expense per pupil in ADA	$2,500	5
Dropout rate	NK	0
Percentage of eligible students who took the ACT	34%	4
Average combined score on ACT	NK	0
Percentage of graduates who enrolled in 2- or 4-year colleges	34%	
Percentage of students who passed the state reading test	99%	
Percentage of students who passed the state math test	97%	
Teacher–student ratio in elementary grades	1:20	10
Teacher–student ratio in secondary grades	1:18	10
Counselor–student ratio in secondary grades	1:460	0
Number of students per music specialist in elementary grades	None	0
Number of students per art specialist in elementary grades	None	
Number of volumes in senior high school library	NK	
Beginning teacher's salary	$18,307	
Maximum teacher's salary	$28,026	
Average years of experience among teachers	11	
Number of students suspended and expelled	NK	
Subjects in which Advanced Placement courses are offered:	None	0

†No response.

FAIR APPRAISAL

Quality of School Leadership
Most school principals are selected because of leadership abilities, and the quality is generally uniform throughout the county. Principal candidates usually are screened by the superintendents, with little or no input from teachers or parents. Principals may have some say in the quality and quantity of resources allotted their schools, but not much.

Parent organizations tend to be effective. An ad hoc group of parents was trying to persuade the School Board at the end of the 1986–87 school year to revise district policy on corporal punishment. The parents want to end the practice of principals and assistant principals spanking students.

Quality of Instruction
Few additional learning opportunities exist for bright students; the instruction for low-achieving students is rated as fair to good. The curriculum for college-bound students also is rated fair to good (no Advanced Placement courses are offered). According to one observer, graduates who received high marks in high school often do not do well at college in competition with students from other districts. The curriculum for students not going to college is considered good. The observers also report the educational needs of minority students are met as well as those of majority students.

Quality of School Environment
The incidence of classroom disruption and vandalism is low. Buildings are in fair condition; the observers blame underfunding by the state. The state provides funds for school construction, but not for maintenance and repair. "A student can be sitting in a classroom with a leaking roof," said one observer, "and watch a new school going up nearby."

SHELBY COUNTY

ADDRESS OF CENTRAL OFFICE:
410 East College Street, Columbiana, AL 25051
ESI:67

STATISTICAL PROFILE	DATA	ESI
Grade organization: K–5/6–8/9–12	†	
Percentage of schools built before 1955	33%	
Total enrollment	13,506	
Average Daily Attendance (ADA)	96%	9
Current expense per pupil in ADA	$3,638	10
Dropout rate	21%	2
Percentage of eligible students who took the ACT	58%	9
Average combined score on ACT	21.2	10
Percentage of graduates who enrolled in 2- or 4-year colleges	55%	
Percentage of students who passed the state reading test	99%	
Percentage of students who passed the state math test	97%	
Teacher–student ratio in elementary grades	1:19	10
Teacher–student ratio in secondary grades	1:17	10
Counselor–student ratio in secondary grades	1:400	2
Number of students per music specialist in elementary grades	None	0
Number of students per art specialist in elementary grades	None	
Number of volumes in senior high school library	5,536	††
Beginning teacher's salary	$18,436	
Maximum teacher's salary	$27,303	
Average years of experience among teachers	10	
Number of students suspended and expelled	NK	
Subjects in which Advanced Placement courses are offered: American History, Biology, Calculus, English Language and Composition, Spanish	5	5

† The pattern is varied now, but this breakdown is the goal for 1990.
††This figure seems quite low, but it is based on the district's statistic of 10 volumes per student (3,875 students in seven high schools).

FAIR APPRAISAL

Quality of School Leadership
Principals are selected for their leadership ability; turnover is not great, so leadership is stable. Teachers and parents have little say in principal selection, but principals in turn have some say in the resources allotted their school. However, as an observer pointed out, "Principals have a list that is a mile long at the start of school, and at the end, the list is about nine-tenths of a mile long."

Parent involvement is generally effective, mostly through PTOs and some PTAs. Also, parents are organized into athletic booster clubs, since money for sports teams comes only from what is raised.

Quality of Instruction
Shelby County is the fastest growing county in the state; consequently, the budget is not keeping up with enrollment. "Schools don't have enough of anything," said one observer. If a school wants a music teacher, for example, the teacher's salary must be paid from donations. The result is that the programs for bright students and low-achieving students are not as good as they should be. The curricula for the college-bound and job-bound are both rated as fair to good.

Quality of School Environment
Classroom disruption and vandalism are not problems in the district, but building maintenance and repair are. The rapid growth is overtaxing buildings that already needed improvements. In some schools, the enrollment is almost 60 percent above the building capacity. There is cause for hope, however; a major referendum (that would also raise school taxes) was being planned for 1987–88.

VESTAVIA HILLS CITY

ADDRESS OF CENTRAL OFFICE:
P.O. Box 20826, Birmingham, AL 35216
ESI:65

STATISTICAL PROFILE	DATA	ESI
Grade organization: K–5/6–8/9–12		
Percentage of schools built before 1955	None†	
Total enrollment	3,399	
Average Daily Attendance (ADA)	96%	9
Current expense per pupil in ADA	$2,376	5
Dropout rate	20%	3
Percentage of eligible students who took the ACT	88%	10
Average combined score on ACT	20.2	7
Percentage of graduates who enrolled in 2- or 4-year colleges	90%	
Percentage of students who passed the state reading test	98%	
Percentage of students who passed the state math test	91%	
Teacher–student ratio in elementary grades	1:20	10
Teacher–student ratio in secondary grades	1:18	10
Counselor–student ratio in secondary grades	1:295	6
Number of students per music specialist in elementary grades	815	0
Number of students per art specialist in elementary grades	None	
Number of volumes in senior high school library	16,000	
Beginning teacher's salary	$18,000††	
Maximum teacher's salary	$28,525	
Average years of experience among teachers	13	
Number of students suspended and expelled	11	
Subjects in which Advanced Placement courses are offered: American History, Biology, Calculus, Chemistry, English Language & Composition	5	5

† The district was created after 1955.
††Teachers who lack some qualifications may start as low as $16,000.

FAIR APPRAISAL

Quality of School Leadership
Observers rate the quality of school leaders very highly. Parents may occasionally be involved in a screening committee. Principals have a say in resource allotment. Parents are very vocal, and they get a fair hearing from district officials. Sometimes parents will go over the heads of the School Board and take their case to the City Council, which controls the purse strings. For example, parent groups have been lobbying for more local funding to meet the demands of the rapidly growing district. One problem is that the Council recently annexed part of Jefferson County. The schools had to accept new students immediately, but the district gets no additional tax money for two years.

Quality of Instruction
The extra programs for bright students are good to excellent, according to the observers. The additional instruction for low-achievers also gets high marks; for example, students have access to a learning lab and to aides. The college-preparatory curriculum is excellent, and the curriculum for students not planning on college is "getting good." "Up until about three years ago," said an observer, "the 10 percent of students who did not go on to college were mostly ignored."

Quality of School Environment
The district experiences little classroom disruption and vandalism. Like most school districts in the area, Vestavia Hills has a problem finding the money to keep school buildings in good repair. Approximately $3 million was set aside in 1987 to build additions to some schools, but these funds will not aid in maintenance and repair.

METROPOLITAN AREA

Boise, ID

Two districts returned Statistical Profiles, and we received Fair Appraisals
alone from two other districts. Districts in this area may
be compared to districts in the Omaha, NE metropolitan area.

AREA AT A GLANCE

SCHOOL DISTRICT	ENROLLMENT	ESI
Boise	21,680	
Caldwell	4,200	71
Meridian	13,000	42
Mountain Home	3,552	

SCHOOL DISTRICT

BOISE

ADDRESS OF CENTRAL OFFICE:
1207 Fort Street, Boise, ID 83702
ESI:None†

STATISTICAL PROFILE	DATA	ESI
Grade organization: Pre-K–K1/1–5/6–9/10–12		
Percentage of schools built before 1955		
Total enrollment		
Average Daily Attendance (ADA)		
Current expense per pupil in ADA		
Dropout rate		
Percentage of eligible students who took the ACT		
Average combined score on ACT		
Percentage of graduates who enrolled in 2- or 4-year colleges		
Percentage of students who passed the state reading test		
Percentage of students who passed the state math test		
Teacher–student ratio in elementary grades		
Teacher–student ratio in secondary grades		
Counselor–student ratio in secondary grades		
Number of students per music specialist in elementary grades		
Number of students per art specialist in elementary grades		
Number of volumes in senior high school library		
Beginning teacher's salary		
Maximum teacher's salary		
Average years of experience among teachers		
Number of students suspended and expelled		
Subjects in which Advanced Placement courses are offered:		

†A Statistical Profile was not received from this district.

FAIR APPRAISAL

Quality of School Leadership
Principals generally are selected for their leadership abilities,
but the quality of leadership varies in the district primarily
because of a lack of lower level administrators. For example,
more supervisors are needed. Teachers and parents have little or
no say in the selection of principals, but principals have some
say in deciding the quantity and quality of resources allotted
them.

Parent groups and other citizens are only sometimes
effective. They are not a major force in decision-making.

Quality of Instruction
The additional learning opportunities available to bright
students are rated fair, but additional instruction for low-
achieving students is said to be good. Special resources teachers
help students with below-average skills and performance. Both
the curriculum for students bound for college and the
curriculum for those heading into the job market are described
as fair.

Quality of School Environment
The level of classroom disruption and vandalism is very low.
However, the quality of building maintenance and repair is only
fair. The primary reason for problems with maintenance and
repair is the lack of necessary funding.

CALDWELL

ADDRESS OF CENTRAL OFFICE:
1101 Cleveland Road, Caldwell, ID 83605
ESI:71

STATISTICAL PROFILE	DATA	ESI
Grade organization: K–3/4–5/6–7/8–9/10–12		
Percentage of schools built before 1955	66%	
Total enrollment	4,200	
Average Daily Attendance (ADA)	97%	10
Current expense per pupil in ADA	$1,726	2
Dropout rate	8%	10
Percentage of eligible students who took the ACT	52%	8
Average combined score on ACT	20.4	8
Percentage of graduates who enrolled in 2- or 4-year colleges	50%	
Percentage of students who passed the state reading test	97%	
Percentage of students who passed the state math test	94%	
Teacher–student ratio in elementary grades	1:20	10
Teacher–student ratio in secondary grades	1:17	10
Counselor–student ratio in secondary grades	1:275	7
Number of students per music specialist in elementary grades	600	3
Number of students per art specialist in elementary grades	None	
Number of volumes in senior high school library	11,000	
Beginning teacher's salary	$13,000	
Maximum teacher's salary	$26,128	
Average years of experience among teachers	14	
Number of students suspended and expelled	58	
Subjects in which Advanced Placement courses are offered: Biology, Calculus, English	3	3

FAIR APPRAISAL

Quality of School Leadership

"We have exceptional principals," said one observer. Principals are chosen for their leadership ability, and the quality is uniform throughout the district (including schools where children of migrant workers are taught). Teachers and parents don't have much say in principal selection, but principals have influence in the distribution of resources.

Schools have PTOs, which tend mostly to be fund-raisers. They do not usually take part in important decision-making. However, a group of parents and other citizens was formed in 1987 to consider a grade reorganization plan that would convert the high school from grades 10–12 to grades 9–12.

Quality of Instruction

The district offers a good program for bright students, but it is limited to a very small group of students. The standards are set too high; some very bright children are screened out. The additional instruction for low-achieving students is rated good to excellent. Special teachers serve students with learning disabilities. However, schools are generally overcrowded and special classes for low-achieving students often are placed in storage areas or other spaces not designed as classrooms. The college-preparatory curriculum is good, but lacks breadth in some areas (e.g. foreign languages). The program for students heading into the job market is not quite as good. Because of good teachers and administrators, the needs of minority students, who are mostly Hispanic, are adequately met.

Quality of School Environment

The incidence of classroom disruption and vandalism is now low, but a few years ago the schools had a problem seasonally. When migrant workers came to the area in the early spring to work in the nearby fields, the level of violence in the schools increased markedly. This condition has eased, due mainly to more counseling with students and a crackdown on fighting.

Most of the school buildings are kept in good condition, but the elementary school attended by most of the migrant workers' children is in poor shape. Water in the basement during 1986–87 destroyed thousands of dollars worth of equipment, including computers used by low-achieving students.

MERIDIAN

ADDRESS OF CENTRAL OFFICE:
911 Meridian Street, Meridian, ID 83642
ESI:42

STATISTICAL PROFILE	DATA	ESI
Grade organization: K–5/6–8/8–12		
Percentage of schools built before 1955	10%	
Total enrollment	13,000	
Average Daily Attendance (ADA)	96%	9
Current expense per pupil in ADA	$1,700	2
Dropout rate	25%	0
Percentage of eligible students who took the ACT	55%	8
Average combined score on ACT	20	6
Percentage of graduates who enrolled in 2- or 4-year colleges	50%	
Percentage of students who passed the state reading test	85%	
Percentage of students who passed the state math test	85%	
Teacher–student ratio in elementary grades	1:26	4
Teacher–student ratio in secondary grades	1:26	2
Counselor–student ratio in secondary grades	1:400	2
Number of students per music specialist in elementary grades	400	7
Number of students per art specialist in elementary grades	None	
Number of volumes in senior high school library	12,000	
Beginning teacher's salary	$12,408	
Maximum teacher's salary	$26,791	
Average years of experience among teachers	17	
Number of students suspended and expelled	260	
Subjects in which Advanced Placement courses are offered: English, American History	2	2

FAIR APPRAISAL

Quality of School Leadership

Principals generally are hired for their leadership ability, and the quality of leadership is generally uniform throughout the district. Principals sometimes rotate among the schools. A screening committee helps select candidates for principals' openings, and teachers have some say in who becomes their principal. The central office considers special requests from principals for special resources.

Parent organizations are quite strong. Parents and other citizens are active in studying district needs, recently including a tax levy proposal.

Quality of Instruction

The district offers a strong program for gifted and talented students through all grades. A special services department is in charge of instruction for the gifted and for low-achieving students. The program for low-achieving students tends to be better at the elementary level than in the high schools. College preparation and work preparation curricula are rated good; the district boasts a relatively large number of semifinalists in the National Merit Scholarship competition.

Quality of School Environment

Meridian is the largest school district in the state (larger than Boise). Therefore, it tends to have more classroom disruption and vandalism than smaller districts, but the level of disturbances is not high (an expulsion–suspension rate of 2 percent is not high). The School Board is behind in school maintenance and repair. A state-imposed ceiling on taxes limits the district's overall budget; consequently, funds for building upkeep are cut first.

MOUNTAIN HOME

ADDRESS OF CENTRAL OFFICE:
P.O. Box 890, Mountain Home, ID 83647
ESI:None†

STATISTICAL PROFILE	DATA	ESI
Grade organization:		
Percentage of schools built before 1955		
Total enrollment		
Average Daily Attendance (ADA)		
Current expense per pupil in ADA		
Dropout rate		
Percentage of eligible students who took the ACT		
Average combined score on ACT		
Percentage of graduates who enrolled in 2- or 4-year colleges		
Percentage of students who passed the state reading test		
Percentage of students who passed the state math test		
Teacher–student ratio in elementary grades		
Teacher–student ratio in secondary grades		
Counselor–student ratio in secondary grades		
Number of students per music specialist in elementary grades		
Number of students per art specialist in elementary grades		
Number of volumes in senior high school library		
Beginning teacher's salary		
Maximum teacher's salary		
Average years of experience among teachers		
Number of students suspended and expelled		
Subjects in which Advanced Placement courses are offered:		

†A Statistical Profile was not received from this district.

FAIR APPRAISAL

Quality of School Leadership

The district selects principals for their leadership ability, and the quality of leadership is uniform throughout the schools. Teachers, parents and other citizens have a major say in principal selection. Candidates appear at a public forum where they may be questioned by all present. Principals, in turn, have a great deal to say about the quality and quantity of resources allotted their schools.

Parents generally are effective in the decision-making process. Usually they make their positions known through local parent–teacher groups.

Quality of Instruction

The program for gifted students is rated excellent, and so is the program for low-achieving students. The curricula for college-bound students and for students heading into the world of work get high marks. The district adequately meets the needs of minority students (mostly Hispanic).

Quality of School Environment

The level of classroom disruption and vandalism is very low, and observers report that buildings are well-maintained and kept in good repair.

Boston, MA

Fifteen school districts completed Statistical Profiles. Fair Appraisals alone
are provided for an additional four districts. Districts in this area
may be compared to districts in the Newark, NJ metropolitan area.

AREA AT A GLANCE

SCHOOL DISTRICT	ENROLLMENT	ESI
Andover	4,718	71
Arlington	4,300	75
Belmont	3,057	67*
Braintree	4,744	62*
Cambridge	7,905	67
Canton	2,610	
Dedham	2,909	60
Easton	3,234	72
Framingham	8,049	71
Lexington	4,564	88
Lynn	11,102	
Natick	4,097	79
Norwood	3,500	64*
Revere	4,848	25
Somerville	6,696	
Wakefield	3,468	
Waltham	5,687	60
Watertown	2,747	60
Wellesley	3,085	89
Winchester	3,000	77

Indicates district misinterpretation of one or more statistics in the ESI. For each misinterpreted statistic, a score of 0 was given instead of a possible score of 0 to 10 points.

ANDOVER

ADDRESS OF CENTRAL OFFICE:
36 Bartlet Street, Andover, MA 01810
ESI:71

STATISTICAL PROFILE	DATA	ESI
Grade organization: K/1–6/7–9/10–12		
Percentage of schools built before 1955	73%	
Total enrollment	4,718	
Average Daily Attendance (ADA)	96%	9
Current expense per pupil in ADA	$3,092	0
Dropout rate	5%	10
Percentage of eligible students who took the SAT	80%	10
Average combined score on SAT	906	5
Percentage of graduates who enrolled in 2- or 4-year colleges	70%	
Percentage of students who passed the state reading test	100%	
Percentage of students who passed the state math test	100%	
Teacher–student ratio in elementary grades	1:24	6
Teacher–student ratio in secondary grades	1:20	8
Counselor–student ratio in secondary grades	1:220	9
Number of students per music specialist in elementary grades	430	7
Number of students per art specialist in elementary grades	430	
Number of volumes in senior high school library	23,500	
Beginning teacher's salary	$16,544	
Maximum teacher's salary	$35,709	
Average years of experience among teachers	20	
Number of students suspended and expelled	NK	
Subjects in which Advanced Placement courses are offered:	7	7
American History, Biology, Calculus, English, European History, French, Spanish		

FAIR APPRAISAL

Quality of School Leadership
Principals are selected for their leadership abilities; teachers normally are involved in the screening of principal candidates. Principals have some say in the resources allotted their school, but, as in nearly all Massachusetts districts, budget constraints resulting from a state referendum do not allow much flexibility.

Parent organizations are sometimes effective in decision-making, but many of their activities are limited to raising extra funds for school equipment and supplies.

Quality of Instruction
The district has a good program for gifted and talented children, but it is described as "nothing special." The additional instruction for low-achieving students is rated as fair, although district officials are "addressing" this need. The curricula for college-bound and job-bound students are termed good.

The district provides a special program for a dozen or so high school students (mostly black) who move to the area temporarily from other parts of the country. They are housed in a dormitory.

Quality of School Environment
Classroom disruption and vandalism are not a problem. School buildings, although most of them are 30 years old or older, are well maintained.

ARLINGTON

ADDRESS OF CENTRAL OFFICE:
869 Massachusetts Avenue, Arlington, MA 02174
ESI:75

STATISTICAL PROFILE	DATA	ESI
Grade organization: K–6/7–8/9–12		
Percentage of schools built before 1955	70%	
Total enrollment	4,300	
Average Daily Attendance (ADA)	95%	8
Current expense per pupil in ADA	$3,504	2
Dropout rate	5%	10
Percentage of eligible students who took the SAT	60%	9
Average combined score on SAT	936	6
Percentage of graduates who enrolled in 2- or 4-year colleges	80%	
Percentage of students who passed the state reading test	95%	
Percentage of students who passed the state math test	94%	
Teacher–student ratio in elementary grades	1:18	10
Teacher–student ratio in secondary grades	1:21	7
Counselor–student ratio in secondary grades	1:250	8
Number of students per music specialist in elementary grades	250	10
Number of students per art specialist in elementary grades	700	
Number of volumes in senior high school library	40,000†	
Beginning teacher's salary	$17,295	
Maximum teacher's salary	$32,691	
Average years of experience among teachers	17	
Number of students suspended and expelled	NK	
Subjects in which Advanced Placement courses are offered:	5	5
American History, Calculus, Computer Science, English Language and Composition, Spanish		

†This figure seems very high; district could not verify when queried.

Quality of School Leadership

Principals are picked for their educational leadership ability, and the quality of leadership does not vary greatly from school to school. Teachers and parents have a great deal to say about who is hired as principal of their school. A screening committee composed of teachers and parents interviews each candidate and advises the superintendent. Principals have some say about resources allotted their school.

The district has a "strong sense of neighborhood," said one observer, and parent effectiveness varies from school to school. However, most principals invite parents to advise them on how to spend a small discretionary fund provided directly by the state (usually less than $5,000).

Quality of Instruction

Additional learning opportunities for gifted students and help for low-achieving students are rated good. In the elementary and middle schools, bright students meet with a special coordinator for 1½ hours each week to receive advanced instruction. Any student with a learning problem can meet with any teacher after school on Mondays, Tuesdays and Thursdays. Teachers stay an extra 45 minutes on those days to give special help. On Wednesday afternoons throughout the school year, teachers are available to meet with parents (students attend in the morning only on Wednesdays).

The college preparatory program is rated good to excellent. Parents are encouraged to help their children select courses. While this is generally a plus, one observer said it is still possible for students to reject courses required for college admission. The program for job preparation is termed good; a regional vocational school offers training in high-tech jobs. The district meets the needs of minority students, including about 60 children bused daily from Boston.

Quality of School Environment

The incidence of classroom disruption and school vandalism is low. School buildings generally are well-maintained, although budget constraints have hurt. As in many Massachusetts communities, major repairs to school buildings often are performed by workers employed by the municipality.

BELMONT

ADDRESS OF CENTRAL OFFICE:
644 Pleasant Street, Belmont, MA 02178
ESI:67*

STATISTICAL PROFILE	DATA	ESI
Grade organization: K–5/6–8/9–12		
Total enrollment	3,057	
Average Daily Attendance (ADA)	90%	3
Current expense per pupil in ADA	$3,537	2
Dropout rate	2%	10
Percentage of eligible students who took the SAT	90%	10
Average combined score on SAT	991	9
Percentage of graduates who enrolled in 2- or 4-year colleges	88%	
Percentage of students who passed the state reading test	89%	
Percentage of students who passed the state math test	89%	
Teacher–student ratio in elementary grades	1:13	10
Teacher–student ratio in secondary grades	1:13	10
Counselor–student ratio in secondary grades	1:200	9
Number of students per music specialist in elementary grades	†	0*
Number of students per art specialist in elementary grades	†	
Number of volumes in senior high school library	16,000	
Beginning teacher's salary	$18,444	
Maximum teacher's salary	$36,998	
Average years of experience among teachers	15	
Number of students suspended and expelled	104	
Subjects in which Advanced Placement courses are offered: American History, Calculus, Computer Science, European History	4	4

†The district misinterpreted these statistics.

Quality of School Leadership
Principals mostly are young men and women hired for their educational leadership ability. Most candidates come from outside the district. Committees that include teachers, parents and other community residents generally meet to interview and rate candidates for principal jobs. Principals have some say in resource allotments.

Parent organizations are an effective influence on decision-making. They were instrumental in passing a proposal to raise more than $10 million for renovations to two elementary schools.

Quality of Instruction
Fair to good is how the observers rate additional learning opportunities for gifted students. Some special help for bright students was cut because of budget restrictions. The college preparatory program is considered good to excellent. With 88 percent of graduates going on to some college, the entire curriculum is geared toward these students. However, the program for students heading into the job market also is rated good.

Quality of School Environment
Classroom disruption and vandalism are not problems in the district. School building maintenance and repair are rated good.

BRAINTREE

ADDRESS OF CENTRAL OFFICE:
482 Washington Street, Braintree, MA 02184
ESI:62*

STATISTICAL PROFILE	DATA	ESI
Grade organization:	†	
Total enrollment	4,744	
Average Daily Attendance (ADA)	95%	8
Current expense per pupil in ADA	$3,870	4
Dropout rate	13%	10
Percentage of eligible students who took the SAT	75%	10
Average combined score on SAT	892	4
Percentage of graduates who enrolled in 2- or 4-year colleges	70%	
Percentage of students who passed the state reading test	98%	
Percentage of students who passed the state math test	98%	
Teacher–student ratio in elementary grades	1:20	10
Teacher–student ratio in secondary grades	1:27	1
Counselor–student ratio in secondary grades	1:26††	0*
Number of students per music specialist in elementary grades	500	5
Number of students per art specialist in elementary grades	668	
Number of volumes in senior high school library	19,000	
Beginning teacher's salary	$15,518	
Maximum teacher's salary	$32,614	
Average years of experience among teachers	14	
Number of students suspended and expelled	297	
Subjects in which Advanced Placement courses are offered: American History, Biology, Calculus, Chemistry, Computer Science, English, European History, French, Physics, Spanish	10	10

† The district misinterpreted this statistic.
††The figure seems exceptionally low and is probably not accurate.

FAIR APPRAISAL

Quality of School Leadership

Most principals are selected from among candidates within the district, and they are picked for their educational leadership ability. Quality of leadership is uniform throughout the district. No special process for screening principal candidates exists, although parents often make their views known about candidates by speaking to members of the School Board. Principals have some say in deciding what resources their school will be allotted.

Parents are instrumental in decision-making. "We have a tradition here," said one observer "that if there's a change being made, parents come out in droves." The League of Women Voters also is active. During the 1987–88 school year, the LWV is expected to study stress on students and teachers in the middle school.

Quality of Instruction

The program for gifted students is considered good. Special assignments in reading and writing are offered to bright students in the lower and middle grades. Additional instruction for low-achieving students also is rated good. The college preparatory curriculum is given high marks and so is the program for students going on to the job market. However, one observer defined the "good" rating in this case as meaning "adequate." Like many of the districts surrounding Boston, Braintree takes part in the METCO project and voluntarily educates minority students bused in from the city.

Quality of School Environment

The level of classroom disruption and vandalism is now considered low, but observers reported some major incidents of vandalism in the recent past, including the "plowing up" of the high school athletic field a couple of years ago. One observer said the School Board accepts reports of vandalism without directing any prevention program. School building maintenance and repair are rated good.

CAMBRIDGE

ADDRESS OF CENTRAL OFFICE:
159 Thorndike Street, Cambridge, MA 02141
ESI:67

STATISTICAL PROFILE	DATA	ESI
Grade organization:	†	
Percentage of schools built before 1955	50%	
Total enrollment	7,905	
Average Daily Attendance (ADA)	91%	4
Current expense per pupil in ADA	$6,852	10
Dropout rate	24%	0
Percentage of eligible students who took the SAT	55%	8
Average combined score on SAT	831	1
Percentage of graduates who enrolled in 2- or 4-year colleges	55%	
Percentage of students who passed the state reading test	85%	
Percentage of students who passed the state math test	84%	
Teacher–student ratio in elementary grades	1:21	9
Teacher–student ratio in secondary grades	1:12	10
Counselor–student ratio in secondary grades	1:116	10
Number of students per music specialist in elementary grades	236	10
Number of students per art specialist in elementary grades	472	
Number of volumes in senior high school library	19,000	
Beginning teacher's salary	$18,466	
Maximum teacher's salary	$34,467	
Average years of experience among teachers	20	
Number of students suspended and expelled	777	
Subjects in which Advanced Placement courses are offered: Biology, Calculus, Chemistry, English, U.S. History	5	5

†The district misinterpreted this statistic.

Quality of School Leadership

Principals are selected for their leadership ability, and the quality of leadership has improved in recent years. A new superintendent "pinpointed" the weaker schools and set out to upgrade their leadership and program. Principal candidates are screened by committees composed of teachers and parents. Principals have some say in how resources are distributed.

Parents are effective in decision-making. As in all Massachusetts districts now, each school has a School Improvement Council that includes parents. The councils help decide how a small amount of discretionary funds will be spent. Also, each elementary school has a paid parent–community liaison. This person is responsible for making the views of parents and other residents known to school officials when important decisions are to be made. Parents played an active role in 1981 when the district devised its voluntary desegregation plan.

Quality of Instruction

Special learning opportunities exist for gifted students primarily in grades 6–8. A strong tutoring program is available to low-achieving students, and the district offers a comprehensive bilingual program in six different languages. The college-preparatory program is rated fair to good. "The district has an excellent arts program," said one observer, "but is a little lax in math and science." The district does not believe in a formal tracking system, so a "college-prep track" does not exist as such. However, students are able to select courses that will prepare them for college. For example, the district has five Advanced Placement courses. Preparation for the world of work is rated good. A special program trains students for restaurant management, and students run a restaurant on the high school campus. The school system adequately meets the needs of a large and diverse minority population.

Quality of School Environment

When the district built a new high school in 1977, people said officials made a mistake including so much glass in the building. They predicted widespread breakage by vandals. But it hasn't happened, and classroom disruption and vandalism generally are not problems. Buildings are kept in good repair and are clean.

CANTON

ADDRESS OF CENTRAL OFFICE:
960 Washington Street, Canton, MA 02021
ESI:None†

STATISTICAL PROFILE	DATA	ESI
Grade organization:		
Percentage of schools built before 1955		
Total enrollment		
Average Daily Attendance (ADA)		
Current expense per pupil in ADA		
Dropout rate		
Percentage of eligible students who took the SAT		
Average combined score on SAT		
Percentage of graduates who enrolled in 2- or 4-year colleges		
Percentage of students who passed the state reading test		
Percentage of students who passed the state math test		
Teacher–student ratio in elementary grades		
Teacher–student ratio in secondary grades		
Counselor–student ratio in secondary grades		
Number of students per music specialist in elementary grades		
Number of students per art specialist in elementary grades		
Number of volumes in senior high school library		
Beginning teacher's salary		
Maximum teacher's salary		
Average years of experience among teachers		
Number of students suspended and expelled		
Subjects in which Advanced Placement courses are offered:		

†A Statistical Profile was not received from this district.

FAIR APPRAISAL

Quality of School Leadership
Principals are hired for their leadership ability, and the quality of leadership is fairly uniform throughout the district. Teachers, parents and other community residents serve on committees that interview candidates for principal. Principals have a major say in how resources are allotted to individual schools.

Parent organizations generally are effective. "Pressure on the School [Board] gets great results when it is organized," said an observer.

Quality of Instruction
Programs for gifted and low-achieving students are rated good. A special teacher is in charge of activities for bright students, and they are eligible to attend classes for gifted students at a nearby private academy. The curricula for college-bound students and those going directly into the work force are considered good. The honors classes are rated excellent.

Quality of School Environment
The level of classroom disruption and vandalism is low. Maintenance and repair of buildings suffer a little because of budget constraints.

DEDHAM

ADDRESS OF CENTRAL OFFICE:
30 Whiting Avenue, Dedham, MA 02026
ESI:60

STATISTICAL PROFILE	DATA	ESI
Grade organization: K–6/7–8/9–12		
Percentage of schools built before 1955	33%	
Total enrollment	2,909	
Average Daily Attendance (ADA)	95%	8
Current expense per pupil in ADA	$3,000	0
Dropout rate	2%	10
Percentage of eligible students who took the SAT	73%	10
Average combined score on SAT	887	4
Percentage of graduates who enrolled in 2- or 4-year colleges	68%	
Percentage of students who passed the state reading test	99%	
Percentage of students who passed the state math test	99%	
Teacher–student ratio in elementary grades	1:20	10
Teacher–student ratio in secondary grades	1:22	6
Counselor–student ratio in secondary grades	1:240	8
Number of students per music specialist in elementary grades	600	3
Number of students per art specialist in elementary grades	600	
Number of volumes in senior high school library	14,000	
Beginning teacher's salary	$18,200	
Maximum teacher's salary	$35,194	
Average years of experience among teachers	15	
Number of students suspended and expelled	35	
Subjects in which Advanced Placement courses are offered:	1	1
Calculus		

FAIR APPRAISAL

Quality of School Leadership
Most principals are selected for their leadership ability, and the quality of leadership is generally uniform throughout the district. Committees of teachers, parents and other administrators screen principal candidates and make recommendations to the superintendent. Principals have some say in how resources are distributed.

Parents are sometimes effective in decision-making. PTAs have minimal influence, and are especially weak at the secondary level.

Quality of Instruction
The School Board expected to hire for the 1987–88 school year a specialist to guide programs for gifted students. Schools have resource rooms to assist low-achieving students. The college-preparatory curriculum is rated fair to good. "There should be more higher-level courses," said an observer (the district offers only one Advanced Placement course). Students who opt for the world of work can attend a good regional vocational school. The district adequately meets the educational needs of minority students.

Quality of School Environment
The level of classroom disruption and vandalism is low, and the quality of building maintenance and repair is rated excellent.

EASTON

ADDRESS OF CENTRAL OFFICE:
Lincoln Street, North Easton, MA 02356
ESI:72

STATISTICAL PROFILE	DATA	ESI
Grade organization: K–5/6/7–9/10–12		
Percentage of schools built before 1955	80%	
Total enrollment	3,234	
Average Daily Attendance (ADA)	96%	9
Current expense per pupil in ADA	$3,007	0
Dropout rate	2%	10
Percentage of eligible students who took the SAT	63%	10
Average combined score on SAT	935	6
Percentage of graduates who enrolled in 2- or 4-year colleges	†	
Percentage of students who passed the state reading test	NK	
Percentage of students who passed the state math test	NK	
Teacher–student ratio in elementary grades	1:22	10
Teacher–student ratio in secondary grades	1:16	10
Counselor–student ratio in secondary grades	1:275	7
Number of students per music specialist in elementary grades	400	7
Number of students per art specialist in elementary grades	400	
Number of volumes in senior high school library	13,065	
Beginning teacher's salary	$19,033	
Maximum teacher's salary	$36,559	
Average years of experience among teachers	14	
Number of students suspended and expelled	35	
Subjects in which Advanced Placement courses are offered: English, Calculus, U.S. History	3	3

†The district misinterpreted this statistic.

FAIR APPRAISAL

Quality of School Leadership
Principals are chosen for their leadership ability, and the quality of leadership does not vary greatly throughout the district. No special means exist for screening principal candidates outside the review by the chief school administrator and School Board. Principals have a great deal to say about how resources are allotted. Indeed, some persons believe certain schools are targeted to get more books, more field trips, and more outside speakers than other schools.

The schools have Parent Advisory Councils that are sometimes effective in making decisions.

Quality of Instruction
What an observer calls "high ability learning" is available for bright students at all levels from grade 3. The instruction for low-achieving students is rated fair to good. The curricula for college-bound students and for students choosing the world of work are rated good. The educational needs of minority students are adequately met.

Quality of School Environment
Classroom disruption and vandalism are not major problems. The quality of building maintenance and repair is good.

FRAMINGHAM

ADDRESS OF CENTRAL OFFICE:
454 Water Street, Framingham, MA 01701
ESI:71

STATISTICAL PROFILE	DATA	ESI
Grade organization: K–6/7–8/9–12		
Percentage of schools built before 1955	21%	
Total enrollment	8,049	
Average Daily Attendance (ADA)	92%	5
Current expense per pupil in ADA	$3,716	3
Dropout rate	13%	10
Percentage of eligible students who took the SAT	92%	10
Average combined score on SAT	933	6
Percentage of graduates who enrolled in 2- or 4-year colleges	80%	
Percentage of students who passed the state reading test	94%	
Percentage of students who passed the state math test	92%	
Teacher–student ratio in elementary grades	1:23	7
Teacher–student ratio in secondary grades	1:15	10
Counselor–student ratio in secondary grades	1:228	8
Number of students per music specialist in elementary grades	460	6
Number of students per art specialist in elementary grades	460	
Number of volumes in senior high school library	7,500	
Beginning teacher's salary	$16,782	
Maximum teacher's salary	$33,678	
Average years of experience among teachers	15	
Number of students suspended and expelled	1,461	
Subjects in which Advanced Placement courses are offered: Biology, Calculus, Chemistry, English, Physics, U.S. History	6	6

FAIR APPRAISAL

Quality of School Leadership
The district generally hires principals for their leadership ability, but there is some question as to whether the quality of leadership is uniform throughout the district. Observers report that the district is roughly divided into north and south sections, with the north section being the more affluent area. Schools in this part of the district sometimes are treated better when it comes to leadership and also to the allotment of resources. Principal candidates usually are screened only by the chief school administrator and other top administrators.

Parent organizations are considered effective. For example, they have studied demographics, class size, building capacity and other factors in connection with a plan for student reassignments.

Quality of Instruction
The programs for gifted students and low-achieving students are rated good. Observers also give high marks to the college-preparatory and job-training curricula. The district partially meets the needs of minority students.

Quality of School Environment
The level of classroom disruption and vandalism is rated low. (However, the district's report of 1,461 suspensions, about 18 percent of the student body, might be considered high.) The quality of building maintenance and repair is rated good, but one observer said both high schools are in need of substantial repairs.

LEXINGTON

ADDRESS OF CENTRAL OFFICE:
1557 Massachusetts Avenue, Lexington, MA 02173
ESI:88

STATISTICAL PROFILE	DATA	ESI
Grade organization: K–5/6–8/9–12		
Percentage of schools built before 1955	25%	
Total enrollment	4,564	
Average Daily Attendance (ADA)	97%	10
Current expense per pupil in ADA	$4,606	7
Dropout rate	3%	10
Percentage of eligible students who took the SAT	93%	10
Average combined score on SAT	1,017	10
Percentage of graduates who enrolled in 2- or 4-year colleges	87%	
Percentage of students who passed the state reading test	97%	
Percentage of students who passed the state math test	95%	
Teacher–student ratio in elementary grades	1:24	6
Teacher–student ratio in secondary grades	1:15	10
Counselor–student ratio in secondary grades	1:230	8
Number of students per music specialist in elementary grades	390	8
Number of students per art specialist in elementary grades	428	
Number of volumes in senior high school library	30,000	
Beginning teacher's salary	$17,900	
Maximum teacher's salary	$38,340	
Average years of experience among teachers	NK	
Number of students suspended and expelled	NK	
Subjects in which Advanced Placement courses are offered:	9	9
American History, Biology, Calculus, Chemistry, English Composition, English Literature, French, Physics, Spanish		

FAIR APPRAISAL

Quality of School Leadership

No new principals have been hired since 1981–82, but principals are normally hired for their leadership ability (although one observer said that a candidate's longevity in the district helps). Screening committees that include administrators, teachers, parents and students interview principal candidates and make recommendations to the superintendent. One observer, speaking of school leadership, said principals are "getting much too old and settled." Principals have some say in the resources that are given their school by the central office.

Parents are effective in influencing school decision-making.

Quality of Instruction

The additional learning opportunities for gifted students are rated good to excellent; the program in the elementary grades is the weakest link. The observers rate as good the instruction for low-achieving students. The curriculum for college-bound students gets very high marks. A wide variety of high-level courses is offered. The high school debating team won its first national championship in 1985–86 and its eighth consecutive state championship. An elementary school math team won first place in the 1985–86 National Continental Mathematics League and the New England Mathematics League. The curriculum for students going into the job market is rated fair to good.

Lexington has taken part in the METCO program for 20 years; in 1986–87, more than 250 minority students from Boston were educated in Lexington schools.

Quality of School Environment

The level of classroom disruption and vandalism is low. The quality of building maintenance and repair is rated fair to good. Voters recently approved a plan to spend $12 million on building renovations and improvements over the next two years.

LYNN

ADDRESS OF CENTRAL OFFICE:
42 Franklin Street, Lynn, MA 01902
ESI:None†

STATISTICAL PROFILE	DATA	ESI
Grade organization:		
Percentage of schools built before 1955		
Total enrollment		
Average Daily Attendance (ADA)		
Current expense per pupil in ADA		
Dropout rate		
Percentage of eligible students who took the SAT		
Average combined score on SAT		
Percentage of graduates who enrolled in 2- or 4-year colleges		
Percentage of students who passed the state reading test		
Percentage of students who passed the state math test		
Teacher–student ratio in elementary grades		
Teacher–student ratio in secondary grades		
Counselor–student ratio in secondary grades		
Number of students per music specialist in elementary grades		
Number of students per art specialist in elementary grades		
Number of volumes in senior high school library		
Beginning teacher's salary		
Maximum teacher's salary		
Average years of experience among teachers		
Number of students suspended and expelled		
Subjects in which Advanced Placement courses are offered:		

†A Statistical Profile was not received from this district.

FAIR APPRAISAL

Quality of School Leadership
Politics ("who you know") plays some part in principal selection. Teachers and parents have hardly any say in principal selection, and principals do not have much say in how resources are disbursed to the schools.

Parents are sometimes effective in decision-making, but they are not a strong influence.

Quality of Instruction
Programs for gifted and low-achieving students are rated as fair, as are the curricula for students going to college and into the world of work. The needs of minority students are not well met.

Quality of School Environment
The level of classroom disruption and vandalism is low, but the quality of building maintenance and repair is considered only fair. One observer attributed the problems in maintenance and repair to "lack of adequate supervision from both principals and the maintenance supervisor."

NATICK

ADDRESS OF CENTRAL OFFICE:
13 East Central Street, Natick, MA 01760
ESI:79

STATISTICAL PROFILE	DATA	ESI
Grade organization: K–5/6–8/9–12		
Percentage of schools built before 1955	40%	
Total enrollment	4,097	
Average Daily Attendance (ADA)	95%	8
Current expense per pupil in ADA	$3,565	2
Dropout rate	3%	10
Percentage of eligible students who took the SAT	62%	10
Average combined score on SAT	1,066	10
Percentage of graduates who enrolled in 2- or 4-year colleges	63%	
Percentage of students who passed the state reading test	98%	
Percentage of students who passed the state math test	98%	
Teacher–student ratio in elementary grades	1:20	10
Teacher–student ratio in secondary grades	1:18	10
Counselor–student ratio in secondary grades	1:200	9
Number of students per music specialist in elementary grades	400	7
Number of students per art specialist in elementary grades	400	
Number of volumes in senior high school library	31,630	
Beginning teacher's salary	$19,000	
Maximum teacher's salary	$35,000	
Average years of experience among teachers	20	
Number of students suspended and expelled	NK	
Subjects in which Advanced Placement courses are offered: Calculus, English, Science	3	3

FAIR APPRAISAL

Quality of School Leadership

Principals are hired because of their educational leadership ability. However, most principals hired recently have been from within the district, so longevity helps. The quality of leadership is uniform throughout the district. Parents and teachers serve on screening committees that interview principal candidates and make recommendations to the superintendent. Principals have a lot to say about the resources allotted their schools.

Parent organizations are very effective. A Parent Coordinating Council was recently active in getting five high school teaching positions retained after the superintendent announced they would be cut because of a slight drop in enrollment. The Council also was instrumental in getting the Town Meeting (where most budget matters are decided in Massachusetts) to restore approximately $100,000 that the town finance committee had sought to slash.

Quality of Instruction

The additional opportunities for gifted students are rated good. For example, bright elementary-school students, beginning in grade 4, can spend part of one day each week getting special instruction at one of the middle schools. Special help also is available to low-achieving students. "Some persons feel too much money is spent on low-achieving students," said one observer. The college-preparatory curriculum is rated high; counselors give students good advice on college preparation. Students going into the job market after graduation are well-prepared. Some internship programs exist with local businesses and industries.

Quality of School Environment

The level of classroom disruption and vandalism is low. School building maintenance and repair are improving. Approximately $3 million was spent recently to renovate the high school; another $3 million will be spent on other schools in the next few years.

NORWOOD

ADDRESS OF CENTRAL OFFICE:
P.O. Box 67, Norwood, MA 02062
ESI:64*

STATISTICAL PROFILE	DATA	ESI
Grade organization: K–6/7–9/10–12		
Percentage of schools built before 1955	50%	
Total enrollment	3,500	
Average Daily Attendance (ADA)	93%	6
Current expense per pupil in ADA	$3,546	2
Dropout rate	7%	10
Percentage of eligible students who took the SAT	85%	10
Average combined score on SAT	900	4
Percentage of graduates who enrolled in 2- or 4-year colleges	80%	
Percentage of students who passed the state reading test	95%	
Percentage of students who passed the state math test	92%	
Teacher–student ratio in elementary grades	1:21	9
Teacher–student ratio in secondary grades	1:22	6
Counselor–student ratio in secondary grades	1:183	10
Number of students per music specialist in elementary grades	†	0*
Number of students per art specialist in elementary grades	†	
Number of volumes in senior high school library	13,428	
Beginning teacher's salary	$16,919	
Maximum teacher's salary	$32,885	
Average years of experience among teachers	20	
Number of students suspended and expelled	NK	
Subjects in which Advanced Placement courses are offered:	7	7
Art, Biology, Chemistry, Computer Science, English, Physics, U.S. History		

†The district misinterpreted this statistic.

Quality of School Leadership
The district chooses principals who have educational leadership ability; quality of leadership is high throughout the district. Teachers and parents have some say in principal selection, and principals have some say in what resources are given to schools.

Parent organizations are effective. Parents recently served with teachers and administrators on a special committee to conduct a needs assessment on early childhood education.

Quality of Instruction
A gifted and talented program exists and is rated good. A new program at the high school, which offers more individual instruction, has added to a good program for low-achieving students. The curricula for college-bound students and work-bound students are rated good.

Quality of School Environment
Classroom disruption and vandalism are not big problems. Renovation of the high school was completed in the spring of 1986; otherwise, maintenance and repair in the district are rated good.

REVERE

ADDRESS OF CENTRAL OFFICE:
101 School Street, Revere, MA 02151
ESI:25

STATISTICAL PROFILE	DATA	ESI
Grade organization: K–8/9–12		
Percentage of schools built before 1955	NK	
Total enrollment	4,848	
Average Daily Attendance (ADA)	90%	3
Current expense per pupil in ADA	$3,360	1
Dropout rate	26%	0
Percentage of eligible students who took the SAT	45%	6
Average combined score on SAT	800	0
Percentage of graduates who enrolled in 2- or 4-year colleges	60%	
Percentage of students who passed the state reading test	95%	
Percentage of students who passed the state math test	96%	
Teacher–student ratio in elementary grades	1:24	6
Teacher–student ratio in secondary grades	1:23	5
Counselor–student ratio in secondary grades	1:337	4
Number of students per music specialist in elementary grades	750	0
Number of students per art specialist in elementary grades	750	
Number of volumes in senior high school library	30,000	
Beginning teacher's salary	$16,258	
Maximum teacher's salary	$35,737	
Average years of experience among teachers	15	
Number of students suspended and expelled	NK	
Subjects in which Advanced Placement courses are offered:	NK	0

Quality of School Leadership

Longevity in the district seems to be an important criterion in principal selection. Most principals are chosen from within the district. Actually, there will not be any hiring of new principals for some time because when the district closed four or five schools four years ago, the principals of those schools were kept on in other jobs. When principalships open up in the future, these persons must be given the positions. Teachers and parents have hardly any say in principal selection, but principals have a great deal to say about the resources allotted their schools.

Parent organizations are effective in the decision-making process. A few years ago, parents were involved in curriculum revision. More recently, parents were influential in pushing the School Board and Town Council into asking the state for help in building a new school to replace an ancient one.

Quality of Instruction

It was expected that the School Board would reinstate in the fall of 1987 a gifted and talented program for grades 5–8 that was phased out four years ago because of budget cuts. The program for low-achieving students is rated fair. Some principals care more than others and push for special help, said one observer. Another observer said the attitude at some schools is "get 'em in and get 'em out." The college-preparatory program is rated good to excellent. However, one observer said guidance counselors discourage some students from aiming high. A case was cited where a student was advised to consider a state four-year college or even a local two-year college, but the student went ahead and applied to and was accepted by a highly competitive private college. The job-preparation curriculum is rated good.

Quality of School Environment

Class disruption and vandalism are not problems. Building maintenance and repair are rated as fair. "We need a plan for preventative maintenance," said one observer.

SOMERVILLE

ADDRESS OF CENTRAL OFFICE:
93 School Street, Somerville, MA 02143
ESI:None†

STATISTICAL PROFILE	DATA	ESI
Grade organization:		
Percentage of schools built before 1955		
Total enrollment		
Average Daily Attendance (ADA)		
Current expense per pupil in ADA		
Dropout rate		
Percentage of eligible students who took the SAT		
Average combined score on SAT		
Percentage of graduates who enrolled in 2- or 4-year colleges		
Percentage of students who passed the state reading test		
Percentage of students who passed the state math test		
Teacher–student ratio in elementary grades		
Teacher–student ratio in secondary grades		
Counselor–student ratio in secondary grades		
Number of students per music specialist in elementary grades		
Number of students per art specialist in elementary grades		
Number of volumes in senior high school library		
Beginning teacher's salary		
Maximum teacher's salary		
Average years of experience among teachers		
Number of students suspended and expelled		
Subjects in which Advanced Placement courses are offered:		

†A Statistical Profile was not received from this district.

FAIR APPRAISAL

Quality of School Leadership

The district hires principals for their educational leadership ability. Teachers and parents have some say in principal selection through interviews, and principals have a great deal to say about how the district's resources are divided among the schools.

Parent organizations are effective; Parent Advisory Councils and PTAs exist at each school.

Quality of Instruction

The additional learning opportunities for gifted students are rated only fair, but additional instruction for low-achieving students is considered excellent. High marks are given to the curricula for college-bound students and those bound for the job market. Speaking of the overall instructional program, an observer said, "This is a parent-involved community; quality has to be good."

Quality of School Environment

The incidence of classroom disruption and vandalism is low, and the quality of building maintenance and repair is rated excellent. "Custodial service is top notch," said an observer.

WAKEFIELD

ADDRESS OF CENTRAL OFFICE:
525 Main Street, Wakefield, MA 01880
ESI:None†

STATISTICAL PROFILE	DATA	ESI
Grade organization:		
Percentage of schools built before 1955		
Total enrollment		
Average Daily Attendance (ADA)		
Current expense per pupil in ADA		
Dropout rate		
Percentage of eligible students who took the SAT		
Average combined score on SAT		
Percentage of graduates who enrolled in 2- or 4-year colleges		
Percentage of students who passed the state reading test		
Percentage of students who passed the state math test		
Teacher–student ratio in elementary grades		
Teacher–student ratio in secondary grades		
Counselor–student ratio in secondary grades		
Number of students per music specialist in elementary grades		
Number of students per art specialist in elementary grades		
Number of volumes in senior high school library		
Beginning teacher's salary		
Maximum teacher's salary		
Average years of experience among teachers		
Number of students suspended and expelled		
Subjects in which Advanced Placement courses are offered:		

†A Statistical Profile was not received from this district.

FAIR APPRAISAL

Quality of School Leadership

Principals are picked for their leadership ability, and the quality of leadership does not vary greatly from school to school. Principal candidates are interviewed at a public meeting by the School Board; parents and other citizens may offer comments and ask questions. Principals have some say in the distribution of resources to their schools.

Parents are effective in decision-making. They make public statements, write letters, and make phone calls to make their voices heard.

Quality of Instruction

An "above-average ability" program exists for bright students in grades 4, 5 and 6, and the high school offers Advanced Placement courses. The college-preparatory curriculum is rated excellent; the program for students entering the world of work is good. Speaking of the overall instructional program, an observer said, "It varies a bit, as everywhere, but generally it is quite competent."

Quality of School Environment

The level of classroom disruption and vandalism is low, and the quality of building maintenance and repair is rated good. Said one observer, "School buildings vary widely in age, but all are kept up, including the beautiful 1847 two-room West Ward School (used only for kindergarten and grade 1)."

WALTHAM

ADDRESS OF CENTRAL OFFICE:
488 Main Street, Waltham, MA 02254
ESI:60

STATISTICAL PROFILE	DATA	ESI
Grade organization: K–5/6–8/9–12		
Percentage of schools built before 1955	85%	
Total enrollment	5,687	
Average Daily Attendance (ADA)	95%	8
Current expense per pupil in ADA	$4,000	4
Dropout rate	2%	10
Percentage of eligible students who took the SAT	60%	10
Average combined score on SAT	860	2
Percentage of graduates who enrolled in 2- or 4-year colleges	53%	
Percentage of students who passed the state reading test	93%	
Percentage of students who passed the state math test	96%	
Teacher–student ratio in elementary grades	1:18	10
Teacher–student ratio in secondary grades	1:20	8
Counselor–student ratio in secondary grades	1:305	5
Number of students per music specialist in elementary grades	725	1
Number of students per art specialist in elementary grades	615	
Number of volumes in senior high school library	22,000	
Beginning teacher's salary	$18,000	
Maximum teacher's salary	$31,286	
Average years of experience among teachers	18	
Number of students suspended and expelled	536	
Subjects in which Advanced Placement courses are offered: Biology, English	2	2

Quality of School Leadership
Principals are selected for their leadership ability, and the quality of leadership does not vary greatly throughout the district. Screening committees of parents and teachers advise on principal candidates. Principals have quite a lot to say about the allotment of resources to the schools.

Parent organizations are considered effective. Sometimes they support the School Board in battles with the town officials, and sometimes they disagree with the School Board and go over its head to town officials.

Quality of Instruction
Gifted students in grades 1–8 take part in an after-school program twice a week offered by the Massachusetts Bay Community College; the program is rated excellent. Additional instruction for low-achieving students is considered good. A revised curriculum that includes more science and history courses has improved the college-preparatory curriculum; observers rate it good to excellent. The district offers its own vocational education program, which is given high marks.

The district adequately meets the educational needs of minority students, most of whom are Hispanic, Haitian or Asian.

Quality of School Environment
Classroom disruption and student vandalism are not problems. A lot of money is being spent on school building improvement. "We're approaching good," said one observer.

WATERTOWN

ADDRESS OF CENTRAL OFFICE:
30 Common Street, Watertown, MA 02172
ESI:60

STATISTICAL PROFILE	DATA	ESI
Grade organization: K–8/9–12	†	
Percentage of schools built before 1955	50%	
Total enrollment	2,747	
Average Daily Attendance (ADA)	92%	5
Current expense per pupil in ADA	$4,500	7
Dropout rate	NK	0
Percentage of eligible students who took the SAT	70%	10
Average combined score on SAT	877	3
Percentage of graduates who enrolled in 2- or 4-year colleges	65%	
Percentage of students who passed the state reading test	99%	
Percentage of students who passed the state math test	99%	
Teacher–student ratio in elementary grades	1:20	10
Teacher–student ratio in secondary grades	1:16	10
Counselor–student ratio in secondary grades	1:220	9
Number of students per music specialist in elementary grades	474	6
Number of students per art specialist in elementary grades	416	
Number of volumes in senior high school library	15,000	
Beginning teacher's salary	$17,035	
Maximum teacher's salary	$32,363	
Average years of experience among teachers	10	
Number of students suspended and expelled	None	
Subjects in which Advanced Placement courses are offered:	None	0

†Three elementary schools are K-6, with seventh and eighth-graders going to the two K-8 schools.

Quality of School Leadership
The district has not hired new principals in at least 15 years, but those in place are considered to have educational leadership ability. Leadership is in a state of flux. In the spring of 1987, the School Board fired the superintendent who had headed the system for 17 years. The dismissal is a symbol of change in the community. The majority of the School Board voting to fire the superintendent consisted mostly of new residents, what one observer called an "overflow" of college-educated persons from nearby Cambridge. The newcomers want more "progressive and creative leadership," said an observer. Parents organizations are very active in the district.

Quality of Instruction
A program for gifted students was added recently. It is rated good as is the additional instruction for low-achieving students. The college-preparatory curriculum is "getting better." Said one observer, "We're still behind some other school districts in the area." Students going into the job market after graduation have good preparation. Minority students are mostly ethnic, including a large population of Armenians. Their educational needs (inlcuding English as a second language) are adequately met.

Quality of School Environment
Classroom disruption and student vandalism are very low. The students are generally well-disciplined both at home and at school. Said an observer, "There is respect for authority." Building maintenance and repair are good; the high school was recently renovated.

WELLESLEY

ADDRESS OF CENTRAL OFFICE:
40 Kingsbury Street, Wellesley, MA 02181
ESI:89

STATISTICAL PROFILE	DATA	ESI
Grade organization: K–5/6–8/9–12		
Percentage of schools built before 1955	63%	
Total enrollment	3,085	
Average Daily Attendance (ADA)	95%	8
Current expense per pupil in ADA	$4,371	6
Dropout rate	2%	10
Percentage of eligible students who took the SAT	90%	10
Average combined score on SAT	1,032	10
Percentage of graduates who enrolled in 2- or 4-year colleges	83%	
Percentage of students who passed the state reading test	99%	
Percentage of students who passed the state math test	98%	
Teacher–student ratio in elementary grades	1:21	9
Teacher–student ratio in secondary grades	1:16	10
Counselor–student ratio in secondary grades	1:223	9
Number of students per music specialist in elementary grades	438	7
Number of students per art specialist in elementary grades	438	
Number of volumes in senior high school library	29,565	
Beginning teacher's salary	$18,562	
Maximum teacher's salary	$40,800	
Average years of experience among teachers	12	
Number of students suspended and expelled	13	
Subjects in which Advanced Placement courses are offered:	10	10
Biology, Calculus, Chemistry, Computer Science, French, German, Latin, Music, Physics, Spanish		

FAIR APPRAISAL

Quality of School Leadership
The district hires principals who demonstrate educational leadership ability; the quality of leadership is uniform throughout the system. Committees that include teachers and parents (and students when a high school principal is being considered) help develop criteria for principal positions and also screen candidates. Principals have some say in resource allottment.

Parent organizations generally are effective in decision-making. They were recently active in devising a new discipline policy. They also lobbied successfully for a high school placement center that gives students career information.

Quality of Instruction
While no formal program for gifted students exists in the elementary schools, high school students have a wide variety of Advanced Placement courses to choose from. Also, the system takes part in the International Baccalaureate program. Additional instruction for low-achieving students is rated good. The schools are "geared" for college, said one observer, and the college-preparatory curriculum is excellent. The job preparation program is considered good.

Quality of School Environment
The level of classroom disruption and student vandalism is low. A recent problem with graffiti at the high school was solved when a group calling itself Students Against Vandalism formed. The schools are properly maintained and kept in good repair.

WINCHESTER

ADDRESS OF CENTRAL OFFICE:
154 Horn Pond Brook Road, Winchester, MA 01890
ESI:77

STATISTICAL PROFILE	DATA	ESI
Grade organization: K–6/7–8/9–12		
Percentage of schools built before 1955	28%	
Total enrollment	3,000	
Average Daily Attendance (ADA)	NK	0
Current expense per pupil in ADA	$3,800	3
Dropout rate	5%	10
Percentage of eligible students who took the SAT	92%	10
Average combined score on SAT	1,018	10
Percentage of graduates who enrolled in 2- or 4-year colleges	85%	
Percentage of students who passed the state reading test	100%	
Percentage of students who passed the state math test	100%	
Teacher–student ratio in elementary grades	1:21	9
Teacher–student ratio in secondary grades	1:21	7
Counselor–student ratio in secondary grades	1:250	8
Number of students per music specialist in elementary grades	280	10
Number of students per art specialist in elementary grades	404	
Number of volumes in senior high school library	13,855	
Beginning teacher's salary	$18,000	
Maximum teacher's salary	$36,000	
Average years of experience among teachers	15	
Number of students suspended and expelled	NK	
Subjects in which Advanced Placement courses are offered:	10	10
Art, Biology, Calculus, Chemistry, English, French, Latin, Physics, Spanish, U.S. History		

FAIR APPRAISAL

Quality of School Leadership
Principals are picked because of their educational leadership ability, and the quality of leadership is uniform throughout the system. Screening committees that include parents and teachers review principal candidates. Principals have some say in what resources their schools receive.

Parent organizations are effective in decision-making.

Quality of Instruction
A mentor program, which brings talented community residents into the schools to meet with students, is one way that gifted students benefit. Reading specialists in every school are part of a good program for low-achieving students. The college-preparatory curriculum is rated excellent. One observer said the curriculum is always under review, with an eye toward improvement. The job-preparation curriculum is termed good.

Few minority families live in the district, but schools are devising an ethnic and cultural awareness program, featuring Spanish and French instruction in the elementary grades.

Quality of School Environment
Classroom disruption and student vandalism are not problems. Recently, however, high school officials had to "tighten up a little" to deal with vandalism. The quality of school building maintenance and repair is rated good.

Buffalo, NY

In the Buffalo area, 11 districts completed the Statistical Profile.
A Fair Appraisal alone is offered for another district. Districts in this area
may be compared to districts in the Rochester, NY Metropolitan Area.

AREA AT A GLANCE

SCHOOL DISTRICT	ENROLLMENT	ESI
Buffalo	46,183	47
Clarence	2,914	72
East Aurora	2,005	
Frontier	5,183	50*
Iroquois	2,695	60
Kenmore–Tonawanda	8,900	73
Lackawana	2,653	52*
Lewiston–Porter	2,749	60
Niagara Falls	9,193	48*
Niagara–Wheatfield	3,295	52*
Orchard Park	4,445	75
Sweet Home	4,245	74

Indicates district misinterpretation of one or more statistics in the ESI. For each misinterpreted statistic, a score of 0 was given instead of a possible score of 0 to 10 points.

BUFFALO

ADDRESS OF CENTRAL OFFICE:
712 City Hall, Buffalo, NY 14202
ESI:47

STATISTICAL PROFILE	DATA	ESI
Grade organization: †		
Percentage of schools built before 1955	78%	
Total enrollment	46,183	
Average Daily Attendance (ADA)	92%	5
Current expense per pupil in ADA	$3,946	0
Dropout rate	NK	0
Percentage of eligible students who took the SAT	48%	7
Average combined score on SAT	853	2
Percentage of graduates who enrolled in 2- or 4-year colleges	60%	
Percentage of students who passed the state reading test	89%	
Percentage of students who passed the state math test	71%	
Teacher–student ratio in elementary grades	1:15	10
Teacher–student ratio in secondary grades	1:13	10
Counselor–student ratio in secondary grades	1:420	1
Number of students per music specialist in elementary grades	229	10
Number of students per art specialist in elementary grades	310	
Number of volumes in senior high school libraries (average)	11,909	
Beginning teacher's salary	$16,720	
Maximum teacher's salary	$32,677	
Average years of experience among teachers	14	
Number of students suspended and expelled	3,035	
Subjects in which Advanced Placement courses are offered: Calculus, Science	2	2

†Grade organization varies: some schools are PK–2 or PK–8, others are K–8 or K–9, some are 3–6 or 3–8, and still others are 5–12 or 9–12.

FAIR APPRAISAL

Quality of School Leadership

As a rule, principals are picked because of their ability as educational leaders. However, some persons of lesser ability get by. "The problem," said one observer, "is that it is difficult getting rid of an unqualified principal due to union resistance." Teachers and parents have little or no say in principal selection. When in office, principals have some say in what resources their schools will receive.

Parents are quite effective in other areas of decision-making. "They do their homework," said one observer; "they know what procedures to follow." Buffalo has been under court supervision for a number of years as part of a desegregation plan, and parents regularly offer the court advice on policy and program.

Quality of Instruction

Buffalo and observers believe it is a much better system than the ESI would indicate. One observer noted that it is one of the few desegregated cities where white families did not flee to the suburbs. The main reason why families stayed is the district's magnet elementary and secondary schools. The magnet schools offer a wide variety of curricula; students are chosen by lottery from among applicants. Gifted students have many enrichment opportunities; also, local colleges offer special programs. The observers rate as very good the additional instruction available to low-achieving students. Both the college-preparatory and job-training curricula are rated good. The district offers one of the few programs in the country that prepares high school students for jobs as air traffic controllers. Observers believe the district adequately meets the needs of "most" minority students.

Quality of School Environment

Classroom disruption and vandalism are not serious problems. "We're not a New York City," said one observer. Many buildings are more than 40 years old and upkeep is difficult. Also, insufficient funds mean some major repairs are put off.

CLARENCE

ADDRESS OF CENTRAL OFFICE:
9625 Main Street, Clarence, NY 14031
ESI:72

STATISTICAL PROFILE	DATA	ESI
Grade organization: K–6/7–8/9–12		
Percentage of schools built before 1955	40%	
Total enrollment	2,914	
Average Daily Attendance (ADA)	95%	8
Current expense per pupil in ADA	$3,928	0
Dropout rate	4%	10
Percentage of eligible students who took the SAT	82%	10
Average combined score on SAT	933	6
Percentage of graduates who enrolled in 2- or 4-year colleges	74%	
Percentage of students who passed the state reading test	100%	
Percentage of students who passed the state math test	98%	
Teacher–student ratio in elementary grades	1:23	7
Teacher–student ratio in secondary grades	1:22	6
Counselor–student ratio in secondary grades	1:264	7
Number of students per music specialist in elementary grades	247	10
Number of students per art specialist in elementary grades	654	
Number of volumes in senior high school library	15,437	
Beginning teacher's salary	$13,899	
Maximum teacher's salary	$39,212	
Average years of experience among teachers	15	
Number of students suspended and expelled	None	
Subjects in which Advanced Placement courses are offered: American History, Biology, Calculus, English, French, Latin, Physics, Spanish	8	8

Quality of School Leadership
The district selects principals who demonstrate educational leadership ability, and the quality of leadership is generally uniform throughout the system. Principal candidates are interviewed by top administrators and the School Board; parents and teachers have hardly any say. Principals go before the School Board to explain special needs.

As one observer put it, in Clarence "the masses speak." Parent committees frequently make recommendations to administrators and the School Board. Parents promoted a new transportation policy that would bus students in lower grades a shorter distance.

Quality of Instruction
Special enrichment programs exist in all schools; also, a special teacher for the gifted and talented regularly visits schools. The observers rate as good the additional instruction available to low-achieving students. They describe the college-preparatory curriculum as excellent. More New York State Regents Scholars come out of Clarence than most districts its size, noted the observers. The preparation for students entering the job market is rated good.

Quality of School Environment
The level of classroom disruption and vandalism is low. The quality of building maintenance and repair is deemed fair to good. Some deterioration has taken place in recent years, but voters were scheduled to decide the fate of a proposed 1987–88 renovation program.

EAST AURORA

ADDRESS OF CENTRAL OFFICE:
430 Main Street, East Aurora, NY 14052
ESI:None†

STATISTICAL PROFILE	DATA	ESI
Grade organization:		
Percentage of schools built before 1955		
Total enrollment		
Average Daily Attendance (ADA)		
Current expense per pupil in ADA		
Dropout rate		
Percentage of eligible students who took the SAT		
Average combined score on SAT		
Percentage of graduates who enrolled in 2- or 4-year colleges		
Percentage of students who passed the state reading test		
Percentage of students who passed the state math test		
Teacher–student ratio in elementary grades		
Teacher–student ratio in secondary grades		
Counselor–student ratio in secondary grades		
Number of students per music specialist in elementary grades		
Number of students per art specialist in elementary grades		
Number of volumes in senior high school library		
Beginning teacher's salary		
Maximum teacher's salary		
Average years of experience among teachers		
Number of students suspended and expelled		
Subjects in which Advanced Placement courses are offered:		

†A Statistical Profile was not received from this district.

Quality of School Leadership
The School Board hires principals who have educational leadership ability; the quality of leadership does not vary greatly in the system. Parents and other citizens may serve on an advisory committee to screen principal candidates if the candidates are from outside the district. If a candidate is from within the system, the person usually is screened by top administrators and School Board only. The principals have a great deal to say about the distribution of resources to the schools.

Parents are sometimes effective in decision-making.

Quality of Instruction
The additional learning opportunities for gifted students are rated good. A special program exists for all grades, and bright high school students can select from a number of Advanced Placement courses. An observer reports "a good variety of elective courses and a good music and drama department." The additional instruction for low-achieving students also is rated good. A pre-first grade helps those students who are not fully prepared after kindergarten. Also, specialists in resource rooms work with students having problems. Both the college-preparatory and job-training curricula are termed good.

Quality of School Environment
Classroom disruption and vandalism are not problems. The quality of building maintenance and repair is called good.

FRONTIER

ADDRESS OF CENTRAL OFFICE:
S4432 Bayview Road, Hamburg, NY 14075
ESI:50*

STATISTICAL PROFILE	DATA	ESI
Grade organization: K–6/7–9/10–12		
Percentage of schools built before 1955	38%	
Total enrollment	5,183	
Average Daily Attendance (ADA)	95%	8
Current expense per pupil in ADA	$4,695	0
Dropout rate	NK	0
Percentage of eligible students who took the SAT	54%	8
Average combined score on SAT	†	0*
Percentage of graduates who enrolled in 2- or 4-year colleges	59%	
Percentage of students who passed the state reading test	95%	
Percentage of students who passed the state math test	78%	
Teacher–student ratio in elementary grades	1:16	10
Teacher–student ratio in secondary grades	1:17	10
Counselor–student ratio in secondary grades	1:458	0
Number of students per music specialist in elementary grades	271	10
Number of students per art specialist in elementary grades	487	
Number of volumes in senior high school library	16,618	
Beginning teacher's salary	$16,664	
Maximum teacher's salary	$41,640	
Average years of experience among teachers	17	
Number of students suspended and expelled	556	
Subjects in which Advanced Placement courses are offered:	4	4
Biology, Calculus, English, French		

†The district supplied an incomplete statistic.

FAIR APPRAISAL

Quality of School Leadership
Generally, principals are selected for their leadership qualities, and the quality is good throughout the district. Teachers and parents have little or no say in principal selection. However, the School Board "makes a concerted effort" to get ideas from principals about their special resource needs.

Parents are effective in decision-making. Recently, they made suggestions concerning the reassignment of students (some buildings have been closed) and class size.

Quality of Instruction
The opportunities for gifted students are rated good; additional instruction for low-achieving students is called average. Both the college-preparatory and job-training curricula are rated good. The district is particularly strong in foreign languages, offering six (including Polish and Russian).

Quality of School Environment
The level of classroom disruption and vandalism is very low, and buildings are mostly kept in very good condition. The School Board has saved up to $100,000 a year in fuel costs by drilling its own gas wells.

IROQUOIS

ADDRESS OF CENTRAL OFFICE:
P.O. Box 32, Elma, NY 14059
ESI:60

STATISTICAL PROFILE	DATA	ESI
Grade Organization: K–5/6–8/9–12		
Percentage of schools built before 1955	83%	
Total enrollment	2,695	
Average Daily Attendance (ADA)	98%	10
Current expense per pupil in ADA	$2,642	0
Dropout rate	NK	0
Percentage of eligible students who took the SAT	75%	10
Average combined score on SAT	949	7
Percentage of graduates who enrolled in 2- or 4-year colleges	74%	
Percentage of students who passed the state reading test	100%	
Percentage of students who passed the state math test	100%	
Teacher–student ratio in elementary grades	1:17	10
Teacher–student ratio in secondary grades	1:15	10
Counselor–student ratio in secondary grades	1:424	1
Number of students per music specialist in elementary grades	303	9
Number of students per art specialist in elementary grades	910	
Number of volumes in senior high school library	11,044	
Beginning teacher's salary	$14,664	
Maximum teacher's salary	$36,402	
Average years of experience among teachers	17	
Number of students suspended and expelled	189	
Subjects in which Advanced Placement courses are offered:	3	3
Biology, Chemistry, English		

FAIR APPRAISAL

Quality of School Leadership
Principals are normally hired from within the system, and internal politics play some role, according to observers. However, principals are considered good leaders, and the quality of leadership is uniform in the system. Principal candidates are screened by top administrators and the School Board; teachers and parents have hardly any voice in the selection. Also, principals don't have much say about the distribution of resources.

Parent organizations are "becoming effective," said an observer. Parents and other citizens are advising more on school spending, and the School Board is paying closer attention.

Quality of Instruction
The program for gifted students is considered excellent, and the additional instruction available to low-achieving students is rated good. Students going to college and students going into the job market are offered equally good curricula. The schools adequately meet the needs of minority students, although they are few in number.

Quality of School Environment
The incidence of disruption and vandalism is low. The quality of building maintenance and repair is fair. "The buildings were let go for 15 years," said an observer. The School Board has now advanced an ambitious renovation project.

KENMORE–TONAWANDA

ADDRESS OF CENTRAL OFFICE:
1500 Colvin Boulevard, Buffalo, NY 14223
ESI:73

STATISTICAL PROFILE	DATA	ESI
Grade organization: K–5/6–8/9–12		
Percentage of schools built before 1955	100%	
Total enrollment	8,900	
Average Daily Attendance (ADA)	95%	8
Current expense per pupil in ADA	$4,700	1
Dropout rate	3%	10
Percentage of eligible students who took the SAT	50%	7
Average combined score on SAT	956	7
Percentage of graduates who enrolled in 2- or 4-year colleges	72%	
Percentage of students who passed the state reading test	97%	
Percentage of students who passed the state math test	97%	
Teacher–student ratio in elementary grades	1:20	10
Teacher–student ratio in secondary grades	1:20	8
Counselor–student ratio in secondary grades	1:300	6
Number of students per music specialist in elementary grades	300	9
Number of students per art specialist in elementary grades	556	
Number of volumes in senior high school libraries (average)	18,000	
Beginning teacher's salary	$17,891	
Maximum teacher's salary	$38,565	
Average years of experience among teachers	22	
Number of students suspended and expelled	940†	
Subjects in which Advanced Placement courses are offered:	7	7
American History, Biology, Calculus, Chemistry, Computer Science, English, Physics		

†Out-of-school suspensions only.

Quality of School Leadership

Principals are selected for their educational leadership abilities, and the quality of leadership is high throughout the system. Principal candidates are screened by top administrators and the School Board; teachers and parents have hardly any say. Principals normally submit their special requests for resources to the central office for consideration.

Parent organizations are mostly effective in school decision-making. They have advised on such matters as school closings, book purchases for school libraries, and the program for gifted students.

Quality of Instruction

Special classes are available for gifted students in elementary and middle schools, and the program is rated good to excellent. The additional instruction available to low-achieving students is rated fair to good. One observer called it "adequate." The curriculum for college-bound students is considered to be good to excellent, and the job preparation program is rated good. Work-study opportunities exist for high school students.

Quality of School Environment

The level of classroom disruption is low, but the incidence of vandalism may be slightly above average. Much of the vandalism consists of graffiti and damage caused by various groups, said an observer. Buildings are kept in good condition.

LACKAWANNA

ADDRESS OF CENTRAL OFFICE:
30 Johnson Street, Buffalo, NY 14218
ESI:52*

STATISTICAL PROFILE	DATA	ESI
Grade Organization: K–4/5–6/7–12		
Percentage of schools built before 1955	60%	
Total enrollment	2,653	
Average Daily Attendance (ADA)	96%	9
Current expense per pupil in ADA	$5,294	4
Dropout rate	10%	10
Percentage of eligible students who took the SAT	51%	8
Average combined score on SAT	†	0*
Percentage of graduates who enrolled in 2- or 4-year colleges	49%	
Percentage of students who passed the state reading test	85%	
Percentage of students who passed the state math test	71%	
Teacher–student ratio in elementary grades	1:22	8
Teacher–student ratio in secondary grades	1:26	2
Counselor–student ratio in secondary grades	1:300	6
Number of students per music specialist in elementary grades	650	2
Number of students per art specialist in elementary grades	650	
Number of volumes in senior high school library	8,630	
Beginning teacher's salary	$15,987	
Maximum teacher's salary	$27,498	
Average years of experience among teachers	16	
Number of students suspended and expelled	57	
Subjects in which Advanced Placement courses are offered: Biology, Calculus, English	3	3

†The district misinterpreted the statistic.

Quality of School Leadership

Usually, principals are selected for their leadership ability; however, most principals are picked from within the district, and internal politics have sometimes been a factor. Leadership is strongest at the elementary school level, an observer noted. Parents and teachers play no role in principal selection. Whether a principal is heard concerning special resource needs depends on his/her clout.

Parent organizations are only occasionally effective in decision-making. Too often, an observer said, parent groups prove to be "rubber stamps" for ideas from administrators or the School Board. Parents apparently have lost some influence as they have lost some hope. The city is economically depressed; thousands of persons lost their jobs when a Bethlehem Steel plant closed, and the unemployment rate is estimated as high as 40 percent.

Quality of Instruction

The opportunities for gifted students are rated good, particularly in the elementary schools. Additional instruction for low-achieving students is termed fair to good, with the elementary schools doing a better job than the secondary grades. The college-preparatory curriculum is called good. It is likely to improve in the years ahead because of a new school for grades 7–12 that includes advanced science labs and a planetarium. Also, a computer lab was scheduled to open in the fall of 1987. These developments may be the "salvation" for students, said one observer, who believes the upgraded curriculum will enable more students to get into college and reduce the number of students competing for the scarce jobs. The job-preparation program is rated fair.

A "dynamite" superintendent is slowly turning things around, said one observer.

Quality of School Environment

Classroom disruption and vandalism are not problems. Buildings are in good condition.

LEWISTON–PORTER

ADDRESS OF CENTRAL OFFICE:
4061 Creek Road, Youngstown, NY 14174
ESI:60

STATISTICAL PROFILE	DATA	ESI
Grade organization: K–5/6–8/9–12		
Percentage of schools built before 1955	50%	
Total enrollment	2,749	
Average Daily Attendance (ADA)	97%	10
Current expense per pupil in ADA	$5,285	4
Dropout rate	18%	5
Percentage of eligible students who took the SAT	60%	10
Average combined score on SAT	899	4
Percentage of graduates who enrolled in 2- or 4-year colleges	72%	
Percentage of students who passed the state reading test	91%	
Percentage of students who passed the state math test	90%	
Teacher–student ratio in elementary grades	1:25	5
Teacher–student ratio in secondary grades	1:25	3
Counselor–student ratio in secondary grades	1:331	4
Number of students per music specialist in elementary grades	274	10
Number of students per art specialist in elementary grades	547	
Number of volumes in senior high school library	11,005	
Beginning teacher's salary	$17,734	
Maximum teacher's salary	$38,997	
Average years of experience among teachers	15	
Number of students suspended and expelled	349	
Subjects in which Advanced Placement courses are offered: American History, Biology, Calculus, Computer Science, English	5	5

FAIR APPRAISAL

Quality of School Leadership

The district chooses principals who have educational leadership ability, and the quality of leadership is uniform in the system. Teachers, parents, and other citizens take part in the initial screening of principal candidates. The central administration pays attention to special requests for resources from principals.

School-community advisory committees are organized in each school. Parent groups were instrumental in establishing an all-day kindergarten several years ago.

Quality of Instruction

An extensive program for gifted students exists at all grade levels, but one observer said the program is better on paper than in reality. Students in grades 7–12 also are eligible to apply for the highly rated gifted program in math offered to students in western New York by the State Univerity of New York at Buffalo. The additional instruction for low-achieving students is rated excellent. A major effort is made to "spot kids with problems before they need a remedial class," said an observer. The college-preparatory curriculum is good to excellent. In addition to Advanced Placement courses, the district takes part in the International Baccalaureate program. Students going directly into the job market are adequately prepared.

Quality of School Environment

Classroom disruption and vandalism are not problems, and buildings are well cared for.

NIAGARA FALLS

ADDRESS OF CENTRAL OFFICE:
P.O. Box 399, Niagara Falls, NY 14302
ESI:48*

STATISTICAL PROFILE	DATA	ESI
Grade organization: K–6/7–8/9–12		
Percentage of schools built before 1955	82%	
Total enrollment	9,193	
Average Daily Attendance (ADA)	91%	4
Current expense per pupil in ADA	$5,593	5
Dropout rate	5%	10
Percentage of eligible students who took the SAT	NK	0
Average combined score on SAT	†	0*
Percentage of graduates who enrolled in 2- or 4-year colleges	†	
Percentage of students who passed the state reading test	96%	
Percentage of students who passed the state math test	88%	
Teacher–student ratio in elementary grades	1:24	6
Teacher–student ratio in secondary grades	1:18	10
Counselor–student ratio in secondary grades	1:350	4
Number of students per music specialist in elementary grades	400	7
Number of students per art specialist in elementary grades	475	
Number of volumes in senior high school libraries (average)	12,720	
Beginning teacher's salary	$15,512	
Maximum teacher's salary	$37,211	
Average years of experience among teachers	18	
Number of students suspended and expelled	NK	
Subjects in which Advanced Placement courses are offered: Calculus, English	2	2

†The district misinterpreted these statistics.

Quality of School Leadership

Most principals are selected from within the district, but educational leadership is still the primary criterion for selecting principals. The new superintendent is a "political animal," said one observer, having served as city manager before being hired as chief school administrator. However, he is considered a good educational leader. A representative of the teachers' union usually helps screen principal candidates along with administrators; parents are not involved. Principals have a say in the way resources are distributed.

Parent organizations are sometimes effective. Parents have served on committees to revise curriculum and report cards.

Quality of Instruction

The extra learning opportunities for gifted students are considered good to excellent. A MERIT program, which features special classes and teachers for bright students, is offered in grades 3–6. The district expects to add a grade each year until it gets into the high school. Observers call the additional instruction offered low-achievers good. Pupil personnel teams recommend remediation for students having learning problems. The teams include parent volunteers who visit the homes of students who are frequently absent without cause. The college-preparatory curriculum is termed fair to good. "We'd like to see more AP courses and other high-level courses," said an observer. The old vocational high school is being incorporated into an expanded academic high school, and the job-preparation curriculum is rated good.

Quality of School Environment

Even though this is a city district, the incidence of class disruption and vandalism is low. Some schools date to the early decades of the century, but observers rate the quality of building maintenance and repair as good.

NIAGARA–WHEATFIELD

ADDRESS OF CENTRAL OFFICE:
2794 Saunders Settlement, Sanborn, NY 14132
ESI:52*

STATISTICAL PROFILE	DATA	ESI
Grade organization: K–5/6–8/9–12		
Percentage of schools built before 1955	0%	
Total enrollment	3,295	
Average Daily Attendance (ADA)	92%	5
Current expense per pupil in ADA	$5,831	7
Dropout rate	†	0*
Percentage of eligible students who took the SAT	42%	5
Average combined score on SAT	921	5
Percentage of graduates who enrolled in 2- or 4-year colleges	57%	
Percentage of students who passed the state reading test	100%	
Percentage of students who passed the state math test	73%	
Teacher–student ratio in elementary grades	1:23	7
Teacher–student ratio in secondary grades	1:19	9
Counselor–student ratio in secondary grades	1:320	5
Number of students per music specialist in elementary grades	363	8
Number of students per art specialist in elementary grades	578	
Number of volumes in senior high school library	9,092	
Beginning teacher's salary	$17,301	
Maximum teacher's salary	$36,821	
Average years of experience among teachers	20	
Number of students suspended and expelled	399	
Subjects in which Advanced Placement courses are offered: Physics	1	1

†The district misinterpreted this statement.

FAIR APPRAISAL

Quality of School Leadership
One observer believes internal politics might sometimes play a role in principal selection, but overall the observers agree that principals demonstrate educational leadership ability. One observer called the superintendent "the most progressive" in Erie County. Neither teachers nor parents play a role in screening principal candidates. Principals are encouraged to voice their special needs to the central administration and School Board.

Parents are active in decision-making. Recently, parents and other citizens served on a task force that recommended two property tax rates for the district, one for business and industry and a lower one for homeowners. The School Board adopted the suggestion by a 6–2 vote (local businesses are still fighting the decision).

Quality of Instruction
Additional learning opportunities for gifted students are rated fair to good. Instruction for low-achieving students is called good. "The tutorial help is great," said an observer. The curriculum for college-bound students is "getting better." The district plans to add two or more Advanced Placement courses, said an observer (physics is the only one listed by the district). The job-training curriculum consists mainly of offerings available through the region's vocational center (called BOCES in New York State).

Quality of School Environment
The level of classroom disruption and vandalism is very low. Buildings are described as being in good to excellent condition.

ORCHARD PARK

ADDRESS OF CENTRAL OFFICE:
3330 Baker Road, Orchard Park, NY 14127
ESI:75

STATISTICAL PROFILE	DATA	ESI
Grade organization:	†	
Percentage of schools built before 1955	50%	
Total enrollment	4,445	
Average Daily Attendance (ADA)	95%	8
Current expense per pupil in ADA	$5,095	3
Dropout rate	8%	10
Percentage of eligible students who took the SAT	73%	10
Average combined score on SAT	916	5
Percentage of graduates who enrolled in 2- or 4-year colleges	76%	
Percentage of students who passed the state reading test	100%	
Percentage of students who passed the state math test	99%	
Teacher–student ratio in elementary grades	1:22	8
Teacher–student ratio in secondary grades	1:16	10
Counselor–student ratio in secondary grades	1:320	5
Number of students per music specialist in elementary grades	270	10
Number of students per art specialist in elementary grades	439	
Number of volumes in senior high school library	15,116	
Beginning teacher's salary	$14,900	
Maximum teacher's salary	$36,450	
Average years of experience among teachers	16	
Number of students suspended and expelled	306	
Subjects in which Advanced Placement courses are offered: American History, Biology, Calculus, English, French, Spanish	6	6

†The district misinterpreted statistic.

FAIR APPRAISAL

Quality of School Leadership
Principals are selected for their leadership ability, and the quality of leadership is uniform throughout the district. Teachers and parents play little or no part in screening principal candidates. Principals have some say in what resources will be allotted their school.

Parent organizations are sometimes effective. According to one observer, "They bother the Board a lot." When teachers went on strike here recently, parent organizations generally supported the teachers.

Quality of Instruction
The program for gifted students is rated good to excellent. Bright students in grades 1–6 can take mini-courses in such subjects as logic, creative writing, and story-telling. Special outings also are offered. Each school has a reading specialist as part of the program to help low-achieving students, and the program is rated good. The curriculum for students heading to college is termed good to excellent; the job-preparation curriculum also is good. Speaking of the latter curriculum, one observer said it prepares students for "real jobs." A work-study program is linked to a local manufacturing company.

Quality of School Environment
Classroom disruption and vandalism are not problems. The upkeep of school buildings is rated good.

SWEET HOME

ADDRESS OF CENTRAL OFFICE:
1901 Sweet Home Road, Buffalo, NY 14221
ESI:74

STATISTICAL PROFILE	DATA	ESI
Grade organization: K–6/7–8/9–12		
Percentage of schools built before 1955	0%	
Total enrollment	4,245	
Average Daily Attendance (ADA)	95%	8
Current expense per pupil in ADA	$4,700	1
Dropout rate	2%	10
Percentage of eligible students who took the SAT	65%	10
Average combined score on SAT	940	6
Percentage of graduates who enrolled in 2- or 4-year colleges	68%	
Percentage of students who passed the state reading test	92%	
Percentage of students who passed the state math test	92%	
Teacher–student ratio in elementary grades	1:14	10
Teacher–student ratio in secondary grades	1:15	10
Counselor–student ratio in secondary grades	1:321	5
Number of students per music specialist in elementary grades	568	4
Number of students per art specialist in elementary grades	568	
Number of volumes in senior high school library	14,807	
Beginning teacher's salary	$17,925	
Maximum teacher's salary	$42,109	
Average years of experience among teachers	23	
Number of students suspended and expelled	150	
Subjects in which Advanced Placement courses are offered:	13	10
American History, Art, Biology, Calculus AB, Calculus BC, Chemistry, Computer Science, English Language, English Literature, European History, Latin, Physics B, Physics C		

FAIR APPRAISAL

Quality of School Leadership

The district picks principals for their educational leadership, and the quality of leadership is uniform in the district. Teachers and parents have little or no say in the screening of principal candidates. Principals have some say in determining what resources their school will receive.

Parent organizations are effective. Said one observer, "They listen to the voice of the parents."

Quality of Instruction

The additional learning opportunities for gifted students are rated excellent. A special program exists at all grade levels. The additional instruction for low-achieving students also is rated excellent. The district offers more than half of the available Advanced Placement courses, and the overall college-preparatory curriculum is termed excellent. Extensive work-student opportunities are available to students heading for the job market, and this curriculum also is rated excellent. In addition to an excellent academic curriculum, the district offers a high-quality sports program, according to observers. The high school's volleyball team holds a national record for most consecutive wins by a high school team in any sport.

Quality of School Environment

As might be expected, the level of classroom disruption and vandalism is very low, and the condition of school buildings is excellent.

Charleston, SC

Most school districts in South Carolina are county districts.
One district in the area supplied a Statistical Profile; Fair Appraisals were received for
three other districts. For comparison, we suggest examining similar districts
in such metropolitan areas as Atlanta, GA and Greensboro, NC.

AREA AT A GLANCE

SCHOOL DISTRICT	ENROLLMENT	ESI
Berkeley County	24,245	
Charleston County	24,900	
Colleton County	6,630	53
Dorchester County #2	11,538	

SCHOOL DISTRICT

BERKELEY COUNTY

ADDRESS OF CENTRAL OFFICE:
P.O. Box 608, Monck's Corner, SC 29461
ESI:None†

STATISTICAL PROFILE	DATA	ESI
Grade organization:		
Percentage of schools built before 1955		
Total enrollment		
Average Daily Attendance (ADA)		
Current expense per pupil in ADA		
Dropout rate		
Percentage of eligible students who took the SAT		
Average combined score on SAT		
Percentage of graduates who enrolled in 2- or 4-year colleges		
Percentage of students who passed the state reading test		
Percentage of students who passed the state math test		
Teacher–student ratio in elementary grades		
Teacher–student ratio in secondary grades		
Counselor–student ratio in secondary grades		
Number of students per music specialist in elementary grades		
Number of students per art specialist in elementary grades		
Number of volumes in senior high school library		
Beginning teacher's salary		
Maximum teacher's salary		
Average years of experience among teachers		
Number of students suspended and expelled		
Subjects in which Advanced Placement courses are offered:		

†A Statistical Profile was not received from this district.

FAIR APPRAISAL

Quality of School Leadership
The School Board chooses principals primarily because of their leadership ability, but the quality of leadership varies within the system. Schools in the lower half of the county, closer to Charleston, tend to have better leadership than schools in the rural upper half of the county. Candidates for principal from within the district must complete a training program. Teachers and parents have hardly any say in the screening of candidates. Principals have some say as to what resources are supplied their school.

Parent organizations are more effective in individual schools than on a district level, although parents helped influence decisions on sex education instruction.

Quality of Instruction
Observers rate learning opportunities for gifted students excellent. The state has mandated a minimum program for gifted students in grades 3–8, but the district has added to that. Students compete in national academic competitions and take part in special classes run by area colleges. On the other hand, instruction for low-achieving students is rated only fair. They get the "least attention," said an observer. The college-preparatory curriclum is considered good, but the job-preparation curriculum is called fair. The schools adequately meet the needs of minority students, observers believe.

Quality of School Environment
The incidence of classroom disruption and vandalism is low. However, some schools, particularly in rural areas, are old and badly in need of repairs.

CHARLESTON COUNTY

ADDRESS OF CENTRAL OFFICE:
**The Center, Hudson and Meeting Streets
Charleston, SC 29403
ESI:None†**

STATISTICAL PROFILE	DATA	ESI
Grade organization:		
Percentage of schools built before 1955		
Total enrollment		
Average Daily Attendance (ADA)		
Current expense per pupil in ADA		
Dropout rate		
Percentage of eligible students who took the SAT		
Average combined score on SAT		
Percentage of graduates who enrolled in 2- or 4-year colleges		
Percentage of students who passed the state reading test		
Percentage of students who passed the state math test		
Teacher–student ratio in elementary grades		
Teacher–student ratio in secondary grades		
Counselor–student ratio in secondary grades		
Number of students per music specialist in elementary grades		
Number of students per art specialist in elementary grades		
Number of volumes in senior high school library		
Beginning teacher's salary		
Maximum teacher's salary		
Average years of experience among teachers		
Number of students suspended and expelled		
Subjects in which Advanced Placement courses are offered:		

†A Statistical Profile was not received from this district.

FAIR APPRAISAL

Quality of School Leadership
Observers differ as to what criteria are primary when picking principals. On the one hand is the view that principals are selected mostly for their educational leadership ability. The other view is that internal politics — how popular the candidate is with top administrators and School Board members — is the main criterion. One observer believes some unqualified principals are hired for rural or mostly black schools. Principal candidates are screened by top administrators and the School Board; teachers and parents are not consulted. Principals do not have much to say about resources their school will get.

Parent organizations are sometimes effective in influencing decision-making by school leaders.

Quality of Instruction
Learning opportunities for gifted students are rated good, thanks mainly to a state reform act of 1984. A new elementary magnet school caters to the brightest students in the district. Observers rate instruction for low-achieving students fair to good, although the same state law has helped in the last year or two. The college-preparatory curriculum is rated good, but one observer complained that "students aren't encouraged strongly enough to enter college-preparatory courses." The curriculum for students entering the job market is rated only fair. Businesses in the county have "adopted" schools and offer support, advice, and speakers.

Quality of School Environment
Classroom disruption and vandalism are not problems in the district. The quality of building maintenance and repair is rated fair to good.

COLLETON COUNTY

ADDRESS OF CENTRAL OFFICE:
P.O. Box 290, Walterboro, SC 29488
ESI:53

STATISTICAL PROFILE	DATA	ESI
Grade organization: K–5/6–8/9–12		
Percentage of schools built before 1955	7%	
Total enrollment	6,630	
Average Daily Attendance (ADA)	96%	9
Current expense per pupil in ADA	2,500	3
Dropout rate	20%	3
Percentage of eligible students who took the SAT	64%	10
Average Combined score on SAT	850	2
Percentage of graduates who enrolled in 2- or 4-year colleges	31%	
Percentage of students who passed the state reading test	62%	
Percentage of students who passed the state math test	62%	
Teacher–student ratio in elementary grades	1:20	10
Teacher–student ratio in secondary grades	1:22	6
Counselor–student ratio in secondary grades	1:395	2
Number of students per music specialist in elementary grades	505	5
Number of students per art specialist in elementary grades	545	
Number of volumes in senior high school library	15,000†	
Beginning teacher's salary	$16,492	
Maximum teacher's salary	$34,716	
Average years of experience among teachers	13	
Number of students suspended and expelled	990	
Subjects in which Advanced Placement courses are offered: American History, Calculus, English	3	

†The district has two high schools, one with 300 students and one with 1,600; the majority of these volumes are in the larger high school.

Quality of School Leadership

The superintendent is elected, but politics do not play a major role in principal selection. While principals are selected primarily for their leadership ability, the quality of leadership varies in the district. The county seat, Walterboro, for example, generally has better principals than schools in more rural areas. Teachers and parents have no say in principal selection. Principals help determine what resources will be allotted to their school.

A School Improvement Council exists in each school (mandated by state law). A council can influence how a small discretionary fund is spent in its school.

Quality of Instruction

The program for gifted students is rated good. "There has been a tremendous improvement in two years," said an observer. Bright students in grades 3–5 attend special classes once a week, and students in grades 6–8 have a two-hour session each week on advanced language and communication skills. The program is moving now into the upper grades. Instruction for low-achieving students is rated fair. The college-preparation curriculum and the job-preparation curriculum are both rated good. Advanced Placement courses were introduced two years ago, and now three courses are offered. The job placement record of the district's vocational school is good.

While the district generally meets the needs of minority students, the real problem is that the district does not meet the needs of rural students — black and white — as well as it does students in Walterboro and surrounding communities.

Quality of School Environment

Classroom disruption and vandalism are about average. However, the quality of school building maintenance and repair is rated fair to poor. The condition of schools is "a disaster," said an observer. "There has been minimal funding for maintenance and repairs, and no overall plan exists. It is a critical problem."

DORCHESTER COUNTY DISTRICT #2

ADDRESS OF CENTRAL OFFICE:
102 Greenwave Boulevard, Summerville, SC 29483
ESI:None†

STATISTICAL PROFILE	DATA	ESI
Grade organization:		
Percentage of schools built before 1955		
Total enrollment		
Average Daily Attendance (ADA)		
Current expense per pupil in ADA		
Dropout rate		
Percentage of eligible students who took the SAT		
Average combined score on SAT		
Percentage of graduates who enrolled in 2- or 4-year colleges		
Percentage of students who passed the state reading test		
Percentage of students who passed the state math test		
Teacher–student ratio in elementary grades		
Teacher–student ratio in secondary grades		
Counselor–student ratio in secondary grades		
Number of students per music specialist in elementary grades		
Number of students per art specialist in elementary grades		
Number of volumes in senior high school library		
Beginning teacher's salary		
Maximum teacher's salary		
Average years of experience among teachers		
Number of students suspended and expelled		
Subjects in which Advanced Placement courses are offered:		

†A Statistical Profile was not received from this district.

FAIR APPRAISAL

Quality of School Leadership

The School Board picks principals who have educational leadership ability, and the quality of leadership is uniform throughout the system. The top administration and School Board screen and choose candidates without advice from teachers and parents. Principals have some say in how resources are distributed to each school.

Parent organizations are sometimes effective in decision-making.

Quality of Instruction

"This district seems particularly geared toward [gifted] students," said an observer, and the program is rated excellent. Instruction for low-achieving students is rated good; remedial labs and tutors are available. Students going to college and students heading for the job market are equally well prepared by excellent curricula. The schools in the district have "an excellent reputation," said an observer.

Quality of School Environment

Classroom disruption and vandalism are not problems. Building maintenance and repair are considered good, but enrollment growth in the district has caused some overcrowding and maintenance problems.

Chicago, IL

In Illinois, and the Chicago Metropolitan Area in particular, separate elementary and high school districts are common. To be able to list a reasonable number of districts in the Chicago area, therefore, we sought information from these separate districts. However, we have combined the information from separate districts serving the same communities so readers could have a better picture of all grades, kindergarten through grade 12, in those communities. For example, the Cicero Elementary (K–8) and Morton High School (9–12) districts are listed together; the Morton High School District is located in and serves Cicero. In a few instances, a high school district also may serve elementary districts in addition to the one listed. When a Profile and Appraisal exist for both the elementary and high school districts, a combined ESI score is given. We received Statistical Profiles from 13 separate districts and another 7 separate districts provided Fair Appraisals only. Illinois does not require tests of reading and math competence. Therefore, all district profiles show NA (not applicable) on the lines requesting those statistics. For comparison, consult the New York and Los Angeles Metropolitan Areas.

AREA AT A GLANCE

SCHOOL DISTRICT	ENROLLMENT	ESI
Chicago (K–12)	430,908	18
Chicago Heights		
Elementary	3,300	
Bloom Township HS	2,063	
Cicero		53
Elementary	6,000	
Morton High School	4,664	
Downers Grove		74
Elementary	4,064	
High School	5,200	
Elmhurst (K–12)	6,256	91
Evanston		
Elementary	6,073	
High School	3,576	
Gary, IN (K–12)	27,196	
Glenview		
Elementary	2,800	
Northfield Township HS	4,494	
Harvey		60
Elementary	3,775	
Thornton Township HS	7,200	
Maywood		
Elementary	5,354	
Proviso Township HS	4,935	
Oak Park		
Elementary	4,656	
Oak Park–River Forest HS	3,438	
Villa Park		
Elementary	3,632	
Dupage High School	4,415	
Wheaton (K–12)	10,185	58

CHICAGO

ADDRESS OF CENTRAL OFFICE:
1819 West Pershing Road, Chicago, IL 60609
ESI:18

STATISTICAL PROFILE	DATA	ESI
Grade organization: †		
Percentage of schools built before 1955	69%	
Total enrollment	430,908	
Average Daily Attendance (ADA)	91%	4
Current expense per pupil in ADA	$3,225	4
Dropout rate	48%	0
Percentage of eligible students who took the ACT	NK	0
Average combined score on ACT	NK	0
Percentage of graduates who enrolled in 2- or 4-year colleges	NK	
Percentage of students who passed the state reading test	NA	
Percentage of students who passed the state math test	NA	
Teacher–student ratio in elementary grades	1:30	0
Teacher–student ratio in secondary grades	1:28	0
Counselor–student ratio in secondary grades	1:450	0
Number of students per music specialist in elementary grades	NK	0
Number of students per art specialist in elementary grades	NK	
Number of volumes in senior high school library	††	
Beginning teacher's salary	$16,016	
Maximum teacher's salary	$34,041	
Average years of experience among teachers	15	
Number of students suspended and expelled	58,346†††	
Subjects in which Advanced Placement courses are offered:	17	10
American History, Art History, Art Studio, Biology, Calculus, Chemistry, Computer Science, English, European History, French Language, French Literature, German, Latin, Music, Physics, Spanish Language, Spanish Literature		

† Grade organization varies.
†† No data were supplied, so no average can be determined.
†††More than half of this number are in-school suspensions.

Quality of School Leadership

In a system as large as Chicago's, almost nothing is uniform or normal for all schools and all sections. A two-year-old state law requires candidates for school administrative positions to demonstrate educational leadership ability for continued certification. Candidates must pass rigorous written and oral exams that include questions related to leadership. However, as one observer pointed out, at least one other consideration in Chicago and other urban districts is racial and ethnic balance among administrators. A local school council first interviews candidates and makes a recommendation to an area superintendent, who must endorse it to the district superintendent. The School Board grants final approval. Both teachers and parents serve on local school councils and, therefore, have much to say about principal selection.

Principals mostly take whatever resources are allotted by the central office (based on a formula). However, principals of magnet schools are able to select up to one-third of their teachers.

Parent organizations are effective in some schools, where principals are especially receptive and willing to share decision-making. However, parents generally are not a major influence.

Quality of Instruction

Chicago is very proud of its magnet schools, which cater to the needs of gifted students. However, throughout the district, the observers rate the opportunities for bright students as fair. Also rated fair is instruction for low-achieving students. Less than half of the schools have federally funded programs to help students with the most severe educational problems, according to observers. The college-preparatory curriculum is "excellent in perhaps 5 of Chicago's 65 public high schools," said one observer. "It is fair or poor in most high schools." Observers assessed the job-preparation curriculum the same way.

They also agreed that the district does not adequately serve the needs of minority students. Of course, minorities in Chicago comprise the majority of the student body.

Quality of School Environment

Classroom disruption and vandalism are problems in some schools, but not all by any means. The quality of building maintenance and repair generally is rated fair to poor. One observer complained that maintenance personnel are paid high wages but perform poorly. As in many districts, budget cutbacks often hurt this area more than any other.

CHICAGO HEIGHTS

ADDRESS OF CENTRAL OFFICE:
Elementary: 16th and Aberdeen Streets
Chicago Heights, IL 60411
Secondary: Bloom Township High School,
10th Street and Dixie Highway,
Chicago Heights, IL 60411
ESI:None†

STATISTICAL PROFILE (secondary only)	DATA	ESI
Grade organization: 9–12		
Percentage of schools built before 1955 (two schools)	50%	
Total enrollment	2,063	
Average Daily Attendance (ADA)	90%	
Current expense per pupil in ADA	$5,521	
Dropout rate	35%	
Percentage of eligible students who took the ACT	60%	
Average combined score on ACT	16.1	
Percentage of graduates who enrolled in 2- or 4-year colleges	60%	
Percentage of students who passed the state reading test	NA	
Percentage of students who passed the state math test	NA	
Teacher–student ratio in elementary grades	NA	
Teacher–student ratio in secondary grades	1:20	
Counselor–student ratio in secondary grades	1:325	
Number of students per music specialist in elementary grades	NA	
Number of students per art specialist in elementary grades	NA	
Number of volumes in senior high school libraries (average)	10,779	
Beginning teacher's salary	$19,268	
Maximum teacher's salary	$41,755	
Average years of experience among teachers	10	
Number of students suspended and expelled	308	
Subjects in which Advanced Placement courses are offered:	None	

†No ESI due to Statistical Profile received for secondary school only.

Quality of School Leadership
Although the quality of educational leadership is generally considered good, observers believe politics are an important criterion in the selection of principals for the elementary schools. A strong mayor controls the School Board and can influence the superintendent of the elementary district, said observers. Consequently, the mayor may have a say in principal selection. Principals at all levels are screened by top administrators and the School Board; teachers and parents have hardly any say. Principals have some say in resource allotment. Among the elementary schools, favored principals and principals of mostly white schools seem to have the most clout, according to observers.

Parents of high school students were instrumental in defeating a recent state proposal to create a K–12 district. However, parent organizations usually are not effective in decision-making.

Quality of Instruction
Additional learning opportunities for gifted students are rated fair to good. Some special classes and field trips are offered in the elementary schools, but not much is available in the high schools. Instruction for low-achieving students, on the other hand, is rated good to excellent. The elementary schools make good use of volunteer tutors and aides, and the program for low achievers at the high schools is "one of the best in the area," said an observer. The college-preparatory curriculum is called fair to good. It is unusual for high schools of this size to offer no Advanced Placement courses. Students going directly into the world of work receive good preparation at a regional vocational school.

Minorities constitute a majority of the enrollment (a strong parochial system attracts many white students), and at least one observer believes the elementary schools do not adequately meet the needs of minority students.

Quality of School Environment
The level of classroom disruption and vandalism is low at all schools. The quality of building maintenance and repair is called fair to good at elementary schools and excellent at the high schools.

CICERO

ADDRESS OF CENTRAL OFFICE:
Elementary: 5110 West 24th Street, Cicero, IL 60650
Secondary: Morton High School, 2423 South Austin
Boulevard, Cicero, IL 60650

ESI:53

STATISTICAL PROFILE (combined)	DATA	ESI
Grade organization: K–8/9–12		
Percentage of schools built before 1955	50%	
Total enrollment	10,664	
Average Daily Attendance (ADA)	92%	5
Current expense per pupil in ADA	$3,595	5
Dropout rate	17%	6
Percentage of eligible students who took the ACT	44%	6
Average combined score on ACT	18.1	4
Percentage of graduates who enrolled in 2- or 4-year colleges	66%	
Percentage of students who passed the state reading test	NA	
Percentage of students who passed the state math test	NA	
Teacher–student ratio in elementary grades	1:24	6
Teacher–student ratio in secondary grades	1:19	9
Counselor–student ratio in secondary grades	1:350	4
Number of students per music specialist in elementary grades	600	3
Number of students per art specialist in elementary grades	600	
Number of volumes in senior high school libraries (average)	35,000	
Beginning teacher's salary	$18,494	
Maximum teacher's salary	$40,869	
Average years of experience among teachers	19	
Number of students suspended and expelled	45†	
Subjects in which Advanced Placement courses are offered:	5	5
American History, Art, Calculus, Foreign Language, Science		

†This is for elementary grades only; the high schools provided no statistic.

FAIR APPRAISAL (combined)

Quality of School Leadership
The School Boards pick principals from within the system on the basis of educational leadership ability. The quality of leadership does not vary much within the systems. Principals are screened by top administrators; teachers and parents have hardly any say. Principals usually have a lot to say about the distribution of resources.

Parent organizations at the elementary level are very effective. They have influenced decisions in recent years on such matters as reassigning students to alleviate overcrowding, restricting students to school during lunch hour, and starting an information program on drugs and alcohol. At the high school level, parent participation is mostly ineffective.

Quality of Instruction
Observers rate as excellent the learning opportunities for gifted students. Bright students in the elementary grades attend a special class once a week; also, computer training is offered in grades 3–6. Low-achieving students are offered much individual attention from tutors, aides and counselors. The curriculum for students going to college is rated fair to good. "A lot of parents complain that students don't get enough high-level courses," said an observer. The curriculum for students going on to jobs also receives a fair to good rating. The schools' record of placing students in jobs is not very good, said an observer.

Quality of School Environment
The incidence of classroom disruption and vandalism is low, and the quality of building maintenance and repair is excellent. "Even the very old schools are well-maintained," said an observer.

DOWNERS GROVE

ADDRESS OF CENTRAL OFFICE:
Elementary: 1860 63rd Street, Downers Grove, IL 60516
Secondary: 1860 63rd Street, Downers Grove, IL 60516

ESI:74

STATISTICAL PROFILE (combined)	DATA	ESI
Grade organization: K–8/9–12		
Percentage of schools built before 1955 (averaged)	45%	
Total enrollment	9,264	
Average Daily Attendance (ADA)	95%	8
Current expense per pupil in ADA	$3,709	6
Dropout rate	6%	10
Percentage of eligible students who took the ACT	70%	10
Average combined score on ACT	20.9	10
Percentage of graduates who enrolled in 2- or 4-year colleges	70%	
Percentage of students who passed the state reading test	NA	
Percentage of students who passed the state math test	NA	
Teacher–student ratio in elementary grades	1:25	5
Teacher–student ratio in secondary grades	1:18	10
Counselor–student ratio in secondary grades	1:325	5
Number of students per music specialist in elementary grades	1,080	0
Number of students per art specialist in elementary grades	None	
Number of volumes in senior high school libraries (average)	27,500	
Beginning teacher's salary (averaged)	$17,550	
Maximum teacher's salary (averaged)	$42,958	
Average years of experience among teachers (averaged)	14	
Number of students suspended and expelled	2,924†	
Subjects in which Advanced Placement courses are offered:	10	10
American History, Biology, Calculus, Chemistry, Computer Science, English, French, German, Physics, Spanish		

†All in high school district.

FAIR APPRAISAL (combined)

Quality of School Leadership
The School Boards pick principals for their leadership ability; the quality of leadership does not vary greatly from school to school. Top administrators screen candidates; teachers and parents are not involved. Principals can influence how resources are allotted. Both districts have new superintendents who are considered "strong leaders" by observers.

Parent organizations are sometimes effective. "They are only heard from on specific issues," said an observer.

Quality of Instruction
Observers rate the additional learning opportunities for gifted students as very good. In the elementary schools, bright students attend special classes once a week. Also, parents of gifted children run an enrichment program affiliated with the school system on Saturday mornings. The high schools offer classes in creativity, leadership and careers, and a special counselor is assigned to gifted students. Instruction for low-achieving students also is rated highly. Remedial classes and tutors are available. College-bound students take part in an excellent curriculum, according to observers. The 10 Advanced Placement courses and various honors and accelerated courses prepare students well. The curriculum for students planning to enter the world of work is termed good. Work-study opportunities are part of this program.

Quality of School Environment
Observers consider the level of classroom disruption and vandalism to be very low, despite of or possibly because of the high school district's report of 2,924 suspensions among a student body of only 5,200. The quality of building maintenance and repair is rated good to excellent.

ELMHURST

ADDRESS OF CENTRAL OFFICE:

145 Arthur Street, Elmhurst, IL 60126

ESI:91

STATISTICAL PROFILE	DATA	ESI
Grade organization: K–5/6–8/9–12		
Percentage of schools built before 1955	66%	
Total enrollment	6,256	
Average Daily Attendance (ADA)	94%	7
Current expense per pupil in ADA	$4,092	8
Dropout rate	6%	10
Percentage of eligible students who took the ACT	65%	10
Average combined score on ACT	20.8	10
Percentage of graduates who enrolled in 2- or 4-year colleges	70%	
Percentage of students who passed the state reading test	NA	
Percentage of students who passed the state math test	NA	
Teacher–student ratio in elementary grades	1:16	10
Teacher–student ratio in secondary grades	1:15	10
Counselor–student ratio in secondary grades	1:250	8
Number of students per music specialist in elementary grades	390	8
Number of students per art specialist in elementary grades	575	
Number of volumes in senior high school library	38,000	
Beginning teacher's salary	$17,630	
Maximum teacher's salary	$40,927	
Average years of experience among teachers	15	
Number of students suspended and expelled	456	
Subjects in which Advanced Placement courses are offered:	11	11
American History, Art, Biology, Calculus, Chemistry, Computer Science, English Language and Composition, English Literature and Composition, French, Music, Spanish		

Quality of School Leadership

Principals are selected for their leadership ability, and the quality of leadership is uniform throughout the system. Teachers interview the top two principal candidates, but parents do not; the superintendent and School Board make the final selection. Principals have some say in how resources will be divided among the schools.

Parent organizations are very effective in decision-making. For example, one school's PTA recently lobbied against redistricting to solve a problem of overcrowding; instead, parents convinced the board to add on to the school. "The School Board is very responsible and responsive," said an observer.

Quality of Instruction

Gifted students are offered special classes once a month; also, French is given after school to children in lower grades. Instruction for low-achieving students is rated good. The curriculum for college-bound students and the curriculum for job-bound students are both rated excellent. Eleven Advanced Placement courses are a very high number for a district this size.

Quality of School Environment

Classroom disruption and vandalism are not problems. The quality of building maintenance and repair is excellent.

EVANSTON

ADDRESS OF CENTRAL OFFICE:
Elementary: 1314 Ridge Avenue,
Evanston, IL 60201
Secondary: 1600 Dodge Avenue,
Evanston, IL 60204
ESI:None†

STATISTICAL PROFILE (elementary only)	DATA	ESI
Grade organization: K–5/6–8		
Percentage of schools built before 1955	71%	
Total enrollment	6,073	
Average Daily Attendance (ADA)	94%	
Current expense per pupil in ADA	$5,189	
Dropout rate	NA	
Percentage of eligible students who took the ACT	NA	
Average combined score on ACT	NA	
Percentage of graduates who enrolled in 2- or 4-year colleges	NA	
Percentage of students who passed the state reading test	NA	
Percentage of students who passed the state math test	NA	
Teacher–student ratio in elementary grades	1:24††	
Teacher–student ratio in secondary grades	NA	
Number of students per music specialist in elementary grades	300	
Number of students per art specialist in elementary grades	350	
Number of volumes in senior high school library	NA	
Beginning teacher's salary	$19,350	
Maximum teacher's salary	$43,150	
Average years of experience among teachers	NK	
Number of students suspended and expelled	89	
Subjects in which Advanced Placement courses are offered:	NA	

† No ESI as Statistical Profile was completed for elementary school only.
††The ratio in grades 6–8 is 1:28.

FAIR APPRAISAL (combined)

Quality of School Leadership
Both districts have new superintendents. Educational leadership ability is the main criterion for principal selection, and the quality of leadership is generally high throughout the system. A couple of elementary school principals are weak, said an observer, but the district has tried to compensate by installing strong vice principals. Top administrators generally screen principal candidates; teachers and parents have hardly any say.

Parent organizations are sometimes effective in decision-making. Parents are capable of putting "political pressure" on the School Boards, said an observer.

Quality of Instruction
Commenting on the learning opportunities for gifted students, one observer said, "That's what the schools do best." Although the program for gifted students is called "uneven" in the elementary grades, the high school program is very highly rated. The district's offering is "due in part to demanding parents," said an observer. Instruction for low-achieving students also is rated highly, although again it tends to be less uniform in the elementary schools. The college-preparatory curriculum is called excellent — "outstanding," said one observer. The high school offers a number of Advanced Placement courses in both the junior and senior years. The curriculum for students going into the job market is rated excellent. Restaurant and hotel management is one of many vocational offerings.

The schools "go to great lengths to answer all the needs" of minority students, said an observer. In the elementary schools in particular, however, the gap in achievement test scores between white and black students is still great.

Quality of School Environment
The level of classroom disruption and vandalism is low. The quality of building maintenance and repair is rated excellent. One observer predicted, however, that maintenance and repair might suffer in the future because of possible budget cutbacks. The schools depend heavily on local property taxes, which in turn depend on property assessments. A reassessment every four years usually results in an increase in tax revenues for the schools, but municipal officials have decided to postpone the next reassessment by one year. It could cause a serious shortfall in tax revenues for the schools.

GARY

ADDRESS OF CENTRAL OFFICE:
620 East Tenth Place, Gary, IN 46402
ESI:None†

STATISTICAL PROFILE	DATA	ESI
Grade organization:		
Percentage of schools built before 1955		
Total enrollment		
Average Daily Attendance (ADA)		
Current expense per pupil in ADA		
Dropout rate		
Percentage of eligible students who took the ACT		
Average combined score on ACT		
Percentage of graduates who enrolled in 2- or 4-year colleges		
Percentage of students who passed the state reading test		
Percentage of students who passed the state math test		
Teacher–student ratio in elementary grades		
Teacher–student ratio in secondary grades		
Counselor–student ratio in secondary grades		
Number of students per music specialist in elementary grades		
Number of students per art specialist in elementary grades		
Number of volumes in senior high school library		
Beginning teacher's salary		
Maximum teacher's salary		
Average years of experience among teachers		
Number of students suspended and expelled		
Subjects in which Advanced Placement courses are offered:		

†A Statistical Profile was not received from this district.

FAIR APPRAISAL

Quality of School Leadership
Principals are chosen for their educational leadership ability, and the quality of leadership does not vary greatly throughout the K–12 system. While parents may later challenge a principal appointment, neither they nor teachers have a say in the selection process. Principals have some say in how resources are allotted to their schools.

Parent organizations are sometimes effective in decision-making, but they are not usually very influential.

Quality of Instruction
One district school is set aside for gifted students, and the program is rated good. On the other hand, instruction for low-achieving students is considered to be only fair. The curriculum for college-bound students is rated good, but the curriculum for students heading into the job market is rated poor.

Minority students comprise a majority of the school population, and the schools are not adequately meeting their needs. The result, said an observer, is that "too often pupils, failing to achieve, drop out of school before graduation." The same observer put some of the blame on parents who "delay interest in their children's progress" until it is too late.

Quality of School Environment
Classroom disruption and vandalism are not major problems. The quality of building maintenance and repair is generally good.

GLENVIEW

ADDRESS OF CENTRAL OFFICE:
Elementary: 1401 Greenwood Road, Glenview, IL 60025
Secondary: Northfield Township High School,
1835 Landwehr Avenue, Glenview, IL 60025
ESI:None†

STATISTICAL PROFILE (elementary only)	DATA	ESI
Grade organization: K–8		
Percentage of schools built before 1955	17%	
Total enrollment	2,800	
Average Daily Attendance (ADA)	98%	
Current expense per pupil in ADA	$4,500	
Dropout rate	NA	
Percentage of eligible students who took the ACT	NA	
Average combined score on ACT	NA	
Percentage of graduates who enrolled in 2- or 4-year colleges	NA	
Percentage of students who passed the state reading test	NA	
Percentage of students who passed the state math test	NA	
Teacher–student ratio in elementary grades	1:22	
Teacher–student ratio in secondary grades	NA	
Counselor–student ratio in secondary grades	NA	
Number of students per music specialist in elementary grades	400	
Number of students per art specialist in elementary grades	400	
Number of volumes in senior high school library	NA	
Beginning teacher's salary	$20,297	
Maximum teacher's salary	$40,830	
Average years of experience among teachers	15	
Number of students suspended and expelled	3	
Subjects in which Advanced Placement courses are offered:	NA	

†No ESI as Statistical Profile was completed only for elementary school.

FAIR APPRAISAL (combined)

Quality of School Leadership
The School Boards hire principals for their educational leadership ability; the quality of leadership is good throughout the systems. Teachers and parents have little say in principal selection. However, principals have some say in how resources will be distributed by the central office.

Parents are considered very effective in decision-making. Most recently, they convinced top administrators and School Board for the high school district to build a new field house.

Quality of Instruction
Additional learning opportunities for both gifted and low-achieving students are rated excellent. Special classes exist, and a Human Potential Center that features a wide range of computer programs and other learning aides is available to students at all learning stages. More than 90 percent of high school graduates go on to higher education, and the college-preparatory curriculum is considered excellent. The rating is good for the job-preparation curriculum.

Quality of School Environment
Classroom disruption and vandalism are not problems. The quality of building maintenance and repair is excellent. "This is a very rich area," said an observer. "If a parent comes to school and notices a tear in the carpet, the carpet will be replaced within a year."

HARVEY

ADDRESS OF CENTRAL OFFICE:
Elementary: 152nd Street and Myrtle Avenue,
Harvey, IL 60426
Secondary: Thornton Township High School,
151st and Broadway, Harvey, IL 60426

ESI:60

STATISTICAL PROFILE (combined)	DATA	ESI
Grade organization: K–5/6–8/9–12		
Percentage of schools built before 1955	†	
Total enrollment	10,975	
Average Daily Attendance (ADA)	92%	5
Current expense per pupil in ADA	$4,255	9
Dropout rate	14%	9
Percentage of eligible students who took the ACT	43%	6
Average combined score on ACT	18.7	4
Percentage of graduates who enrolled in 2- or 4-year colleges	NK	
Percentage of students who passed the state reading test	NA	
Percentage of students who passed the state math test	NA	
Teacher–student ratio in elementary grades	1:21	9
Teacher–student ratio in secondary grades	1:22	6
Counselor–student ratio in secondary grades	NK	0
Number of students per music specialist in elementary grades	539	5
Number of students per art specialist in elementary grades	629	
Number of volumes in senior high school libraries (average)	18,334	
Beginning teacher's salary (averaged)	$16,254	
Maximum teacher's salary (averaged)	$43,000	
Average years of experience among teachers (median)	17	
Number of students suspended and expelled	600	
Subjects in which Advanced Placement courses are offered:	7	7
Biology, Calculus, Chemistry, Computer Science, English Language and Composition, French, German		

†One percent of the elementary and middle schools were built before 1955 and two out of three senior high schools.

FAIR APPRAISAL (combined)

Quality of School Leadership
Educational leadership ability is the primary criterion for judging principal candidates, and the quality of leadership is uniform. Teachers and parents have hardly any say in the principal selection process. Principals have some say in resource disbursement.

Parents are sometimes effective in decision-making, more so at the elementary level than in the high school district.

Quality of Instruction
Special programs for gifted students are rated good, as is additional instruction available to low-achieving students. The curriculum for college-bound students and the curriculum for job-bound students are considered good; the vocational training is particularly extensive.

Minority students constitute a majority of the student population, and observers believe their educational needs are adequately met.

Quality of School Environment
The incidence of classroom disruption and vandalism is low, and the quality of building maintenance and repair is good. The high school district in particular does an excellent job of upkeep.

MAYWOOD

ADDRESS OF CENTRAL OFFICE:
Elementary: 1133 South Eighth Avenue,
Maywood, IL 60153
Secondary: Proviso Township High School, 807 South
First Avenue, Maywood, IL 60153

ESI:None†

STATISTICAL PROFILE (secondary only)	DATA	ESI
Grade organization: 9–12		
Percentage of schools built before 1955	50%††	
Total enrollment	4,935	
Average Daily Attendance (ADA)	89%	
Current expense per pupil in ADA	$4,341	
Dropout rate	28%	
Percentage of eligible students who took the ACT	57%	
Average combined score on ACT	21.5	
Percentage of graduates who enrolled in 2- or 4-year colleges	65%	
Percentage of students who passed the state reading test	NA	
Percentage of students who passed the state math test	NA	
Teacher–student ratio in elementary grades	NA	
Teacher–student ratio in secondary grades	1:21	
Counselor–student ratio in secondary grades	1:300	
Number of students per music specialist in elementary grades	NA	
Number of students per art specialist in elementary grades	NA	
Number of volumes in senior high school libraries (average)	25,000	
Beginning teacher's salary	$21,300 †††	
Maximum teacher's salary	$50,198 †††	
Average years of experience among teachers	12	
Number of students suspended and expelled	100	
Subjects in which Advanced Placement courses are offered:	4	
English, Calculus, Chemistry, Physics		

† No ESI as Statistical Profile was completed only for secondary school.
†† The district has two schools.
†††These are 1986–87 statistics.

FAIR APPRAISAL (combined)

Quality of School Leadership
Most principals are chosen for their educational leadership ability, and the quality of leadership is generally high throughout the districts. However, internal politics have been a factor in some selection. Principal candidates are screened by top administrators; teachers and parents are not involved. Principals have some say about the allotment of resources.

Parent organizations are sometimes effective. Parents tend to be more active at the secondary level than in the elementary schools, a switch from the norm in most districts.

Quality of Instruction
Additional learning opportunities for gifted students are good at the high school, but fair to poor in the elementary schools. "The program at the elementary level is half-hearted," said an observer. Even when students are identified as bright, they sometimes have trouble getting into the program. Instruction for low-achieving students is called "unsatisfactory." The curriculum for students going to college is good, but the curriculum for students heading into the job market is termed fair to poor.

Minority students constitute a majority in the district, and observers believe the schools are not adequately meeting their educational needs.

Quality of School Environment
The level of classroom disruption and vandalism is about average, but the quality of building maintenance and repair is rated only fair.

OAK PARK

ADDRESS OF CENTRAL OFFICE:
Elementary: 970 Madison Avenue, Oak Park, IL 60302
Secondary: 201 North Scoville Avenue,
Oak Park, IL 60302
ESI:None†

STATISTICAL PROFILE	DATA	ESI
Grade organization:		
Percentage of schools built before 1955		
Total enrollment		
Average Daily Attendance (ADA)		
Current expense per pupil in ADA		
Dropout rate		
Percentage of eligible students who took the ACT		
Average combined score on ACT		
Percentage of graduates who enrolled in 2- or 4-year colleges		
Percentage of students who passed the state reading test		
Percentage of students who passed the state math test		
Teacher–student ratio in elementary grades		
Teacher–student ratio in secondary grades		
Counselor–student ratio in secondary grades		
Number of students per music specialist in elementary grades		
Number of students per art specialist in elementary grades		
Number of volumes in senior high school library		
Beginning teacher's salary		
Maximum teacher's salary		
Average years of experience among teachers		
Number of students suspended and expelled		
Subjects in which Advanced Placement courses are offered:		

†A Statistical Profile was not received from this district.

FAIR APPRAISAL (combined)

Quality of School Leadership
Principals are chosen primarily for their educational leadership ability, and the quality of leadership is uniform throughout the system. Top administrators screen principal candidates for the elementary district, but teacher and parent representatives are asked to voice their views of finalists among the candidates. Principals of the elementary schools have some say in deciding how resources will be distributed among the schools. (The high school district has one school, and the superintendent and principal are the same person.) Parent organizations are called effective in decision-making.

Quality of Instruction
Additional learning opportunities are available for gifted students in both districts, and the programs are rated good. One thing bright students in the high school get involved in is a special class that studies the stock market, even investing money earned by students. Instruction for low-achieving students is called good. The curriculum for college-bound students is rated excellent; the high school offers a number of Advanced Placement courses. The preparation for students entering the job market is good.

Quality of School Environment
Classroom disruption and vandalism are not problems. The quality of building maintenance and repair is rated good to excellent.

VILLA PARK

ADDRESS OF CENTRAL OFFICE:
Elementary: 255 West Vermont Street,
Villa Park, IL 60181
Secondary: Dupage High School (Willow Brook),
1250 South Ardmore Avenue, Villa Park, IL 60181
ESI:None†

STATISTICAL PROFILE (elementary only)	DATA	ESI
Grade organization: K–5/6–8		
Percentage of schools built before 1955	86%	
Total enrollment	3,209	
Average Daily Attendance (ADA)	88%	
Current expense per pupil in ADA	$3,632	
Dropout rate	NA	
Percentage of eligible students who took the ACT	NA	
Average combined score on ACT	NA	
Percentage of graduates who enrolled in 2- or 4-year colleges	NA	
Percentage of students who passed the state reading test	NA	
Percentage of students who passed the state math test	NA	
Teacher–student ratio in elementary grades	1:26	
Teacher–student ratio in secondary grades	1:28 ††	
Counselor–student ratio in secondary grades	1:500††	
Number of students per music specialist in elementary grades	700	
Number of students per art specialist in elementary grades	700	
Number of volumes in senior high school library	NA	
Beginning teacher's salary	$17,352	
Maximum teacher's salary	$36,493	
Average years of experience among teachers	14	
Number of students suspended and expelled	30	
Subjects in which Advanced Placement courses are offered:	NA	

† No ESI as Statistical Profile was completed only for elementary schools.
††These figures are for grades 6–8.

FAIR APPRAISAL (combined)

Quality of School Leadership
The School Boards select principals on the basis of their educational leadership ability; the quality of leadership is high throughout the schools. Parents and teachers have little say in screening principal candidates. However, principals can influence the allotment of resources to the various schools.

Parent organizations are sometimes effective in decision-making. Parents tried to impress both sides with the need for compromise in a three-week-long teachers' strike in the fall of 1986, but were largely unsuccessful. However, parents are believed to have had some influence in the superintendent's decision to retire when a replacement is found (at least by the 1988–89 school year).

Quality of Instruction
Programs for the gifted and low-achievers are rated good. The curricula for college-bound and job-bound students also are rated good. Students in the high school district scored 20.7 on the ACT in 1985–86, which is above the state average of 19.2. Vocational education is provided mostly by a regional center. The ADA is unusually low.

Quality of School Environment
The level of classroom disruption and vandalism is low, and the quality of building maintenance and repair is good.

WHEATON

ADDRESS OF CENTRAL OFFICE:
130 West Park Avenue, Wheaton, IL 60187
ESI:58

STATISTICAL PROFILE	DATA	ESI
Grade organization: K–5/6–8/9–12		
Percentage of schools built before 1955	38%	
Total enrollment	10,185	
Average Daily Attendance (ADA)	95%	8
Current expense per pupil in ADA	$3,317	4
Dropout rate	6%	10
Percentage of eligible students who took the ACT	42%	6
Average combined score on ACT	22.1	10
Percentage of graduates who enrolled in 2- or 4-year colleges	74%	
Percentage of students who passed the state reading test	NA	
Percentage of students who passed the state math test	NA	
Teacher–student ratio in elementary grades	1:23	7
Teacher–student ratio in secondary grades	1:20	8
Counselor–student ratio in secondary grades	1:404	1
Number of students per music specialist in elementary grades	1,588	0
Number of students per art specialist in elementary grades	1,588	
Number of volumes in senior high school library	31,176	
Beginning teacher's salary	$18,125	
Maximum teacher's salary	$39,640	
Average years of experience among teachers	17	
Number of students suspended and expelled	NK	
Subjects in which Advanced Placement courses are offered: Calculus, English, Foreign Language, Physics	4	4

Quality of School Leadership

The school board generally hires principals for their educational leadership ability, and the quality of leadership is high throughout the system. Indeed, one principal won a state award several years ago as an outstanding administrator. Candidates for principal are screened by top administrators; parents and teachers are not involved. Principals' specific needs are considered by central administration and School Board.

Parents and other citizens are effective in decision-making. When district officials four years ago wanted to close the high school and generally contract the system, parent groups got almost 7,000 persons to sign petitions that persuaded the School Board to change its mind about the district's future.

Quality of Instruction

The program for gifted students at all levels is rated good — "better than most." One observer gave a lot of credit to a strong group of parents of gifted children. The program includes a couple of teachers especially for the gifted. Instruction for low-achieving students is rated fair to good. Parents of low-achieving students do not apply pressure on district officials as do parents of bright children, said an observer. Also, students who need help most are least likely to stay after school to take advantage of an elective extra period the high school offers, said an observer. College-bound students can take advantage of a good curriculum, but students moving into the job market fare a little worse. The vocational education program doesn't get the attention the college-preparatory curiculum does, said an observer, mainly because the majority of parents and other citizens think "everybody's" going to college. They tend to forget about the 24 percent of students who don't.

Quality of School Environment

Classroom disruption and vandalism are not problems. However, the quality of school building maintenance and repair is rated fair to poor. One observer estimated district officials are "eight years behind" in making needed repairs and improvements. As much as $27 million may be needed to catch up.

Cincinnati, OH

We received Statistical Profiles from ten districts in the Cincinnati Metropolitan Area,
including nearby Kentucky, and Fair Appraisals alone from two other districts.
Ohio does not have required competency tests in reading and math. Therefore, all Ohio
district profiles show *NA* (not applicable) on the lines requesting those statistics.
For comparison, you may wish to examine districts in the Cleveland and
Columbus Metropolitan Areas in Ohio and the Louisville Metropolitan Area in Kentucky.

AREA AT A GLANCE

SCHOOL DISTRICT	ENROLLMENT	ESI
Campbell County, KY	4,158	45
Cincinnati	52,002	47*
Covington, KY	5,937	39*
Greenhills–Forest Park	5,061	77
Hamilton	10,698	36
Kenton County, KY	10,745	51
Middletown	16,000	76
Mount Healthy	4,900	31
Norwood	38,041	
Oak Hills	7,324	63
Southwest	3,431	65
Sycamore	5,118	

Indicates district misinterpretation of one or more statistics in the ESI. For each misinterpreted statistic, a score of 0* was given instead of a possible score of 0 to 10 points.

CAMPBELL COUNTY

ADDRESS OF CENTRAL OFFICE:
101 Orchard Lane, Alexandria, KY 41001
ESI:45

STATISTICAL PROFILE	DATA	ESI
Grade organization: †		
Percentage of schools built before 1955	62%	
Total enrollment	4,158	
Average Daily Attendance (ADA)	95%	8
Current expense per pupil in ADA	$2,030	1
Dropout rate	25%	0
Percentage of eligible students who took the ACT	44%	6
Average combined score on ACT	19.7	5
Percentage of graduates who enrolled in 2- or 4-year colleges	40%	
Percentage of students who passed the state reading test	90%	
Percentage of students who passed the state math test	94%	
Teacher–student ratio in elementary grades	1:21	9
Teacher–student ratio in secondary grades	1:18	10
Counselor–student ratio in secondary grades	1:400	2
Number of students per music specialist in elementary grades	1,000	0
Number of students per art specialist in elementary grades	2,000	
Number of volumes in senior high school library	10,326	
Beginning teacher's salary	$14,704	
Maximum teacher's salary	$24,625	
Average years of experience among teachers	15	
Number of students suspended and expelled	128	
Subjects in which Advanced Placement courses are offered: American History, Calculus, English, French, Physics	5	5

FAIR APPRAISAL

Quality of School Leadership
Principals are chosen for their educational leadership ability, and the quality of leadership is high throughout the system. Teachers and parents have little or no say in the selection of principals. Principals have some influence on how resources will be allotted to the schools.

Parent organizations generally are effective in their influence on district decision-making. For example, an observer said, parents have a great deal to say about what holidays will be observed in the school calendar.

Quality of Instruction
Gifted students in the middle schools are grouped for part of the day to receive special instruction, and the program is rated excellent. The additional instruction for low-achieving students is called good. Both the curriculum for the college-bound student and the curriculum for the job-bound student are considered good.

Quality of School Environment
The incidence of classroom disruption and vandalism is very low. School officials simply "don't permit it," said an observer. Vandals are sent to juvenile court. The quality of building maintenance and repair is good. New windows were recently installed in the high school and two middle schools.

CINCINNATI

ADDRESS OF CENTRAL OFFICE:
230 East Ninth Street, Cincinnati, OH 45202
ESI:47*

STATISTICAL PROFILE	DATA	ESI
Grade organization: K–6/7–8/9–12		
Percentage of schools built before 1955	50%	
Total enrollment	52,002	
Average Daily Attendance (ADA)	91%	4
Current expense per pupil in ADA	$3,650	9
Dropout rate	34%	0
Percentage of eligible students who took the ACT	25%	2
Average combined score on ACT	†	0*
Percentage of graduates who enrolled in 2- or 4-year colleges	61%	
Percentage of students who passed the state reading test	NA	
Percentage of students who passed the state math test	NA	
Teacher–student ratio in elementary grades	1:20	10
Teacher–student ratio in secondary grades	1:17	10
Counselor–student ratio in secondary grades	1:394	2
Number of students per music specialist in elementary grades	810	0
Number of students per art specialist in elementary grades	850	
Beginning teacher's salary	$16,372	
Maximum teacher's salary	$36,336	
Average years of experience among teachers	14	
Number of students suspended and expelled	10,516††	
Subjects in which Advanced Placement courses are offered: American History, Art History, Art Studio General, Biology, Calculus AB, Calculus BC, Chemistry, English Language & Composition, English Literature & Composition, European History, French Language, French Literature, German Language, Latin-Vergil, Music, Physics B, Physics-Mechanics, Physics-Electricity, Spanish	19	19

† The district misinterpreted the statistics.

††Students suspended or expelled more than once are counted for each penalty.

Quality of School Leadership

One observer is favorably impressed by the leadership quality of the new superintendent. Observers also believe the district hires principals for their educational leadership ability, and the quality of leadership is generally good throughout the district. Parents and teachers are not involved in screening principal candidates. Principals have some say, however, in how resources are apportioned to the schools.

Parent organizations are sometimes effective influencing decision-making. Parents and other citizens, for example, are included in a task force devising a long-range plan for the district.

Quality of Instruction

Three schools have received Awards of Excellence from the U.S. Department of Education. The district offers such special programs as a School for Creative and Performing Arts; Academy of Physical Education; and bilingual education in seven languages, beginning in the primary grades. Observers rate the learning opportunities for gifted students as good. The additional instruction for low-achieving students is not quite as good, but, said an observer, the district is making a "great effort" to improve instruction. Overall, the college-preparatory curriculum is termed good; indeed, there is a special college-prep high school (Walnut Hills), which accounts for many of the Advanced Placement courses. One complaint from an observer is that not enough students are counseled into the college-prep curriculum and too few students take high-level courses. The curriculum for students planning on jobs after graduation is called fair to good.

The needs of minority students are not adquately met, according to the observers. However, the district is making progress under a court desegregation order. Racial balance is scheduled to be achieved by 1991.

Quality of School Environment

Even though this is a medium-sized district, observers consider the level of classroom disruption and vandalism to be low. One observer credited the low incidence to increased discipline (see statistic for suspensions and expulsions). The quality of building maintenance and repair is rated good. A special tax levy in 1984 was earmarked for repairs and improvements.

COVINGTON

ADDRESS OF CENTRAL OFFICE:
25 East Seventh Street, Covington, KY 41011
ESI:39*

STATISTICAL PROFILE	DATA	ESI
Grade organization: K–7/8–12		
Percentage of schools built before 1955	67%	
Total enrollment	5,937	
Average Daily Attendance (ADA)	93%	6
Current expense per pupil in ADA	$2,340	3
Dropout rate	38%	0
Percentage of eligible students who took the ACT	81%	10
Average combined score on ACT	16.3	0
Percentage of graduates who enrolled in 2- or 4-year colleges	34%	
Percentage of students who passed the state reading test	95%	
Percentage of students who passed the state math test	95%	
Teacher–student ratio in elementary grades	1:19	10
Teacher–student ratio in secondary grades	1:13	10
Counselor–student ratio in secondary grades	1:600	0
Number of students per music specialist in elementary grades	1,000	0
Number of students per art specialist in elementary grades	1,000	
Number of volumes in senior high school library	12,000	
Beginning teacher's salary	$15,400	
Maximum teacher's salary	$26,800	
Average years of experience among teachers	14	
Number of students suspended and expelled	486	
Subjects in which Advanced Placement courses are offered:	†	0*

†The district misinterpreted this statistic.

FAIR APPRAISAL

Quality of School Leadership
The School Board appoints principals who have educational leadership ability, and the quality of leadership is uniform in the district. Teachers and parents have no say in principal selection, and principals do not have much say in how resources are apportioned.

Parent organizations are rarely effective in influencing decision-making by school officials.

Quality of Instruction
Gifted and talented students in grades 4–6 are mostly grouped at one elementary school; the program at this level and at the high school is rated good. However, low-achieving students do not fare as well; the level of additional instruction available to them is called fair to poor. "They are not getting the individual attention they deserve," said an observer. The curricula for students going to college and those entering the job market are rated good.

Quality of School Environment
The level of classroom disruption and vandalism is very low, and the quality of building maintenance and repair is good.

GREENHILLS–FOREST PARK

ADDRESS OF CENTRAL OFFICE:
1215 West Kemper Road, Cincinnati, OH 45240
ESI:77

STATISTICAL PROFILE	DATA	ESI
Grade organization: K–5/6–8/9–12		
Percentage of schools built before 1955	10%	
Total enrollment	5,061	
Average Daily Attendance (ADA)	94%	7
Current expense per pupil in ADA	$3,330	8
Dropout rate	2%	10
Percentage of eligible students who took the ACT	87%	10
Average combined score on ACT	19.9	5
Percentage of graduates who enrolled in 2- or 4-year colleges	63%	
Percentage of students who passed the state reading test	NA	
Percentage of students who passed the state math test	NA	
Teacher–student ratio in elementary grades	1:16	10
Teacher–student ratio in secondary grades	1:18	10
Counselor–student ratio in secondary grades	1:290	6
Number of students per music specialist in elementary grades	300	9
Number of students per art specialist in elementary grades	300	
Number of volumes in senior high school library	10,459	
Beginning teacher's salary	$16,800	
Maximum teacher's salary	$36,000	
Average years of experience among teachers	15	
Number of students suspended and expelled	229	
Subjects in which Advanced Placement courses are offered:	2	2
Calculus, English		

FAIR APPRAISAL

Quality of School Leadership
Principals are selected for their ability as educational leaders, and the quality of leadership is good throughout the system. Parents and teachers have hardly any say in principal selection, but principals have some say in how resources are distributed.

The district recently completed a year-long study on future directions that involved hundreds of residents. A parent advisory council is an ongoing influence on decision-making.

Quality of Instruction
Both the program for gifted students and the program for low-achieving students receive a good rating. Computer instruction for bright students begins in kindergarten. The district was one of the first in the area to adopt a competency-based program that provides additional tutoring for students having difficulty. The observers rate the college-preparatory curriculum good and the curriculum for students entering the job market as excellent. A regional vocational school offers instruction in such special fields as aviation and chef training.

Quality of School Environment
Classroom disruption and vandalism are not problems. Building maintenance and repair are rated good to excellent.

HAMILTON

ADDRESS OF CENTRAL OFFICE:
P.O. Box 627, Hamilton, OH 45012
ESI:36

STATISTICAL PROFILE	DATA	ESI
Grade organization: K–6/7–9/10–12		
Percentage of schools built before 1955	53%	
Total enrollment	10,698	
Average Daily Attendance (ADA)	90%	3
Current expense per pupil in ADA	$2,682	5
Dropout rate	22%	1
Percentage of eligible students who took the ACT	10%	0
Average combined score on ACT	17.7	4
Percentage of graduates who enrolled in 2- or 4-year colleges	22%	
Percentage of students who passed the state reading test	NA	
Percentage of students who passed the state math test	NA	
Teacher–student ratio in elementary grades	1:26	4
Teacher–student ratio in secondary grades	1:26	2
Counselor–student ratio in secondary grades	1:289	6
Number of students per music specialist in elementary grades	418	7
Number of students per art specialist in elementary grades	899	
Number of volumes in senior high school library	12,000	
Beginning teacher's salary	$15,475	
Maximum teacher's salary	$32,497	
Average years of experience among teachers	13	
Number of students suspended and expelled	4,621	
Subjects in which Advanced Placement courses are offered: Calculus, Chemistry, English, Physics	4	4

FAIR APPRAISAL

Quality of School Leadership
The School Board appoints principals who show educational leadership ability; the quality of leadership in the system is generally uniform. Teachers and parents do not take part in screening principal candidates. Principals have some say in how resources are allotted to schools.

Parent organizations are effective influences on decision-making. For example, parents were influential in getting the School Board to adopt computer literacy and gifted programs.

Quality of Instruction
Programs for gifted and low-achieving students are rated good. In addition to special instruction for bright students during school hours, the district runs a voluntary enrichment program on Saturdays. Observers term as good the curricula for students going to college and students going into the world of work. The vocational education curriculum is "getting better all the time," said an observer. District students have access to "state-of-the-art" equipment, some of it better than what local industries have.

Quality of School Environment
District administrators have emphasized school discipline in recent years, and it has paid off in lowering the level of classroom disruption and vandalism. (Also note the exceptionally high number of suspensions and expulsions.) The quality of building maintenance and repair is poor, but "getting better." A tax levy for more than $10 million was passed recently, and a major repair and improvement program is underway. The work is scheduled for completion by the end of the decade.

KENTON COUNTY

ADDRESS OF CENTRAL OFFICE:
5533 Madison Pike, Independence, KY 41051
ESI:51

STATISTICAL PROFILE	DATA	ESI
Grade organization: K–6/7–8/9–12		
Percentage of schools built before 1955	50%	
Total enrollment	10,745	
Average Daily Attendance (ADA)	94%	7
Current expense per pupil in ADA	$2,122	2
Dropout rate	19%	4
Percentage of eligible students who took the ACT	53%	8
Average combined score on ACT	18.3	4
Percentage of graduates who enrolled in 2- or 4-year colleges	52%	
Percentage of students who passed the state reading test	NK	
Percentage of students who passed the state math test	NK	
Teacher–student ratio in elementary grades	1:27	3
Teacher–student ratio in secondary grades	1:17	10
Counselor–student ratio in secondary grades	1:550	0
Number of students per music specialist in elementary grades	490	6
Number of students per art specialist in elementary grades	None	
Number of volumes in senior high school library	13,121	
Beginning teacher's salary	$14,610	
Maximum teacher's salary	$25,807	
Average years of experience among teachers	12	
Number of students suspended and expelled	229	
Subjects in which Advanced Placement courses are offered: American History, Biology, Calculus, Chemistry, English, French, Spanish	7	7

FAIR APPRAISAL

Quality of School Leadership
Principals are selected primarily for their educational leadership ability, and the quality of leadership does not vary greatly from school to school. Teachers and parents have no say in screening principal candidates, but principals have a great deal to say about the distribution of district resources.

Parent organizations are sometimes effective in their influence on decision-making.

Quality of Instruction
The program for gifted children is rated excellent. Bright students in the intermediate grades are bused twice a week to two or three different locations for special instruction. At least one teacher is designated at each elementary school to work with low-achieving students, and the effort is rated good. The curriculum for college-bound students is called excellent, and the curriculum for the job-bound is rated good.

Quality of School Environment
A sophisticated security system has been installed to protect schools when they are vacant, and the level of classroom disruption and vandalism has gone down. The quality of building maintenance and repair is good.

MIDDLETOWN

ADDRESS OF CENTRAL OFFICE:
1515 Girard Avenue, Middletown, OH 45044
ESI:76

STATISTICAL PROFILE	DATA	ESI
Grade organization: K–6/7–8/9–12		
Percentage of schools built before 1955	50%	
Total enrollment	10,000	
Average Daily Attendance (ADA)	97%	10
Current expense per pupil in ADA	$3,812	10
Dropout rate	10%	10
Percentage of eligible students who took the ACT	50%	8
Average combined score on ACT	18.7	4
Percentage of graduates who enrolled in 2- or 4-year colleges	52%	
Percentage of students who passed the state reading test	NA	
Percentage of students who passed the state math test	NA	
Teacher–student ratio in elementary grades	1:21	9
Teacher–student ratio in secondary grades	1:16	10
Counselor–student ratio in secondary grades	1:400	2
Number of students per music specialist in elementary grades	130	10
Number of students per art specialist in elementary grades	130	
Number of volumes in senior high school library	30,353	
Beginning teacher's salary	$17,129	
Maximum teacher's salary	$36,056	
Average years of experience among teachers	15	
Number of students suspended and expelled	890	
Subjects in which Advanced Placement courses are offered: Biology, Calculus, English	3	3

FAIR APPRAISAL

Quality of School Leadership
The School Board appoints principals who demonstrate educational leadership ability; the quality of leadership does not vary greatly throughout the system. While principals primarily are screened by top administrators, letters of recommendation are accepted from teachers and parents. Principals have some say in the allotment of resources.

Parents are considered effective influences on decision-making. Principals meet monthly with parent leaders.

Quality of Instruction
Gifted students in grades 4–6 have special instruction five hours per week, and opportunities exist also for students in higher grades. The program is rated good, as is the instruction available to low-achieving students. The high school has strong foreign language and science courses, and the performing arts program is considered exceptional. Extensive vocational courses make the curriculum for students going into the world of work a good one.

Quality of School Environment
Classroom disruption and vandalism are not problems. "The appearance of some buildings could be improved with more adequate custodial services," said an observer; nevertheless, the quality of building maintenance and repair is considered good.

MT. HEALTHY

ADDRESS OF CENTRAL OFFICE:
7615 Harrison Avenue, Cincinnati, OH 45231
ESI:31

STATISTICAL PROFILE	DATA	ESI
Grade organization: K–6/7–8/9–12		
Percentage of schools built before 1955	40%	
Total enrollment	4,900	
Average Daily Attendance (ADA)	96%	9
Current expense per pupil in ADA	$2,706	5
Dropout rate	25%	0
Percentage of eligible students who took the ACT	31%	4
Average combined score on ACT	17	0
Percentage of graduates who enrolled in 2- or 4-year colleges	52%	
Percentage of students who passed the state reading test	NA	
Percentage of students who passed the state math test	NA	
Teacher–student ratio in elementary grades	1:25	5
Teacher–student ratio in secondary grades	1:23	5
Counselor–student ratio in secondary grades	1:367	3
Number of students per music specialist in elementary grades	2,500	0
Number of students per art specialist in elementary grades	2,500	
Number of volumes in senior high school library	16,000	
Beginning teacher's salary	$14,800	
Maximum teacher's salary	$32,165	
Average years of experience among teachers	14	
Number of students suspended and expelled	335	
Subjects in which Advanced Placement courses are offered:	None	0

FAIR APPRAISAL

Quality of School Leadership
Most principals are hired from the ranks of district teachers, but their educational leadership ability is the primary criterion for their selection. The quality of leadership does not vary greatly from school to school. Teachers and parents usually have a representative on the committee that interviews final candidates. Principals have some say in deciding how resources will be divided among the schools.

Parents are sometimes effective in their influence on district decision-making. A standing parent advisory committee is the main voice of parents.

Quality of Instruction
The additional learning opportunities for gifted students are rated poor. "There are none to speak of," said an observer. The additional instruction for low-achieving students is given a fair rating. The college-preparatory curriculum is considered good, and the curriculum that prepares students for the world of work is rated excellent. A regional vocational education school offers a wide variety of up-to-date vocational courses.

Quality of School Environment
The level of classroom disruption and student vandalism is low. The district is in the midst of "repairing and revamping" the schools, and the quality of maintenance and repair is rated good to excellent.

NORWOOD

ADDRESS OF CENTRAL OFFICE:
2132 Williams Avenue, Norwood, OH 45212
ESI:None†

STATISTICAL PROFILE	DATA	ESI
Grade organization:		
Percentage of schools built before 1955		
Total enrollment		
Average Daily Attendance (ADA)		
Current expense per pupil in ADA		
Dropout rate		
Percentage of eligible students who took the ACT		
Average combined score on ACT		
Percentage of graduates who enrolled in 2- or 4-year college		
Percentage of students who passed the state reading test		
Percentage of students who passed the state math test		
Teacher–student ratio in elementary grades		
Teacher–student ratio in secondary grades		
Counselor–student ratio in secondary grades		
Number of students per music specialist in elementary grades		
Number of students per art specialist in elementary grades		
Number of volumes in senior high school library		
Beginning teacher's salary		
Maximum teacher's salary		
Average years of experience among teachers		
Number of students suspended and expelled		
Subjects in which Advanced Placement courses are offered:		

†A Statistical Profile was not received from this district.

FAIR APPRAISAL

Quality of School Leadership

The School Board seeks principals who have educational leadership ability; the quality of leadership is generally uniform throughout the district. Parents and teachers do not have a say in principal selection, but principals have some say in how resources are allotted to the schools.

Parent organizations are sometimes effective in their influence on policy decisions.

Quality of Instruction

The program for gifted students is rated good. One feature is a volunteer after-school science project in which studetns build robots. Additional instruction for low-achieving students is rated fair to good. Both the curriculum for college-bound and the curriculum for job-bound students are given a fair rating.

Quality of School Environment

Classroom disruption and vandalism are not problems. Money has been tight in the district, and the budget for maintenance and repair has suffered. As a result, the quality of building maintenance and repair is rated only fair. The situation may worsen because of the closing of a General Motors plant, the city's largest employer.

OAK HILLS

ADDRESS OF CENTRAL OFFICE:
6479 Bridgetown Road, Cincinnati, OH 45248
ESI:63

STATISTICAL PROFILE	DATA	ESI
Grade organization: K–6/7–9/10–12		
Percentage of schools built before 1955	37%	
Total enrollment	7,324	
Average Daily Attendance (ADA)	95%	8
Current expense per pupil in ADA	$2,868	5
Dropout rate	3%	10
Percentage of eligible students who took the ACT	53%	8
Average combined score on ACT	19.9	5
Percentage of graduates who enrolled in 2- or 4-year colleges	60%	
Percentage of students who passed the state reading test	NA	
Percentage of students who passed the state math test	NA	
Teacher–student ratio in elementary grades	1:25	5
Teacher–student ratio in secondary grades	1:19	9
Counselor–student ratio in secondary grades	1:364	3
Number of students per music specialist in elementary grades	462	6
Number of students per art specialist in elementary grades	528	
Number of volumes in senior high school library	18,600	
Beginning teacher's salary	$16,497	
Maximum teacher's salary	$35,644	
Average years of experience among teachers	15	
Number of students suspended and expelled	NK	
Subjects in which Advanced Placement courses are offered:	4	4
American History, Calculus, Chemistry, English		

FAIR APPRAISAL

Quality of School Leadership

Educational leadership ability is the primary criterion for choosing a principal, and the quality of educational leadership does not vary greatly from school to school. Teachers have some say in principal selection, but parents do not. Principals have some influence in how resources will be divided among the schools.

Parent organizations are sometimes effective in decision-making.

Quality of Instruction

The programs for gifted students and low-achieving students are rated good, although observers think each program can be improved. The college-preparatory curriculum is in "pretty good shape," but observers would like to see more Advanced Placement courses. The vocational education curriculum is considered excellent.

Quality of School Environment

The incidence of classroom disruption and vandalism is low. The quality of building maintenance and repair has been poor, but it is starting to improve. Two recent tax levies earmarked funds for school building improvements.

SOUTHWEST

ADDRESS OF CENTRAL OFFICE:
230 South Elm Street, Harrison, OH 45030
ESI:65

STATISTICAL PROFILE	DATA	ESI
Grade organization: K–6/7–8/9–12		
Percentage of schools built before 1955	71%	
Total enrollment	3,431	
Average Daily Attendance (ADA)	94%	7
Current expense per pupil in ADA	$2,643	4
Dropout rate	7%	10
Percentage of eligible students who took the ACT	55%	8
Average combined score on ACT	21.1	10
Percentage of graduates who enrolled in 2- or 4-year colleges	51%	
Percentage of students who passed the state reading test	NA	
Percentage of students who passed the state math test	NA	
Teacher–student ratio in elementary grades	1:23	7
Teacher–student ratio in secondary grades	1:20	8
Counselor–student ratio in secondary grades	1:319	5
Number of students per music specialist in elementary grades	598	4
Number of students per art specialist in elementary grades	598	
Number of volumes in senior high school library	13,074	
Beginning teacher's salary	$16,350†	
Maximum teacher's salary	$36,403†	
Average years of experience among teachers	10	
Number of students suspended and expelled	NK	
Subjects in which Advanced Placement courses are offered: American History, English	2	2

†These are 1986–87 statistics.

FAIR APPRAISAL

Quality of School Leadership
The School Board hires principals for their educational leadership ability. The quality of leadership is uniform throughout the system. Parents and teachers have no say in principal selection; however, principals have some say in how resources are divided among the schools.

Parents and other residents influence school decisions through citizens advisory committees at each school.

Quality of Instruction
Grouping for special instruction is the main feature of a gifted program rated excellent. The additional instruction for low-achieving students is rated good. The district is adding more Advanced Placement courses, but the current curriculum for college-bound students is considered excellent. Preparation for the job market is termed good.

Quality of School Environment
The level of classroom disruption and vandalism is low now, but six years ago there were problems at some schools. As part of a beefed-up security system, a family lives in a mobile home on the property of each of two schools. The quality of building maintenance and repair is fair. Some schools get more attention than others, said an observer. The schools that have been mostly overlooked are those which were hit hardest by vandalism.

SYCAMORE

ADDRESS OF CENTRAL OFFICE:
4881 Cooper Road, Cincinnati, OH 45242
ESI:None†

STATISTICAL PROFILE	DATA	ESI
Grade organization:		
Percentage of schools built before 1955		
Total enrollment		
Average Daily Attendance (ADA)		
Current expense per pupil in ADA		
Dropout rate		
Percentage of eligible students who took the ACT		
Average combined score on ACT		
Percentage of graduates who enrolled in 2- or 4-year college		
Percentage of students who passed the state reading test		
Percentage of students who passed the state math test		
Teacher–student ratio in elementary grades		
Teacher–student ratio in secondary grades		
Counselor–student ratio in secondary grades		
Number of students per music specialist in elementary grades		
Number of students per art specialist in elementary grades		
Number of volumes in senior high school library		
Beginning teacher's salary		
Maximum teacher's salary		
Average years of experience among teachers		
Number of students suspended and expelled		
Subjects in which Advanced Placement courses are offered:		

†A Statistical Profile was not received from this district.

FAIR APPRAISAL

Quality of School Leadership
Internal politics were a factor in principal selection in the past, but observers believe principals are now chosen for their educational leadership ability. Also, the quality of leadership does not vary greatly from school to school. Parents and teachers do not have a voice in principal selection, although one observer thinks that may change in the future. Principals have some say on what resources will be allotted their school.

Parent organizations are effective in influencing decisions. A planning commission has brought together parents and other citizens to study future goals and objectives.

Quality of Instruction
The district prides itself on designing an individual educational plan for each child, and it is reviewed every two years. Consequently, both the program for gifted students and the program for low-achieving students are rated excellent. The curricula for college-bound students and job-bound students are rated good to excellent.

Quality of School Environment
Classroom disruption and vandalism are not problems. The quality of building maintenance and repair is excellent.

Cleveland, OH

We received Statistical Profiles from eighteen districts in the Cleveland Metropolitan Area, and Fair Appraisals alone from one additional district. Ohio does not have required competency tests in reading and math. Therefore, all profiles show *NA* (not applicable) on the lines requesting those statistics. For comparison, you may wish to examine districts in the Cincinnati and Columbus Metropolitan Areas in Ohio.

AREA AT A GLANCE

SCHOOL DISTRICT	ENROLLMENT	ESI
Akron	34,688	30
Bay Village	2,633	84
Bedford	4,074	65
Chardon	2,633	53
Cleveland	73,806	29
Cleveland Heights–University Heights	8,500	40*
Crestwood	2,615	50
Cuyahoga Falls	6,110	54
Elyria	9,906	
Euclid	5,429	75
Mayfield	3,157	86
Medina	4,815	69
North Olmsted	4,649	75
Revere	2,527	69
Shaker Heights	5,013	82
Solon	3,028	76
South Euclid–Lyndhurst	4,207	86
Strongsville	5,770	69
Westlake	3,199	78

Indicates district misinterpretation of one or more statistics in the ESI. For each misinterpreted statistic, a score of 0 was given instead of a possible score of 0 to 10 points.

AKRON

ADDRESS OF CENTRAL OFFICE:
70 North Broadway, Akron, OH 44308
ESI:30

STATISTICAL PROFILE	DATA	ESI
Grade organization: †		
Percentage of schools built before 1955	78%	
Total enrollment	34,688	
Average Daily Attendance (ADA)	95%	8
Current expense per pupil in ADA	$3,135	7
Dropout rate	13%	10
Percentage of eligible students who took the ACT	NK	0
Average combined score on ACT	NK	0
Percentage of graduates who enrolled in 2- or 4-year colleges	48%	
Percentage of students who passed the state reading test	NA	
Percentage of students who passed the state math test	NA	
Teacher–student ratio in elementary grades	1:25	5
Teacher–student ratio in secondary grades	NK	0
Counselor–student ratio in secondary grades	NK	0
Number of students per music specialist in elementary grades	NK	0
Number of students per art specialist in elementary grades	NK	
Number of volumes in senior high school library	10,700	
Beginning teacher's salary	$17,820	
Maximum teacher's salary	$36,680	
Average years of experience among teachers	16	
Number of students suspended and expelled	4,405	
Subjects in which Advanced Placement courses are offered:	None	0

†The district misinterpreted this statistic.

FAIR APPRAISAL

Quality of School Leadership
The district has had the same superintendent for 21 years, and he "runs a tight ship." He also greatly influences who will become a principal. However, observers believe most principals are chosen for their educational leadership ability, and the quality of leadership is generally uniform throughout the system. Teachers and parents do not get involved in screening principal candidates. Principals have some say in the distribution of district resources.

While some districts in the country are reporting a decrease in parental involvement, observers here say parents and other citizens are more involved now than they were just a few years ago. They influenced the School Board to propose a new school to voters. The proposition passed.

Quality of Instruction
The additional learning opportunities for gifted children are rated good to fair. Extra help is available mostly at the elementary school level. Additional instruction for low-achieving students is called good. In the high school, low-achieving students are required to attend a special program designed for them. The college-preparatory curriculum is rated good, but quality varies from high school to high school (eight high schools). The lack of Advanced Placement courses in a district of this size is unusual. The job-preparation curriculum is considered very good. Its Distributive Education program (preparing students mostly for retail jobs) has received a number of awards.

Quality of School Environment
The level of classroom disruption and vandalism is low, and the school buildings are kept in good condition.

BAY VILLAGE

ADDRESS OF CENTRAL OFFICE:
377 Dover Center Road, Bay Village, OH 44140
ESI:84

STATISTICAL PROFILE	DATA	ESI
Grade organization: K–2/3–5/6–8/9–12		
Percentage of schools built before 1955	75%	
Total enrollment	2,633	
Average Daily Attendance (ADA)	94%	7
Current expense per pupil in ADA	$3,600	9
Dropout rate	5%	10
Percentage of eligible students who took the ACT	78%	10
Average combined score on ACT	21.5	10
Percentage of graduates who enrolled in 2- or 4-year colleges	85%	
Percentage of students who passed the state reading test	NA	
Percentage of students who passed the state math test	NA	
Teacher–student ratio in elementary grades	1:22	8
Teacher–student ratio in secondary grades	1:14	10
Counselor–student ratio in secondary grades	1:250	8
Number of students per music specialist in elementary grades	512	
Number of students per art specialist in elementary grades	512	5
Number of volumes in senior high school library	16,824	
Beginning teacher's salary	$16,000	
Maximum teacher's salary	$37,119	
Average years of experience among teachers	NK	
Number of students suspended and expelled	83	
Subjects in which Advanced Placement courses are offered:	7	7
American History, Calculus, Computer Science, English, French, Physics, Spanish		

FAIR APPRAISAL

Quality of School Leadership
The School Board hires principals who have educational leadership ability; the quality of leadership is good throughout the district. Teachers and parents have some say in screening principal candidates. The central administration and School Board honor the special requests of school principals if possible, say the observers.

A parent–citizens committee is very effective in decision-making, having studied and made recommendations regarding tax levies, staffing, curriculum, and building use.

Quality of Instruction
Gifted students in grades 4 and 5 devote one day a week to special instruction at a middle school. At the middle and high schools, high level courses are available to bright students. The additional instruction for low-achieving students is rated good, although, as one observer put it, a student gets a better deal if he/she is labeled learning disabled. The curriculum for students heading to college (most of those who graduate) is rated very good to excellent. The job-preparation curriculum also is good, but one observer complained that some parents will not let a child take vocational courses because they won't accept the fact that he/she doesn't want to go to college.

Quality of School Environment
Classroom disruption and vandalism are not problems. Two tax levy proposals were defeated in 1986–87; a new proposal was scheduled to go before voters in 1987–88. Some funds will be earmarked for maintenance and repair, although observers now rate the condition of schools as good.

BEDFORD

ADDRESS OF CENTRAL OFFICE:
475 Northfield Road, Bedford, OH 44146
ESI:65

STATISTICAL PROFILE	DATA	ESI
Grade organization: K–2/3–5/6–8/9–12		
Percentage of schools built before 1955	11%	
Total enrollment	4,074	
Average Daily Attendance (ADA)	96%	9
Current expense per pupil in ADA	$4,500	10
Dropout rate	NK	0
Percentage of eligible students who took the ACT	51%	8
Average combined score on ACT	17.6	3
Percentage of graduates who enrolled in 2- or 4-year colleges	52%	
Percentage of students who passed the state reading test	NA	
Percentage of students who passed the state math test	NA	
Teacher–student ratio in elementary grades	1:25	5
Teacher–student ratio in secondary grades	1:17	10
Counselor–student ratio in secondary grades	1:280	6
Number of students per music specialist in elementary grades	300	9
Number of students per art specialist in elementary grades	336	
Number of volumes in senior high school library	13,500	
Beginning teacher's salary	$17,531	
Maximum teacher's salary	$33,975	
Average years of experience among teachers	17	
Number of students suspended and expelled	964	
Subjects in which Advanced Placement courses are offered: American History, Calculus, Computer Science, English, Science	5	5

Quality of School Leadership
Decisions on hiring principals are based 70 percent on the candidates' educational leadership ability and 30 percent on internal politics, but the quality of leadership is good. Parents and teachers have hardly any say in screening principal candidates. Principals, on the other hand, have some say in how resources will be allotted to the schools.

Parents are effective in decision-making. For example, when the School Board was going to make drastic cuts in the budget for instruction of gifted and talented children, parent groups were successful in persuading the School Board to reinstate some of the funds.

Quality of Instruction
Additional learning opportunities are available to gifted students from grade 6 through high school, and the program is rated good. Also called good is instruction for low-achieving students. The college-preparatory curriculum is called excellent, although students did not score very high on the 1986 ACT. The job-preparation curriculum is rated good to excellent.

Quality of School Environment
The incidence of classroom disruption and vandalism is low, and the quality of building maintenance and repair is good.

CHARDON

ADDRESS OF CENTRAL OFFICE:
428 North Street, Chardon, OH 44024
ESI:53

STATISTICAL PROFILE	DATA	ESI
Grade organization: K–5/6–8/9–12		
Percentage of schools built before 1955	40%	
Total enrollment	2,633	
Average Daily Attendance (ADA)	95%	8
Current expense per pupil in ADA	$2,887	5
Dropout rate	5%	10
Percentage of eligible students who took the ACT	60%	9
Average combined score on ACT	NK	0
Percentage of graduates who enrolled in 2- or 4-year colleges	54%	
Percentage of students who passed the state reading test	NA	
Percentage of students who passed the state math test	NA	
Teacher–student ratio in elementary grades	1:27	3
Teacher–student ratio in secondary grades	1:20	8
Counselor–student ratio in secondary grades	1:414	1
Number of students per music specialist in elementary grades	576	4
Number of students per art specialist in elementary grades	719	
Number of volumes in senior high school library	11,843	
Beginning teacher's salary	$16,700	
Maximum teacher's salary	$34,068	
Average years of experience among teachers	12	
Number of students suspended and expelled	605	
Subjects in which Advanced Placement courses are offered: American History, Calculus, Chemistry, English European History	5	5

Quality of School Leadership
The leadership ability of the superintendent is labeled "superlative." Principals are appointed primarily for their educational leadership ability, and the quality of leadership does not vary greatly from school to school. Teachers and parents do not take part in screening principal candidates. Principals do have a say in resource allocations.

Parent effectiveness is a mixed bag. "The trend is toward more involvement," said an observer, but some parent groups still devote most of their time to fund-raising.

Quality of Instruction
The additional opportunities for gifted children range from excellent in the elementary grades to good at the middle and high schools. In grades 2–5, the brightest students take one day a week away from regular classes to work in the district's learning resource room. Additional instruction for low-achieving students is rated good, but one observer noted that the students who get the most help are those whom teachers perceive as having low ability. If a student is thought to have ability, but is not achieving as well as teachers expect, he or she may get little help, said the observer. The curricula for college-bound students and job-bound students are rated good to excellent.

Quality of School Environment
The discipline policy is tough. At the middle school, parents of students who have been given in-school suspension must come to the school and spend the day with their child. A consequence of the policy is that classroom disruption and vandalism are not problems. The quality of building maintenance and repair is good, thanks to a new program that has concentrated on the oldest buildings.

CLEVELAND

ADDRESS OF CENTRAL OFFICE:
1380 East Sixth Street, Cleveland, OH 44114
ESI:29

STATISTICAL PROFILE	DATA	ESI
Grade organization: †		
Percentage of schools built before 1955	48%	
Total enrollment	73,806	
Average Daily Attendance (ADA)	86%	0
Current expense per pupil in ADA	$4,640	10
Dropout rate	NK	0
Percentage of eligible students who took the ACT	26%	3
Average combined score on ACT	12.3	0
Percentage of graduates who enrolled in 2- or 4-year colleges	NK	
Percentage of students who passed the state reading test	NA	
Percentage of students who passed the state math test	NA	
Teacher–student ratio in elementary grades	1:21	9
Teacher–student ratio in secondary grades	1:29	0
Counselor–student ratio in secondary grades	1:400	2
Number of students per music specialist in elementary grades	1,249	0
Number of students per art specialist in elementary grades	1,482	
Number of volumes in senior high school library	12,642	
Beginning teacher's salary	$17,678	
Maximum teacher's salary	$37,457	
Average years of experience among teachers	16	
Number of students suspended and expelled	15,043	
Subjects in which Advanced Placement courses are offered: American History, Biology, Calculus, English, European History	5	5

†There is variation at the elementary school level: K–3, K–4 and K–6, but the upper grades are uniform: 6–8/9–12

Quality of School Leadership

The district is paying more attention to the educational leadership ability of principals, but the system was quite political in the past. "The current superintendent believes in the principal as a strong educational leader," said an observer. The district was scheduled to replace 38 principals in 1987–88. The reason is that 1986–87 was a "buy-out" year, when the district encouraged early retirements of principals and teachers to "weed out deadwood and cut costs" (retirees are at or near the top of the salary scale). The quality of educational leadership varies greatly from school to school. Cleveland is under court order to desegregate and the court now requires that parents help screen principal candidates along with central administrators. Principals have much say about the use of resources. The district is decentralized; principals have some of the authority central administrators have in other districts. For example, a principal can decide how to spend about 10 percent of his/her school budget. Also, principals can make other decisions concerning resources. In fact, one observer believes decentralization has gone too far. "The district could advocate the use of calculators in math classes, for example, but a principal could elect not to buy calculators for his/her school."

Parent organizations are not very influential for a number of reasons. One is that desegregation has required transporting students across town in many instances. Their parents, who may lack transportation, have trouble getting to meetings at their school. Also, schools are rarely open in late afternoon or evening for meetings of parents because the local custodial union charges time and a half for after-school meetings.

Quality of Instruction

Additional learning opportunities for gifted children have been "watered down" over the years and the program is now rated fair. Even the city's magnet schools are of varying quality. One example, said an observer, is that the magnet high school for science doesn't get any more money than a comprehensive high school. Additional instruction for low-achieving students is rated fair to good. The curriculum for college-bound students is considered fair to good. According to one observer who had access to a 1986 district report, only 45 percent of seventh-graders graduate from high school, and only 34 percent of high school graduates go to college. The job-training curriculum is getting better. Until recently, said observers, training was out-of-date.

The district is trying to meet the needs of all students, but is not succeeding very well. While minorities constitute a majority of the student body, the problem is not one of race but of income, said an observer. Most of the children who are left in the district — white, black or Hispanic — are from poor families.

Quality of School Environment

The level of classroom disruption and vandalism is on the high side. One reason is that ninth-graders entered the high schools for the first time in 1986–87, and there was much "jockeying" for position and macho power. Also, because 1986–87 was a "buy-out" year, some principals and teachers who were scheduled to retire lost interest and enthusiasm during the school year, said an observer. The quality of maintenance and repair is getting better, but has a long way to go. At a high school that is not quite 12 years old, the gym was condemned because of severe buckling in the floor. Voters were scheduled to consider a bond issue in the late summer of 1987 that would allocate $60 million for building improvements.

CLEVELAND HEIGHTS–UNIVERSITY HEIGHTS

ADDRESS OF CENTRAL OFFICE:
2155 Miramar Boulevard, Cleveland, OH 44118
ESI:40*

STATISTICAL PROFILE	DATA	ESI
Grade organization: K–5/6–8/9–12		
Percentage of schools built before 1955	67%	
Total enrollment	8,500	
Average Daily Attendance (ADA)	94%	7
Current expense per pupil in ADA	$4,702	10
Dropout rate	†	0*
Percentage of eligible students who took the ACT	†	0*
Average combined score on ACT	†	0*
Percentage of graduates who enrolled in 2- or 4-year colleges	75%	
Percentage of students who passed the state reading test	NA	
Percentage of students who passed the state math test	NA	
Teacher–student ratio in elementary grades	1:23	7
Teacher–student ratio in secondary grades	1:25	3
Counselor–student ratio in secondary grades	1:250	8
Number of students per music specialist in elementary grades	500	5
Number of students per art specialist in elementary grades	900	
Number of volumes in senior high school library	35,000	
Beginning teacher's salary	$17,900	
Maximum teacher's salary	$39,000	
Average years of experience among teachers	14	
Number of students suspended and expelled	671	
Subjects in which Advanced Placement courses are offered:	None	0

†The district misinterpreted this statistic.

FAIR APPRAISAL

Quality of School Leadership
Principals are selected for their educational leadership ability, and the quality of leadership is generally uniform throughout the system. Teachers and parents are not involved in screening the principals. Principals do have a say on how the central office disburses district resources.

Parents influence decisions mainly through membership on School Board advisory committees and attendance at Board meetings.

Quality of Instruction
Additional learning opportunities for gifted students are rated good to excellent. In the elementary schools, especially bright students are excused from their regular schedule once a week to attend special enrichment classes. Individual tutoring helps low-achievers, and the program is rated good. The college-preparatory curriculum is called good. For readers who thought it unusual for a district this size not to have one Advanced Placement course, be advised the observers noted that some AP courses (unspecified) were scheduled to be introduced in 1987–88. The curriculum for students going directly into the job market also is rated good.

For the most part, the district meets the educational needs of minority students. However, the high school student council has complained that the schools aren't doing as much as they could do; it is urging a greater effort by district officials.

Quality of School Environment
The level of classroom disruption and vandalism is low, and the quality of building maintenance and repair is good.

CRESTWOOD

ADDRESS OF CENTRAL OFFICE:
4565 West Prospect Street, Mantua, OH 44255
ESI:50

STATISTICAL PROFILE	DATA	ESI
Grade organization: K–4/5–8/9–12		
Percentage of schools built before 1955	64%	
Total enrollment	2,615	
Average Daily Attendance (ADA)	95%	8
Current expense per pupil in ADA	$3,100	4
Dropout rate	12%	10
Percentage of eligible students who took the ACT	35%	4
Average combined score on ACT	20.1	6
Percentage of graduates who enrolled in 2- or 4-year colleges	35%	
Percentage of students who passed the state reading test	NA	
Percentage of students who passed the state math test	NA	
Teacher–student ratio in elementary grades	1:24	6
Teacher–student ratio in secondary grades	1:22	6
Counselor–student ratio in secondary grades	1:425	1
Number of students per music specialist in elementary grades	500	5
Number of students per art specialist in elementary grades	None	
Number of volumes in senior high school library	NK	
Beginning teacher's salary	$15,800	
Maximum teacher's salary	$31,442	
Average years of experience among teachers	10	
Number of students suspended and expelled	NK	
Subjects in which Advanced Placement courses are offered:	None	0

FAIR APPRAISAL

Quality of School Leadership
The School Board selects principals for their educational leadership ability, and the quality of leadership doesn't vary greatly from school to school. Although teachers and parents have no say in principal selection, principals have some say in deciding how resources will be allotted to the schools.

Parents have only occasional influence over district decision-making.

Quality of Instruction
Additional opportunities for gifted students are rated good. Bright students are excused from regular classes once a week for special instruction. The program for low-achieving students also is considered good; remedial reading instruction is available in all grades. The college-preparatory and job-preparation curricula are rated good.

Quality of School Environment
The level of classroom disruption and vandalism is low. The quality of building maintenance and repair is called fair to good. While work is continually being done, said an observer, the district never seems to "catch up" with the needs.

CUYAHOGA FALLS

ADDRESS OF CENTRAL OFFICE:
431 Stowe Street, Cuyahoga Falls, OH 44221
ESI:54

STATISTICAL PROFILE	DATA	ESI
Grade organization: K–5/6–8/9–12		
Percentage of schools built before 1955	64%	
Total enrollment	6,110	
Average Daily Attendance (ADA)	95%	8
Current expense per pupil in ADA	$1,698	0
Dropout rate	12%	10
Percentage of eligible students who took the ACT	57%	9
Average combined score on ACT	19.5	5
Percentage of graduates who enrolled in 2- or 4-year colleges	66%	
Percentage of students who passed the state reading test	NA	
Percentage of students who passed the state math test	NA	
Teacher–student ratio in elementary grades	1:24	6
Teacher–student ratio in secondary grades	1:21	7
Counselor–student ratio in secondary grades	1:380	2
Number of students per music specialist in elementary grades	529	5
Number of students per art specialist in elementary grades	529	
Number of volumes in senior high school library	24,324	
Beginning teacher's salary	$15,000	
Maximum teacher's salary	$30,300	
Average years of experience among teachers	15	
Number of students suspended and expelled	NK	
Subjects in which Advanced Placement courses are offered: Calculus, Chemistry	2	2

Quality of School Leadership
Educational leadership ability is the main criterion used when selecting principals, and the quality of educational leadership is uniform throughout the system. Parents and teachers are not involved in principal selection, but principals have some way in how district resources are allocated.

Parent organizations generally are effective in district decision-making. "We have a strong PTA in the district," said an observer, and the School Board looks to the PTA as being representative of parents.

Quality of Instruction
The program for gifted students is rated fair to good now, but up until a couple of years ago gifted students were mostly "overlooked." Project Excel offers bright students enrichment activities after school and on Saturdays. The rating is good for additional instruction for low-achieving students. While the college-preparatory curriculum is considered good, one observer noted that preparation in science is weak. A regional vocational school provides excellent training for the job market, observers said.

Quality of School Environment
Classroom disruption and vandalism are not problems. The quality of building maintenance and repair is considered fair to good. The district has a ten-year building improvement plan that was initially funded by a five-year tax levy. Unfortunately, as of Fall 1987, voters had not yet approved a tax levy to fund the final five years. Also, a program to remove asbestos from buildings took money away from normal upkeep.

ELYRIA

ADDRESS OF CENTRAL OFFICE:
4710 Griswold Road, Elyria, OH 44035
ESI:None†

STATISTICAL PROFILE	DATA	ESI
Grade organization:		
Percentage of schools built before 1955		
Total enrollment		
Average Daily Attendance (ADA)		
Current expense per pupil in ADA		
Dropout rate		
Percentage of eligible students who took the ACT		
Average combined score on ACT		
Percentage of graduates who enrolled in 2- or 4-year college		
Percentage of students who passed the state reading test		
Percentage of students who passed the state math test		
Teacher–student ratio in elementary grades		
Teacher–student ratio in secondary grades		
Counselor–student ratio in secondary grades		
Number of students per music specialist in elementary grades		
Number of students per art specialist in elementary grades		
Number of volumes in senior high school library		
Beginning teacher's salary		
Maximum teacher's salary		
Average years of experience among teachers		
Number of students suspended and expelled		
Subjects in which Advanced Placement courses are offered:		

†A Statistical Profile was not received from this district.

Quality of School Leadership
Educational leadership ability is what the School Board mainly looks for in principal candidates, but longevity in the system helps. The quality of leadership is generally high throughout the system. Teachers and parents have no official role in screening candidates, but they make their views known. Principals have a great deal of influence on how the district distributes resources to the schools.

The influence of parents in decision-making is sometimes effective; they and other citizens work from time to time on advisory committees.

Quality of Instruction
Observers rate the opportunities for gifted students as excellent. Classes for especially bright students are offered at all grade levels, and a nearby community college gives "credits in escrow" to high school students who complete courses there. Additional instruction for low-achieving students is considered good. Tutors are available at most schools. On Monday and Thursday evenings the high school library becomes a "homework center," where teachers assist students who are having problems. The curricula for college-bound students and job-bound students are rated excellent.

Quality of School Environment
The incidence of classroom disruption and vandalism is low, and building maintenance and repair are rated good to excellent.

EUCLID

ADDRESS OF CENTRAL OFFICE:
651 East 222nd Street, Euclid, OH 44123
ESI:75

STATISTICAL PROFILE	DATA	ESI
Grade organization: K–6/7–8/9–12		
Percentage of schools built before 1955	73%	
Total enrollment	5,429	
Average Daily Attendance (ADA)	95%	8
Current expense per pupil in ADA	$4,768	10
Dropout rate	23%	0
Percentage of eligible students who took the ACT	50%	7
Average combined score on ACT	18.8	4
Percentage of graduates who enrolled in 2- or 4-year colleges	65%	
Percentage of students who passed the state reading test	NA	
Percentage of students who passed the state math test	NA	
Teacher–student ratio in elementary grades	1:21	9
Teacher–student ratio in secondary grades	1:19	9
Counselor–student ratio in secondary grades	1:239	8
Number of students per music specialist in elementary grades	299	10
Number of students per art specialist in elementary grades	672	
Number of volumes in senior high school library	26,251	
Beginning teacher's salary	$17,330	
Maximum teacher's salary	$37,953	
Average years of experience among teachers	17	
Number of students suspended and expelled	1,806	
Subjects in which Advanced Placement courses are offered:	10	10
American History, Biology, Calculus, Chemistry, English, European History, French, German, Physics, Spanish		

FAIR APPRAISAL

Quality of School Leadership
A new superintendent does things differently, but for many years internal politics were important in principal selection. Because of favorites, said an observer, some persons were appointed principals when they lacked the proper training for the position. Educational leadership ability is now the primary criterion. As a result of past practices, however, the quality of leadership may vary significantly from school to school. Teachers and parents have hardly any say in the selection of principals. Principals, however, do have a say on what resources they will receive from the central office.

Parents' influence on school decisions is sometimes effective. They and other citizens played a major part in advising district officials concerning the recent closing of three elementary schools, the creation of a new magnet school, and the reassignment of students.

Quality of Instruction
Additional opportunities for gifted students are rated good. In the elementary schools, bright students are excused from their regular schedule once a week to attend special classes. The program for low-achieving students also is rated good. Although the curriculum for students going to college is considered good, one observer thought the district should allow more students to take high-level courses. The curriculum for students heading into the world of work is considered good.

Quality of School Environment
Classroom disruption and vandalism are not problems, and the quality of building maintenance and repair is good.

MAYFIELD

ADDRESS OF CENTRAL OFFICE:
784 Som Center Road, Mayfield, OH 44143
ESI:86

STATISTICAL PROFILE	DATA	ESI
Grade organization: K–6/7–12		
Percentage of schools built before 1955	40%	
Total enrollment	3,157	
Average Daily Attendance (ADA)	98%	10
Current expense per pupil in ADA	$4,893	10
Dropout rate	10%	10
Percentage of eligible students who took the ACT	80%	10
Average combined score on ACT	19.9	5
Percentage of graduates who enrolled in 2- or 4-year colleges	60%	
Percentage of students who passed the state reading test	NA	
Percentage of students who passed the state math test	NA	
Teacher–student ratio in elementary grades	1:20	10
Teacher–student ratio in secondary grades	1:13	10
Counselor–student ratio in secondary grades	1:300	6
Number of students per music specialist in elementary grades	450	6
Number of students per art specialist in elementary grades	450	
Number of volumes in senior high school library	34,845	
Beginning teacher's salary	$20,136	
Maximum teacher's salary	$43,823	
Average years of experience among teachers	16	
Number of students suspended and expelled	16	
Subjects in which Advanced Placement courses are offered:	9	9
American Government, American History, Calculus, Chemistry, Computer Science, English, European History, French, Spanish		

FAIR APPRAISAL

Quality of School Leadership
Principals are picked for their educational leadership ability. The quality of leadership does not vary greatly from school to school. Parents and teachers have little or no say in principal selection, but principals have some influence over the district resources they receive.

Parent organizations are quite effective; parents are out in large numbers at all School Board meetings.

Quality of Instruction
Observers give the program for gifted students a good rating, and additional instruction for low-achieving students is rated very good. The curricula for college-bound students and job-bound students are considered very good. A new, non-profit, private foundation is raising money to help "promote excellence." A seventh-grader who successfully completed an eleventh-grade math course was given a small cash award that he can save for college or perhaps use to attend a math tournament. Plaques have been purchased for each school, and the names of teachers and students who win awards for excellence will be inscribed.

Quality of School Environment
Classroom disruption and vandalism are not problems, and buildings are well-maintained and kept in good repair.

MEDINA

ADDRESS OF CENTRAL OFFICE:
P.O. Box 408, Medina, OH 44258
ESI:69

STATISTICAL PROFILE	DATA	ESI
Grade organization: K–6/7–8/9–12		
Percentage of schools built before 1955	17%	
Total enrollment	4,815	
Average Daily Attendance (ADA)	96%	9
Current expense per pupil in ADA	$3,494	9
Dropout rate	10%	10
Percentage of eligible students who took the ACT	33%	4
Average combined score on ACT	21.2	10
Percentage of graduates who enrolled in 2- or 4-year colleges	57%	
Percentage of students who passed the state reading test	NA	
Percentage of students who passed the state math test	NA	
Teacher–student ratio in elementary grades	1:24	5
Teacher–student ratio in secondary grades	1:24	4
Counselor–student ratio in secondary grades	1:320	5
Number of students per music specialist in elementary grades	300	9
Number of students per art specialist in elementary grades	600	
Number of volumes in senior high school library	17,300	
Beginning teacher's salary	$17,900	
Maximum teacher's salary	$36,140	
Average years of experience among teachers	12	
Number of students suspended and expelled	328	
Subjects in which Advanced Placement courses are offered: American History, Biology, Calculus, English	4	4

FAIR APPRAISAL

Quality of School Leadership
The School Board measures principal candidates by their educational leadership ability; the quality of leadership is uniform in the system. Parents and teachers have no say in principal selection, but principals have a say in deciding how district resources will be used.

Parents and other citizens are most influential when they sit as members of a standing committee that advises the superintendent on policy issues.

Quality of Instruction
Observers rate additional opportunities for gifted children as good and additional instruction for low-achieving students as fair. The college-preparatory curriculum is considered excellent, and a county-wide vocational education curriculum is rated very good.

Quality of School Environment
The level of classroom disruption and vandalism is very low. The quality of building maintenance and repair is very high.

NORTH OLMSTED

ADDRESS OF CENTRAL OFFICE:
27253 Butternut Ridge, North Olmsted, OH 44070
ESI:75

STATISTICAL PROFILE	DATA	ESI
Grade organization: K–5/6–8/9–12		
Percentage of schools built before 1955	14%	
Total enrollment	4,649	
Average Daily Attendance (ADA)	94%	7
Current expense per pupil in ADA	$3,849	10
Dropout rate	11%	10
Percentage of eligible students who took the ACT	72%	10
Average combined score on ACT	20	6
Percentage of graduates who enrolled in 2- or 4-year colleges	69%	
Percentage of students who passed the state reading test	NA	
Percentage of students who passed the state math test	NA	
Teacher–student ratio in elementary grades	1:22	8
Teacher–student ratio in secondary grades	1:18	10
Counselor–student ratio in secondary grades	1:365	3
Number of students per music specialist in elementary grades	554	4
Number of students per art specialist in elementary grades	554	
Number of volumes in senior high school library	20,884	
Beginning teacher's salary	$17,580	
Maximum teacher's salary	$44,027	
Average years of experience among teachers	15	
Number of students suspended and expelled	189	
Subjects in which Advanced Placement courses are offered: American History, Biology, Calculus AB, Calculus BC, Chemistry, English, Physics	7	7

FAIR APPRAISAL

Quality of School Leadership
The School Board hires principals primarily for their educational leadership ability, and the quality of leadership does not vary greatly from school to school. Teachers and parents have hardly any say in selecting principals, but principals have some say in deciding how the district will allot resources to each school.

Parents are occasionally effective in their influence on policy; however, according to an observer, they primarily are concerned with fund-raising.

Quality of Instruction
Additional learning opportunities for gifted students are rated good to excellent. The district's Odyssey of the Mind team won a world championship, and the Advanced Study Program for gifted and talented students was listed as an "exemplary" program by the North Central Association of Colleges and Schools. Additional instruction for low-achieving students is considered good. An excellent rating is given the college-preparatory curriculum. The high school recently was named one of the top 100 high schools in the country by the U.S. Department of Education. The Forest Elementary School was chosen as being among the top 210 elementary schools by the department. The job-training curriculum is very good; students attend a regional vocational education center.

Quality of School Environment
The level of classroom disruption and vandalism is very low. The quality of building maintenance and repair is good.

REVERE

ADDRESS OF CENTRAL OFFICE:
P.O. Box 176, Bath, OH 44210
ESI:69

STATISTICAL PROFILE	DATA	ESI
Grade organization: K–2/3–6/7–8/9–12		
Percentage of schools built before 1955	40%	
Total enrollment	2,527	
Average Daily Attendance (ADA)	94%	7
Current expense per pupil in ADA	$3,100	7
Dropout rate	4%	10
Percentage of eligible students who took the ACT	77%	10
Average combined score on ACT	19.7	5
Percentage of graduates who enrolled in 2- or 4-year colleges	67%	
Percentage of students who passed the state reading test	NA	
Percentage of students who passed the state math test	NA	
Teacher–student ratio in elementary grades	1:26	4
Teacher–student ratio in secondary grades	1:22	6
Counselor–student ratio in secondary grades	1:317	5
Number of students per music specialist in elementary grades	371	8
Number of students per art specialist in elementary grades	445	
Number of volumes in senior high school library	9,230	
Beginning teacher's salary	$15,975	
Maximum teacher's salary	$31,758	
Average years of experience among teachers	12	
Number of students suspended and expelled	75	
Subjects in which Advanced Placement courses are offered: American History, Biology, Calculus, Chemistry, English, European History, Physics	7	7

FAIR APPRAISAL

Quality of School Leadership

Educational leadership ability is what the School Board primarily looks for in principal candidates, and the quality of leadership is high throughout the system. Although parents and teachers have no say in principal selection, principals have some influence over the distribution of district resources.

Parents and other citizens serve frequently on a future planning committee that makes policy recommendations to the central administration and School Board. PTAs also are active. "There's quite a lot of parental involvement here," said an observer.

Quality of Instruction

Voters defeated a tax levy in 1986 that caused the district to drop some elements of its program for gifted students; however, the additional learning opportunities for bright students are still rated good. Also considered good is the additional instruction for low-achieving students. The curriculum for students going to college is rated excellent, and the curriculum for students heading for the job market is called good. One observer believes more students would take advantage of the vocational educational program if their parents were aware that more than 30 percent of graduates do not go to college (the observer had guessed the percentage of graduates going to college was between 80 and 90 percent).

Quality of School Environment

The level of classroom disruption and vandalism is low, and the quality of building maintenance and repair is fair to good. A bond issue two years ago helped, said an observer, but the district had gotten behind and is still trying to catch up.

SHAKER HEIGHTS

ADDRESS OF CENTRAL OFFICE:

15600 Parkland Drive, Shaker Heights, OH 44120
ESI:82

STATISTICAL PROFILE	DATA	ESI
Grade organization: K–6/7–8/9–12		
Percentage of schools built before 1955	91%	
Total enrollment	5,013	
Average Daily Attendance (ADA)	93%	6
Current expense per pupil in ADA	$5,300	10
Dropout rate	3%	10
Percentage of eligible students who took the SAT	58%	9
Average combined score on SAT	985†	8
Percentage of graduates who enrolled in 2- or 4-year colleges	84%	
Percentage of students who passed the state reading test	NA	
Percentage of students who passed the state math test	NA	
Teacher–student ratio in elementary grades	1:19	10
Teacher–student ratio in secondary grades	1:22	6
Counselor–student ratio in secondary grades	1:235	8
Number of students per music specialist in elementary grades	417	7
Number of students per art specialist in elementary grades	835	
Number of volumes in senior high school library	28,000	
Beginning teacher's salary	$20,081††	
Maximum teacher's salary	$46,301	
Average years of experience among teachers	13	
Number of students suspended and expelled	20	
Subjects in which Advanced Placement courses are offered:	8	8
American Government, Calculus, English, European History, French, Latin, Physics, Spanish		

† The ACT score was not known. This is the average combined SAT score.
††This statistic is for 1986–87.

FAIR APPRAISAL

Quality of School Leadership

Educational leadership ability is the primary criterion in principal selection. The quality of leadership does not vary greatly from school to school. Parents and teachers interview principal candidates during the screening process. Students are included if the candidate is for the position of high school principal. Also, principals are influential in deciding how the resources of the district will be allotted to the schools.

The influence parents have on policy is very effective. For example, parents were very involved in a recent reorganization that closed four schools and reassigned students. Also, parents of minority students work with district officials to solve problems facing minorities.

Quality of Instruction

Magnet elementary schools specializing in computer science, physical sciences and language arts are part of an excellent program for gifted students. Additional instruction for low-achieving students is considered very good. "The district is constantly monitoring the program in order to improve it," said an observer. The college-preparatory curriculum is rated excellent (a record number of graduates who had sought entrance to Harvard University were accepted for early admission). The high school is regularly listed as an outstanding secondary school by the U.S. Department of Education. Elementary and middle schools also have been cited for excellence. The curriculum for students going directly into the job market is considered good.

The district adequately meets the educational needs of minority students, but successful racial integration is never taken for granted. For example, said an observer, the district helps black and white students at the high school to maintain and build on interracial friendships made in the elementary schools.

Quality of School Environment

The incidence of classroom disruption and vandalism is low. The quality of building maintenance and repair is excellent.

SOLON

ADDRESS OF CENTRAL OFFICE:
33675 Solon Road, Cleveland, OH 44139
ESI:76

STATISTICAL PROFILE	DATA	ESI
Grade organization: K–4/5–6/7–8/9–12		
Percentage of schools built before 1955	20%	
Total enrollment	3,028	
Average Daily Attendance (ADA)	94%	7
Current expense per pupil in ADA	$4,400	10
Dropout rate	1%	10
Percentage of eligible students who took the ACT	95%	10
Average combined score on ACT	20	6
Percentage of graduates who enrolled in 2- or 4-year colleges	84%	
Percentage of students who passed the state reading test	NA	
Percentage of students who passed the state math test	NA	
Teacher–student ratio in elementary grades	1:18	10
Teacher–student ratio in secondary grades	1:13	10
Counselor–student ratio in secondary grades	1:372	3
Number of students per music specialist in elementary grades	500	5
Number of students per art specialist in elementary grades	500	
Number of volumes in senior high school library	15,000	
Beginning teacher's salary	$18,400	
Maximum teacher's salary	$41,795	
Average years of experience among teachers	16	
Number of students suspended and expelled	352	
Subjects in which Advanced Placement courses are offered: Biology, Calculus, Chemistry, English, Physics	5	5

FAIR APPRAISAL

Quality of School Leadership
Principals are chosen for their educational leadership ability; the quality of leadership does not vary greatly from school to school. Although parents and teachers have no say in principal selection, principals influence the quantity and quality of resources their school will receive.

Parent organizations' influence is sometimes effective. Their primary role seems to be to help pass tax levies.

Quality of Instruction
The programs for gifted students and low-achieving students are rated good. So are the curricula for college-bound and job-bound students. The high school recently set up a print shop to train students in that field. Business education is reported to be very good.

Quality of School Environment
Classroom disruption and vandalism are not problems. The quality of building maintenance and repair is good.

SOUTH EUCLID–LYNDHURST

ADDRESS OF CENTRAL OFFICE:
5044 Mayfield Road, Cleveland, OH 44124
ESI:86

STATISTICAL PROFILE	DATA	ESI
Grade organization: K–6/7–8/9–12		
Percentage of schools built before 1955	88%	
Total enrollment	4,207	
Average Daily Attendance (ADA)	99%	10
Current expense per pupil in ADA	$4,568	10
Dropout rate	2%	10
Percentage of eligible students who took the ACT	70%	10
Average combined score on ACT	22.7	10
Percentage of graduates who enrolled in 2- or 4-year colleges	70%	
Percentage of students who passed the state reading test	NA	
Percentage of students who passed the state math test	NA	
Teacher–student ratio in elementary grades	1:16	10
Teacher–student ratio in secondary grades	1:18	10
Counselor–student ratio in secondary grades	1:311	5
Number of students per music specialist in elementary grades	405	7
Number of students per art specialist in elementary grades	675	
Number of volumes in senior high school library	85,000†	
Beginning teacher's salary	$18,251	
Maximum teacher's salary	$39,265	
Average years of experience among teachers	16	
Number of students suspended and expelled	500	
Subjects in which Advanced Placement courses are offered: American Government, Calculus, Computer Science, English	4	4

†This figure seems unusually high and is questionable; verification was not possible.

FAIR APPRAISAL

Quality of School Leadership
Most principals are selected for their leadership abilities. The quality of leadership does not vary greatly from school to school.

Parents and teachers have hardly any say in principal selection, but principals have some say in resource distribution.

Parent organizations are considered effective. "Parents are very vocal in this community," said an observer.

Quality of Instruction
Additional learning opportunities for gifted students are rated good, but the program exists mostly in the secondary grades. Opportunities at the elementary level are "not much," according to an observer. The secondary school program includes internships with local businesses and professional persons. The additional instruction for low-achieving students is called good. The curricula for students planning on college and for those heading into the job market are both rated excellent.

Quality of School Environment
The level of classroom disruption and vandalism is very low. Although most of the buildings are more than 30 years old, the quality of maintenance and repair is termed excellent.

STRONGSVILLE

ADDRESS OF CENTRAL OFFICE:
13200 Pearl Road, Cleveland, OH 44136
ESI:69

STATISTICAL PROFILE	DATA	ESI
Grade organization: K–6/7–9/10–12		
Percentage of schools built before 1955	10%	
Total enrollment	5,770	
Average Daily Attendance (ADA)	95%	8
Current expense per pupil in ADA	$2,811	5
Dropout rate	8%	10
Percentage of eligible students who took the ACT	75%	10
Average combined score on ACT	20.2	7
Percentage of graduates who enrolled in 2- or 4-year colleges	66%	
Percentage of students who passed the state reading test	NA	
Percentage of students who passed the state math test	NA	
Teacher–student ratio in elementary grades	1:22	8
Teacher–student ratio in secondary grades	1:22	6
Counselor–student ratio in secondary grades	1:353	3
Number of students per music specialist in elementary grades	355	8
Number of students per art specialist in elementary grades	499	
Number of volumes in senior high school library	11,719	
Beginning teacher's salary	$16,360	
Maximum teacher's salary	$38,197	
Average years of experience among teachers	10	
Number of students suspended and expelled	529	
Subjects in which Advanced Placement courses are offered: American History, Calculus, English, Physics	4	4

FAIR APPRAISAL

Quality of School Leadership
Observers believe the School Board hires principals primarily because of their educational leadership ability. The quality of leadership does not vary greatly from school to school. Parents and teachers do not screen principal candidates, but principals do influence the distribution of district resources.

Quality of Instruction
Fair to good is how the additional learning opportunities for gifted students are rated. Instruction for low-achieving students is termed fair. The curriculum for students going to college is called good, while the curriculum for students moving into the world of work is rated fair.

Quality of School Environment
Classroom disruption and vandalism are not problems, but the quality of building maintenance and repair is called poor. "Our buildings are in terrible condition," said an observer, who blamed the poor upkeep on repeated defeats of recent tax levy propositions.

WESTLAKE

ADDRESS OF CENTRAL OFFICE:
2260 Dover Center Road, Cleveland, OH 44145
ESI:78

STATISTICAL PROFILE	DATA	ESI
Grade organization: K–6/7–9/10–12		
Percentage of schools built before 1955	28%	
Total enrollment	3,199	
Average Daily Attendance (ADA)	92%	5
Current expense per pupil in ADA	$3,875	10
Dropout rate	2%	10
Percentage of eligible students who took the ACT	88%	10
Average combined score on ACT	21	10
Percentage of graduates who enrolled in 2- or 4-year colleges	82%	
Percentage of students who passed the state reading test	NA	
Percentage of students who passed the state math test	NA	
Teacher–student ratio in elementary grades	1:25	5
Teacher–student ratio in secondary grades	1:20	8
Counselor–student ratio in secondary grades	1:290	6
Number of students per music specialist in elementary grades	182	10
Number of students per art specialist in elementary grades	400	
Number of volumes in senior high school library	NK	
Beginning teacher's salary	$17,152	
Maximum teacher's salary	$38,592	
Average years of experience among teachers	15	
Number of students suspended and expelled	NK	
Subjects in which Advanced Placement courses are offered: Biology, Calculus, Chemistry, European History	4	4

FAIR APPRAISAL

Quality of School Leadership
Educational leadership ability is what the School Board primarily looks for in principal candidates. The quality of leadership is generally high throughout the district. Although parents and teachers have no say in choosing principals, principals have some say in deciding what resources will be allotted their school.

"We're in the throes of change," said one observer about the district. The district is expanding, and professional and business people moving in are changing a once mostly rural district into a more suburban one. As a consequence, said the observer, parents are demanding a greater role in decision-making than they have had in the past. "The schools still look to parents primarily for fund-raising," the observer said, but district officials are beginning to see the need to "look to parents also for advice."

Quality of Instruction
Additional learning opportunities for gifted students are good. Special instruction is built in to the regular curriculum; therefore, students are not taken out of regular classes once a week. Additional instruction for low-achieving students also is rated good. The curricula for college-bound and job-bound students are considered good.

Quality of School Environment
The incidence of classroom disruption and vandalism is very low, and the condition of school buildings is good. "Things are pretty well taken care of," said an observer.

METROPOLITAN AREA

Columbus, OH

Eight districts returned Statistical Profiles in the Columbus Metropolitan Area.
Fair Appraisals alone were received from another four districts. Ohio does not
have required competency tests in reading and math. Therefore, all profiles show NA
(not applicable) on the lines requesting those statistics. For comparison,
we suggest looking at districts in the Cincinnati and Cleveland Metropolitan Areas in Ohio.

AREA AT A GLANCE

SCHOOL DISTRICT	ENROLLMENT	ESI
Columbus	66,823	55*
Dublin	5,268	
Delaware	3,620	
Gahanna–Jefferson	5,201	70
Groveport–Madison	5,954	58
Lancaster	7,030	
Southwest Licking	2,852	62
South Western	16,034	57
Teays Valley	2,666	43*
Upper Arlington	5,106	69*
Whitehall	3,401	
Worthington	8,330	62*

Indicates district misinterpretation of one or more statistics in the ESI. For each misinterpreted statistic, a score of 0 was given instead of a possible score of 0 to 10 points.

COLUMBUS

ADDRESS OF CENTRAL OFFICE:
270 East State Street, Columbus, OH 43215
ESI:55*

STATISTICAL PROFILE	DATA	ESI
Grade organization: K–5/6–8/9–12		
Percentage of schools built before 1955	45%	
Total enrollment	66,823	
Average Daily Attendance (ADA)	91%	4
Current expense per pupil in ADA	$3,767	10
Dropout rate	6%	10
Percentage of eligible students who took the ACT	54%	8
Average combined score on ACT	17.4	2
Percentage of graduates who enrolled in 2- or 4-year colleges	38%	
Percentage of students who passed the state reading test	NA	
Percentage of students who passed the state math test	NA	
Teacher–student ratio in elementary grades	1:19†	10
Teacher–student ratio in secondary grades	†	0*
Counselor–student ratio in secondary grades	1:400	2
Number of students per music specialist in elementary grades	††	
Number of students per art specialist in elementary grades	††	
Number of volumes in senior high school libraries (average)	9,357	
Beginning teacher's salary	$18,525†††	
Maximum teacher's salary	$37,463†††	
Average years of experience among teachers	13	
Number of students suspended and expelled	21,101	
Subjects in which Advanced Placement courses are offered:	9	9
American History, Calculus, Chemistry, English Literature, European History, French, German, Physics, Spanish		

† The only available ratio is this districtwide one, which includes all grades.

†† Over a three-year period, beginning 1987–88, the district will add music and art specialists to the elementary schools.

†††These are 1986–87 statistics.

FAIR APPRAISAL

Quality of School Leadership
Educational leadership ability is the primary criterion used in choosing principals, but the quality of leadership varies greatly from school to school in the city. According to one observer, "The administration recognizes this as a problem." As a consequence, several leadership training programs have been started. Parents and teachers have little or no say in principal selection. Principals have some influence over the distribution of resources to the schools.

Parents are sometimes effective, but their advice and opinions are rarely sought.

Quality of Instruction
Observers rate additional learning opportunities for gifted students as good. They may get better, according to district plans. Beginning in 1987–88, the program for gifted and talented students is scheduled to be expanded. Also, the district is scheduled to create more alternative (magnet) elementary schools concentrating on such specialities as math and science, international studies, the arts, and others. An attempt is being made to improve additional instruction for low-achieving students, which is now rated fair to good. Tutors are available, and a special dropout prevention project is underway. The curricula for college-bound students and job-bound students are termed good. New alternative (magnet) middle schools are expected to improve the college-preparatory program, with emphasis on math and science, foreign languages, reading, and other subjects.

"Improvement has been made with programs to combat youth alienation and reduce the dropout rate," said an observer, who thinks the district generally meets the educational needs of minority students.

Quality of School Environment
The level of classroom disruption and vandalism is low. The quality of building maintenance and repair, however, is rated fair. "There is a need for a building improvement levy to address repair and maintenance costs of $16 million," said an observer.

DUBLIN

ADDRESS OF CENTRAL OFFICE:
62 West Bridge Street, Dublin, OH 43017
ESI:None†

STATISTICAL PROFILE	DATA	ESI
Grade organization:		
Percentage of schools built before 1955		
Total enrollment		
Average Daily Attendance (ADA)		
Current expense per pupil in ADA		
Dropout rate		
Percentage of eligible students who took the ACT		
Average combined score on ACT		
Percentage of graduates who enrolled in 2- or 4-year college		
Percentage of students who passed the state reading test		
Percentage of students who passed the state math test		
Teacher–student ratio in elementary grades		
Teacher–student ratio in secondary grades		
Counselor–student ratio in secondary grades		
Number of students per music specialist in elementary grades		
Number of students per art specialist in elementary grades		
Number of volumes in senior high school library		
Beginning teacher's salary		
Maximum teacher's salary		
Average years of experience among teachers		
Number of students suspended and expelled		
Subjects in which Advanced Placement courses are offered:		

†A Statistical Profile was not received from this district.

FAIR APPRAISAL

Quality of School Leadership
Popularity in the school or community and longevity are important criteria affecting the choice of principals by the School Board. One reason is that parents in the "best" (high-income) sections pressure the central administration to get the "best" principals, according to an observer. Parents and teachers have hardly any say in principal selection, but principals have a great deal of influence over the allotment of resources to their school.

The influence by parent organizations on decision-making is minimal.

Quality of Instruction
The district has a good enrichment program for gifted students, and instruction for low-achieving students also is rated good. The college-preparatory curriculum is considered excellent, while the job-preparation curriculum is rated good ("not enough emphasis on vocational education").

Quality of School Environment
Classroom disruption and vandalism are not problems. The quality of building maintenance and repair is excellent.

DELAWARE

ADDRESS OF CENTRAL OFFICE:
248 North Washington Street, Delaware, OH 43015
ESI:None†

STATISTICAL PROFILE	DATA	ESI
Grade organization:		
Percentage of schools built before 1955		
Total enrollment		
Average Daily Attendance (ADA)		
Current expense per pupil in ADA		
Dropout rate		
Percentage of eligible students who took the ACT		
Average combined score on ACT		
Percentage of graduates who enrolled in 2- or 4-year college		
Percentage of students who passed the state reading test		
Percentage of students who passed the state math test		
Teacher–student ratio in elementary grades		
Teacher–student ratio in secondary grades		
Counselor–student ratio in secondary grades		
Number of students per music specialist in elementary grades		
Number of students per art specialist in elementary grades		
Number of volumes in senior high school library		
Beginning teacher's salary		
Maximum teacher's salary		
Average years of experience among teachers		
Number of students suspended and expelled		
Subjects in which Advanced Placement courses are offered:		

†A Statistical Profile was not received from this district.

FAIR APPRAISAL

Quality of School Leadership
Principals are selected primarily for their educational leadership ability, but there is some variance among the schools in the quality of leadership. Parents and teachers influence principal selection informally, but have no specific role in the process. Principals have some say in how the district's resources are distributed.

Parent organizations are only occasionally effective influencing district decision-making. Parents are hardly ever asked their opinion, said an observer.

Quality of Instruction
Additional learning opportunities for gifted students are rated good, but an observer complains that some students who should be included are not. Additional instruction for low-achieving students is rated fair. The curricula for students going to college and students going into the job market are rated excellent.

Quality of School Environment
The level of classroom disruption and vandalism is low, and the quality of building maintenance and repair is good.

GAHANNA-JEFFERSON

ADDRESS OF CENTRAL OFFICE:
160 Hamilton Road, Gahanna, OH 43230
ESI:70

STATISTICAL PROFILE	DATA	ESI
Grade organization: K–5/6–8/9–12		
Percentage of schools built before 1955	30%	
Total enrollment	5,201	
Average Daily Attendance (ADA)	95%	8
Current expense per pupil in ADA	$3,308	8
Dropout rate	2%	10
Percentage of eligible students who took the ACT	55%	8
Average combined score on ACT	20.9	10
Percentage of graduates who enrolled in 2- or 4-year colleges	63%	
Percentage of students who passed the state reading test	NA	
Percentage of students who passed the state math test	NA	
Teacher–student ratio in elementary grades	1:23	7
Teacher–student ratio in secondary grades	1:23	5
Counselor–student ratio in secondary grades	1:344	4
Number of students per music specialist in elementary grades	318	9
Number of students per art specialist in elementary grades	455	
Number of volumes in senior high school library	17,200	
Beginning teacher's salary	$16,300	
Maximum teacher's salary	$33,578	
Average years of experience among teachers	12	
Number of students suspended and expelled	NK	
Subjects in which Advanced Placement courses are offered: American History	1	1

FAIR APPRAISAL

Quality of School Leadership

Principals are selected mostly for their educational leadership ability, but one observer believes a candidate's popularity is considered a little more than it should be. However, the quality of leadership is generally uniform throughout the system. Parents and teachers are not involved in screening principal candidates, but principals have some say about the distribution of district resources among the schools.

Parents are occasionally effective. One observer complained that parents don't have enough influence.

Quality of Instruction

Additional learning opportunities for gifted students are rated good. An enrichment program, that excuses gifted students from regular classes at least once a week to attend special instruction, begins in grade 3. Additional instruction for low-achieving students is rated fair to good. The curricula for college-bound students and job-bound students are rated fair.

Quality of School Environment

The incidence of classroom disruption and vandalism is low, and the quality of building maintenance and repair is good.

GROVEPORT-MADISON

ADDRESS OF CENTRAL OFFICE:
5055 South Hamilton Road, Groveport, OH 43125
ESI:58

STATISTICAL PROFILE	DATA	ESI
Grade organization: K–5/6–8/9/10–12		
Percentage of schools built before 1955	20%	
Total enrollment	5,945	
Average Daily Attendance (ADA)	96%	9
Current expense per pupil in ADA	$2,661	4
Dropout rate	20%	3
Percentage of eligible students who took the ACT	52%	8
Average combined score on ACT	19.2	5
Percentage of graduates who enrolled in 2- or 4-year colleges	49%	
Percentage of students who passed the state reading test	NA	
Percentage of students who passed the state math test	NA	
Teacher–student ratio in elementary grades	1:21	9
Teacher–student ratio in secondary grades	1:19	9
Counselor–student ratio in secondary grades	1:397	2
Number of students per music specialist in elementary grades	539	5
Number of students per art specialist in elementary grades	539	
Number of volumes in senior high school library	17,610	
Beginning teacher's salary	$15,000	
Maximum teacher's salary	$36,705	
Average years of experience among teachers	12	
Number of students suspended and expelled	343	
Subjects in which Advanced Placement courses are offered: Biology, Chemistry, English, French	4	4

FAIR APPRAISAL

Quality of School Leadership

Principals are selected mostly for their educational leadership ability, and the quality of leadership is generally uniform throughout the system. Parents and teachers do not take part in screening principal candidates, but principals have some influence over the resources allotted to their school.

Parents are sometimes effective influencing decisions made by school officials. For example, they promoted the idea of a latch-key program for children whose parents are not at home after school. They also have helped to pass recent tax levies.

Quality of Instruction

Additional learning opportunities for gifted students are rated fair to good, while instruction for low-achieving students is considered good to excellent. A new pre-kindergarten program is designed to help youngsters who might have learning difficulties later on. The curriculum for students going to college is rated fair to good. "It's not where I'd like to see it," said an observer. The job-preparation curriculum is seen as good to excellent. "This is a blue-collar area," said an observer, "and many parents don't think of their children going on to college."

Quality of School Environment

Classroom disruption and vandalism are not problems. The quality of building maintenance and repair is good now, but it tends to "go up and down," said an observer.

LANCASTER

ADDRESS OF CENTRAL OFFICE:
345 East Mulberry Street, Lancaster, OH 43130
ESI:None†

STATISTICAL PROFILE	DATA	ESI
Grade organization:		
Percentage of schools built before 1955		
Total enrollment		
Average Daily Attendance (ADA)		
Current expense per pupil in ADA		
Dropout rate		
Percentage of eligible students who took the ACT		
Average combined score on ACT		
Percentage of graduates who enrolled in 2- or 4-year college		
Percentage of students who passed the state reading test		
Percentage of students who passed the state math test		
Teacher–student ratio in elementary grades		
Teacher–student ratio in secondary grades		
Counselor–student ratio in secondary grades		
Number of students per music specialist in elementary grades		
Number of students per art specialist in elementary grades		
Number of volumes in senior high school library		
Beginning teacher's salary		
Maximum teacher's salary		
Average years of experience among teachers		
Number of students suspended and expelled		
Subjects in which Advanced Placement courses are offered:		

†A Statistical Profile was not received from this district.

FAIR APPRAISAL

Quality of School Leadership
The School Board hires principals who display educational leadership ability. The quality of leadership does not vary greatly from school to school. Teachers are involved in screening principal candidates, and parents are included at a public hearing to question finalists for the position of superintendent. Principals have a great deal to say about the way district resources are divided among the schools.

Parents are effective influencing decision-making, mainly at public meetings of the School Board.

Quality of Instruction
An enrichment program for gifted students, which is rated good, extends from the third grade to the ninth. Especially bright high school students can take courses for no cost at the local branch of the State University. Additional instruction for low-achieving students is called excellent; a number of special classes are available. The curriculum for students going on to college is considered excellent, and the job-preparation curriculum is rated good.

Quality of School Environment
Observers consider the level of classroom disruption and vandalism to be high; the district places disruptive students in special classes. The quality of building maintenance and repair is excellent.

SOUTHWEST LICKING

ADDRESS OF CENTRAL OFFICE:
P.O. Box 400, Kirkersville, OH 43033
ESI:62

STATISTICAL PROFILE	DATA	ESI
Grade organization: K–5/6–8/9–12		
Percentage of schools built before 1955	60%	
Total enrollment	2,852	
Average Daily Attendance (ADA)	94%	7
Current expense per pupil in ADA	$2,691	5
Dropout rate	2%	10
Percentage of eligible students who took the ACT	43%	6
Average combined score on ACT	18.4	4
Percentage of graduates who enrolled in 2- or 4-year colleges	45%	
Percentage of students who passed the state reading test	NA	
Percentage of students who passed the state math test	NA	
Teacher–student ratio in elementary grades	1:21	9
Teacher–student ratio in secondary grades	1:19	9
Counselor–student ratio in secondary grades	1:340	4
Number of students per music specialist in elementary grades	395	8
Number of students per art specialist in elementary grades	592	
Number of volumes in senior high school library	11,121	
Beginning teacher's salary	$15,500	
Maximum teacher's salary	$32,240	
Average years of experience among teachers	11	
Number of students suspended and expelled	158	
Subjects in which Advanced Placement courses are offered:	None	0

FAIR APPRAISAL

Quality of School Leadership
Principals are hired because of their educational leadership ability, and the quality of leadership does not vary greatly from school to school. Parents and teachers do not screen principal candidates. However, principals have a say in deciding how resources will be allotted to their school. Parent groups are effective influencing district decisions. In recent years, a large group of parents formed the Academic Boosters Club (ABC), and they were instrumental in getting more emphasis on science and math and reading improvement.

Quality of Instruction
Additional opportunities for gifted and talented students are recent and are rated fair. Additional instruction for low-achieving students is said to be fair to good. The college-preparatory curriculum is rated good and the job-preparation curriculum is called fair.

Quality of School Environment
The level of classroom disruption and vandalism is low. The quality of building maintenance and repair is excellent.

SOUTH WESTERN

ADDRESS OF CENTRAL OFFICE:
2975 Kingston Avenue, Grove City, OH 43123
ESI:57

STATISTICAL PROFILE	DATA	ESI
Grade organization: K–5/6–8/9–12		
Percentage of schools built before 1955	25%	
Total enrollment	16,034	
Average Daily Attendance (ADA)	94%	7
Current expense per pupil in ADA	$3,024	6
Dropout rate	26%	0
Percentage of eligible students who took the ACT	32%	4
Average combined score on ACT	19.9	5
Percentage of graduates who enrolled in 2- or 4-year colleges	52%	
Percentage of students who passed the state reading test	NA	
Percentage of students who passed the state math test	NA	
Teacher–student ratio in elementary grades	1:23	7
Teacher–student ratio in secondary grades	1:19	9
Counselor–student ratio in secondary grades	1:345	4
Number of students per music specialist in elementary grades	244	10
Number of students per art specialist in elementary grades	394	
Number of volumes in senior high school libraries (average)	11,460	
Beginning teacher's salary	$17,100	
Maximum teacher's salary	$39,422	
Average years of experience among teachers	10	
Number of students suspended and expelled	2,160	
Subjects in which Advanced Placement courses are offered: American History, Art, Calculus, Chemistry, Physics	5	5

FAIR APPRAISAL

Quality of School Leadership

Educational leadership ability is the main criterion for principal selection, and the quality of leadership is generally uniform in the system. Parents and teachers take no part in screening principal candidates. Principals, however, have some say as to what resources their school will receive.

Parents are sometimes effective influencing policy decisions. Recently, parents helped decide a new grading system that gives greater weight to grades in tougher, more advanced courses.

Quality of Instruction

An enrichment program for gifted students, in which students are excused one day a week for special instruction, is rated good. A new remedial program has improved instruction for low-achieving students. The college-preparatory curriculum has gone from fair to good, said an observer, largely because students are now able to take a wider variety of high-level courses. A strong vocational program is designed for students not going to college.

The district adequately meets the needs of minority students, said observers, although integration mostly occurs in the middle and high schools.

Quality of School Environment

The level of classroom disruption and vandalism is low. A recent tax levy for school improvements and additions has raised the quality of building maintenance and repair.

TEAYS VALLEY

ADDRESS OF CENTRAL OFFICE:
385 Circleville Avenue, Ashville, OH 43103
ESI:43*

STATISTICAL PROFILE	DATA	ESI
Grade organization: K–5/6–8/9–12		
Percentage of schools built before 1955	60%	
Total enrollment	2,666	
Average Daily Attendance (ADA)	94%	7
Current expense per pupil in ADA	$2,379	3
Dropout rate	†	0*
Percentage of eligible students who took the ACT	22%	2
Average combined score on ACT	18	4
Percentage of graduates who enrolled in 2- or 4-year colleges	31%	
Percentage of students who passed the state reading test	NA	
Percentage of students who passed the state math test	NA	
Teacher–student ratio in elementary grades	1:23	7
Teacher–student ratio in secondary grades	1:17	10
Counselor–student ratio in secondary grades	1:448	0
Number of students per music specialist in elementary grades	373	8
Number of students per art specialist in elementary grades	None	
Number of volumes in senior high school library	7,769	
Beginning teacher's salary	$16,100	
Maximum teacher's salary	$29,780	
Average years of experience among teachers	11	
Number of students suspended and expelled	69	
Subjects in which Advanced Placement courses are offered: English, Chemistry	2	2

†The district misinterpreted this statistic.

FAIR APPRAISAL

Quality of School Leadership

The School Board chooses principals primarily for their educational leadership ability, and the quality of leadership does not vary greatly from school to school. Although parents and teachers have no say in principal selection, principals have some say in how resources will be allotted their school.

Parents are sometimes effective influencing district decisions, but mostly they are involved in fund-raising and sports boosting.

Quality of Instruction

Additional learning opportunities for gifted students are rated good. The program is relatively new, but it includes a special teacher for gifted students. The district offers Olympics of the Mind for especially bright students, and it sponsors occasional student debates on weighty topics. Instruction for low-achieving students is rated fair to good. Students at all levels are expected to benefit from a recent innovation called Period Zero. Students who want to fit in a social studies course or driver education or something else before the regular school day begins can come early for instruction. The curricula for college-bound students and job-bound students are called fair to good.

Quality of School Environment

The level of classroom disruption and vandalism is said to be low, which is a considerable improvement over the past when district students had the reputation of being "the worst" in the county. Students now "care more," said an observer. The quality of building maintenance and repair is good.

UPPER ARLINGTON

ADDRESS OF CENTRAL OFFICE:
1950 North Mallway, Upper Arlington, OH 43221
ESI:69*

STATISTICAL PROFILE	DATA	ESI
Grade organization: K–5/6–8/9–12		
Percentage of schools built before 1955	43%	
Total enrollment	5,106	
Average Daily Attendance (ADA)	92%	5
Current expense per pupil in ADA	$4,138	10
Dropout rate	1%	10
Percentage of eligible students who took the ACT	90%	10
Average combined score on ACT	22.7	10
Percentage of graduates who enrolled in 2- or 4-year colleges	90%	
Percentage of students who passed the state reading test	NA	
Percentage of students who passed the state math test	NA	
Teacher–student ratio in elementary grades	1:22	8
Teacher–student ratio in secondary grades	1:20	8
Counselor–student ratio in secondary grades	†	0*
Number of students per music specialist in elementary grades	†	0*
Number of students per art specialist in elementary grades	†	
Number of volumes in senior high school library	19,000	
Beginning teacher's salary	$17,415	
Maximum teacher's salary	$48,359	
Average years of experience among teachers	14	
Number of students suspended and expelled	300	
Subjects in which Advanced Placement courses are offered: American History, Biology, Calculus, Chemistry, Computer Science, English, French, Physics	8	8

†The district misinterpreted these statistics.

FAIR APPRAISAL

Quality of School Leadership
Principals are picked because of their educational leadership ability, and the quality of leadership is uniform throughout the system. Parents and teachers have no formal role to play in principal selection, but they may voice their opinions through channels. Principals have some say in how district resources are allotted to the schools.

Parent groups are sometimes effective influencing district decision-making.

Quality of Instruction
A special teacher for the gifted instructs very bright elementary school students at weekly sessions, and the overall program is rated good. Additional instruction for low-achieving students also is rated good. The curricula for students going on to college and for those going into the job market are termed excellent.

Quality of School Environment
Observers consider the level of classroom disruption and vandalism to be low. A special tax levy recently passed is expected to improve the condition of school buildings.

WHITEHALL

ADDRESS OF CENTRAL OFFICE:
625 South Yearling Road, Whitehall, OH 43213
ESI:None†

STATISTICAL PROFILE	DATA	ESI
Grade organization:		
Percentage of schools built before 1955		
Total enrollment		
Average Daily Attendance (ADA)		
Current expense per pupil in ADA		
Dropout rate		
Percentage of eligible students who took the ACT		
Average combined score on ACT		
Percentage of graduates who enrolled in 2- or 4-year college		
Percentage of students who passed the state reading test		
Percentage of students who passed the state math test		
Teacher–student ratio in elementary grades		
Teacher–student ratio in secondary grades		
Counselor–student ratio in secondary grades		
Number of students per music specialist in elementary grades		
Number of students per art specialist in elementary grades		
Number of volumes in senior high school library		
Beginning teacher's salary		
Maximum teacher's salary		
Average years of experience among teachers		
Number of students suspended and expelled		
Subjects in which Advanced Placement courses are offered:		

†A Statistical Profile was not received from this district.

FAIR APPRAISAL

Quality of School Leadership
Popularity in school and community is an important factor in principal selection. Nevertheless, the quality of educational leadership does not vary greatly from school to school. Parents and teaches do not screen principal candidates, but they may make their views of candidates known to the School Board. Principals do influence the way district resources are distributed to the schools.

Parents are sometimes effective influencing policy decisions in the district.

Quality of Instruction
Additional learning opportunities for gifted students and additional instruction for low-achieving students are rated excellent. The college-preparatory curriculum and the job-preparation curriculum are considered good.

Quality of School Environment
The incidence of classroom disruption and vandalism is low, and the quality of building maintenance and repair is high.

WORTHINGTON

ADDRESS OF CENTRAL OFFICE:
752 High Street, Worthington, OH 43085
ESI:62*

STATISTICAL PROFILE	DATA	ESI
Grade organization: †		
Percentage of schools built before 1955	32%	
Total enrollment	8,330	
Average Daily Attendance (ADA)	97%	10
Current expense per pupil in ADA	$3,502	10
Dropout rate	1%	10
Percentage of eligible students who took the ACT	71%	10
Average combined score on ACT	††	0*
Percentage of graduates who enrolled in 2- or 4-year colleges	75%	
Percentage of students who passed the state reading test	NA	
Percentage of students who passed the state math test	NA	
Teacher–student ratio in elementary grades	1:23	7
Teacher–student ratio in secondary grades	1:25	3
Counselor–student ratio in secondary grades	1:329	4
Number of students per music specialist in elementary grades	500	5
Number of students per art specialist in elementary grades	500	
Number of volumes in senior high school library	22,000	
Beginning teacher's salary	$18,347	
Maximum teacher's salary	$43,356	
Average years of experience among teachers	11	
Number of students suspended and expelled	137	
Subjects in which Advanced Placement courses are offered: Calculus, English Literature, European History	3	3

† The district misinterpreted this statistic.
††The district inadvertently left answer space blank; an asterisk (*) has been added to its ESI score.

FAIR APPRAISAL

Quality of School Leadership
Internal politics are a factor in principal selection, according to observers, but they also agree that the quality of educational leadership is generally uniform throughout the system. Parents and teachers generally are included on the teams that interview principal candidates. Principals have a great deal to say about the division of district resources, with principals having much autonomy within their building.

Parents' influence on decision-making in the district is termed effective. Parents and other citizens often take part in administrative study groups that discuss and make suggestions concerning current issues.

Quality of Instruction
Additional learning opportunities for gifted students and additional instruction for low-achieving students are considered good. Observers rate as excellent the curriculum for students planning on college. On the other hand, the curriculum for students preparing for the job market is considered fair "but improving."

Quality of School Environment
Classroom disruption and vandalism are not problems. The quality of building maintenance and repair is called good, but the high school is overcrowded.

METROPOLITAN AREA

Dallas–Fort Worth, TX

Seventeen districts in the Dallas-Fort Worth Metropolitan Area completed Statistical Profiles; we received a Fair Appraisal alone from one other district. Districts in this area can be compared with districts in the Houston and San Antonio Metropolitan Areas in Texas. Note, however, that San Antonio does not have a single city district.

AREA AT A GLANCE

SCHOOL DISTRICT	ENROLLMENT	ESI
Carrollton-Farmers Branch	15,106	62
Dallas	132,388	38
Duncanville	9,500	63
Eagle-Mt. Saginaw	4,408	48
Fort Worth	63,778	29*
Garland	34,213	39
Grand Prairie	16,032	33*
Grapevine-Colleyville	6,043	54
Highland Park	4,050	74
Hurst-Euless-Bedford	17,600	42
Irving	21,186	61
Lancaster	4,055	40
Mansfield	5,986	37
Mesquite	22,000	44
Plano	27,512	
Richardson	33,381	60
White Settlement	3,500	28
Wilmer Hutchins	4,154	33

Indicates district misinterpretation of one or more statistics in the ESI. For each misinterpreted statistic, a score of 0 was given instead of a possible score of 0 to 10 points.

CARROLLTON–FARMERS BRANCH

ADDRESS OF CENTRAL OFFICE:
P.O. Box 110186, Carrollton, TX 75011
ESI:62

STATISTICAL PROFILE	DATA	ESI
Grade organization: K–6/7–8/9–12		
Percentage of schools built before 1955	15%	
Total enrollment	15,106	
Average Daily Attendance (ADA)	96%	9
Current expense per pupil in ADA	$3,600	7
Dropout rate	15%	8
Percentage of eligible students who took the SAT	40%	5
Average combined score on SAT	941	6
Percentage of graduates who enrolled in 2- or 4-year colleges	51%	
Percentage of students who passed the state reading test	96%	
Percentage of students who passed the state math test	96%	
Teacher–student ratio in elementary grades	1:18	10
Teacher–student ratio in secondary grades	1:17	10
Counselor–student ratio in secondary grades	1:400	2
Number of students per music specialist in elementary grades	521	5
Number of students per art specialist in elementary grades	None	
Number of volumes in senior high school library	NK	
Beginning teacher's salary	$19,376	
Maximum teacher's salary	$37,653	
Average years of experience among teachers	10	
Number of students suspended and expelled	280	
Subjects in which Advanced Placement courses are offered:	None	0

FAIR APPRAISAL

Quality of School Leadership

Although the quality of educational leadership among principals is generally uniform throughout the district, an observer believes district officials also consider a principal's ability to be a disciplinarian. This might be due in part to the deaths in 1986–87 of several students who were reported to have been high on drugs or drunk on alcohol. Parents and teachers do not get involved in the screening of principal candidates. Principals have some say in deciding how resources will be divided among the schools.

Parents are sometimes an effective influence on district policy decisions. Recently, they have strongly advocated a stronger policy to curb drugs and alcohol use.

Quality of Instruction

The program for gifted students is rated excellent, with special instruction beginning in grade 1. Additional instruction for low-achieving students is considered good, with many such students being served at a special learning center. The curricula for college-bound students and job-bound students are rated good, although it is unusual for a district of this size not to offer any Advanced Placement courses.

Quality of School Environment

The level of classroom disruption and vandalism is "average." The quality of building maintenance and repair is considered excellent.

DALLAS

ADDRESS OF CENTRAL OFFICE:
3700 Ross Avenue, Dallas, TX 75204
ESI:38

STATISTICAL PROFILE	DATA	ESI
Grade organization: K–6/7–8/9–12		
Percentage of schools built before 1955	45%	
Total enrollment	132,388	
Average Daily Attendance (ADA)	94%	7
Current expense per pupil in ADA	$4,932	10
Dropout rate	58%	0
Percentage of eligible students who took the SAT	35%	4
Average combined score on SAT	813	0
Percentage of graduates who enrolled in 2- or 4-year colleges	56%	
Percentage of students who passed the state reading test	89%	
Percentage of students who passed the state math test	86%	
Teacher–student ratio in elementary grades	1:24	6
Teacher–student ratio in secondary grades	1:27	1
Counselor–student ratio in secondary grades	1:500	0
Number of students per music specialist in elementary grades	76,482	0
Number of students per art specialist in elementary grades	76,482	
Number of volumes in senior high school library	†	
Beginning teacher's salary	$19,000	
Maximum teacher's salary	$31,000	
Average years of experience among teachers	12	
Number of students suspended and expelled	15,318	
Subjects in which Advanced Placement courses are offered: American History, Art, Biology, Calculus, Chemistry, Computer Science, English, French, German, Latin, Music, Physics, Spanish	13	10

†The statistic provided by the district is 16–20 books per student.

Quality of School Leadership

Although popularity and longevity are sometimes factors in principal selection, observers believe educational leadership ability is the primary criterion used in appointing principals. The observers also agree that the quality of educational leadership varies in the district, but, as one observer put it, "there is no real pattern." For example, principals of lesser ability are not necessarily assigned to schools that have the largest enrollment of minority or low-achieving students. Parents and teachers do not screen principal candidates. However, one observer noted that parents are sometimes instrumental in getting a "poor" principal moved from their children's school. Principals have some say in the division of district resources. Recently, they were given greater authority to choose teachers and other personnel assigned to their school.

Parents are often effective influencing policy decisions. They primarily make their views known through monthly "cluster" meetings with the superintendent.

Quality of Instruction

Additional learning opportunities for gifted students are rated excellent. In addition to an extensive gifted and talented program for students in grades 4–12, there are magnet schools emphasizing different academic subjects. Additional instruction for low-achieving students, on the other hand, is given a fair rating. Although the percentage of students going to college is not high, the college-preparatory curriculum is considered excellent. The curriculum for those students going into the job market (44% of graduates) is rated fair.

The observers believe the district is not adequately meeting the educational needs of minority students (predominantly Hispanic and black). However, one observer said it is important to note "the excellent academic and career-oriented programs, the high achievement of many students of all races, and the good parental involvement and community support."

Quality of School Environment

Overall, the level of classroom disruption and vandalism is low, but, as one observer put it, some schools "are a mess." The quality of building maintenance and repair is fair. "The district has 180 schools," said an observer, "and they have trouble keeping up."

DUNCANVILLE

ADDRESS OF CENTRAL OFFICE:
802 South Main Street, Duncanville, TX 75137
ESI:63

STATISTICAL PROFILE	DATA	ESI
Grade organization: K–4/5–6/7–8/9–12		
Percentage of schools built before 1955	10%	
Total enrollment	9,500	
Average Daily Attendance (ADA)	96%	9
Current expense per pupil in ADA	$3,100	4
Dropout rate	3%	10
Percentage of eligible students who took the SAT	62%	10
Average combined score on SAT	922	5
Percentage of graduates who enrolled in 2- or 4-year colleges	80%	
Percentage of students who passed the state reading test	98%	
Percentage of students who passed the state math test	96%	
Teacher–student ratio in elementary grades	1:24	6
Teacher–student ratio in secondary grades	1:20	8
Counselor–student ratio in secondary grades	1:500	0
Number of students per music specialist in elementary grades	500	5
Number of students per art specialist in elementary grades	None	
Number of volumes in senior high school library	25,000	
Beginning teacher's salary	$18,700	
Maximum teacher's salary	$32,100	
Average years of experience among teachers	9	
Number of students suspended and expelled	200	
Subjects in which Advanced Placement courses are offered: American History, Biology, Calculus, Chemistry, English, Government & Politics	6	6

FAIR APPRAISAL

Quality of School Leadership

The School Board selects principals primarily for their educational leadership ability. The quality of leadership does not vary greatly from school to school. Parents and teachers are not part of the formal screening of principal candidates, but they are able to voice their opinions at open meetings. Principals have some say in how the district's resources will be divided among the schools.

Parents have a "strong voice," according to an observer, and are an effective influence over policy decisions.

Quality of Instruction

The program for gifted students is rated good. Usually, especially bright students take one special class a day. The program begins in the lower grades. Low-achieving students often are able to attend classes that are smaller than the norm, where they are able to get more individual attention. Therefore, additional instruction for low-achieving students is rated good. The curriculum for students going to college is termed good, and the curriculum for students heading into the job market is called excellent.

Quality of School Environment

The level of classroom disruption and vandalism is low, and the quality of building maintenance and repair is excellent.

EAGLE–MT. SAGINAW

ADDRESS OF CENTRAL OFFICE:
P.O. Box 79160, Fort Worth, TX 76179
ESI:48

STATISTICAL PROFILE	DATA	ESI
Grade organization: Pre-K–6/7–8/9–12		
Percentage of schools built before 1955	1%	
Total enrollment	4,408	
Average Daily Attendance (ADA)	95%	8
Current expense per pupil in ADA	$1,490	0
Dropout rate	8%	10
Percentage of eligible students who took the SAT	43%	6
Average combined score on SAT	880	3
Percentage of graduates who enrolled in 2- or 4-year colleges	66%	
Percentage of students who passed the state reading test	92%	
Percentage of students who passed the state math test	95%	
Teacher–student ratio in elementary grades	1:21	9
Teacher–student ratio in secondary grades	1:17	10
Counselor–student ratio in secondary grades	1:440	0
Number of students per music specialist in elementary grades	831	0
Number of students per art specialist in elementary grades	831	
Number of volumes in senior high school library	17,803	
Beginning teacher's salary	$18,150	
Maximum teacher's salary	$32,470	
Average years of experience among teachers	10	
Number of students suspended and expelled	26	
Subjects in which Advanced Placement courses are offered: Calculus, Physics	2	2

FAIR APPRAISAL

Quality of School Leadership

The School Board appoints principals mainly on the basis of their educational leadership ability, and the quality of leadership does not vary greatly from school to school. Parents and teachers do not take part in the screening of principal candidates, but principals have some say in deciding how the resources of the district will be allotted to each school.

Parents are sometimes effective influencing policy decisions, but not often.

Quality of Instruction

Additional learning opportunities for gifted students are rated good to excellent, with a special program in the elementary schools and honors courses in the middle and high schools. Special classes also exist for slow learners. The curricula for college-bound students and job-bound students are termed good. One observer noted that a number of families in the district moved there from Fort Worth because of the caliber of education.

Quality of School Environment

The incidence of classroom disruption and vandalism is very low, and the quality of building maintenance and repair is excellent.

FORT WORTH

ADDRESS OF CENTRAL OFFICE:
3210 West Lancaster, Fort Worth, TX 76107
ESI:29*

STATISTICAL PROFILE	DATA	ESI
Grade organization: K–5/6–8/9–12		
Percentage of schools built before 1955	62%	
Total enrollment	63,778	
Average Daily Attendance (ADA)	94%	7
Current expense per pupil in ADA	$3,028	4
Dropout rate	31%	0
Percentage of eligible students who took the SAT	33%	4
Average combined score on SAT	830	1
Percentage of graduates who enrolled in 2- or 4-year colleges	53%	
Percentage of students who passed the state reading test	90%	
Percentage of students who passed the state math test	87%	
Teacher–student ratio in elementary grades	1:23	7
Teacher–student ratio in secondary grades	1:26	2
Counselor–student ratio in secondary grades	1:438	0
Number of students per music specialist in elementary grades	†	0*
Number of students per art specialist in elementary grades	†	
Number of volumes in senior high school libraries (average)	16,660	
Beginning teacher's salary	$19,100	
Maximum teacher's salary	$36,066	
Average years of experience among teachers	9	
Number of students suspended and expelled	NK	
Subjects in which Advanced Placement courses are offered: American History, Calculus, English, Foreign Language (unspecified)	4	4

†The district misinterpreted these statistics.

Quality of School Leadership

Years spent in the district and popularity seem to be almost as important criteria as educational leadership ability when it comes to choosing principals. Also, observers report that the quality of educational leadership varies greatly from school to school. The quality of leadership at a school "depends on the affluence of the neighborhood" served by the school, said an observer. Parents and teachers have little say about principal selection; however, principals have some say about the distribution of district resources.

Parent groups are not considered effective influencing district policy decisions.

Quality of Instruction

Additional learning opportunities for gifted students are considered good. In addition to special programs for gifted students, magnet schools that specialize in various subjects cater to very bright students. Observers rate additional instruction for low-achieving students as fair, but tutors are mandated for failing students. The college-preparatory curriculum is considered fair to good; the curriculum for students going into the job market is rated fair.

The observers believe the district does not adequately meet the needs of minority students, and one observer said the problem is that minority students tend to be taught by the least able teachers and placed in the most inferior buildings.

Quality of School Environment

The level of classroom disruption and vandalism is on the high side, but not a major problem. The quality of building maintenance and repair is rated fair to good.

GARLAND

ADDRESS OF CENTRAL OFFICE:
P.O. Box 461547, Garland, TX 75046
ESI:39

STATISTICAL PROFILE	DATA	ESI
Grade organization: K–5/6–8/9–12		
Percentage of schools built before 1955	9%	
Total enrollment	34,213	
Average Daily Attendance (ADA)	93%	6
Current expense per pupil in ADA	$2,947	3
Dropout rate	NK	0
Percentage of eligible students who took the SAT	41%	6
Average combined score on SAT	887	4
Percentage of graduates who enrolled in 2- or 4-year colleges	NK	
Percentage of students who passed the state reading test	89%	
Percentage of students who passed the state math test	89%	
Teacher–student ratio in elementary grades	1:21	9
Teacher–student ratio in secondary grades	1:25	3
Counselor–student ratio in secondary grades	1:500	0
Number of students per music specialist in elementary grades	502	5
Number of students per art specialist in elementary grades	None	
Number of volumes in senior high school library	27,500	
Beginning teacher's salary	$19,300	
Maximum teacher's salary	$29,700	
Average years of experience among teachers	14	
Number of students suspended and expelled	984	
Subjects in which Advanced Placement courses are offered: American History, Biology, Calculus	3	3

Quality of School Leadership

For the most part, principals are selected because of their educational leadership ability, although the internal "old boy" politics sometimes have been a factor. The quality of leadership does not vary greatly throughout the system. Parents and teachers have no formal role in principal selection. Principals have some say in how resources are allotted to their school, but not much.

Parent organizations are sometimes effective at an individual school, but seldom do they influence policy decisions for the district.

Quality of Instruction

Much has been done in the last three years to improve the learning opportunities for gifted students, and in 1987–88 several magnet schools were opened to give bright students the chance to specialize in a particular subject area. Additional instruction for low-achieving students is rated fair. Also rated fair is the curriculum for students going to college. The curriculum for job-bound students, however, is good.

The district is under court order to desegregate through a freedom of choice plan (students can attend their neighborhood school or any other school in the district). The jury is out on whether the schools are adequately meeting the educational needs of minority students. Said one observer, "They're trying like hell!"

Quality of School Environment

Classroom disruption and vandalism are not problems. The quality of building maintenance and repair is fair to good.

GRAND PRAIRIE

ADDRESS OF CENTRAL OFFICE:
P.O. Box 1170, Grand Prairie, TX 75053
ESI:33*

STATISTICAL PROFILE	DATA	ESI
Grade organization: K–5/6–8/9–12		
Percentage of schools built before 1955	35%	
Total enrollment	16,032	
Average Daily Attendance (ADA)	97%	10
Current expense per pupil in ADA	$3,108	4
Dropout rate	24%	0
Percentage of eligible students who took the SAT	25%	2
Average combined score on SAT	843	1
Percentage of graduates who enrolled in 2- or 4-year colleges	40%	
Percentage of students who passed the state reading test	93%	
Percentage of students who passed the state math test	91%	
Teacher–student ratio in elementary grades	1:22	8
Teacher–student ratio in secondary grades	1:25	3
Counselor–student ratio in secondary grades	1:400	2
Number of students per music specialist in elementary grades	†	0*
Number of students per art specialist in elementary grades	None	
Number of volumes in senior high school libraries (average)	17,186	
Beginning teacher's salary	$18,000	
Maximum teacher's salary	$32,900	
Average years of experience among teachers	10	
Number of students suspended and expelled	44	
Subjects in which Advanced Placement courses are offered: English, Calculus, Chemistry	3	3

†The district misinterpreted this statistic.

Quality of School Leadership

Longevity and popularity are considerations when hiring principals, but educational leadership ability remains the number one criterion. The quality of leadership is generally uniform throughout the system. Parents and teachers have little or no say in the selection of principals. Principals complete a needs assessment for their school each year, said an observer, and their needs are honored insofar as possible.

Parent groups have a strong, loud voice, and the School Board generally pays attention. When the board and the central administration wanted to change high school graduation day to Sunday afternoon, parents complained and won.

Quality of Instruction

Additional instruction for gifted students in grades 1–5 is offered two or three times a week by a special teacher, and the overall program for gifted students is rated good. Also considered good is the additional instruction for low-achieving students. The curriculum for students bound for college is fair to good, and the curriculum for students going into the job market is good.

The district is beginning to meet minority students' needs, "but there's still a way to go." One forward step has been an increase in English as a Second Language (ESL) classes for Hispanic children beginning at the pre-kindergarten level.

Quality of School Environment

The incidence of classroom disruption and vandalism is low. The quality of building maintenance and repair is rated fair to good. A new superintendent is intent on improving the physical plant.

GRAPEVINE–COLLEYVILLE

ADDRESS OF CENTRAL OFFICE:
3051 West Highway 26, Grapevine, TX 76051
ESI:54

STATISTICAL PROFILE	DATA	ESI
Grade organization: †		
Percentage of schools built before 1955	13%	
Total enrollment	6,043	
Average Daily Attendance (ADA)	97%	10
Current expense per pupil in ADA	$3,000	4
Dropout rate	NK	0
Percentage of eligible students who took the SAT	60%	9
Average Combined score on SAT	906	4
Percentage of graduates who enrolled in 2- or 4-year colleges	79%	
Percentage of students who passed the state reading test	93%	
Percentage of students who passed the state math test	94%	
Teacher–student ratio in elementary grades	1:18	10
Teacher–student ratio in secondary grades	1:18	10
Counselor–student ratio in secondary grades	1:402	1
Number of students per music specialist in elementary grades	600	3
Number of students per art specialist in elementary grades	None	
Number of volumes in senior high school library	14,000	
Beginning teacher's salary	$19,000	
Maximum teacher's salary	$31,600	
Average years of experience among teachers	10	
Number of students suspended and expelled	325	
Subjects in which Advanced Placement courses are offered: American History, Biology, English	3	3

†The district misinterpreted this statistic.

Quality of School Leadership

The School Board mostly considers a candidate's ability as an educational leader when hiring a principal, but longevity in the district helps. However, the quality of leadership is uniform throughout the system. Parents and teachers are able to state their opinions regarding principal candidates. Principals also influence the central administration about the allotment of resources to the schools.

Parents are sometimes effective influencing school policy decisions.

Quality of Instruction

Additional learning opportunities for gifted students and additional instruction for low-achieving students are rated good. Also termed good is the college-preparatory curriculum. The observers rate the curriculum for job-bound students as fair.

Quality of School Environment

The level of classroom disruption and vandalism is very low, and the quality of building maintenance and repair is good.

HIGHLAND PARK

ADDRESS OF CENTRAL OFFICE:
7015 Westchester Drive, Dallas, TX 75205
ESI:74

STATISTICAL PROFILE	DATA	ESI
Grade organization: K–5/6–8/9–12		
Percentage of schools built before 1955	100%	
Total enrollment	4,050	
Average Daily Attendance (ADA)	95%	8
Current expense per pupil in ADA	$4,200	10
Dropout rate	NK	0
Percentage of eligible students who took the SAT	97%	10
Average combined score on SAT	972	8
Percentage of graduates who enrolled in 2- or 4-year colleges	96%	
Percentage of students who passed the state reading test	100%	
Percentage of students who passed the state math test	100%	
Teacher–student ratio in elementary grades	1:14	10
Teacher–student ratio in secondary grades	1:15	10
Counselor–student ratio in secondary grades	1:355	3
Number of students per music specialist in elementary grades	400	7
Number of students per art specialist in elementary grades	400	
Number of volumes in senior high school library	28,829	
Beginning teacher's salary	$20,000	
Maximum teacher's salary	$38,000	
Average years of experience among teachers	13	
Number of students suspended and expelled	NK	
Subjects in which Advanced Placement courses are offered:	8	8
American History, Biology, Calculus, Chemistry, English, French, Physics, Spanish		

FAIR APPRAISAL

Quality of School Leadership
Educational leadership ability is the primary criterion the School Board uses in selecting principals, although seniority in the system helps. The quality of leadership does not vary greatly from school to school. Parents and teachers are able to express their views on principal candidates. Principals have a great deal to say about the distribution of district resources to the schools.

Parent organizations have influenced district officials to start a drug education program, but otherwise parental influence is spotty.

Quality of Instruction
Observers rate additional learning opportunities for gifted students and additional instruction for low-achieving students as good. The college preparatory curriculum is considered excellent, but the curriculum for students going directly into the job market is rated fair.

Quality of School Environment
The level of classroom disruption and vandalism is very low, and the quality of building maintenance and repair is very high.

SCHOOL DISTRICT

HURST–EULESS–BEDFORD

ADDRESS OF CENTRAL OFFICE:
1849 Central Drive, Bedford, TX 76046
ESI:42

STATISTICAL PROFILE	DATA	ESI
Grade organization: K–6/7–9/10–12		
Percentage of schools built before 1955	4%	
Total enrollment	17,600	
Average Daily Attendance (ADA)	97%	10
Current expense per pupil in ADA	$3,409	5
Dropout rate	NK	0
Percentage of eligible students who took the SAT	55%	8
Average combined score on SAT	914	5
Percentage of graduates who enrolled in 2- or 4-year colleges	84%	
Percentage of students who passed the state reading test	98%	
Percentage of students who passed the state math test	97%	
Teacher–student ratio in elementary grades	1:23	7
Teacher–student ratio in secondary grades	1:24	4
Counselor–student ratio in secondary grades	1:567	0
Number of students per music specialist in elementary grades	800	0
Number of students per art specialist in elementary grades	800	
Number of volumes in senior high school libraries (average)	21,907	
Beginning teacher's salary	$19,500	
Maximum teacher's salary	$36,758	
Average years of experience among teachers	15	
Number of students suspended and expelled	670	
Subjects in which Advanced Placement courses are offered:	3	3
American History, English, Government and Politics		

FAIR APPRAISAL

Quality of School Leadership
Educational leadership ability is the primary criterion for choosing a principal, but popularity and longevity in the district also are considered. The quality of leadership does not vary greatly from school to school. Principals are almost always chosen from among candidates within the system; parents and teachers do not help in the selection process. Principals, however, make their views known about the allotment of district resources to the schools.

Parent organizations are only sometimes effective influencing district policy decisions.

Quality of Instruction
Most schools have programs for gifted and talented students, and although program quality varies from school to school, the overall effort is rated good. Additional instruction for low-achieving students is termed fair. Observers believe the curricula for college-bound and work-bound students are good. The district is noted in the area for its first-rate computer instruction.

Quality of School Environment
Classroom disruption and vandalism are not problems, and the quality of building maintenance and repair is good.

IRVING

ADDRESS OF CENTRAL OFFICE:
P.O. Box 2637, Irving, TX 75061
ESI:61

STATISTICAL PROFILE	DATA	ESI
Grade organization: K–5/6–8/9–12		
Percentage of schools built before 1955	22%	
Total enrollment	21,186	
Average Daily Attendance (ADA)	97%	10
Current expense per pupil in ADA	$3,383	6
Dropout rate	38%	0
Percentage of eligible students who took the SAT	53%	8
Average combined score on SAT	900	4
Percentage of graduates who enrolled in 2- or 4-year colleges	80%	
Percentage of students who passed the state reading test	96%	
Percentage of students who passed the state math test	96%	
Teacher–student ratio in elementary grades	1:19	10
Teacher–student ratio in secondary grades	1:18	10
Counselor–student ratio in secondary grades	1:338	4
Number of students per music specialist in elementary grades	619	3
Number of students per art specialist in elementary grades	1,239	
Number of volumes in senior high school libraries (average)	23,380	
Beginning teacher's salary	$20,200	
Maximum teacher's salary	$34,400	
Average years of experience among teachers	12	
Number of students suspended and expelled	1,562	
Subjects in which Advanced Placement courses are offered: American History, Biology, Calculus, Chemistry, English, Physics	6	6

Quality of School Leadership
Educational leadership ability is a major criterion used by the School Board when measuring a principal candidate, but popularity and longevity in the system also are considerations. Observers complain that quality of leadership varies greatly from school to school. Furthermore, said one observer, "little is done about poor principals." Parents and teachers play no formal part in the screening of principal candidates. Principals, on the other hand, have some say in how the district divides resources among the schools.

Parent influence in decision-making is sometimes effective.

Quality of Instruction
A good program for gifted students is offered at all grade levels, but additional instruction for low-achieving students is rated fair. The observers also rate as good the curricula for students going on to college and for students going directly into the world of work. The district offers something for all students, said an observer, but everything offered is not equally good. Some students "fall through the cracks," said the observer.

Quality of School Environment
The level of classroom disruption and vandalism is low. The quality of building maintenance and repair is rated good.

LANCASTER

ADDRESS OF CENTRAL OFFICE:
P.O. Box 400, Lancaster, TX 75146
ESI:40

STATISTICAL PROFILE	DATA	ESI
Grade organization: K–4/5–6/7–8/9–12		
Percentage of schools built before 1955	14%	
Total enrollment	4,055	
Average Daily Attendance (ADA)	97%	10
Current expense per pupil in ADA	$3,151	4
Dropout rate	30%	0
Percentage of eligible students who took the SAT	39%	5
Average combined score on SAT	826	0
Percentage of graduates who enrolled in 2- or 4-year colleges	45%	
Percentage of students who passed the state reading test	89%	
Percentage of students who passed the state math test	89%	
Teacher–student ratio in elementary grades	1:20	10
Teacher–student ratio in secondary grades	1:23	5
Counselor–student ratio in secondary grades	1:425	1
Number of students per music specialist in elementary grades	520	5
Number of students per art specialist in elementary grades	520	
Number of volumes in senior high school library	13,000	
Beginning teacher's salary	$17,400	
Maximum teacher's salary	$29,900	
Average years of experience among teachers	10	
Number of students suspended and expelled	189	
Subjects in which Advanced Placement courses are offered:	None	0

Quality of School Leadership
Although popularity and longevity are factors in principal selection, educational leadership ability is the primary criterion, and the quality of leadership does not vary greatly from school to school. Parents and teachers have little to say about principal selection, but principals have more to say about the quantity and quality of resources allotted their school.

Parent organizations are not very effective influencing policy decisions.

Quality of Instruction
Additional opportunities for gifted students are rated good, but additional instruction for low-achieving students is considered to be fair. Rated good are the curricula for students going to college and for students going into the job world.

Quality of School Environment
The incidence of classroom disruption and vandalism is very low. The quality of building maintenance and repair is good.

MANSFIELD

ADDRESS OF CENTRAL OFFICE:
609 East Broad Street, Mansfield, TX 76063
ESI:37

STATISTICAL PROFILE	DATA	ESI
Grade organization: †		
Percentage of schools built before 1955	8%	
Total enrollment	5,986	
Average Daily Attendance (ADA)	93%	6
Current expense per pupil in ADA	$2,340	0
Dropout rate	NK	0
Percentage of eligible students who took the SAT	62%	10
Average combined score on SAT	883	4
Percentage of graduates who enrolled in 2- or 4-year colleges	58%	
Percentage of students who passed the state reading test	NK	
Percentage of students who passed the state math test	NK	
Teacher–student ratio in elementary grades	1:22	8
Teacher–student ratio in secondary grades	1:25	3
Counselor–student ratio in secondary grades	1:460	0
Number of students per music specialist in elementary grades	620	3
Number of students per art specialist in elementary grades	None	
Number of volumes in senior high school library	13,500	
Beginning teacher's salary	$17,200	
Maximum teacher's salary	$30,100	
Average years of experience among teachers	10	
Number of students suspended and expelled	105	
Subjects in which Advanced Placement courses are offered: American History, Calculus, English	3	3

†The district misinterpreted the statistic.

FAIR APPRAISAL

Quality of School Leadership

For the most part, principals are selected for their educational leadership ability, and the quality of leadership is uniform throughout the system. Parents and teachers do not have a say in principal selection, but principals help determine how resources will be divided among the schools.

Parents are effective influencing school decisions. Recently, parents persuaded district officials to build temporary facilities at an overcrowded school rather than bus students to another school.

Quality of Instruction

Additional learning opportunities for gifted students are rated excellent, with special classes and special teachers beginning in the elementary grades. The additional instruction for low-achieving students also is rated excellent. The curricula for students going on to college and going into the job market are rated good.

Quality of School Environment

Classroom disruption is not a problem, but vandalism is. While vandalism is not a major problem now, said an observer, it is getting to be one. The quality of building maintenance and repair is fair to good.

MESQUITE

ADDRESS OF CENTRAL OFFICE:
405 East Davis Street, Mesquite, TX 75149
ESI:44

STATISTICAL PROFILE	DATA	ESI
Grade organization: K–6/7–8/9–12		
Percentage of schools built before 1955	3%	
Total enrollment	22,000	
Average Daily Attendance (ADA)	95%	8
Current expense per pupil in ADA	$3,000	4
Dropout rate	20%	3
Percentage of eligible students who took the SAT	30%	3
Average combined score on SAT	908	4
Percentage of graduates who enrolled in 2- or 4-year colleges	50%	
Percentage of students who passed the state reading test	97%	
Percentage of students who passed the state math test	93%	
Teacher–student ratio in elementary grades	1:21	9
Teacher–student ratio in secondary grades	1:21	7
Counselor–student ratio in secondary grades	1:556	0
Number of students per music specialist in elementary grades	500	5
Number of students per art specialist in elementary grades	1,200	
Number of volumes in senior high school library	†	
Beginning teacher's salary	$19,500	
Maximum teacher's salary	$38,500	
Average years of experience among teachers	9	
Number of students suspended and expelled	488	
Subjects in which Advanced Placement courses are offered: English	1	1

†The district's statistic is 12 volumes per student.

FAIR APPRAISAL

Quality of School Leadership

Popularity and longevity count in principal selection, and the quality of leadership varies greatly from school to school. According to an observer, the "good" principals go to schools in the "wealthy neighborhoods." Parents and teachers have no say in principal selection, but principals have some say about the resources they will get from the central office.

Parent organizations sometimes are able to influence school decisions, but not often.

Quality of Instruction

Special programs in most schools make the learning opportunities for gifted students good. However, additional instruction for low-achieving students is said to be fair. Students going to college are offered a good curriculum, but the curriculum for students going into the job market is fair.

Quality of School Environment

The level of classroom disruption and vandalism is low. The quality of building maintenance and repair is good.

PLANO

ADDRESS OF CENTRAL OFFICE:
1517 Avenue H, Plano, TX 75074
ESI:None†

STATISTICAL PROFILE	DATA	ESI
Grade organization:		
Percentage of schools built before 1955		
Total enrollment		
Average Daily Attendance (ADA)		
Current expense per pupil in ADA		
Dropout rate		
Percentage of eligible students who took the SAT		
Average Combined score on SAT		
Percentage of graduates who enrolled in 2- or 4-year colleges		
Percentage of students who passed the state reading test		
Percentage of students who passed the state math test		
Teacher–student ratio in elementary grades		
Teacher–student ratio in secondary grades		
Counselor–student ratio in secondary grades		
Number of students per music specialist in elementary grades		
Number of students per art specialist in elementary grades		
Number of volumes in senior high school library		
Beginning teacher's salary		
Maximum teacher's salary		
Average years of experience among teachers		
Number of students suspended and expelled		
Subjects in which Advanced Placement courses are offered:		

†A Statistical Profile was not received from this district.

FAIR APPRAISAL

Quality of School Leadership
Most principals are selected for their educational leadership ability, and the quality of leadership does not vary greatly from school to school. Teachers help to draft the qualifications of principal candidates; parents, however, have no say in principal selection. Principals have a great deal to say about the district resources allotted their school.

Parents are sometimes effective influencing decision-making by school officials.

Quality of Instruction
Gifted students are excused from regular classes at least once a week in the elementary grades for special instruction. The overall program is called excellent. Remedial reading and math classes have provided more individual attention for low-achieving students. The curriculum for college-bound students is rated excellent, and the curriculum for students heading for the job market is termed good.

Quality of School Environment
The level of classroom disruption and vandalism is very low, and the quality of building maintenance and repair is good.

RICHARDSON

ADDRESS OF CENTRAL OFFICE:
400 South Greenville Avenue, Richardson, TX 75081
ESI:60

STATISTICAL PROFILE	DATA	ESI
Grade organization: K–6/7–9/10–12		
Percentage of schools built before 1955	4%	
Total enrollment	33,381	
Average Daily Attendance (ADA)	99%	10
Current expense per pupil in ADA	$1,909	0
Dropout rate	NK	0
Percentage of eligible students who took the SAT	73%	10
Average combined score on SAT	906	4
Percentage of graduates who enrolled in 2- or 4-year colleges	NK	
Percentage of students who passed the state reading test	93%	
Percentage of students who passed the state math test	96%	
Teacher–student ratio in elementary grades	1:23	7
Teacher–student ratio in secondary grades	1:22	6
Counselor–student ratio in secondary grades	1:297	6
Number of students per music specialist in elementary grades	318	9
Number of students per art specialist in elementary grades	650	
Number of volumes in senior high school libraries (average)	23,848	
Beginning teacher's salary	$19,571	
Maximum teacher's salary	$41,175	
Average years of experience among teachers	NK	
Number of students suspended and expelled	605	
Subjects in which Advanced Placement courses are offered:	8	8
American History, Biology, Calculus AB, Calculus BC, Chemistry, English, European History, Physics		

FAIR APPRAISAL

Quality of School Leadership
Most principals are selected for their educational leadership ability, and the quality of leadership does not vary greatly from school to school. However, one observer noted that some principals are better managers than they are educational leaders. Teachers help screen candidates for principal positions, but parents play no part. Principals have quite a lot of influence in the distribution of district resources.

Parents are sometimes effective influencing decision-making by school officials. Primarily, they serve on advisory committees.

Quality of Instruction
Additional learning opportunities for gifted students are rated excellent. At lower grade levels, gifted students are excused from regular classes at least once a week for special instruction. Additional instruction for low-achieving students is considered fair to good. The college-preparatory curriculum is termed excellent, and the job-preparation curriculum is rated good.

Quality of School Environment
The incidence of classroom disruption and vandalism is very low, and the quality of building maintenance and repair is excellent.

WHITE SETTLEMENT

ADDRESS OF CENTRAL OFFICE:
P.O. Box 5187, White Settlement, TX 76108
ESI:28

STATISTICAL PROFILE	DATA	ESI
Grade organization: K–5/6–8/9–12		
Percentage of schools built before 1955	20%	
Total enrollment	3,500	
Average Daily Attendance (ADA)	96%	9
Current expense per pupil in ADA	$1,488	0
Dropout rate	NK	0
Percentage of eligible students who took the SAT	30%	3
Average combined score on SAT	875	3
Percentage of graduates who enrolled in 2- or 4-year colleges	24%	
Percentage of students who passed the state reading test	89%	
Percentage of students who passed the state math test	85%	
Teacher–student ratio in elementary grades	1:22	8
Teacher–student ratio in secondary grades	1:25	3
Counselor–student ratio in secondary grades	1:400	2
Number of students per music specialist in elementary grades	1,500	0
Number of students per art specialist in elementary grades	1,500	
Number of volumes in senior high school library	NK	
Beginning teacher's salary	$17,000	
Maximum teacher's salary	$30,092	
Average years of experience among teachers	13	
Number of students suspended and expelled	NK	
Subjects in which Advanced Placement courses are offered:	None	0

FAIR APPRAISAL

Quality of School Leadership
Most principals are hired for their educational leadership ability, and the quality of leadership is generally uniform from school to school. Parents and teachers have no say in the principal selection process, but principals have some say about the resources allotted to their school.

A new housing development in the district has resulted, on occasion, in unproductive competition between parents of the older section of the district and parents who have just moved in. Parents of the district could be more effective if they would "get together on issues of mutual interest," said an observer.

Quality of Instruction
The additional learning opportunities for gifted students are fair; the additional instruction for low-achieving students is good. Students planning on college receive a fair to poor preparation, although an observer believes the district is trying to improve the curriculum. The preparation of job-bound students is good.

Many families in the district do not have a history of members going to college, said an observer; hence, they don't put the necessary pressure on district officials to upgrade the program for gifted students and the college-preparatory curriculum (less than a quarter of graduates go on to college).

Quality of School Environment
The level of classroom disruption and vandalism tends to be on the high side. However, building maintenance and repair is considered excellent.

WILMER HUTCHINS

ADDRESS OF CENTRAL OFFICE:
3829 East Illinois Avenue, Dallas, TX 75216
ESI:33

STATISTICAL PROFILE	DATA	ESI
Grade organization: K–6/7–8/9–12		
Percentage of schools built before 1955	90%	
Total enrollment	4,154	
Average Daily Attendance (ADA)	94%	7
Current expense per pupil in ADA	NK	0
Dropout rate	10%	10
Percentage of eligible students who took the SAT	10	0
Average combined score on SAT	800	0
Percentage of graduates who enrolled in 2- or 4-year colleges	25%	
Percentage of students who passed the state reading test	73%	
Percentage of students who passed the state math test	55%	
Teacher–student ratio in elementary grades	1:24	6
Teacher–student ratio in secondary grades	1:29	0
Counselor–student ratio in secondary grades	1:200	10
Number of students per music specialist in elementary grades	None	0
Number of students per art specialist in elementary grades	None	0
Number of volumes in senior high school library	NK	
Beginning teacher's salary	$17,400	
Maximum teacher's salary	$25,380	
Average years of experience among teachers	15	
Number of students suspended and expelled	50	
Subjects in which Advanced Placement courses are offered:	None	0

FAIR APPRAISAL

Quality of School Leadership
Principals are chosen more on the basis of internal politics than because of their ability as educational leaders, and the quality of leadership varies greatly from school to school. Parents and teachers do not take part in screening principal candidates, and principals do not have much to say about the distribution of district resources.

Parent organizations tend not to be very effective because parents in the southern part of the district, who are mostly white, and parents in the northern section, who are mostly black, don't often work together for the same causes.

Quality of Instruction
Additional learning opportunities for gifted students and additional instruction for low-achieving students are rated poor. The college-preparatory curriculum also is rated poor. "Some of our graduates have tried to enter college when they couldn't even read or write," said an observer. The curriculum for students going into the job world is considered fair to good.

Minority students' needs are not being adequately met, said observers, and neither are those of most other students.

Quality of School Environment
The level of classroom disruption and vandalism is high. The quality of building maintenance and repair is good, despite the fact that most buildings are more than 30 years old.

Dayton, OH

Five districts in the Dayton Metropolitan Area completed the Statistical Profile.
Ohio does not have required competency tests in reading and math. Therefore, all profiles
show *NA* (not applicable) on the lines requesting those statistics. Districts in this area may
be compared to districts in the Cincinnati and Columbus, OH Metropolitan Areas.

AREA AT A GLANCE

SCHOOL DISTRICT	ENROLLMENT	ESI
Centerville	6,808	68
Dayton	29,536	38
Kettering	7,692	70
Miamisburg	4,200	63
Xenia	6,200	45

CENTERVILLE

ADDRESS OF CENTRAL OFFICE:
111 Virginia Avenue, Dayton, OH 45459
ESI:68

STATISTICAL PROFILE	DATA	ESI
Grade organization: K–5/6–8/9–12		
Percentage of schools built before 1955	86%	
Total enrollment	6,808	
Average Daily Attendance (ADA)	94%	7
Current expense per pupil in ADA	$3,453	8
Dropout rate	1%	10
Percentage of eligible students who took the ACT	90%	10
Average combined score on ACT	21.1	10
Percentage of graduates who enrolled in 2- or 4-year colleges	84%	
Percentage of students who passed the state reading test	NA	
Percentage of students who passed the state math test	NA	
Teacher–student ratio in elementary grades	1:18	10
Teacher–student ratio in secondary grades	1:22	6
Counselor–student ratio in secondary grades	1:417	1
Number of students per music specialist in elementary grades	675	1
Number of students per art specialist in elementary grades	675	
Number of volumes in senior high school library	21,424	
Beginning teacher's salary	$17,350	
Maximum teacher's salary	$35,525	
Average years of experience among teachers	15	
Number of students suspended and expelled	141	
Subjects in which Advanced Placement courses are offered: American History, Calculus, English, Foreign Language, Science	5	5

FAIR APPRAISAL

Quality of School Leadership

For the most part, principals are hired because of their educational leadership ability, and the quality of leadership does not vary greatly from school to school. Parents and teachers have hardly any say in principal selection. Principals have some say about the quality and quantity of resources given to their school.

Parents are sometimes effective influencing decision-making. They have their most clout as members of interaction councils that meet once a month at each school. Teachers and administrators also are members of the councils.

Quality of Instruction

Additional learning opportunitites for gifted students are rated good to excellent. Special classes are available , and the Olympics of the Mind is designed for very bright students. The only criticism comes from an observer who said the program can only accommodate about half the students who qualify. Additional instruction for low-achieving students is rated good, although one observer was afraid some students with low IQs who are not labeled handicapped "fall through the cracks." The college-preparatory curriculum is rated excellent, and the job-preparation curriculum is termed good. Students in the district's office-education program have won awards in state and regional competitions.

Observers differ over whether the schools adequately meet the needs of minority students. One person thinks the schools spend more time getting black students into sports than into a good academic program. Another observer said most minority students are from Asian and Mid-eastern countries and do quite well after instruction in English.

Quality of School Environment

The incidence of classroom disruption and vandalism is low, and the quality of building maintenance and repair is good.

DAYTON

ADDRESS OF CENTRAL OFFICE:
348 West First Street, Dayton, OH 45402
ESI:38

STATISTICAL PROFILE	DATA	ESI
Grade organization: K–6/7–9/10–12		
Percentage of schools built before 1955	78%	
Total enrollment	29,536	
Average Daily Attendance (ADA)	89%	2
Current expense per pupil in ADA	$4,242	10
Dropout rate	34%	0
Percentage of eligible students who took the ACT	NK	0
Average combined score on ACT	NK	0
Percentage of graduates who enrolled in 2- or 4-year colleges	33%	
Percentage of students who passed the state reading test	NA	
Percentage of students who passed the state math test	NA	
Teacher–student ratio in elementary grades	1:28	2
Teacher–student ratio in secondary grades	1:33	0
Counselor–student ratio in secondary grades	1:221	9
Number of students per music specialist in elementary grades	334	9
Number of students per art specialist in elementary grades	522	
Number of volumes in senior high school library	8,518	
Beginning teacher's salary	$15,490	
Maximum teacher's salary	$31,922	
Average years of experience among teachers	13	
Number of students suspended and expelled	2,770†	
Subjects in which Advanced Placement courses are offered	6	6
American Government, American History, Calculus, Chemistry, English, Physics		

†This figure does not include in-school suspensions.

Quality of School Leadership
Educational leadership ability is now the primary attribute the School Board looks for in principal candidates. Until a few years ago politics was the most important consideration. The quality of leadership does not vary greatly from school to school. Parents and teachers have no say in principal selection, but principals can influence the distribution of resources to the schools.

Parents are sometimes effective influencing policy decisions. A community education council formed a few years ago has given parents and other citizens a strong voice in decision-making.

Quality of Instruction
Special classes in grades 3 through 7 have made the additional opportunities for gifted students excellent, in the opinion of observers. Remediation for low-achieving students also is considered excellent. The curricula for students going to college and into jobs after graduation are rated good. However, one observer thinks the vocational education courses don't always prepare students for existing jobs.

The observers think the schools have not done as well by minority students as they might. One observer said the district has focused more on achieving racial balance than on the academic needs of minority students. Another observer said the schools need to have higher expectations for minority students.

Quality of School Environment
Classroom disruption and vandalism are problems in the schools. One observer noted that assaults by students against other students and teachers had increased by more than 25% from 1976 to 1986. The quality of building maintenance and repair is considered good.

KETTERING

ADDRESS OF CENTRAL OFFICE:
3750 Far Hills Avenue, Dayton, OH 45429
ESI:70

STATISTICAL PROFILE	DATA	ESI
Grade organization: K–6/7–9/10–12		
Percentage of schools built before 1955	30%	
Total enrollment	7,692	
Average Daily Attendance (ADA)	94%	7
Current expense per pupil in ADA	$3,614	9
Dropout rate	12%	10
Percentage of eligible students who took the ACT	32%	4
Average combined score on ACT	20.7	9
Percentage of graduates who enrolled in 2- or 4-year colleges	74%	
Percentage of students who passed the state reading test	NA	
Percentage of students who passed the state math test	NA	
Teacher–student ratio in elementary grades	1:22	8
Teacher–student ratio in secondary grades	1:17	10
Counselor–student ratio in secondary grades	1:317	5
Number of students per music specialist in elementary grades	372	8
Number of students per art specialist in elementary grades	512	
Number of volumes in senior high school library	24,067	
Beginning teacher's salary	$16,067	
Maximum teacher's salary	$41,841	
Average years of experience among teachers	18	
Number of students suspended and expelled	387	
Subjects in which Advanced Placement courses are offered:	None	0

FAIR APPRAISAL

Quality of School Leadership
Longevity and popularity are key criteria for principal selection, and the quality of educational leadership among principals varies greatly from school to school. Parents and teachers play no part in principal selection, but principals have some say about the allotment of district resources to the schools.

Parents are not considered effective influencing decision-making.

Quality of Instruction
The program for gifted students is rated good, as is additional instruction for low-achieving students. The curriculum for students going on to college is considered good, and the curriculum for students entering the world of work is rated excellent.

Quality of School Environment
The incidence of classroom disruption and vandalism is low. The quality of building maintenance and repair is fair. The district badly needs a tax levy to cover overdue repairs to buildings, said an observer.

MIAMISBURG

ADDRESS OF CENTRAL OFFICE:
Sixth Street at Park Avenue, Miamisburg, OH 45342
ESI:63

STATISTICAL PROFILE	DATA	ESI
Grade organization: K–6/7–8/9–10/12		
Percentage of schools built before 1955	20%	
Total enrollment	4,200	
Average Daily Attendance (ADA)	95%	8
Current expense per pupil in ADA	$2,800	6
Dropout rate	10%	10
Percentage of eligible students who took the ACT	48%	7
Average combined score on ACT	20	6
Percentage of graduates who enrolled in 2- or 4-year colleges	57%	
Percentage of students who passed the state reading test	NA	
Percentage of students who passed the state math test	NA	
Teacher–student ratio in elementary grades	1:24	6
Teacher–student ratio in secondary grades	1:21	7
Counselor–student ratio in secondary grades	1:300	6
Number of students per music specialist in elementary grades	500	5
Number of students per art specialist in elementary grades	500	
Number of volumes in senior high school library	50,000†	
Beginning teacher's salary	$16,050	
Maximum teacher's salary	$34,000	
Average years of experience among teachers	16	
Number of students suspended and expelled	126††	
Subjects in which Advanced Placement courses are offered: American History, English	2	2

† This seems an unusually high number.
†† This number is approximate.

FAIR APPRAISAL

Quality of School Leadership
Principals are hired primarily for their educational leadership ability, and the quality of leadership is generally uniform in the district. Both teachers and parents interview principal candidates. Principals have some influence over the resources their school gets; they also have complete authority to administer a small contingency fund allotted each school.

Parents are an effective influence on decision-making. Recent examples have been recommendations from parents and other citizens regarding school boundary redrawing and school building improvements.

Quality of Instruction
Additional learning opportunities for gifted students and additional instruction for low-achieving students are rated good. Also considered good is the college-preparatory curriculum. The preparation given students planning on entering the world of work is rated excellent.

Quality of School Environment
The level of classroom disruption and vandalism is low, and the quality of building maintenance and repair is excellent.

XENIA

ADDRESS OF CENTRAL OFFICE:
578 East Market Street, Xenia, OH 45385
ESI:45

STATISTICAL PROFILE	DATA	ESI
Grade organization: K–6/7–9/10–12		
Percentage of schools built before 1955	20%	
Total enrollment	6,200	
Average Daily Attendance (ADA)	94%	7
Current expense per pupil in ADA	$2,600	4
Dropout rate	20%	3
Percentage of eligible students who took the ACT	5%	0
Average combined score on ACT	19.9	5
Percentage of graduates who enrolled in 2- or 4-year colleges	40%	
Percentage of students who passed the state reading test	NA	
Percentage of students who passed the state math test	NA	
Teacher–student ratio in elementary grades	1:25	5
Teacher–student ratio in secondary grades	1:23	5
Counselor–student ratio in secondary grades	1:325	5
Number of students per music specialist in elementary grades	100	10
Number of students per art specialist in elementary grades	None	
Number of volumes in senior high school library	20,864	
Beginning teacher's salary	$15,150	
Maximum teacher's salary	$33,027	
Average years of experience among teachers	14	
Number of students suspended and expelled	NK	
Subjects in which Advanced Placement courses are offered: English	1	1

Quality of School Leadership

Most principals are picked because of their educational leadership ability, and the quality of leadership does not vary greatly from school to school. Parents and teachers do not take part in screening principal candidates, but principals have some say in how district resources are divided among the schools.

Parents are effective influences on decision-making. They and other citizens work best through a citizens advisory council.

Quality of Instruction

Gifted students in the elementary grades are excused from regular classes two or three times a week to attend special enrichment classes. The overall program for gifted students, which extends into the upper grades, is rated excellent. Additional instruction for low-achieving students is called good. Also considered good are the curricula for college-bound students and job-bound students.

Quality of School Environment

The incidence of classroom disruption and vandalism is low. The quality of building maintenance and repair is fair but due to get better. After many defeats, a special tax levy to cover building improvements was passed recently.

Denver, CO

Five districts in the Denver Metropolitan Area completed Statistical Profiles; Fair Appraisals only were received for two additional districts. Colorado does not require competency tests in reading and math. Therefore, all profiles show *NA* (not applicable) on the lines requesting those statistics. The Denver Metropolitan Area might be compared to the Oklahoma City Metropolitan Area.

AREA AT A GLANCE

SCHOOL DISTRICT	ENROLLMENT	ESI
Aurora–Adams–Arapahoe	25,356	59
Boulder Valley	20,448	63
Brighton	4,200	52
Cherry Creek	26,500	67*
Denver	60,282	53
Jefferson County	75,939	
Littleton	15,958	

Indicates district misinterpretation of one or more statistics in the ESI. For each misinterpreted statistic, a score of 0 was given instead of a possible score of 0 to 10 points.

AURORA–ADAMS–ARAPAHOE

ADDRESS OF CENTRAL OFFICE:
1085 Peoria Street, Aurora, CO 80011
ESI:59

STATISTICAL PROFILE	DATA	ESI
Grade organization: K–5/6–8/9–12		
Percentage of schools built before 1955	7%	
Total enrollment	25,356	
Average Daily Attendance (ADA)	92%	5
Current expense per pupil in ADA	$3,649	5
Dropout rate	17%	6
Percentage of eligible students who took the ACT	33%	4
Average combined score on ACT	18.8	5
Percentage of graduates who enrolled in 2- or 4-year colleges	55%	
Percentage of students who passed the state reading test	NA	
Percentage of students who passed the state math test	NA	
Teacher–student ratio in elementary grades	1:22	8
Teacher–student ratio in secondary grades	1:20	8
Counselor–student ratio in secondary grades	1:284	6
Number of students per music specialist in elementary grades	384	8
Number of students per art specialist in elementary grades	577	
Number of volumes in senior high school library	14,210	
Beginning teacher's salary	$16,305	
Maximum teacher's salary	$43,554	
Average years of experience among teachers	11	
Number of students suspended and expelled	NK	
Subjects in which Advanced Placement courses are offered: American History, Art, Calculus, English	4	4

FAIR APPRAISAL

Quality of School Leadership

Educational leadership ability is what the School Board primarily looks for in principal candidates, and the quality of leadership is generally uniform in the district. Teachers and parents have no say in the selection of principals, but principals have some say in how resources are divided among the schools.

Parent organizations are sometimes effective influencing school decisions.

Quality of Instruction

Additional opportunities for gifted students extend through all grades and are considered good. Additional instruction for low-achieving students also is rated good. Specialists try to head off learning problems early by offering extra help to low-achievers in kindergarten and grade 1. The curricula for college-bound students and job-bound students are rated excellent.

Quality of School Environment

Classroom disruption and vandalism are not problems. The quality of building maintenance and repair is excellent.

BOULDER VALLEY

ADDRESS OF CENTRAL OFFICE:
6500 East Arapahoe, Boulder, CO 80303
ESI:63

STATISTICAL PROFILE	DATA	ESI
Grade organization: †		
Percentage of schools built before 1955	31%	
Total enrollment	20,448	
Average Daily Attendance (ADA)	92%	5
Current expense per pupil in ADA	$4,079	4
Dropout rate	NK	0
Percentage of eligible students who took the ACT	65%	10
Average combined score on ACT	22.1	10
Percentage of graduates who enrolled in 2- or 4-year colleges	NK	
Percentage of students who passed the state reading test	NA	
Percentage of students who passed the state math test	NA	
Teacher–student ratio in elementary grades	1:25	5
Teacher–student ratio in secondary grades	1:20	8
Counselor–student ratio in secondary grades	1:263	7
Number of students per music specialist in elementary grades	348	9
Number of students per art specialist in elementary grades	637	
Number of volumes in senior high school library	15,848	
Beginning teacher's salary	$17,606	
Maximum teacher's salary	$41,061	
Average years of experience among teachers	14	
Number of students suspended and expelled	350	
Subjects in which Advanced Placement courses are offered: American History, Calculus AB, Calculus BC, Computer Science, English	5	5

†The district has two organizational patterns: K–5/6–8/9–12 and K–6/7–9/10–12.

FAIR APPRAISAL

Quality of School Leadership

A new superintendent has been selected and the School Board has hired a number of new principals; the primary criterion for their selection was educational leadership ability. The quality of leadership is uniform throughout the district. Committees that include parents and teachers help select principals by interviewing candidates who are finalists and making recommendations to the superintendent. Principals have some say, but not much, in the distribution of resources among the schools.

Parents are quite effective influencing school policy decisions. They and other citizens serve on a variety of advisory committees.

Quality of Instruction

Observers believe the additional learning opportunities for gifted students are fair. The district has a program, said an observer, but there is not much to it. Gifted students go on better field trips than other students, the observer said, but there is little extra instruction in high-level thinking and analytical skills and few opportunities for expression of creative genius. Also rated fair is the additional instruction for low-achieving students. The curriculum for college-bound students is considered excellent. "That is what the district does best," said an observer. The job-preparation curriculum is good.

Quality of School Environment

Classroom disruption and vandalism are not problems; the quality of building maintenance and repair is good.

BRIGHTON

ADDRESS OF CENTRAL OFFICE:
630 South Eighth Avenue, Brighton, CO 80601
ESI:52

STATISTICAL PROFILE	DATA	ESI
Grade organization: K–5/6–8/9–12		
Percentage of schools built before 1955	80%	
Total enrollment	4,200	
Average Daily Attendance (ADA)	93%	6
Current expense per pupil in ADA	$3,400	4
Dropout rate	8%	10
Percentage of eligible students who took the ACT	35%	4
Average combined score on ACT	19.6	5
Percentage of graduates who enrolled in 2- or 4-year colleges	45%	
Percentage of students who passed the state reading test	NA	
Percentage of students who passed the state math test	NA	
Teacher–student ratio in elementary grades	1:26	4
Teacher–student ratio in secondary grades	1:23	5
Counselor–student ratio in secondary grades	1:350	4
Number of students per music specialist in elementary grades	400	7
Number of students per art specialist in elementary grades	None	
Number of volumes in senior high school library	NK	
Beginning teacher's salary	$17,500	
Maximum teacher's salary	$39,000	
Average years of experience among teachers	6	
Number of students suspended and expelled	NK	
Subjects in which Advanced Placement courses are offered: Calculus, English, Science	3	3

FAIR APPRAISAL

Quality of School Leadership
The School looks for principal candidates who show educational leadership ability, and the quality of leadership does not vary greatly from school to school. Parents and teachers interview principal candidates and make their recommendations to the superintendent. Principals have some say in how district resources are divided among the schools.

Parent organizations are sometimes effective influencing school policy decisions.

Quality of Instruction
Additional learning opportunities for gifted students are rated fair, and additional instruction for low-achieving students is rated good. The latter program features small-group tutoring. The curriculum for college-bound students is considered good, but the curriculum for students heading for the job market is only fair.

Observers believe the district could do more for minority students. Although the dropout rate is not very high (8%), "a disproportionate number of dropouts are minority students," said an observer.

Quality of School Environment
The level of classroom disruption and vandalism is considered low, and the quality of building maintenance and repair is good.

CHERRY CREEK

ADDRESS OF CENTRAL OFFICE:
4700 South Yosemite Street, Englewood, CO 80111
ESI:67*

STATISTICAL PROFILE	DATA	ESI
Grade organization: K–6/7–8/9–12		
Percentage of schools built before 1955	5%	
Total enrollment	26,500	
Average Daily Attendance (ADA)	95%	8
Current expense per pupil in ADA	$3,754	5
Dropout rate	6%	10
Percentage of eligible students who took the ACT	76%	10
Average combined score on ACT	21.1	10
Percentage of graduates who enrolled in 2- or 4-year colleges	80%	
Percentage of students who passed the state reading test	NA	
Percentage of students who passed the state math test	NA	
Teacher–student ratio in elementary grades	1:20	10
Teacher–student ratio in secondary grades	1:19	9
Counselor–student ratio in secondary grades	1:450	0
Number of students per music specialist in elementary grades	†	0*
Number of students per art specialist in elementary grades	†	
Number of volumes in senior high school library	29,000	
Beginning teacher's salary	$17,720	
Maximum teacher's salary	$45,552	
Average years of experience among teachers	8	
Number of students suspended and expelled	NK	
Subjects in which Advanced Placement courses are offered: American History, Calculus, English, Foreign Language (unspecified), Science (unspecified)	5	5

†The district misinterpreted these statistics.

FAIR APPRAISAL

Quality of School Leadership
Most principals are chosen because of their educational leadership ability, and the quality of leadership is generally uniform from school to school. Parents and teachers have no say in principal selection, but principals have a voice in deciding what resources their school will get.

Parent organizations are very active and do influence decision-making. Recently, parents prevented the School Board from moving grade 6 into the middle schools.

Quality of Instruction
Additional learning opportunities for gifted students are called excellent. They begin in the elementary grades and include enrichment activities during and after school. Additional instruction for low-achieving students is good. Students going to college have an excellent curriculum. Those planning on jobs after graduation have a good curriculum. The district does not put as "much effort" into job preparation, said an observer.

Quality of School Environment
The incidence of classroom disruption and vandalism is very low. The quality of maintenance and repair is considered very good.

DENVER

ADDRESS OF CENTRAL OFFICE:
900 Grant Street, Denver, CO 80203
ESI:53

STATISTICAL PROFILE	DATA	ESI
Grade organization: Pre-K–6/7–8/9–12		
Percentage of schools built before 1955	46%	
Total enrollment	60,282	
Average Daily Attendance (ADA)	92%	5
Current expense per pupil in ADA	$3,967	7
Dropout rate	40%	0
Percentage of eligible students who took the ACT	41%	6
Average combined score on ACT	18.1	4
Percentage of graduates who enrolled in 2- or 4-year colleges	53%	
Percentage of students who passed the state reading test	NA	
Percentage of students who passed the state math test	NA	
Teacher–student ratio in elementary grades	1:24	6
Teacher–student ratio in secondary grades	1:18	10
Counselor–student ratio in secondary grades	1:290	6
Number of students per music specialist in elementary grades	None	0
Number of students per art specialist in elementary grades	None	
Number of volumes in senior high school library	17,011	
Beginning teacher's salary	$16,882	
Maximum teacher's salary	$41,600	
Average years of experience among teachers	16	
Number of students suspended and expelled	8,359	
Subjects in which Advanced Placement courses are offered: American History, Biology, Calculus, Chemistry, English, European History, French, Physics, Spanish	9	9

FAIR APPRAISAL

Quality of School Leadership

Most principals are hired because of their educational leadership ability. However, there is some variation in quality of leadership among the schools. One observer complained that schools in neighborhoods with a high proportion of minority students "tend not to have the same high quality leadership." Parents and teachers serve on committees that interview finalists for principal positions. Principals can influence the distribution of district resources to the schools.

Parent organizations are an effective voice in school decision-making. The PTA Council meets weekly with the superintendent.

Quality of Instruction

The observers rate as excellent the additional learning opportunities for gifted students and additional instruction for low-achieving students. Gifted and talented instruction exists in each school, and a special Challenge program offers gifted students in each of four sections of the city still more enrichment opportunities. Also, Denver University provides advanced studies for especially bright students. Three achievement centers offer extra help to low-achieving students. The curricula for students going on to college and students heading for the world of work are rated good.

Observers believe the district adequately meets the needs of minority students, despite a very high dropout rate and an observer's admission that "test scores may not corroborate" the claim.

Quality of School Environment

The level of classroom disruption and vandalism is low, and the quality of building maintenance and repair is good.

JEFFERSON COUNTY

ADDRESS OF CENTRAL OFFICE:
1829 Denver West Drive, Golden, CO 80401
ESI:None†

STATISTICAL PROFILE	DATA	ESI
Grade organization:		
Percentage of schools built before 1955		
Total enrollment		
Average Daily Attendance (ADA)		
Current expense per pupil in ADA		
Dropout rate		
Percentage of eligible students who took the ACT		
Average combined score on ACT		
Percentage of graduates who enrolled in 2- or 4-year colleges		
Percentage of students who passed the state reading test		
Percentage of students who passed the state math test		
Teacher–student ratio in elementary grades		
Teacher–student ratio in secondary grades		
Counselor–student ratio in secondary grades		
Number of students per music specialist in elementary grades		
Number of students per art specialist in elementary grades		
Number of volumes in senior high school library		
Beginning teacher's salary		
Maximum teacher's salary		
Average years of experience among teachers		
Number of students suspended and expelled		
Subjects in which Advanced Placement courses are offered:		

†A Statistical Profile was not received from this district.

FAIR APPRAISAL

Quality of School Leadership
Leadership has undergone change in the last couple of years, according to observers, and new principals have been hired primarily for their educational leadership and management abilities. Because of past hiring practices based more on a candidate's seniority and internal politics, the quality of leadership varies greatly from school to school. Parents and teachers play no role in principal selection. Principals have very little to say about the division of district resources among the schools.

Parents and other citizens sit on a number of advisory committees, and their influence is generally effective. According to one observer, "the district rested on its laurels and good reputation until it deteriorated; the comeback is now in progress."

Quality of Instruction
Additional opportunities for gifted students are rated good to excellent, and additional instruction for low-achieving students is rated fair to good. The curricula for college-bound students and job-bound students are rated good to excellent.

Quality of School Environment
Classroom disruption and vandalism are not problems. The quality of building maintenance and repair is good.

LITTLETON

ADDRESS OF CENTRAL OFFICE:
5776 South Crocker Street, Littleton, CO 80120
ESI:None†

STATISTICAL PROFILE	DATA	ESI
Grade organization:		
Percentage of schools built before 1955		
Total enrollment		
Average Daily Attendance (ADA)		
Current expense per pupil in ADA		
Dropout rate		
Percentage of eligible students who took the ACT		
Average combined score on ACT		
Percentage of graduates who enrolled in 2- or 4-year colleges		
Percentage of students who passed the state reading test		
Percentage of students who passed the state math test		
Teacher–student ratio in elementary grades		
Teacher–student ratio in secondary grades		
Counselor–student ratio in secondary grades		
Number of students per music specialist in elementary grades		
Number of students per art specialist in elementary grades		
Number of volumes in senior high school library		
Beginning teacher's salary		
Maximum teacher's salary		
Average years of experience among teachers		
Number of students suspended and expelled		
Subjects in which Advanced Placement courses are offered:		

†A Statistical Profile was not received from this district.

FAIR APPRAISAL

Quality of School Leadership
Principals are selected from candidates outside the district as well as from within, and educational leadership ability is the primary criterion used in principal selection. The quality of leadership is generally uniform throughout the system. Parents and teachers have very little to say about principal selection. However, principals can influence the allotment of resources to their school.

Parents are sometimes effective influencing decision-making. Recently, they prevented a school closing.

Quality of Instruction
Additional learning opportunities for gifted students are rated fair. "The program has been hurt by budget cuts," said an observer, "and is not as good as it could or should be." Additional instruction for low-achieving students is considered good. "A greater effort is made" for these students, said an observer. The curriculum for students going on to college is rated good to excellent, and the curriculum for students heading into the job market is fair to good. A regional vocational education center serves the district.

Quality of School Environment
The level of classroom disruption and vandalism is low, and the quality of building maintenance and repair is rated fair to good.

Detroit, MI

Twenty districts completed Statistical Profiles. Fair Appraisals alone
were received for and additional four districts. Districts in this area
might be compared to districts in the Minneapolis–St. Paul, MN Metropolitan Area.

AREA AT A GLANCE

SCHOOL DISTRICT	ENROLLMENT	ESI
Avondale	2,632	50
Birmingham	7,453	
Bloomfield Hills	6,033	93
Chippewa Valley	8,286	52
Dearborn	12,463	67
Farmington	10,500	83
Ferndale	4,823	33
Grosse Pointe	7,380	77
Highland Park	6,854	17
L'Anse Creuse	7,464	43
Lake Shore	3,912	59*
Lincoln Park	6,375	14*
Livonia	16,608	33
Madison	2,940	43
Northville	3,368	
Plymouth–Canton	15,500	50
Royal Oak	8,169	
Southfield	8,608	65
Taylor	13,900	
Troy	10,823	67
Warren Woods	2,946	43
Waterford	11,990	41
Wayne–Westland	17,682	43
West Bloomfield	4,526	61

Indicates district misinterpretation of one or more statistics in the ESI. For each misinterpreted statistic, a score of 0 was given instead of a possible score of 0 to 10 points.

AVONDALE

ADDRESS OF CENTRAL OFFICE:
2950 Waukegan Avenue, Pontiac, MI 48057
ESI:50

STATISTICAL PROFILE	DATA	ESI
Grade organization: K–12†		
Percentage of schools built before 1955	50%	
Total enrollment	2,632	
Average Daily Attendance (ADA)	93%	6
Current expense per pupil in ADA	$3,240	0
Dropout rate	13%	10
Percentage of eligible students who took the ACT	44%	6
Average combined score on ACT	20.0	6
Percentage of graduates who enrolled in 2- or 4-year colleges	50%	
Percentage of students who passed the state reading test	84%	
Percentage of students who passed the state math test	79%	
Teacher–student ratio in elementary grades	1:22 ††	8
Teacher–student ratio in secondary grades	1:19 ††	9
Counselor–student ratio in secondary grades	1:380††	2
Number of students per music specialist in elementary grades	630††	3
Number of students per art specialist in elementary grades	630††	
Number of volumes in senior high school library	17,800	
Beginning teacher's salary	$18,536††	
Maximum teacher's salary	$38,095††	
Average years of experience among teachers	16†	
Number of students suspended and expelled	151	
Subjects in which Advanced Placement courses are offered:	None	0

†The district misinterpreted this statistic.
††1986–87 statistics.

FAIR APPRAISAL

Quality of School Leadership
Principals are hired because of their educational leadership ability, and the quality of leadership is generally uniform throughout the system. Parents and teachers do not help select principals, but principals have some say in the distribution of resources to their school.

Parent committees are often used to study district policies and practices.

Quality of Instruction
A program for gifted students was started in 1985–86 and is now rated fair to good. Additional instruction for low-achieving students is minimal (mostly what is required by law), and the program is considered only fair. The college preparatory curriculum is becoming good, according to observers; new high-level courses are being added. The curriculum for students going into the job market is rated good. The district has its own vocational education programs, but students also attend a regional center.

Quality of School Environment
The level of classroom disruption and student vandalism is low; the quality of building maintenance and repair is good. The district is growing. New housing development and industry have increased the wealth of the district, enabling the School Board to "improve the curriculum and renovate buildings that had been neglected for years," according to an observer.

BIRMINGHAM

ADDRESS OF CENTRAL OFFICE:
550 West Merrill Street, Birmingham, MI 48012
ESI:None†

STATISTICAL PROFILE	DATA	ESI
Grade organization:		
Percentage of schools built before 1955		
Total enrollment		
Average Daily Attendance (ADA)		
Current expense per pupil in ADA		
Dropout rate		
Percentage of eligible students who took the ACT		
Average combined score on ACT		
Percentage of graduates who enrolled in 2- or 4-year colleges		
Percentage of students who passed the state reading test		
Percentage of students who passed the state math test		
Teacher–student ratio in elementary grades		
Teacher–student ratio in secondary grades		
Counselor–student ratio in secondary grades		
Number of students per music specialist in elementary grades		
Number of students per art specialist in elementary grades		
Number of volumes in senior high school library		
Beginning teacher's salary		
Maximum teacher's salary		
Average years of experience among teachers		
Number of students suspended and expelled		
Subjects in which Advanced Placement courses are offered:		

†A Statistical Profile was not received from this district.

FAIR APPRAISAL

Quality of School Leadership
The School Board hires principals who demonstrate educational leadership ability, and the quality of leadership does not vary greatly from school to school. Parents and teachers interview principal candidates. Principals have a great deal to say about the allotment of resources to the schools, and each principal has a small discretionary fund to use as he/she sees fit.

Parent organizations are an effective influence on school policy decisions. PTAs have a strong voice, and members of community education councils often sit on committees studying school policies and practices.

Quality of Instruction
Additional learning opportunities for gifted students are rated good. A special program is available at all levels. Considered good to excellent is additional instruction for low-achieving students. A Learning Resource Center provides special help. The curricula for students going to college and students going into the job market are rated excellent. More than 80 percent of graduates enroll in two or four-year colleges, said an observer.

Quality of School Environment
The level of classroom disruption and student vandalism is low, and the quality of building maintenance and repair is good.

BLOOMFIELD HILLS

ADDRESS OF CENTRAL OFFICE:
P.O. Box 816, Bloomfield Hills, MI 48013
ESI:93

STATISTICAL PROFILE	DATA	ESI
Grade organization: K–5/6–8/9–12		
Percentage of schools built before 1955	25%	
Total enrollment	6,033†	
Average Daily Attendance (ADA)	93%	6
Current expense per pupil in ADA	$5,270	10
Dropout rate	1%	10
Percentage of eligible students who took the ACT	79%	10
Average combined score on ACT	22.0	10
Percentage of graduates who enrolled in 2- or 4-year colleges	90%	
Percentage of students who passed the state reading test	NK	
Percentage of students who passed the state math test	NK	
Teacher–student ratio in elementary grades	1:17	10
Teacher–student ratio in secondary grades	1:16	10
Counselor–student ratio in secondary grades	1:249	8
Number of students per music specialist in elementary grades	307	9
Number of students per art specialist in elementary grades	358	
Number of volumes in senior high school library	23,000	
Beginning teacher's salary	$17,367	
Maximum teacher's salary	$43,408	
Average years of experience among teachers	12	
Number of students suspended and expelled	226	
Subjects in which Advanced Placement courses are offered:	13	10
American History, Art, Biology, Calculus, Chemistry, Computer Science, English Literature, European History, French, Latin, Music, Physics, Spanish		

†1986–87 statistic.

FAIR APPRAISAL

Quality of School Leadership
For the most part, principals are selected for their educational leadership ability, although popularity and longevity are sometimes factors. The quality of leadership does not vary greatly from school to school. Teachers and parents help in the screening of principal candidates. Also, principals have much to say about how district resources are divided among the schools.

Parents are effective influencing school decision-making. Parents have been involved, for example, in new learning experiments and in changes in transportation routes.

Quality of Instruction
Additional learning opportunities for gifted students are considered good, as is additional instruction for low-achieving students. Each elementary school has a special resource teacher working with low-achievers. At the high school, an experimental program is aiding so-called "at risk" students (potential dropouts). The curriculum for college-bound students is rated excellent, and the curriculum for students going into the job market is rated good.

Quality of School Environment
Classroom disruption and student vandalism are not problems. The quality of building maintenance and repair is considered good to excellent.

CHIPPEWA VALLEY

ADDRESS OF CENTRAL OFFICE:
19120 Cass Avenue, Mount Clemens, MI 48044
ESI:52

STATISTICAL PROFILE	DATA	ESI
Grade organization: K–5/6–8/9–12		
Percentage of schools built before 1955	0%	
Total enrollment	8,286	
Average Daily Attendance (ADA)	94%	7
Current expense per pupil in ADA	$3,049	0
Dropout rate	15%	8
Percentage of eligible students who took the ACT	50%	7
Average combined score on ACT	19	5
Percentage of graduates who enrolled in 2- or 4-year colleges	55%	
Percentage of students who passed the state reading test	89%	
Percentage of students who passed the state math test	85%	
Teacher–student ratio in elementary grades	1:21	9
Teacher–student ratio in secondary grades	1:21	7
Counselor–student ratio in secondary grades	1:380	2
Number of students per music specialist in elementary grades	500	5
Number of students per art specialist in elementary grades	500	
Number of volumes in senior high school library	21,685	
Beginning teacher's salary	$18,020	
Maximum teacher's salary	$41,037	
Average years of experience among teachers	11	
Number of students suspended and expelled	130	
Subjects in which Advanced Placement courses are offered:	2	2
American History, English		

FAIR APPRAISAL

Quality of School Leadership
Generally, the School Board selects principals for their educational leadership ability; however, longevity and popularity are also factors. The quality of leadership is generally uniform throughout the district. Parents and teachers do not take part in the selection of principals. On the other hand, principals influence the distribution of district resources.

Parent organizations are effective influences on school policy decisions. For example, the reading incentive program at the elementary schools was instigated by parents.

Quality of Instruction
Additional learning opportunities for gifted students and additional instruction for low-achieving students are rated good. Community volunteers are used to help tutor low-achievers. The curricula for students going to college and students going into the world of work are considered excellent.

Quality of School Environment
The level of classroom disruption and student vandalism is low, and the quality of building maintenance repair is good.

DEARBORN

ADDRESS OF CENTRAL OFFICE:
4824 Lois Avenue, Dearborn, MI 48126
ESI:67

STATISTICAL PROFILE	DATA	ESI
Grade organization: K–12†		
Percentage of schools built before 1955	100%	
Total enrollment	12,463	
Average Daily Attendance (ADA)	95%	8
Current expense per pupil in ADA	$4,520	7
Dropout rate	3%	10
Percentage of eligible students who took the ACT	64%	10
Average combined score on ACT	18.7	4
Percentage of graduates who enrolled in 2- or 4-year colleges	69%	
Percentage of students who passed the state reading test	81%	
Percentage of students who passed the state math test	71%	
Teacher–student ratio in elementary grades	1:23	7
Teacher–student ratio in secondary grades	1:21	7
Counselor–student ratio in secondary grades	1:263	7
Number of students per music specialist in elementary grades	400	7
Number of students per art specialist in elementary grades	400	
Number of volumes in senior high school libraries (average)	2,400	
Beginning teacher's salary	$16,845	
Maximum teacher's salary	$38,900	
Average years of experience among teachers	15	
Number of students suspended and expelled	1,100	
Subjects in which Advanced Placement courses are offered:	None	0

†The district misinterpreted this statistic.

Quality of School Leadership
The School Board looks primarily for educational leadership ability in principal candidates. The quality of leadership does not vary greatly from school to school. PTA officers and union members have some say in the selection of principals, and principals have some say in how district resources are allotted to the schools.

Parent organizations are only sometimes effective influencing school policy decisions. "They're kiss-fanny groups basically," said one observer.

Quality of Instruction
Additional learning opportunities for gifted students are known as the "Ignite Program," but, according to observers, not much igniting is going on. Instruction is minimal and class-cutting is common. The program is rated fair to poor. Considered good is additional instruction for low-achieving students. "Great efforts are made to keep kids from falling through the cracks," said an observer. The curricula for college-bound and job-bound students are rated good.

Quality of School Environment
Classroom disruption and student vandalism are not problems, and the quality of building maintenance and repair is considered excellent.

FARMINGTON

ADDRESS OF CENTRAL OFFICE:
32500 Shiawassee Street, Farmington, MI 48024
ESI:83

STATISTICAL PROFILE	DATA	ESI
Grade organization: K–5/6–8/9–12		
Percentage of schools built before 1955	20%	
Total enrollment	10,500	
Average Daily Attendance (ADA)	98%	10
Current expense per pupil in ADA	$5,261	10
Dropout rate	3%	10
Percentage of eligible students who took the ACT	60%	9
Average Combined score on ACT	21	10
Percentage of graduates who enrolled in 2- or 4-year colleges	70%	
Percentage of students who passed the state reading test	90%	
Percentage of students who passed the state math test	88%	
Teacher–student ratio in elementary grades	1:24	6
Teacher–student ratio in secondary grades	1:22	6
Counselor–student ratio in secondary grades	1:250	8
Number of students per music specialist in elementary grades	150	10
Number of students per art specialist in elementary grades	150	
Number of volumes in senior high school library (average)	14,000	
Beginning teacher's salary	$20,000	
Maximum teacher's salary	$40,000	
Average years of experience among teachers	15	
Number of students suspended and expelled	NK	
Subjects in which Advanced Placement courses are offered:	4	4
American History, Calculus, English, Science		

Quality of School Leadership
Principals are hired primarily for their educational leadership ability, although popularity and seniority are factors. The quality of leadership does not vary greatly from school to school. Parents and teachers do not screen principal candidates, but principals have quite a bit of influence over the distribution of district resources.

Overall, parents are not very effective influencing school policy decisions.

Quality of Instruction
Additional learning opportunities for gifted students are rated fair to good. Special instruction for gifted students is "almost negligible" at the elementary level, said an observer, but better at the middle and high schools. Additional instruction for low-achieving students is considered good. Rated excellent are the curricula for college-bound students and those heading into the job market.

Quality of School Environment
Classroom disruption and student vandalism are not problems, and the quality of building maintenance and repair is good to excellent.

FERNDALE

ADDRESS OF CENTRAL OFFICE:
725 Pinecrest Avenue, Detroit, MI 48220
ESI:33

STATISTICAL PROFILE	DATA	ESI
Grade organization: K–12†		
Percentage of schools built before 1955	10%	
Total enrollment	4,823	
Average Daily Attendance (ADA)	NK	0
Current expense per pupil in ADA	$3,759	3
Dropout rate	NK	0
Percentage of eligible students who took the ACT	NK	0
Average combined score on ACT	NK	0
Percentage of graduates who enrolled in 2- or 4-year colleges	61%	
Percentage of students who passed the state reading test	NK	
Percentage of students who passed the state math test	NK	
Teacher–student ratio in elementary grades	1:22	8
Teacher–student ratio in secondary grades	1:24	4
Counselor–student ratio in secondary grades	1:350	4
Number of students per music specialist in elementary grades	285	10
Number of students per art specialist in elementary grades	642	
Number of volumes in senior high school library	20,000	
Beginning teacher's salary	$18,098	
Maximum teacher's salary	$35,464	
Average years of experience among teachers	14	
Number of students suspended and expelled	NK	
Subjects in which Advanced Placement courses are offered:	4	4
Calculus, English, German, Science		

†The district misinterpreted this statistic.

Quality of School Leadership

The School Board mainly looks for educational leadership ability in principal candidates, but the quality of leadership nevertheless varies greatly from school to school. According to an observer, the variation occurs because "low-income neighborhoods tend to get the least able principals." Parents and teachers do not screen principal candidates. However, principals have some say in how the district divides its resources among the schools.

Parent organizations are effective influencing school policy decisions. For example, parents successfully petitioned the School Board to save some music programs after a recent budget reduction.

Quality of Instruction

Additional learning opportunities for gifted students and additional instruction for low-achieving students are rated good. Also considered good are the curricula for college-bound students and for those going into the world of work. One observer complained that improvement is needed in academic counseling.

Quality of School Environment

Classroom disruption tends to be on the high side, but varies from school to school. The quality of building maintenance and repair is rated fair to good.

GROSSE POINTE

ADDRESS OF CENTRAL OFFICE:
389 St. Clair, Grosse Pointe, MI 48230
ESI:77

STATISTICAL PROFILE	DATA	ESI
Grade organization: K–5/6–8/9–12		
Percentage of schools built before 1955	80%	
Total enrollment	7,380	
Average Daily Attendance (ADA)	95%	8
Current expense per pupil in ADA	$5,100	10
Dropout rate	NK	0
Percentage of eligible students who took the ACT	87%	10
Average combined score on ACT	21.3	10
Percentage of graduates who enrolled in 2- or 4-year colleges	85%	
Percentage of students who passed the state reading test	94%	
Percentage of students who passed the state math test	87%	
Teacher–student ratio in elementary grades	1:22	8
Teacher–student ratio in secondary grades	1:18	10
Counselor–student ratio in secondary grades	1:261	7
Number of students per music specialist in elementary grades	463	6
Number of students per art specialist in elementary grades	594	
Number of volumes in senior high school library	39,000	
Beginning teacher's salary	$18,514	
Maximum teacher's salary	$41,144	
Average years of experience among teachers	NK	
Number of students suspended and expelled	NK	
Subjects in which Advanced Placement courses are offered:	8	8
American History, Calculus, Chemistry, English, European History, French, German, Spanish		

Quality of School Leadership

Principals are selected primarily for their educational leadership ability. The quality of leadership does not vary greatly from school to school. Parents and teachers serve on committees screening principal candidates. Principals have much to say about the allotment of resources to their school.

Parents and other citizens are involved in school decision-making through committees appointed by the School Board. Also, PTOs are quite effective.

Quality of Instruction

Programs for gifted students exist at all levels and are rated excellent. Additional instruction for low-achieving students is considered good. Learning resource rooms are used by low-achieving students. The college preparatory curriculum is rated excellent, and the curriculum for students going into the job market is considered good. Many parents volunteer to work in the schools as aides and tutors.

Quality of School Environment

Classroom disruption and student vandalism are not problems. The quality of building maintenance and repair is considered good.

HIGHLAND PARK

ADDRESS OF CENTRAL OFFICE:
20 Bartlett Street, Highland Park, MI 48203
ESI:17

STATISTICAL PROFILE	DATA	ESI
Grade organization: K–12†		
Percentage of schools built before 1955	56%	
Total enrollment	6,854	
Average Daily Attendance (ADA)	88%	1
Current expense per pupil in ADA	$3,402	1
Dropout rate	40%	0
Percentage of eligible students who took the SAT	35%	4
Average combined score on SAT	695	0
Percentage of graduates who enrolled in 2- or 4-year colleges	66%	
Percentage of students who passed the state reading test	66%	
Percentage of students who passed the state math test	46%	
Teacher–student ratio in elementary grades	1:28	2
Teacher–student ratio in secondary grades	1:24	4
Counselor–student ratio in secondary grades	1:320	5
Number of students per music specialist in elementary grades	None	0
Number of students per art specialist in elementary grades	None	
Number of volumes in senior high school libraries (average)	19,500	
Beginning teacher's salary	$15,656††	
Maximum teacher's salary	$34,666††	
Average years of experience among teachers	12	
Number of students suspended and expelled	1,638	
Subjects in which Advanced Placement courses are offered:	None	0

† The district misinterpreted this statistic.
††1986–87 statistics.

Quality of School Leadership
A candidate's popularity is an important criterion in the selection of a principal, but the quality of leadership does not seem to vary greatly from school to school. Parents and teachers have no say in principal selection, but principals have some say in the distribution of district resources to the schools.

Parent organizations are not very effective influencing school policy.

Quality of Instruction
Money has been a problem for the district, and programs have suffered. The additional learning opportunities for gifted students are rated fair; additional instruction for low-achieving students is considered good. Getting fair marks from observers are the curricula for college-bound students and for those heading into the job market. One observer criticized counseling for students not planning on college.

According to the observers, the district is not adequately meeting the educational needs of minority students. "I don't think they take the time to teach," said an observer.

Quality of School Environment
Classroom disruption and student vandalism tend to be on the high side. Purse snatchings have been reported at the high school. The quality of building maintenance and repair is considered good.

L'ANSE CREUSE

ADDRESS OF CENTRAL OFFICE:
36727 Jefferson Avenue, Mount Clemens, MI 48045
ESI:43

STATISTICAL PROFILE	DATA	ESI
Grade organization: K–6/7–8/9–12		
Percentage of schools built before 1955	25%	
Total enrollment	7,464	
Average Daily Attendance (ADA)	97%	10
Current expense per pupil in ADA	$3,485	2
Dropout rate	16%	7
Percentage of eligible students who took the ACT	33%	4
Average combined score on ACT	19.1	5
Percentage of graduates who enrolled in 2- or 4-year colleges	28%	
Percentage of students who passed the state reading test	87%	
Percentage of students who passed the state math test	93%	
Teacher–student ratio in elementary grades	1:27	3
Teacher–student ratio in secondary grades	1:24	4
Counselor–student ratio in secondary grades	1:310	5
Number of students per music specialist in elementary grades	855	0
Number of students per art specialist in elementary grades	1,140	
Number of volumes in senior high school library	14,000	
Beginning teacher's salary	$17,522	
Maximum teacher's salary	$39,135	
Average years of experience among teachers	14	
Number of students suspended and expelled	306	
Subjects in which Advanced Placement courses are offered: American History, Calculus, Computer Science	3	3

FAIR APPRAISAL

Quality of School Leadership
Principals are hired because of their educational leadership ability, and the quality of leadership is generally uniform throughout the system. Parents and teachers serve on a committee to select a superintendent, but they have less say in principal selection. Principals, on the other hand, have a great deal to say about how resources will be divided among the schools.

Parents are very effective influencing school policy decisions. Parents and other citizens serve on curriculum and finance committees. "I think someone moving in can feel ownership with the schools," said an observer.

Quality of Instruction
Additional learning opportunities for gifted students are rated good and getting better. Additional instruction for low-achieving students is considered fair but on the verge of improvement. The curriculum for college-bound students is good, and the curriculum for students going into the world of work is rated excellent.

Quality of School Environment
The level of classroom disruption and student vandalism is very low, and the quality of building maintenance and repair is good.

LAKE SHORE

ADDRESS OF CENTRAL OFFICE:
30401 Taylor Road, St. Clair Shores, MI 48082
ESI:59*

STATISTICAL PROFILE	DATA	ESI
Grade organization: K–8/9–12		
Percentage of schools built before 1955	0%	
Total enrollment	3,912	
Average Daily Attendance (ADA)	94%	7
Current expense per pupil in ADA	$3,852	3
Dropout rate	10%	10
Percentage of eligible students who took the ACT	50%	7
Average combined score on ACT	19.1	5
Percentage of graduates who enrolled in 2- or 4-year colleges	49%	
Percentage of students who passed the state reading test	82%	
Percentage of students who passed the state math test	73%	
Teacher–student ratio in elementary grades	1:23	7
Teacher–student ratio in secondary grades	1:19	9
Counselor–student ratio in secondary grades	†	0*
Number of students per music specialist in elementary grades	140	10
Number of students per art specialist in elementary grades	721	
Number of volumes in senior high school library	26,000	
Beginning teacher's salary	$18,009	
Maximum teacher's salary	$33,134	
Average years of experience among teachers	14	
Number of students suspended and expelled	602	
Subjects in which Advanced Placement courses are offered: English	1	1

†The district supplied an inappropriate statistic.

FAIR APPRAISAL

Quality of School Leadership
Most principals are hired for their educational leadership ability, but popularity has been an important factor in some cases. The quality of leadership does not vary greatly from school to school. Parents and teachers do not screen principal candidates. Principals have some say, but not much, in how resources will be allotted to their school.

Parents and other citizens sit on various advisory committees, and parent organizations play "an active role in getting people elected to the School Board."

Quality of Instruction
Additional opportunities for gifted students are rated good, but additional instruction for low-achieving students is considered fair. The college preparatory curriculum is considered good, and the curriculum for students preparing for the job world is rated excellent.

Quality of School Environment
Classroom disruption and vandalism are not problems. The quality of building maintenance and repair is rated good; even old buildings are in good shape.

LINCOLN PARK

ADDRESS OF CENTRAL OFFICE:
145 Southfield Road, Lincoln Park, MI 48146
ESI:14*

STATISTICAL PROFILE	DATA	ESI
Grade organization: K–7/8–12		
Percentage of schools built before 1955	91%	
Total enrollment	6,375	
Average Daily Attendance (ADA)	85%	0
Current expense per pupil in ADA	$2,628	0
Dropout rate	18%	5
Percentage of eligible students who took the ACT	22%	2
Average combined score on ACT	†	0*
Percentage of graduates who enrolled in 2- or 4-year colleges	30%	
Percentage of students who passed the state reading test	NK	
Percentage of students who passed the state math test	NK	
Teacher–student ratio in elementary grades	1:25	5
Teacher–student ratio in secondary grades	1:29	0
Counselor–student ratio in secondary grades	1:400	2
Number of students per music specialist in elementary grades	None	0
Number of students per art specialist in elementary grades	None	
Number of volumes in senior high school library	23,025	
Beginning teacher's salary	$18,524	
Maximum teacher's salary	$35,580	
Average years of experience among teachers	8	
Number of students suspended and expelled	450	
Subjects in which Advanced Placement courses are offered:	None	0

†The district supplied an inappropriate statistic.

FAIR APPRAISAL

Quality of School Leadership
The School Board looks for educational leadership ability in principal candidates, and the quality of leadership is generally uniform from school to school. Parents and teachers do not screen principal candidates, but principals have some influence over how resources are used in the district.

Parent organizations are sometimes effective influencing school policy decisions. Although they worked hard to get a tax levy passed in 1986–1987, they "spend most of their time raising funds," said an observer.

Quality of Instruction
The program for gifted students was started in 1986–1987 in grades 4–7, and is rated good. Also considered good is additional instruction for low-achieving students. The curricula for college-bound students and job-bound students are rated fair.

Quality of School Environment
The incidence of classroom disruption and student vandalism is low, and the quality of building maintenance and repair is excellent.

LIVONIA

ADDRESS OF CENTRAL OFFICE:
15125 Farmington Road, Livonia, MI 48154
ESI:33

STATISTICAL PROFILE	DATA	ESI
Grade organization: K–6/7–8/9–12		
Percentage of schools built before 1955	1%	
Total enrollment	16,608	
Average Daily Attendance (ADA)	NK	0
Current expense per pupil in ADA	NK	0
Dropout rate	NK	0
Percentage of eligible students who took the ACT	60%	9
Average combined score on ACT	19.7	5
Percentage of graduates who enrolled in 2- or 4-year colleges	72%	
Percentage of students who passed the state reading test	NK	
Percentage of students who passed the state math test	NK	
Teacher–student ratio in elementary grades	1:25	5
Teacher–student ratio in secondary grades	1:24	4
Counselor–student ratio in secondary grades	1:307	5
Number of students per music specialist in elementary grades	744	1
Number of students per art specialist in elementary grades	744	
Number of volumes in senior high school library	25,189	
Beginning teacher's salary	$19,405	
Maximum teacher's salary	$39,198	
Average years of experience among teachers	18	
Number of students suspended and expelled	NK	
Subjects in which Advanced Placement courses are offered:	4	4
American History, Calculus, Chemistry, English		

FAIR APPRAISAL

Quality of School Leadership
Principals are selected primarily for their educational leadership ability. The quality of leadership does not vary greatly from school to school. Parents and teachers do not screen principal candidates, but principals have some say in the distribution of district resources.

Although Livonia is supposed to have the largest PTA membership in the state, parents are only sometimes effective influencing school policy decisions.

Quality of Instruction
Additional learning opportunities for gifted students are called excellent at all grade levels. High school students gifted in the performing arts gather at one high school for enrichment. Additional instruction for low-achieving students also is considered excellent. The college preparatory curriculum is considered excellent, and the curriculum for job-bound students is rated good. The Career Center offers instruction in home construction and various trades.

The district has been able to maintain a quality educational program, observers believe, despite the trauma of enrollment shrinking from 40,000 to 16,608 over a dozen years or so.

Quality of School Environment
Classroom disruption and student vandalism are not problems. The quality of building maintenance and repair is good.

MADISON

ADDRESS OF CENTRAL OFFICE:
25421 Alger, Madison Heights, MI 48071
ESI:43

STATISTICAL PROFILE	DATA	ESI
Grade organization: K–12†		
Percentage of schools built before 1955	20%	
Total enrollment	2,940	
Average Daily Attendance (ADA)	92%	5
Current expense per pupil in ADA	$3,500	2
Dropout rate	20%	3
Percentage of eligible students who took the ACT	85%	10
Average combined score on ACT	NK	0
Percentage of graduates who enrolled in 2- or 4-year colleges	40%	
Percentage of students who passed the state reading test	85%	
Percentage of students who passed the state math test	83%	
Teacher–student ratio in elementary grades	1:21	9
Teacher–student ratio in secondary grades	1:23	5
Counselor–student ratio in secondary grades	1:350	4
Number of students per music specialist in elementary grades	500	5
Number of students per art specialist in elementary grades	500	
Number of volumes in senior high school library	NK	
Beginning teacher's salary	$19,313	
Maximum teacher's salary	$41,344	
Average years of experience among teachers	22	
Number of students suspended and expelled	20	
Subjects in which Advanced Placement courses are offered:	None	0

†The district misinterpreted this statistic.

FAIR APPRAISAL

Quality of School Leadership
Principals are hired because of their educational leadership ability, and the quality of leadership is generally uniform throughout the district. Parents and teachers do not screen principal candidates. Principals, on the other hand, have some say in how resources are divided among the schools.

Parent organizations are sometimes influential in school decision-making.

Quality of Instruction
Additional learning opportunities for gifted students are rated fair. The program is relatively new. Considered good is additional instruction for low-achieving students. The curriculum for college-bound students is rated fair to good, and the curriculum for students bound for the job market is considered good.

The district is considered financially poor compared with most other districts in the area. According to an observer, "They do the best they can with what they have."

Quality of School Environment
Classroom disruption and student vandalism are not problems, and the quality of building maintenance and repair is considered good.

NORTHVILLE

ADDRESS OF CENTRAL OFFICE:
501 West Main Street, Northville, MI 48167
ESI:None†

STATISTICAL PROFILE	DATA	ESI
Grade organization:		
Percentage of schools built before 1955		
Total enrollment		
Average Daily Attendance (ADA)		
Current expense per pupil in ADA		
Dropout rate		
Percentage of eligible students who took the ACT		
Average combined score on ACT		
Percentage of graduates who enrolled in 2- or 4-year colleges		
Percentage of students who passed the state reading test		
Percentage of students who passed the state math test		
Teacher–student ratio in elementary grades		
Teacher–student ratio in secondary grades		
Counselor–student ratio in secondary grades		
Number of students per music specialist in elementary grades		
Number of students per art specialist in elementary grades		
Number of volumes in senior high school library		
Beginning teacher's salary		
Maximum teacher's salary		
Average years of experience among teachers		
Number of students suspended and expelled		
Subjects in which Advanced Placement courses are offered:		

†A Statistical Profile was not received from this district.

FAIR APPRAISAL

Quality of School Leadership
The School Board picks principals who demonstrate educational leadership ability, and the quality of leadership is generally uniform throughout the system. Parents and teachers do not have a say in principal selection, but principals have some say about the allotment of resources to their school.

Parent advisory committees are considered effective influencing school policy decisions.

Quality of Instruction
Additional learning opportunities for gifted students and additional instruction for low-achieving students are rated only fair. Considered good are the curricula for college-bound students going into the world of work.

Quality of School Environment
The incidence of classroom disruption and student vandalism is low, and the quality of building maintenance and repair is considered good.

PLYMOUTH–CANTON

ADDRESS OF CENTRAL OFFICE:
454 South Harvey Street, Plymouth, MI 48170
ESI:50

STATISTICAL PROFILE	DATA	ESI
Grade organization: K–5/6–8/9–12		
Percentage of schools built before 1955	16%	
Total enrollment	15,500	
Average Daily Attendance (ADA)	95%	8
Current expense per pupil in ADA	$3,329	1
Dropout rate	12%	10
Percentage of eligible students who took the SAT	34%	4
Average combined score on SAT	972	8
Percentage of graduates who enrolled in 2- or 4-year colleges	58%	
Percentage of students who passed the state reading test	88%	
Percentage of students who passed the state math test	81%	
Teacher–student ratio in elementary grades	1:23	7
Teacher–student ratio in secondary grades	1:22	6
Counselor–student ratio in secondary grades	1:345	4
Number of students per music specialist in elementary grades	865	0
Number of students per art specialist in elementary grades	865	
Number of volumes in senior high school libraries (average)	19,290	
Beginning teacher's salary	$18,696	
Maximum teacher's salary	$39,200	
Average years of experience among teachers	11	
Number of students suspended and expelled	NK	
Subjects in which Advanced Placement courses are offered: American History, Calculus	2	2

FAIR APPRAISAL

Quality of School Leadership
Principals are hired primarily because of their educational leadership ability, but the School Board also looks for candidates who are able to communicate well with parents and other taxpayers. The quality of leadership is generally uniform throughout the system. Teachers, but not parents, are included on committees screening principal candidates. Principals have a great deal of influence over the distribution of district resources.

Parent organizations and citizen advisory committees are effective influencing school policy decisions.

Quality of Instruction
Special classes exist for gifted students; also, gifted students can attend satellite centers for enrichment opportunities. Observers rate the program excellent, and one observer said it is among the top programs in the area. Additional instruction for low-achieving students is rated fair to good. Curricula for college-bound students and job-bound students are rated excellent and good respectively. The vocational education program includes culinary arts, a dental clinic, and training in day-care management.

Quality of School Environment
The level of student vandalism is low, but classroom disruption is a problem in some schools. The quality of building maintenance and repair is good.

ROYAL OAK

ADDRESS OF CENTRAL OFFICE:
1123 Lexington Boulevard, Royal Oak, MI 48073
ESI:None†

STATISTICAL PROFILE	DATA	ESI
Grade organization:		
Percentage of schools built before 1955		
Total enrollment		
Average Daily Attendance (ADA)		
Current expense per pupil in ADA		
Dropout rate		
Percentage of eligible students who took the ACT		
Average combined score on ACT		
Percentage of graduates who enrolled in 2- or 4-year colleges		
Percentage of students who passed the state reading test		
Percentage of students who passed the state math test		
Teacher–student ratio in elementary grades		
Teacher–student ratio in secondary grades		
Counselor–student ratio in secondary grades		
Number of students per music specialist in elementary grades		
Number of students per art specialist in elementary grades		
Number of volumes in senior high school library		
Beginning teacher's salary		
Maximum teacher's salary		
Average years of experience among teachers		
Number of students suspended and expelled		
Subjects in which Advanced Placement courses are offered:		

†A Statistical Profile was not received from this district.

FAIR APPRAISAL

Quality of School Leadership
Principals are hired because of their educational leadership ability, and the quality of leadership is generally uniform from school to school. Parents and teachers do not take part in screening principal candidates. Principals, however, influence how the district distributes resources to the schools.

Parent organizations are generally effective influencing school policy decisions; the PTA is described as being "very strong."

Quality of Instruction
Additional learning opportunities for gifted students and additional instruction for low-achieving students are described as good to excellent. The program for gifted students seems to be weighted mostly in favor of students in the upper grades. The curricula for college-bound students and for students going into the job market are rated highly. The district offers many "skilled labor classes," said an observer.

Quality of School Environment
The level of classroom disruption and student vandalism is considered low, and the quality of building repair and maintenance is called excellent.

SOUTHFIELD

ADDRESS OF CENTRAL OFFICE:
24661 Lasher Road, Southfield, MI 48034
ESI:65

STATISTICAL PROFILE	DATA	ESI
Grade organization: K–5/6–8/9–12		
Percentage of schools built before 1955	6%	
Total enrollment	8,608	
Average Daily Attendance (ADA)	92%	5
Current expense per pupil in ADA	$6,004	10
Dropout rate	8%	10
Percentage of eligible students who took the SAT	20%	1
Average combined score on SAT	980	8
Percentage of graduates who enrolled in 2- or 4-year colleges	78%	
Percentage of students who passed the state reading test	97%	
Percentage of students who passed the state math test	96%	
Teacher–student ratio in elementary grades	1:22	8
Teacher–student ratio in secondary grades	1:27	1
Counselor–student ratio in secondary grades	1:240	8
Number of students per music specialist in elementary grades	372	8
Number of students per art specialist in elementary grades	454	
Number of volumes in senior high school library	23,264	
Beginning teacher's salary	$20,039	
Maximum teacher's salary	$41,461	
Average years of experience among teachers	16	
Number of students suspended and expelled	NK	
Subjects in which Advanced Placement courses are offered:	6	6
American History, Calculus, Computer Science, English, Foreign Language, Science		

FAIR APPRAISAL

Quality of School Leadership
The School Board looks for principal candidates who have educational leadership ability. The quality of leadership is generally uniform throughout the district. Parents and teachers do not screen principal candidates. Principals have some say in determining what resources are allotted their school.

The School Board and administrators pay attention to parents, said observers. One way in which parents are most influential is through an advisory council that meets regularly with district officials to discuss policies and practices.

Quality of Instruction
Additional learning opportunities for gifted students are rated good. In addition to the special classes offered in the schools, gifted high school students can earn credits for courses taken at nearby colleges. Additional instruction for low-achieving students also is rated good. The curriculum for college-bound students is termed excellent. The International Baccalaureate program is offered in addition to a number of Advanced Placement courses. The curriculum for job-bound students is rated good.

Quality of School Environment
The incidence of classroom disruption and student vandalism is generally low, but one observer said the district's proximity to Detroit accounted for more problems than a typical suburban school district might have. The quality of building maintenance and repair is excellent.

TAYLOR

ADDRESS OF CENTRAL OFFICE:
23033 North Line Street, Taylor, MI 48180
ESI:None†

STATISTICAL PROFILE	DATA	ESI
Grade organization:		
Percentage of schools built before 1955		
Total enrollment		
Average Daily Attendance (ADA)		
Current expense per pupil in ADA		
Dropout rate		
Percentage of eligible students who took the ACT		
Average combined score on ACT		
Percentage of graduates who enrolled in 2- or 4-year colleges		
Percentage of students who passed the state reading test		
Percentage of students who passed the state math test		
Teacher–student ratio in elementary grades		
Teacher–student ratio in secondary grades		
Counselor–student ratio in secondary grades		
Number of students per music specialist in elementary grades		
Number of students per art specialist in elementary grades		
Number of volumes in senior high school library		
Beginning teacher's salary		
Maximum teacher's salary		
Average years of experience among teachers		
Number of students suspended and expelled		
Subjects in which Advanced Placement courses are offered:		

†A Statistical Profile was not received from this district.

FAIR APPRAISAL

Quality of School Leadership
Principal candidates must have educational leadership ability and experience in order to be considered. The quality of leadership in the district is generally uniform from school to school. Parents and teachers do not take part in principal selection, but principals have some say about the distribution of district resources.

Parent organizations are sometimes effective influencing school policy decisions.

Quality of Instruction
Additional learning opportunities for gifted students and additional instruction for low-achieving students are rated fair. Also rated fair are the curricula for students preparing for college and students preparing for the world of work.

Quality of School Environment
Classroom disruption and student vandalism are not problems. However, repeated defeats of tax levies "have hindered building maintenance and repair," according to an observer. The condition of buildings, therefore, is considered to be only fair.

TROY

ADDRESS OF CENTRAL OFFICE:
4400 Livernois, Troy, MI 48098
ESI:67

STATISTICAL PROFILE	DATA	ESI
Grade organization: K–5/6–8/9–12		
Percentage of schools built before 1955	8%	
Total enrollment	10,823	
Average Daily Attendance (ADA)	97%	10
Current expense per pupil in ADA	$3,842	3
Dropout rate	16%	7
Percentage of eligible students who took the ACT	75%	10
Average combined score on ACT	21	10
Percentage of graduates who enrolled in 2- or 4-year colleges	77%	
Percentage of students who passed the state reading test	92%	
Percentage of students who passed the state math test	88%	
Teacher–student ratio in elementary grades	1:23	7
Teacher–student ratio in secondary grades	1:23	5
Counselor–student ratio in secondary grades	1:310	5
Number of students per music specialist in elementary grades	457	6
Number of students per art specialist in elementary grades	701	
Number of volumes in senior high school libraries (average)	13,680	
Beginning teacher's salary	$18,056	
Maximum teacher's salary	$42,348	
Average years of experience among teachers	10	
Number of students suspended and expelled	325	
Subjects in which Advanced Placement courses are offered: American History, Biology, Chemistry, English Literature and Composition	4	4

FAIR APPRAISAL

Quality of School Leadership
The School Board picks principals who demonstrate educational leadership ability, and the quality of leadership is considered uniform throughout the system. Parents and teachers help screen principal candidates, and principals have a say in deciding how district resources will be apportioned. One observer commended the superintendent and other key administrators for "outstanding leadership" that sets a high tone for the entire system.

Parents and other citizens are very effective influencing school policy decisions. A number of ongoing committees involve parents and others in studying policies and practices. Said one observer, "I'm a former teacher, and I've never seen such active parents."

Quality of Instruction
Additional learning opportunites for gifted students are rated excellent. Said one observer, "I've watched the program grow from nothing to excellence." One observer complained, however, that the district determines gifted students by grade point average rather than test scores. Additional instruction for low-achieving students is considered good. Also rated good are the curricula for college-bound students and for those going into the job market.

Quality of School Environment
Classroom disruption and student vandalism are not problems. The quality of building maintenance and repair is good, but has just arrived at this point. A recent bond issue has enabled the district to make up for years of neglect. Also, one observer said that buildings on the west side of the district are in worse shape than those on the east side.

WARREN WOODS

ADDRESS OF CENTRAL OFFICE:
27100 Schoenherr Road, Warren, MI 48093
ESI:43

STATISTICAL PROFILE	DATA	ESI
Grade organization: K–12†		
Percentage of schools built before 1955	0%	
Total enrollment	2,946	
Average Daily Attendance (ADA)	92%	5
Current expense per pupil in ADA	$4,982	9
Dropout rate	5%	10
Percentage of eligible students who took the ACT	48%	7
Average combined score on ACT	18.4	4
Percentage of graduates who enrolled in 2- or 4-year colleges	52%	
Percentage of students who passed the state reading test	85%	
Percentage of students who passed the state math test	80%	
Teacher–student ratio in elementary grades	1:26	4
Teacher–student ratio in secondary grades	1:28	0
Counselor–student ratio in secondary grades	1:400	1
Number of students per music specialist in elementary grades	1,061	0
Number of students per art specialist in elementary grades	1,061	
Number of volumes in senior high school library	18,701	
Beginning teacher's salary	$17,588	
Maximum teacher's salary	$35,709	
Average years of experience among teachers	17	
Number of students suspended and expelled	102	
Subjects in which Advanced Placement courses are offered: Biology, Chemistry, English	3	3

†The district misinterpreted this statistic.

FAIR APPRAISAL

Quality of School Leadership
While longevity or seniority helps, principals are chosen primarily because of their educational leadership ability. Also, the quality of leadership does not vary greatly from school to school. Parents and teachers do not help select principals. Principals, on the other hand, do have some say in how resources are allotted to their school.

Sometimes the School Board has made "decisions hastily," said an observer, and "parents have stepped in and convinced them to reconsider." Another observer said, "When parents want something, they're effective."

Quality of Instruction
Additional learning opportunities for gifted students are called good, with the program being better in the elementary grades than in the upper grades. Rated fair is additional instruction for low-achieving students. The curricula for college-bound students and for those bound for the job market are rated good.

Quality of School Environment
Classroom disruption and student vandalism are not problems, and the quality of building maintenance and repair is rated good.

WATERFORD

ADDRESS OF CENTRAL OFFICE:
P.O. Box 547, Waterford, MI 48095
ESI:41

STATISTICAL PROFILE	DATA	ESI
Grade organization: K–6/7–9/10–12		
Percentage of schools built before 1955	15%	
Total enrollment	11,990	
Average Daily Attendance (ADA)	90%	3
Current expense per pupil in ADA	$3,100	0
Dropout rate	21%	2
Percentage of eligible students who took the ACT	35%	4
Average combined score on ACT	19.2	5
Percentage of graduates who enrolled in 2- or 4-year colleges	50%	
Percentage of students who passed the state reading test	85%	
Percentage of students who passed the state math test	88%	
Teacher–student ratio in elementary grades	1:25	5
Teacher–student ratio in secondary grades	1:30	0
Counselor–student ratio in secondary grades	1:300	5
Number of students per music specialist in elementary grades	340	9
Number of students per art specialist in elementary grades	781	
Number of volumes in senior high school libraries (average)	12,144	
Beginning teacher's salary	$19,000	
Maximum teacher's salary	$40,000	
Average years of experience among teachers	15	
Number of students suspended and expelled	NK	
Subjects in which Advanced Placement courses are offered: American Government, Biology, Calculus, Chemistry, English, French, Physics, Spanish	8	8

Quality of School Leadership
The School Board hires principals who demonstrate educational leadership ability; however, seniority also is considered. The quality of leadership does not vary greatly from school to school. Screening of principal candidates does not include parents and teachers. Principals are able to influence distribution of district resources.

Quality of Instruction
Additional learning opportunities for gifted students are rated good and improving. The program spans all grades. Also rated good is additional instruction for low-achieving students. The curricula for students preparing for college and for those preparing for jobs are considered good.

Quality of School Environment
The level of classroom disruption and student vandalism is low, and the quality of building maintenance and repair is good.

WAYNE–WESTLAND

ADDRESS OF CENTRAL OFFICE:
36745 Marquette Street, Westland, MI 48185
ESI:43

STATISTICAL PROFILE	DATA	ESI
Grade organization: K–12†		
Percentage of schools built before 1955	20%	
Total enrollment	17,682	
Average Daily Attendance (ADA)	95%	8
Current expense per pupil in ADA	$3,350	1
Dropout rate	15%	8
Percentage of eligible students who took the ACT	80%	10
Average combined score on ACT	20.5	8
Percentage of graduates who enrolled in 2- or 4-year colleges	32%	
Percentage of students who passed the state reading test	85%	
Percentage of students who passed the state math test	80%	
Teacher–student ratio in elementary grades	1:28	2
Teacher–student ratio in secondary grades	1:29	0
Counselor–student ratio in secondary grades	1:300	6
Number of students per music specialist in elementary grades	800	0
Number of students per art specialist in elementary grades	800	
Number of volumes in senior high school libraries (average)	13,345	
Beginning teacher's salary	$18,967	
Maximum teacher's salary	$38,073	
Average years of experience among teachers	15	
Number of students suspended and expelled	NK	
Subjects in which Advanced Placement courses are offered:	None	0

†The district misinterpreted this statistic.

Quality of School Leadership
The superintendent personally selects principals and recommends them to the School Board, which almost always accepts the recommendations. While the superintendent wants principals who have educational leadership ability, an observer said, the superintendent "also considers longevity and popularity." Parents and teachers have no say in the selection process. Principals have a little say in what resources are allotted their school.

The gifted program was started largely at the request of parent groups, and their influence is generally effective.

Quality of Instruction
The program for gifted students is rated excellent, but additional instruction for low-achieving students is considered only fair. The curricula for students going to college and students going into the job market are termed excellent. An observer called the district's vocational-technical center "the finest in the state."

Quality of School Environment
Classroom disruption and student vandalism are not problems. However, lack of necessary funds (a recent bond issue was defeated) has hurt the quality of building maintenance and repair. Said an observer, "Some of the buildings are falling apart."

WEST BLOOMFIELD

ADDRESS OF CENTRAL OFFICE:

3250 Commerce Road, Keego Harbor, MI 48033

ESI:61

STATISTICAL PROFILE	DATA	ESI
Grade organization: K–5/6–8/9–12		
Percentage of schools built before 1955	50%	
Total enrollment	4,526	
Average Daily Attendance (ADA)	95%	8
Current expense per pupil in ADA	$4,420	7
Dropout rate	22%	1
Percentage of eligible students who took the ACT	40%	5
Average combined score on ACT	19.8	5
Percentage of graduates who enrolled in 2- or 4-year colleges	75%	
Percentage of students who passed the state reading test	NK	
Percentage of students who passed the state math test	NK	
Teacher–student ratio in elementary grades	1:23	7
Teacher–student ratio in secondary grades	1:19	9
Counselor–student ratio in secondary grades	1:259	7
Number of students per music specialist in elementary grades	326	9
Number of students per art specialist in elementary grades	391	
Number of volumes in senior high school library	20,000	
Beginning teacher's salary	$18,432	
Maximum teacher's salary	$42,648	
Average years of experience among teachers	15	
Number of students suspended and expelled	517	
Subjects in which Advanced Placement courses are offered: Art, English, Science	3	3

FAIR APPRAISAL

Quality of School Leadership

Principals are selected for their educational leadership ability, and the quality of leadership does not vary greatly from school to school. Parents and teachers have no say in principal selection, but principals have some say in how resources are allotted to the schools.

Parent organizations are sometimes effective influencing school policy decisions.

Quality of Instruction

Additional learning opportunities for gifted students are rated good, as is additional instruction for low-achieving students. The college preparatory curriculum is termed excellent, and the curriculum for students preparing for the world of work is rated good.

Observers disagree over how well the district serves a large number of students from Asian and Middle Eastern countries. One observer said the district shows "a lot of sensitivity;" another observer criticized the district for "lack of preparation and understanding."

Quality of School Environment

The incidence of classroom disruption and student vandalism is low. The quality of building maintenance and repair is fair to good.

Fort Lauderdale, FL

Florida's school districts are county districts. The Fort Lauderdale
Metropolitan Area is primarily served by the Broward County School
District. For comparisons, we suggest consulting the listings for
Miami and Tampa-St. Petersburg Metropolitan Areas in Florida.

AREA AT A GLANCE

SCHOOL DISTRICT	ENROLLMENT	ESI
Broward County	126,000	28

BROWARD COUNTY

ADDRESS OF CENTRAL OFFICE:
1320 Southwest Fourth Street,
Fort Lauderdale, FL 33322
ESI:28

STATISTICAL PROFILE	DATA	ESI
Grade organization: K–5/6–8/9–12		
Percentage of schools built before 1955	14%	
Total enrollment	126,000	
Average Daily Attendance (ADA)	93%	6
Current expense per pupil in ADA	$3,337	0
Dropout rate	NK	0
Percentage of eligible students who took the SAT	NK	0
Average combined score on SAT	884	3
Percentage of graduates who enrolled in 2- or 4-year colleges	60%	
Percentage of students who passed the state reading test	91%	
Percentage of students who passed the state math test	86%	
Teacher–student ratio in elementary grades	1:26	4
Teacher–student ratio in secondary grades	1:28	0
Counselor–student ratio in secondary grades	1:311	5
Number of students per music specialist in elementary grades	NK	0
Number of students per art specialist in elementary grades	1,058	
Number of volumes in senior high school library	21,760	
Beginning teacher's salary	$20,150	
Maximum teacher's salary	$34,796	
Average years of experience among teachers	13	
Number of students suspended and expelled	NK	
Subjects in which Advanced Placement courses are offered:	17	10

American History, Art Studio, Art Studies, Biology,
Calculus, Chemistry, Computer Science, English
Language & Composition, European History, French,
German, Latin, Music Theory, Physics B, Physics
Mechanical, Spanish Language, Spanish Literature

Quality of School Leadership

Principals are chosen primarily because of their educational leadership ability; however, the quality of leadership varies greatly from school to school. Some principals close to retirement "seem to have lost interest," said one observer. Another observer noted that schools "where parents are most vocal and demanding" seem to get the most able principals. Parents and teachers do not have a say in principal selection, but principals have some say about the distribution of district resources.

Parents are sometimes effective influencing decision-making, but their efforts vary greatly from school to school. They have the least impact on decisions affecting the district as a whole.

Quality of Instruction

Additional opportunities for gifted students generally are rated good, but one observer thinks the program is not adequate. Additional instruction for low-achieving students is termed fair to poor. The curriculum for students going on to college is considered fair, but the curriculum for students planning on entering the job market is rated good. In addition to a typical high school vocational education program, the district also operates a trade/technical school for young men and women who want to specialize or learn more advanced skills after high school.

The district is not adequately meeting the educational needs of minority students. One observer believes "the needs of black students may be accommodated, but the district is still not meeting the needs of Hispanic students" moving into the county from the Miami area.

Quality of School Environment

The level of classroom disruption and vandalism is low. The quality of building maintenance and repair, on the other hand, is fair to poor. Broward is in the midst of a major population boom in the western part of the county. School buildings there are overcrowded, while in the eastern portion, along the coast, enrollment is still decreasing. With meager funds available, an oberver said, the district "tried to keep up" with growth in the west by putting up portable classrooms and making other temporary provisions. In the end, the observer said, the district "spent its limited resources, but could not keep up with the expansion in the west and, meanwhile, allowed school buildings in the east to become dilapidated." A bond issue for $819 million was approved in June, 1987 to pay for needed repairs and to build new facilities over a 10-year period.

METROPOLITAN AREA

Greensboro/Winston-Salem, NC

Five districts in the Greensboro — Winston-Salem Metropolitan Area completed the
Statistical Profile, and a Fair Appraisal alone was received from one other district.
The Greensboro/Winston-Salem Metropolitan Area can be compared with the
Norfolk–Virginia Beach Metropolitan Area in Virginia and the Nashville Metropolitan Area in Tennessee.

AREA AT A GLANCE

SCHOOL DISTRICT	ENROLLMENT	ESI
Greensboro	21,743	
Guilford County	23,780	43
High Point	8,380	42
Randolph County	13,741	12*
Rockingham County	3,779	42
Winston-Salem/ Forsyth County	38,847	70

Indicates district misinterpretation of one or more statistics in the ESI. For each misinterpreted statistic, a score of 0 was given instead of a possible score of 0 to 10 points.

GREENSBORO

ADDRESS OF CENTRAL OFFICE:
712 North Eugene Street, Greensboro, NC 27401
ESI:None†

STATISTICAL PROFILE	DATA	ESI
Grade organization:		
Percentage of schools built before 1955		
Total enrollment		
Average Daily Attendance (ADA)		
Current expense per pupil in ADA		
Dropout rate		
Percentage of eligible students who took the SAT		
Average combined score on SAT		
Percentage of graduates who enrolled in 2- or 4-year colleges		
Percentage of students who passed the state reading test		
Percentage of students who passed the state math test		
Teacher–student ratio in elementary grades		
Teacher–student ratio in secondary grades		
Counselor–student ratio in secondary grades		
Number of students per music specialist in elementary grades		
Number of students per art specialist in elementary grades		
Number of volumes in senior high school library		
Beginning teacher's salary		
Maximum teacher's salary		
Average years of experience among teachers		
Number of students suspended and expelled		
Subjects in which Advanced Placement courses are offered:		

†A Statistical Profile was not received from this district.

Quality of School Leadership

An effort is made to select principals who have educational leadership ability, but popularity and "perceived power" are considerations in some appointments. Because of this situation, the quality of leadership varies greatly from school to school. Parents and teachers play no formal role in principal selection, but they sometimes informally express their views on candidates. Principals have some say in the distribution of district resources, mainly through budgets they submit to the central administration.

Parent organizations are sometimes effective influencing school decisions. They have been concerned primarily with school closings.

Quality of Instruction

Additional learning opportunities for gifted students are rated fair to good. The program is less effective at the elementary level than at the secondary level. One way in which very bright high school students (and others, too) are benefitted is through a special school set up to teach those subjects that individual schools can't because of insufficient students. For example, at one of the district's four high schools, two or three gifted students might want to study Russian, or perhaps astronomy in depth. Their school cannot offer the class because of too few students. However, the special school might round up a dozen or more students from the four high schools and be able to offer the course. While the district offers remedial instruction, the additional instruction for low-achieving students is rated only fair. The curriculum for students going on to college is considered good, and the curriculum for students heading for the job market is rated fair.

Minority students' educational needs are not adequately met, according to the observers. The main problem is that students are put on "tracks" in the early grades, and many minority students are placed on a low-level track that does not prepare them for college if they should later choose to go. "It is extremely difficult for students to get off a track," said an observer, "and, therefore, a number of potentially able minority students are poorly prepared."

Quality of School Environment

The level of classroom disruption and vandalism is low, and the quality of building maintenance and repair is good.

GUILFORD COUNTY

ADDRESS OF CENTRAL OFFICE:
120 Franklin Boulevard, Greensboro, NC 27401
ESI:43

STATISTICAL PROFILE	DATA	ESI
Grade organization: K–5/6–8/9–12		
Percentage of schools built before 1955	23%	
Total enrollment	23,780	
Average Daily Attendance (ADA)	97%	10
Current expense per pupil in ADA	$2,995	4
Dropout rate	22%	1
Percentage of eligible students who took the SAT	57%	9
Average combined score on SAT	860	2
Percentage of graduates who enrolled in 2- or 4-year colleges	67%	
Percentage of students who passed the state reading test	97%	
Percentage of students who passed the state math test	95%	
Teacher–student ratio in elementary grades	1:25	5
Teacher–student ratio in secondary grades	1:29	0
Counselor–student ratio in secondary grades	1:390	2
Number of students per music specialist in elementary grades	1,018	0
Number of students per art specialist in elementary grades	None	
Number of volumes in senior high school libraries (average)	12,360	
Beginning teacher's salary	$16,886	
Maximum teacher's salary	$28,865	
Average years of experience among teachers	13	
Number of students suspended and expelled	868	
Subjects in which Advanced Placement courses are offered:	10	10
American History, Art Studio, Biology, Calculus, Chemistry, English Language & Composition, English Literature & Composition, European History, French, Spanish		

FAIR APPRAISAL

Quality of School Leadership

Principals are chosen primarily for their educational leadership ability, and the quality of leadership is generally uniform throughout the county. However, the tenure system prevents the dismissal of some less able principals, and they may be shuffled from one school to another and in and out of supervisory posts in the central office. Parents and teachers do not take part in screening principal candidates. Principals have a limited voice in deciding how the district's resources will be distributed among the schools.

Parents and other citizens are an effective influence on district decision-making. Not only is the District Council of PTAs a strong voice, but dozens of parents, business and community leaders, and representatives of colleges in the area have joined teachers and administrators for an ongoing, extensive examination of all aspects of the system. The coalition, known as Century Alliance, already has been influential in up-grading the high school curriculum.

Quality of Instruction

Observers rate the opportunities for gifted students as excellent, thanks to an overhaul of the program during the last two years. Prior to the revision, said an observer, bright students in the lower grades were excused from regular classes for part of a day and given "busy work." The enrichment is now much more productive, the observer said. Instruction for low-achieving students is good. The curriculum for students going on to college is considered excellent. Again, a major revision broadened the curriculum and added more high-level courses. The curriculum for students planning on jobs after graduation is good, but, according to an observer, "needs improvement."

Observers believe the district adequately meets the educational needs of minority students. Students are not bused for integration, but, according to an observer, neighborhood schools are, for the most part, naturally integrated.

Quality of School Environment

The level of classroom disruption and vandalism is very low, and the quality of building maintenance and repair is termed good to excellent.

HIGH POINT

ADDRESS OF CENTRAL OFFICE:
P.O. Box 789, High Point, NC 27261
ESI:42

STATISTICAL PROFILE	DATA	ESI
Grade organization: K–5/6–8/9–12		
Percentage of schools built before 1955	25%	
Total enrollment	8,380	
Average Daily Attendance (ADA)	95%	8
Current expense per pupil in ADA	$2,970	4
Dropout rate	36%	0
Percentage of eligible students who took the SAT	65%	10
Average combined score on SAT	842	1
Percentage of graduates who enrolled in 2- or 4-year colleges	64%	
Percentage of students who passed the state reading test	99%	
Percentage of students who passed the state math test	99%	
Teacher–student ratio in elementary grades	1:24	6
Teacher–student ratio in secondary grades	1:26	2
Counselor–student ratio in secondary grades	1:300	6
Number of students per music specialist in elementary grades	700	1
Number of students per art specialist in elementary grades	700	
Number of volumes in senior high school library	†	
Beginning teacher's salary	$17,906	
Maximum teacher's salary	$30,861	
Average years of experience among teachers	15	
Number of students suspended and expelled	1,851	
Subjects in which Advanced Placement courses are offered: American History, Biology, Calculus, English	4	4

†The district did not supply a statistic, but stated that the figure meets regional accrediting standards.

Quality of School Leadership

The School Board hires principals mostly for their educational leadership ability. The quality of leadership is uniform from school to school. Parents and teachers do not take part in screening principal candidates. However, principals have some say in the allotment of resources to their school.

Parent organizations are sometimes effective influencing school decisions.

Quality of Instruction

Additional learning opportunities for gifted students are rated good. One observer felt the gifted program in the elementary grades needs to emphasize math and science more than it does. Observers rate as excellent additional instruction for low-achieving students. The curricula for college-bound students and job-bound students are considered good. "A number of students have gained early admission to first-rate colleges," said an observer.

High Point consists mostly of low-income and high-income families, said an observer, with not too many families in the middle-income category. However, the observer said, students from low-income families have "the same learning opportunities and resources as students from high-income families."

Quality of School Environment

Classroom disruption and vandalism are not problems. The quality of building maintenance and repair is good.

RANDOLPH COUNTY

ADDRESS OF CENTRAL OFFICE:
2222 Fayetteville Street, Asheboro, NC 27203
ESI:12*

STATISTICAL PROFILE	DATA	ESI
Grade organization: †		
Percentage of schools built before 1955	26%	
Total enrollment	13,741	
Average Daily Attendance (ADA)	95%	8
Current expense per pupil in ADA	$2,191	0
Dropout rate	37%	0
Percentage of eligible students who took the SAT	10%	0
Average combined score on SAT	††	0*
Percentage of graduates who enrolled in 2- or 4-year colleges	35%	
Percentage of students who passed the state reading test	98%	
Percentage of students who passed the state math test	96%	
Teacher–student ratio in elementary grades	1:26	4
Teacher–student ratio in secondary grades	1:31	0
Counselor–student ratio in secondary grades	1:493	0
Number of students per music specialist in elementary grades	800	0
Number of students per art specialist in elementary grades	600	
Number of volumes in senior high school library	10,955	
Beginning teacher's salary	$16,700	
Maximum teacher's salary	$27,730	
Average years of experience among teachers	9	
Number of students suspended and expelled	478	
Subjects in which Advanced Placement courses are offered:	None	0

† The district has three patterns: K–3/4–5/6–8/9–12, K–5/6–8/9–12 and K–8/9–12.
††The district misinterpreted this statistic.

FAIR APPRAISAL

Quality of School Leadership
Most principals hired by the district demonstrate educational leadership ability, and the quality of leadership does not vary greatly from school to school. Parents and teachers do not screen principal candidates, but principals have some voice in deciding what resources their school will get.

Parent organizations are sometimes effective influencing school decisions. Most recently, they were influential in getting the district to adopt a middle school concept (grades 6–8).

Quality of Instruction
Additional learning opportunities for gifted students are considered good, and so is the additional instruction for low-achieving students. The college-preparatory curriculum is rated good, and the curriculum for students preparing for jobs is called excellent.

Quality of School Environment
The level of classroom disruption and vandalism tends to be on the high side; vandalism is more serious than classroom disruption. The quality of building maintenance and repair is good.

ROCKINGHAM COUNTY

ADDRESS OF CENTRAL OFFICE:
P.O. Box 8, Wentworth, NC 27375
ESI:42

STATISTICAL PROFILE	DATA	ESI
Grade organization: K–6/7–8/9–12		
Percentage of schools built before 1955	85%	
Total enrollment	3,779	
Average Daily Attendance (ADA)	94%	7
Current expense per pupil in ADA	$2,566	1
Dropout rate	42%	0
Percentage of eligible students who took the SAT	33%	4
Average combined score on SAT	828	1
Percentage of graduates who enrolled in 2- or 4-year colleges	63%	
Percentage of students who passed the state reading test	94%	
Percentage of students who passed the state math test	92%	
Teacher–student ratio in elementary grades	1:19	9
Teacher–student ratio in secondary grades	1:16	10
Counselor–student ratio in secondary grades	1:327	4
Number of students per music specialist in elementary grades	608	3
Number of students per art specialist in elementary grades	None	
Number of volumes in senior high school library	12,000	
Beginning teacher's salary	$16,700	
Maximum teacher's salary	$27,730	
Average years of experience among teachers	18	
Number of students suspended and expelled	348	
Subjects in which Advanced Placement courses are offered:	3	3
Calculus, English, European History		

FAIR APPRAISAL

Quality of School Leadership
Most principals have been hired because of their educational leadership ability, and the quality of leadership does not vary greatly from school to school. Parents and teachers do not take part in principal selection. However, principals have some say on how resources are allotted to the schools.

Parent organizations are sometimes influential in district decision-making.

Quality of Instruction
There are some special classes for gifted students, and the additional opportunities for gifted students are rated good. The additional instruction for low-achieving students is fair. Also considered fair is the curriculum for college-bound students. However, the curriculum for students preparing for the job market is rated good.

Quality of School Environment
The incidence of classroom disruption and vandalism is low, but the quality of building maintenance and repair is fair. "The district doesn't have the money to keep up with major repairs," said an observer.

WINSTON-SALEM/FORSYTH COUNTY

ADDRESS OF CENTRAL OFFICE:
P.O. Box 2513, Winston-Salem, NC 27102
ESI:70

STATISTICAL PROFILE	DATA	ESI
Grade organization: K–5/6–8/9–12		
Percentage of schools built before 1955	23%	
Total enrollment	38,847	
Average Daily Attendance (ADA)	96%	9
Current expense per pupil in ADA	$3,339	5
Dropout rate	15%	8
Percentage of eligible students who took the SAT	53%	8
Average combined score on SAT	840	1
Percentage of graduates who enrolled in 2- or 4-year colleges	67%	
Percentage of students who passed the state reading test	99%	
Percentage of students who passed the state math test	99%	
Teacher–student ratio in elementary grades	1:13	10
Teacher–student ratio in secondary grades	1:18	10
Counselor–student ratio in secondary grades	1:400	2
Number of students per music specialist in elementary grades	400	7
Number of students per art specialist in elementary grades	None	
Number of volumes in senior high school libraries (average)	14,494	
Beginning teacher's salary	$18,000	
Maximum teacher's salary	$31,540	
Average years of experience among teachers	9	
Number of students suspended and expelled	6,053	
Subjects in which Advanced Placement courses are offered:	21	10
American History, Art History, Art Studio (Drawing), Art Studio (General), Biology, Calculus AB, Calculus BC, Chemistry, English Language & Composition, English Literature & Composition, European History, French Language, French Literature, German Language, German Literature, Latin, Music Listening & Literature, Music Theory, Physics C (Mechanics), Spanish Language, Spanish Literature		

Quality of School Leadership

The School Board hires principals who demonstrate educational leadership ability, and the quality of leadership does not vary greatly from school to school. Parents have no say in principal selection, but principals have some say in resource distribution.

Parent organizations are sometimes effective influencing the decisions of school officials.

Quality of Instruction

Additional learning opportunities for gifted students are rated excellent. Most schools have at least one class designed for academically gifted students. In the past, gifted students were completely separated from other students in all classes. That has changed so that only the "super gifted" are in classes with only their peers; most gifted students mix at least half the school day with other students. Additional instruction for low-achieving students is fair. It's a problem "they haven't worked out yet," said an observer. The college-preparatory curriculum is considered excellent, and the curriculum for students going into the world of work is rated good. The district has an excellent career center, an observer said, "but students must get there on their own. If a student does not have a car or someone to drive him/her, the student cannot attend; there is no busing."

Quality of School Environment

Classroom disruption and vandalism are not problems, but the quality of building maintenance and repair is rated only fair. At least three schools are in "very bad shape." The School Board was considering a bond issue for needed improvements in 1987–88.

METROPOLITAN AREA

Houston, TX

Eleven districts in the Houston Metropolitan Area completed Statistical Profiles.
Districts in this area can be compared with districts in the Dallas and San Antonio, TX
Metropolitan Areas. Note, however, that San Antonio does not have a single city district.

AREA AT A GLANCE

SCHOOL DISTRICT	ENROLLMENT	ESI
Alvin	9,280	43
Cypress–Fairbanks	32,035	44
Deer Park	8,815	58
Galena Park	13,500	41
Goose Creek	16,611	59
Houston	193,889	30
Humble	16,814	42
Katy	15,978	70
Pasadena	35,000	48
Spring Branch	24,626	39
Tomball	4,250	64

ALVIN

ADDRESS OF CENTRAL OFFICE:
605 West House Street, Alvin, TX 77511
ESI:43

STATISTICAL PROFILE	DATA	ESI
Grade organization: K–3/4–6/7–8/9–12		
Percentage of schools built before 1955	5%	
Total enrollment	9,280	
Average Daily Attendance (ADA)	95%	8
Current expense per pupil in ADA	$2,080	0
Dropout rate	27%	0
Percentage of eligible students who took the SAT	62%	10
Average combined score on SAT	965	7
Percentage of graduates who enrolled in 2- or 4-year colleges	62%	
Percentage of students who passed the state reading test	NK	
Percentage of students who passed the state math test	NK	
Teacher–student ratio in elementary grades	1:24	6
Teacher–student ratio in secondary grades	1:19	9
Counselor–student ratio in secondary grades	1:499	0
Number of students per music specialist in elementary grades	601	3
Number of students per art specialist in elementary grades	1,053	
Number of volumes in senior high school library	27,400	
Beginning teacher's salary	$19,400	
Maximum teacher's salary	$30,100	
Average years of experience among teachers	7	
Number of students suspended and expelled	347	
Subjects in which Advanced Placement courses are offered:	None	0

FAIR APPRAISAL

Quality of School Leadership

The School Board primarily considers educational leadership ability when judging candidates for principal. The quality of leadership is generally good and uniform throughout the system. Parents and teachers may informally make their views known about principal candidates, but they take no part in screening candidates. Principals, however, have a great deal to say about the manner in which resources are distributed to the schools.

Parent organizations are sometimes effective influencing decision-making.

Quality of Instruction

Additional learning opportunities for gifted students are rated excellent. An enriched curriculum and special classes are offered. Additional instruction for low-achieving students also is considered excellent. The program features a number of "one-on-one relationships," said an observer. The curricula for college-bound students and job-bound students are rated good.

Quality of School Environment

The level of classroom disruption and vandalism is low, and the quality of building maintenance and repair is excellent.

CYPRESS–FAIRBANKS

ADDRESS OF CENTRAL OFFICE:
P.O. Box 40040, Houston, TX 77240
ESI:44

STATISTICAL PROFILE	DATA	ESI
Grade organization: K–5/6–8/9–12		
Percentage of schools built before 1955	5%	
Total enrollment	32,035	
Average Daily Attendance (ADA)	93%	6
Current expense per pupil in ADA	$3,962	3
Dropout rate	NK	0
Percentage of eligible students who took the SAT	58%	9
Average combined score on SAT	905	4
Percentage of graduates who enrolled in 2- or 4-year colleges	56%	
Percentage of students who passed the state reading test	98%	
Percentage of students who passed the state math test	99%	
Teacher–student ratio in elementary grades	1:17	10
Teacher–student ratio in secondary grades	1:16	10
Counselor–student ratio in secondary grades	1:400	2
Number of students per music specialist in elementary grades	None	0
Number of students per art specialist in elementary grades	None	0
Number of volumes in senior high school libraries (average)	32,000	
Beginning teacher's salary	$19,000	
Maximum teacher's salary	$32,700	
Average years of experience among teachers	8	
Number of students suspended and expelled	458	
Subjects in which Advanced Placement courses are offered:	None	0

FAIR APPRAISAL

Quality of School Leadership

Internal politics play a major part in principal selection; the "old boy network" is very much in operation, said one person. Because of this, the quality of leadership varies greatly. Parents and teachers have no say in principal selection, but principals exercise some influence over resource distribution.

Parent organizations are not effective influencing school policy decisions. The main reason, an observer said, is that the School Board "pays little attention to them."

Quality of Instruction

Additional learning opportunities for gifted students are fair to good, while additional instruction for low-achieving students is rated good to excellent. An observer praised the program for low-achieving students because it is designed to help students reach higher academic standards; the district does not have "dummy classes," that consist of watered-down courses, an observer said. The curriculum for college-bound students is considered fair to good. It is unusual for a district of this size not to offer any Advanced Placement courses. The curriculum for students preparing for a job after graduation is called good. Particularly strong are vocational courses in agriculture.

Quality of School Environment

Classroom disruption and vandalism are not problems. The quality of building maintenance and repair is excellent. Most of the school buildings have been constructed within the last 10 years as the population mushroomed in a once rural region. Not only are the buildings new, but one observer described them as "gorgeous."

DEER PARK

ADDRESS OF CENTRAL OFFICE:
203 Ivy Street, Deer Park, TX 77536
ESI:58

STATISTICAL PROFILE	DATA	ESI
Grade organization: K–5/6–8/9–12		
Percentage of schools built before 1955	25%	
Total enrollment	8,815	
Average Daily Attendance (ADA)	94%	7
Current expense per pupil in ADA	$4,270	10
Dropout rate	11%	10
Percentage of eligible students who took the ACT	25%	2
Average combined score on ACT	19†	5
Percentage of graduates who enrolled in 2- or 4-year colleges	52%	
Percentage of students who passed the state reading test	98%	
Percentage of students who passed the state math test	98%	
Teacher–student ratio in elementary grades	1:22	8
Teacher–student ratio in secondary grades	1:25	3
Counselor–student ratio in secondary grades	1:500	0
Number of students per music specialist in elementary grades	327	9
Number of students per art specialist in elementary grades	None	0
Number of volumes in senior high school libraries (average)	17,450	
Beginning teacher's salary	$22,500	
Maximum teacher's salary	$34,700	
Average years of experience among teachers	12	
Number of students suspended and expelled	204	
Subjects in which Advanced Placement courses are offered: American History, Calculus, English, Science	4	4

†Most Texas districts report SAT scores. The average composite ACT score for the state in 1985–86 was 17.1.

FAIR APPRAISAL

Quality of School Leadership

Principals are mostly selected for their educational ability. Turnover of principals is not great; many of them have been in the system for a number of years. The quality of leadership is generally uniform throughout the system. Teachers and parents do not screen principal candidates. Principals have some say, but not much, in how district resources are divided among the schools. A new superintendent was scheduled to be hired in 1987–88.

Parents and other citizens are generally effective influencing school decisions. The School Board is receptive to suggestions and constructive criticism, said an observer. The assistant superintendent meets regularly with a parent-citizen advisory committee.

Quality of Instruction

Additional learning opportunities for gifted students and additional instruction for low-achieving students are rated excellent. Special classes help in both situations. The curricula for students going on to college and those heading into the world of work are considered good. The quality instruction is attributed to the district's wealth by one observer. Many major industries keep revenue high but homeowners' taxes low. Teachers' salaries are among the highest in the state.

Quality of School Environment

The level of classroom disruption and vandalism is very low, and the quality of building maintenance and repair is excellent. "The buildings and grounds are beautiful," said an observer. Both high schools have swimming pools.

GALENA PARK

ADDRESS OF CENTRAL OFFICE:
P.O. Box 565, Galena Park, TX 77547
ESI:41

STATISTICAL PROFILE	DATA	ESI
Grade organization: Pre-K–5/6–8/9–12		
Percentage of schools built before 1955	63%	
Total enrollment	13,500	
Average Daily Attendance (ADA)	95%	8
Current expense per pupil in ADA	$2,948	3
Dropout rate	NK	0
Percentage of eligible students who took the SAT	23%	2
Average combined score on SAT	880	3
Percentage of graduates who enrolled in 2- or 4-year colleges	39%	
Percentage of students who passed the state reading test	95%	
Percentage of students who passed the state math test	94%	
Teacher–student ratio in elementary grades	1:20	10
Teacher–student ratio in secondary grades	1:17	10
Counselor–student ratio in secondary grades	1:365	3
Number of students per music specialist in elementary grades	723	1
Number of students per art specialist in elementary grades	None	0
Number of volumes in senior high school libraries (average)	19,963	
Beginning teacher's salary	$19,200	
Maximum teacher's salary	$30,370	
Average years of experience among teachers	10	
Number of students suspended and expelled	598	
Subjects in which Advanced Placement courses are offered: English	1	1

FAIR APPRAISAL

Quality of School Leadership

Principals are hired primarily because of their educational ability, and the quality of leadership is generally uniform throughout the system. While parents and teachers have no say in principal selection, principals have some say (mainly through budget requests) about the allotment of district resources.

Parent organizations are sometimes effective in school decision-making.

Quality of Instruction

Additional learning opportunities for gifted students and additional instruction for low-achieving students are rated good. Also considered good are the curricula preparing students for college and for the world of work. A regional vocational education center is considered outstanding.

Quality of School Environment

The level of classroom disruption and vandalism is low, and the quality of building maintenance and repair is good.

GOOSE CREEK

ADDRESS OF CENTRAL OFFICE:
P.O. Box 30, Baytown, TX 77522
ESI:59

STATISTICAL PROFILE	DATA	ESI
Grade organization: K–5/6–8/9–12		
Percentage of schools built before 1955	80%	
Total enrollment	16,611	
Average Daily Attendance (ADA)	96%	9
Current expense per pupil in ADA	$4,327	10
Dropout rate	22%	1
Percentage of eligible students who took the SAT	48%	7
Average combined score on SAT	874	4
Percentage of graduates who enrolled in 2- or 4-year colleges	59%	
Percentage of students who passed the state reading test	85%	
Percentage of students who passed the state math test	82%	
Teacher–student ratio in elementary grades	1:18	10
Teacher–student ratio in secondary grades	1:19	9
Counselor–student ratio in secondary grades	1:550	0
Number of students per music specialist in elementary grades	325	9
Number of students per art specialist in elementary grades	325	
Number of volumes in senior high school libraries (average)	35,350	
Beginning teacher's salary	$22,000	
Maximum teacher's salary	$37,100	
Average years of experience among teachers	11	
Number of students suspended and expelled	840	
Subjects in which Advanced Placement courses are offered:	None	0

FAIR APPRAISAL

Quality of School Leadership
Primarily, principals are hired because of their educational leadership ability; the quality of leadership does not vary greatly from school to school. Teachers and parents are not involved in the screening of principal candidates, but principals are somewhat involved in deciding how the district's resources will be divided among the schools.

Parents are sometimes effective in school decision-making.

Quality of Instruction
Even in kindergarten, students are initially screened to determine who might be gifted. Starting in grade 3, gifted students are separated from other students and attend special classes as a group (except for art, music and some nonacademic subjects such as physical education). The program is rated excellent. Considered good is additional instruction for low-achieving students. The curricula for students going on to college and for those going into the world of work are rated excellent. A special school enables potential dropouts who already have jobs to continue their education; classes are adjusted to students' work schedules.

Quality of School Environment
The incidence of classroom disruption and vandalism is low. A strong policy on discipline guides teachers and administrators step by step. Although many of the buildings are old, the quality of maintenance and repair is excellent. One observer was worried this condition could change if future budget cuts are made, which is feared.

HOUSTON

ADDRESS OF CENTRAL OFFICE:
3830 Richmond Avenue, Houston, TX 77027
ESI:30

STATISTICAL PROFILE	DATA	ESI
Grade organization: K–5/6–8/9–12		
Percentage of schools built before 1955	43%	
Total enrollment	193,889	
Average Daily Attendance (ADA)	95%	8
Current expense per pupil in ADA	$2,908	3
Dropout rate	40%	0
Percentage of eligible students who took the SAT	37%	5
Average combined score on SAT	862	2
Percentage of graduates who enrolled in 2- or 4-year colleges	40%	
Percentage of students who passed the state reading test	91%	
Percentage of students who passed the state math test	89%	
Teacher–student ratio in elementary grades	1:24	6
Teacher–student ratio in secondary grades	1:28	0
Counselor–student ratio in secondary grades	1:500	0
Number of students per music specialist in elementary grades	500	5
Number of students per art specialist in elementary grades	1,000	
Number of volumes in senior high school library	†	
Beginning teacher's salary	$19.100	
Maximum teacher's salary	$33,180	
Average years of experience among teachers	13	
Number of students suspended and expelled	9,794	
Subjects in which Advanced Placement courses are offered:	None	1

†The district's statistic here is a minimum of 10 volumes per student.

Quality of School Leadership

Major factors in principal selection are a candidate's "race or ethnic background and his/her popularity in the community served by the school," according to observers. Once hired, the principal's prior involvement in the community can "sometimes work to the advantage of the students, but not always," said an observer, particularly if educational leadership ability has been largely overlooked. The quality of leadership varies greatly from school to school. Parents and teachers are not involved in the principal selection process, but principals have quite a lot to say about how resources are allotted to the schools.

Parent organizations are not very effective influencing school decisions.

Quality of Instruction

Additional learning opportunities for gifted students are rated excellent. In addition to special classes, exceptionally bright students at all grade levels can profit from enriched instruction at a variety of magnet schools, concentrating on such subjects as math, science and the arts. Additional instruction for low-achieving students is rated fair to poor. College preparation varies widely throughout the system, but overall observers consider the curriculum good to excellent. The curriculum for students preparing for the job market is fair.

The district does not adequately meet the educational needs of minority students, who comprise 84 percent of the school population. One observer pointed out, however, that "failure to meet many students' educational needs has more to do with which school students attend rather than whether they are black, Hispanic or white."

Quality of School Environment

While some schools have had problems with disruptive students, overall, the observers said, the level of classroom disruption and vandalism is on the low side. The quality of building maintenance and repair is good, especially for a district of this size.

HUMBLE

ADDRESS OF CENTRAL OFFICE:
P.O. Box 2000, Humble, TX 77347
ESI:42

STATISTICAL PROFILE	DATA	ESI
Grade organization: K–5/6–8/9–12		
Percentage of schools built before 1955	5%	
Total enrollment	16,814	
Average Daily Attendance (ADA)	96%	9
Current expense per pupil in ADA	$3,249	5
Dropout rate	NK	0
Percentage of eligible students who took the SAT	NK	0
Average combined score on SAT	915	5
Percentage of graduates who enrolled in 2- or 4-year colleges	70%	
Percentage of students who passed the state reading test	95%	
Percentage of students who passed the state math test	95%	
Teacher–student ratio in elementary grades	1:22	8
Teacher–student ratio in secondary grades	1:21	7
Counselor–student ratio in secondary grades	1:365	3
Number of students per music specialist in elementary grades	627	3
Number of students per art specialist in elementary grades	None	
Number of volumes in senior high school libraries (average)	15,989	
Beginning teacher's salary	$19,000	
Maximum teacher's salary	$29,000	
Average years of experience among teachers	10	
Number of students suspended and expelled	4†	
Subjects in which Advanced Placement courses are offered: Calculus, English	2	2

†This statistic seems unusually low.

FAIR APPRAISAL

Quality of School Leadership
Principals are hired mainly because of their educational leadership ability, and the quality of leadership does not vary greatly from school to school. Parents and teachers do not screen principal candidates. Principals, however, have some say about the distribution of the district's resources.

Parents are sometimes effective influencing school policy decisions.

Quality of Instruction
Special classes help make the program for gifted students excellent. Additional instruction for low-achieving students is considered fair to good. The college-preparatory curriculum is rated excellent, and the curriculum for students planning on jobs after graduation is called good.

Quality of School Environment
The level of classroom disruption and vandalism is low, and the quality of building maintenance and repair is good. Many schools have been built in the last 10 years.

KATY

ADDRESS OF CENTRAL OFFICE:
P.O. Box 159, Katy, TX 77492
ESI:70

STATISTICAL PROFILE	DATA	ESI
Grade organization: †		
Percentage of schools built before 1955	16%	
Total enrollment	15,978	
Average Daily Attendance (ADA)	96%	9
Current expense per pupil in ADA	$4,609	10
Dropout rate	3%	10
Percentage of eligible students who took the SAT	64%	10
Average combined score on SAT	888	4
Percentage of graduates who enrolled in 2- or 4-year colleges	70%	
Percentage of students who passed the state reading test	95%	
Percentage of students who passed the state math test	95%	
Teacher–student ratio in elementary grades	1:21	9
Teacher–student ratio in secondary grades	1:17	10
Counselor–student ratio in secondary grades	1:400	2
Number of students per music specialist in elementary grades	546	5
Number of students per art specialist in elementary grades	764	
Number of volumes in senior high school libraries (average)	15,856	
Beginning teacher's salary	$19,200	
Maximum teacher's salary	$31,800	
Average years of experience among teachers	5	
Number of students suspended and expelled	19††	
Subjects in which Advanced Placement courses are offered: American Government	1	1

† This district misinterpreted this statistic.
††This figure seems unusually low.

FAIR APPRAISAL

Quality of School Leadership
The School Board hires principals primarily because of their educational leadership ability, and the quality of leadership does not vary greatly from school to school. Parents and teachers do not take part in the screening of principal candidates. Principals, however, have some influence over the distribution of resources to the schools.

Parent organizations are effective influencing policy decisions. An advisory committee composed of parents and other citizens meets regularly with the superintendent.

Quality of Instruction
Gifted students in the elementary grades are excused from regular classes one day a week for special instruction; honors classes are available at the middle and high schools. Overall, additional learning opportunities for gifted students are rated good. Also considered good is additional instruction for low-achieving students. A fairly new tutorial program has "greatly improved" this instruction, said an observer. The curricula for students going to college and for students entering the job market are called good. The vocational education program has a "good record for job-placement," said an observer.

Quality of School Environment
Classroom disruption and vandalism are not problems, and the quality of building and maintenance is good. Because of an expanding enrollment, the district has built a number of new schools in the last ten years.

PASADENA

ADDRESS OF CENTRAL OFFICE:
P.O. Box 1799, Pasadena, TX 77501
ESI:48

STATISTICAL PROFILE	DATA	ESI
Grade organization: †		
Percentage of schools built before 1955	33%	
Total enrollment	35,000	
Average Daily Attendance (ADA)	97%	10
Current expense per pupil in ADA	$3,002	4
Dropout rate	NK	0
Percentage of eligible students who took the SAT	42%	6
Average combined score on SAT	893	4
Percentage of graduates who enrolled in 2- or 4-year colleges	45%	
Percentage of students who passed the state reading test	95%	
Percentage of students who passed the state math test	95%	
Teacher–student ratio in elementary grades	1:21	9
Teacher–student ratio in secondary grades	1:19	9
Counselor–student ratio in secondary grades	1:472	0
Number of students per music specialist in elementary grades	454	6
Number of students per art specialist in elementary grades	None	
Number of volumes in senior high school libraries (average)	30,000	
Beginning teacher's salary	$20,000	
Maximum teacher's salary	$34,000	
Average years of experience among teachers	11	
Number of students suspended and expelled	559	
Subjects in which Advanced Placement courses are offered:	None	0

†The district misinterpreted the statistic.

Quality of School Leadership
For the most part, principals are selected for their educational leadership ability. The quality of leadership does not vary greatly throughout the system. Parents and teachers have no say in screening principal candidates, but principals have a great deal to say about the way the district's resources are divided among the schools.

Parents are generally an effective influence on school decision-making. Groups of students, parents and other community residents meet regularly with the superintendent.

Quality of Instruction
Additional opportunities for gifted students and additional instruction for low-achieving students are rated good. A goal for 1987–88 is to better identify those students who are potential dropouts and low-achievers and "give them the necessary help earlier in their school life," said an observer. The college-preparatory curriculum is considered good (although it is unusual for a district of this size not to offer any Advanced Placement courses), and the curriculum for students heading for the job market is called good to excellent.

Quality of School Environment
The level of classroom disruption and vandalism has "decreased significantly" since the district created the Guidance Center and added some police officers to patrol buildings and grounds, according to observers. The Guidance Center is where disruptive students are sent. The quality of building maintenance and repair is good.

SPRING BRANCH

ADDRESS OF CENTRAL OFFICE:
P.O. Box 19432, Houston, TX 77224
ESI:39

STATISTICAL PROFILE	DATA	ESI
Grade organization: †		
Percentage of schools built before 1955	NK	
Total enrollment	24,626	
Average Daily Attendance (ADA)	95%	8
Current expense per pupil in ADA	$4,224	10
Dropout rate	NK	0
Percentage of eligible students who took the SAT	NK	0
Average combined score on SAT	953	7
Percentage of graduates who enrolled in 2- or 4-year colleges	80%	
Percentage of students who passed the state reading test	80%	
Percentage of students who passed the state math test	81%	
Teacher–student ratio in elementary grades	1:22	8
Teacher–student ratio in secondary grades	1:22	6
Counselor–student ratio in secondary grades	NK	0
Number of students per music specialist in elementary grades	NK	0
Number of students per art specialist in elementary grades	NK	
Number of volumes in senior high school library	NK	
Beginning teacher's salary	$19,000	
Maximum teacher's salary	$46,410	
Average years of experience among teachers	NK	
Number of students suspended and expelled	NK	
Subjects in which Advanced Placement courses are offered:	None	0

†The district misinterpreted this statistic.

FAIR APPRAISAL

Quality of School Leadership

In the immediate past, internal politics (allegiance to the superintendent) played a major role in principal selection. However, a new superintendent is hiring principals primarily on the basis of educational leadership ability. As a consequence of past policies, said the observers, the quality of leadership varies greatly from school to school and from section to section. "Watch out for the schools north of Interstate #10," said an observer, because they tend to have the least able administrators.

Parents and teachers do not aid in screening principal candidates, and principals have very little influence over how district resources will be allotted.

Parents are sometimes effective influencing policy decisions by school officials.

Quality of Instruction

Additional learning opportunities for gifted students are rated good, although one observer complained that a "rigid" tracking system prevents some "late-bloomers" from being included in the program. Additional instruction for low-achieving students is rated fair to poor. Although the district does not offer any Advanced Placement courses, more than 20 honors courses are offered in the high schools, and the college-preparatory curriculum is considered good. The curriculum preparing students for the world of work also is rated good.

Observers believe the district does not adequately meet the educational needs of minority students. The district "does not direct sufficient resources to schools with high minority enrollments," said an observer.

Quality of School Environment

The level of classroom disruption and vandalism is on the low side, but problems exist in some schools. The quality of building maintenance and repair is excellent.

TOMBALL

ADDRESS OF CENTRAL OFFICE:
221 West Main Street, Tomball, TX 77375
ESI:64

STATISTICAL PROFILE	DATA	ESI
Grade organization: Pre-K–6/7–8/9–12		
Percentage of schools built before 1955	50%	
Total enrollment	4,250	
Average Daily Attendance (ADA)	98%	10
Current expense per pupil in ADA	$3,646	7
Dropout rate	7%	10
Percentage of eligible students who took the SAT	65%	10
Average combined score on SAT	863	2
Percentage of graduates who enrolled in 2- or 4-year colleges	65%	
Percentage of students who passed the state reading test	99%	
Percentage of students who passed the state math test	99%	
Teacher–student ratio in elementary grades	1:20	10
Teacher–student ratio in secondary grades	1:20	8
Counselor–student ratio in secondary grades	1:300	6
Number of students per music specialist in elementary grades	700	1
Number of students per art specialist in elementary grades	700	
Number of volumes in senior high school library	18,000	
Beginning teacher's salary	$19,540	
Maximum teacher's salary	$30,000	
Average years of experience among teachers	13	
Number of students suspended and expelled	50	
Subjects in which Advanced Placement courses are offered:	None	0

Quality of School Leadership
Although longevity helps, according to one observer, most principals are hired because they exhibit ability as an educational leader. The quality of leadership is generally uniform throughout the system. Teachers and parents have little say about principal selection, and principals have little to say about the division of district resources among the schools.

Parent organizations are not very effective influencing school policy decisions.

Quality of Instruction
Additional learning opportunities for gifted students are considered good. In the elementary grades, exceptionally bright students are excused from regular classes for part of a day to take enriched instruction. Additional instruction for low-achieving students is rated fair, "but getting better." A recent federal grant is expected to increase the remedial instruction and student counseling. Observers think the college-preparatory curriculum is fair and the curriculum for students going into the job market is good.

Quality of School Environment
The level of classroom disruption and vandalism is low, and the quality of building maintenance and repair is excellent.

METROPOLITAN AREA

Indianapolis, IN

Completed Statistical Profiles were received from six districts, and Fair Appraisals alone were received for three districts. Districts in this area can be compared with those in the Cincinnati and Columbus, OH Metropolitan Areas.

AREA AT A GLANCE

SCHOOL DISTRICT	ENROLLMENT	ESI
Carmel Clay	7,342	
Franklin	3,400	54
Greenfield	3,600	57
Indianapolis	50,628	44
Lawrence Township	9,137	68
Perry Township	11,398	55*
Plainfield	2,833	
Warren Township	9,089	52
Washington Township	9,564	

Indicates district misinterpretation of one or more statistics in the ESI. For each misinterpreted statistic, a score of 0 was given instead of a possible score of 0 to 10 points.

CARMEL CLAY

ADDRESS OF CENTRAL OFFICE:
5201 East 131st Street, Carmel, IN 46032
ESI:None†

STATISTICAL PROFILE	DATA	ESI
Grade organization:		
Percentage of schools built before 1955		
Total enrollment		
Average Daily Attendance (ADA)		
Current expense per pupil in ADA		
Dropout rate		
Percentage of eligible students who took the SAT		
Average combined score on SAT		
Percentage of graduates who enrolled in 2- or 4-year colleges		
Percentage of students who passed the state reading test		
Percentage of students who passed the state math test		
Teacher–student ratio in elementary grades		
Teacher–student ratio in secondary grades		
Counselor–student ratio in secondary grades		
Number of students per music specialist in elementary grades		
Number of students per art specialist in elementary grades		
Number of volumes in senior high school library		
Beginning teacher's salary		
Maximum teacher's salary		
Average years of experience among teachers		
Number of students suspended and expelled		
Subjects in which Advanced Placement courses are offered:		

†A Statistical Profile was not received from this district.

FAIR APPRAISAL

Quality of School Leadership
The School Board hires principals mainly on the basis of their educational leadership ability, and the quality of leadership does not vary greatly from school to school. Parents and teachers may informally voice their opinions about principal candidates, but they do not screen candidates. Principals exercise considerable influence over the personnel assigned to their school, but have less say about material resources.

Parent organizations are very active and have some influence over school policy.

Quality of Instruction
Additional learning opportunities for gifted students are rated excellent. The district has a "most able program," said one observer. Additional instruction for low-achieving students is considered good. The curriculum for students preparing for college is excellent, according to observers, and the curriculum for students preparing for the world of work is good.

Quality of School Environment
The incidence of classroom disruption and vandalism is very low, and the quality of building maintenance and repair is excellent.

FRANKLIN

ADDRESS OF CENTRAL OFFICE:
998 Grizzly Cub Drive, Franklin, IN 46131
ESI:54

STATISTICAL PROFILE	DATA	ESI
Grade organization: †		
Percentage of schools built before 1955	42%	
Total enrollment	3,400	
Average Daily Attendance (ADA)	95%	8
Current expense per pupil in ADA	$1,945	0
Dropout rate	20%	3
Percentage of eligible students who took the SAT	49%	7
Average combined score on SAT	865	3
Percentage of graduates who enrolled in 2- or 4-year colleges	40%	
Percentage of students who passed the state reading test	91%	
Percentage of students who passed the state math test	92%	
Teacher–student ratio in elementary grades	1:21	9
Teacher–student ratio in secondary grades	1:19	9
Counselor–student ratio in secondary grades	1:250	8
Number of students per music specialist in elementary grades	500	5
Number of students per art specialist in elementary grades	500	
Number of volumes in senior high school library	15,994	
Beginning teacher's salary	$16,200	
Maximum teacher's salary	$29,440	
Average years of experience among teachers	14	
Number of students suspended and expelled	21	
Subjects in which Advanced Placement courses are offered: American History, English	2	2

†The district misinterpreted this statistic.

Quality of School Leadership

Principals are selected for their educational leadership ability, and the quality of leadership does not vary greatly from school to school (even though the elementary schools are roughly divided between small country schools and larger suburban schools). Parents and teachers do screen principal candidates and make recommendations to the superintendent and School Board. Principals have some say in how the district's resources will be divided among the schools.

Parent organizations' influence over decision-making by school leaders is generally effective. Parents, for example, successfully lobbied for a gifted and talented program and for changes in transportation routes so that students living out in the country were not on the buses so long.

Quality of Instruction

The gifted and talented program began in 1985–86. Since then it has been expanded, and now includes a full-time coordinator and teacher. The program is rated good and potentially excellent. Also considered good is additional instruction for low-achieving students. The curriculum for college-bound students is good and "improving." The curriculum for students heading for the job market is rated good; local vocational education has won some state awards.

Quality of School Environment

The level of classroom disruption and vandalism is very low, and the quality of building maintenance and repair is excellent.

GREENFIELD

ADDRESS OF CENTRAL OFFICE:
1 Courthouse Plaza, Greenfield, IN 46140
ESI:57

STATISTICAL PROFILE	DATA	ESI
Grade organization: K–6/7–8/9–12		
Percentage of schools built before 1955	30%	
Total enrollment	3,600	
Average Daily Attendance (ADA)	97%	10
Current expense per pupil in ADA	$1,800	0
Dropout rate	6%	10
Percentage of eligible students who took the SAT	60%	9
Average combined score on SAT	855	2
Percentage of graduates who enrolled in 2- or 4-year colleges	68%	
Percentage of students who passed the state reading test	92%	
Percentage of students who passed the state math test	92%	
Teacher–student ratio in elementary grades	1:22	8
Teacher–student ratio in secondary grades	1:26	2
Counselor–student ratio in secondary grades	1:350	4
Number of students per music specialist in elementary grades	325	9
Number of students per art specialist in elementary grades	500	
Number of volumes in senior high school library	9,477	
Beginning teacher's salary	$15,000	
Maximum teacher's salary	$29,450	
Average years of experience among teachers	11	
Number of students suspended and expelled	435	
Subjects in which Advanced Placement courses are offered: Chemistry, English, Foreign Language	3	3

Quality of School Leadership

The School Board hires principals who demonstrate educational leadership ability. The quality of leadership is uniform from school to school. Parents and teachers do not take part in the screening of principal candidates. However, principals have some influence over the distribution of district resources.

Parent organizations are sometimes effective influencing school policy decisions.

Quality of Instruction

Additional learning opportunities for gifted students are rated good. Local schools have special classes, but the county also has pooled state funds earmarked for gifted and talented to create project VISION, which offers gifted students in four small districts, including Greenfield, a variety of enrichment programs during the year. Additional instruction for low-achieving students also is considered good. The curricula for college-bound students and job-bound students are rated good.

Quality of School Environment

Classroom disruption and vandalism are not problems. The quality of building maintenance and repair is good.

INDIANAPOLIS

ADDRESS OF CENTRAL OFFICE:
120 East Walnut Street, Indianapolis, IN 46204
ESI:44

STATISTICAL PROFILE	DATA	ESI
Grade organization: †		
Percentage of schools built before 1955	60%	
Total enrollment	50,628	
Average Daily Attendance (ADA)	89%	2
Current expense per pupil in ADA	$3,515	8
Dropout rate	14%	9
Percentage of eligible students who took the SAT	30%	3
Average combined score on SAT	768	0
Percentage of graduates who enrolled in 2- or 4-year colleges	43%	
Percentage of students who passed the state reading test	70%	
Percentage of students who passed the state math test	70%	
Teacher–student ratio in elementary grades	1:26	4
Teacher–student ratio in secondary grades	1:28	0
Counselor–student ratio in secondary grades	1:389	2
Number of students per music specialist in elementary grades	332	9
Number of students per art specialist in elementary grades	437	
Number of volumes in senior high school libraries (average)	31,279	
Beginning teacher's salary	$16,167	
Maximum teacher's salary	$34,396	
Average years of experience among teachers	14	
Number of students suspended and expelled	7,057	
Subjects in which Advanced Placement courses are offered: American History, Biology, Calculus, Chemistry, Computer Science, English, Foreign Language	7	7

†The district misinterpreted this statistic.

FAIR APPRAISAL

Quality of School Leadership

Educational leadership ability is the primary criterion for selecting principals, but the School Board also considers race; racial balance is an important goal. The quality of leadership varies from school to school. The district used to require a principal candidate to have first served as a vice principal, but, according to an observer, "this is not always true at present." Parents and teachers do not screen principal candidates. Principals have some say in how district resources are allotted, but most of the disbursement is by formula.

A district-wide parents' advisory council meets twice a month with the superintendent and other district officials, and parental influence is generally considered effective.

Quality of Instruction

Additional learning opportunities for gifted students are rated good. Not only are there special classes, but students in middle and high schools may opt for a magnet school. The magnet schools emphasize science, math, performing arts, foreign languages and health professions. One observer said the only fault with the program is that because of its effort to maintain racial balance, "a number of gifted white students remain on waiting lists." Additional instruction for low-achieving students also is considered good. The curricula for college-bound students and job-bound students are rated fair to good.

The district tries very hard to meet the educational needs of minority students, but, according to an observer, "minority students generally do less well in the system."

Quality of School Environment

Classroom disruption and vandalism tend to be on the high side. A task force composed of district officials, parents, and other citizens was appointed in 1986 to study the problem; they had not made recommendations as of the start of the 1987–88 school year. The quality of building maintenance and repair is good, even though many of the buildings are quite old.

LAWRENCE TOWNSHIP

ADDRESS OF CENTRAL OFFICE:

7601 East 56th Street, Indianapolis, IN 46226
ESI:68

STATISTICAL PROFILE	DATA	ESI
Grade organization: K–5/6–8/9–12		
Percentage of schools built before 1955	27%	
Total enrollment	9,137	
Average Daily Attendance (ADA)	95%	8
Current expense per pupil in ADA	$2,600	4
Dropout rate	5%	10
Percentage of eligible students who took the SAT	69%	10
Average combined score on SAT	905	4
Percentage of graduates who enrolled in 2- or 4-year colleges	85%	
Percentage of students who passed the state reading test	90%	
Percentage of students who passed the state math test	90%	
Teacher–student ratio in elementary grades	1:21	9
Teacher–student ratio in secondary grades	1:18	10
Counselor–student ratio in secondary grades	1:340	4
Number of students per music specialist in elementary grades	495	6
Number of students per art specialist in elementary grades	495	
Number of volumes in senior high school library	17,500	
Beginning teacher's salary	$17,275	
Maximum teacher's salary	$33,929	
Average years of experience among teachers	12	
Number of students suspended and expelled	768	
Subjects in which Advanced Placement courses are offered: American History, Biology, Calculus	3	3

FAIR APPRAISAL

Quality of School Leadership
The School Board hires principals who demonstrate educational leadership ability, and the quality of leadership is uniform from school to school. Parents and teachers do not take part in selecting principals. However, principals have some say in how the resources of the district are divided among the schools.

Parent effectiveness in decision-making varies significantly from school to school.

Quality of Instruction
A special program for gifted students begins in grade 3. Also, a magnet school that concentrates on math and science caters primarily to exceptionally bright students in the elementary grades. The overall program is rated excellent. Observers call the additional instruction for low-achieving students good. The curriculum for college-bound students is considered excellent, and the curriculum for those preparing for the world of work is good.

Lawrence Township is one of several districts surrounding Indianapolis that receives a relatively small number of minority students from the city each day under a court desegregation order.

Quality of School Environment
Classroom disruption and vandalism are not problems. The quality of building maintenance and repair is good.

PERRY TOWNSHIP

ADDRESS OF CENTRAL OFFICE:
1130 East Epler Avenue, Indianapolis, IN 46227
ESI:55*

STATISTICAL PROFILE	DATA	ESI
Grade organization: K–5/6–8/9–12		
Percentage of schools built before 1955	7%	
Total enrollment	11,398	
Average Daily Attendance (ADA)	77%†	0*
Current expense per pupil in ADA	$3,374	8
Dropout rate	21%	2
Percentage of eligible students who took the SAT	51%	8
Average combined score on SAT	888	4
Percentage of graduates who enrolled in 2- or 4-year colleges	53%	
Percentage of students who passed the state reading test	91%	
Percentage of students who passed the state math test	91%	
Teacher–student ratio in elementary grades	1:20	10
Teacher–student ratio in secondary grades	1:18	10
Counselor–student ratio in secondary grades	1:258	7
Number of students per music specialist in elementary grades	460	6
Number of students per art specialist in elementary grades	460	
Number of volumes in senior high school libraries (average)	21,100	
Beginning teacher's salary	$17,700	
Maximum teacher's salary	$35,650	
Average years of experience among teachers	17	
Number of students suspended and expelled	630	
Subjects in which Advanced Placement courses are offered:	None	0

†This statistic was computed using figures supplied by the district, but it is exceptionally low and is probably inaccurate.

FAIR APPRAISAL

Quality of School Leadership
Principals are selected primarily for their educational leadership ability. The quality of leadership is generally uniform in the district's elementary and middle schools, but it varies greatly between the two high schools, according to an observer. Parents and teachers do not take part in the selection of principals, but principals have some influence over the distribution of resources to the schools.

Parent organizations are sometimes effective influencing school policy decisions.

Quality of Instruction
Additional learning opportunities for gifted students are rated good. Some enrichment courses are offered, and gifted students go on field trips more often than most students and to more interesting places. Also rated good is the additional instruction for low-achieving students. A writing lab and a reading lab help students who are having difficulty. The curriculum for college-bound students is considered excellent, but the curriculum for students preparing for the world of work is called fair.

Perry Township is included in a mandatory desegregation program in the area in which some minority students from the city are bused daily to schools in suburban districts.

Quality of School Environment
The incidence of classroom disruption and vandalism is very low and the quality of building maintenance and repair is good.

PLAINFIELD

ADDRESS OF CENTRAL OFFICE:
985 South Longfellow Drive, Plainfield, IN 46168
ESI:None†

STATISTICAL PROFILE	DATA	ESI
Grade organization:		
Percentage of schools built before 1955		
Total enrollment		
Average Daily Attendance (ADA)		
Current expense per pupil in ADA		
Dropout rate		
Percentage of eligible students who took the ACT		
Average combined score on ACT		
Percentage of graduates who enrolled in 2- or 4-year colleges		
Percentage of students who passed the state reading test		
Percentage of students who passed the state math test		
Teacher–student ratio in elementary grades		
Teacher–student ratio in secondary grades		
Counselor–student ratio in secondary grades		
Number of students per music specialist in elementary grades		
Number of students per art specialist in elementary grades		
Number of volumes in senior high school library		
Beginning teacher's salary		
Maximum teacher's salary		
Average years of experience among teachers		
Number of students suspended and expelled		
Subjects in which Advanced Placement courses are offered:		

†A Statistical Profile was not received from this district.

FAIR APPRAISAL

Quality of School Leadership
Principals are hired mostly for their educational leadership ability, and the quality of leadership does not vary greatly from school to school. Parents and teachers do not screen principal candidates. Principals, on the other hand, have a great deal to say about the allotment of district resources to the schools.

Parent organizations are quite effective influencing school policy decisions. Recently, the Parent-Teacher Organization recommended a drug awareness program for the elementary grades that was adopted by the School Board.

Quality of Instruction
Computers play an important part in special classes for gifted students, and the program is rated excellent. Additional instruction for low-achieving students is called good. The curricula for college-bound students and job-bound students are considered good. An observer complains that the district places "too much stress on sports and not enough on science."

Quality of School Environment
Classroom disruption and vandalism are not problems, and the quality of building maintenance and repair is good.

WARREN TOWNSHIP

ADDRESS OF CENTRAL OFFICE:
9301 East 18th Street, Indianapolis, IN 46229
ESI:52

STATISTICAL PROFILE	DATA	ESI
Grade organization: K–6/7–9/10–12		
Percentage of schools built before 1955	1%	
Total enrollment	9,089	
Average Daily Attendance (ADA)	97%	10
Current expense per pupil in ADA	$3,259	4
Dropout rate	29%	0
Percentage of eligible students who took the SAT	56%	9
Average combined score on SAT	874	3
Percentage of graduates who enrolled in 2- or 4-year colleges	49%	
Percentage of students who passed the state reading test	†	
Percentage of students who passed the state math test	†	
Teacher–student ratio in elementary grades	1:21	9
Teacher–student ratio in secondary grades	1:22	6
Counselor–student ratio in secondary grades	1:350	4
Number of students per music specialist in elementary grades	410	7
Number of students per art specialist in elementary grades	410	
Number of volumes in senior high school library	22,269	
Beginning teacher's salary	$18,000	
Maximum teacher's salary	$38,160	
Average years of experience among teachers	15	
Number of students suspended and expelled	384	
Subjects in which Advanced Placement courses are offered:	None	0

†The district supplied incorrect data.

FAIR APPRAISAL

Quality of School Leadership

The School Board hires principals who demonstrate educational leadership ability, and the quality of leadership does not vary greatly from school to school. Parents and teachers are asked to serve on committees that screen principal candidates. Also, principals have some influence over the resources allotted their schools.

The School Board is receptive to suggestions and constructive criticisms, and influence by parents organizations is sometimes effective.

Quality of Instruction

The district is still in the early stages of providing meaningful learning opportunities for gifted students, and observers rate the program as fair. Instruction for low-achieving students is considered good. The curriculum for students going to college and the curriculum for students bound for the world of work are rated good. A Career Center offers a wide variety of courses and programs for students not college-bound. These include work-study in a greenhouse and a day-care center.

A small number of minority students are bused daily into the district from Indianapolis.

Quality of School Environment

Classroom disruption and vandalism are not problems, and the quality of building and maintenance and repair are considered excellent.

WASHINGTON TOWNSHIP

ADDRESS OF CENTRAL OFFICE:
3801 East 79th Street, Indianapolis, IN 46240
ESI:None†

STATISTICAL PROFILE	DATA	ESI
Grade organization:		
Percentage of schools built before 1955		
Total enrollment		
Average Daily Attendance (ADA)		
Current expense per pupil in ADA		
Dropout rate		
Percentage of eligible students who took the ACT		
Average combined score on ACT		
Percentage of graduates who enrolled in 2- or 4-year colleges		
Percentage of students who passed the state reading test		
Percentage of students who passed the state math test		
Teacher–student ratio in elementary grades		
Teacher–student ratio in secondary grades		
Counselor–student ratio in secondary grades		
Number of students per music specialist in elementary grades		
Number of students per art specialist in elementary grades		
Number of volumes in senior high school library		
Beginning teacher's salary		
Maximum teacher's salary		
Average years of experience among teachers		
Number of students suspended and expelled		
Subjects in which Advanced Placement courses are offered:		

†A Statistical Profile was not received from this district.

FAIR APPRAISAL

Quality of School Leadership

For the most part, principals are selected for their educational leadership ability, and the quality of leadership is generally uniform throughout the system. Parents and teachers do not play a formal role in screening principal candidates. Principals have some say in what resources the district will allot their school.

Parent organizations' influence in decision-making is considered effective. A districtwide planning committee meets monthly and makes an annual report with recommendations to the superintendent and School Board. Another committee composed of parents and other citizens screens candidates for the School Board, and the ones they recommend usually win.

Quality of Instruction

The additional learning opportunities for gifted students are rated excellent. Two elementary schools are geared primarily toward bright students who can succeed at independent study. The additional instruction for low-achieving students is considered good to excellent. Learning centers in the elementary schools help. The curricula for college-bound students and job-bound students are excellent. A self-directed learning program for high school students called Learning Unlimited was begun by a grant from the Kettering Foundation and is highly rated.

The district participates in the desegregation plan involving the city of Indianapolis, and a small number of minority students are bused to the schools each day.

Quality of School Environment

The incidence of classroom disruption and vandalism is low and the quality of building maintenance and repair is excellent.

Kansas City, MO

Nine districts completed Statistical Profiles, and Fair Appraisals alone were received from three other districts. Districts in this Metropolitan Area may be compared with those in the St. Louis, MO Metropolitan Area.

AREA AT A GLANCE

SCHOOL DISTRICT	ENROLLMENT	ESI
Blue Valley, KS	5,913	55
Center	2,873	67
Grandview	5,277	70
Independence	11,081	41
Kansas City, KS	23,223	29
Kansas City, MO	36,451	
Liberty	3,900	69
North Kansas City	15,367	
Olathe, KS	12,060	73
Park Hill	6,406	
Raytown	8,439	72
Shawnee Mission, KS	30,600	84

BLUE VALLEY, KS

ADDRESS OF CENTRAL OFFICE:
P.O. Box 23901, Shawnee Mission, KS 66223
ESI:55

STATISTICAL PROFILE	DATA	ESI
Grade organization: K–5/6–8/9–12		
Percentage of schools built before 1955	10%	
Total enrollment	5,913	
Average Daily Attendance (ADA)	NK	0
Current expense per pupil in ADA	NK	0
Dropout rate	28%	0
Percentage of eligible students who took the ACT	76%	10
Average combined score on ACT	21.2	10
Percentage of graduates who enrolled in 2- or 4-year colleges	80%	
Percentage of students who passed the state reading test	96%	
Percentage of students who passed the state math test	90%	
Teacher–student ratio in elementary grades	1:20	10
Teacher–student ratio in secondary grades	1:25	3
Counselor–student ratio in secondary grades	1:237	8
Number of students per music specialist in elementary grades	400	7
Number of students per art specialist in elementary grades	400	
Number of volumes in senior high school library	13,800	
Beginning teacher's salary	$17,800†	
Maximum teacher's salary	$37,736†	
Average years of experience among teachers	NK	
Number of students suspended and expelled	NK	
Subjects in which Advanced Placement courses are offered: American Government, American History, Calculus, English, French, German, Spanish	7	7

†These are 1986–87 statistics.

FAIR APPRAISAL

Quality of School Leadership
Principals are selected for their educational leadership ability, and the quality of leadership does not vary greatly from school to school. While parents have no say in the selection of principals, principals have some influence over the distribution of district resources to the schools.

An advisory council of parents and other citizens meets regularly with the superintendent and is generally an effective influence on school policy decisions.

Quality of Instruction
Additional learning opportunities for gifted students are rated good to excellent, and additional instruction for low-achieving students is called good. The curriculum for college-bound students is excellent, and the preparation for students not going to college is considered good.

Quality of School Environment
The level of classroom disruption and vandalism is very low, and the quality of building maintenance and repair is good.

CENTER

ADDRESS OF CENTRAL OFFICE:
8701 Holmes Road, Kansas City, MO 64131
ESI:67

STATISTICAL PROFILE	DATA	ESI
Grade organization: K–6/7–8/9–12		
Percentage of schools built before 1955	33%	
Total enrollment	2,873	
Average Daily Attendance (ADA)	90%	3
Current expense per pupil in ADA	$4,272	10
Dropout rate	19%	4
Percentage of eligible students who took the ACT	67%	10
Average combined score on ACT	18.8	4
Percentage of graduates who enrolled in 2- or 4-year colleges	75%	
Percentage of students who passed the state reading test	96%	
Percentage of students who passed the state math test	92%	
Teacher–student ratio in elementary grades	1:14	10
Teacher–student ratio in secondary grades	1:14	10
Counselor–student ratio in secondary grades	1:338	4
Number of students per music specialist in elementary grades	346	9
Number of students per art specialist in elementary grades	461	
Number of volumes in senior high school library	13,542	
Beginning teacher's salary	$17,550	
Maximum teacher's salary	$36,680	
Average years of experience among teachers	13	
Number of students suspended and expelled	224	
Subjects in which Advanced Placement courses are offered: Biology, Calculus, Chemistry	3	3

FAIR APPRAISAL

Quality of School Leadership
The School Board looks for principals who have educational leadership ability. The quality of leadership is generally uniform throughout the schools. Teachers and parents help screen principal candidates, and principals exercise some influence on how district resources are allotted to the schools.

Parent organizations are sometimes effective influencing school policy decisions.

Quality of Instruction
Additional learning opportunities for gifted students are rated good, and additional instruction for low-achieving students is termed fair. The curriculum for students planning on college is good, while the curriculum preparing students for the world of work is considered fair. The high school is particularly strong in art, band music, debating, and graphic arts, according to observers.

Quality of School Environment
Classroom disruption and vandalism are not problems. The quality of building maintenance and repair is good.

GRANDVIEW

ADDRESS OF CENTRAL OFFICE:
724 Main Street, Grandview, MO 64030
ESI:70

STATISTICAL PROFILE	DATA	ESI
Grade organization: K–6/7–9/10–12		
Percentage of schools built before 1955	40%	
Total enrollment	5,277	
Average Daily Attendance (ADA)	92%†	5
Current expense per pupil in ADA	$3,556	8
Dropout rate	13%	10
Percentage of eligible students who took the ACT	48%	7
Average combined score on ACT	18.9	5
Percentage of graduates who enrolled in 2- or 4-year colleges	45%	
Percentage of students who passed the state reading test	100%	
Percentage of students who passed the state math test	54%	
Teacher–student ratio in elementary grades	1:21	9
Teacher–student ratio in secondary grades	1:18	10
Counselor–student ratio in secondary grades	1:225	9
Number of students per music specialist in elementary grades	409	7
Number of students per art specialist in elementary grades	409	
Number of volumes in senior high school library	21,256	
Beginning teacher's salary	$16,200	
Maximum teacher's salary	$33,210	
Average years of experience among teachers	15	
Number of students suspended and expelled	164	
Subjects in which Advanced Placement courses are offered:	None	0

†This statistic is Average Daily Membership (ADM) rather than ADA.

FAIR APPRAISAL

Quality of School Leadership
Principals normally are selected because of their educational leadership ability, and the quality of leadership does not vary greatly from school to school. Parents and teachers have an informal say on principal candidates, but do not conduct interviews. Principals are able to influence the distribution of resources to the schools.

Parent organizations are sometimes effective influencing school decision-making.

Quality of Instruction
Additional learning opportunities for gifted students are called excellent, and the additional instruction for low-achieving students is termed good. However, readers should take note of the low score on the state competency test in math. Observers rate the college-preparatory curriculum excellent. While no Advanced Placement courses were offered as of 1986–87, district officials plan to add one or more in the near future. The curriculum for students entering the world of work is considered good.

Quality of School Environment
The incidence of classroom disruption and vandalism is very low; the quality of building maintenance and repair is called excellent.

INDEPENDENCE

ADDRESS OF CENTRAL OFFICE:
1231 South Windsor Street, Independence, MO 64055
ESI:41

STATISTICAL PROFILE	DATA	ESI
Grade organization: K–6/7–8/9–12		
Percentage of schools built before 1955	35%	
Total enrollment	11,081	
Average Daily Attendance (ADA)	91%	4
Current expense per pupil in ADA	$2,783	7
Dropout rate	26%	0
Percentage of eligible students who took the ACT	40%	5
Average combined score on ACT	19.2	5
Percentage of graduates who enrolled in 2- or 4-year colleges	48%†	
Percentage of students who passed the state reading test	98%	
Percentage of students who passed the state math test	89%	
Teacher–student ratio in elementary grades	1:24	6
Teacher–student ratio in secondary grades	1:23	5
Counselor–student ratio in secondary grades	1:329	4
Number of students per music specialist in elementary grades	500	5
Number of students per art specialist in elementary grades	600	
Number of volumes in senior high school libraries (average)	15,870	
Beginning teacher's salary	$15,100	
Maximum teacher's salary	$30,672	
Average years of experience among teachers	15	
Number of students suspended and expelled	NK	
Subjects in which Advanced Placement courses are offered:	None	0

FAIR APPRAISAL

Quality of School Leadership
Principals are selected primarily for their educational leadership ability, and the quality of leadership does not vary greatly from school to school. Parents and teachers do not take part in principal selection, but principals have some say about how resources are allotted to their school.

Parent organizations are sometimes effective influencing school leaders.

Quality of Instruction
A good program for gifted students exists in grades 7–12, but it is just being introduced into the elementary schools. A special school for low-achieving students and "problem" students leads observers to rate the additional instruction for low-achievers as excellent. The curriculum for college-bound students is considered good, and the curriculum for students heading for the world of work is called fair.

Quality of School Environment
The level of classroom disruption and vandalism is low, and the quality of building maintenance and repair is good.

KANSAS CITY, KS

ADDRESS OF CENTRAL OFFICE:
625 Minnesota Avenue, Kansas City, KS 66101
ESI:29

STATISTICAL PROFILE	DATA	ESI
Grade organization: K–5/6–8/9–12		
Percentage of schools built before 1955	NK	
Total enrollment	23,223	
Average Daily Attendance (ADA)	92%	5
Current expense per pupil in ADA	$2,712	5
Dropout rate	26%	0
Percentage of eligible students who took the ACT	40%	5
Average combined score on ACT	17	0
Percentage of graduates who enrolled in 2- or 4-year colleges	NK	
Percentage of students who passed the state reading test	72%	
Percentage of students who passed the state math test	80%	
Teacher–student ratio in elementary grades	1:23	7
Teacher–student ratio in secondary grades	1:23	5
Counselor–student ratio in secondary grades	1:450	0
Number of students per music specialist in elementary grades	None	0
Number of students per art specialist in elementary grades	None	
Number of volumes in senior high school libraries (average)	17,682	
Beginning teacher's salary	$17,600	
Maximum teacher's salary	$32,580	
Average years of experience among teachers	12	
Number of students suspended and expelled	6,201	
Subjects in which Advanced Placement courses are offered: American History, English	2	2

Quality of School Leadership

Principals now are hired mainly because of their educational leadership ability. However, until a year ago, when a new superintendent came in, most principals were selected because they were part of an "old boy network." As a result of past practices, the quality of leadership varies greatly from school to school. "Some principals are just riding out until retirement," said an observer. Parents and teachers do not take part in screening principal candidates. However, principals have some say in what resources will be given their school. High school principals (five) have more clout than elementary school principals.

The School Board and new superintendent are open to public inquiries and constructive criticism, but parent organizations remain only sometimes influential in district policy-making.

Quality of Instruction

Additional learning opportunities for gifted students are rated good. Exceptionally bright students in the elementary schools are included in a county cooperative program. Personnel for the gifted program are very experienced. Additional instruction for low-achieving students is called good and getting better. A magnet school serving college-bound students in grades 8–12 (part of a court-ordered desegregation plan) has helped improve the college-preparatory curriculum (now rated good). The district has reacted to low scores on the ACT by enrolling students in special workshops that prepare them for the test. The curriculum that prepares students who are not going to college (the majority of students) is termed only fair and in need of improvement.

Quality of School Environment

The level of classroom disruption and vandalism is on the high side. At least one security guard is posted at each high school. The quality of building maintenance and repair is excellent. Many new schools were built in recent years, and even the old ones have been kept in very good shape.

KANSAS CITY, MO

ADDRESS OF CENTRAL OFFICE:
1211 McGee, Kansas City, MO 64106
ESI:None†

STATISTICAL PROFILE	DATA	ESI
Grade organization:		
Percentage of schools built before 1955		
Total enrollment		
Average Daily Attendance (ADA)		
Current expense per pupil in ADA		
Dropout rate		
Percentage of eligible students who took the ACT		
Average combined score on ACT		
Percentage of graduates who enrolled in 2- or 4-year colleges		
Percentage of students who passed the state reading test		
Percentage of students who passed the state math test		
Teacher–student ratio in elementary grades		
Teacher–student ratio in secondary grades		
Counselor–student ratio in secondary grades		
Number of students per music specialist in elementary grades		
Number of students per art specialist in elementary grades		
Number of volumes in senior high school library		
Beginning teacher's salary		
Maximum teacher's salary		
Average years of experience among teachers		
Number of students suspended and expelled		
Subjects in which Advanced Placement courses are offered:		

†A Statistical Profile was not received from this district.

Quality of School Leadership

In the past, principals were selected mainly for their ability to be disciplinarians, and most were chosen from within the district. Now, principal candidates must demonstrate educational leadership ability. Also, the state Department of Education now requires persons who would be school principals to spend several days at a "leadership academy." Because of past practices, the quality of leadership varies greatly from school to school. Parents and teachers have had no part in principal selection, but they may be part of the interviewing process at new magnet schools being created. Principals have little to say about the general distribution of district resources, but, as part of a court desegregation order, most schools have received $75,000 to $100,000, which principals, together with parents and other citizens, decide how to use.

Each school has an advisory committee. Some are more active than others, but districtwide, parent organizations tend to be only sometimes influential in school decision-making.

Quality of Instruction

Kansas City is embarking on one of the most ambitious magnet school programs in the country. By 1991, 43 of the 71 schools will be magnet schools, specializing in math, science, the performing arts, foreign languages, and other subjects. One observer wonders whether the district will become oversaturated with magnet schools. Additional learning opportunities for gifted students are now rated fair to good. Additional instruction for low-achieving students is rated fair, despite many efforts by the district, including before and after school tutoring. The curricula for college-bound students and job-bound students are rated fair (one of the magnet high schools will be designed for college-bound students). Vocational education was termed a "disaster" by one observer, who rated it poor.

Quality of School Environment

The level of classroom disruption and student vandalism varies greatly from school to school. In some schools, the problem is minimal, while other schools are called a "zoo" or a "circus." The quality of building maintenance and repair is fair, but improving. The court enforcing the desegregation plan has directed that several hundreds of millions of dollars (mostly state aid) be spent on building improvements and renovations.

LIBERTY

ADDRESS OF CENTRAL OFFICE:
14 South Main Street, Liberty, MO 64068
ESI:69

STATISTICAL PROFILE	DATA	ESI
Grade organization: K/1–6/7–9/10–12		
Percentage of schools built before 1955	37%	
Total enrollment	3,900	
Average Daily Attendance (ADA)	96%	9
Current expense per pupil in ADA	$3,290	6
Dropout rate	2%	10
Percentage of eligible students who took the ACT	55%	8
Average combined score on ACT	19.7	5
Percentage of graduates who enrolled in 2- or 4-year colleges	57%	
Percentage of students who passed the state reading test	96%	
Percentage of students who passed the state math test	87%	
Teacher–student ratio in elementary grades	1:16	10
Teacher–student ratio in secondary grades	1:17	10
Counselor–student ratio in secondary grades	1:310	5
Number of students per music specialist in elementary grades	492	6
Number of students per art specialist in elementary grades	650	
Number of volumes in senior high school library	16,141	
Beginning teacher's salary	$16,200	
Maximum teacher's salary	$29,430	
Average years of experience among teachers	13	
Number of students suspended and expelled	473	
Subjects in which Advanced Placement courses are offered:	None	0

FAIR APPRAISAL

Quality of School Leadership

The School Board looks for principals who demonstrate educational leadership ability; the quality of leadership is generally uniform throughout the system. Parents and teachers do not take part in principal selection. However, principals have a lot to say about the division of district resources among the schools.

Parent organizations are more influential in decision-making now than they were two years ago. New changes in administration have made the system more open to suggestions and constructive criticism from parents and other citizens.

Quality of Instruction

A "good" program for gifted students that begins at grade 4 is now being expanded into grades 7, 8, and 9. Additional instruction for low-achieving students is considered fair. College preparation is rated excellent, and job preparation is called good.

Quality of School Environment

The level of classroom disruption and vandalism is low, and the quality of building maintenance and repair is excellent.

NORTH KANSAS CITY

ADDRESS OF CENTRAL OFFICE:
2000 Northeast 46th Street, North Kansas City, MO 64116
ESI:None†

STATISTICAL PROFILE	DATA	ESI
Grade organization: K–5/6–8/9–12		
Percentage of schools built before 1955		
Total enrollment		
Average Daily Attendance (ADA)		
Current expense per pupil in ADA		
Dropout rate		
Percentage of eligible students who took the SAT		
Average combined score on SAT		
Percentage of graduates who enrolled in 2- or 4-year colleges		
Percentage of students who passed the state reading test		
Percentage of students who passed the state math test		
Teacher–student ratio in elementary grades		
Teacher–student ratio in secondary grades		
Counselor–student ratio in secondary grades		
Number of students per music specialist in elementary grades		
Number of students per art specialist in elementary grades		
Number of volumes in senior high school library		
Beginning teacher's salary		
Maximum teacher's salary		
Average years of experience among teachers		
Number of students suspended and expelled		
Subjects in which Advanced Placement courses are offered:		

†A Statistical Profile was not received from this district.

FAIR APPRAISAL

Quality of School Leadership

Principals are picked because of their educational leadership ability; the quality of leadership is high throughout the system. Parents, other citizens, and teachers all take part in screening and recommending principal candidates. The district was reorganized a few years ago, and resources now are more evenly distributed, with principals having much to say about the allotment of resources.

Parent organizations are influential in decision-making at individual schools and districtwide.

Quality of Instruction

Additional learning opportunities for gifted students are rated good. A program begins in the elementary grades. One feature in the higher grades is the opportunity to take courses for credit at nearby colleges. Additional instruction for low-achieving students also is considered good. Remedial reading instruction is available through grade 8. The curricula for college-bound students and for those going on to the world of work are rated good.

Quality of School Environment

Classroom disruption and vandalism are not problems. The quality of building maintenance and repair is good.

OLATHE, KS

ADDRESS OF CENTRAL OFFICE:
P.O. Box 2000, Olathe, KS 66061
ESI:73

STATISTICAL PROFILE	DATA	ESI
Grade organization: K–6/7–9/10–12		
Percentage of schools built before 1955	15%	
Total enrollment	12,060	
Average Daily Attendance (ADA)	96%	9
Current expense per pupil in ADA	$3,369	8
Dropout rate	8%	10
Percentage of eligible students who took the ACT	60%	9
Average combined score on ACT	20.1	6
Percentage of graduates who enrolled in 2- or 4-year colleges	75%	
Percentage of students who passed the state reading test	86%	
Percentage of students who passed the state math test	88%	
Teacher–student ratio in elementary grades	1:21	8
Teacher–student ratio in secondary grades	1:17	10
Counselor–student ratio in secondary grades	1:339	4
Number of students per music specialist in elementary grades	302	9
Number of students per art specialist in elementary grades	1,391	
Number of volumes in senior high school libraries (average)	18,500	
Beginning teacher's salary	$17,800	
Maximum teacher's salary	$35,066	
Average years of experience among teachers	10	
Number of students suspended and expelled	169	
Subjects in which Advanced Placement courses are offered:	None	0

FAIR APPRAISAL

Quality of School Leadership

The district hires principals with educational leadership ability, and the quality of leadership does not vary greatly from school to school. Parents and teachers do not play a part in principal selection. Principals have some say in what district resources will be allotted their school.

"Parental involvement is low," said an observer, for two reasons. Most parents and teachers are content to leave important decisions to a strong superintendent who "dominates" the system. The other reason, according to the observer, is that the district is divided into two parts—one with new, young families and the other with well-established families. "The new parents do not seem too interested in school affairs."

Quality of Instruction

Special classes from kindergarten through high school constitute an excellent program for gifted students. However, additional instruction for low-achieving students is rated fair. "It's just the basic minimum," said an observer. The college preparatory curriculum is considered excellent, and the curriculum for students preparing for jobs is termed good.

While the percentage of minority students is low, observers believe the district does little to insure that minority students' educational needs are adequately met.

Quality of School Environment

Classroom disruption and vandalism are not problems. The quality of building maintenance and repair is excellent.

PARK HILL

ADDRESS OF CENTRAL OFFICE:
7703 Northwest Berry Road, Kansas City, MO 64153
ESI:None†

STATISTICAL PROFILE	DATA	ESI
Grade organization:		
Percentage of schools built before 1955		
Total enrollment		
Average Daily Attendance (ADA)		
Current expense per pupil in ADA		
Dropout rate		
Percentage of eligible students who took the ACT		
Average combined score on ACT		
Percentage of graduates who enrolled in 2- or 4-year colleges		
Percentage of students who passed the state reading test		
Percentage of students who passed the state math test		
Teacher–student ratio in elementary grades		
Teacher–student ratio in secondary grades		
Counselor–student ratio in secondary grades		
Number of students per music specialist in elementary grades		
Number of students per art specialist in elementary grades		
Number of volumes in senior high school library		
Beginning teacher's salary		
Maximum teacher's salary		
Average years of experience among teachers		
Number of students suspended and expelled		
Subjects in which Advanced Placement courses are offered:		

†A Statistical Profile was not received from this district.

FAIR APPRAISAL

Quality of School Leadership

Principals are hired because of their educational leadership ability, and the quality of leadership is uniform in the district. Parents and teachers do not help screen principal candidates, but principals have a say in the way district resources are divided among the schools.

Parents' influence over school policy is generally effective. Parents and other citizens serve on a number of committees that advise the administration and School Board.

Quality of Instruction

Gifted students in all grades are periodically excused from regular classes so they can attend special enrichment classes, and the program is rated good. Also called good is the additional instruction for low-achieving students. Here also, students are excused from regular classes when they need the help of special teachers. The curricula for college-bound and job-bound students are rated good.

Quality of School Environment

The incidence of classroom disruption and student vandalism is very low. The quality of building maintenance and repair is rated excellent.

RAYTOWN

ADDRESS OF CENTRAL OFFICE:
10500 East 60th Terrace, Kansas City, MO 64133
ESI:72

STATISTICAL PROFILE	DATA	ESI
Grade organization: K–5/6–8/9–12		
Percentage of schools built before 1955	73%	
Total enrollment	8,439	
Average Daily Attendance (ADA)	92%	5
Current expense per pupil in ADA	$3,993	10
Dropout rate	5%	10
Percentage of eligible students who took the ACT	49%	7
Average combined score on ACT	19.5	5
Percentage of graduates who enrolled in 2- or 4-year colleges	60%	
Percentage of students who passed the state reading test	99%	
Percentage of students who passed the state math test	99%	
Teacher–student ratio in elementary grades	1:14	10
Teacher–student ratio in secondary grades	1:15	10
Counselor–student ratio in secondary grades	1:316	5
Number of students per music specialist in elementary grades	487	6
Number of students per art specialist in elementary grades	487	
Number of volumes in senior high school library	18,173	
Beginning teacher's salary	$16,750	
Maximum teacher's salary	$33,416	
Average years of experience among teachers	21	
Number of students suspended and expelled	NK	
Subjects in which Advanced Placement courses are offered:	4	4
Biology, Calculus, English, Physics		

FAIR APPRAISAL

Quality of School Leadership

The School Board seeks out principals who have educational leadership ability; the quality of leadership is generally uniform from school to school. Parents and teachers can voice their opinions about principal candidates, and principals are involved in deciding how the district's resources are distributed.

The PTA is very involved in decision-making, which, according to an observer, is relatively unusual for the area. Parents proposed a drug education program before one was needed, said an observer, and some other districts used it as a model.

Quality of Instruction

Additional learning opportunities for gifted students are rated good, and additional instruction for low-achieving students is termed excellent. Also considered excellent is the curriculum for college-bound students. The curriculum preparing students for the world of work is called good.

Quality of School Environment

Classroom disruption and student vandalism are not problems. The quality of building maintenance and repair is termed good to excellent.

SHAWNEE MISSION, KS

ADDRESS OF CENTRAL OFFICE:
7235 Antioch Road, Shawnee Mission, KS 66204
ESI:84

STATISTICAL PROFILE	DATA	ESI
Grade organization: K–6/7–8/9–12		
Percentage of schools built before 1955	16%	
Total enrollment	30,600	
Average Daily Attendance (ADA)	94%	7
Current expense per pupil in ADA	$3,185	7
Dropout rate	3%	10
Percentage of eligible students who took the ACT	70%	10
Average combined score on ACT	21.1	10
Percentage of graduates who enrolled in 2- or 4-year colleges	83%	
Percentage of students who passed the state reading test	91%	
Percentage of students who passed the state math test	86%	
Teacher–student ratio in elementary grades	1:22	8
Teacher–student ratio in secondary grades	1:19	9
Counselor–student ratio in secondary grades	1:260	7
Number of students per music specialist in elementary grades	365	8
Number of students per art specialist in elementary grades	482	
Number of volumes in senior high school libraries (average)	30,000	
Beginning teacher's salary	$17,733	
Maximum teacher's salary	$37,329	
Average years of experience among teachers	11	
Number of students suspended and expelled	4,251	
Subjects in which Advanced Placement courses are offered:	8	8
American History, Biology, Calculus, Chemistry, English, European History, French, Spanish		

FAIR APPRAISAL

Quality of School Leadership

The School Board hires principals who demonstrate educational leadership ability. The quality of leadership does not vary from school to school. Parents and teachers have no formal role to play in screening principal candidates. Principals, however, have some influence over the distribution of district resources.

Parent organizations are active at many individual schools, but districtwide parents are only sometimes effective influencing policy decisions.

Quality of Instruction

Additional learning opportunities for gifted students are considered excellent. The district is divided into four sections, and each section has a school to which gifted students in that area are sent for a few hours each week for enrichment. Additional instruction for low-achieving students is rated good. The college preparatory curriculum is rated excellent, and the curriculum for students heading for the job market is called fair to good. A new vocational center just getting started should improve job preparation.

Quality of School Environment

The incidence of classroom disruption and student vandalism is low, and the quality of building maintenance and repair is considered good.

Los Angeles– Orange County, CA

Fourteen districts completed the Statistical Profiles, and another five districts are represented by Fair Appraisals alone. The California State Department of Education requires competency tests in reading and math, but allows local districts to develop their own test questions. Because of possible variations in the testing, no scores are listed. Instead, all district profiles show *NA* (not applicable) on the lines requesting the test data. Districts in this area may be compared to districts in the Chicago, IL Metropolitan Area.

AREA AT A GLANCE

SCHOOL DISTRICT	ENROLLMENT	ESI
ABC	21,323	
Arcadia	7,427	50
Bellflower	9,273	20
Charter Oak	5,329	
Claremont	5,723	54
Downey	14,457	43
Duarte	4,400	30
Glendale	20,500	44*
Glendora	5,575	47*
Las Virgenes	8,250	51
Los Angeles	578,760	28*
Montebello	29,644	
Newport–Mesa	16,215	38
Palos Verdes Peninsula	10,200	53
Pasadena	22,300	23
Pomona	24,000	29
San Marino	2,750	60
Santa Ana	36,314	
Torrance	19,435	

Indicates district misinterpretation of one or more statistics in the ESI. For each misinterpreted statistic, a score of 0 was given instead of a possible score of 0 to 10 points.

ABC

ADDRESS OF CENTRAL OFFICE:
16700 Norwalk Boulevard, Cerritos, CA 90701
ESI:None†

STATISTICAL PROFILE	DATA	ESI
Grade organization:		
Percentage of schools built before 1955		
Total enrollment		
Average Daily Attendance (ADA)		
Current expense per pupil in ADA		
Dropout rate		
Percentage of eligible students who took the SAT		
Average combined score on SAT		
Percentage of graduates who enrolled in 2- or 4-year colleges		
Percentage of students who passed the state reading test		
Percentage of students who passed the state math test		
Teacher–student ratio in elementary grades		
Teacher–student ratio in secondary grades		
Counselor–student ratio in secondary grades		
Number of students per music specialist in elementary grades		
Number of students per art specialist in elementary grades		
Number of volumes in senior high school library		
Beginning teacher's salary		
Maximum teacher's salary		
Average years of experience among teachers		
Number of students suspended and expelled		
Subjects in which Advanced Placement courses are offered:		

†A Statistical Profile was not received from this district.

FAIR APPRAISAL

Quality of School Leadership

Most principals are hired because of their educational leadership ability, and the quality of leadership is generally uniform throughout the schools. However, one observer complained that some principals seem more concerned "with image than with the needs of their students." Parents and teachers have some influence over principal selection, but not much. Principals also have some say in how resources are allotted to the schools.

Parent organizations are sometimes effective influencing school decisions.

Quality of Instruction

Additional learning opportunities for gifted students are rated excellent, but most of the program seems to be in the high school. Additional instruction for low-achieving students is good. College-bound students have an excellent program, according to observers, and the curriculum for students going into the job market is good.

Quality of School Environment

Classroom disruption and student vandalism are not problems, and the quality of building maintenance and repair is good.

ARCADIA

ADDRESS OF CENTRAL OFFICE:
234 Campus Drive, Arcadia, CA 91006
ESI:50

STATISTICAL PROFILE	DATA	ESI
Grade organization: †		
Percentage of schools built before 1955	70%	
Total enrollment	7,427	
Average Daily Attendance (ADA)	99%	10
Current expense per pupil in ADA	$2,943	2
Dropout rate	7%	10
Percentage of eligible students who took the SAT	61%	10
Average combined score on SAT	951	7
Percentage of graduates who enrolled in 2- or 4-year colleges	84%	
Percentage of students who passed the state reading test	NA	
Percentage of students who passed the state math test	NA	
Teacher–student ratio in elementary grades	1:28	2
Teacher–student ratio in secondary grades	1:29	0
Counselor–student ratio in secondary grades	1:508	0
Number of students per music specialist in elementary grades	None	0
Number of students per art specialist in elementary grades	None	
Number of volumes in senior high school library	39,500	
Beginning teacher's salary	$21,684	
Maximum teacher's salary	$39,320	
Average years of experience among teachers	14	
Number of students suspended and expelled	369	
Subjects in which Advanced Placement courses are offered:	9	9
Art History, American Government, American History, Calculus AV, Calculus BC, Chemistry, English, Physics, Spanish		

†The district misinterpreted this statistic.

FAIR APPRAISAL

Quality of School Leadership

The School Board looks for principals who have educational leadership ability, and the quality of leadership is generally uniform throughout the system. Teachers have influence in principal selection; parents do not. Principals have some say about the allotment of district resources to their school.

Parent organizations are very active and vocal, and they are listened to by district administrators and the School Board.

Quality of Instruction

Learning opportunities for gifted students are rated excellent. Neighboring universities offer enrichment courses in addition to those provided by the schools. Additional instruction for low-achieving students is considered fair. An observer said more remedial teachers are needed. The curriculum for students going to college is rated excellent, but the curriculum for students entering the job market is considered only fair.

While observers feel the district meets the needs of most minority students, they are concerned that the schools may not be quite prepared for a major influx of students from Asian countries.

Quality of School Environment

The level of classroom disruption and student vandalism is low, according to observers, but parent groups are concerned about a drug problem and increasing friction between some Asian and white students. The quality of building maintenance and repair is good.

BELLFLOWER

ADDRESS OF CENTRAL OFFICE:
16703 South Clark Avenue, Bellflower, CA 90706
ESI:20

STATISTICAL PROFILE	DATA	ESI
Grade organization: †		
Percentage of schools built before 1955	60%	
Total enrollment	9,273	
Average Daily Attendance (ADA)	94%	7
Current expense per pupil in ADA	$2,388	0
Dropout rate	22%	1
Percentage of eligible students who took the SAT	45%	6
Average combined score on SAT	846	1
Percentage of graduates who enrolled in 2- or 4-year colleges	44%	
Percentage of students who passed the state reading test	NA	
Percentage of students who passed the state math test	NA	
Teacher–student ratio in elementary grades	1:30	0
Teacher–student ratio in secondary grades	1:30	0
Counselor–student ratio in secondary grades	1:467	0
Number of students per music specialist in elementary grades	2,650	0
Number of students per art specialist in elementary grades	None	
Number of volumes in senior high school libraries (average)	17,740	
Beginning teacher's salary	$20,490	
Maximum teacher's salary	$37,040	
Average years of experience among teachers	17	
Number of students suspended and expelled	584	
Subjects in which Advanced Placement courses are offered:	5	5
American Government, American History, Calculus, English, Spanish		

†The district misinterpreted this statistic.

FAIR APPRAISAL

Quality of School Leadership
Principals are selected primarily for their educational leadership ability. The quality of leadership is generally uniform throughout the system. Parents and teachers play no part in principal selection, but principals have some say in deciding how district resources will be divided among the schools.

Parent organizations are effective influences on school policy decisions.

Quality of Instruction
Additional learning opportunities for gifted students and additional instruction for low-achieving students are rated good. Also considered good are the curricula for college-bound students and for students heading into the world of work. As part of a campaign against dropouts, the district has adopted a very tough truancy policy. Parents who allow their children to cut school for a long period can expect to be taken to court.

Quality of School Environment
The incidence of classroom disruption and student vandalism is very low. The quality of building maintenance and repair is considered good.

CHARTER OAK

ADDRESS OF CENTRAL OFFICE:
P.O. Box 9, Covina, CA 91723
ESI:None†

STATISTICAL PROFILE	DATA	ESI
Grade organization:		
Percentage of schools built before 1955		
Total enrollment		
Average Daily Attendance (ADA)		
Current expense per pupil in ADA		
Dropout rate		
Percentage of eligible students who took the SAT		
Average combined score on SAT		
Percentage of graduates who enrolled in 2- or 4-year colleges		
Percentage of students who passed the state reading test		
Percentage of students who passed the state math test		
Teacher–student ratio in elementary grades		
Teacher–student ratio in secondary grades		
Counselor–student ratio in secondary grades		
Number of students per music specialist in elementary grades		
Number of students per art specialist in elementary grades		
Number of volumes in senior high school library		
Beginning teacher's salary		
Maximum teacher's salary		
Average years of experience among teachers		
Number of students suspended and expelled		
Subjects in which Advanced Placement courses are offered:		

†A Statistical Profile was not received from this district.

FAIR APPRAISAL

Quality of School Leadership
The School Board seeks principals who demonstrate educational leadership ability. The quality of leadership does not vary greatly from school to school. Parents and teachers have hardly any say on principal selections. Principals, however, have some influence over the resources allotted their school.

Parent organizations are not very strong, and their influence in policy decisions is minimal.

Quality of Instruction
Additional learning opportunities for gifted students are rated good, and additional instruction for low-achieving students is considered excellent. Each elementary school has a reading specialist to help low-achievers. The curricula for college-bound students and job-bound students are rated good.

Quality of School Environment
The level of classroom disruption and student vandalism is considered on the high side. "The vandalism problem has increased in recent years," said an observer. The quality of building maintenance and repair is good.

CLAREMONT

ADDRESS OF CENTRAL OFFICE:
2080 North Mountain Avenue, Claremont, CA 91711
ESI:54

STATISTICAL PROFILE	DATA	ESI
Grade organization: K–6/7–8/9–12		
Percentage of schools built before 1955	25%	
Total enrollment	5,723	
Average Daily Attendance (ADA)	98%	10
Current expense per pupil in ADA	$3,305	4
Dropout rate	10%	10
Percentage of eligible students who took the SAT	50%	7
Average combined score on SAT	941	6
Percentage of graduates who enrolled in 2- or 4-year colleges	89%	
Percentage of students who passed the state reading test	NA	
Percentage of students who passed the state math test	NA	
Teacher–student ratio in elementary grades	1:32	0
Teacher–student ratio in secondary grades	1:33	0
Counselor–student ratio in secondary grades	1:341	4
Number of students per music specialist in elementary grades	563	4
Number of students per art specialist in elementary grades	None	
Number of volumes in senior high school library	17,000	
Beginning teacher's salary	$22,790	
Maximum teacher's salary	$39,675	
Average years of experience among teachers	13	
Number of students suspended and expelled	252	
Subjects in which Advanced Placement courses are offered:	9	9
American History, Calculus, Chemistry, Computer Science, English Language & Composition, English Literature and Composition, French, German, Spanish		

FAIR APPRAISAL

Quality of School Leadership
Principals are hired because of their educational leadership ability, and the quality of leadership does not vary greatly from school to school. Parents and teachers help screen principal candidates. Also, principals have a say in the distribution of district resources to the schools.

A district advisory committee is an effective influence on district policies. Its most recent task was to study the district's desegregation policy and make recommendations.

Quality of Instruction
Additional learning opportunities for gifted students are considered excellent, and additional instruction for low-achieving students is rated good. The curriculum for college-bound students is considered excellent, but the curriculum preparing students for the world of work is rated fair.

Quality of School Environment
Classroom disruption and student vandalism are not problems. The quality of building maintenance and repair is termed fair, mainly because of budget cuts.

DOWNEY

ADDRESS OF CENTRAL OFFICE:
P.O. Box 75, Downey, CA 90341
ESI:43

STATISTICAL PROFILE	DATA	ESI
Grade organization: K–5/6–8/9–12		
Percentage of schools built before 1955	50%	
Total enrollment	14,457	
Average Daily Attendance (ADA)	97%	10
Current expense per pupil in ADA	$3,100	3
Dropout rate	11%	10
Percentage of eligible students who took the SAT	87%	10
Average combined score on SAT	926	6
Percentage of graduates who enrolled in 2- or 4-year colleges	62%	
Percentage of students who passed the state reading test	NA	
Percentage of students who passed the state math test	NA	
Teacher–student ratio in elementary grades	1:28	2
Teacher–student ratio in secondary grades	1:32	0
Counselor–student ratio in secondary grades	1:400	2
Number of students per music specialist in elementary grades	None	0
Number of students per art specialist in elementary grades	None	
Number of volumes in senior high school libraries (average)	15,000	
Beginning teacher's salary	$23,465	
Maximum teacher's salary	$41,655	
Average years of experience among teachers	12	
Number of students suspended and expelled	110†	
Subjects in which Advanced Placement courses are offered:	None	0

†These are all expulsions and are the result of a very strict policy on drug abuse.

FAIR APPRAISAL

Quality of School Leadership
Principals are hired because of their educational leadership ability, and the quality of leadership is mostly uniform from school to school. Teachers and parents have no say in principal selection, but principals influence what district resources their school will receive.

A variety of parent support groups exist in the district, and they are generally effective influences on decision-making.

Quality of Instruction
Additional learning opportunities for gifted students are rated as good, and additional instruction for low-achieving students is considered excellent. The curricula for college-bound students and for students going on to the world of work are rated good.

Quality of School Environment
The level of classroom disruption and student vandalism is low. The quality of building maintenance and repair is considered fair. However, the district is planning necessary building renovations.

DUARTE

ADDRESS OF CENTRAL OFFICE:
1427 Buena Vista Avenue, Duarte, CA 91010
ESI:30

STATISTICAL PROFILE	DATA	ESI
Grade organization: K–6/7–8/9–12		
Percentage of schools built before 1955	80%	
Total enrollment	4,400	
Average Daily Attendance (ADA)	97%	10
Current expense per pupil in ADA	$3,255	4
Dropout rate	44%	0
Percentage of eligible students who took the SAT	26%	3
Average combined score on SAT	777	0
Percentage of graduates who enrolled in 2- or 4-year colleges	20%	
Percentage of students who passed the state reading test	NA	
Percentage of students who passed the state math test	NA	
Teacher–student ratio in elementary grades	1:27	3
Teacher–student ratio in secondary grades	1:24	4
Counselor–student ratio in secondary grades	1:333	5
Number of students per music specialist in elementary grades	3,200	0
Number of students per art specialist in elementary grades	None	
Number of volumes in senior high school library	19,800	
Beginning teacher's salary	$22,220	
Maximum teacher's salary	$42,300	
Average years of experience among teachers	14	
Number of students suspended and expelled	3,221†	
Subjects in which Advanced Placement courses are offered: Chemistry	1	1

†This figure seems extremely high given the total enrollment.

FAIR APPRAISAL

Quality of School Leadership

Principals are hired primarily for their educational leadership ability, and the quality of leadership does not vary greatly from school to school. Parents and teachers have some say in principal selection, mostly expressing informal opinions. Principals, however, have a great deal to say about how resources are allotted the schools.

Parent organizations are an effective influence on school decision-making.

Quality of Instruction

Additional learning opportunities for gifted students and additional instruction for low-achieving students are rated good. Also rated good are the curricula for students going to college and for students not planning on college.

Quality of School Environment

The level of classroom disruption and student vandalism is low, and the quality of building maintenance and repair is good.

SCHOOL DISTRICT

GLENDALE

ADDRESS OF CENTRAL OFFICE:
223 North Jackson Street, Glendale, CA 91206
ESI:44*

STATISTICAL PROFILE	DATA	ESI
Grade organization: K–6/7–9/10–12		
Percentage of schools built before 1955	70%	
Total enrollment	20,500	
Average Daily Attendance (ADA)	99%	10
Current expense per pupil in ADA	$2,600	1
Dropout rate	6%	10
Percentage of eligible students who took the SAT	78%	10
Average combined score on SAT	919	5
Percentage of graduates who enrolled in 2- or 4-year colleges	67%	
Percentage of students who passed the state reading test	NA	
Percentage of students who passed the state math test	NA	
Teacher–student ratio in elementary grades	1:30	0
Teacher–student ratio in secondary grades	1:32	0
Counselor–student ratio in secondary grades	1:544	0
Number of students per music specialist in elementary grades	†	0
Number of students per art specialist in elementary grades	†	
Number of volumes in senior high school library	18,000	
Beginning teacher's salary	$21,684	
Maximum teacher's salary	$38,788	
Average years of experience among teachers	18	
Number of students suspended and expelled	1,092	
Subjects in which Advanced Placement courses are offered: American History, Calculus, Chemistry, English, French, German, Physics, Spanish	8	8

†The district supplied an inappropriate statistic.

FAIR APPRAISAL

Quality of School Leadership

The School Board hires principals who demonstrate educational leadership ability; the quality of leadership does not vary greatly from school to school. Teachers and parents have an informal say in the selection of principals. Principals also have some say in the distribution of district resources.

Parent organizations are sometimes effective influencing school decisions.

Quality of Instruction

Additional learning opportunities for gifted students and additional instruction for low-achieving students are rated good. Gifted students in grades 3–12 receive three hours of enrichment per week. Also considered good is the curriculum for college-bound students. The curriculum for students not planning on college is rated fair.

Quality of School Environment

Classroom disruption and student vandalism are not problems. However, the quality of building maintenance and repair is rated poor. "Most of the schools are over 30 years old," said an observer, "and the district has not had the money to regularly repair them."

GLENDORA

ADDRESS OF CENTRAL OFFICE:
500 North Lorraine Avenue, Glendora, CA 91740
ESI:47*

STATISTICAL PROFILE	DATA	ESI
Grade organization: †		
Percentage of schools built before 1955	10%	
Total enrollment	5,575	
Average Daily Attendance (ADA)	99%	10
Current expense per pupil in ADA	$2,557	0
Dropout rate	5%	10
Percentage of eligible students who took the SAT	52%	8
Average combined score on SAT	††	0*
Percentage of graduates who enrolled in 2- or 4-year colleges	NK	
Percentage of students who passed the state reading test	NA	
Percentage of students who passed the state math test	NA	
Teacher–student ratio in elementary grades	1:25	5
Teacher–student ratio in secondary grades	1:21	7
Counselor–student ratio in secondary grades	1:395	2
Number of students per music specialist in elementary grades	2,428	0
Number of students per art specialist in elementary grades	None	
Number of volumes in senior high school library	19,000	
Beginning teacher's salary	$18,425	
Maximum teacher's salary	$36,757	
Average years of experience among teachers	16	
Number of students suspended and expelled	459	
Subjects in which Advanced Placement courses are offered: American History, Calculus, English, Foreign Language, Physics	5	5

† The district misinterpreted this statistic.
††The district supplied an inappropriate statistic.

FAIR APPRAISAL

Quality of School Leadership

Principals today are hired mainly because of their ability as educational leaders. However, some principals who have been in the system a while were part of an "old boy" network, and their leadership ability is not as good, according to observers. Parents and teachers have little say in the selection of principals, but principals have some say in the allocation of district resources.

Parent organizations are effective influencing school decision-making.

Quality of Instruction

Additional learning opportunities for gifted students and additional instruction for low-achieving students are rated fair. The problem is the lack of funding, said the observers. Considered good are the curricula for the college-bound and for students bound for the world of work. Work experience programs are part of the latter curriculum.

Quality of School Environment

The level of classroom disruption and student vandalism is low. The quality of building maintenance and repair is excellent.

LAS VIRGENES

ADDRESS OF CENTRAL OFFICE:
30961 West Agoura Road, Thousand Oaks, CA 91361
ESI:51

STATISTICAL PROFILE	DATA	ESI
Grade organization: K–5/6–8/9–12		
Percentage of schools built before 1955	8%	
Total enrollment	8,250	
Average Daily Attendance (ADA)	98%	10
Current expense per pupil in ADA	$3,503	5
Dropout rate	5%	10
Percentage of eligible students who took the SAT	964	7
Average combined score on SAT	61%	10
Percentage of graduates who enrolled in 2- or 4-year colleges	85%	
Percentage of students who passed the state reading test	NA	
Percentage of students who passed the state math test	NA	
Teacher–student ratio in elementary grades	1:30	0
Teacher–student ratio in secondary grades	1:30	0
Counselor–student ratio in secondary grades	1:595	0
Number of students per music specialist in elementary grades	None	0
Number of students per art specialist in elementary grades	None	0
Number of volumes in senior high school library	34,287	
Beginning teacher's salary	$22,200	
Maximum teacher's salary	$36,700	
Average years of experience among teachers	15	
Number of students suspended and expelled	799	
Subjects in which Advanced Placement courses are offered: American History, Calculus AB, Calculus BC, Chemistry, Computer Science, English Literature and Composition, French, Physics B, Spanish	9	9

FAIR APPRAISAL

Quality of School Leadership

Principals are hired for their educational leadership ability, and the quality of leadership is generally uniform throughout the system. Parents and teachers have hardly any say in principal selection, although principals have some say in the allotment of resources to the schools.

Parent organizations are effective influencing school decisions.

Quality of Instruction

Additional learning opportunities for gifted students are rated fair, and additional instruction for low-achieving students is considered good. The latter program is funded better than the gifted program, said an observer. The curriculum for students going to college and the curriculum for students heading for the world of work are rated good.

Quality of School Environment

The level of classroom disruption and student vandalism is low, but the quality of building maintenance and repair is fair. Money has been cut from the maintenance and repair budget.

LOS ANGELES

ADDRESS OF CENTRAL OFFICE:

P.O. Box 3307 — Terminal Annex, Los Angeles, CA 90051

ESI:28

STATISTICAL PROFILE	DATA	ESI
Grade organization: K–5/6–7/8/9–12		
Percentage of schools built before 1955	77%	
Total enrollment	578,760	
Average Daily Attendance (ADA)	95%	8
Current expense per pupil in ADA	77,103	3
Dropout rate	34%	0
Percentage of eligible students who took the SAT	34%	4
Average combined score on SAT	†	0*
Percentage of graduates who enrolled in 2- or 4-year colleges	NK	
Percentage of students who passed the state reading test	NA	
Percentage of students who passed the state math test	NA	
Teacher–student ratio in elementary grades	1:33	0
Teacher–student ratio in secondary grades	1:36	0
Counselor–student ratio in secondary grades	1:358	3
Number of students per music specialist in elementary grades	††	0*
Number of students per art specialist in elementary grades	†††	
Number of volumes in senior high school libraries (average)	17,000	
Beginning teacher's salary	$20,297	
Maximum teacher's salary	$35,384	
Average years of experience among teachers	15	
Number of students suspended and expelled	77,626††††	
Subjects in which Advanced Placement courses are offered: 23 out of 25 are offered	23	10

†   The district supplied an inappropriate statistic.

††   46 specialists are on site in some of 410 elementary schools, and 66 specialists travel to other schools.

††† There are no art specialists; classroom teachers provide instruction.

††††Of this number, 686 are expulsions.

Quality of School Leadership

Internal politics and racial balance are important factors in choosing a school principal, sometimes more important than demonstrated educational leadership ability, according to the observers. Consequently, the quality of leadership varies greatly from school to school. Teachers and parents have little or no say in principal selection, and principals have little say in how district resources are allotted to the schools.

Parent organizations are sometimes effective influencing school decisions.

Quality of Instruction

Budget constraints limit the number who can be identified and served by the gifted program, but for those who are admitted, the observers rate the program good. Magnet schools are part of the program at the secondary level. Considered fair is additional instruction for low-achieving students. The curriculum for college preparation is rated fair to good, but the quality varies greatly among the 49 senior high schools. The curriculum for students not planning on college is rated fair to poor; again, quality varies greatly from school to school.

Observers agree that the schools are not adequately meeting the needs of minority students. "There is a tremendous need for competent bilingual teachers of Spanish, Korean, Thai, Tagolog (Phillipines), Armenian, and many other languages," said one observer.

Quality of School Environment

Generally, the level of classroom disruption and student vandalism is on the high side, although the problems vary from school to school. The quality of building maintenance and repair is rated fair. "There is a huge backlog of deferred maintenance throughout the district," said an observer.

MONTEBELLO

ADDRESS OF CENTRAL OFFICE:
123 South Montebello Boulevard, CA 90640
ESI:None†

STATISTICAL PROFILE	DATA	ESI
Grade organization:		
Percentage of schools built before 1955		
Total enrollment		
Average Daily Attendance (ADA)		
Current expense per pupil in ADA		
Dropout rate		
Percentage of eligible students who took the SAT		
Average combined score on SAT		
Percentage of graduates who enrolled in 2- or 4-year colleges		
Percentage of students who passed the state reading test		
Percentage of students who passed the state math test		
Teacher–student ratio in elementary grades		
Teacher–student ratio in secondary grades		
Counselor–student ratio in secondary grades		
Number of students per music specialist in elementary grades		
Number of students per art specialist in elementary grades		
Number of volumes in senior high school library		
Beginning teacher's salary		
Maximum teacher's salary		
Average years of experience among teachers		
Number of students suspended and expelled		
Subjects in which Advanced Placement courses are offered:		

†A Statistical Profile was not received from this school.

FAIR APPRAISAL

Quality of School Leadership
Most principals are selected because of their ability as educational leaders. However, the high-income areas of the district seem to get the most qualified leaders, said an observer. Parents and teachers do not interview principal candidates. Principals have a great deal to say about the distribution of resources to the schools.

Parent organizations are sometimes effective as an influence on school policy-making. PTA representatives regularly attend School Board meetings.

Quality of Instruction
Additional learning opportunities for gifted students are rated excellent, but there is "a fear," said an observer, that a cutback in funding might scale down the program. Additional instruction for low-achieving students also is considered excellent. The curricula for students going to college and for those going into the job market are rated good.

Quality of School Environment
Classroom disruption and student vandalism are not problems, and the quality of building maintenance and repair is good.

NEWPORT–MESA

ADDRESS OF CENTRAL OFFICE:
P.O. Box 1368, Newport Beach, CA 92663
ESI:38

STATISTICAL PROFILE	DATA	ESI
Grade organization: †		
Percentage of schools built before 1955	25%	
Total enrollment	16,215	
Average Daily Attendance (ADA)	99%	10
Current expense per pupil in ADA	$3,482	5
Dropout rate	26%	0
Percentage of eligible students who took the SAT	45%	6
Average combined score on SAT	953	7
Percentage of graduates who enrolled in 2- or 4-year colleges	85%	
Percentage of students who passed the state reading test	NA	
Percentage of students who passed the state math test	NA	
Teacher–student ratio in elementary grades	1:27	3
Teacher–student ratio in secondary grades	1:29	0
Counselor–student ratio in secondary grades	1:430	0
Number of students per music specialist in elementary grades	1,200	0
Number of students per art specialist in elementary grades	None	0
Number of volumes in senior high school libraries (average)	28,250	
Beginning teacher's salary	$20,265	
Maximum teacher's salary	$43,160	
Average years of experience among teachers	20	
Number of students suspended and expelled	1,065	
Subjects in which Advanced Placement courses are offered:	7	7
American History, Art, Calculus, Computer Science, English, Foreign Language (unspecified), Science (unspecified)		

†The district misinterpreted this statistic.

FAIR APPRAISAL

Quality of School Leadership
Principals are selected primarily for their educational leadership ability, and the quality of leadership does not vary greatly from school to school. Parents and teachers have no say in the principal selection process, but principals have some say in the allotment of resources to their school.

Parent advisory councils meet regularly with principals and are effective as an influence on decision-making.

Quality of Instruction
Additional learning opportunities for gifted students are rated fair to good, and additional instruction for low-achieving students is considered fair. The curriculum for students planning on college is termed excellent, but the curriculum for students not planning on college is rated only fair.

Quality of School Environment
The incidence of classroom disruption and student vandalism is very low, but the quality of building maintenance and repair is fair. "They are doing a good job with the money they have," said an observer.

PALOS VERDES

ADDRESS OF CENTRAL OFFICE:
3801 Via La Selva, Palos Verdes, CA 90274
ESI:53

STATISTICAL PROFILE	DATA	ESI
Grade organization: K–5/6–8/9–12		
Percentage of schools built before 1955	70%	
Total enrollment	10,200	
Average Daily Attendance (ADA)	98%	10
Current expense per pupil in ADA	$3,000	3
Dropout rate	5%	10
Percentage of eligible students who took the SAT	75%	10
Average combined score on SAT	1,000	9
Percentage of graduates who enrolled in 2- or 4-year colleges	90%	
Percentage of students who passed the state reading test	NA	
Percentage of students who passed the state math test	NA	
Teacher–student ratio in elementary grades	1:29	1
Teacher–student ratio in secondary grades	1:30	0
Counselor–student ratio in secondary grades	1:450	0
Number of students per music specialist in elementary grades	None	0
Number of students per art specialist in elementary grades	None	
Number of volumes in senior high school library	NK	
Beginning teacher's salary	$21,000	
Maximum teacher's salary	$38,500	
Average years of experience among teachers	17	
Number of students suspended and expelled	2	
Subjects in which Advanced Placement courses are offered:	25†	10

†Total number of available AP courses.

FAIR APPRAISAL

Quality of School Leadership

The School Board primarily hires principals with educational leadership ability. The quality of leadership is generally uniform throughout the system. Parents and teachers have hardly any say in the selection of principals, but principals have some say in the allotment of resources to the schools.

Parent organizations are effective influencing school policies.

Quality of Instruction

Additional learning opportunities for gifted students and additional instruction for low-achieving students are rated good. The curriculum for students planning on college is excellent (all the Advanced Placement courses are offered). However, the curriculum for students not planning on college is called fair to poor.

Quality of School Environment

The level of classroom disruption and student vandalism is very low, and the quality of building maintenance and repair is good.

PASADENA

ADDRESS OF CENTRAL OFFICE:
351 South Hudson Avenue, Pasadena, CA 91109
ESI:23

STATISTICAL PROFILE	DATA	ESI
Grade organization: K–5/6–8/9–12		
Percentage of schools built before 1955	90%	
Total enrollment	22,300	
Average Daily Attendance (ADA)	98%	10
Current expense per pupil in ADA	$2,581	1
Dropout rate	30%	0
Percentage of eligible students who took the SAT	38%	5
Average combined score on SAT	NK	0
Percentage of graduates who enrolled in 2- or 4-year colleges	75%	
Percentage of students who passed the state reading test	NA	
Percentage of students who passed the state math test	NA	
Teacher–student ratio in elementary grades	1:30	0
Teacher–student ratio in secondary grades	1:28	0
Counselor–student ratio in secondary grades	1:400	2
Number of students per music specialist in elementary grades	None	0
Number of students per art specialist in elementary grades	None	
Number of volumes in senior high school libraries (average)	28,000	
Beginning teacher's salary	$21,660	
Maximum teacher's salary	$41,940	
Average years of experience among teachers	17	
Number of students suspended and expelled	1,568	
Subjects in which Advanced Placement courses are offered: American History, Biology, English Literature, French, Spanish	5	5

FAIR APPRAISAL

Quality of School Leadership

Internal politics are a factor in principal selection, but educational leadership ability remains the primary consideration. There are some major variations in the quality of leadership, mainly because "the same standards are not used for everyone," said an observer. Parents and teachers have no say in principal selection, and principals have little say in the way district resources are used.

Parent organizations are occasionally effective influencing school decision-making.

Quality of Instruction

Additional learning opportunities for gifted students are rated good, but additional instruction for low-achieving students is considered fair. The curriculum for students bound for college is termed good, but the curriculum for students not planning on colleges is rated fair.

The observers do not believe the district is adequately meeting the educational needs of minority students.

Quality of School Environment

The level of classroom disruption and student vandalism is on the low side (barely), but the quality of building maintenance and repair is fair. "Many of the buildings are old," said an observer.

POMONA

ADDRESS OF CENTRAL OFFICE:
P.O. Box 2900, Pomona, CA 91769
ESI:29

STATISTICAL PROFILE	DATA	ESI
Grade organization: Pre-K/K–6/7–8/9–12		
Percentage of schools built before 1955	31%	
Total enrollment	24,000	
Average Daily Attendance (ADA)	98%	10
Current expense per pupil in ADA	$3,293	4
Dropout rate	42%	0
Percentage of eligible students who took the SAT	33%	4
Average combined score on SAT	760	0
Percentage of graduates who enrolled in 2- or 4-year colleges	48%	
Percentage of students who passed the state reading test	NA	
Percentage of students who passed the state math test	NA	
Teacher–student ratio in elementary grades	1:32	0
Teacher–student ratio in secondary grades	1:28	0
Counselor–student ratio in secondary grades	1:500	0
Number of students per music specialist in elementary grades	245	10
Number of students per art specialist in elementary grades	1,400	
Number of volumes in senior high school libraries (average)	15,300	
Beginning teacher's salary	$20,265	
Maximum teacher's salary	$40,079	
Average years of experience among teachers	20	
Number of students suspended and expelled	2,255	
Subjects in which Advanced Placement courses are offered: Calculus	1	1

FAIR APPRAISAL

Quality of School Leadership
Principals are chosen primarily for their ability as educational leaders. The quality of educational leadership is generally uniform from school to school. Parents and teachers serve on committees that screen principal candidates, and principals have a great deal to say about the distribution of district resources among the schools.

Parent organizations are not very effective influencing school decisions.

Quality of Instruction
The program for gifted students is rated good, but the money crunch means the district must "fight to keep it," said an observer. Additional instruction for low-achieving students is considered fair. The curricula for students planning on college and for those not planning on college are rated good. The district offers a good adult program that includes instruction leading to the equivalent of a high school diploma.

Quality of School Environment
The level of classroom disruption and student vandalism tend to be on the high side, and the quality of building maintenance and repair is fair.

SAN MARINO

ADDRESS OF CENTRAL OFFICE:
1665 West Drive, San Marino, CA 91108
ESI:60

STATISTICAL PROFILE	DATA	ESI
Grade organization: †		
Percentage of schools built before 1955	100%	
Total enrollment	2,750	
Average Daily Attendance (ADA)	99%	10
Current expense per pupil in ADA	$3,425	5
Dropout rate	1%	10
Percentage of eligible students who took the SAT	85%	10
Average combined score on SAT	1,012	10
Percentage of graduates who enrolled in 2- or 4-year colleges	99%	
Percentage of students who passed the state reading test	NA	
Percentage of students who passed the state math test	NA	
Teacher–student ratio in elementary grades	1:26	4
Teacher–student ratio in secondary grades	1:24	4
Counselor–student ratio in secondary grades	1:380	2
Number of students per music specialist in elementary grades	None	0
Number of students per art specialist in elementary grades	None	
Number of volumes in senior high school library	24,000	
Beginning teacher's salary	$20,680	
Maximum teacher's salary	$39,560	
Average years of experience among teachers	14	
Number of students suspended and expelled	27	
Subjects in which Advanced Placement courses are offered: Calculus, English, French Language and Literature, Spanish Language and Literature, Studio Art	5	5

†The district misinterpreted this statistic.

FAIR APPRAISAL

Quality of School Leadership
Principals are hired because of their educational leadership ability; the quality of leadership is generally uniform throughout the system. Parents and teachers help select principals, and principals have a great deal to say about the allotment of district resources.

Parent organizations are effective as an influence on district policy.

Quality of Instruction
Additional learning opportunities for gifted students are rated excellent, and the additional instruction for low-achieving students is considered fair. The curriculum for students going to college is called excellent, but the curriculum for students not planning on college is rated fair.

Quality of School Environment
The incidence of classroom disruption and student vandalism is very low. However, the quality of building maintenance and repair is only fair to poor. The secondary schools "need much repair," said one observer. Another observer expressed the problem faced by this and many other California districts: "The money is for people, and the staff is terrific, but the roofs leak."

SANTA ANA

ADDRESS OF CENTRAL OFFICE:
1405 North French Street, Santa Ana, CA 92701
ESI:None†

STATISTICAL PROFILE	DATA	ESI
Grade organization:		
Percentage of schools built before 1955		
Total enrollment		
Average Daily Attendance (ADA)		
Current expense per pupil in ADA		
Dropout rate		
Percentage of eligible students who took the SAT		
Average combined score on SAT		
Percentage of graduates who enrolled in 2- or 4-year colleges		
Percentage of students who passed the state reading test		
Percentage of students who passed the state math test		
Teacher–student ratio in elementary grades		
Teacher–student ratio in secondary grades		
Counselor–student ratio in secondary grades		
Number of students per music specialist in elementary grades		
Number of students per art specialist in elementary grades		
Number of volumes in senior high school library		
Beginning teacher's salary		
Maximum teacher's salary		
Average years of experience among teachers		
Number of students suspended and expelled		
Subjects in which Advanced Placement courses are offered:		

†A Statistical Profile was not received from this district.

FAIR APPRAISAL

Quality of School Leadership
Longevity is a consideration, but most principals are hired primarily because they have ability as educational leaders. The quality of leadership does not vary greatly from school to school. Parents and teachers do not screen principal candidates. Principals have some say in the allotment of resources to the schools.

Parent organizations are sometimes effective as an influence on school policy.

Quality of Instruction
Special schools and classes for gifted students make the program an excellent one, but additional instruction for low-achieving students is rated only fair. The curriculum for students heading for college is rated good to excellent, and the curriculum for students not planning on college is said to be fair to good.

Quality of School Environment
Classroom disruption and student vandalism are not problems, and the quality of building maintenance and repair is good.

TORRANCE

ADDRESS OF CENTRAL OFFICE:
2335 Plaza del Amo, Torrance, CA 90509
ESI:None†

STATISTICAL PROFILE	DATA	ESI
Grade organization:		
Percentage of schools built before 1955		
Total enrollment		
Average Daily Attendance (ADA)		
Current expense per pupil in ADA		
Dropout rate		
Percentage of eligible students who took the SAT		
Average combined score on SAT		
Percentage of graduates who enrolled in 2- or 4-year colleges		
Percentage of students who passed the state reading test		
Percentage of students who passed the state math test		
Teacher–student ratio in elementary grades		
Teacher–student ratio in secondary grades		
Counselor–student ratio in secondary grades		
Number of students per music specialist in elementary grades		
Number of students per art specialist in elementary grades		
Number of volumes in senior high school library		
Beginning teacher's salary		
Maximum teacher's salary		
Average years of experience among teachers		
Number of students suspended and expelled		
Subjects in which Advanced Placement courses are offered:		

†A Statistical Profile was not received from this district.

FAIR APPRAISAL

Quality of School Leadership
Principals are hired primarily for their educational leadership ability, and the quality of leadership is generally uniform throughout the system. Parents and teachers do not help screen principal candidates, but principals have some say in the division of district resources.

Parent organizations are effective influencing school decision-making. "The PTA is very strong and well-respected by district officials," said one observer.

Quality of Instruction
Additional learning opportunities for gifted students are rated excellent. Special classes in grades 3–6 stress critical thinking skills. Additional instruction for low-achieving students is termed good. The program features remedial and lab work with special teachers. The curricula for students planning on college and for those students not planning on college are considered excellent.

Quality of School Environment
Classroom disruption and student vandalism are not problems, and the quality of building mantenance and repair is good.

Louisville, KY

Kentucky is served primarily by county school districts. Two of the three county school systems serving the Louisville Metropolitan Area completed a Statistical Profile. Districts in this area may be compared to districts in the Memphis, TN Metropolitan Area.

AREA AT A GLANCE

SCHOOL DISTRICT	ENROLLMENT	ESI
Jefferson County	92,470	39
Oldham County	6,400	53

JEFFERSON COUNTY

ADDRESS OF CENTRAL OFFICE:
P.O. Box 34020, Louisville, KY 40232
ESI:39

STATISTICAL PROFILE	DATA	ESI
Grade organization: K–5/6–8/9–12		
Percentage of schools built before 1955	31%	
Total enrollment	92,000	
Average Daily Attendance (ADA)	93%	6
Current expense per pupil in ADA	$2,988	6
Dropout rate	39%	0
Percentage of eligible students who took the ACT	41%	6
Average combined score on ACT	17.8	0
Percentage of graduates who enrolled in 2- or 4-year colleges	NK	
Percentage of students who passed the state reading test	85%	
Percentage of students who passed the state math test	91%	
Teacher–student ratio in elementary grades	1:25	5
Teacher–student ratio in secondary grades	1:22	6
Counselor–student ratio in secondary grades	1:401	1
Number of students per music specialist in elementary grades	1,050	0
Number of students per art specialist in elementary grades	1,050	
Number of volumes in senior high school libraries (average)	18,874	
Beginning teacher's salary	$14,024	
Maximum teacher's salary	$27,950	
Average years of experience among teachers	14	
Number of students suspended and expelled	4,513	
Subjects in which Advanced Placement courses are offered:	9	9
American History, Art Studio, Biology, Calculus, Chemistry, French, German, Physics, Spanish		

FAIR APPRAISAL

Quality of School Leadership
Most principals are selected for their educational leadership ability, and the quality of leadership is generally uniform throughout the district. Parents and teachers assist top administrators in interviewing principal candidates. Principals also have some say in the allotment of district resources to the schools.

Parent organizations are sometimes effective influencing school policy decisions.

Quality of Instruction
A variety of magnet schools specializing in math, science, the arts and other subjects help make additional learning opportunities for gifted students excellent. However, additional instruction for low-achieving students is rated only fair. The curriculum for college-bound students is considered good, but the curriculum for students going into the job market is only fair. An observer believes "students would get more out of the educational program if less emphasis were placed upon college preparation, especially since the majority of students do not plan on college."

Quality of School Environment
Classroom disruption and student vandalism are not considered problems, and the quality of maintenance and repair is rated good.

OLDHAM COUNTY

ADDRESS OF CENTRAL OFFICE:
P.O. Box 207, La Grange, KY 40031
ESI:53

STATISTICAL PROFILE	DATA	ESI
Grade organization: K–5/6–8/9–12		
Percentage of schools built before 1955	15%	
Total enrollment	6,400	
Average Daily Attendance (ADA)	96%	9
Current expense per pupil in ADA	$2,081	2
Dropout rate	14%	9
Percentage of eligible students who took the ACT	68%	10
Average combined score on ACT	19	5
Percentage of graduates who enrolled in 2- or 4-year colleges	57%	
Percentage of students who passed the state reading test	95%	
Percentage of students who passed the state math test	95%	
Teacher–student ratio in elementary grades	1:23	7
Teacher–student ratio in secondary grades	1:27	1
Counselor–student ratio in secondary grades	1:520	0
Number of students per music specialist in elementary grades	550	4
Number of students per art specialist in elementary grades	550	
Number of volumes in senior high school library	25,000	
Beginning teacher's salary	$14,477	
Maximum teacher's salary	$25,266	
Average years of experience among teachers	12	
Number of students suspended and expelled	331	
Subjects in which Advanced Placement courses are offered:	6	6
American History, Calculus, Computer Science, English, French, Science (unspecified)		

FAIR APPRAISAL

Quality of School Leadership
Principals are hired because of their educational leadership ability. The quality of leadership does not vary greatly from school to school. However, parents and teachers have no say in principal selection, but principals do have some influence over the distribution of district resources.

Parent organizations are not very influential, mainly "because the superintendent is so strong," according to an observer.

Quality of Instruction
The district is growing rapidly (the population of the county doubled from 1970 to 1978), and many schools are over capacity. A consequence has been the elimination of parts of many programs. For example, additional learning opportunities for gifted students are now rated fair, and additional instruction for low-achieving students is fair to poor. To date, the high school has not been adversely affected by the rapid rise in enrollment, and the curriculum for the college-bound is considered excellent. Rated good is the job-preparation curriculum for those not going to college.

Quality of School Environment
The level of classroom disruption and student vandalism is very low, and the quality of building maintenance and repair is very high.

Memphis, TN

Except for the city of Memphis, the Metropolitan Area is composed of county districts. One of these county districts is in Mississippi. Two county districts and the city of Memphis completed Statistical Profiles. Mississippi did not require competency tests in reading and math at the time of our survey. Therefore, the Statistical Profile for De Soto County, MS shows *NA* (not applicable) on those lines requesting competency test results. This area's districts might be compared to those in the Louisville, KY Metropolitan Area.

AREA AT A GLANCE

SCHOOL DISTRICT	ENROLLMENT	ESI
De Soto County, MS	12,442	40
Memphis	107,054	33
Shelby County	29,951	53

SCHOOL DISTRICT

DE SOTO COUNTY

ADDRESS OF CENTRAL OFFICE:
655 Holly Springs Street, Hernando, MS 38632
ESI:40

STATISTICAL PROFILE	DATA	ESI
Grade organization: K–4/5–8/9–12		
Percentage of schools built before 1955	20%	
Total enrollment	12,442	
Average Daily Attendance (ADA)	96%	9
Current expense per pupil in ADA	$1,928	4
Dropout rate	22%	1
Percentage of eligible students who took the ACT	40%	5
Average combined score on ACT	15.4	0
Percentage of graduates who enrolled in 2- or 4-year colleges	40%	
Percentage of students who passed the state reading test	NA	
Percentage of students who passed the state math test	NA	
Teacher–student ratio in elementary grades	1:20	10
Teacher–student ratio in secondary grades	1:19	9
Counselor–student ratio in secondary grades	1:750	0
Number of students per music specialist in elementary grades	None	0
Number of students per art specialist in elementary grades	None	
Number of volumes in senior high school library	†	
Beginning teacher's salary	$15,375	
Maximum teacher's salary	$23,725	
Average years of experience among teachers	8	
Number of students suspended and expelled	484	
Subjects in which Advanced Placement courses are offered: English, Science	2	2

†The district uses the statistic of 10 volumes per student.

FAIR APPRAISAL

Quality of School Leadership
Principals in recent years have been hired primarily because of their educational leadership ability, but some longtime principals were hired "because of internal politics or popularity," said an observer. Consequently, the quality of leadership varies greatly from school to school. "Each year the team of principals gets stronger and stronger," said an observer. Parents and teachers do not help select principals. On the other hand, principals have some say about the resources allotted their school.

Parent groups are becoming more and more involved in decision-making.

Quality of Instruction
Additional learning opportunities for gifted students are rated excellent in grades 2 through 12. Students meet two or three hours a week with a teacher of gifted students. The one complaint an observer had was that the gifted program "concentrates on academic subjects and nearly ignores the creative arts." Additional instruction for low-achieving students is considered good. The curricula for college-bound students and for those going to a job are rated good.

Quality of School Environment
Classroom disruption and student vandalism are not problems, and the quality of building and maintenance is good. The district has an ongoing building program.

MEMPHIS

ADDRESS OF CENTRAL OFFICE:
2597 Avery Avenue, Memphis, TN 38112
ESI:33

STATISTICAL PROFILE	DATA	ESI
Grade organization: K–6/7–9/10–12		
Percentage of schools built before 1955	38%	
Total enrollment	107,054	
Average Daily Attendance (ADA)	98%	10
Current expense per pupil in ADA	$2,597	6
Dropout rate	NK	0
Percentage of eligible students who took the ACT	10%	0
Average combined score on ACT	14.7	0
Percentage of graduates who enrolled in 2- or 4-year colleges	54%	
Percentage of students who passed the state reading test	99%	
Percentage of students who passed the state math test	99%	
Teacher–student ratio in elementary grades	1:25	5
Teacher–student ratio in secondary grades	1:26	2
Counselor–student ratio in secondary grades	1:387	2
Number of students per music specialist in elementary grades	1,000	0
Number of students per art specialist in elementary grades	None	
Number of volumes in senior high school libraries (average)	13,560	
Beginning teacher's salary	$17,550	
Maximum teacher's salary	$33,175	
Average years of experience among teachers	12	
Number of students suspended and expelled	NK	
Subjects in which Advanced Placement courses are offered:	8	8
American History, Art, Biology, Calculus, Chemistry, Computer Science, English, Physics		

Quality of School Leadership

Most principals are selected for their educational leadership ability, and the quality of leadership is generally uniform throughout the system. However, "some principals nearing retirement are not as effective as they should be," according to an observer. The district has a leadership training program for persons wishing to become principals. Parents and teachers do not take part in the screening of candidates, but principals have some say in how district resources are allotted to the schools.

Parent organizations are not particularly effective. However, individual parents and small ad hoc groups of parents are listened to and can effect change.

Quality of Instruction

Additional learning opportunities for gifted students are considered excellent. Exceptionally bright children in the elementary grades have special enrichment classes one or two times a week. Additional instruction of low-achieving students is good to excellent. Rated excellent is the curriculum for the college-bound students; the instruction for students heading into the job market is good. A feature of the Memphis schools that has attracted national attention is the optional school program offered at 27 elementary and junior high schools. Each program specializes in an academic discipline, career field, or the creative arts.

"The schools are doing a good job," an observer said, but the district is still not fully meeting the educational needs of minority students.

Quality of School Environment

The level of classroom disruption and vandalism is low. The quality of building maintenance and repair is fair to poor.

SHELBY COUNTY

ADDRESS OF CENTRAL OFFICE:
160 South Hollywood Street, Memphis, TN 38112
ESI:53

STATISTICAL PROFILE	DATA	ESI
Grade organization: K–8/9–12		
Percentage of schools built before 1955	44%	
Total enrollment	29,951	
Average Daily Attendance (ADA)	95%	8
Current expense per pupil in ADA	$2,025	3
Dropout rate	29%	0
Percentage of eligible students who took the ACT	76%	10
Average combined score on ACT	19.2	5
Percentage of graduates who enrolled in 2- or 4-year colleges	NK	
Percentage of students who passed the state reading test	100%	
Percentage of students who passed the state math test	100%	
Teacher–student ratio in elementary grades	1:22	8
Teacher–student ratio in secondary grades	1:20	8
Counselor–student ratio in secondary grades	1:488	0
Number of students per music specialist in elementary grades	742	1
Number of students per art specialist in elementary grades	865	
Number of volumes in senior high school libraries (average)	17,170	
Beginning teacher's salary	$17,560	
Maximum teacher's salary	$32,070	
Average years of experience among teachers	15	
Number of students suspended and expelled	707†	
Subjects in which Advanced Placement courses are offered: American Government, American History, Biology, Calculus, Chemistry, Computer Science, English, French, Physics, Spanish)	10	10

†Does not include in-school suspensions.

FAIR APPRAISAL

Quality of School Leadership

Most principals are hired for their educational leadership ability, and the quality of leadership is generally uniform throughout the system. However, the quality of leadership varies somewhat because individual school boards have applied different hiring standards over the years. Parents and teachers do not take part in the selection of principals. Also, principals do not have much say in how the district's resources are divided among the schools.

Parent organizations are effective "only when they're angry," said an observer. They recently got angry over late hours at a school, 9AM to 4PM, and the hours were promptly changed to 8AM to 3PM.

Quality of Instruction

Additional learning opportunities for gifted students are rated good, but additional instruction for low-achieving students is considered only fair ("just the minimum"). The curriculum for college-bound students is good, but the job-preparation curriculum is termed fair.

Quality of School Environment

Classroom disruption and student vandalism are not problems, and the quality of building maintenance and repair is good. However, many schools are overcrowded. Two schools scheduled to open at the start of the 1987–88 school year were already at capacity.

Miami, FL

Florida operates county school systems. The Dade County school district
serves the Miami Metropolitan Area (also see Fort Lauderdale, FL).
We received a Fair Appraisal alone for the Dade County school district.

AREA AT A GLANCE

SCHOOL DISTRICT	ENROLLMENT	ESI
Dade County	236,127	

SCHOOL DISTRICT

DADE COUNTY

ADDRESS OF CENTRAL OFFICE:
1450 Northeast 2nd Ave., Miami, FL 33132
ESI:None†

STATISTICAL PROFILE	DATA	ESI
Grade organization:		
Percentage of schools built before 1955		
Total enrollment		
Average Daily Attendance (ADA)		
Current expense per pupil in ADA		
Dropout rate		
Percentage of eligible students who took the SAT		
Average combined score on SAT		
Percentage of graduates who enrolled in 2- or 4-year colleges		
Percentage of students who passed the state reading test		
Percentage of students who passed the state math test		
Teacher–student ratio in elementary grades		
Teacher–student ratio in secondary grades		
Counselor–student ratio in secondary grades		
Number of students per music specialist in elementary grades		
Number of students per art specialist in elementary grades		
Number of volumes in senior high school library		
Beginning teacher's salary		
Maximum teacher's salary		
Average years of experience among teachers		
Number of students suspended and expelled		
Subjects in which Advanced Placement courses are offered:		

†A Statistical Profile was not received from this district.

FAIR APPRAISAL

Quality of School Leadership

Most principals are hired because of their educational leadership
ability, but the quality of leadership may vary greatly from school to
school. According to an observer, "some sections of the district (often
but not always low-income areas) have less-able principals." Parents
and teachers have no say in principal selection, although they may play
a role in having a principal removed. Principals exercise some influence
over the distribution of district resources to the schools.

Parent organizations are sometimes effective influencing policy
decisions.

Quality of Instruction

Additional learning opportunities for gifted students are rated fair to
poor, but additional instruction for low-achieving students is
considered excellent. One observer complained that the district claims
it has trouble fully funding the gifted program. The curriculum for
students planning on college is excellent, but the curriculum for
students preparing for the world of work is rated only fair.

Miami in particular has a large number of Spanish-speaking and
black students, but observers believe the district still adequately meets
the educational needs of minority students.

Quality of School Environment

Classroom disruption and student vandalism are not major problems,
but the quality of building maintenance and repair is termed only fair.

Milwaukee, WI

Eight districts completed Statistical Profiles, and Fair Appraisals alone are provided for two more districts. Wisconsin does not have state tests in reading and math. Therefore, *NA* (not applicable) follows the lines requesting those test data. Districts in this area may be compared to districts in the Minneapolis-St. Paul, MN Metropolitan Area.

AREA AT A GLANCE

SCHOOL DISTRICT	ENROLLMENT	ESI
Elmbrook	6,513	67
Greenfield	2,969	58
Kettle Moraine	3,326	66
Milwaukee	92,558	23
New Berlin	4,341	68
Oconomowoc	4,306	56
Racine	21,080	34
South Milwaukee	3,500	
Wauwatosa	6,208	
West Allis–West Milwaukee	8,049	72

ELMBROOK

ADDRESS OF CENTRAL OFFICE:
2430 North Pilgrim Road, Brookfield, WI 53005
ESI:67

STATISTICAL PROFILE	DATA	ESI
Grade organization: K–6/7–8/9–12		
Percentage of schools built before 1955	22%	
Total enrollment	6,513	
Average Daily Attendance (ADA)	88%	1
Current expense per pupil in ADA	$4,404	4
Dropout rate	2%	10
Percentage of eligible students who took the ACT	66%	10
Average combined score on ACT	21.3	10
Percentage of graduates who enrolled in 2- or 4-year colleges	85%	
Percentage of students who passed the state reading test	NA	
Percentage of students who passed the state math test	NA	
Teacher–student ratio in elementary grades	1:24	6
Teacher–student ratio in secondary grades	1:10	10
Counselor–student ratio in secondary grades	1:300	6
Number of students per music specialist in elementary grades	220	10
Number of students per art specialist in elementary grades	440	
Number of volumes in senior high school libraries (average)	23,350	
Beginning teacher's salary	$17,822	
Maximum teacher's salary	$37,407	
Average years of experience among teachers	NK	
Number of students suspended and expelled	200	
Subjects in which Advanced Placement courses are offered:	None	0

FAIR APPRAISAL

Quality of School Leadership
Principals are selected for their educational leadership ability; the quality of leadership is generally uniform throughout the system. Parents and teachers play no formal role in principal selection. However, principals greatly influence how the district distributes resources to the schools.

Parent organizations are sometimes effective influencing school policy decisions. For example, parents were influential in getting an extra computer class for junior high students.

Quality of Instruction
Additional learning opportunities for gifted students are rated good, and so is additional instruction for low-achieving students. At the high school level, in particular, low-achieving students receive one-on-one tutoring. The curriculum for college-bound students is rated excellent. The high schools offer a number of advanced courses (*not* Advanced Placement). The curriculum for students going into the world of work is considered good.

Quality of School Environment
The level of classroom disruption and student vandalism is very low, and the quality of building maintenance and repair is good to excellent.

GREENFIELD

ADDRESS OF CENTRAL OFFICE:
3200 West Barnard Avenue, Milwaukee, WI 53221
ESI:58

STATISTICAL PROFILE	DATA	ESI
Grade organization: K–6/7–8/9–12		
Percentage of schools built before 1955	50%	
Total enrollment	2,969	
Average Daily Attendance (ADA)	97%	10
Current expense per pupil in ADA	$4,400	7
Dropout rate	16%	7
Percentage of eligible students who took the ACT	30%	3
Average combined score on ACT	20.4	8
Percentage of graduates who enrolled in 2- or 4-year colleges	55%	
Percentage of students who passed the state reading test	NA	
Percentage of students who passed the state math test	NA	
Teacher–student ratio in elementary grades	1:23	7
Teacher–student ratio in secondary grades	1:25	3
Counselor–student ratio in secondary grades	1:350	4
Number of students per music specialist in elementary grades	320	9
Number of students per art specialist in elementary grades	425	
Number of volumes in senior high school library	24,109	
Beginning teacher's salary	$16,188	
Maximum teacher's salary	$33,183	
Average years of experience among teachers	15	
Number of students suspended and expelled	811	
Subjects in which Advanced Placement courses are offered:	None	0

FAIR APPRAISAL

Quality of School Leadership
Principals are hired on the basis of their educational leadership ability. The quality of leadership does not vary greatly from school to school. Parents and teachers have little say in the selection of principals. However, principals have quite a lot to say about how resources will be divided among the schools.

Parent organizations are sometimes effective influencing school decision-making.

Quality of Instruction
The program for gifted students, according to an observer, is "great" in the elementary and middle schools and still being developed at the high school. Overall, observers rate it good. Additional instruction for low-achieving students also is rated good. The curricula for students preparing for college and for those preparing for jobs are considered excellent.

The district has almost doubled the number of minority students it accepts on a voluntary basis from Milwaukee, although the number is still relatively small.

Quality of School Environment
The level of classroom disruption and student vandalism is low, but the quality of building maintenance and repair is only fair. Observers report that older buildings are badly in need of renovations. Lack of funding has prevented the district from doing all it would like to do.

KETTLE MORAINE

ADDRESS OF CENTRAL OFFICE:
P.O. Box 39, Wales, WI 53183
ESI:66

STATISTICAL PROFILE	DATA	ESI
Grade organization: K–12†		
Percentage of schools built before 1955	43%	
Total enrollment	3,326	
Average Daily Attendance (ADA)	96%	9
Current expense per pupil in ADA	$3,817	4
Dropout rate	8%	10
Percentage of eligible students who took the ACT	34%	4
Average combined score on ACT	19.9	5
Percentage of graduates who enrolled in 2- or 4-year colleges	73%	
Percentage of students who passed the state reading test	NA	
Percentage of students who passed the state math test	NA	
Teacher–student ratio in elementary grades	1:25	5
Teacher–student ratio in secondary grades	1:14	10
Counselor–student ratio in secondary grades	1:289	6
Number of students per music specialist in elementary grades	175	10
Number of students per art specialist in elementary grades	175	
Number of volumes in senior high school library	13,156	
Beginning teacher's salary	$16,945	
Maximum teacher's salary	$33,534	
Average years of experience among teachers	10	
Number of students suspended and expelled	301	
Subjects in which Advanced Placement courses are offered: American History, Chemistry, English	3	3

†The district misinterpreted this statistic.

FAIR APPRAISAL

Quality of School Leadership

Principals are chosen because of their educational leadership ability, and the quality of leadership is generally uniform throughout the system. Teachers and parents take no part in screening principal candidates. Principals, on the other hand, influence the distribution of district resources.

Parents are called on regularly to study issues and advise on policy, according to observers.

Quality of Instruction

Additional learning opportunities for gifted students are rated good and "improving." Also rated good is additional instruction for low-achieving students. "They really look out for the slow learner," said an observer. The college preparatory curriculum is considered excellent, and one observer. The college preparatory curriculum is considered excellent, and one observer had high praise for the guidance counselors. Rated good is the curriculum for students preparing for the world of work. "They have a good co-op program," said an observer.

Quality of School Environment

Observers differ on the level of classroom disruption and student vandalism. On the one hand, the level was said to be very low, but another observer commented that vandalism is high, particularly at the high school. All agree that the quality of building maintenance and repair is good.

MILWAUKEE

ADDRESS OF CENTRAL OFFICE:
5225 West Vliet Street, Milwaukee, WI 53208
ESI:23

STATISTICAL PROFILE	DATA	ESI
Grade organization: K–5/6–8/9–12		
Percentage of schools built before 1955	59%	
Total enrollment	92,558	
Average Daily Attendance (ADA)	90%	3
Current expense per pupil in ADA	$4,477†	7
Dropout rate	54%	0
Percentage of eligible students who took the SAT	NK	0
Average combined score on SAT	832	1
Percentage of graduates who enrolled in 2- or 4-year colleges	43%	
Percentage of students who passed the state reading test	NA	
Percentage of students who passed the state math test	NA	
Teacher–student ratio in elementary grades	1:27	3
Teacher–student ratio in secondary grades	1:28	0
Counselor–student ratio in secondary grades	1:450	0
Number of students per music specialist in elementary grades	1,000	0
Number of students per art specialist in elementary grades	1,000	
Number of volumes in senior high school libraries (average)	17,500	
Beginning teacher's salary	$17,496	
Maximum teacher's salary	$23,598	
Average years of experience among teachers	15	
Number of students suspended and expelled	9,354	
Subjects in which Advanced Placement courses are offered:	9	9
American History, Art, Biology, Calculus, Computer Science, English, European History, Music, Spanish		

†This figure was based on average daily membership (ADM).

Quality of School Leadership

The School Board looks for educational leadership ability in principal candidates, but racial balance is an important concern. The observers believe the quality of leadership varies greatly from school to school. The "best" principals seem to be reserved for high schools, particularly the magnet schools. Parents and teachers do not have a part in principal selection, but principals have some say in how district resources are allotted to each school. The district is considering a site management plan that would give principals more control over the running of their school.

Parent groups are generally effective influences on district decision-making. The PTA has been responsible for initiating "many new groups in inner city schools," said an observer.

Quality of Instruction

Additional learning opportunities for gifted children are rated good. A program exists at all grade levels, and talented students in academic subjects and the arts can do very well at a variety of special or magnet schools. Additional instruction for low-achieving students is considered only fair. The curricula for college-bound and job-bound students are good.

Observers believe the district does not adequately meet the educational needs of minority students. "Smaller class size, more individual tutoring, and greater parent involvement would help."

Quality of School Environment

Classroom disruption and student vandalism are generally on the low side, but problems exist at some schools. The quality of building maintenance and repair is rated as good to excellent.

NEW BERLIN

ADDRESS OF CENTRAL OFFICE:
4333 South Sunny Slope Road, New Berlin, WI 53151
ESI:68

STATISTICAL PROFILE	DATA	ESI
Grade organization: K–6/7–8/9–12		
Percentage of schools built before 1955	33%	
Total enrollment	4,341	
Average Daily Attendance (ADA)	95%	8
Current expense per pupil in ADA	$5,411	10
Dropout rate	2%	10
Percentage of eligible students who took the ACT	20%	1
Average combined score on ACT	20.5	8
Percentage of graduates who enrolled in 2- or 4-year colleges	82%	
Percentage of students who passed the state reading test	NA	
Percentage of students who passed the state math test	NA	
Teacher–student ratio in elementary grades	1:21	9
Teacher–student ratio in secondary grades	1:21	7
Counselor–student ratio in secondary grades	1:290	6
Number of students per music specialist in elementary grades	400	7
Number of students per art specialist in elementary grades	670	
Number of volumes in senior high school library	23,149	
Beginning teacher's salary	$18,410	
Maximum teacher's salary	$37,760	
Average years of experience among teachers	18	
Number of students suspended and expelled	207	
Subjects in which Advanced Placement courses are offered: Biology, Chemistry	2	2

FAIR APPRAISAL

Quality of School Leadership

Principals are selected mostly for their educational leadership ability. However, observers noted that seniority also is a factor, and one observer complained that few women are hired. The quality of leadership does not vary greatly from school to school. Parents and teachers do not screen principal candidates, but principals have influence over the distribution of district resources. Principals are rotated from school to school.

Parent organizations have influence in district policy-making. For example, parents opposed an all-day kindergarten proposed by district officials; the plan was dropped.

Quality of Instruction

Many learning opportunities for gifted students exist at all grade levels, and the program is rated excellent. Additional instruction for low-achieving students is considered good. Tutoring and resource rooms are used; "strong parent volunteer effort" is helpful, said an observer. The curriculum for college-bound students is rated excellent, and the curriculum for students going on to the world of work is called good.

Quality of School Environment

The incidence of classroom disruption and student vandalism is low. The district has a plan to discourage vandalism: Unused money earmarked for repairing damage caused by vandalism finances special outings for students. The quality of building maintenance and repair is good to excellent.

OCONOMOWOC

ADDRESS OF CENTRAL OFFICE:
7077 Brown Street, Oconomowoc, WI 53066
ESI:56

STATISTICAL PROFILE	DATA	ESI
Grade organization: K–6/7–8/9–12		
Percentage of schools built before 1955	50%	
Total enrollment	4,306	
Average Daily Attendance (ADA)	87%	0
Current expense per pupil in ADA	$3,799	4
Dropout rate	12%	10
Percentage of eligible students who took the ACT	60%	9
Average combined score on ACT	20.0	6
Percentage of graduates who enrolled in 2- or 4-year colleges	62%	
Percentage of students who passed the state reading test	NA	
Percentage of students who passed the state math test	NA	
Teacher–student ratio in elementary grades	1:21	9
Teacher–student ratio in secondary grades	1:24	4
Counselor–student ratio in secondary grades	1:300	6
Number of students per music specialist in elementary grades	369	8
Number of students per art specialist in elementary grades	263	
Number of volumes in senior high school library	17,000	
Beginning teacher's salary	$18,100	
Maximum teacher's salary	$34,020	
Average years of experience among teachers	19	
Number of students suspended and expelled	45	
Subjects in which Advanced Placement courses are offered:	None	0

FAIR APPRAISAL

Quality of School Leadership

The School Board seeks principals who evidence educational leadership ability, and the quality of leadership does not vary greatly from school to school. Parents and teachers play no part in screening principals, but principals have some say about the disbursement of district resources to the schools.

Parent organizations are very effective influencing school policy decisions. The School Board and administration "really listen to parents," said an observer. "They care about parental involvement and encourage it."

Quality of Instruction

Observers rate as fair the additional learning opportunities available to gifted students. The program is good at the upper levels, said one observer, but not very strong at the elementary level. Additional instruction for low-achieving students is considered excellent (many extra teachers and aides). The curricula for college-bound students and job-bound students are rated excellent, although one observer thought there was "room for improvement in counseling."

Quality of School Environment

The level of classroom disruption and vandalism is low, and the quality of building maintenance and repair is good.

RACINE

ADDRESS OF CENTRAL OFFICE:
2220 Northwestern Avenue, Racine, WI 53404
ESI:34

STATISTICAL PROFILE	DATA	ESI
Grade organization: K–5/6–8/9–12		
Percentage of schools built before 1955	56%	
Total enrollment	21,080	
Average Daily Attendance (ADA)	93%	6
Current expense per pupil in ADA	$4,159	5
Dropout rate	NK	0
Percentage of eligible students who took the ACT	17%	1
Average combined score on ACT	20.1	6
Percentage of graduates who enrolled in 2- or 4-year colleges	52%	
Percentage of students who passed the state reading test	NA	
Percentage of students who passed the state math test	NA	
Teacher–student ratio in elementary grades	1:24	6
Teacher–student ratio in secondary grades	NK	0
Counselor–student ratio in secondary grades	1:350	4
Number of students per music specialist in elementary grades	693	2
Number of students per art specialist in elementary grades	913	
Number of volumes in senior high school libraries (average)	24,500	
Beginning teacher's salary	$16,900	
Maximum teacher's salary	$33,082	
Average years of experience among teachers	NK	
Number of students suspended and expelled	1,012†	
Subjects in which Advanced Placement courses are offered: American History, Calculus, English, Science	4	4

†Does not include in-school suspensions.

Quality of School Leadership
Most principals hired have demonstrated educational leadership ability, and the quality of leadership does not vary greatly throughout the system. Parents and teachers do not screen principal candidates. Principals have some say in how district resources will be allotted to the schools.

Parent organizations are sometimes effective in their influence over school policy decisions. One observer thought parental involvement at the middle and high schools was not strong.

Quality of Instruction
Observers rate additional learning opportunities for gifted students as excellent. A special school for gifted students exists; also, magnet schools for the upper grades offer enrichment for especially bright students. Additional instruction for low-achieving students also is rated excellent. The district "works very hard to raise each student's achievement to the standards set for all students," said an observer. The college preparatory curriculum is considered excellent, and the curriculum for students heading into the job market is called good.

Committees composed of administrators, teachers and parents select textbooks in all subjects.

Quality of School Environment
Classroom disruption and student vandalism are not problems, although some schools report more incidents than other schools. The quality of building maintenance and repair is good.

SOUTH MILWAUKEE

ADDRESS OF CENTRAL OFFICE:
1001 Fifteenth Avenue, South Milwaukee, WI 53172
ESI:None†

STATISTICAL PROFILE	DATA	ESI
Grade organization:		
Percentage of schools built before 1955		
Total enrollment		
Average Daily Attendance (ADA)		
Current expense per pupil in ADA		
Dropout rate		
Percentage of eligible students who took the ACT		
Average combined score on ACT		
Percentage of graduates who enrolled in 2- or 4-year colleges		
Percentage of students who passed the state reading test		
Percentage of students who passed the state math test		
Teacher–student ratio in elementary grades		
Teacher–student ratio in secondary grades		
Counselor–student ratio in secondary grades		
Number of students per music specialist in elementary grades		
Number of students per art specialist in elementary grades		
Number of volumes in senior high school library		
Beginning teacher's salary		
Maximum teacher's salary		
Average years of experience among teachers		
Number of students suspended and expelled		
Subjects in which Advanced Placement courses are offered:		

†A Statistical Profile was not received from this district.

Quality of School Leadership
The School Board hires principals who demonstrate educational leadership ability, and the quality of leadership is generally uniform throughout the district. Parents and teachers have little say in principal selection. Principals, however, have some say in how district resources are distributed.

Parent organizations are sometimes effective influencing school decision-making.

Quality of Instruction
Additional learning opportunities for gifted students and additional instruction for low-achieving students are rated fair. Considered excellent, however, are the curricula for college-bound students and for those heading into the job market.

Quality of School Environment
The level of classroom disruption and student vandalism is low, and the quality of building maintenance and repair is excellent.

WAUWATOSA

ADDRESS OF CENTRAL OFFICE:
12121 West North Avenue, Wauwatosa, WI 53226
ESI:None†

STATISTICAL PROFILE	DATA	ESI
Grade organization:		
Percentage of schools built before 1955		
Total enrollment		
Average Daily Attendance (ADA)		
Current expense per pupil in ADA		
Dropout rate		
Percentage of eligible students who took the ACT		
Average combined score on ACT		
Percentage of graduates who enrolled in 2- or 4-year colleges		
Percentage of students who passed the state reading test		
Percentage of students who passed the state math test		
Teacher–student ratio in elementary grades		
Teacher–student ratio in secondary grades		
Counselor–student ratio in secondary grades		
Number of students per music specialist in elementary grades		
Number of students per art specialist in elementary grades		
Number of volumes in senior high school library		
Beginning teacher's salary		
Maximum teacher's salary		
Average years of experience among teachers		
Number of students suspended and expelled		
Subjects in which Advanced Placement courses are offered:		

†A Statistical Profile was not received from this district.

FAIR APPRAISAL

Quality of School Leadership
Principals are hired based on their educational leadership ability, and the quality of leadership does not vary greatly from school to school. Parents and teachers assist in interviewing principal candidates. Principals are very influential in deciding how district resources are distributed among the schools. An observer praised the district's administrators as being "the best in the area."

Parent organizations exercise effective influence in district decision-making.

Quality of Instruction
A program for gifted students that spans all grade levels is rated good, as is additional instruction for low-achieving students. The curricula for college-bound students and for those planning on jobs after graduation are considered excellent.

Quality of School Environment
Classroom disruption and student vandalism are not problems, and the quality of building maintenance and repair is rated good to excellent.

WEST ALLIS–WEST MILWAUKEE

ADDRESS OF CENTRAL OFFICE:
9333 West Lincoln Avenue, West Allis, WI 53227
ESI:72

STATISTICAL PROFILE	DATA	ESI
Grade organization: K–6/7–8/9–12		
Percentage of schools built before 1955	53%	
Total enrollment	9,049	
Average Daily Attendance (ADA)	93%	6
Current expense per pupil in ADA	$4,891	9
Dropout rate	16%	7
Percentage of eligible students who took the ACT	47%	7
Average combined score on ACT	20.6	9
Percentage of graduates who enrolled in 2- or 4-year colleges	45%	
Percentage of students who passed the state reading test	NA	
Percentage of students who passed the state math test	NA	
Teacher–student ratio in elementary grades	1:26	4
Teacher–student ratio in secondary grades	1:13	10
Counselor–student ratio in secondary grades	1:246	8
Number of students per music specialist in elementary grades	278	10
Number of students per art specialist in elementary grades	148	
Number of volumes in senior high school library	50,000	
Beginning teacher's salary	$17,900	
Maximum teacher's salary	$38,411	
Average years of experience among teachers	14	
Number of students suspended and expelled	272	
Subjects in which Advanced Placement courses are offered:	2†	2
English, European History		

†International Baccalaureate classes are offered in 18 subjects.

FAIR APPRAISAL

Quality of School Leadership
The School Board hires principals based primarily on their educational leadership ability. The quality of leadership does not vary greatly from school to school. Parents and teachers do not screen principal candidates, but may informally influence selection. Principals have some say as to what resources will be allotted their school.

Cooperation between parents and school administrators is good, and parents' influence in decision-making is usually effective.

Quality of Instruction
Additional learning opportunities for gifted students and additional instruction for low-achieving students are rated good. The college preparatory curriculum is called excellent; International Baccalaureate classes are offered in 18 subjects. The curriculum preparing students for the world of work is considered good.

Quality of School Environment
The incidence of classroom disruption and student vandalism is low, and the quality of building maintenance and repair is excellent.

Minneapolis – St. Paul, MN

Twenty districts completed Statistical Profiles, and Fair Appraisals alone are provided for an additional four districts. Minnesota does not have state tests of reading and math. Therefore, *NA* (not applicable) follows the lines requesting those data. The average dropout rate for Minnesota is only 9%, but the ESI scoring for this statistic has not been adjusted to facilitate comparable ESI's nationwide. Districts in this area may be compared to those in the Milwaukee, WI Metropolitan Area.

AREA AT A GLANCE

SCHOOL DISTRICT	ENROLLMENT	ESI
Bloomington	12,317	71
Burnsville–Eagan–Savage	9,047	50
Centennial	3,158	
Eden Prairie	4,457	48
Forest Lake	6,563	
Fridley	2,703	42
Hastings	4,550	58
Hopkins	6,697	75
Hudson, WI	2,731	
Inver Grove	3,488	34*
Lakeville	3,327	49*
Minneapolis	38,483	37*
Minnetonka	5,400	56
Mounds View	11,164	41*
North St. Paul–Maplewood–Oakdale	8,185	38
Osseo	18,000	45
Prior Lake	2,986	76
Richfield	4,630	55
Rosemount	15,785	56
Roseville	6,199	26*
St. Louis Park	4,105	62
St. Paul	32,382	44
Westonka	2,655	42*
White Bear Lake	7,711	

Indicates district misinterpretation of one or more statistics in the ESI. For each misinterpreted statistic, a score of 0 was given instead of a possible score of 0 to 10 points.

BLOOMINGTON

ADDRESS OF CENTRAL OFFICE:
8900 Portland Avenue, Bloomington, MN 55420
ESI:71

STATISTICAL PROFILE	DATA	ESI
Grade organization: K–6/7–9/10–12		
Percentage of schools built before 1955	12%	
Total enrollment	12,317	
Average Daily Attendance (ADA)	96%	9
Current expense per pupil in ADA	$4,375	8
Dropout rate	3%	10
Percentage of eligible students who took the SAT	53%	8
Average combined score on SAT	1,071	10
Percentage of graduates who enrolled in 2- or 4-year colleges	70%	
Percentage of students who passed the state reading test	NA	
Percentage of students who passed the state math test	NA	
Teacher–student ratio in elementary grades	1:27	3
Teacher–student ratio in secondary grades	1:21	7
Counselor–student ratio in secondary grades	1:500	0
Number of students per music specialist in elementary grades	240	10
Number of students per art specialist in elementary grades	None	
Number of volumes in senior high school libraries (average)	22,500	
Beginning teacher's salary	$19,396	
Maximum teacher's salary	$40,919	
Average years of experience among teachers	19	
Number of students suspended and expelled	534	
Subjects in which Advanced Placement courses are offered: American History, Biology, Calculus, English, European History, French	6	6

FAIR APPRAISAL

Quality of School Leadership
For the most part, principals are hired based on their educational leadership ability, and the quality of leadership is generally uniform throughout the system. Parents and teachers do not screen principal candidates. Principals have some say in how district resources are divided among the schools.

Parent organizations are not very effective influencing school policy decisions.

Quality of Instruction
Special classes exist for gifted students at all levels, and the program is rated excellent. The additional instruction for low-achieving students is considered good, although one observer complained that more could be done for these students. The college preparatory curriculum is rated excellent, and the curriculum for students going into the job market is rated good. One of the district's high schools and one elementary school have been designated schools of excellence by the U.S. Department of Education.

Quality of School Environment
The level of classroom disruption and student vandalism is low, and the quality of building maintenance and repair is excellent.

BURNSVILLE–EAGAN–SAVAGE

ADDRESS OF CENTRAL OFFICE:
100 River Ridge Court, Burnsville, MN 55337
ESI:50

STATISTICAL PROFILE	DATA	ESI
Grade organization: K–6/7–9/10–12		
Percentage of schools built before 1955	8%	
Total enrollment	9,047	
Average Daily Attendance (ADA)	95%	8
Current expense per pupil in ADA	NK	0
Dropout rate	8%	10
Percentage of eligible students who took the ACT	40%	5
Average combined score on ACT	NK	0
Percentage of graduates who enrolled in 2- or 4-year colleges	†	
Percentage of students who passed the state reading test	NA	
Percentage of students who passed the state math test	NA	
Teacher–student ratio in elementary grades	1:20	10
Teacher–student ratio in secondary grades	1:20	8
Counselor–student ratio in secondary grades	1:450	0
Number of students per music specialist in elementary grades	450	6
Number of students per art specialist in elementary grades	1,100	
Number of volumes in senior high school library	30,000	
Beginning teacher's salary	$19,000	
Maximum teacher's salary	$43,830	
Average years of experience among teachers	14	
Number of students suspended and expelled	120	
Subjects in which Advanced Placement courses are offered: American History, Calculus, English	3	3

†The district supplied an inappropriate statistic.

FAIR APPRAISAL

Quality of School Leadership
Although seniority is a factor, principals are hired mostly for their educational leadership ability. The quality of leadership does not vary greatly from school to school. Parents and teachers do not screen principal candidates. Principals have some say in how district resources are allotted to the schools.

"Parents often are the impetus for change," said an observer. Another observer said district officials are "very interested in parental involvement."

Quality of Instruction
Additional learning opportunities for gifted students have "grown tremendously," according to an observer, and they are rated excellent. However, one observer thought the gifted program was "a little weak in the sciences." Additional instruction for low-achieving students is rated fair to good, the program being stronger in the elementary grades than at the high school. Another observer thought the program was "limited in scope." The curriculum for college-bound students is considered excellent, and the curriculum for students preparing for the job world is rated good. The district offers excellent business training, said an observer.

Quality of School Environment
Classroom disruption and student vandalism are not problems, and the quality of building maintenance and repair is excellent.

CENTENNIAL

ADDRESS OF CENTRAL OFFICE:
4707 North Road, Circle Pines, MN 55014
ESI:None†

STATISTICAL PROFILE	DATA	ESI
Grade organization:		
Percentage of schools built before 1955		
Total enrollment		
Average Daily Attendance (ADA)		
Current expense per pupil in ADA		
Dropout rate		
Percentage of eligible students who took the ACT		
Average combined score on ACT		
Percentage of graduates who enrolled in 2- or 4-year colleges		
Percentage of students who passed the state reading test		
Percentage of students who passed the state math test		
Teacher–student ratio in elementary grades		
Teacher–student ratio in secondary grades		
Counselor–student ratio in secondary grades		
Number of students per music specialist in elementary grades		
Number of students per art specialist in elementary grades		
Number of volumes in senior high school library		
Beginning teacher's salary		
Maximum teacher's salary		
Average years of experience among teachers		
Number of students suspended and expelled		
Subjects in which Advanced Placement courses are offered:		

†A Statistical Profile was not received from this district.

FAIR APPRAISAL

Quality of School Leadership
Seniority is an important consideration in principal selection, but the quality of leadership is generally uniform throughout the system. Parents and teachers take no part in principal selection. Also, principals have little say about the distribution of district resources.

Parent organizations are not very effective influencing school policy decisions.

Quality of Instruction
Additional learning opportunities for gifted students and additional instruction for low-achieving students are rated only fair. Also considered fair is the curriculum preparing students for college. The only good rating goes to the curriculum for students preparing for the job market.

Quality of School Environment
The level of classroom disruption and student vandalism is very low, but the quality of building maintenance and repair is considered fair to poor. "Many times schools begin in the fall and the carpeting is the only clean item in the classroom," complained an observer.

EDEN PRAIRIE

ADDRESS OF CENTRAL OFFICE:
8100 School Road, Eden Prairie, MN 55344
ESI:48

STATISTICAL PROFILE	DATA	ESI
Grade organization: K–5/6–8/9–12		
Percentage of schools built before 1955	25%	
Total enrollment	4,457	
Average Daily Attendance (ADA)	97%	10
Current expense per pupil in ADA	$3,531	4
Dropout rate	2%	10
Percentage of eligible students who took the ACT	60%	9
Average combined score on ACT	20.1	6
Percentage of graduates who enrolled in 2- or 4-year colleges	80%	
Percentage of students who passed the state reading test	NA	
Percentage of students who passed the state math test	NA	
Teacher–student ratio in elementary grades	1:25	5
Teacher–student ratio in secondary grades	1:27	1
Counselor–student ratio in secondary grades	1:460	0
Number of students per music specialist in elementary grades	590	4
Number of students per art specialist in elementary grades	590	
Number of volumes in senior high school library	14,462	
Beginning teacher's salary	$20,062	
Maximum teacher's salary	$42,181	
Average years of experience among teachers	9	
Number of students suspended and expelled	NK	
Subjects in which Advanced Placement courses are offered:	3	3
Calculus, Chemistry, English		

FAIR APPRAISAL

Quality of School Leadership
The School Board hires principals who demonstrate educational leadership ability, and the quality of leadership is uniform throughout the system. Parents and other citizens serve on a screening committee that interviews principal candidates. Principals have considerable influence over the allotment of district resources to the schools.

Parent groups are extremely active and very effective influencing district policies and practices. "Parents are involved on committees that make sure every student learns up to his/her potential," said one observer. Another observer said parents have resolved elementary school boundary disputes.

Quality of Instruction
Additional learning opportunities for gifted students are rated excellent. "Lots of time, money and taxes keep it good," an observer said about the program. Additional instruction for low-achieving students is rated good. Observers said the district program for low-achieving students is being "worked on" and is "improving." The curriculum for college-bound students is considered excellent, and the curriculum for students preparing for the job world is rated good. One observer praised district officials for their fairness. "If there are budget cuts," said the observer, "they are made on a fair basis, and programs are reinstated when funds become available."

Quality of School Environment
Classroom disruption and student vandalism are not problems, and the quality of building maintenance and repair is excellent.

FOREST LAKE

ADDRESS OF CENTRAL OFFICE:
6100 North 210th Street, Forest Lake, MN 55025
ESI:None†

STATISTICAL PROFILE	DATA	ESI
Grade organization:		
Percentage of schools built before 1955		
Total enrollment		
Average Daily Attendance (ADA)		
Current expense per pupil in ADA		
Dropout rate		
Percentage of eligible students who took the SAT		
Average combined score on SAT		
Percentage of graduates who enrolled in 2- or 4-year colleges		
Percentage of students who passed the state reading test		
Percentage of students who passed the state math test		
Teacher–student ratio in elementary grades		
Teacher–student ratio in secondary grades		
Counselor–student ratio in secondary grades		
Number of students per music specialist in elementary grades		
Number of students per art specialist in elementary grades		
Number of volumes in senior high school library		
Beginning teacher's salary		
Maximum teacher's salary		
Average years of experience among teachers		
Number of students suspended and expelled		
Subjects in which Advanced Placement courses are offered:		

†A Statistical Profile was not received from this district.

FAIR APPRAISAL

Quality of School Leadership
Principals are hired because of their educational leadership ability, and the quality of leadership does not vary greatly from school to school. Parents and teachers do not screen principal candidates. However, principals have much to say about the division of resources among the schools.

Parent organizations are sometimes effective influences on school decision-making.

Quality of Instruction
Additional learning opportunities for gifted students and additional instruction for low-achieving students are rated good. Also considered good is the college preparatory curriculum. The curriculum preparing students for the job world is only fair.

Quality of School Environment
The incidence of classroom disruption and student vandalism is low, and the quality of building maintenance and repair is excellent.

FRIDLEY

ADDRESS OF CENTRAL OFFICE:
6000 West Moore Lake Drive, Fridley, MN 55432
ESI:42

STATISTICAL PROFILE	DATA	ESI
Grade organization: K–5/6–8/9–12		
Percentage of schools built before 1955	0%	
Total enrollment	2,703	
Average Daily Attendance (ADA)	95%	8
Current expense per pupil in ADA	$4,513	9
Dropout rate	10%	10
Percentage of eligible students who took the ACT	10%	0
Average combined score on ACT	NK	0
Percentage of graduates who enrolled in 2- or 4-year colleges	55%	
Percentage of students who passed the state reading test	NA	
Percentage of students who passed the state math test	NA	
Teacher–student ratio in elementary grades	1:25	5
Teacher–student ratio in secondary grades	1:22	6
Counselor–student ratio in secondary grades	1:440	0
Number of students per music specialist in elementary grades	584	4
Number of students per art specialist in elementary grades	1,168	
Number of volumes in senior high school library	21,550	
Beginning teacher's salary	$19,368	
Maximum teacher's salary	$37,800	
Average years of experience among teachers	17	
Number of students suspended and expelled	None	0
Subjects in which Advanced Placement courses are offered:	None	0

FAIR APPRAISAL

Quality of School Leadership
Principals are selected primarily for their ability as educational leaders, and the quality of leadership is generally uniform throughout the district. Parents and teachers do not help screen principal candidates. Principals, however, have some say in what resources will be allotted their school.

Parent advisory boards are effective influences on school policy decisions. Parents were instrumental in getting the School Board to restore funds cut from extracurricular sports.

Quality of Instruction
Additional learning opportunities for gifted students are rated good. "Parent support has kept the program going when funds were short," said an observer. Additional instruction for low-achieving students is considered fair. One observer said there is no "early intervention" with preschoolers, and another observer said the program for low-achievers is also weak at the other end—in the high school. The curricula for college-bound students and job-bound students are rated good.

Quality of School Environment
The level of student vandalism is very low, but at least one observer complained the classroom disruption was a problem in some schools. The quality of building maintenance and repair is good.

HASTINGS

ADDRESS OF CENTRAL OFFICE:
9th & Vermillion Streets, Hastings, MN 55033
ESI:58

STATISTICAL PROFILE	DATA	ESI
Grade organization: K–5/6–8/9–12		
Percentage of schools built before 1955	0%	
Total enrollment	4,550	
Average Daily Attendance (ADA)	95%	8
Current expense per pupil in ADA	$3,641	4
Dropout rate	8%	10
Percentage of eligible students who took the ACT	54%	8
Average combined score on ACT	19.5	5
Percentage of graduates who enrolled in 2- or 4-year colleges	40%	
Percentage of students who passed the state reading test	NA	
Percentage of students who passed the state math test	NA	
Teacher–student ratio in elementary grades	1:23	7
Teacher–student ratio in secondary grades	1:21	7
Counselor–student ratio in secondary grades	1:390	2
Number of students per music specialist in elementary grades	437	7
Number of students per art specialist in elementary grades	None	0
Number of volumes in senior high school library	21,800	
Beginning teacher's salary	$18,180	
Maximum teacher's salary	$35,060	
Average years of experience among teachers	12	
Number of students suspended and expelled	270	
Subjects in which Advanced Placement courses are offered:	None	0

Quality of School Leadership
The School Board hires principals who have demonstrated ability as educational leaders. The quality of leadership does not vary greatly from school to school. Parents and teachers serve on committees that screen principal candidates, and principals (along with teachers) have considerable influence over the distribution of resources to the schools.

Parents helped get approval for a recent referendum for a new elementary school, and parent groups generally are effective influencing district decision-making. Parent advisory groups are at each school. "It's a real responsive district," said an observer.

Quality of Instruction
Additional opportunities for gifted students are rated excellent. Gifted students are normally grouped together, and resource rooms are used to challenge and stimulate students. Additional instruction for low-achieving students is also considered excellent. Curricula for college-bound students and for those heading into the world of work are rated good. Parent volunteers are used frequently as aides and tutors.

Quality of School Environment
Classroom disruption and student vandalism are not problems, and the quality of building maintenance and repair is excellent.

HOPKINS

ADDRESS OF CENTRAL OFFICE:
1001 Highway #7, Hopkins, MN 55343
ESI:75

STATISTICAL PROFILE	DATA	ESI
Grade organization: K–6/7–9/10–12		
Percentage of schools built before 1955	33%	
Total enrollment	6,697	
Average Daily Attendance (ADA)	97%	10
Current expense per pupil in ADA	$5,234	10
Dropout rate	2%	10
Percentage of eligible students who took the SAT	30%	3
Average combined score on SAT	1,016	10
Percentage of graduates who enrolled in 2- or 4-year colleges	77%	
Percentage of students who passed the state reading test	NA	
Percentage of students who passed the state math test	NA	
Teacher–student ratio in elementary grades	1:19	10
Teacher–student ratio in secondary grades	1:18	10
Counselor–student ratio in secondary grades	1:468	0
Number of students per music specialist in elementary grades	352	8
Number of students per art specialist in elementary grades	None†	
Number of volumes in senior high school libraries (average)	30,000	
Beginning teacher's salary	$20,000	
Maximum teacher's salary	$42,104	
Average years of experience among teachers	NK	
Number of students suspended and expelled	1††	
Subjects in which Advanced Placement courses are offered: American Government, American History, English, European History	4	4

† See Fair Appraisal.
††Does not include suspensions.

Quality of School Leadership
Principals are selected primarily for their educational leadership ability, and the quality of leadership is generally uniform throughout the system. Parents and teachers usually assist in screening principal candidates. Principals have a great deal to say about where district resources will go.

"Schools work real closely with parents," said an observer, and parent organizations are effective.

Quality of Instruction
Additional learning opportunities for gifted students are rated excellent. Additional instruction for low-achieving students is considered good. Computer drill and practice are used extensively. The curriculum for students preparing for college is termed excellent. All three high schools have been cited for excellence by the U.S. Department of Education. One high school produced 14 National Merit Scholarship finalists in 1985, the largest number of any public high school in the state. The curriculum for students not planning on college also is rated excellent.

Although the elementary schools do not have art specialists, the art program conducted by classroom teachers was cited by the J. Paul Getty Center for Education in the Arts as one of seven exemplary programs in the nation.

Quality of School Environment
The incidence of classroom disruption and student vandalism is low, and the quality of building maintenance and repair is good.

HUDSON, WI

ADDRESS OF CENTRAL OFFICE:
416 St. Croix Street, Hudson, WI 54016
ESI:None†

STATISTICAL PROFILE	DATA	ESI
Grade organization:		
Percentage of schools built before 1955		
Total enrollment		
Average Daily Attendance (ADA)		
Current expense per pupil in ADA		
Dropout rate		
Percentage of eligible students who took the SAT		
Average combined score on SAT		
Percentage of graduates who enrolled in 2- or 4-year colleges		
Percentage of students who passed the state reading test		
Percentage of students who passed the state math test		
Teacher–student ratio in elementary grades		
Teacher–student ratio in secondary grades		
Counselor–student ratio in secondary grades		
Number of students per music specialist in elementary grades		
Number of students per art specialist in elementary grades		
Number of volumes in senior high school library		
Beginning teacher's salary		
Maximum teacher's salary		
Average years of experience among teachers		
Number of students suspended and expelled		
Subjects in which Advanced Placement courses are offered:		

†A Statistical Profile was not received from this district.

FAIR APPRAISAL

Quality of School Leadership
The School Board picks principals for their educational leadership ability, and the quality of leadership does not vary greatly from school to school. Parents and teachers do not screen principal candidates, and principals have little influence over the distribution of resources to the schools.

Parent organizations are sometimes effective influencing school decision-making.

Quality of Instruction
Additional learning opportunities for gifted students and additional instruction for low-achieving students are rated fair. The curriculum for students preparing for college is considered good to excellent, while the curriculum for students moving into the job market is rated good.

Quality of School Environment
The level of classroom disruption and student vandalism is very low, and the quality of building maintenace and repair is excellent.

INVER GROVE

ADDRESS OF CENTRAL OFFICE:
9875 Inver Grove Trail, St. Paul, MN 55075
ESI:34*

STATISTICAL PROFILE	DATA	ESI
Grade organization: K–6/7–9/10–12		
Percentage of schools built before 1955	NK	
Total enrollment	3,488	
Average Daily Attendance (ADA)	95%	8
Current expense per pupil in ADA	$2,175	0
Dropout rate	9%	10
Percentage of eligible students who took the SAT	50%	7
Average combined score on SAT	NK	0
Percentage of graduates who enrolled in 2- or 4-year colleges	49%	
Percentage of students who passed the state reading test	NA	
Percentage of students who passed the state math test	NA	
Teacher–student ratio in elementary grades	1:26	4
Teacher–student ratio in secondary grades	1:27	1
Counselor–student ratio in secondary grades	†	0*
Number of students per music specialist in elementary grades	570	4
Number of students per art specialist in elementary grades	None	0
Number of volumes in senior high school library	15,000	
Beginning teacher's salary	$20,000	
Maximum teacher's salary	$37,465	
Average years of experience among teachers	NK	
Number of students suspended and expelled	NK	
Subjects in which Advanced Placement courses are offered:	None	0

†The district supplied an inappropriate statistic.

FAIR APPRAISAL

Quality of School Leadership
Principals are hired primarily because they show ability as educational leaders, and the quality of leadership is generally uniform throughout the system. Teachers help screen principal candidates, but parents do not. Principals have some say in how much of the district's resources their school will receive.

Parent organizations are sometimes effective influencing school policy decisions at the elementary level, but are "virtually non-existent" at the high school. One observer complained that students' morale at the high school is very low. "The kids don't have any backing," said the observer. "We are laughed at around the area. Administrators are aware of the problem, but other things get in the way."

Quality of Instruction
The program for gifted students is rated fair. Additional instruction for low-achieving students is considered good. Observers complimented the director of the latter program, although they agree that improvement is still needed. The curriculua for college-bound students and for those preparing for the world of work are good.

Quality of School Environment
Classroom disruption and student vandalism are not problems. The quality of building maintenance and repair is rated fair. Lack of money and planning are blamed.

LAKEVILLE

ADDRESS OF CENTRAL OFFICE:
8670 West 210th Street, Lakeville, MN 55044
ESI:49*

STATISTICAL PROFILE	DATA	ESI
Grade organization: K–6/7–9/10–12		
Percentage of schools built before 1955	0%	
Total enrollment	3,327	
Average Daily Attendance (ADA)	96%	9
Current expense per pupil in ADA	$2,350	0
Dropout rate	3%	10
Percentage of eligible students who took the ACT	30%	3
Average combined score on ACT	†	0*
Percentage of graduates who enrolled in 2- or 4-year colleges	73%	
Percentage of students who passed the state reading test	NA	
Percentage of students who passed the state math test	NA	
Teacher–student ratio in elementary grades	1:20 ††	10
Teacher–student ratio in secondary grades	1:19††	9
Counselor–student ratio in secondary grades	1:433††	0
Number of students per music specialist in elementary grades	527	5
Number of students per art specialist in elementary grades	None	
Number of volumes in senior high school library	11,500	
Beginning teacher's salary	$19,215	
Maximum teacher's salary	$35,354	
Average years of experience among teachers	14	
Number of students suspended and expelled	NK	
Subjects in which Advanced Placement courses are offered: Calculus, Chemistry, Computer Science	3	3

†The district supplied an inappropriate statistic.
††1986–87 statistics.

FAIR APPRAISAL

Quality of School Leadership
The School Board looks for principal candidates who demonstrate educational leadership ability. The quality of leadership does not vary greatly from school to school, although one observer believes the leadership is somewhat better at the elementary level. Parents and teachers do not screen principal candidates, but principals exercise some influence over the distribution of district resources.

A parent advisory council meets monthly with district officials and is influential in decisions on curriculum, textbooks, and other matters.

Quality of Instruction
Additional learning opportunities for gifted students are rated fair, and additional instruction for low-achieving students is called good. The curriculum for students preparing for college is rated good, although one observer believes the high school is weak in math instruction. The curriculum for students preparing for jobs after graduation is rated good.

Quality of School Environment
The level of classroom disruption and student vandalism is low, and the quality of building maintenance and repair is fair to good.

MINNEAPOLIS

ADDRESS OF CENTRAL OFFICE:

807 Northeast Broadway, Minneapolis, MN 55413
ESI:37*

STATISTICAL PROFILE	DATA	ESI
Grade organization: †		
Percentage of schools built before 1955	66%	
Total enrollment	38,483	
Average Daily Attendance (ADA)	91%	4
Current expense per pupil in ADA	$4,333	8
Dropout rate	25%	0
Percentage of eligible students who took the SAT	15%	0
Average combined score on SAT	1,002	9
Percentage of graduates who enrolled in 2- or 4-year colleges	76%	
Percentage of students who passed the state reading test	NA	
Percentage of students who passed the state math test	NA	
Teacher–student ratio in elementary grades	1:24	6
Teacher–student ratio in secondary grades	1:25	3
Counselor–student ratio in secondary grades	1:400	2
Number of students per music specialist in elementary grades	††	0*
Number of students per art specialist in elementary grades	††	
Number of volumes in senior high school library	NK	
Beginning teacher's salary	$19,157	
Maximum teacher's salary	$41,809	
Average years of experience among teachers	14	
Number of students suspended and expelled	3,987	
Subjects in which Advanced Placement courses are offered: American History, Calculus, Computer Science, English, Science	5	5

† Different patterns exist, although the common one is PreK–6/7–8/9–12.
††The district supplied an inappropriate statistic.

Quality of School Leadership

Although seniority and popularity are factors, most principals are selected because of their educational leadership ability. The quality of leadership does not vary greatly from school to school. Parents and teachers (and students when the high school is involved) help screen candidates for principal. Principals, for their part, have some say in what resources are allotted their school.

Parent organizations are generally effective. For example, parents were not pleased with some aspects of the curriculum, so they suggested revisions that were later adopted by the School Board.

Quality of Instruction

Additional learning opportunities for gifted students, including some magnet schools of excellence, are rated good, as is the additional instruction for low-achieving students. Speaking of the latter program, an observer said, "There's a good program delivered to students who are serious about education." The curriculum for college-bound students is rated excellent, and the curriculum for job-bound students is considered good.

Observers believe the district is adequately meeting the educational needs of minority students (many of them from migrant families). "We have early intervention programs for students who need help," said an observer.

Quality of School Environment

Classroom disruption and student vandalism are not problems, and the quality of building maintenance and repair is good.

MINNETONKA

ADDRESS OF CENTRAL OFFICE:
261 School Avenue, Excelsior, MN 55311
ESI:56

STATISTICAL PROFILE	DATA	ESI
Grade organization: K–4/5–6/7–8/9–12		
Percentage of schools built before 1955	NK	
Total enrollment	5,400	
Average Daily Attendance (ADA)	95%	8
Current expense per pupil in ADA	$3,975	6
Dropout rate	11%	10
Percentage of eligible students who took the SAT	76%	10
Average combined score on SAT	994	9
Percentage of graduates who enrolled in 2- or 4-year colleges	75%	
Percentage of students who passed the state reading test	NA	
Percentage of students who passed the state math test	NA	
Teacher–student ratio in elementary grades	1:25	5
Teacher–student ratio in secondary grades	1:27	1
Counselor–student ratio in secondary grades	1:500	0
Number of students per music specialist in elementary grades	446	7
Number of students per art specialist in elementary grades	None	0
Number of volumes in senior high school library	18,000	
Beginning teacher's salary	$20,000	
Maximum teacher's salary	$43,400	
Average years of experience among teachers	17	
Number of students suspended and expelled	75	
Subjects in which Advanced Placement courses are offered:	None	0

FAIR APPRAISAL

Quality of School Leadership
Principals are hired because of their educational leadership ability, and the quality of leadership is generally uniform throughout the system. Parents and teachers help screen principal candidates. Also, principals have some say about the division of resources among the schools.

Parents are mostly an effective influence on district policies. Recently, parents came up with a plan for reopening and making best use of a closed school. Board members (most of whom were once parent volunteers in the schools) are receptive to parents and other citizens.

Quality of Instruction
Additional learning opportunities for gifted students are rated good, and additional instruction for low-achieving students is termed excellent. The latter program is a top priority for the district, said observers. Parent volunteers are used extensively to help low-achieving students. The curriculum for students planning on college is rated excellent (graduation standards were raised recently), and the curriculum for those students not planning on college is rated good.

The district's instruction in English as a second language is considered outstanding by the observers.

Quality of School Environment
The incidence of classroom disruption and student vandalism is low, and the quality of building maintenance and repair is good.

MOUNDS VIEW

ADDRESS OF CENTRAL OFFICE:
2959 North Hamline Avenue, Mounds View, MN 55113
ESI:41*

STATISTICAL PROFILE	DATA	ESI
Grade organization: K–6/7–8/9–12		
Percentage of schools built before 1955	17%	
Total enrollment	11,164	
Average Daily Attendance (ADA)	95%	8
Current expense per pupil in ADA	$3,470	4
Dropout rate	5%	10
Percentage of eligible students who took the ACT	22%	2
Average combined score on ACT	20.5	8
Percentage of graduates who enrolled in 2- or 4-year colleges	60%	
Percentage of students who passed the state reading test	NA	
Percentage of students who passed the state math test	NA	
Teacher–student ratio in elementary grades	1:26	4
Teacher–student ratio in secondary grades	1:24	4
Counselor–student ratio in secondary grades	1:454	0
Number of students per music specialist in elementary grades	†	0*
Number of students per art specialist in elementary grades	†	
Number of volumes in senior high school libraries (average)	24,000	
Beginning teacher's salary	$18,014††	
Maximum teacher's salary	$43,747††	
Average years of experience among teachers	18	
Number of students suspended and expelled	279	
Subjects in which Advanced Placement courses are offered: Calculus	1	1

† The district supplied an inappropriate statistic.
††1986–87 statistics.

FAIR APPRAISAL

Quality of School Leadership
The School Board looks for principal candidates who have educational leadership ability, and the quality of leadership does not vary greatly throughout the system. Parents and teachers help select principals by screening candidates. Also, principals have some say about the allotment of district resources to the schools.

Parent advisory committees are effective influencing school policy decisions, although, according to observers, the central administration is more receptive to parents than is the School Board.

Quality of Instruction
The program for gifted students is rated good. Exceptionally bright students are excused from regular classes during the week to attend special enrichment classes. According to one observer, the program "has come a long way in the last several years." Additional instruction for low-achieving students is rated good, although one observer wondered if students who are "a bit below average" are getting enough attention. The curricula for college-bound students and job-bound students are considered good.

Quality of School Environment
Classroom disruption and student vandalism are not problems, and the quality of building maintenance and repair is good.

NORTH ST. PAUL–MAPLEWOOD–OAKDALE

ADDRESS OF CENTRAL OFFICE:
2055 East Larpenteur Avenue, Maplewood, MN 55109
ESI:38

STATISTICAL PROFILE	DATA	ESI
Grade organization: K–5/6–8/9–12		
Percentage of schools built before 1955	23%	
Total enrollment	8,185	
Average Daily Attendance (ADA)	92%	5
Current expense per pupil in ADA	$4,068	7
Dropout rate	NK	0
Percentage of eligible students who took the ACT	25%	2
Average combined score on ACT	20.4	8
Percentage of graduates who enrolled in 2- or 4-year colleges	64%	
Percentage of students who passed the state reading test	NA	
Percentage of students who passed the state math test	NA	
Teacher–student ratio in elementary grades	1:25	5
Teacher–student ratio in secondary grades	1:27	1
Counselor–student ratio in secondary grades	1:467	0
Number of students per music specialist in elementary grades	250	10
Number of students per art specialist in elementary grades	None	0
Number of volumes in senior high school library	25,000	
Beginning teacher's salary	$19,848	
Maximum teacher's salary	$40,609	
Average years of experience among teachers	16	
Number of students suspended and expelled	350	
Subjects in which Advanced Placement courses are offered:	None	0

Quality of School Leadership

Principal candidates must demonstrate ability in educational leadership, and the quality of leadership is generally uniform throughout the system. Parents and teachers serve on committees that screen principal candidates. Principals have a great deal to say about how the district allots resources to the schools.

A parent council for the district meets monthly to consider issues and make recommendations to district officials.

Quality of Instruction

Approximately the top 5 percent of students K-12 are designated gifted and take part in a program that is rated excellent. Also rated excellent is the additional instruction for low-achieving students. The curricula for college-bound students and for those preparing for jobs are considered good.

This was the first district in the state to require students to pass district competency tests in reading and math in order to graduate. Also, all schools are included in an educational improvement program that is based on effective schools research.

Quality of School Environment

The level of classroom disruption and student vandalism is very low, and the quality of building maintenance and repair is good.

OSSEO

ADDRESS OF CENTRAL OFFICE:
P.O. Box 327, Osseo, MN 55369
ESI:45

STATISTICAL PROFILE	DATA	ESI
Grade organization: K–6/7–9/10–12		
Percentage of schools built before 1955	10%	
Total enrollment	18,000	
Average Daily Attendance (ADA)	96%	9
Current expense per pupil in ADA	$3,350	3
Dropout rate	5%	10
Percentage of eligible students who took the ACT	36%	5
Average combined score on ACT	21.1	10
Percentage of graduates who enrolled in 2- or 4-year colleges	46%	
Percentage of students who passed the state reading test	NA	
Percentage of students who passed the state math test	NA	
Teacher–student ratio in elementary grades	1:25	5
Teacher–student ratio in secondary grades	1:25	3
Counselor–student ratio in secondary grades	NK	0
Number of students per music specialist in elementary grades	NK	0
Number of students per art specialist in elementary grades	None	0
Number of volumes in senior high school libraries (average)	25,000	
Beginning teacher's salary	$19,340	
Maximum teacher's salary	$40,000	
Average years of experience among teachers	12	
Number of students suspended and expelled	None	0
Subjects in which Advanced Placement courses are offered:	None	0

Quality of School Leadership

Although seniority is a factor, principals are hired primarily for their educational leadership ability. Furthermore, the quality of leadership does not vary greatly from school to school. Parents and teachers may influence principal selection on an informal basis. Principals, however, have a lot of influence over the distribution of district resources.

"The district has gone a very long way in involving the community in all areas," said an observer. Parental influence on district decision-making is considered effective.

Quality of Instruction

Additional learning opportunities for gifted students are rated good, and additional instruction for low-achieving students is considered excellent. Concerning the gifted program, an observer said it is "on the way to excellence; they have a department working on it, and they're working hard at improving the program at the upper grades." The college preparatory curriculum is considered good, and the curriculum for students not planning to attend college is called excellent. The vocational education program involves area businesses and industries to a great degree.

Quality of School Environment

The level of classroom disruption and student vandalism is low, and the quality of building maintenance and repair is excellent. A $30-million bond issue for building improvements was passed recently.

PRIOR LAKE

ADDRESS OF CENTRAL OFFICE:
P.O. Box 539, Prior Lake, MN 55372
ESI:76

STATISTICAL PROFILE	DATA	ESI
Grade organization: K–3/4–6/7–8/9–12		
Percentage of schools built before 1955	0%	
Total enrollment	2,986	
Average Daily Attendance (ADA)	98%	10
Current expense per pupil in ADA	$2,900	1
Dropout rate	7%	10
Percentage of eligible students who took the SAT	67%	10
Average combined score on SAT	1,041	10
Percentage of graduates who enrolled in 2- or 4-year colleges	68%	
Percentage of students who passed the state reading test	NA	
Percentage of students who passed the state math test	NA	
Teacher–student ratio in elementary grades	1:20	10
Teacher–student ratio in secondary grades	1:16	10
Counselor–student ratio in secondary grades	1:325	5
Number of students per music specialist in elementary grades	350	8
Number of students per art specialist in elementary grades	600	
Number of volumes in senior high school library	11,000	
Beginning teacher's salary	$19,200	
Maximum teacher's salary	$36,900	
Average years of experience among teachers	15	
Number of students suspended and expelled	448	
Subjects in which Advanced Placement courses are offered: Calculus, English	2	2

FAIR APPRAISAL

Quality of School Leadership
Educational leadership ability is the primary criterion for principal selection, and the quality of leadership in the district is generally uniform. Teachers, but not parents, are involved in principal selection. Principals have some influence over the distribution of resources to their school.

Parent organizations are sometimes effective influencing school decision-making.

Quality of Instruction
Gifted students normally are grouped together for instruction, and the program is rated good. Additional instruction for low-achieving students is rated fair. The curricula for college-bound students and for those not planning on college are considered good.

Quality of School Environment
Classroom disruption and student vandalism are not problems, and the quality of building maintenance and repair is rated excellent.

RICHFIELD

ADDRESS OF CENTRAL OFFICE:
7001 Harriet Avenue, South Richfield, MN 55423
ESI:55

STATISTICAL PROFILE	DATA	ESI
Grade organization: K–3/4–6/7–8/9–12		
Percentage of schools built before 1955	40%	
Total enrollment	4,630	
Average Daily Attendance (ADA)	95%	8
Current expense per pupil in ADA	$4,997	10
Dropout rate	10%	1
Percentage of eligible students who took the ACT	30%	3
Average combined score on ACT	20.7	9
Percentage of graduates who enrolled in 2- or 4-year colleges	70%	
Percentage of students who passed the state reading test	NA	
Percentage of students who passed the state math test	NA	
Teacher–student ratio in elementary grades	1:24	6
Teacher–student ratio in secondary grades	1:25	3
Counselor–student ratio in secondary grades	1:396	2
Number of students per music specialist in elementary grades	560	4
Number of students per art specialist in elementary grades	None	0
Number of volumes in senior high school library	24,000	
Beginning teacher's salary	$19,263	
Maximum teacher's salary	$41,763	
Average years of experience among teachers	21	
Number of students suspended and expelled	285	
Subjects in which Advanced Placement courses are offered:	None	0

FAIR APPRAISAL

Quality of School Leadership
Principals are selected primarily because of their ability as educational leaders, and the quality of leadership does vary from school to school. Parents and teachers do not help screen principal candidates. However, principals have some say about the allotment of resources to their school.

Parent organizations are sometimes effective influencing policy decisions. Recently, for example, parents worked out a system for supervising students at after-school social functions.

Quality of Instruction
Additional learning opportunities for gifted students are rated excellent. "They really do search out qualified students," said an observer; "then the curriculum follows through." Additional instruction for low-achieving students is considered good. Observers rate as excellent the curricula for college-bound students and for students bound for the job market.

Quality of School Environment
Classroom disruption and student vandalism are not problems, and the quality of building maintenance and repair is excellent.

ROSEMOUNT

ADDRESS OF CENTRAL OFFICE:
14445 Diamond Path, Rosemount, MN 55068
ESI:56

STATISTICAL PROFILE	DATA	ESI
Grade organization: K–5/6–8/9–12		
Percentage of schools built before 1955	6%	
Total enrollment	15,785	
Average Daily Attendance (ADA)	89%	2
Current expense per pupil in ADA	$2,593	0
Dropout rate	2%	10
Percentage of eligible students who took the SAT	60%	9
Average combined score on SAT	1,041	10
Percentage of graduates who enrolled in 2- or 4-year colleges	63%	
Percentage of students who passed the state reading test	NA	
Percentage of students who passed the state math test	NA	
Teacher–student ratio in elementary grades	1:25	5
Teacher–student ratio in secondary grades	1:21	7
Counselor–student ratio in secondary grades	1:500	0
Number of students per music specialist in elementary grades	645	3
Number of students per art specialist in elementary grades	None	0
Number of volumes in senior high school library	2,050†	
Beginning teacher's salary	$19,700	
Maximum teacher's salary	$36,700	
Average years of experience among teachers	NK	
Number of students suspended and expelled	507	
Subjects in which Advanced Placement courses are offered: Art, Biology, Calculus, Chemistry, English, French, German, Music Theory, Physics, Spanish	10	10

†This statistic seems unusually low and is probably inaccurate.

FAIR APPRAISAL

Quality of School Leadership
Educational leadership ability is certainly an important consideration in principal selection, but observers complain that selection is based too much on internal politics ("who you know"). Because of this influence, observers believe the quality of leadership is not as uniform in the system as it should be. Parents and teachers do not screen principal candidates. However, principals have a great deal to say about the division of resources among the schools.

Parent organizations are sometimes effective influencing school decision-making.

Quality of Instruction
Additional learning opportunities for gifted students and additional instruction for low-achieving students are rated good. The curriculum that prepares students for college is considered excellent, and the curriculum that prepares students for the job market is rated good.

Quality of School Environment
The incidence of classroom disruption and student vandalism is very low, and the quality of building maintenance and repair is good to excellent.

ROSEVILLE

ADDRESS OF CENTRAL OFFICE:

1251 West County Road, B2, Roseville, MN 55113
ESI:26*

STATISTICAL PROFILE	DATA	ESI
Grade organization: K–6/7–9/10–12		
Percentage of schools built before 1955	20%	
Total enrollment	6,199	
Average Daily Attendance (ADA)	95%	8
Current expense per pupil in ADA	$3,065	1
Dropout rate	NK	0
Percentage of eligible students who took the SAT	9%	0
Average combined score on SAT	1,009	10
Percentage of graduates who enrolled in 2- or 4-year colleges	70%	
Percentage of students who passed the state reading test	NA	
Percentage of students who passed the state math test	NA	
Teacher–student ratio in elementary grades	1:25	5
Teacher–student ratio in secondary grades	1:26	2
Counselor–student ratio in secondary grades	1:560	0
Number of students per music specialist in elementary grades	†	0*
Number of students per art specialist in elementary grades	†	
Number of volumes in senior high school library	30,000	
Beginning teacher's salary	$19,546	
Maximum teacher's salary	$39,467	
Average years of experience among teachers	16	
Number of students suspended and expelled	NK	
Subjects in which Advanced Placement courses are offered:	None	0

†The district supplied an inappropriate statistic.

FAIR APPRAISAL

Quality of School Leadership

Newly hired principals have been selected primarily because of their educational leadership ability. However, some older principals see their job more as a building manager, said observers, and for that reason the quality of leadership varies markedly from school to school. Parents and teachers serve on committees that screen principal candidates; they provide written evaluations for each candidate. Principals have some say about the allotment of resources to the schools.

Parent organizations are generally effective influencing school policy decisions. The PTA Coordinating Council has been working on a policy that could enhance parental influence with the School Board and central administration.

Quality of Instruction

Additional learning opportunities for gifted students are rated fair. Most of the enrichment activities for gifted students take place after school, according to observers. Considered good is additional instruction for low-achieving students. "The district is making an effort for students at risk to make sure they aren't lost," said an observer. The college preparatory curriculum is considered good, but the curriculum preparing non-college bound students is only called fair.

Quality of School Environment

Observers report classroom disruption and vandalism are fairly high in schools (particularly secondary schools) at the west end of the district and low in schools at the east end. The quality of building maintenance and repair is considered fair. The main problems are money and planning. Said an observer, "The district is in trouble because of mismanagement of money."

ST. LOUIS PARK

ADDRESS OF CENTRAL OFFICE:
6425 West 33rd Street, Minneapolis, MN 55426
ESI:62

STATISTICAL PROFILE	DATA	ESI
Grade organization: K–3/4–6/7–8/9–12		
Percentage of schools built before 1955	16%	
Total enrollment	4,105	
Average Daily Attendance (ADA)	94%	7
Current expense per pupil in ADA	$5,432†	10
Dropout rate	4%	10
Percentage of eligible students who took the ACT	15%	0
Average combined score on ACT	20	6
Percentage of graduates who enrolled in 2- or 4-year colleges	65%	
Percentage of students who passed the state reading test	NA	
Percentage of students who passed the state math test	NA	
Teacher–student ratio in elementary grades	1:25	5
Teacher–student ratio in secondary grades	1:25	3
Counselor–student ratio in secondary grades	1:263	7
Number of students per music specialist in elementary grades	237	10
Number of students per art specialist in elementary grades	1,661	
Number of volumes in senior high school library	32,000	
Beginning teacher's salary	$20,754	
Maximum teacher's salary	$43,468	
Average years of experience among teachers	22	
Number of students suspended and expelled	83	
Subjects in which Advanced Placement courses are offered: American History, Calculus, English, European History	4	4

†This statistic is suspect; it may include spending on capital expenses and debt service.

FAIR APPRAISAL

Quality of School Leadership
Principals are hired who demonstrate ability as educational leaders. The quality of leadership is uniform throughout the system. Parents and teachers are involved in principal selection; in fact, finalists submit to general public questioning. Principals have a great deal to say about the allotment of district resources, and the system is moving toward decentralization, which would mean more local authority for principals.

Parent advisory councils are mostly effective influences in district decision-making.

Quality of Instruction
Additional learning opportunities for gifted students are rated excellent, and additional instruction for low-achieving students is called good. "There's a good program to keep kids from dropping out," said an observer. The curriculum for students planning on college is termed excellent, and the curriculum for students not planning on college is rated good. The district is one of 16 technology demonstration sites in the state.

The observers do not believe the district is adequately meeting the educational needs of minority students, who mostly speak a language other than English. The program to teach English as a second language "needs improvement," said one observer.

Quality of School Environment
The level of classroom disruption and student vandalism is generally low, although more of a problem is reported at the high school. The quality of building maintenance and repair is excellent.

ST. PAUL

ADDRESS OF CENTRAL OFFICE:
360 Colbourne Street, St. Paul, MN 55102
ESI:44

STATISTICAL PROFILE	DATA	ESI
Grade organization: K–6/7–8/9–12		
Percentage of schools built before 1955	58%	
Total enrollment	32,382	
Average Daily Attendance (ADA)	92%	5
Current expense per pupil in ADA	$4,640	9
Dropout rate	NK	0
Percentage of eligible students who took the ACT	21%	2
Average combined score on ACT	17.6	3
Percentage of graduates who enrolled in 2- or 4-year colleges	52%	
Percentage of students who passed the state reading test	NA	
Percentage of students who passed the state math test	NA	
Teacher–student ratio in elementary grades	1:24	6
Teacher–student ratio in secondary grades	1:27	1
Counselor–student ratio in secondary grades	1:227	8
Number of students per music specialist in elementary grades	481	6
Number of students per art specialist in elementary grades	2,105	
Number of volumes in senior high school libraries (average)	22,166	
Beginning teacher's salary	$19,868	
Maximum teacher's salary	$40,519	
Average years of experience among teachers	15	
Number of students suspended and expelled	1,696	
Subjects in which Advanced Placement courses are offered: American History, Calculus, English, Science	4	4

FAIR APPRAISAL

Quality of School Leadership
Principals are hired mainly for their educational leadership ability, and the quality of leadership does not vary greatly from school to school. Parents and teachers do not interview principal candidates. Principals, however, have some say in how resources of the district will be used.

Parent organizations' influence in district decision-making is sometimes effective.

Quality of Instruction
"Choices, programs and enrichment, as well as new challenges, are available for students who are actually gifted," said an observer, and the program is rated excellent. Considered only fair is additional instruction for low-achieving students. The curriculum for college-bound students is rated excellent, and the curriculum for students not planning on college is termed good.

The district still has a way to go before it adequately meets the educational needs of minority students. "Good teachers are working hard to develop instructional methods to satisfy the needs of children," said an observer, but so far it hasn't been quite enough.

Quality of School Environment
The level of classroom disruption and student vandalism tends to be on the high side, although "getting better." The quality of building maintenance and repair is rated fair. Many schools were built 20 or 30 years ago and "now are needing repair." Unfortunately, the money spent has been insufficient, according to observers.

WESTONKA

ADDRESS OF CENTRAL OFFICE:
5600 Lynwood Boulevard, Mound, MN 55364
ESI:42*

STATISTICAL PROFILE	DATA	ESI
Grade organization: K–5/6–8/9–12		
Percentage of schools built before 1955	25%	
Total enrollment	2,655	
Average Daily Attendance (ADA)	93%	6
Current expense per pupil in ADA	$4,387	8
Dropout rate	29%	0
Percentage of eligible students who took the SAT	10%	0
Average combined score on SAT	†	0*
Percentage of graduates who enrolled in 2- or 4-year colleges	60%	
Percentage of students who passed the state reading test	NA	
Percentage of students who passed the state math test	NA	
Teacher–student ratio in elementary grades	1:21	9
Teacher–student ratio in secondary grades	1:21	7
Counselor–student ratio in secondary grades	1:325	5
Number of students per music specialist in elementary grades	400	7
Number of students per art specialist in elementary grades	490	
Number of volumes in senior high school library	14,000	
Beginning teacher's salary	$18,500	
Maximum teacher's salary	$34,764	
Average years of experience among teachers	17	
Number of students suspended and expelled	210	
Subjects in which Advanced Placement courses are offered:	None	0

†The district misinterpreted this statistic.

FAIR APPRAISAL

Quality of School Leadership
For the most part, principals are selected because of their educational leadership ability, and the quality of leadership does not vary greatly from school to school. One observer complained, however, that "some principals seem to be given more favorable consideration because of internal politics." Parents and teachers do not help select principals. On the other hand, principals have a lot to say about the distribution of resources to the schools.

Parent organizations are sometimes effective influencing school decisions. Recently, parents were largely responsible for getting voters to approve a tax levy that had been defeated previously.

Quality of Instruction
Additional learning opportunities for gifted students are rated fair to good. "They could do more," said an observer. Observers disagree on the quality of the additional instruction for low-achieving students, but generally they rate the program fair to good. The curricula for college-bound students and for those not planning on college are considered good.

Quality of School Environment
The level of classroom disruption and student vandalism is low, and the quality of building maintenance and repair is excellent.

WHITE BEAR LAKE

ADDRESS OF CENTRAL OFFICE:
2399 Cedar Avenue, White Bear Lake, MN 55110
ESI:None†

STATISTICAL PROFILE	DATA	ESI
Grade organization:		
Percentage of schools built before 1955		
Total enrollment		
Average Daily Attendance (ADA)		
Current expense per pupil in ADA		
Dropout rate		
Percentage of eligible students who took the SAT		
Average combined score on SAT		
Percentage of graduates who enrolled in 2- or 4-year colleges		
Percentage of students who passed the state reading test		
Percentage of students who passed the state math test		
Teacher–student ratio in elementary grades		
Teacher–student ratio in secondary grades		
Counselor–student ratio in secondary grades		
Number of students per music specialist in elementary grades		
Number of students per art specialist in elementary grades		
Number of volumes in senior high school library		
Beginning teacher's salary		
Maximum teacher's salary		
Average years of experience among teachers		
Number of students suspended and expelled		
Subjects in which Advanced Placement courses are offered:		

†A Statistical Profile was not received from this district.

FAIR APPRAISAL

Quality of School Leadership
The School Board hires principals who demonstrate educational leadership ability, and the quality of leadership is generally uniform throughout the system. Parents and teachers serve on committees that screen candidates for principal. Also, principals have much influence in how resources are divided among the schools.

PTA's are effective influencing school decision-making. Parents are involved in long-term planning and curriculum review.

Quality of Instruction
Additional learning opportunities for gifted students are rated good. Enrichment programs are offered in all schools; exceptionally bright high school students can take courses for credit at a nearby college. Additional instruction for low-achieving students also is rated good. Large numbers of parent volunteers serve as tutors and aides. The college preparatory curriculum is considered excellent, and the curriculum for students not going on to college is rated good to excellent.

Quality of School Environment
Classroom disruption and student vandalism are not problems, and the quality of building maintenance and repair is good.

Nashua, NH

Four school districts in the Nashua area submitted Statistical Profiles.
New Hampshire does not give state competency tests in reading and math.
Therefore, NA (not applicable) is noted on lines requesting those data. Districts
in this area may be compared to those in the Boston, MA or Rochester, NY Metropolitan Areas.

AREA AT A GLANCE

SCHOOL DISTRICT	ENROLLMENT	ESI
Merrimack	3,870	53*
Milford	2,452	55
Nashua	10,480	68
Salem	3,800	54

Indicates district misinterpretation of one or more statistics in the ESI. For each misinterpreted statistic, a score of 0 was given instead of a possible score of 0 to 10 points.

SCHOOL DISTRICT

MERRIMACK

ADDRESS OF CENTRAL OFFICE:
36 McElwain Street, Merrimack, NH 03054
ESI:53*

STATISTICAL PROFILE	DATA	ESI
Grade organization: 1–5/6–8/9–12		
Percentage of schools built before 1955	80%	
Total enrollment	3,870	
Average Daily Attendance (ADA)	93%	6
Current expense per pupil in ADA	$2,700	3
Dropout rate	NK	0
Percentage of eligible students who took the SAT	100%	10
Average combined score on SAT	935	6
Percentage of graduates who enrolled in 2- or 4-year colleges	53%	
Percentage of students who passed the state reading test	NA	
Percentage of students who passed the state math test	NA	
Teacher–student ratio in elementary grades	1:23	7
Teacher–student ratio in secondary grades	1:19	10
Counselor–student ratio in secondary grades	1:250	8
Number of students per music specialist in elementary grades	†	0*
Number of students per art specialist in elementary grades	†	
Number of volumes in senior high school library	40,000	
Beginning teacher's salary	$14,250	
Maximum teacher's salary	$26,000	
Average years of experience among teachers	8	
Number of students suspended and expelled	201	
Subjects in which Advanced Placement courses are offered: Calculus, English, Science	3	3

†The district misinterpreted this statistic.

FAIR APPRAISAL

Quality of School Leadership
Principals are hired based on demonstration of educational leadership ability, and the quality of leadership does not vary greatly from school to school. Although teachers and parents have little say in the selection of principals, principals have some say on the distribution of district resources.

Parent organizations are sometimes an effective influence on school policy decisions, but mostly they are concerned with "recreational things."

Quality of Instruction
The district enters its third year of a gifted and talented program in 1987–88, but the program already is considered excellent. Additional instruction for low-achieving students is rated good. The curriculum preparing students for college also is rated excellent, and the curriculum for students not planning on college is considered good. One problem with the latter program is that insufficient state funding sometimes results in the district cutting transportation to a regional vocational center.

Quality of School Environment
The level of classroom disruption and student vandalism is low, and the quality of building maintenance and repair is rated good to excellent.

MILFORD

ADDRESS OF CENTRAL OFFICE:
Elm Street, Milford, NH 03055
ESI:55

STATISTICAL PROFILE	DATA	ESI
Grade organization: †		
Percentage of schools built before 1955	40%	
Total enrollment	2,452	
Average Daily Attendance (ADA)	95%	8
Current expense per pupil in ADA	$2,432	2
Dropout rate	NK	0
Percentage of eligible students who took the SAT	60%	9
Average combined score on SAT	NK	0
Percentage of graduates who enrolled in 2- or 4-year colleges	68%	
Percentage of students who passed the state reading test	NA	
Percentage of students who passed the state math test	NA	
Teacher–student ratio in elementary grades	1:20	10
Teacher–student ratio in secondary grades	1:18	10
Counselor–student ratio in secondary grades	1:288	6
Number of students per music specialist in elementary grades	356	8
Number of students per art specialist in elementary grades	712	
Number of volumes in senior high school library	8,425	
Beginning teacher's salary	$16,500††	
Maximum teacher's salary	$31,440††	
Average years of experience among teachers	9	
Number of students suspended and expelled	NK	
Subjects in which Advanced Placement courses are offered: French, Latin	2	2

† The district misinterpreted this statistic.
††1987–88 statistics.

FAIR APPRAISAL

Quality of School Leadership
For the most part, principals are picked because of their ability as educational leaders. However, internal politics and popularity are important factors. Generally, the quality of leadership is uniform throughout the district. Parents and teachers have little or no say on principal selection, but principals have some say in how much of the district's resources are allotted their school.

Parent organizations are not very effective influencing school policy decisions.

Quality of Instruction
The learning opportunities for gifted students are very good at the elementary and senior high levels, but not as good in the middle school. Overall, however, the program is rated good. The additional instruction for low-achieving students is considered excellent, as are the curricula for students planning on college and for students entering the job market after graduation.

Quality of School Environment
The incidence of classroom disruption and student vandalism is low, and the quality of building maintenance and repair is good.

NASHUA

ADDRESS OF CENTRAL OFFICE:
P.O. Box 687, Nashua, NH 03061
ESI:68

STATISTICAL PROFILE	DATA	ESI
Grade organization: K–6/7–9/10–12†		
Percentage of schools built before 1955	37%	
Total enrollment	10,480	
Average Daily Attendance (ADA)	94%	7
Current expense per pupil in ADA	$2,800	4
Dropout rate	20%	3
Percentage of eligible students who took the SAT	55%	8
Average combined score on SAT	925	5
Percentage of graduates who enrolled in 2- or 4-year colleges	55%	
Percentage of students who passed the state reading test	NA	
Percentage of students who passed the state math test	NA	
Teacher–student ratio in elementary grades	1:18	10
Teacher–student ratio in secondary grades	1:17	10
Counselor–student ratio in secondary grades	1:300	6
Number of students per music specialist in elementary grades	465	6
Number of students per art specialist in elementary grades	465	
Number of volumes in senior high school libraries (average)	20,000	
Beginning teacher's salary	$15,900	
Maximum teacher's salary	$30,588	
Average years of experience among teachers	13	
Number of students suspended and expelled	350	
Subjects in which Advanced Placement courses are offered: American History, Biology, Calculus, Chemistry, Computer Science, English, European History, French, Spanish	9	9

†Most New Hampshire districts do not have a kindergarten, but some have a year of readiness (R) for 6-year-olds not yet ready for first grade.

FAIR APPRAISAL

Quality of School Leadership
The School Board looks for principals who demonstrate educational leadership ability, although seniority is a factor when principals are chosen from within the ranks. The quality of leadership does not vary greatly from school to school. Parents and teachers do not interview principal candidates, but they may make their opinions known informally. Principals have some influence over the distribution of district resources.

"Parents are a strong lobbying force," said an observer. Parents have been particularly active in lobbying for a kindergarten, and the School Board has approved one for 1988–89.

Quality of Instruction
The learning opportunities for gifted students are rated fair to good. The program is still in development. Additional instruction for low-achieving students is considered good. The college preparatory curriculum is rated excellent, and the curriculum for students not planning on college is called good.

Quality of School Environment
The level of classroom disruption and student vandalism is low, and the quality of building maintenance and repair is good.

SALEM

ADDRESS OF CENTRAL OFFICE:
206 Main Street, Salem, NH 03079
ESI:54

STATISTICAL PROFILE	DATA	ESI
Grade organization: 1–6/7–8/9–12		
Percentage of schools built before 1955	50%	
Total enrollment	3,800	
Average Daily Attendance (ADA)	94%	7
Current expense per pupil in ADA	$3,862†	9
Dropout rate	NK	0
Percentage of eligible students who took the SAT	58%	9
Average combined score on SAT	NK	0
Percentage of graduates who enrolled in 2- or 4-year colleges	56%	
Percentage of students who passed the state reading test	NA	
Percentage of students who passed the state math test	NA	
Teacher–student ratio in elementary grades	1:22	8
Teacher–student ratio in secondary grades	1:18	10
Counselor–student ratio in secondary grades	1:300	6
Number of students per music specialist in elementary grades	535	5
Number of students per art specialist in elementary grades	None	
Number of volumes in senior high school library	11,725	
Beginning teacher's salary	$14,324	
Maximum teacher's salary	$29,103	
Average years of experience among teachers	14	
Number of students suspended and expelled	873	
Subjects in which Advanced Placement courses are offered:	None	0

†1986–87 figures.

FAIR APPRAISAL

Quality of School Leadership
Although popularity is a factor, principals are hired mostly based on their educational leadership ability. Also, the quality of leadership does not vary greatly from school to school. Parents and teachers do not screen principal candidates, but principals have some influence over the allotment of district resources.

Parent organizations are sometimes influential in district decision-making. Recently, parents organized to thwart district plans to close two elementary schools.

Quality of Instruction
Additional learning opportunities for gifted students are rated fair to poor. The program is "almost non-existent," said an observer. Additional instruction for low-achieving students, on the other hand, is considered good to excellent. "We do that right," said an observer. The curricula for college-bound students and for those not planning on college are termed good.

Quality of School Environment
Classroom disruption and student vandalism are not problems, and the quality of building maintenance and repair is good.

METROPOLITAN AREA

Nashville, TN

Tennessee operates mostly county school systems; there are several
in the Nashville Metropolitan Area. We received a Fair Appraisal alone
from one district, Sumner County.

AREA AT A GLANCE

SCHOOL DISTRICT	ENROLLMENT	ESI
Sumner County	18,452	

SCHOOL DISTRICT

SUMNER COUNTY

ADDRESS OF CENTRAL OFFICE:
117 E. Winchester, Gallatin, TN 37066
ESI:None†

STATISTICAL PROFILE	DATA	ESI
Grade organization:		
Percentage of schools built before 1955		
Total enrollment		
Average Daily Attendance (ADA)		
Current expense per pupil in ADA		
Dropout rate		
Percentage of eligible students who took the SAT		
Average combined score on SAT		
Percentage of graduates who enrolled in 2- or 4-year colleges		
Percentage of students who passed the state reading test		
Percentage of students who passed the state math test		
Teacher–student ratio in elementary grades		
Teacher–student ratio in secondary grades		
Counselor–student ratio in secondary grades		
Number of students per music specialist in elementary grades		
Number of students per art specialist in elementary grades		
Number of volumes in senior high school library		
Beginning teacher's salary		
Maximum teacher's salary		
Average years of experience among teachers		
Number of students suspended and expelled		
Subjects in which Advanced Placement courses are offered:		

†A Statistical Profile was not received from this district.

FAIR APPRAISAL

Quality of School Leadership

Principals are hired mostly for their educational leadership
ability, and the quality of leadership is generally uniform
throughout the system. However, an observer pointed out that
in a district which covers 500 square miles and has nearly 19,000
students, some variation in the quality of leadership exists. The
leadership at the middle and senior high school levels is
consistently good, the observer said. Parents and teachers do
not take part in principal selection, but principals have much to
say about the resources allotted to the schools. The
superintendent is elected, and the district recently changed to a
seven-member elected school board.

Parent organizations are sometimes effective influencing
policy decisions. However, according to an observer, most
PTAs and PTOs concentrate on fund-raising. A new citizens'
task force was scheduled to be formed at the start of the 1987–88
school year.

Quality of Instruction

Additional learning opportunities for gifted students are rated
excellent, and additional instruction for low-achieving students
is considered good. Tutoring is available before and after
school. The curriculum for college-bound students is rated
good, and the curriculum for job-bound students is called
excellent. "Excellent vocational programs are available through
the district," said an observer.

Quality of School Environment

Classroom disruption and student vandalsim are not problems.
The quality of building maintenance and repair is considered
fair. The School Board submits its budget for approval to the
County Commission, and the County Commission, according
to an observer, has reduced funds that would have been used for
building maintenance and repair.

Nassau & Suffolk Counties, NY

Twenty-seven school districts completed Statistical Profiles, and Fair Appraisals alone were received for two other districts. Nassau & Suffolk counties are considered a separate metropolitan area, but districts in this area should be compared with districts in the New York City and Newark, NJ Metropolitan Areas.

AREA AT A GLANCE

SCHOOL DISTRICT	ENROLLMENT	ESI
Amityville	3,000	80
Brentwood	12,346	78
Brookhaven–Comsewogue	3,829	61
Commack	6,121	72*
Deer Park	3,914	70
East Islip	4,500	67
Farmingdale	5,763	86
Glen Cove	2,814	67*
Great Neck	5,600	81*
Hauppauge	4,387	72*
Hempstead	5,540	12*
Herricks	3,275	95
Hewlett–Woodmere	2,959	87
Hicksville	4,799	67*
Island Trees	2,400	82
Kings Park	3,644	85
Lindenhurst	6,611	64
Lynbrook	2,495	92
Miller Place	2,603	68*
North Babylon	5,000	81
Port Washington	4,057	91
Riverhead	3,704	54*
Rockville Center	3,200	82
Roosevelt	3,032	49
Seaford	2,602	80
Smithtown	8,700	
Three Village	7,523	88
Westbury	2,740	
West Islip	5,471	76*

Indicates district misinterpretation of one or more statistics in the ESI. For each misinterpreted statistic, a score of 0 was given instead of a possible score of 0 to 10 points.

AMITYVILLE

ADDRESS OF CENTRAL OFFICE:
Park Avenue & Ireland Place, Amityville, NY 11701
ESI:80

STATISTICAL PROFILE	DATA	ESI
Grade organization: Pre-K-K/1–5/6–9/10–12		
Percentage of schools built before 1955	40%	
Total enrollment	3,000†	
Average Daily Attendance (ADA)	92%	5
Current expense per pupil in ADA	$7,000	10
Dropout rate	10%	10
Percentage of eligible students who took the SAT	67%	10
Average combined score on SAT	834	1
Percentage of graduates who enrolled in 2- or 4-year colleges	70%	
Percentage of students who passed the state reading test	100%	
Percentage of students who passed the state math test	100%	
Teacher–student ratio in elementary grades	1:20 †	10
Teacher–student ratio in secondary grades	1:12 †	10
Counselor–student ratio in secondary grades	1:187†	10
Number of students per music specialist in elementary grades	250†	10
Number of students per art specialist in elementary grades	300†	
Number of volumes in senior high school library	22,722†	
Beginning teacher's salary	$20,583†	
Maximum teacher's salary	$46,009†	
Average years of experience among teachers	15†	
Number of students suspended and expelled	NK	
Subjects in which Advanced Placement courses are offered: American History, Biology, Calculus, English	4	4

†1986–87 statistic.

FAIR APPRAISAL

Quality of School Leadership
Most principals are hired because of their educational leadership ability, although internal politics and longevity are factors. The quality of leadership generally is uniform throughout the system. Parents and teachers have no say in principal selection, but principals have some say in how the resources of the district are distributed.

Parents organizations are sometimes effective influencing school decision-making.

Quality of Instruction
Additional learning opportunities for gifted students and additional instruction for low-achieving students are rated fair. On the other hand, the curricula for college-bound students and for those not going to college are considered good.

Quality of School Environment
The level of classroom disruption and student vandalism is low, and the quality of building maintenance and repair is fair to good.

BRENTWOOD

ADDRESS OF CENTRAL OFFICE:
Third Avenue & Fourth Street, Brentwood, NY 11717
ESI:78

STATISTICAL PROFILE	DATA	ESI
Grade organization: K–6/7–9/10–12		
Percentage of schools built before 1955	25%	
Total enrollment	12,346	
Average Daily Attendance (ADA)	92%	5
Current expense per pupil in ADA	$6,903	10
Dropout rate	10%	10
Percentage of eligible students who took the SAT	63%	10
Average combined score on SAT	920	5
Percentage of graduates who enrolled in 2- or 4-year colleges	58%	
Percentage of students who passed the state reading test	100%	
Percentage of students who passed the state math test	100%	
Teacher–student ratio in elementary grades	1:20	10
Teacher–student ratio in secondary grades	1:18	10
Counselor–student ratio in secondary grades	1:291	6
Number of students per music specialist in elementary grades	359	8
Number of students per art specialist in elementary grades	509	
Number of volumes in senior high school libraries (average)	26,000	
Beginning teacher's salary	$19,304	
Maximum teacher's salary	$47,922	
Average years of experience among teachers	17	
Number of students suspended and expelled	705	
Subjects in which Advanced Placement courses are offered: Calculus, Chemistry, Computer Science, English	4	4

FAIR APPRAISAL

Quality of School Leadership
The School Board hires principals primarily for their ability as educational leaders, and the quality of leadership does not vary greatly from school to school. Parents and teachers have little say in principal selection, but principals have some say in the allotment of resources to the schools.

Parent organizations are sometimes effective influencing district policy.

Quality of Instruction
Additional learning opportunities for gifted students are rated fair, and additional instruction for low-achieving students is rated good. Reading and math labs help the low-achieving students. The college preparatory curriculum is considered fair, but the curriculum preparing students for the world of work is considered good.

Quality of School Environment
Classroom disruption and student vandalsim are not problems, and the quality of building maintenance and repair is good.

BROOKHAVEN–COMSEWOGUE

ADDRESS OF CENTRAL OFFICE:
499 Jayne Boulevard, Port Jefferson Station, NY 11776

ESI:61

STATISTICAL PROFILE	DATA	ESI
Grade organization: K–6/7–8/9–12		
Percentage of schools built before 1955	NK	
Total enrollment	3,829	
Average Daily Attendance (ADA)	95%	8
Current expense per pupil in ADA	$4,150	0
Dropout rate	3%	10
Percentage of eligible students who took the SAT	NK	0
Average combined score on SAT	NK	0
Percentage of graduates who enrolled in 2- or 4-year colleges	64%	
Percentage of students who passed the state reading test	98%	
Percentage of students who passed the state math test	99%	
Teacher–student ratio in elementary grades	1:14	10
Teacher–student ratio in secondary grades	1:16	10
Counselor–student ratio in secondary grades	1:250	7
Number of students per music specialist in elementary grades	200	10
Number of students per art specialist in elementary grades	410	
Number of volumes in senior high school library	30,000	
Beginning teacher's salary	$20,258	
Maximum teacher's salary	$47,457	
Average years of experience among teachers	12	
Number of students suspended and expelled	180	
Subjects in which Advanced Placement courses are offered: American History, Art, Calculus, English, Music, Science	6	6

FAIR APPRAISAL

Quality of School Leadership

The School Board seeks principals with proven educational leadership ability; the quality of leadership is generally uniform throughout the system. Parents and teachers serve on committees that screen principal candidates. Also, principals influence the distribution of resources to the schools.

Parent organizations are sometimes effective influencing school policy decisions. For example, parents influence school scheduling.

Quality of Instruction

Additional learning opportunities for gifted students are rated good. These students are excused from regular classes to attend enrichment classes; special offerings also are available during the summer. Additional instruction for low-achieving students is called fair. The curricula for college-bound students and for those heading into the job market are considered good.

Quality of School Environment

Classroom disruption and student vandalism are not problems, but the quality of building maintenance and repair is only fair. However, a bond issue passed in 1987 should help complete needed repairs.

COMMACK

ADDRESS OF CENTRAL OFFICE:
P.O. Box 150, Commack, NY 11725

ESI:72*

STATISTICAL PROFILE	DATA	ESI
Grade organization: K–5/6–8/9–12		
Percentage of schools built before 1955	5%	
Total enrollment	6,121	
Average Daily Attendance (ADA)	94%	7
Current expense per pupil in ADA	$8,600	10
Dropout rate	4%	10
Percentage of eligible students who took the SAT	98%	10
Average combined score on SAT	†	0*
Percentage of graduates who enrolled in 2- or 4-year colleges	92%	
Percentage of students who passed the state reading test	97%	
Percentage of students who passed the state math test	93%	
Teacher–student ratio in elementary grades	1:23	7
Teacher–student ratio in secondary grades	1:23	5
Counselor–student ratio in secondary grades	1:240	8
Number of students per music specialist in elementary grades	240	10
Number of students per art specialist in elementary grades	365	
Number of volumes in senior high school library	50,000	
Beginning teacher's salary	$21,177	
Maximum teacher's salary	$51,858	
Average years of experience among teachers	19	
Number of students suspended and expelled	10	
Subjects in which Advanced Placement courses are offered: Calculus, French, German, Science, Spanish	5	5

†The district supplied an inappropriate statistic.

FAIR APPRAISAL

Quality of School Leadership

Principals are selected primarily for their educational leadership ability, and the quality of leadership is generally uniform throughout the district. Parents and teachers have some say in principal selection, and principals have some say in how resources of the district are used.

Parent organizations are effective as an influence in district decision-making. "Parent participation is unusually strong," said an observer. Parents have influenced policy on such matters as health and safety, cultural arts, child abuse, and bringing in outside speakers and programs.

Quality of Instruction

Gifted students in the elementary grades are transported to a central class a few times a week for enrichment, and the program for gifted students is rated good. Additional instruction for low-achieving students, on the other hand, is considered fair. "We need a lot more help for under-achievers," said an observer. The curriculum for students preparing for college is rated good, but the curriculum for students heading for the world of work is only called fair.

Quality of School Environment

The incidence of classroom disruption and student vandalism is low, but the quality of building maintenance and repair is rated only fair. Day-to-day maintenance is okay, said an observer, but "major repairs often go a long time untended."

DEER PARK

ADDRESS OF CENTRAL OFFICE:
1881 Deer Park Avenue, Deer Park, NY 11729
ESI:70

STATISTICAL PROFILE	DATA	ESI
Grade organization: K–3/4–6/7–9/10–12		
Percentage of schools built before 1955	1%	
Total enrollment	3,914	
Average Daily Attendance (ADA)	92%	5
Current expense per pupil in ADA	$8,122	10
Dropout rate	11%	10
Percentage of eligible students who took the SAT	64%	10
Average combined score on SAT	837	1
Percentage of graduates who enrolled in 2- or 4-year colleges	62%	
Percentage of students who passed the state reading test	94%	
Percentage of students who passed the state math test	85%	
Teacher–student ratio in elementary grades	1:16	10
Teacher–student ratio in secondary grades	1:12	10
Counselor–student ratio in secondary grades	1:229	8
Number of students per music specialist in elementary grades	462	6
Number of students per art specialist in elementary grades	500	
Number of volumes in senior high school library	17,982	
Beginning teacher's salary	$18,922	
Maximum teacher's salary	$46,114	
Average years of experience among teachers	17	
Number of students suspended and expelled	986	
Subjects in which Advanced Placement courses are offered:	None	0

FAIR APPRAISAL

Quality of School Leadership

Principals are selected primarily for their educational leadership ability, and the quality of leadership does not vary greatly from school to school. Parents and teachers have hardly any say in principal selection, but principals have a great deal to say about how resources are used.

Parent organizations are sometimes effective influencing school policy decisions. PTA Council representatives meet monthly with the superintendent.

Quality of Instruction

Additional learning opportunities for gifted students are rated good; the program in the elementary grades is self-contained in classrooms. Additional instruction for low-achieving students is also considered good. The curricula for college-bound students and for those not going to college are rated good as well.

Quality of School Environment

The level of classroom disruption and student vandalism is very low, and the quality of building maintenance and repair is good.

EAST ISLIP

ADDRESS OF CENTRAL OFFICE:
8 Laurel Avenue, East Islip, NY 11730
ESI:67

STATISTICAL PROFILE	DATA	ESI
Grade organization: K–6/7–8/9–12		
Percentage of schools built before 1955	NK	
Total enrollment	4,500	
Average Daily Attendance (ADA)	96%	9
Current expense per pupil in ADA	$5,200	3
Dropout rate	12%	10
Percentage of eligible students who took the SAT	70%	10
Average combined score on SAT	903	4
Percentage of graduates who enrolled in 2- or 4-year colleges	68%	4
Percentage of students who passed the state reading test	100%	
Percentage of students who passed the state math test	100%	
Teacher–student ratio in elementary grades	1:23	7
Teacher–student ratio in secondary grades	1:24	4
Counselor–student ratio in secondary grades	1:300	6
Number of students per music specialist in elementary grades	200	10
Number of students per art specialist in elementary grades	200	
Number of volumes in senior high school library	25,000	
Beginning teacher's salary	$21,000	
Maximum teacher's salary	$52,000	
Average years of experience among teachers	22	
Number of students suspended and expelled	20	
Subjects in which Advanced Placement courses are offered: American History, Calculus, Foreign Language, Science	4	4

FAIR APPRAISAL

Quality of School Leadership

Principals are chosen for their educational leadership ability; the quality of leadership does not vary greatly throughout the system. Parents and teachers have hardly any say in principal selection, but principals have some influence over the distribution of district resources.

Parent organizations are sometimes an effective influence on school decision-making. Generally, parents and school administrators work well with each other.

Quality of Instruction

A separate class for gifted students in grades 5 and 6, and grouping at higher grade levels make the learning opportunities for gifted students good, said observers. Additional instruction for low-achieving students also is rated good. The curriculum for college-bound students is considered excellent, while the curriculum for students not planning on college is rated good.

Quality of School Environment

The level of classroom disruption and student vandalism is low, and the quality of building maintenance and repair is excellent.

NASSAU & SUFFOLK COUNTIES, NY • 229

FARMINGDALE

ADDRESS OF CENTRAL OFFICE:
Van Cott Avenue, Farmingdale, NY 11735
ESI:86

STATISTICAL PROFILE	DATA	ESI
Grade organization: K–6/7–8/9–12		
Percentage of schools built before 1955	33%	
Total enrollment	5,763	
Average Daily Attendance (ADA)	94%	7
Current expense per pupil in ADA	$6,967	10
Dropout rate	7%	10
Percentage of eligible students who took the SAT	97%	10
Average combined score on SAT	910	5
Percentage of graduates who enrolled in 2- or 4-year colleges	74%	
Percentage of students who passed the state reading test	95%	
Percentage of students who passed the state math test	98%	
Teacher–student ratio in elementary grades	1:14	10
Teacher–student ratio in secondary grades	1:10	10
Counselor–student ratio in secondary grades	1:270	7
Number of students per music specialist in elementary grades	164	10
Number of students per art specialist in elementary grades	466	
Number of volumes in senior high school library	24,000	
Beginning teacher's salary	$17,948	
Maximum teacher's salary	$44,444	
Average years of experience among teachers	18	
Number of students suspended and expelled	132	
Subjects in which Advanced Placement courses are offered: American History, Art, Calculus, English, French, Science, Spanish	7	7

FAIR APPRAISAL

Quality of School Leadership

The School Board picks principals who demonstrate educational leadership ability, and the quality of leadership is generally uniform throughout the system. Parents and teachers have hardly any say in principal selection, but principals have some say in how the district's resources are allotted to the schools.

Parent organizations are effective influencing school policy issues. Parents are generally consulted regularly by the superintendent, said an observer.

Quality of Instruction

Additional learning opportunities for gifted students are considered excellent. In the elementary schools, students are excused from regular classes to attend enrichment classes. Additional instruction for low-achieving students is also considered excellent. The college preparatory curriculum is called excellent, while the curriculum for students not planning on college is rated good.

Quality of School Environment

The level of classroom disruption and student vandalism is very low, and the quality of building maintenance and repair is good.

GLEN COVE

ADDRESS OF CENTRAL OFFICE:
Dosoris Lane, Glen Cove, NY 11542
ESI:67*

STATISTICAL PROFILE	DATA	ESI
Grade organization: Pre-K/K–5/6–8/9–12		
Percentage of schools built before 1955	57%	
Total enrollment	2,814	
Average Daily Attendance (ADA)	94%	7
Current expense per pupil in ADA	NK	0
Dropout rate	4%	10
Percentage of eligible students who took the SAT	100%	10
Average combined score on SAT	†	0*
Percentage of graduates who enrolled in 2- or 4-year colleges	74%	
Percentage of students who passed the state reading test	93%	
Percentage of students who passed the state math test	94%	
Teacher–student ratio in elementary grades	1:19	10
Teacher–student ratio in secondary grades	1:20	8
Counselor–student ratio in secondary grades	1:242	8
Number of students per music specialist in elementary grades	110	10
Number of students per art specialist in elementary grades	201	
Number of volumes in senior high school library	20,000	
Beginning teacher's salary	$20,239	
Maximum teacher's salary	$46,853	
Average years of experience among teachers	NK	
Number of students suspended and expelled	NK	
Subjects in which Advanced Placement courses are offered: American History, Calculus, English, Science (unspecified)	4	4

†The district supplied an inappropriate statistic.

FAIR APPRAISAL

Quality of School Leadership

Principals are hired primarily for their ability as educational leaders. The quality of leadership does not vary greatly from school to school. Teachers have some say in principal selection; parents do not. Principals have a great deal to say about the division of district resources.

Parent organizations are effective influencing district policies. Parents recently were concerned about security at the elementary schools, and they made their case before district officials. Officials agreed with parents, and now it is not so easy for outsiders to enter the buildings.

Quality of Instruction

Additional learning opportunities for gifted students and additional instruction for low-achieving students are rated good. Gifted students in the lower grades have enrichment in all academic subjects. The curriculum for students planning on college is considered good, but the curriculum for students not planning on college is rated only fair. The district has a strong program in English as a second language for Hispanic students.

Quality of School Environment

Classroom disruption and student vandalism are not problems. The quality of building maintenance and repair is rated good. A lack of funds in past years has hurt capital improvement, said observers.

GREAT NECK

ADDRESS OF CENTRAL OFFICE:
345 Lakeville Road, Great Neck, NY 11021
ESI:81*

STATISTICAL PROFILE	DATA	ESI
Grade organization: K–5/6–8/9–12		
Percentage of schools built before 1955	67%	
Total enrollment	5,600	
Average Daily Attendance (ADA)	93%	6
Current expense per pupil in ADA	$9,470	10
Dropout rate	4%	10
Percentage of eligible students who took the SAT	87%	10
Average combined score on SAT	1,025	10
Percentage of graduates who enrolled in 2- or 4-year colleges	92%	
Percentage of students who passed the state reading test	79%	
Percentage of students who passed the state math test	66%	
Teacher–student ratio in elementary grades	1:13	10
Teacher–student ratio in secondary grades	1:11	10
Counselor–student ratio in secondary grades	1:173	10
Number of students per music specialist in elementary grades	537	5
Number of students per art specialist in elementary grades	429	
Number of volumes in senior high school library	51,000	
Beginning teacher's salary	$20,505	
Maximum teacher's salary	$47,388	
Average years of experience among teachers	NK	
Number of students suspended and expelled	NK	
Subjects in which Advanced Placement courses are offered:	†	0*

†The district indicated an attachment to its profile, but it was not supplied.

FAIR APPRAISAL

Quality of School Leadership
The School Board seeks principals who evidence educational leadership ability, and the quality of leadership does not vary greatly from school to school. Parents and teachers, and in some cases, students, interview principal candidates as part of the selection process. Principals also have a great deal to say about the allotment of resources to the schools.

Parent organizations are effective influencing school decision-making. For example, it was parent study and pressure that resulted in the first written curriculum for the elementary grades, said an observer.

Quality of Instruction
In the elementary grades, gifted students have an individual plan for enrichment, and the overall learning opporunities for gifted students are rated excellent. Called good is instruction for low-achieving students. Each school has its own psychologist. At the secondary level, teachers are available after school to give extra help to low-achievers. The college-preparatory curriculum is rated excellent, and the curriculum for job-bound students is considered good.

Quality of School Environment
The level of classroom disruption and student vandalism is very low and the quality of building maintenance and repair is very high.

HAUPPAUGE

ADDRESS OF CENTRAL OFFICE:
600 Town Line Road, Hauppauge, NY 11788
ESI:72*

STATISTICAL PROFILE	DATA	ESI
Grade organization: K–6/7–8/9–12		
Percentage of schools built before 1955	20%	
Total enrollment	4,387	
Average Daily Attendance (ADA)	94%	7
Current expense per pupil in ADA	$6,476	10
Dropout rate	6%	10
Percentage of eligible students who took the SAT	81%	10
Average combined score on SAT	957	7
Percentage of graduates who enrolled in 2- or 4-year colleges	80%	
Percentage of students who passed the state reading test	100%	
Percentage of students who passed the state math test	100%	
Teacher–student ratio in elementary grades	1:15	10
Teacher–student ratio in secondary grades	1:14	10
Counselor–student ratio in secondary grades	1:240	8
Number of students per music specialist in elementary grades	††	0*
Number of students per art specialist in elementary grades	††	
Number of volumes in senior high school library	47,307	
Beginning teacher's salary	$18,188	
Maximum teacher's salary	$43,512	
Average years of experience among teachers	19	
Number of students suspended and expelled	326	
Subjects in which Advanced Placement courses are offered:	None†	0

†See Fair Appraisal.
††The district supplied an inappropriate statistic.

FAIR APPRAISAL

Quality of School Leadership
Internal politics are a factor in principal selection, although educational leadership ability is still a primary criterion for selection. The quality of leadership varies markedly between elementary and secondary levels, with internal politics being more influential at the lower level, according to observers. Parents and teachers have hardly any say in principal selection, but principals have some say in how district resources are used in the schools.

Quality of Instruction
Additional learning opportunities for gifted students and additional instruction for low-achieving students is rated good. Although the district does not offer Advanced Placement courses, it does offer some 70 college credits for college-level courses. The curriculum that prepares students for college is considered good, as is the curriculum for students entering the job market.

Quality of School Environment
The incidence of classroom disruption and student vandalism is low, and the quality of building maintenance and repair is good.

HEMPSTEAD

ADDRESS OF CENTRAL OFFICE:
185 Peninsula Boulevard, Hempstead, NY 11550
ESI:12*

STATISTICAL PROFILE	DATA	ESI
Grade organization: †		
Percentage of schools built before 1955	90%	
Total enrollment	5,540	
Average Daily Attendance (ADA)	85%	0
Current expense per pupil in ADA	††	0*
Dropout rate	29%	0
Percentage of eligible students who took the SAT	20%	1
Average combined score on SAT	††	0*
Percentage of graduates who enrolled in 2- or 4-year colleges	70%	
Percentage of students who passed the state reading test	62%	
Percentage of students who passed the state math test	44%	
Teacher–student ratio in elementary grades	1:26	4
Teacher–student ratio in secondary grades	1:35	0
Counselor–student ratio in secondary grades	1:340	4
Number of students per music specialist in elementary grades	††	0
Number of students per art specialist in elementary grades	††	
Number of volumes in senior high school library	25,000	
Beginning teacher's salary	$21,939	
Maximum teacher's salary	$50,588	
Average years of experience among teachers	5	
Number of students suspended and expelled	228	
Subjects in which Advanced Placement courses are offered: Calculus, English, Science	3	3

†The district misinterpreted this statistic.
††The district provided an inappropriate statistic.

FAIR APPRAISAL

Quality of School Leadership
Although educational leadership ability is considered in principal selection, other criteria, such as internal politics and popularity, are very important factors. While the quality of leadership is fairly strong at the secondary level, it is called "spotty" elsewhere. Parents and teachers have hardly any say in principal selection, but principals have some say in the allotment of resources to their school.

Parents are sometimes effective in influencing school decision-making.

Quality of Instruction
Additional learning opportunities for gifted students and additional instruction for low-achieving students are rated fair. Also considered only fair are the curricula for college-bound students and for students heading into the job market. Observers feel the district is not adequately meeting the needs of minority students, who constitute a majority of the student body. "The financing is adequate," said an observer, "but families are relatively poor and student test scores are among the area's lowest."

Quality of School Environment
The level of classroom disruption and student vandalism tend to be on the high side, but the quality of building maintenance and repair is good.

HERRICKS

ADDRESS OF CENTRAL OFFICE:
Shelter Rock Road, New Hyde Park, NY 11040
ESI:95

STATISTICAL PROFILE	DATA	ESI
Grade organization: K–5/6–8/9–12		
Percentage of schools built before 1955	100%	
Total enrollment	3,275	
Average Daily Attendance (ADA)	95%	8
Current expense per pupil in ADA	$8,750	10
Dropout rate	1%	10
Percentage of eligible students who took the SAT	88%	10
Average combined score on SAT	994	9
Percentage of graduates who enrolled in 2- or 4-year colleges	83%	
Percentage of students who passed the state reading test	98%	
Percentage of students who passed the state math test	99%	
Teacher–student ratio in elementary grades	1:16	10
Teacher–student ratio in secondary grades	1:11	10
Counselor–student ratio in secondary grades	1:205	9
Number of students per music specialist in elementary grades	225	10
Number of students per art specialist in elementary grades	430	
Number of volumes in senior high school library	NK	
Beginning teacher's salary	$21,532	
Maximum teacher's salary	$46,403	
Average years of experience among teachers	15	
Number of students suspended and expelled	106	
Subjects in which Advanced Placement courses are offered: American History, Biology, Calculus AB, Calculus BC, Chemistry, English Literature, French, Physics, Spanish	9	9

FAIR APPRAISAL

Quality of School Leadership
Principals are hired mainly for their educational leadership ability, and the quality of leadership does not vary greatly throughout the system. However, one observer noted there is variation among principals in educational philosophy. Parents and teachers have some say in principal selection, mostly on an informal basis. Principals have a great deal to say about the allotment of district resources to the schools. Observers credit a new superintendent with "turning the district around."
Parent organizations are sometimes effective as an influence in school decision-making.

Quality of Instruction
Additional learning opportunities for gifted students and additional instruction for low-achieving students are rated good. Observers call the gifted program "incredible," offering a broad range of opportunities in addition to classroom instruction. Resource rooms at the elementary level and special instruction in the high school aid low-achievers. The curriculum for students going on to college is called good, while the curriculum for students heading for the world of work is only rated as fair.

Quality of School Environment
The level of classroom disruption and student vandalism is low, but the quality of building repair and maintenance is fair. A recent bond issue, however, should help a "critically needed long-range building plan."

HEWLETT–WOODMERE

ADDRESS OF CENTRAL OFFICE:
P.O. Box 27, Hewlett, NY 11557
ESI:87

STATISTICAL PROFILE	DATA	ESI
Grade organization: Pre-K–K/1–5/6–8/9–12		
Percentage of schools built before 1955	100%	
Total enrollment	2,959	
Average Daily Attendance (ADA)	97%	10
Current expense per pupil in ADA	$6,500	10
Dropout rate	3%	10
Percentage of eligible students who took the SAT	93%	10
Average combined score on SAT	993	9
Percentage of graduates who enrolled in 2- or 4-year colleges	93%	
Percentage of students who passed the state reading test	98%	
Percentage of students who passed the state math test	98%	
Teacher–student ratio in elementary grades	1:23	7
Teacher–student ratio in secondary grades	1:25	3
Counselor–student ratio in secondary grades	1:235	8
Number of students per music specialist in elementary grades	190	10
Number of students per art specialist in elementary grades	570	
Number of volumes in senior high school library	20,122	
Beginning teacher's salary	$19,600	
Maximum teacher's salary	$44,200	
Average years of experience among teachers	17	
Number of students suspended and expelled	77	
Subjects in which Advanced Placement courses are offered:	10	10
American History, Biology, Calculus AB, Calculus BC, Chemistry, Computer Science, English Literature and Composition, French, Physics, Spanish		

FAIR APPRAISAL

Quality of School Leadership
The School Board looks for principals who demonstrate educational leadership ability; the quality of leadership is generally uniform throughout the system. Parents and teachers have hardly any say in principal selection, but principals influence the distribution of resources to the schools.

Parent organizations are sometimes effective influencing school policy decisions.

Quality of Instruction
The gifted program in the elementary schools is "marvelous," said an observer. Gifted students are grouped in special classes. One of the courses offered to gifted students is criminal justice. Overall, the program is rated excellent. Additional instruction for low-achieving students, on the other hand, is rated only fair. The college preparatory curriculum is considered excellent, but the curriculum for students not planning on college is deemed only fair.

One observer said the district may be "tempted to rest on its laurels and assume that students do well."

Quality of School Environment
Classroom disruption and student vandalism are low, and the quality of building maintenance and repair is excellent.

HICKSVILLE

ADDRESS OF CENTRAL OFFICE:
Division Avenue, Hicksville, NY 11801
ESI:67*

STATISTICAL PROFILE	DATA	ESI
Grade organization: K–6/7–9/10–12		
Percentage of schools built before 1955	80%	
Total enrollment	4,799	
Average Daily Attendance (ADA)	98%	10
Current expense per pupil in ADA	$8,110	10
Dropout rate	4%	10
Percentage of eligible students who took the SAT	NK	0
Average combined score on SAT	†	0*
Percentage of graduates who enrolled in 2- or 4-year colleges	66%	
Percentage of students who passed the state reading test	92%	
Percentage of students who passed the state math test	94%	
Teacher–student ratio in elementary grades	1:21	9
Teacher–student ratio in secondary grades	1:13	10
Counselor–student ratio in secondary grades	1:190	10
Number of students per music specialist in elementary grades	528	5
Number of students per art specialist in elementary grades	775	
Number of volumes in senior high school library	42,140††	
Beginning teacher's salary	$18,114	
Maximum teacher's salary	$42,731	
Average years of experience among teachers	15	
Number of students suspended and expelled	1,030	
Subjects in which Advanced Placement courses are offered:	3	3
American History, English, Science		

†The district supplied an inappropriate statistic.
††This statistic seems unusually high and may be incorrect.

FAIR APPRAISAL

Quality of School Leadership
Principals are selected for their educational leadership ability, and the quality of leadership is generally uniform throughout the system. Parents and teachers have little or no formal say in principal selection. Principals, however, influence the allotment of resources to the schools.

Parent organizations are sometimes effective influencing school policy decisions. Parents meet monthly with the superintendent, and they were influential regarding school redistricting.

Quality of Instruction
Additional learning opportunities for gifted students are rated excellent, and additional instruction for low-achieving students is considered good. Also rated good are the curricula for students going to college and for those not planning on college.

Quality of School Environment
Classroom disruption and student vandalism are not problems, and the quality of building maintenance and repair is good.

ISLAND TREES

ADDRESS OF CENTRAL OFFICE:
Owl Place, Island Trees 3, Levittown, NY 11756
ESI:82

STATISTICAL PROFILE	DATA	ESI
Grade organization: K–6/7–9/10–12		
Percentage of schools built before 1955	83%	
Total enrollment	2,400	
Average Daily Attendance (ADA)	95%	8
Current expense per pupil in ADA	$7,341	10
Dropout rate	10%	10
Percentage of eligible students who took the SAT	44%	6
Average combined score on SAT	896	4
Percentage of graduates who enrolled in 2- or 4-year colleges	53%	
Percentage of students who passed the state reading test	100%	
Percentage of students who passed the state math test	88%	
Teacher–student ratio in elementary grades	1:14	10
Teacher–student ratio in secondary grades	1:11	10
Counselor–student ratio in secondary grades	1:300	6
Number of students per music specialist in elementary grades	262	10
Number of students per art specialist in elementary grades	550	
Number of volumes in senior high school library	14,951	
Beginning teacher's salary	$19,260	
Maximum teacher's salary	$45,261	
Average years of experience among teachers	20	
Number of students suspended and expelled	51	
Subjects in which Advanced Placement courses are offered: American History, Biology, Calculus, English, European History, French, Latin, Spanish	8	8

FAIR APPRAISAL

Quality of School Leadership
The School Board hires principals who demonstrate an ability for educational leadership, and the quality of leadership is generally uniform throughout the system. Parents and teachers have an informal say about principal selection, and principals have some say about the way district resources are used.

Parent organizations are sometimes effective influencing school policy decisions.

Quality of Instruction
Additional learning opportunities for gifted students are rated good, while additional instruction for low-achieving students is considered fair. The curricula for students bound for college and students bound for the world of work are both rated good.

Quality of School Environment
Classroom disruption and student vandalism are not problems, and the quality of building maintenance and repair is good.

KINGS PARK

ADDRESS OF CENTRAL OFFICE:
Kohr Road, Kings Park, NY 11754
ESI:85

STATISTICAL PROFILE	DATA	ESI
Grade organization: K–6/7–9/10–12		
Percentage of schools built before 1955	25%	
Total enrollment	3,644	
Average Daily Attendance (ADA)	95%	8
Current expense per pupil in ADA	$7,165	10
Dropout rate	8%	10
Percentage of eligible students who took the SAT	87%	10
Average combined score on SAT	955	7
Percentage of graduates who enrolled in 2- or 4-year colleges	77%	
Percentage of students who passed the state reading test	100%	
Percentage of students who passed the state math test	100%	
Teacher–student ratio in elementary grades	1:16	10
Teacher–student ratio in secondary grades	1:12	10
Counselor–student ratio in secondary grades	1:217	9
Number of students per music specialist in elementary grades	280	10
Number of students per art specialist in elementary grades	561	
Number of volumes in senior high school library	22,228	
Beginning teacher's salary	$19,126	
Maximum teacher's salary	$47,631	
Average years of experience among teachers	18	
Number of students suspended and expelled	121	
Subjects in which Advanced Placement courses are offered: American History, Calculus, English, Science	4	4

FAIR APPRAISAL

Quality of School Leadership
Principals are hired mostly for their educational leadership ability. The quality of leadership does not vary greatly from school to school, although there is variation among educational philosophies. Parents and teachers do not interview principal candidates. Principals have some say about the allotment of resources to the schools.

Parent organizations are sometimes effective influencing school decision-making.

Quality of Instruction
Additional learning opportunities for gifted students and additional instruction for low-achieving students are rated good. Also considered good are the curricula for the college-bound students and for the job-bound students.

Quality of School Environment
Classroom disruption and student vandalism are not problems, and the quality of building maintenance and repair is good.

LINDENHURST

ADDRESS OF CENTRAL OFFICE:
350 Daniel Street, Lindenhurst, NY 11757
ESI:64

STATISTICAL PROFILE	DATA	ESI
Grade organization: K–6/7–8/9–12		
Percentage of schools built before 1955	9%	
Total enrollment	6,611	
Average Daily Attendance (ADA)	91%	4
Current expense per pupil in ADA	$6,744	10
Dropout rate	16%	7
Percentage of eligible students who took the SAT	54%	8
Average combined score on SAT	880	3
Percentage of graduates who enrolled in 2- or 4-year colleges	52%	
Percentage of students who passed the state reading test	87%	
Percentage of students who passed the state math test	82%	
Teacher–student ratio in elementary grades	1:22	8
Teacher–student ratio in secondary grades	1:24	4
Counselor–student ratio in secondary grades	1:300	6
Number of students per music specialist in elementary grades	189	10
Number of students per art specialist in elementary grades	300	
Number of volumes in senior high school library	25,646	
Beginning teacher's salary	$18,300	
Maximum teacher's salary	$42,517	
Average years of experience among teachers	19	
Number of students suspended and expelled	206	
Subjects in which Advanced Placement courses are offered:	4	4
Biology, Calculus, Computer Science, English		

FAIR APPRAISAL

Quality of School Leadership
Most principals are selected because of their educational leadership ability, but the quality of leadership nevertheless varies greatly from school to school. One observer said the better quality principals are assigned to those schools where parents are most vocal. Parents and teachers do not screen principal candidates, but the principals have some say about the distribution of school resources.

Parent organizations are sometimes effective influencing school policy decisions.

Quality of Instruction
Additional learning opportunities for gifted students are rated good, while additional instruction for low-achieving students is considered only fair. The curricula for students going to college and for students not planning on college are both rated good.

Quality of School Environment
The level of classroom disruption and student vandalism is low, and the quality of building maintenance and repair is good.

LYNBROOK

ADDRESS OF CENTRAL OFFICE:
Atlantic Avenue, Lynbrook, NY 11563
ESI:92

STATISTICAL PROFILE	DATA	ESI
Grade organization: K–5/6–8/9–12		
Percentage of schools built before 1955	71%	
Total enrollment	2,495	
Average Daily Attendance (ADA)	94%	7
Current expense per pupil in ADA	$8,165	10
Dropout rate	2%	10
Percentage of eligible students who took the SAT	84%	10
Average combined score on SAT	954	8
Percentage of graduates who enrolled in 2- or 4-year colleges	82%	
Percentage of students who passed the state reading test	NK	
Percentage of students who passed the state math test	NK	
Teacher–student ratio in elementary grades	1:12	10
Teacher–student ratio in secondary grades	1:11	10
Counselor–student ratio in secondary grades	1:186	10
Number of students per music specialist in elementary grades	140	10
Number of students per art specialist in elementary grades	328	
Number of volumes in senior high school library	13,770	
Beginning teacher's salary	$19,340	
Maximum teacher's salary	$46,316	
Average years of experience among teachers	16	
Number of students suspended and expelled	16	
Subjects in which Advanced Placement courses are offered:	7	7
American History, Biology, Calculus, English,		
European History, French, Spanish		

FAIR APPRAISAL

Quality of School Leadership
Principals are hired primarily for their educational leadership ability; the quality of leadership does not vary greatly from school to school. Parents and teachers have some say, informally, in principal selection, and principals have some say in how the district's resources are allotted to the schools.

Quality of Instruction
Additional learning opportunities for gifted students are rated good, as is the additional instruction for low-achieving students. The curriculum for students preparing for college is considered excellent, but the curriculum for students not planning on college is rated only fair.

Quality of School Environment
Classroom disruption and student vandalism are not problems. The quality of building maintenance and repair is good.

MILLER PLACE

ADDRESS OF CENTRAL OFFICE:
191 North Country Road, Miller Place, NY 11764
ESI:68*

STATISTICAL PROFILE	DATA	ESI
Grade organization: K–3/4–6/7–8/9–12		
Percentage of schools built before 1955	25%	
Total enrollment	2,603	
Average Daily Attendance (ADA)	94%	7
Current expense per pupil in ADA	$6,508	10
Dropout rate	8%	10
Percentage of eligible students who took the SAT	79%	10
Average combined score on SAT	887	4
Percentage of graduates who enrolled in 2- or 4-year colleges	77%	
Percentage of students who passed the state reading test	100%	
Percentage of students who passed the state math test	100%	
Teacher–student ratio in elementary grades	1:24	6
Teacher–student ratio in secondary grades	1:14	10
Counselor–student ratio in secondary grades	1:283	6
Number of students per music specialist in elementary grades	†	0*
Number of students per art specialist in elementary grades	†	
Number of volumes in senior high school library	9,555	
Beginning teacher's salary	$18,584	
Maximum teacher's salary	$45,094	
Average years of experience among teachers	10	
Number of students suspended and expelled	102	
Subjects in which Advanced Placement courses are offered: Calculus, English, European History, French, Spanish	5	5

†The district supplied an inappropriate statistic.

FAIR APPRAISAL

Quality of School Leadership
Principals for the most part are selected for their ability as educational leaders; the quality of leadership is uniform throughout the system. Parents and teachers have hardly any say in principal selection, but principals have some say in how resources are allotted to their school.

Parent organizations are sometimes effective influencing school decision-making.

Quality of Instruction
Additional learning opportunities for gifted students are rated good, and so is additional instruction for low-achieving students. A foster grandparents program is particularly helpful for at-risk children, said an observer. The curricula for college-bound students and for those not planning on college are considered good.

Quality of School Environment
The incidence of classroom disruption and student vandalism is low; the quality of building maintenance and repair is good.

NORTH BABYLON

ADDRESS OF CENTRAL OFFICE:
5 Jardine Place, Babylon, NY 11703
ESI:81

STATISTICAL PROFILE	DATA	ESI
Grade organization: K–6/7–9/10–12		
Percentage of schools built before 1955	25%	
Total enrollment	5,000	
Average Daily Attendance (ADA)	94%	7
Current expense per pupil in ADA	$8,000	10
Dropout rate	14%	9
Percentage of eligible students who took the SAT	75%	10
Average combined score on SAT	835	1
Percentage of graduates who enrolled in 2- or 4-year colleges	72%	
Percentage of students who passed the state reading test	98%	
Percentage of students who passed the state math test	95%	
Teacher–student ratio in elementary grades	1:15	10
Teacher–student ratio in secondary grades	1:15	10
Counselor–student ratio in secondary grades	1:216	9
Number of students per music specialist in elementary grades	265	10
Number of students per art specialist in elementary grades	796	
Number of volumes in senior high school library	29,116	
Beginning teacher's salary	$18,060	
Maximum teacher's salary	$43,360	
Average years of experience among teachers	17	
Number of students suspended and expelled	1,264	
Subjects in which Advanced Placement courses are offered: American History, Biology, Calculus, English, European History	5	5

FAIR APPRAISAL

Quality of School Leadership
The School Board looks for principals with educational leadership ability, and the quality of leadership is generally uniform throughout the system. Parents and teachers have hardly any say in principal selection, but principals have some influence over the distribution of district resources.

Parent organizations are effective influencing school policy decisions. Parents meet regularly with administrators, and they have been particularly influential in decisions about redistricting.

Quality of Instruction
Additional learning opportunities for gifted students are good, but additional instruction for low-achieving students is only fair. The gifted program emphasizes enrichment in creative writing, science and the arts. The curriculum for college-bound students and the curriculum for job-bound students are both considered good.

Quality of School Environment
Classroom disruption and student vandalism are not problems. The quality of building maintenance and repair is generally good, but one school, "in a predominantly black area, is not kept up well," said an observer.

PORT WASHINGTON

ADDRESS OF CENTRAL OFFICE:
100 Campus Drive, Port Washington, NY 11050
ESI:91

STATISTICAL PROFILE	DATA	ESI
Grade organization: K–6/7–8/9–12		
Percentage of schools built before 1955	88%	
Total enrollment	4,057	
Average Daily Attendance (ADA)	95%	8
Current expense per pupil in ADA	$8,704	10
Dropout rate	3%	10
Percentage of eligible students who took the SAT	89%	10
Average combined score on SAT	1,000	9
Percentage of graduates who enrolled in 2- or 4-year colleges	88%	
Percentage of students who passed the state reading test	84%	
Percentage of students who passed the state math test	83%	
Teacher–student ratio in elementary grades	1:20	10
Teacher–student ratio in secondary grades	1:21	7
Counselor–student ratio in secondary grades	1:175	10
Number of students per music specialist in elementary grades	437	7
Number of students per art specialist in elementary grades	437	
Number of volumes in senior high school library	26,000	
Beginning teacher's salary	$21,725	
Maximum teacher's salary	$50,135	
Average years of experience among teachers	16	
Number of students suspended and expelled	3	
Subjects in which Advanced Placement courses are offered:	16	10
American History, Biology, Calculus AB, Calculus BC, Chemistry, English Language, English Literature, European History, French, Latin (Virgil), Latin (Catullus), Physics C, Physics (magnetism and electricity), Spanish Language, Spanish Literature		

Quality of School Leadership
Principals are hired because of their educational leadership ability, and the quality of leadership does not vary greatly from school to school. Parents and teachers sit on committees that help screen principal candidates. Also, principals have some influence over the use of district resources.

Parent organizations are effective as an influence on district policy. "Parents' presence and opinions certainly are respected," said an observer.

Quality of Instruction
Additional learning opportunities for gifted students are rated excellent. Students in elementary grades are excused from regular classes to attend enrichment classes. At the high school level, one guidance counselor serves only very bright students. Additional instruction for low-achieving students is rated good. Observers find the college preparatory curriculum excellent. For its size, the district offers a large number of Advanced Placement courses. The curriculum for students not planning on college is rated good.

Observers agree that the district's high academic standards have made for a first-rate educational program. However, they believe more could be done for the bright students who don't achieve their potential.

Quality of School Environment
Classroom disruption and student vandalism are not problems. However, the quality of building maintenance and repair is rated only fair. A new superintendent is giving this problem "priority attention," said an observer.

RIVERHEAD

ADDRESS OF CENTRAL OFFICE:
700 Osborne Avenue, Riverhead, NY 11901
ESI:54*

STATISTICAL PROFILE	DATA	ESI
Grade organization: †		
Percentage of schools built before 1955	28%	
Total enrollment	3,704	
Average Daily Attendance (ADA)	92%	5
Current expense per pupil in ADA	$5,061	2
Dropout rate	46%	0
Percentage of eligible students who took the SAT	84%	10
Average combined score on SAT	††	0*
Percentage of graduates who enrolled in 2- or 4-year colleges	50%	
Percentage of students who passed the state reading test	89%	
Percentage of students who passed the state math test	64%	
Teacher–student ratio in elementary grades	1:22	8
Teacher–student ratio in secondary grades	1:23	5
Counselor–student ratio in secondary grades	1:250	8
Number of students per music specialist in elementary grades	200	10
Number of students per art specialist in elementary grades	200	
Number of volumes in senior high school library	16,000	
Beginning teacher's salary	$18,721	
Maximum teacher's salary	$42,271	
Average years of experience among teachers	12	
Number of students suspended and expelled	291	
Subjects in which Advanced Placement courses are offered:	6	6
American History, Biology, Calculus, Chemistry, Computer Science, English		

†The district misinterpreted this statistic.
††The district supplied an inappropriate statistic.

Quality of School Leadership
The School Board generally seeks out principals who show ability as educational leaders. However, past hiring practices have resulted in some major variations in the quality of leadership. "Some principals who have been in the system a long time were hired more on the basis of other criteria, such as longevity," said one observer. Parents and teachers have hardly any say in principal selection, but principals have some say in how resources will be allotted to their school.

Parent organizations are sometimes effective influencing school decisions, but, according to observers, the strong superintendent is not very responsible to parent opinions.

Quality of Instruction
Additional learning opportunities for gifted students are rated good. The program is particularly strong in math and science. Additional instruction for low-achieving students is only rated fair. The college preparatory curriculum is good, but the curriculum for students not planning on college is called fair. One observer complained about insufficient and ineffective guidance at the high school.

Quality of School Environment
The level of classroom disruption and student vandalism is low, and the quality of building maintenance and repair is good.

ROCKVILLE CENTER

ADDRESS OF CENTRAL OFFICE:
Shepherd Street, Rockville Center, NY 11570
ESI:82

STATISTICAL PROFILE	DATA	ESI
Grade organization: †		
Percentage of schools built before 1955	100%	
Total enrollment	3,200	
Average Daily Attendance (ADA)	96%	9
Current expense per pupil in ADA	$5,300	4
Dropout rate	8%	10
Percentage of eligible students who took the SAT	82%	10
Average combined score on SAT	971	8
Percentage of graduates who enrolled in 2- or 4-year colleges	89%	
Percentage of students who passed the state reading test	100%	
Percentage of students who passed the state math test	100%	
Teacher–student ratio in elementary grades	1:22	8
Teacher–student ratio in secondary grades	1:20	8
Counselor–student ratio in secondary grades	1:200	9
Number of students per music specialist in elementary grades	200	10
Number of students per art specialist in elementary grades	700	
Number of volumes in senior high school library	19,500	
Beginning teacher's salary	$20,330	
Maximum teacher's salary	$50,639	
Average years of experience among teachers	14	
Number of students suspended and expelled	241	
Subjects in which Advanced Placement courses are offered:	6	6
American History, Biology, Calculus, Chemistry,		
Computer Science, English		

†The district misinterpreted this statistic.

FAIR APPRAISAL

Quality of School Leadership

Principals are hired primarily for their educational leadership ability, and the quality of leadership does not vary greatly from school to school. Parents and teachers help interview principal candidates, and principals have a great deal to say about the allotment of district resources to the schools.

Parent organizations are effective as an influence on school policy. For example, parents were largely responsible for the assignment of a full-time nurse at each elementary school.

Quality of Instruction

Additional learning opportunities for gifted students are rated good. At the elementary level, students are excused from regular classes to attend enrichment programs. Additional instruction for low-achieving students also is rated good. Study skills groups and resource rooms are all used to help the low-achievers. The curriculum for students bound for college is considered excellent, while the curriculum for students headed for the world of work is rated good. One observer spoke of the "highly motivated community" that demands quality education.

Quality of School Environment

Classroom disruption and student vandalism are not problems. The quality of building maintenance and repair is good. A major building "up-dating" program is underway.

ROOSEVELT

ADDRESS OF CENTRAL OFFICE:
240 Denton Place, Roosevelt, NY 11575
ESI:49

STATISTICAL PROFILE	DATA	ESI
Grade organization: †		
Percentage of schools built before 1955	60%	
Total enrollment	3,032	
Average Daily Attendance (ADA)	97%	10
Current expense per pupil in ADA	$4,009	0
Dropout rate	27%	0
Percentage of eligible students who took the SAT	56%	9
Average combined score on SAT	665	0
Percentage of graduates who enrolled in 2- or 4-year colleges	63%	
Percentage of students who passed the state reading test	88%	
Percentage of students who passed the state math test	58%	
Teacher–student ratio in elementary grades	1:12	10
Teacher–student ratio in secondary grades	1:14	10
Counselor–student ratio in secondary grades	1:200	9
Number of students per music specialist in elementary grades	None	0
Number of students per art specialist in elementary grades	None	0
Number of volumes in senior high school library	21,984	
Beginning teacher's salary	$14,863	
Maximum teacher's salary	$36,683	
Average years of experience among teachers	13	
Number of students suspended and expelled	2,063	
Subjects in which Advanced Placement courses are offered:	1	1
American History		

†The district misinterpreted this statistic.

FAIR APPRAISAL

Quality of School Leadership

According to the observers, internal politics, popularity and longevity are more important criteria than educational leadership ability when it comes to picking principals. Consequently, the quality of leadership varies greatly from school to school. Parents and teachers have no say in principal selection, and principals have little to say about the way resources are used.

Parent organizations are generally ineffective as an influence over district policy. A new superintendent took office in June 1987, and observers believe the system may change for the better.

Quality of Instruction

Additional learning opportunities for gifted students and additional instruction for low-achieving students are rated poor. The curriculum for college-bound students and the curriculum for students not planning on college are both considered only fair.

One observer, commenting on the system, said simply, "It is not good."

Quality of School Environment

The incidence of classroom disruption and student vandalism is low, but the quality of building maintenance and repair is only fair to poor.

SEAFORD

ADDRESS OF CENTRAL OFFICE:
1600 Washington Avenue, Seaford, NY 11783
ESI:80

STATISTICAL PROFILE	DATA	ESI
Grade organization: K–5/6–8/9–12		
Percentage of schools built before 1955	0%	
Total enrollment	2,602	
Average Daily Attendance (ADA)	91%	4
Current expense per pupil in ADA	$7,214	10
Dropout rate	10%	10
Percentage of eligible students who took the SAT	80%	10
Average combined score on SAT	925	5
Percentage of graduates who enrolled in 2- or 4-year colleges	75%	
Percentage of students who passed the state reading test	100%	
Percentage of students who passed the state math test	100%	
Teacher–student ratio in elementary grades	1:19	10
Teacher–student ratio in secondary grades	1:15	10
Counselor–student ratio in secondary grades	1:258	6
Number of students per music specialist in elementary grades	263	10
Number of students per art specialist in elementary grades	526	
Number of volumes in senior high school library	14,861	
Beginning teacher's salary	$18,694	
Maximum teacher's salary	$40,698	
Average years of experience among teachers	15	
Number of students suspended and expelled	123	
Subjects in which Advanced Placement courses are offered: American History, Calculus, Computer Science, French, Spanish	5	5

FAIR APPRAISAL

Quality of School Leadership
Principals are hired for their educational leadership ability, and the quality of leadership is generally uniform throughout the system. Parents and teachers have hardly any say in principal selection, but principals have some say about the division of district resources.

Parent organizations are sometimes effective influencing district policy.

Quality of Instruction
Additional learning opportunities for gifted students and additional instruction for low-achieving students are both rated fair. Also considered fair are the curricula for college-bound students and for students not planning on college.
The district has been operating on an "austerity" budget, which one observer blames for a less than adequate educational program.

Quality of School Environment
Classroom disruption and student vandalism are not problems. The quality of building maintenance and repair is good.

SMITHTOWN

ADDRESS OF CENTRAL OFFICE:
26 New York Avenue, Smithtown, NY 11787
ESI:None†

STATISTICAL PROFILE	DATA	ESI
Grade organization:		
Percentage of schools built before 1955		
Total enrollment		
Average Daily Attendance (ADA)		
Current expense per pupil in ADA		
Dropout rate		
Percentage of eligible students who took the SAT		
Average combined score on SAT		
Percentage of graduates who enrolled in 2- or 4-year colleges		
Percentage of students who passed the state reading test		
Percentage of students who passed the state math test		
Teacher–student ratio in elementary grades		
Teacher–student ratio in secondary grades		
Counselor–student ratio in secondary grades		
Number of students per music specialist in elementary grades		
Number of students per art specialist in elementary grades		
Number of volumes in senior high school library		
Beginning teacher's salary		
Maximum teacher's salary		
Average years of experience among teachers		
Number of students suspended and expelled		
Subjects in which Advanced Placement courses are offered:		

†A Statistical Profile was not received from this district.

FAIR APPRAISAL

Quality of School Leadership
Although longevity is a factor, most principals are selected for their educational leadership ability. The quality of leadership is generally uniform throughout the system. Parents and teachers do not take part in screening principal candidates. Principals, however, have some say in how resources are used by the schools.

PTA representatives meet monthly with the superintendent, and parent organizations generally are an effective influence on school decision-making.

Quality of Instruction
Additional learning opportunities for gifted students are rated good to excellent. The program begins in grade 2. Additional instruction for low-achieving students is considered good, and each building has a "well-staffed" learning center for remedial and tutorial work. The curriculum for students heading for college is considered excellent, while the curriculum for students not planning on college is termed good.

Quality of School Environment
The incidence of classroom disruption and student vandalism is very low, and the quality of building maintenance and repair is good.

THREE VILLAGE

ADDRESS OF CENTRAL OFFICE:
Nicoll Road, East Setauket, NY 11733
ESI:88

STATISTICAL PROFILE	DATA	ESI
Grade organization: K–6/7–9/10–12		
Percentage of schools built before 1955	12%	
Total enrollment	7,523	
Average Daily Attendance (ADA)	94%	7
Current expense per pupil in ADA	$5,977	4
Dropout rate	6%	10
Percentage of eligible students who took the SAT	78%	10
Average combined score on SAT	994	9
Percentage of graduates who enrolled in 2- or 4-year colleges	87%	
Percentage of students who passed the state reading test	98%	
Percentage of students who passed the state math test	99%	
Teacher–student ratio in elementary grades	1:14	10
Teacher–student ratio in secondary grades	1:14	10
Counselor–student ratio in secondary grades	1:210	9
Number of students per music specialist in elementary grades	309	9
Number of students per art specialist in elementary grades	392	
Number of volumes in senior high school library	28,000	
Beginning teacher's salary	$18,070	
Maximum teacher's salary	$46,432	
Average years of experience among teachers	14	
Number of students suspended and expelled	532	
Subjects in which Advanced Placement courses are offered:	11	10
American History, Biology, Calculus AB, Calculus BC, Chemistry, Computer Science, English, European History, French, Physics, Spanish		

Quality of School Leadership
Most principals are hired because of their educational leadership ability, but internal politics is a factor, according to observers. The observers also question whether the standards of educational leadership set for the district are met by all principals. Teachers have a great deal to say about principal selection; parents get in on the tail end of the process and may question the candidate who is considered the finalist. Principals have some influence over the distribution of district resources.

Parent organizations are sometimes effective influencing school decisions.

Quality of Instruction
Additional learning opportunities for gifted students are rated good. Gifted students in the elementary schools are grouped and transported to special classes for instruction. One observer reported that a number of parents complain that "many bright students are not selected for the program because of extremely high standards." Additional instruction for low-achieving students is considered good. The curriculum for college-bound students is considered excellent, while the curriculum for students not planning on college is rated only fair. "This is definitely a college-oriented school system," said one observer.

Quality of School Environment
The level of classroom disruption and student vandalism is low, and the quality of building maintenance and repair is good.

WESTBURY

ADDRESS OF CENTRAL OFFICE:
Jericho Turnpike and Hitchcock Lane, Westbury, NY 11590
ESI:None†

STATISTICAL PROFILE	DATA	ESI
Grade organization:		
Percentage of schools built before 1955		
Total enrollment		
Average Daily Attendance (ADA)		
Current expense per pupil in ADA		
Dropout rate		
Percentage of eligible students who took the SAT		
Average combined score on SAT		
Percentage of graduates who enrolled in 2- or 4-year colleges		
Percentage of students who passed the state reading test		
Percentage of students who passed the state math test		
Teacher–student ratio in elementary grades		
Teacher–student ratio in secondary grades		
Counselor–student ratio in secondary grades		
Number of students per music specialist in elementary grades		
Number of students per art specialist in elementary grades		
Number of volumes in senior high school library		
Beginning teacher's salary		
Maximum teacher's salary		
Average years of experience among teachers		
Number of students suspended and expelled		
Subjects in which Advanced Placement courses are offered:		

†A Statistical Profile was not received from this district.

Quality of School Leadership
The School Board seeks principals who demonstrate educational leadership ability, and the quality of leadership does not vary greatly from school to school. Parents and teachers have some say in principal selection in an informal way, and principals have some say in how resources are allotted to the schools.

Parent organizations are sometimes effective as an influence on school policy-making.

Quality of Instruction
Additional learning opportunities for gifted students are rated fair, while additional instruction for low-achieving students is considered good. The curriculum that prepares students for college is rated fair, but the curriculum for students not planning on college is considered good.

The district is not adequately meeting the needs of minority students, who constitute a majority of the enrollment, according to observers. Test scores are low.

Quality of School Environment
The incidence of classroom disruption and student vandalism is low, and the quality of building maintenance and repair is good.

WEST ISLIP

ADDRESS OF CENTRAL OFFICE:
Sherman Avenue, West Islip, NY 11795
ESI:76*

STATISTICAL PROFILE	DATA	ESI
Grade organization: K–6/7–9/10–12		
Percentage of schools built before 1955	10%	
Total enrollment	5,471	
Average Daily Attendance (ADA)	95%	8
Current expense per pupil in ADA	$7,093	10
Dropout rate	5%	10
Percentage of eligible students who took the SAT	66%	10
Average combined score on SAT	917	5
Percentage of graduates who enrolled in 2- or 4-year colleges	36%	
Percentage of students who passed the state reading test	93%	
Percentage of students who passed the state math test	84%	
Teacher–student ratio in elementary grades	1:21	9
Teacher–student ratio in secondary grades	1:14	10
Counselor–student ratio in secondary grades	1:340	4
Number of students per music specialist in elementary grades	†	0*
Number of students per art specialist in elementary grades	†	
Number of volumes in senior high school library	17,230	
Beginning teacher's salary	$17,750	
Maximum teacher's salary	$41,083	
Average years of experience among teachers	15	
Number of students suspended and expelled	286	
Subjects in which Advanced Placement courses are offered: American History, Biology, Calculus, Computer Science, English Composition & Literature, European History, French, Physics, Spanish	9	9

†The district supplied an inappropriate statistic.

FAIR APPRAISAL

Quality of School Leadership
Principals are hired primarily for their educational leadership ability, and the quality of leadership is generally uniform throughout the system. Parents and teachers have hardly any say in principal selection, but principals have some say about the allotment of resources to their school.

"Parent organizations, by expressing concern and pressure, generally make an impact on policies and practices of individual schools," said one observer.

Quality of Instruction
Additional learning opportunities for gifted students and additional instruction for low-achieving students are both rated good. The program for gifted students is "limited" in the elementary grades, the observers said, but is "more extensive in upper grades." The college preparatory curriculum is rated excellent, while the curriculum for students not going to college is considered good.

Quality of School Environment
The level of classroom disruption and student vandalism is low, and the quality of building maintenance and repair is good.

Newark, NJ

Fourteen districts supplied Statistical Profiles, and Fair Appraisals alone were received from two other districts. Districts in this area should be compared with those in the New York City and Nassau–Suffolk Counties, NY Metropolitan Areas.

AREA AT A GLANCE

SCHOOL DISTRICT	ENROLLMENT	ESI
Belleville	4,033	57
Bloomfield	5,262	56*
Hillside	2,974	46
Irvington	9,020	39
Kearny	4,500	53
Livingston	4,100	66*
Middletown Township	10,260	64
Monroe	2,559	68
Montclair	5,263	43
Morris	4,396	90
New Brunswick	4,950	
North Brunswick	3,401	71
Scotch Plains–Fanwood	3,974	75*
South Orange–Maplewood	4,946	86
Union City	8,000	
Woodbridge	10,556	73

Indicates district misinterpretation of one or more statistics in the ESI. For each misinterpreted statistic, a score of 0 was given instead of a possible score of 0 to 10 points.

BELLEVILLE

ADDRESS OF CENTRAL OFFICE:
190 Cortland Street, Belleville, NJ 07109
ESI:57

STATISTICAL PROFILE	DATA	ESI
Grade organization: K–6/7–8/9–12		
Percentage of schools built before 1955	78%	
Total enrollment	4,033	
Average Daily Attendance (ADA)	92%	5
Current expense per pupil in ADA	$3,400	0
Dropout rate	12%	10
Percentage of eligible students who took the SAT	47%	7
Average combined score on SAT	813	0
Percentage of graduates who enrolled in 2- or 4-year colleges	46%	
Percentage of students who passed the state reading test	79%	
Percentage of students who passed the state math test	78%	
Teacher–student ratio in elementary grades	1:20	10
Teacher–student ratio in secondary grades	1:22	6
Counselor–student ratio in secondary grades	1:200	9
Number of students per music specialist in elementary grades	500	5
Number of students per art specialist in elementary grades	500	
Number of volumes in senior high school library	17,250	
Beginning teacher's salary	$19,000	
Maximum teacher's salary	$38,300	
Average years of experience among teachers	10	
Number of students suspended and expelled	495	
Subjects in which Advanced Placement courses are offered: Calculus, English, French, Italian, Spanish	5	5

FAIR APPRAISAL

Quality of School Leadership
Principals are hired mainly for their leadership ability, and the quality of leadership is generally uniform throughout the system. Parents and teachers do not screen principal candidates, although principals have some say in the allotment of resources to the schools.

Parent organizations are sometimes effective influencing school policies.

Quality of Instruction
Additional learning opportunities for gifted students are rated good, while additional instruction for low-achieving students is considered fair. Also rated fair is the curriculum for students planning on college. The curriculum for students not planning on college is rated excellent.

Quality of School Environment
The level of classroom disruption and student vandalism is very low, and the quality of building maintenance and repair is good.

BLOOMFIELD

ADDRESS OF CENTRAL OFFICE:
155 Broad Street, Bloomfield, NJ 07003
ESI:56*

STATISTICAL PROFILE	DATA	ESI
Grade organization: †		
Percentage of schools built before 1955	15%	
Total enrollment	5,262	
Average Daily Attendance (ADA)	94%	7
Current expense per pupil in ADA	$5,156	4
Dropout rate	7%	10
Percentage of eligible students who took the SAT	60%	9
Average combined score on SAT	††	0*
Percentage of graduates who enrolled in 2- or 4-year colleges	48%	
Percentage of students who passed the state reading test	91%	
Percentage of students who passed the state math test	87%	
Teacher–student ratio in elementary grades	1:22	8
Teacher–student ratio in secondary grades	1:25	3
Counselor–student ratio in secondary grades	1:175	10
Number of students per music specialist in elementary grades	621	3
Number of students per art specialist in elementary grades	587	
Number of volumes in senior high school library	32,329	
Beginning teacher's salary	$19,781	
Maximum teacher's salary	$37,500	
Average years of experience among teachers	15	
Number of students suspended and expelled	1	
Subjects in which Advanced Placement courses are offered: English, Mathematics	2	2

† The district misinterpreted this statistic.
††The district supplied an inappropriate statistic.

FAIR APPRAISAL

Quality of School Leadership
The School Board hires principals who demonstrate educational leadership ability, although internal politics is a factor, and the quality of leadership does not vary greatly from school to school. Parents and teachers have hardly any say in principal selection. However, principals have a lot to say about how district resources are distributed.

Parent organizations are not effective as an influence on school policy.

Quality of Instruction
Additional learning opportunities for gifted students and additional instruction for low-achieving students are both rated fair. Also considered fair are the curricula for students going to college and for those students heading into the job market.

Quality of School Environment
The level of classroom disruption and student vandalism are on the high side. The quality of building maintenance and repair is fair.

HILLSIDE

ADDRESS OF CENTRAL OFFICE:
195 Virginia Street, Hillside, NJ 07205
ESI:46

STATISTICAL PROFILE	DATA	ESI
Grade organization: K–8/9–12		
Percentage of schools built before 1955	100%	
Total enrollment	2,974	
Average Daily Attendance (ADA)	84%	0
Current expense per pupil in ADA	$4,588	1
Dropout rate	34%	0
Percentage of eligible students who took the SAT	61%	10
Average combined score on SAT	739	0
Percentage of graduates who enrolled in 2- or 4-year colleges	55%	
Percentage of students who passed the state reading test	82%	
Percentage of students who passed the state math test	72%	
Teacher–student ratio in elementary grades	1:22	8
Teacher–student ratio in secondary grades	1:12	10
Counselor–student ratio in secondary grades	1:220	9
Number of students per music specialist in elementary grades	350	8
Number of students per art specialist in elementary grades	700	
Number of volumes in senior high school library	21,978	
Beginning teacher's salary	$18,500	
Maximum teacher's salary	$40,000	
Average years of experience among teachers	14	
Number of students suspended and expelled	1,466	
Subjects in which Advanced Placement courses are offered:	None	0

FAIR APPRAISAL

Quality of School Leadership
Most principals are hired because of their educational leadership ability, and the quality of leadership is generally uniform throughout the system. However, one observer pointed out that "a lack of standard policies causes some undesirable differences among schools." Parents and teachers have hardly any say about the selection of principals, but principals have some say about the way district resources are allocated. "Basically," said one observer, "school leaders of individual schools have tried very hard to grow, to develop innovative programs."

Parent organizations are sometimes effective influencing district policy.

Quality of Instruction
Additional learning opportunities for gifted students are rated as good. "It is a very innovative enrichment program, starting in grade 3," said an observer. Additional instruction for low-achieving students is considered good, also. "Project Homework" matches teachers and low-achievers in a tutorial setting. The curriculum preparing students for college is rated good, while the curriculum for students not planning on college is considered fair.

Quality of School Environment
The incidence of classroom disruption and student vandalism is low, and the quality of building maintenance and repair is excellent.

IRVINGTON

ADDRESS OF CENTRAL OFFICE:
1150 Springfield Avenue, Irvington, NJ 07111
ESI:39

STATISTICAL PROFILE	DATA	ESI
Grade organization: K–6/7–8/9–12		
Percentage of schools built before 1955	0%	
Total enrollment	9,020†	
Average Daily Attendance (ADA)	92%†	5
Current expense per pupil in ADA	$2,635	0
Dropout rate	38%	0
Percentage of eligible students who took the SAT	30%	3
Average combined score on SAT	629	0
Percentage of graduates who enrolled in 2- or 4-year colleges	31%	
Percentage of students who passed the state reading test	43%	
Percentage of students who passed the state math test	16%	
Teacher–student ratio in elementary grades	1:26 †	4
Teacher–student ratio in secondary grades	1:14 †	10
Counselor–student ratio in secondary grades	1:285†	6
Number of students per music specialist in elementary grades	314	9
Number of students per art specialist in elementary grades	314	
Number of volumes in senior high school library	30,635	
Beginning teacher's salary	$19,900	
Maximum teacher's salary	$41,000	
Average years of experience among teachers	7	
Number of students suspended and expelled	792	
Subjects in which Advanced Placement courses are offered:	2	2
Calculus, English		

†1986–87 statistics.

FAIR APPRAISAL

Quality of School Leadership
Principals are hired mainly for their ability as educational leaders, and the quality of leadership is generally uniform throughout the system. Parents and teachers have little or no say in principal selection, and principals do not have much say in how resources are distributed.

Parent organizations are mostly ineffective as an influence on district decision-making.

Quality of Instruction
Additional learning opportunities for gifted students and additional instruction for low-achieving students are rated fair. The curricula for college-bound students and for job-bound students are both considered good.

Quality of School Environment
The level of classroom disruption and student vandalism is very low, and the quality of building maintenance and repair is good.

KEARNY

ADDRESS OF CENTRAL OFFICE:
336 Devon Street, Kearny, NJ 07032
ESI:53

STATISTICAL PROFILE	DATA	ESI
Grade organization: K–6/7–8/9–12		
Percentage of schools built before 1955	71%	
Total enrollment	4,500	
Average Daily Attendance (ADA)	96%	9
Current expense per pupil in ADA	$4,200	0
Dropout rate	NK	0
Percentage of eligible students who took the SAT	66%	10
Average combined score on SAT	850	2
Percentage of graduates who enrolled in 2- or 4-year colleges	55%	
Percentage of students who passed the state reading test	85%	
Percentage of students who passed the state math test	75%	
Teacher–student ratio in elementary grades	1:18	10
Teacher–student ratio in secondary grades	1:22	6
Counselor–student ratio in secondary grades	1:250	8
Number of students per music specialist in elementary grades	375	8
Number of students per art specialist in elementary grades	900	
Number of volumes in senior high school libraries (average)	NK	
Beginning teacher's salary	$18,500	
Maximum teacher's salary	$37,255	
Average years of experience among teachers	17	
Number of students suspended and expelled	NK	
Subjects in which Advanced Placement courses are offered:	None	0

FAIR APPRAISAL

Quality of School Leadership

The School Board looks for principals with educational leadership ability, and the quality of leadership does not vary greatly from school to school. Parents and teachers do not help screen principal candidates, but principals have some influence over the use of district resources.

Parent organizations are mostly ineffective influencing school decisions.

Quality of Instruction

Additional learning opportunities for gifted students are rated fair. The program "could be better in the elementary grades," said an observer. Additional instruction for low-achieving students is called good. The curriculum preparing students for college and the curriculum preparing students for the world of work are both considered excellent.

Quality of School Environment

Classroom disruption and student vandalism are not problems, and the quality of building maintenance and repair is good.

LIVINGSTON

ADDRESS OF CENTRAL OFFICE:
11 Foxcroft Drive, Livingston, NJ 07039
ESI:66*

STATISTICAL PROFILE	DATA	ESI
Grade organization: K–5/6–8/9–12		
Percentage of schools built before 1955	62%	
Total enrollment	4,100	
Average Daily Attendance (ADA)	99%	10
Current expense per pupil in ADA	$5,260	4
Dropout rate	5%	10
Percentage of eligible students who took the SAT	NK	0
Average combined score on SAT	988	9
Percentage of graduates who enrolled in 2- or 4-year colleges	93%	
Percentage of students who passed the state reading test	96%	
Percentage of students who passed the state math test	90%	
Teacher–student ratio in elementary grades	1:24	6
Teacher–student ratio in secondary grades	1:12	10
Counselor–student ratio in secondary grades	1:213	9
Number of students per music specialist in elementary grades	†	0*
Number of students per art specialist in elementary grades	†	
Number of volumes in senior high school library	27,000	
Beginning teacher's salary	$19,500	
Maximum teacher's salary	$41,000	
Average years of experience among teachers	21	
Number of students suspended and expelled	90	
Subjects in which Advanced Placement courses are offered:	8	8
American History, Biology, Calculus, Chemistry, Computer Science, English, French, Spanish		

†The district supplied an inappropriate statistic.

FAIR APPRAISAL

Quality of School Leadership

Principals are hired primarily because of their educational leadership ability, and the quality of leadership is generally uniform throughout the system. Parents and teachers have some involvement in principal selection, and the school's PTA president helps make a final decision on the principal for that school. Principals have a lot to say about the way district resources are used.

Parent organizations are very effective influencing school decision-making.

Quality of Instruction

Additional learning opportunities for gifted students are rated excellent. Students are excused from regular classes for enrichment. The program begins in grade 2. Additional instruction for low-achieving students is called good. The college preparatory curriculum is considered excellent. Because of a heavy concentration on college-bound students, the curriculum for students not planning on college is weak. Observers rate it fair to poor.

Quality of School Environment

Classroom disruption and student vandalism are not problems; the quality of building maintenance and repair is good.

MIDDLETOWN TOWNSHIP

ADDRESS OF CENTRAL OFFICE:
59 Tindall Road, Middletown, NJ 07748
ESI:64

STATISTICAL PROFILE	DATA	ESI
Grade organization: K–5/6–8/9–12		
Percentage of schools built before 1955	53%	
Total enrollment	10,260	
Average Daily Attendance (ADA)	94%	7
Current expense per pupil in ADA	$4,085	0
Dropout rate	10%	10
Percentage of eligible students who took the SAT	95%	10
Average combined score on SAT	913	5
Percentage of graduates who enrolled in 2- or 4-year colleges	72%	
Percentage of students who passed the state reading test	89%	
Percentage of students who passed the state math test	78%	
Teacher–student ratio in elementary grades	1:22	8
Teacher–student ratio in secondary grades	1:14	10
Counselor–student ratio in secondary grades	1:234	8
Number of students per music specialist in elementary grades	592	4
Number of students per art specialist in elementary grades	592	
Number of volumes in senior high school libraries (average)	31,651	
Beginning teacher's salary	$18,500	
Maximum teacher's salary	$42,221	
Average years of experience among teachers	15	
Number of students suspended and expelled	5,890	
Subjects in which Advanced Placement courses are offered: Chemistry, Physics	2	2

FAIR APPRAISAL

Quality of School Leadership
Principals are selected for their educational leadership ability; the quality of leadership does not vary greatly from school to school. Parents and teachers have hardly any say in principal selection, but principals have some say in the allocation of district resources.

Parent organizations are effective influencing school decisions.

Quality of Instruction
Additional learning opportunities for gifted students are rated good, while additional instruction for low-achieving students is rated only fair to poor. The curriculum for students going to college is rated good to excellent, but the curriculum for students not planning on college is considered fair to good.

Quality of School Environment
The level of classroom disruption and student vandalism is low, and the quality of building maintenance and repair is good.

MONROE

ADDRESS OF CENTRAL OFFICE:
Jamesburg–Englishtown Road, Jamesburg, NJ 08831
ESI:68

STATISTICAL PROFILE	DATA	ESI
Grade organization: †		
Percentage of schools built before 1955	40%	
Total enrollment	2,559	
Average Daily Attendance (ADA)	94%	7
Current expense per pupil in ADA	$3,749	0
Dropout rate	1%	10
Percentage of eligible students who took the SAT	62%	10
Average combined score on SAT	864	2
Percentage of graduates who enrolled in 2- or 4-year colleges	67%	
Percentage of students who passed the state reading test	96%	
Percentage of students who passed the state math test	98%	
Teacher–student ratio in elementary grades	1:12	10
Teacher–student ratio in secondary grades	1:12	10
Counselor–student ratio in secondary grades	1:177	10
Number of students per music specialist in elementary grades	418	7
Number of students per art specialist in elementary grades	418	
Number of volumes in senior high school library	12,000	
Beginning teacher's salary	$19,100	
Maximum teacher's salary	$34,650	
Average years of experience among teachers	11	
Number of students suspended and expelled	NK	
Subjects in which Advanced Placement courses are offered: American History, Biology	2	2

†The district misinterpreted this statistic.

FAIR APPRAISAL

Quality of School Leadership
Principals are selected based on demonstrated ability as educational leaders, and the quality of leadership is generally uniform throughout the system. Parents and teachers have little to do with principal selection, but principals have something to say about the allocation of resources to the schools.

Parent organizations are effective as an influence on school decision-making. Members of the PTA council meet monthly with the superintendent.

Quality of Instruction
Additional learning opportunities for gifted students are rated excellent. Students in the lower grades are excused from regular classes to attend enrichment programs. Additional instruction for low-achieving students is considered good; remedial services and resource rooms are featured. The curriculum for students planning on college is rated excellent, while the curriculum for students planning on the world of work after graduation is rated good.

Quality of School Environment
Classroom disruption and student vandalism are not problems, and the quality of building maintenance and repair is good.

MONTCLAIR

ADDRESS OF CENTRAL OFFICE:
22 Valley Road, Montclair, NJ 07042
ESI:43

STATISTICAL PROFILE	DATA	ESI
Grade organization: Pre-K–5/6–8/9–12		
Percentage of schools built before 1955	100%	
Total enrollment	5,263	
Average Daily Attendance (ADA)	92%	5
Current expense per pupil in ADA	$4,140	0
Dropout rate	NK	0
Percentage of eligible students who took the SAT	80%	10
Average combined score on SAT	908	5
Percentage of graduates who enrolled in 2- or 4-year colleges	82%	
Percentage of students who passed the state reading test	88%	
Percentage of students who passed the state math test	79%	
Teacher–student ratio in elementary grades	1:25	5
Teacher–student ratio in secondary grades	1:14	10
Counselor–student ratio in secondary grades	1:250	8
Number of students per music specialist in elementary grades	None	0
Number of students per art specialist in elementary grades	None	0
Number of volumes in senior high school library	33,000	
Beginning teacher's salary	$19,450	
Maximum teacher's salary	$39,680	
Average years of experience among teachers	16	
Number of students suspended and expelled	162	
Subjects in which Advanced Placement courses are offered:	None	0

FAIR APPRAISAL

Quality of School Leadership
The School Board looks for principals who have ability as educational leaders, and the quality of leadership does not vary greatly from school to school. Parents and teachers have little to say about principal selection, although parents informally may influence the selection. Principals, on the other hand, have a lot to say about the distribution of district resources.

Parent organizations are effective influencing school policy decisions. Parent representatives have monthly meetings with the superintendent.

Quality of Instruction
Magnet secondary schools are a followup to the elementary program for gifted students, and additional learning opportunities for gifted students are rated excellent. Additional instruction for low-achieving students is considered good. The curriculum for college-bound students is called excellent, while the curriculum for students not planning on college is termed good.

Quality of School Environment
Classroom disruption and student vandalism are not problems, and the quality of building maintenance and repair is good.

MORRIS

ADDRESS OF CENTRAL OFFICE:
Normandy Parkway, Morristown, NJ 07960
ESI:90

STATISTICAL PROFILE	DATA	ESI
Grade organization: K–3/4–6/7–8/9–12		
Percentage of schools built before 1955	50%	
Total enrollment	4,396	
Average Daily Attendance (ADA)	94%	7
Current expense per pupil in ADA	$6,008	8
Dropout rate	4%	10
Percentage of eligible students who took the SAT	78%	10
Average combined score on SAT	930	6
Percentage of graduates who enrolled in 2- or 4-year colleges	81%	
Percentage of students who passed the state reading test	98%	
Percentage of students who passed the state math test	98%	
Teacher–student ratio in elementary grades	1:20	10
Teacher–student ratio in secondary grades	1:12	10
Counselor–student ratio in secondary grades	1:215	9
Number of students per music specialist in elementary grades	242	10
Number of students per art specialist in elementary grades	483	
Number of volumes in senior high school library	37,031	
Beginning teacher's salary	$20,535	
Maximum teacher's salary	$43,810	
Average years of experience among teachers	15	
Number of students suspended and expelled	73	
Subjects in which Advanced Placement courses are offered:	10	10
American History, Biology, Chemistry, Computer Science, English, French Literature, French Language, Physics, Spanish Language, Spanish Literature		

FAIR APPRAISAL

Quality of School Leadership
Principals are hired primarily because they evidence ability as educational leaders. The quality of leadership is generally uniform throughout the system. Parents and teachers serve on committees that screen principal candidates; also, principals have some influence in the allocation of district resources to the schools.

Parent organizations are effective influencing school policy matters. Parent leaders meet monthly with the superintendent.

Quality of Instruction
Additional learning opportunities for gifted students are rated excellent. Special programs exist in math, science, creative arts and computer science. Additional instruction for low-achieving students also is rated excellent, with each school having a resource room and remedial teachers. The curricula for college-bound students and job-bound students are both termed excellent.

Quality of School Environment
Classroom disruption and student vandalism are not problems, and the quality of building maintenance and repair is good.

NEW BRUNSWICK

ADDRESS OF CENTRAL OFFICE:
24 Bayard Street, New Brunswick, NJ 08901
ESI:None†

STATISTICAL PROFILE	DATA	ESI
Grade organization:		
Percentage of schools built before 1955		
Total enrollment		
Average Daily Attendance (ADA)		
Current expense per pupil in ADA		
Dropout rate		
Percentage of eligible students who took the SAT		
Average combined score on SAT		
Percentage of graduates who enrolled in 2- or 4-year colleges		
Percentage of students who passed the state reading test		
Percentage of students who passed the state math test		
Teacher–student ratio in elementary grades		
Teacher–student ratio in secondary grades		
Counselor–student ratio in secondary grades		
Number of students per music specialist in elementary grades		
Number of students per art specialist in elementary grades		
Number of volumes in senior high school library		
Beginning teacher's salary		
Maximum teacher's salary		
Average years of experience among teachers		
Number of students suspended and expelled		
Subjects in which Advanced Placement courses are offered:		

†A Statistical Profile was not received from this district.

FAIR APPRAISAL

Quality of School Leadership
Principals are hired primarily for their educational leadership ability, and the quality of leadership does not vary greatly from school to school. Parents and teachers have no say in principal selection, but principals have some say in resources disbursement.

Parent organizations are ineffective influencing school decision-making.

Quality of Instruction
Additional learning opportunities for gifted students are rated good, but additional instruction for low-achieving students is considered poor. The curriculum for students going to college is rated fair, while the curriculum for students not planning on college is considered poor.

Quality of School Environment
The level of classroom disruption and student vandalism are on the high side, but the quality of building maintenance and repair is good.

NORTH BRUNSWICK

ADDRESS OF CENTRAL OFFICE:
Maple Meade Building, Old George's Road, North Brunswick, NJ 08902
ESI:71

STATISTICAL PROFILE	DATA	ESI
Grade organization: †		
Percentage of schools built before 1955	17%	
Total enrollment	3,401	
Average Daily Attendance (ADA)	94%	7
Current expense per pupil in ADA	$4,000	0
Dropout rate	2%	10
Percentage of eligible students who took the SAT	85%	10
Average combined score on SAT	942	6
Percentage of graduates who enrolled in 2- or 4-year colleges	75%	
Percentage of students who passed the state reading test	91%	
Percentage of students who passed the state math test	83%	
Teacher–student ratio in elementary grades	1:14	10
Teacher–student ratio in secondary grades	1:12	10
Counselor–student ratio in secondary grades	1:296	6
Number of students per music specialist in elementary grades	300	9
Number of students per art specialist in elementary grades	300	
Number of volumes in senior high school library	30,000	
Beginning teacher's salary	$19,000	
Maximum teacher's salary	$37,575	
Average years of experience among teachers	13	
Number of students suspended and expelled	1	
Subjects in which Advanced Placement courses are offered: American History, Calculus, English	3	3

†The district misinterpreted this statistic.

FAIR APPRAISAL

Quality of School Leadership
The School Board hires principals primarily for their educational leadership ability; the quality of leadership is generally uniform throughout the system. Parents and teachers have hardly any say in principal selection, but principals have some say in how resources are allotted to the schools.

"Administrators turn to parent groups as a sounding board," said one observer, speaking of the influence of such groups. Parents play a "big role" in deciding issues, said the observer.

Quality of Instruction
The program for gifted students is rated good; at the elementary level, students are excused from regular classes for enrichment. The additional instruction for low-achieving students is considered excellent. "A lot of people move here because the programs for under-achievers are so good," said one observer. The curricula for students planning on college and for those going on to the world of work are rated good. Observers talked of teachers with good educational credentials who also are "warm and caring."

Quality of School Environment
Classroom disruption and student vandalism are not problems. The quality of building maintenance and repair is excellent.

SCOTCH PLAINS–FANWOOD

ADDRESS OF CENTRAL OFFICE:
Evergreen and Cedar Streets, Scotch Plains, NJ 07076
ESI:75*

STATISTICAL PROFILE	DATA	ESI
Grade organization: K–5/6–8/9–12		
Percentage of schools built before 1955	25%	
Total enrollment	3,974	
Average Daily Attendance (ADA)	95%	8
Current expense per pupil in ADA	$5,432	5
Dropout rate	4%	10
Percentage of eligible students who took the SAT	90%	10
Average combined score on SAT	†	0*
Percentage of graduates who enrolled in 2- or 4-year colleges	71%	
Percentage of students who passed the state reading test	93%	
Percentage of students who passed the state math test	84%	
Teacher–student ratio in elementary grades	1:20	10
Teacher–student ratio in secondary grades	1:18	10
Counselor–student ratio in secondary grades	1:190	10
Number of students per music specialist in elementary grades	360	8
Number of students per art specialist in elementary grades	567	
Number of volumes in senior high school library	20,000	
Beginning teacher's salary	$19,710	
Maximum teacher's salary	$45,390	
Average years of experience among teachers	15	
Number of students suspended and expelled	NK	
Subjects in which Advanced Placement courses are offered: American History, Calculus, English, European History	4	4

†The district supplied an inappropriate statistic.

Quality of School Leadership
Principals are appointed because they evidence ability as educational leaders, and the quality of leadership is generally uniform throughout the system. Parents and teachers do not take part in screening principals. Principals have some say in how resources are allotted their school.

Parent organizations are not effective as an influence on school policy.

Quality of Instruction
Additional learning opportunities for gifted students are rated good, and additional instruction for low-achieving students also is rated good. The curricula for students planning on college and for students not planning on college are both rated good.

Quality of School Environment
The level of classroom disruption and student vandalism is very low, and the quality of building maintenance and repair is good.

SOUTH ORANGE–MAPLEWOOD

ADDRESS OF CENTRAL OFFICE:
525 Academy Street, Maplewood, NJ 07040
ESI:86

STATISTICAL PROFILE	DATA	ESI
Grade organization: K–5/6–8/9–12		
Percentage of schools built before 1955	100%	
Total enrollment	4,946	
Average Daily Attendance (ADA)	95%	8
Current expense per pupil in ADA	$5,558	6
Dropout rate	9%	10
Percentage of eligible students who took the SAT	85%	10
Average combined score on SAT	970	8
Percentage of graduates who enrolled in 2- or 4-year colleges	82%	
Percentage of students who passed the state reading test	94%	
Percentage of students who passed the state math test	82%	
Teacher–student ratio in elementary grades	1:22	8
Teacher–student ratio in secondary grades	1:13	10
Counselor–student ratio in secondary grades	1:224	9
Number of students per music specialist in elementary grades	239	10
Number of students per art specialist in elementary grades	460	
Number of volumes in senior high school library	31,000	
Beginning teacher's salary	$18,500	
Maximum teacher's salary	$40,550	
Average years of experience among teachers	17	
Number of students suspended and expelled	213	
Subjects in which Advanced Placement courses are offered: American History, Art, Calculus, English, Foreign Language, Music	7	7

Quality of School Leadership
The School Board looks for principals who show ability as educational leaders, and the quality of leadership does not vary greatly from school to school. Parents and teachers have little to say about principal selection, but principals have some influence over the allocation of resources.

Parent organizations are sometimes effective as an influence in school policy.

Quality of Instruction
Additional learning opportunities for gifted students and additional instruction for low-achieving students are both rated good. The curriculum preparing students for college is termed good, but an observer pointed out that the average student "probably finds it less appropriate and helpful than the above-average student." The curriculum for students not going to college is only called fair.

Quality of School Environment
The level of classroom disruption and student vandalism is low, but the quality of building maintenance and repair is only fair. "Many of the buildings are not kept clean," said an observer.

UNION CITY

ADDRESS OF CENTRAL OFFICE:
3912 Bergen Turnpike, Union City, NJ 07087
ESI:None†

STATISTICAL PROFILE	DATA	ESI
Grade organization:		
Percentage of schools built before 1955		
Total enrollment		
Average Daily Attendance (ADA)		
Current expense per pupil in ADA		
Dropout rate		
Percentage of eligible students who took the SAT		
Average combined score on SAT		
Percentage of graduates who enrolled in 2- or 4-year colleges		
Percentage of students who passed the state reading test		
Percentage of students who passed the state math test		
Teacher–student ratio in elementary grades		
Teacher–student ratio in secondary grades		
Counselor–student ratio in secondary grades		
Number of students per music specialist in elementary grades		
Number of students per art specialist in elementary grades		
Number of volumes in senior high school library		
Beginning teacher's salary		
Maximum teacher's salary		
Average years of experience among teachers		
Number of students suspended and expelled		
Subjects in which Advanced Placement courses are offered:		

†A Statistical Profile was not received from this district.

FAIR APPRAISAL

Quality of School Leadership
Principals are hired primarily for their educational leadership ability, and the quality of leadership is generally uniform throughout the system. Parents and teachers have little to say about principal selection, but principals have a lot to say about the use of district resources.

Parent organizations are considered effective as an influence on district policy.

Quality of Instruction
Additional learning opportunities for gifted students and additional instruction for low-achieving students are both rated excellent. Also rated excellent is the curriculum preparing students for college. The curriculum for students not planning on college is considered good.

Quality of School Environment
Classroom disruption and student vandalism are not problems, and the quality of building maintenance and repair is good.

WOODBRIDGE

ADDRESS OF CENTRAL OFFICE:
P.O. Box 429, Woodbridge, NJ 07095
ESI:73

STATISTICAL PROFILE	DATA	ESI
Grade organization: K–6/7–8/9–12		
Percentage of schools built before 1955	6%	
Total enrollment	10,556	
Average Daily Attendance (ADA)	93%	6
Current expense per pupil in ADA	$4,429	0
Dropout rate	5%	10
Percentage of eligible students who took the SAT	65%	10
Average combined score on SAT	1,133	10
Percentage of graduates who enrolled in 2- or 4-year colleges	70%	
Percentage of students who passed the state reading test	93%	
Percentage of students who passed the state math test	84%	
Teacher–student ratio in elementary grades	1:17	10
Teacher–student ratio in secondary grades	1:13	10
Counselor–student ratio in secondary grades	1:250	8
Number of students per music specialist in elementary grades	308	9
Number of students per art specialist in elementary grades	617	
Number of volumes in senior high school library	16,000	
Beginning teacher's salary	$18,500	
Maximum teacher's salary	$35,029	
Average years of experience among teachers	20	
Number of students suspended and expelled	2%	
Subjects in which Advanced Placement courses are offered:	None	0

FAIR APPRAISAL

Quality of School Leadership
The School Board picks principals for their educational leadership ability, and the quality of leadership is generally uniform throughout the system. Parents and teachers do not screen principal candidates. Principals, however, have a say in the allotment of resources to their school.

Parent organizations are effective influencing school policy decisions. "Parents have a lot of power in some schools," said an observer.

Quality of Instruction
"We have come a long, long way," said an observer speaking of the program for gifted students, which the observers rated excellent. Elementary students are excused from regular classes to attend enrichment classes. Additional instruction for low-achieving students is considered good. Also rated good are the curricula for students planning on college and for students planning on the world of work.

Quality of School Environment
Classroom disruption and student vandalism are not problems, and the quality of building maintenance and repair is good.

New Orleans, LA

Louisiana operates mostly county (parish) school districts. We received completed Statistical Profiles from three districts and a Fair Appraisal alone from another district. Districts in this area might be compared to districts in the Memphis, TN Metropolitan Area.

AREA AT A GLANCE

SCHOOL DISTRICT	ENROLLMENT	ESI
Jefferson Parish	56,060	33
New Orleans	84,164	
St. Charles Parish	8,176	69
St. Tammany Parish	26,292	26

SCHOOL DISTRICT

JEFFERSON PARISH

ADDRESS OF CENTRAL OFFICE:
501 Manhatten, Harvey, LA 70058
ESI:33

STATISTICAL PROFILE	DATA	ESI
Grade organization: K–12†		
Percentage of schools built before 1955	40%	
Total enrollment	56,060	
Average Daily Attendance (ADA)	94%	7
Current expense per pupil in ADA	$2,768	4
Dropout rate	47%	0
Percentage of eligible students who took the ACT	36%	5
Average combined score on ACT	16.2	0
Percentage of graduates who enrolled in 2- or 4-year colleges	34%	
Percentage of students who passed the state reading test	90%	
Percentage of students who passed the state math test	91%	
Teacher–student ratio in elementary grades	1:27	3
Teacher–student ratio in secondary grades	1:27	0
Counselor–student ratio in secondary grades	1:479	0
Number of students per music specialist in elementary grades	175	10
Number of students per art specialist in elementary grades	None	
Number of volumes in senior high school library	20,000	
Beginning teacher's salary	$15,503	
Maximum teacher's salary	$24,919	
Average years of experience among teachers	9	
Number of students suspended and expelled	7,979	
Subjects in which Advanced Placement courses are offered: American History, Biology, Calculus, English	4	4

†The district misinterpreted this statistic.

FAIR APPRAISAL

Quality of School Leadership

Principals are hired mostly because of their educational leadership ability, but it is difficult for a person within the system to become a principal without the support of the School Board member representing the section of the district where the candidate is employed. Also, according to an observer, the quality of leadership varies greatly from school to school. "It used to be terribly, terribly political," said the observer, "and some principals hired more than 15 years ago may be better politicians than educators." Parents and teachers have no say in principal selection, but principals are becoming influential in deciding how resources will be allotted among the schools.

Parent organizations are quite effective influencing school policy.

Quality of Instruction

Additional instruction for gifted students is given almost as much attention as special education for handicapped students. Exceptionally bright students are evaluated, and instruction is tailored to their gifts. The program is rated excellent. Additional instruction for low-achieving students is considered good. Also rated good are curricula for college-bound students and job-bound students.

Quality of School Environment

The level of classroom disruption and student vandalism is low. The quality of building maintenance and repair varies greatly throughout the district. Some old buildings, particularly those in low-income areas, are "decrepit."

NEW ORLEANS

ADDRESS OF CENTRAL OFFICE:
4100 Touro Steet, New Orleans, LA 70122
ESI:None†

STATISTICAL PROFILE	DATA	ESI
Grade organization:		
Percentage of schools built before 1955		
Total enrollment		
Average Daily Attendance (ADA)		
Current expense per pupil in ADA		
Dropout rate		
Percentage of eligible students who took the SAT		
Average combined score on SAT		
Percentage of graduates who enrolled in 2- or 4-year colleges		
Percentage of students who passed the state reading test		
Percentage of students who passed the state math test		
Teacher–student ratio in elementary grades		
Teacher–student ratio in secondary grades		
Counselor–student ratio in secondary grades		
Number of students per music specialist in elementary grades		
Number of students per art specialist in elementary grades		
Number of volumes in senior high school library		
Beginning teacher's salary		
Maximum teacher's salary		
Average years of experience among teachers		
Number of students suspended and expelled		
Subjects in which Advanced Placement courses are offered:		

†A Statistical Profile was not received from this district.

FAIR APPRAISAL

Quality of School Leadership
Although many principals demonstrate educational leadership ability, internal politics are an important factor in principal selection. Because of this, the quality of leadership varies from school to school. Parents and teachers have no say in principal selection, but principals have some influence over the distribution of district resources.

Parents' influence in decision-making is sometimes effective, but at some schools, said an observer, there is no parental involvement.

Quality of Instruction
Additional opportunities for gifted students are rated good. Parents of very bright students comprise a strong lobby, and their efforts have helped to establish special classes. On the other hand, additional instruction for low-achieving students is considered fair to poor. "There is nothing available beyond Chapter I," said an observer. (Chapter I refers to a federal compensatory education program for low-income children.) The curriculum for students going to college is rated good. "Large classes and limited materials" hinder the program, said an observer. The curriculum for students preparing for the job market is called fair.

The schools do not adequately meet the needs of minority students, observers said.

Quality of School Environment
The incidence of classroom disruption and student vandalism is on the low side districtwide, but greater problems exist at some schools. The quality of building maintenance and repair ranges from fair to good. Insufficient funding is a problem.

ST. CHARLES PARISH

ADDRESS OF CENTRAL OFFICE:
P.O. Box 46, Luling, LA 70070
ESI:69

STATISTICAL PROFILE	DATA	ESI
Grade organization: K–3/4–6/7–8/9–12		
Percentage of schools built before 1955	20%	
Total enrollment	8,176	
Average Daily Attendance (ADA)	95%	8
Current expense per pupil in ADA	$3,500	8
Dropout rate	9%	10
Percentage of eligible students who took the ACT	60%	9
Average combined score on ACT	17.7	0
Percentage of graduates who enrolled in 2- or 4-year colleges	50%	
Percentage of students who passed the state reading test	90%	
Percentage of students who passed the state math test	85%	
Teacher–student ratio in elementary grades	1:18	10
Teacher–student ratio in secondary grades	1:18	10
Counselor–student ratio in secondary grades	1:419	1
Number of students per music specialist in elementary grades	577	4
Number of students per art specialist in elementary grades	445	
Number of volumes in senior high school library	13,382	
Beginning teacher's salary	$16,504	
Maximum teacher's salary	$24,060	
Average years of experience among teachers	12	
Number of students suspended and expelled	746	
Subjects in which Advanced Placement courses are offered:	9	9
American History, Biology, Calculus, Chemistry, Computer Science, English, European History, French, Spanish		

FAIR APPRAISAL

Quality of School Leadership
The School Board hires principals primarily for their educational leadership ability, and the quality of leadership is generally uniform throughout the district. Parents and teachers do not take part in principal selection. However, principals have some say in the allotment of resources to their school.

Parent organizations are sometimes effective influencing decision-making in the schools.

Quality of Instruction
Additional learning opportunities for gifted students and additional instruction for low-achieving students are rated good. The college-preparatory curriculum is excellent, and the curriculum for students heading for the world of work is considered good.

Quality of School Environment
Classroom disruption and student vandalism are not problems. The quality of building maintenance and repair is rated good.

ST. TAMMANY PARISH

ADDRESS OF CENTRAL OFFICE:
P.O. Box 940, Covington, LA 70434
ESI:26

STATISTICAL PROFILE	DATA	ESI
Grade organization: K–12†		
Percentage of schools built before 1955	29%	
Total enrollment	26,292	
Average Daily Attendance (ADA)	90%	3
Current expense per pupil in ADA	$2,663	4
Dropout rate	NK	0
Percentage of eligible students who took the ACT	74%	10
Average combined score on ACT	18.6	4
Percentage of graduates who enrolled in 2- or 4-year colleges	56%	
Percentage of students who passed the state reading test	95%	
Percentage of students who passed the state math test	94%	
Teacher–student ratio in elementary grades	1:29	1
Teacher–student ratio in secondary grades	1:30	0
Counselor–student ratio in secondary grades	1:465	0
Number of students per music specialist in elementary grades	None	0
Number of students per art specialist in elementary grades	None	
Number of volumes in senior high school library	††	
Beginning teacher's salary	$16,194	
Maximum teacher's salary	$31,376	
Average years of experience among teachers	10	
Number of students suspended and expelled	2,717	
Subjects in which Advanced Placement courses are offered: American History, Calculus, English, Foreign Language	4	4

† The district misinterpreted this statistic.
††The district supplied the statistic 10 volumes per student.

FAIR APPRAISAL

Quality of School Leadership

Principals now are selected primarily for their educational leadership ability. However, in the past, according to an observer, "politics and favoritism strongly entered into the decision." Therefore, the quality of leadership varies greatly from school to school. Parents and teachers do not screen principal candidates. However, principals have a great deal to say about the way district resources are divided among the schools.

The influence of parent organizations in school policy decisions is sometimes effective.

Quality of Instruction

Additional learning opportunities for gifted students are rated fair, and additional instruction for low-achieving students is called good. The curriculum for college-bound students is rated fair to good. "The quality of preparation for college depends upon which high school a student attends," said an observer. The curriculum that prepares students for the job market is also considered fair. An observer believes the district is taking "some positive steps" toward improving the overall curriculum. For example, the curriculum is becoming more standardized throughout the system, and a master teaching program was established recently.

Quality of School Environment

The level of classroom disruption and student vandalism is on the low side, and the quality of building maintenance and repair is good.

New York City

Fifteen school districts completed Statistical Profiles, and Fair Appraisals are provided for another two districts. Districts in this area should be compared with districts in the Nassau–Suffolk Counties, NY and Newark, NJ Metropolitan Areas.

AREA AT A GLANCE

SCHOOL DISTRICT	ENROLLMENT	ESI
Bergenfield, NJ	3,315	74
East Ramapo, NY	10,425	70*
Greenwich, CT	6,758	75*
Mamaroneck, NY	3,906	88
New Rochelle, NY	7,400	82
North Bergen, NJ	5,300	76
Norwalk, CT	9,901	
Paramus, NJ	3,500	89
Parsippany–Troy Hills, NJ	6,563	51*
Port Chester, NY	2,618	72
Ridgewood, NJ	4,696	86
Scarsdale, NY	3,783	
Teaneck, NJ	4,476	77*
Wayne, NJ	6,439	57*
White Plains, NY	4,979	88
Yonkers, NY	18,619	70
Yorktown, NY	3,129	78

Indicates district misinterpretation of one or more statistics in the ESI. For each misinterpreted statistic, a score of 0 was given instead of a possible score of 0 to 10 points.

BERGENFIELD

ADDRESS OF CENTRAL OFFICE:
100 South Prospect Avenue, Bergenfield, NJ 07621
ESI:74

STATISTICAL PROFILE	DATA	ESI
Grade organization: K–6/7–8/9–12		
Percentage of schools built before 1955	86%	
Total enrollment	3,315	
Average Daily Attendance (ADA)	94%	7
Current expense per pupil in ADA	$5,316	4
Dropout rate	3%	10
Percentage of eligible students who took the SAT	64%	10
Average combined score on SAT	862	3
Percentage of graduates who enrolled in 2- or 4-year colleges	64%	
Percentage of students who passed the state reading test	93%	
Percentage of students who passed the state math test	81%	
Teacher–student ratio in elementary grades	1:15	10
Teacher–student ratio in secondary grades	1:12	10
Counselor–student ratio in secondary grades	1:287	6
Number of students per music specialist in elementary grades	539	5
Number of students per art specialist in elementary grades	425	
Number of volumes in senior high school library	26,000	
Beginning teacher's salary	$18,500	
Maximum teacher's salary	$43,500	
Average years of experience among teachers	18	
Number of students suspended and expelled	82	
Subjects in which Advanced Placement courses are offered: American History, Art Studio, Calculus, Chemistry, English, French, German, Physics, Spanish	9	9

FAIR APPRAISAL

Quality of School Leadership
Principals are selected for their educational leadership ability. However, the observers cite major differences among principals in the system. For example, some principals are "against parental involvement in school affairs," said one observer. Parents and teachers have little say in the selection of principals, but principals have a great deal of influence on how the resources of the district are distributed.

Parent organizations are sometimes effective influencing school policy decisions.

Quality of Instruction
Additional learning opportunities for gifted students are rated good, while additional instruction for low-achieving students is termed fair. The curriculum for students going to college is considered good, but the curriculum for students not bound for college is rated fair.

Quality of School Environment
The level of classroom disruption and student vandalism is very low, and the quality of building maintenance and repair is very high.

EAST RAMAPO

ADDRESS OF CENTRAL OFFICE:
50A South Amin Street, Spring Valley, NY 10977
ESI:70*

STATISTICAL PROFILE	DATA	ESI
Grade organization: K–3/4–6/7–9/10–12		
Percentage of schools built before 1955	NK	
Total enrollment	10,425	
Average Daily Attendance (ADA)	92%	5
Current expense per pupil in ADA	$7,834	10
Dropout rate	5%	10
Percentage of eligible students who took the SAT	64%	10
Average combined score on SAT	†	0*
Percentage of graduates who enrolled in 2- or 4-year colleges	84%	
Percentage of students who passed the state reading test	95%	
Percentage of students who passed the state math test	87%	
Teacher–student ratio in elementary grades	1:22	8
Teacher–student ratio in secondary grades	1:25	3
Counselor–student ratio in secondary grades	1:300	6
Number of students per music specialist in elementary grades	300	9
Number of students per art specialist in elementary grades	500	
Number of volumes in senior high school library	20,000	
Beginning teacher's salary	$21,268	
Maximum teacher's salary	$53,024	
Average years of experience among teachers	12	
Number of students suspended and expelled	557	
Subjects in which Advanced Placement courses are offered: American History, Biology, Calculus, Chemistry, European History, French, German, Physics, Spanish	9	9

†The district supplied an inappropriate statistic.

FAIR APPRAISAL

Quality of School Leadership
Most principals are selected because of their ability as educational leaders, and the quality of leadership does not vary greatly from school to school. One observer said, however, that the district has had more success picking principals from outside the system than from within. Teacher and parents serve on committees that screen principal candidates. Principals have a great deal to say about how the resources of the district are used.

Parent organizations are effective influencing district decision-making. "Liaison" exists between PTAs and school leaders on all important issues.

Quality of Instruction
Observers rate additional learning opportunities for gifted students as good, but they point out that the program is much more effective at the secondary level than in the elementary schools. Also considered good is additional instruction for low-achieving students. A new program for pre-school children is designed to head off underachievement. The college preparatory curriculum is called excellent, while the curriculum for students not heading for college is termed good.

Quality of School Environment
The incidence of classroom disruption and student vandalism is very low, and the quality of building maintenance and repair is very high.

GREENWICH, CT

ADDRESS OF CENTRAL OFFICE:
290 Greenwich Avenue, Greenwich, CT 06830
ESI:75*

STATISTICAL PROFILE	DATA	ESI
Grade organization: K–6/7–9/10–12		
Percentage of schools built before 1955	71%	
Total enrollment	6,758	
Average Daily Attendance (ADA)	96%	9
Current expense per pupil in ADA	$4,836	6
Dropout rate	NK	0
Percentage of eligible students who took the SAT	84%	10
Average combined score on SAT	†	0*
Percentage of graduates who enrolled in 2- or 4-year colleges	74%	
Percentage of students who passed the state reading test	100%	
Percentage of students who passed the state math test	98%	
Teacher–student ratio in elementary grades	1:20	10
Teacher–student ratio in secondary grades	1:15	10
Counselor–student ratio in secondary grades	1:192	10
Number of students per music specialist in elementary grades	245	10
Number of students per art specialist in elementary grades	359	
Number of volumes in senior high school library	54,493††	
Beginning teacher's salary	$18,219	
Maximum teacher's salary	$42,139	
Average years of experience among teachers	13	
Number of students suspended and expelled	NK	
Subjects in which Advanced Placement courses are offered:	11	10
American History, Biology, Calculus AB, Calculus BC, Chemistry, Computer Science, English, French, Physics B, Physics C, Spanish		

† The district supplied an inappropriate statistic.
††This seems to be an unusually high number.

FAIR APPRAISAL

Quality of School Leadership
The School Board picks principals who demonstrate educational leadership ability, and the quality of leadership is generally uniform throughout the system. Parents and teachers have no direct say in the principal selection, but they may make their views known informally. Principals, on the other hand, have a lot to say about the distribution of district resources.

Parent organizations are effective as influences on district policy-making.

Quality of Instruction
Additional learning opportunities for gifted students and additional instruction for low-achieving students are both rated excellent. Also considered excellent are the curricula for students heading for college and for those not planning on college. Observers had high praise for the teaching staff.

Quality of School Environment
The level of classroom disruption and student vandalism is low, and the quality of building maintenance and repair is good.

MAMARONECK

ADDRESS OF CENTRAL OFFICE:
1000 West Boston Post Road, Mamaroneck, NY 10543
ESI:88

STATISTICAL PROFILE	DATA	ESI
Grade organization: K–6/7–8/9–12		
Percentage of schools built before 1955	16%	
Total enrollment	3,906	
Average Daily Attendance (ADA)	95%	8
Current expense per pupil in ADA	$8,116	10
Dropout rate	NK	0
Percentage of eligible students who took the SAT	83%	10
Average combined score on SAT	1,022	10
Percentage of graduates who enrolled in 2- or 4-year colleges	82%	
Percentage of students who passed the state reading test	100%	
Percentage of students who passed the state math test	100%	
Teacher–student ratio in elementary grades	1:14	10
Teacher–student ratio in secondary grades	1:12	10
Counselor–student ratio in secondary grades	1:183	10
Number of students per music specialist in elementary grades	241	10
Number of students per art specialist in elementary grades	403	
Number of volumes in senior high school library	46,000†	
Beginning teacher's salary	$20,583	
Maximum teacher's salary	$46,562	
Average years of experience among teachers	17	
Number of students suspended and expelled	57	
Subjects in which Advanced Placement courses are offered:	16	10
American History, Biology, Calculus AB, Calculus BC, Chemistry, Computer Science, English, European History, French Language, French Literature, Latin (Virgil), Latin (Lyric), Music, Physics, Spanish, Studio Art		

†This seems to be an unusually high number.

FAIR APPRAISAL

Quality of School Leadership
The School Board hires principals who demonstrate ability as educational leaders. The quality of leadership does not vary greatly from school to school. Parents and teachers help screen principal candidates. Also, principals have a great deal of influence over the allocation of resources to the schools.

Parent organizations are an effective influence on school decisions. "Parents have always been seen as allies, not adversaries," said one observer.

Quality of Instruction
Additional learning opportunities for gifted students are rated excellent. Special classes for gifted students begin in grade 4. Additional instruction for low-achieving students is considered good. Remedial programs are particularly strong at the elementary level. The curricula for students planning on college and for students not planning on college are both considered excellent.

Quality of School Environment
Classroom disruption and student vandalism are not problems, and the quality of building maintenance and repair is excellent.

NEW ROCHELLE

ADDRESS OF CENTRAL OFFICE:
575 North Avenue, New Rochelle, NY 10801
ESI:82

STATISTICAL PROFILE	DATA	ESI
Grade organization: K–6/7–9/10–12		
Percentage of schools built before 1955	56%	
Total enrollment	7,400	
Average Daily Attendance (ADA)	92%	5
Current expense per pupil in ADA	$8,502	10
Dropout rate	8%	10
Percentage of eligible students who took the SAT	80%	10
Average combined score on SAT	1,053	10
Percentage of graduates who enrolled in 2- or 4-year colleges	67%	
Percentage of students who passed the state reading test	98%	
Percentage of students who passed the state math test	97%	
Teacher–student ratio in elementary grades	1:22	8
Teacher–student ratio in secondary grades	1:25	3
Counselor–student ratio in secondary grades	1:231	8
Number of students per music specialist in elementary grades	374	8
Number of students per art specialist in elementary grades	553	
Number of volumes in senior high school library	25,526	
Beginning teacher's salary	$20,149	
Maximum teacher's salary	$46,697	
Average years of experience among teachers	20	
Number of students suspended and expelled	200	
Subjects in which Advanced Placement courses are offered:	12	10
American History, Biology, Calculus AB, Calculus BC, Chemistry, Computer Science, English Composition and Literature, European History, French Language, Latin, Physics B, Spanish Literature		

Quality of School Leadership
Principals are selected primarily because of their educational leadership ability, and the quality of leadership is generally uniform throughout the system. Parents and teachers have a part in principal selection, and principals have a lot to say about the distribution of the district's resources.

Parent organizations are effective influencing school decision-making. They have been particularly influencial in recent school reorganization plans.

Quality of Instruction
Additional learning opportunities for gifted students are rated excellent. Gifted students in grades 5 and 6 spend all their time in special classes; the program is modified to half day in other grades. The additional instruction for low-achieving students also is considered excellent. The high school has won national recognition, and the curriculum for college-bound students is rated excellent. The curriculum for students not planning on college is considered good.

Quality of School Environment
The incidence of classroom disruption and student vandalism is low, and the quality of building maintenance and repair is considered good.

NORTH BERGEN

ADDRESS OF CENTRAL OFFICE:
7317 Kennedy Boulevard, North Bergen, NJ 07047
ESI:76

STATISTICAL PROFILE	DATA	ESI
Grade organization: K–8/9–12		
Percentage of schools built before 1955	72%	
Total enrollment	5,300	
Average Daily Attendance (ADA)	90%	3
Current expense per pupil in ADA	$5,302	4
Dropout rate	4%	10
Percentage of eligible students who took the SAT	85%	10
Average combined score on SAT	875	3
Percentage of graduates who enrolled in 2- or 4-year colleges	62%	
Percentage of students who passed the state reading test	84%	
Percentage of students who passed the state math test	72%	
Teacher–student ratio in elementary grades	1:21	9
Teacher–student ratio in secondary grades	1:13	10
Counselor–student ratio in secondary grades	1:200	9
Number of students per music specialist in elementary grades	211	10
Number of students per art specialist in elementary grades	450	
Number of volumes in senior high school library	23,000	
Beginning teacher's salary	$18,500	
Maximum teacher's salary	$43,571	
Average years of experience among teachers	18	
Number of students suspended and expelled	1,000	
Subjects in which Advanced Placement courses are offered:	8	8
American History, Calculus, English, French, German, Latin, Science, Spanish		

Quality of School Leadership
Most principals are hired because of their educational leadership ability. However, there is wide variation among elementary schools and school policies. "There is no central policy," said an observer. Parents and teachers have no say in principal selection, but principals have some say in how resources are allotted to the schools.

Parent organizations are sometimes effective influencing school policies.

Quality of Instruction
Additional learning opportunities for gifted students are rated good, while additional instruction for low-achieving students is considered fair. The curricula for college-bound students and job-bound students are both rated good.

Quality of School Environment
The level of classroom disruption and student vandalism is low, and the quality of building maintenance and repair is fair.

NORWALK

ADDRESS OF CENTRAL OFFICE:
105 Main Street, Norwalk, CT 06852
ESI:None†

STATISTICAL PROFILE	DATA	ESI
Grade organization:		
Percentage of schools built before 1955		
Total enrollment		
Average Daily Attendance (ADA)		
Current expense per pupil in ADA		
Dropout rate		
Percentage of eligible students who took the SAT		
Average combined score on SAT		
Percentage of graduates who enrolled in 2- or 4-year colleges		
Percentage of students who passed the state reading test		
Percentage of students who passed the state math test		
Teacher–student ratio in elementary grades		
Teacher–student ratio in secondary grades		
Counselor–student ratio in secondary grades		
Number of students per music specialist in elementary grades		
Number of students per art specialist in elementary grades		
Number of volumes in senior high school library		
Beginning teacher's salary		
Maximum teacher's salary		
Average years of experience among teachers		
Number of students suspended and expelled		
Subjects in which Advanced Placement courses are offered:		

†A Statistical Profile was not received from this district.

FAIR APPRAISAL

Quality of School Leadership
Principals are hired based on their educational leadership ability, and the quality of leadership does not vary greatly from school to school. Parents and teachers take part in screening principal candidates. Also, principals have a great deal to say about the division of district resources.

Parent organizations are effective influencing school policy. The current PTA council is "very strong," said an observer.

Quality of Instruction
Additional learning opportunities for gifted students are rated good, as is additional instruction for low-achieving students. The curricula for students bound for college and for students bound for the world of work are both rated good.

Quality of School Environment
Classroom disruption and student vandalism are not problems, and the quality of building maintenance and repair is good.

PARAMUS

ADDRESS OF CENTRAL OFFICE:
145 Spring Valley Road, Paramus, NJ 07652
ESI:89

STATISTICAL PROFILE	DATA	ESI
Grade organization: †		
Percentage of schools built before 1955	0%	
Total enrollment	3,500	
Average Daily Attendance (ADA)	98%	10
Current expense per pupil in ADA	$5,500	5
Dropout rate	1%	10
Percentage of eligible students who took the SAT	70%	10
Average combined score on SAT	909	5
Percentage of graduates who enrolled in 2- or 4-year colleges	73%	
Percentage of students who passed the state reading test	96%	
Percentage of students who passed the state math test	82%	
Teacher–student ratio in elementary grades	1:15	10
Teacher–student ratio in secondary grades	1:12	10
Counselor–student ratio in secondary grades	1:200	9
Number of students per music specialist in elementary grades	250	10
Number of students per art specialist in elementary grades	600	
Number of volumes in senior high school library	27,000	
Beginning teacher's salary	$18,500	
Maximum teacher's salary	$46,900	
Average years of experience among teachers	22	
Number of students suspended and expelled	50	
Subjects in which Advanced Placement courses are offered:	10	10
American History, Art History, Biology, Calculus, Chemistry, English, French, German, Physics, Spanish		

†The district misinterpreted this statistic.

FAIR APPRAISAL

Quality of School Leadership
The School Board hires principals who evidence educational leadership ability, and the quality of leadership is generally uniform throughout the system. Parents and teachers have some say in principal selection, mostly informal expression of views. Principals, however, have significant influence over the use of district resources.

Parent organizations are an effective influence in district decision-making.

Quality of Instruction
Gifted students in the lower grades are excused from regular classes to attend enrichment classes, and the overall program is rated excellent. Additional instruction for low-achieving students is considered good. Also rated good is the curriculum for students planning on college. The curriculum for job-bound students is called excellent.

Quality of School Environment
The level of classroom disruption and student vandalism is low, and the quality of building maintenance and repair is good.

PARSIPPANY-TROY HILLS

ADDRESS OF CENTRAL OFFICE:
P.O. Box 52, Parsippany, NJ 07054
ESI:51*

STATISTICAL PROFILE	DATA	ESI
Grade organization: K–5/6–8/9–12		
Percentage of schools built before 1955	17%	
Total enrollment	6,563	
Average Daily Attendance (ADA)	95%	8
Current expense per pupil in ADA	$4,094	0
Dropout rate	8%	10
Percentage of eligible students who took the SAT	75%	10
Average combined score on SAT	†	0*
Percentage of graduates who enrolled in 2- or 4-year colleges	75%	
Percentage of students who passed the state reading test	93%	
Percentage of students who passed the state math test	89%	
Teacher–student ratio in elementary grades	1:22	8
Teacher–student ratio in secondary grades	NK	0
Counselor–student ratio in secondary grades	1:230	8
Number of students per music specialist in elementary grades	745	1
Number of students per art specialist in elementary grades	745	
Number of volumes in senior high school library	22,000	
Beginning teacher's salary	$17,100	
Maximum teacher's salary	$37,600	
Average years of experience among teachers	NK	
Number of students suspended and expelled	153	
Subjects in which Advanced Placement courses are offered:	6	6
American History, Art, Calculus, English,		
Foreign Langugage, Science		

†The district supplied an inappropriate statistic.

FAIR APPRAISAL

Quality of School Leadership
Principals are hired for their educational leadership ability, and the quality of leadership does not vary greatly from school to school. Parents and teachers have some say in principal selection, but it is mainly an informal expression of views. Principals, on the other hand, have influence over the allocation of resources to the schools.

Parent organizations are effective influencing school policy decisions. PTA representatives meet regularly with the superintendent and School Board members.

Quality of Instruction
Additional learning opportunities for gifted students and additional instruction for low-achieving students are rated fair. The curriculum for students planning on college is considered excellent, while the curriculum for students not planning on college is rated only fair to good.

Quality of School Environment
The level of classroom disruption and student vandalism is low, and the quality of building maintenance and repair is called good.

PORT CHESTER

ADDRESS OF CENTRAL OFFICE:
P.O. Box 246, Port Chester, NY 10573
ESI:72

STATISTICAL PROFILE	DATA	ESI
Grade organization: K–5/6–8/9–12		
Percentage of schools built before 1955	50%	
Total enrollment	2,618	
Average Daily Attendance (ADA)	96%	9
Current expense per pupil in ADA	$5,362	4
Dropout rate	13%	10
Percentage of eligible students who took the SAT	47%	7
Average combined score on SAT	841	1
Percentage of graduates who enrolled in 2- or 4-year colleges	62%	
Percentage of students who passed the state reading test	57%	
Percentage of students who passed the state math test	79%	
Teacher–student ratio in elementary grades	1:20	10
Teacher–student ratio in secondary grades	1:20	8
Counselor–student ratio in secondary grades	1:256	7
Number of students per music specialist in elementary grades	269	10
Number of students per art specialist in elementary grades	None	0
Number of volumes in senior high school library	16,000	
Beginning teacher's salary	$19,180	
Maximum teacher's salary	$44,298	
Average years of experience among teachers	NK	
Number of students suspended and expelled	NK	
Subjects in which Advanced Placement courses are offered:	6	6
American History, Biology, Calculus, Chemistry,		
English, Physics		

FAIR APPRAISAL

Quality of School Leadership
Ordinarily, principals are hired because of their ability as educational leaders. However, observers report racial imbalance in the schools, including an "insufficient number" of minority principals. Parents and teachers have some say in principal selection, but in an informal way. Principals also have some say concerning the distribution of district resources.

Parent organizations are sometimes effective influencing school decision-making.

Quality of Instruction
Additional learning opportunities for gifted students are rated good. Students in the elementary grades are excused from regular classes to attend enrichment programs. Additional instruction for low-achieving students is considered fair. Also rated fair are the curricula for students planning on college and for students preparing for the job market.

The district does not adequately meet the educational needs of minority students, according to observers. "The quality of instruction is not there in the schools serving minority students," said an observer.

Quality of School Environment
The level of classroom disruption and student vandalism is low, and the quality of building maintenance and repair is fair to good.

RIDGEWOOD

ADDRESS OF CENTRAL OFFICE:
49 Cottage Place, Ridgewood, NJ 07451
ESI:86

STATISTICAL PROFILE	DATA	ESI
Grade organization: K–5/6–8/9–12		
Percentage of schools built before 1955	65%	
Total enrollment	4,696	
Average Daily Attendance (ADA)	96%	9
Current expense per pupil in ADA	$5,034	3
Dropout rate	2%	10
Percentage of eligible students who took the SAT	89%	10
Average combined score on SAT	1,064	10
Percentage of graduates who enrolled in 2- or 4-year colleges	87%	
Percentage of students who passed the state reading test	97%	
Percentage of students who passed the state math test	96%	
Teacher–student ratio in elementary grades	1:19	10
Teacher–student ratio in secondary grades	1:14	10
Counselor–student ratio in secondary grades	1:194	10
Number of students per music specialist in elementary grades	350	8
Number of students per art specialist in elementary grades	350	
Number of volumes in senior high school library	16,019	
Beginning teacher's salary	$20,200	
Maximum teacher's salary	$46,825	
Average years of experience among teachers	17	
Number of students suspended and expelled	162	
Subjects in which Advanced Placement courses are offered:	6	6
American History, Calculus, Computer Science, English, Foreign Language, Science		

FAIR APPRAISAL

Quality of School Leadership

Principals are selected primarily for their educational leadership ability, and the quality of leadership does not vary greatly from school to school. Parents and teachers have little say in principal selection, although principals have some say in how district resources are allotted.

Parent organizations are sometimes effective influencing school policy.

Quality of Instruction

Additional learning opportunities for gifted students are rated good, although the program seems stronger in the upper grades than it does in the elementary grades. Additional instruction for low-achieving students is considered only fair. The curriculum for students planning on college is considered excellent, while the curriculum for students not planning on college is rated good.

Quality of School Environment

The incidence of classroom disruption and student vandalism is low, and the quality of building maintenance and repair is good.

SCARSDALE

ADDRESS OF CENTRAL OFFICE:
Brewster Road, Scarsdale, NY 10583
ESI:None†

STATISTICAL PROFILE	DATA	ESI
Grade organization:		
Percentage of schools built before 1955		
Total enrollment		
Average Daily Attendance (ADA)		
Current expense per pupil in ADA		
Dropout rate		
Percentage of eligible students who took the SAT		
Average combined score on SAT		
Percentage of graduates who enrolled in 2- or 4-year colleges		
Percentage of students who passed the state reading test		
Percentage of students who passed the state math test		
Teacher–student ratio in elementary grades		
Teacher–student ratio in secondary grades		
Counselor–student ratio in secondary grades		
Number of students per music specialist in elementary grades		
Number of students per art specialist in elementary grades		
Number of volumes in senior high school library		
Beginning teacher's salary		
Maximum teacher's salary		
Average years of experience among teachers		
Number of students suspended and expelled		
Subjects in which Advanced Placement courses are offered:		

†A Statistical Profile was not received from this district.

FAIR APPRAISAL

Quality of School Leadership

Popularity is a factor in principal selection, but most principals demonstrate educational leadership ability. Parents and teachers do not screen principal candidates, but principals have some say in how resources are allocated to the schools. Parent organizations are not effective influencing school policy.

Quality of Instruction

Additional learning opportunities for gifted students and additional instruction for low-achieving students are rated good. Also considered good is the curriculum for students planning on college. The curriculum for students not planning on college is rated fair.

Quality of School Environment

The level of classroom disruption and student vandalism is low, and the quality of building maintenance and repair is fair.

TEANECK

ADDRESS OF CENTRAL OFFICE:
1 Merrison Street, Teaneck, NJ 07666
ESI:77*

STATISTICAL PROFILE	DATA	ESI
Grade organization: K–2/3–5/6–8/9–12		
Percentage of schools built before 1955	100%	
Total enrollment	4,476	
Average Daily Attendance (ADA)	93%	6
Current expense per pupil in ADA	$7,300	10
Dropout rate	7%	10
Percentage of eligible students who took the SAT	85%	10
Average combined score on SAT	†	0*
Percentage of graduates who enrolled in 2- or 4-year colleges	79%	
Percentage of students who passed the state reading test	85%	
Percentage of students who passed the state math test	92%	
Teacher–student ratio in elementary grades	1:23	7
Teacher–student ratio in secondary grades	1:20	8
Counselor–student ratio in secondary grades	1:185	10
Number of students per music specialist in elementary grades	400	7
Number of students per art specialist in elementary grades	400	
Number of volumes in senior high school library	30,000	
Beginning teacher's salary	$18,500	
Maximum teacher's salary	$43,286	
Average years of experience among teachers	NK	
Number of students suspended and expelled	34	
Subjects in which Advanced Placement courses are offered: American History, Biology, Calculus, Chemistry, Computer Science, English, French, Physics, Spanish	9	9

†The district supplied an inappropriate statistic.

Quality of School Leadership
Internal politics and longevity are factors in principal selection, although educational leadership ability is still the primary criterion. Observers believe the quality of leadership is better in the elementary schools than at the secondary level. Parents and teachers do not help screen principal candidates. Principals have some say in the allocation of district resources.

Parent organizations are effective influencing school decision-making when "they have cared a great deal and researched well."

Quality of Instruction
Additional learning opportunities for gifted students are rated excellent. The program at the elementary level has been redesigned to cater more to the very brightest students. Additional instruction for low-achieving students is considered good, although an observer pointed out that "more needs to be done at the secondary level." The curriculum for college-bound students is rated excellent, but the curriculum for students not planning on college is termed only fair to poor. "The standards are very high for college-bound students," said one observer, "including high and low-achievers."

Quality of School Environment
The level of classroom disruption and student vandalism is low, and the quality of building maintenance and repair is good.

WAYNE

ADDRESS OF CENTRAL OFFICE:
50 Nellis Drive, Wayne, NJ 07470
ESI:57*

STATISTICAL PROFILE	DATA	ESI
Grade organization: †		
Percentage of schools built before 1955	NK	
Total enrollment	6,439	
Average Daily Attendance (ADA)	95%	5
Current expense per pupil in ADA	$4,881	2
Dropout rate	2%	10
Percentage of eligible students who took the SAT	NK	0
Average combined score on SAT	††	0*
Percentage of graduates who enrolled in 2- or 4-year colleges	76%	
Percentage of students who passed the state reading test	91%	
Percentage of students who passed the state math test	81%	
Teacher–student ratio in elementary grades	1:20	10
Teacher–student ratio in secondary grades	1:15	10
Counselor–student ratio in secondary grades	1:230	8
Number of students per music specialist in elementary grades	219	10
Number of students per art specialist in elementary grades	482	
Number of volumes in senior high school libraries (average)	25,864	
Beginning teacher's salary	$18,500	
Maximum teacher's salary	$37,528	
Average years of experience among teachers	15	
Number of students suspended and expelled	121	
Subjects in which Advanced Placement courses are offered: Calculus, English	2	2

† The district misinterpreted this statistic.
††The district supplied an inappropriate statistic.

Quality of School Leadership
Principals are hired primarily because of their educational leadership ability, and the quality of leadership does not vary greatly from school to school. Parents and teachers have hardly any say in principal selection, but principals have a great deal to say about resource distribution.

Parent organizations are considered sometimes effective.

Quality of Instruction
Additional learning opportunities for gifted students are rated excellent. Gifted elementary students beginning in grade 4, go to a central location for special instruction. Additional instruction for low-achieving students is rated good. Some students with learning problems may be excused from regular classes so they may receive special help. The college-bound curriculum is termed excellent, but the job-bound curriculum is rated only fair.

Quality of School Environment
Classroom disruption and student vandalism are not problems, but the quality of building maintenance and repair ranges between fair and good.

WHITE PLAINS

ADDRESS OF CENTRAL OFFICE:
5 Homeside Lane, White Plains, NY 10605
ESI:88

STATISTICAL PROFILE	DATA	ESI
Grade organization: K–4/5–6/7–8/9–12		
Percentage of schools built before 1955	88%	
Total enrollment	4,979	
Average Daily Attendance (ADA)	92%	5
Current expense per pupil in ADA	$11,500	10
Dropout rate	5%	10
Percentage of eligible students who took the SAT	60%	9
Average combined score on SAT	912	5
Percentage of graduates who enrolled in 2- or 4-year colleges	70%	
Percentage of students who passed the state reading test	100%	
Percentage of students who passed the state math test	100%	
Teacher–student ratio in elementary grades	1:13	10
Teacher–student ratio in secondary grades	1:10	10
Counselor–student ratio in secondary grades	1:180	10
Number of students per music specialist in elementary grades	225	10
Number of students per art specialist in elementary grades	310	
Number of volumes in senior high school library	35,805	
Beginning teacher's salary	$21,883	
Maximum teacher's salary	$54,823	
Average years of experience among teachers	12	
Number of students suspended and expelled	380	
Subjects in which Advanced Placement courses are offered:	9	9
American History, Biology, Calculus, Chemistry, Computer Science, English, French, Physics, Spanish		

Quality of School Leadership

The School Board seeks principals who show ability as educational leaders, and the quality of leadership is generally uniform throughout the system. Parents and teachers sit on committees that screen principal candidates. Also, principals have a lot to say about the disbursement of district resources.

Parent organizations are effective influencing school decision-making. Parents serve on a variety of district study and advisory committees.

Quality of Instruction

The program for gifted students begins in the elementary grades, where students are excused from regular classes so they can attend enrichment classes. The overall program is rated excellent. Additional instruction for low-achieving students is considered good. The curriculum for students who are college-bound is termed excellent, while the curriculum for students planning on work after graduation is considered good.

Observers think the district could do better in educating minority students. Minority students are not scoring as well as they should on standardized tests, said one observer.

Quality of School Environment

The incidence of classroom disruption and student vandalism is very low, and the quality of building maintenance and repair is good.

YONKERS

ADDRESS OF CENTRAL OFFICE:
145 Palmer Road, Yonkers, NY 10701
ESI:70

STATISTICAL PROFILE†	DATA	ESI
Grade organization: PreK–6/7–9/10–12		
Percentage of schools built before 1955	68%	
Total enrollment	18,619	
Average Daily Attendance (ADA)	87%	0
Current expense per pupil in ADA	$7,599	10
Dropout rate	11%	10
Percentage of eligible students who took the SAT	54%	8
Average combined score on SAT	796	0
Percentage of graduates who enrolled in 2- or 4-year colleges	54%	
Percentage of students who passed the state reading test	91%	
Percentage of students who passed the state math test	89%	
Teacher–student ratio in elementary grades	1:24	6
Teacher–student ratio in secondary grades	1:16	10
Counselor–student ratio in secondary grades	1:192	10
Number of students per music specialist in elementary grades	368	8
Number of students per art specialist in elementary grades	657	
Number of volumes in senior high school library	29,140	
Beginning teacher's salary	$19,163	
Maximum teacher's salary	$44,494	
Average years of experience among teachers	16	
Number of students suspended and expelled	NK	
Subjects in which Advanced Placement courses are offered: American History, Art, Biology, Calculus, Chemistry, Computer Science, English, Physics	8	8

†All statistics are 1986–87.

FAIR APPRAISAL

Quality of School Leadership
Principals are selected because of their educational leadership ability; the quality of leadership does not vary greatly from school to school. Parents and teachers have little say in the selection of principals. However, principals have some say about resource allotment.

Parent organizations are effective as an influence on district policy. PTA leaders meet regularly with the superintendent.

Quality of Instruction
Additional learning opportunities for gifted students are rated good; the program is required to have minority representation by court order. Additional instruction for low-achieving students is considered good. The college-bound curriculum is rated good, but the job-bound curriculum is considered fair.

The district's desegregation plan is only a couple of years old, and observers report that the educational needs of minority students are not yet adequately met.

Quality of School Environment
Classroom disruption and student vandalism are not problems. Building maintenance and repair are good.

YORKTOWN

ADDRESS OF CENTRAL OFFICE:
2723 Crompond Road, Yorktown Heights, NY 10598
ESI:78

STATISTICAL PROFILE	DATA	ESI
Grade organization: K–3/4–5/6–8/9–12		
Percentage of schools built before 1955	1%	
Total enrollment	3,129	
Average Daily Attendance (ADA)	95%	8
Current expense per pupil in ADA	$6,458	10
Dropout rate	1%	10
Percentage of eligible students who took the SAT	82%	10
Average combined score on SAT	943	6
Percentage of graduates who enrolled in 2- or 4-year colleges	77%	
Percentage of students who passed the state reading test	100%†	
Percentage of students who passed the state math test	100%†	
Teacher–student ratio in elementary grades	1:26†	4
Teacher–student ratio in secondary grades	1:20†	8
Counselor–student ratio in secondary grades	1:238	8
Number of students per music specialist in elementary grades	254†	10
Number of students per art specialist in elementary grades	433†	
Number of volumes in senior high school library	18,381	
Beginning teacher's salary	$20,243†	
Maximum teacher's salary	$44,433†	
Average years of experience among teachers	17†	
Number of students suspended and expelled	352	
Subjects in which Advanced Placement courses are offered: American History, Calculus, Chemistry, English	4	4

†1986–87 statistics.

FAIR APPRAISAL

Quality of School Leadership
The School Board chooses principals because of their ability as educational leaders. The quality of leadership is generally uniform throughout the system. Parents and teachers have some informal say in principal selection, and principals have a great deal of influence over the allotment of resources.

Parent organizations are sometimes effective as an influence in district decision-making.

Quality of Instruction
Additional learning opportunities for gifted students are rated excellent. Students are excused from regular classes in the elementary grades to attend enrichment courses in critical thinking and problem solving. Additional instruction for low-achieving students is considered good. Also rated good are the curricula for students planning on college and for those not planning on college.

Quality of School Environment
The incidence of classroom disruption and student vandalism is very low, and the quality of building maintenance and repair is good.

Norfolk–
Newport News, VA

Completed Statistical Profiles were received from six districts.
The districts in this area may be compared to districts in
the Greensboro–Winston-Salem, NC Metropolitan Area.

AREA AT A GLANCE

SCHOOL DISTRICT	ENROLLMENT	ESI
Chesapeake	26,328	46
Hampton	20,400	56
Isle of Wight County	4,002	46
Newport News	26,600	50
Norfolk	35,600	46
Portsmouth	18,658	30*

Indicates district misinterpretation of one or more statistics in the ESI. For each misinterpreted statistic, a score of 0 was given instead of a possible score of 0 to 10 points.

CHESAPEAKE

ADDRESS OF CENTRAL OFFICE:
P.O. Box 15204, Chesapeake, VA 23320
ESI:46

STATISTICAL PROFILE	DATA	ESI
Grade organization: †		
Percentage of schools built before 1955	10%	
Total enrollment	26,328	
Average Daily Attendance (ADA)	89%	2
Current expense per pupil in ADA	$3,579	7
Dropout rate	19%	4
Percentage of eligible students who took the SAT	38%	5
Average combined score on SAT	826	0
Percentage of graduates who enrolled in 2- or 4-year colleges	64%	
Percentage of students who passed the state reading test	100%	
Percentage of students who passed the state math test	100%	
Teacher–student ratio in elementary grades	1:23	7
Teacher–student ratio in secondary grades	1:23	5
Counselor–student ratio in secondary grades	1:282	6
Number of students per music specialist in elementary grades	590	4
Number of students per art specialist in elementary grades	1,243	
Number of volumes in senior high school library	††	
Beginning teacher's salary	$18,500	
Maximum teacher's salary	$27,479	
Average years of experience among teachers	18	
Number of students suspended and expelled	3†††	
Subjects in which Advanced Placement courses are offered:	6	6
American History, Biology, Calculus AB, Calculus BC,		
English, European History		

† The district has more than one pattern, for example: K–4/5–6/7–8/9–12 and K–6/7–9/10–12.
†† The district supplied the statistic of 10 volumes per student.
†††Does not include suspensions.

Quality of School Leadership
Principals are hired because they have ability as educational leaders, and the quality of leadership is generally uniform throughout the system. However, one observer noted that "parents who band together and demand an excellent principal are more likely to get the most able person than a school where parents accept whomever is assigned." Parents and teachers do not screen principal candidates. Principals have some say about the division of district resources.

Parent groups are very active and quite influential in decision-making. For example, parents got a program on child abuse taught in the schools; they also review textbooks.

Quality of Instruction
Additional learning opportunities for gifted students are rated excellent. The program begins in the early grades. Additional instruction for low-achieving students is rated good. The curriculum for college-bound students is called excellent, while the curriculum for students not planning on college is rated good.

Quality of School Environment
The level of classroom disruption and student vandalism is low, and the quality of building maintenance and repair is good.

HAMPTON

ADDRESS OF CENTRAL OFFICE:
P.O. Box 4217, Hampton, VA 23664
ESI:56

STATISTICAL PROFILE	DATA	ESI
Grade organization: †		
Percentage of schools built before 1955	17%	
Total enrollment	20,400	
Average Daily Attendance (ADA)	95%	8
Current expense per pupil in ADA	$3,400	6
Dropout rate	25%	0
Percentage of eligible students who took the SAT	53%	8
Average combined score on SAT	842	1
Percentage of graduates who enrolled in 2- or 4-year colleges	48%	
Percentage of students who passed the state reading test	97%	
Percentage of students who passed the state math test	95%	
Teacher–student ratio in elementary grades	1:21	9
Teacher–student ratio in secondary grades	1:18	10
Counselor–student ratio in secondary grades	1:350	4
Number of students per music specialist in elementary grades	877	0
Number of students per art specialist in elementary grades	None	
Number of volumes in senior high school library	21,500	
Beginning teacher's salary	$19,000	
Maximum teacher's salary	$31,116	
Average years of experience among teachers	14	
Number of students suspended and expelled	8,245	
Subjects in which Advanced Placement courses are offered:	10	10
American History, Biology, Calculus BC, Chemistry,		
Computer Science, English (Language and Composition),		
English (Literature and Composition) French, Physics,		
Spanish		

†The district misinterpreted this statistic.

Quality of School Leadership
Principals are hired based on their educational leadership ability, and the quality of leadership does not vary greatly from school to school. Teachers may occasionally help screen principal candidates, but parents do not. Principals have some say about how resources will be divided among the schools.

Parents organizations are sometimes an effective influence in district decision-making.

Quality of Instruction
Additional learning opportunities for gifted students are rated fair to good. A standout of the program is a regional magnet school that offers advanced programs in the sciences to junior and seniors in high school. Each student is assigned a mentor, some of whom are scientists from a nearby NASA research facility. Additional instruction for low-achieving students is called good. Another magnet school, this one for elementary grades, offers "a lot of individual attention to students and helps low-achievers," according to an observer. The curricula for college-bound students and job-bound students are rated good and fair respectively.

Quality of School Environment
The incidence of classroom disruption and student vandalism is low, and the quality of building maintenance and repair is rated fair to good.

ISLE OF WIGHT COUNTY

ADDRESS OF CENTRAL OFFICE:
P.O. Box 78, Isle of Wight, VA 23397
ESI:46

STATISTICAL PROFILE	DATA	ESI
Grade organization: K–7/8–12		
Percentage of schools built before 1955	17%	
Total enrollment	4,002	
Average Daily Attendance (ADA)	95%	8
Current expense per pupil in ADA	$3,655	8
Dropout rate	33%	0
Percentage of eligible students who took the SAT	NK	0
Average combined score on SAT	777	0
Percentage of graduates who enrolled in 2- or 4-year colleges	44%	
Percentage of students who passed the state reading test	99%	
Percentage of students who passed the state math test	98%	
Teacher–student ratio in elementary grades	1:17	10
Teacher–student ratio in secondary grades	1:15	10
Counselor–student ratio in secondary grades	1:296	6
Number of students per music specialist in elementary grades	572	4
Number of students per art specialist in elementary grades	839	
Number of volumes in senior high school library	24,051	
Beginning teacher's salary	$16,400	
Maximum teacher's salary	$27,805	
Average years of experience among teachers	NK	
Number of students suspended and expelled	NK	
Subjects in which Advanced Placement courses are offered:	None	0

FAIR APPRAISAL

Quality of School Leadership

The School Board seeks principals who demonstrate educational leadership ability, and the quality of leadership is generally uniform throughout the system. Parents and teachers do not help screen principal candidates. Principals have some say, but not much, concerning the allotment of resources to the schools.

Parent organizations are not very effective influencing district policy decisions. "Parents tend not to get involved," said an observer.

Quality of Instruction

Additional learning opportunities for gifted students are rated good, while additional instruction for low-achieving students is considered fair. "Some students get promoted before they are ready," said an observer. The college preparatory curriculum is rated good, and the curriculum for students not planning on college is considered fair to good. One observer complained that the latter program lacks the parent support it needs and deserves.

Quality of School Environment

The level of classroom disruption and student vandalism is low, and the quality of building maintenance and repair is good.

NEWPORT NEWS

ADDRESS OF CENTRAL OFFICE:
P.O. Box 6130, Newport News, VA 23606
ESI:50

STATISTICAL PROFILE	DATA	ESI
Grade organization: K–5/6–8/9–12		
Percentage of schools built before 1955	30%	
Total enrollment	26,600	
Average Daily Attendance (ADA)	93%	6
Current expense per pupil in ADA	$3,476	7
Dropout rate	16%	7
Percentage of eligible students who took the SAT	53%	8
Average combined score on SAT	857	2
Percentage of graduates who enrolled in 2- or 4-year colleges	60%	
Percentage of students who passed the state reading test	96%	
Percentage of students who passed the state math test	97%	
Teacher–student ratio in elementary grades	1:25	5
Teacher–student ratio in secondary grades	1:18	10
Counselor–student ratio in secondary grades	1:301	5
Number of students per music specialist in elementary grades	1,131	0
Number of students per art specialist in elementary grades	1,193	
Number of volumes in senior high school library	25,000	
Beginning teacher's salary	$19,000	
Maximum teacher's salary	$33,095	
Average years of experience among teachers	16	
Number of students suspended and expelled	1,198	
Subjects in which Advanced Placement courses are offered:	None	0

FAIR APPRAISAL

Quality of School Leadership

Principals are selected primarily for their educational leadership ability, and the quality of leadership does not vary greatly from school to school. Parents and teachers do not help screen principal candidates. Principals, however, have some influence over the resources assigned their school.

Parent organizations are sometimes effective influencing school decision-making. The School Board makes a genuine effort to listen to parents' suggestions and constructive criticisms, said one observer.

Quality of Instruction

A special school for gifted students helps make the program an excellent one in the view of observers. Additional instruction for low-achieving students is considered good to excellent. The curricula for students planning on college and for students not planning on college are both termed good.

Quality of School Environment

Classroom disruption and student vandalism are not problems, and the quality of building maintenance and repair is good to excellent.

NORFOLK

ADDRESS OF CENTRAL OFFICE:
P.O. Box 1357, Norfolk, VA 23501
ESI:46

STATISTICAL PROFILE	DATA	ESI
Grade organization: K–5/6–8/9–12		
Percentage of schools built before 1955	56%	
Total enrollment	35,600	
Average Daily Attendance (ADA)	92%	5
Current expense per pupil in ADA	$3,570	7
Dropout rate	28%	0
Percentage of eligible students who took the SAT	30%	3
Average combined score on SAT	804	0
Percentage of graduates who enrolled in 2- or 4-year colleges	72%	
Percentage of students who passed the state reading test	99%	
Percentage of students who passed the state math test	99%	
Teacher–student ratio in elementary grades	1:18	10
Teacher–student ratio in secondary grades	1:21	7
Counselor–student ratio in secondary grades	1:347	4
Number of students per music specialist in elementary grades	800	0
Number of students per art specialist in elementary grades	1,500	
Number of volumes in senior high school library	21,000	
Beginning teacher's salary	$18,500	
Maximum teacher's salar	$33,070	
Average years of experience among teachers	22	
Number of students suspended and expelled	6,685	
Subjects in which Advanced Placement courses are offered:	14	10
American History, Art History, Biology, Calculus, Computer Science, English, European History, French, German, Latin, Music, Physics, Spanish, Studio Art		

Quality of School Leadership

Longevity and popularity are factors in principal selection, but principals are hired primarily because they demonstrate ability as educational leaders. Also, the quality of leadership is generally uniform throughout the system, except that one observer complained that "principals do not receive enough on-the-job training." Teachers and parents have almost no role to play in principal selection, but principals are able to influence how the district's resources are divided among the schools.

Parent organizations are effective voices in district decision-making. The PTA has worked for guidance counselors in elementary schools, and it helped established school health clinics.

Quality of Instruction

The program for gifted students is implemented "vigorously," said an observer, and it is rated excellent. The program "challenges children on several levels," said another observer. Additional instruction for low-achieving students is considered good. Also rated good are the curricula for students going to college and for students heading into the job market after graduation. "The system is very conscientious about evaluating special needs and acting upon the evaluations," said an observer.

Quality of School Environment

The incidence of classroom disruption and student vandalism is low. However building maintenance and repair are rated only fair. Insufficient funding is given as the principal cause of problems.

PORTSMOUTH

ADDRESS OF CENTRAL OFFICE:
P.O. Box 998, Portsmouth, VA 23705
ESI:30*

STATISTICAL PROFILE	DATA	ESI
Grade organization: K–6/7–8/9–12		
Percentage of schools built before 1955	33%	
Total enrollment	18,658	
Average Daily Attendance (ADA)	94%	7
Current expense per pupil in ADA	$2,873	4
Dropout rate	36%	0
Percentage of eligible students who took the SAT	11%	0
Average combined score on SAT	764	0
Percentage of graduates who enrolled in 2- or 4-year colleges	68%	
Percentage of students who passed the state reading test	99%	
Percentage of students who passed the state math test	98%	
Teacher–student ratio in elementary grades	1:25	5
Teacher–student ratio in secondary grades	1:19	9
Counselor–student ratio in secondary grades	1:303	5
Number of students per music specialist in elementary grades	None†	0*
Number of students per art specialist in elementary grades	None†	
Number of volumes in senior high school library	21,111	
Beginning teacher's salary	$18,009	
Maximum teacher's salary	$30,802	
Average years of experience among teachers	17	
Number of students suspended and expelled	2,736	
Subjects in which Advanced Placement courses are offered:	None	0

†Music and art are taught by a ''unified arts team''.

Quality of School Leadership
Principals are hired primarily because of their educational leadership ability, and the quality of leadership is generally uniform throughout the system. Parents and teachers do not screen principal candidates. Principals, however, have some influence over the allotment of district resources.

Parent organizations are sometimes effective influencing school policies. "The administration listens to parents' concerns and will act on them," said an observer.

Quality of Instruction
Additional learning opportunities for gifted students are rated fair. The program "has gone down hill recently," said an observer. "Some parents are concerned that there's not enough offered," said another observer. Additional instruction for low-achieving students is considered good. Also rated good are curricula for students going on to college and for students not planning on college.

Quality of School Environment
Classroom disruption and student vandalism are on the high side, according to observers. "Stealing is at an all-time high," said one observer. Lack of funding is blamed for the fair quality of building maintenance and repair.

Oklahoma City, OK

Five districts completed Statistical Profiles. Oklahoma does not require state competency tests in reading and mathematics. Therefore, NA (not applicable) appears on lines requesting those statistics. Districts in this area may be compared with those in the Denver, CO Metropolitan Area.

AREA AT A GLANCE

SCHOOL DISTRICT	ENROLLMENT	ESI
Edmond	11,051	67
Midwest City	16,000	52*
Moore	15,691	56
Norman	10,027	69
Oklahoma City	40,139	27

Indicates district misinterpretation of one or more statistics in the ESI. For each misinterpreted statistic, a score of 0 was given instead of a possible score of 0 to 10 points.

SCHOOL DISTRICT

EDMOND

ADDRESS OF CENTRAL OFFICE:
1216 South Rankin, Edmond, OK 73034
ESI:67

STATISTICAL PROFILE	DATA	ESI
Grade organization: K–5/6–8/9–10/11–12		
Percentage of schools built before 1955	25%	
Total enrollment	11,051	
Average Daily Attendance (ADA)	93%	6
Current expense per pupil in ADA	$2,400	3
Dropout rate	9%	10
Percentage of eligible students who took the ACT	86%	10
Average combined score on ACT	20.9	10
Percentage of graduates who enrolled in 2- or 4-year colleges	89%	
Percentage of students who passed the state reading test	NA	
Percentage of students who passed the state math test	NA	
Teacher–student ratio in elementary grades	1:18	10
Teacher–student ratio in secondary grades	1:20	8
Counselor–student ratio in secondary grades	1:409	1
Number of students per music specialist in elementary grades	590	4
Number of students per art specialist in elementary grades	1,700	
Number of volumes in senior high school library	16,000	
Beginning teacher's salary	$17,497	
Maximum teacher's salary	$27,823	
Average years of experience among teachers	10	
Number of students suspended and expelled	67	
Subjects in which Advanced Placement courses are offered:	5	5
American History, Calculus, English, Foreign Language, Science		

FAIR APPRAISAL

Quality of School Leadership
Popularity, longevity and internal politics are all important criteria in principal selection, and the quality of leadership suffers a little as a result, according to observers. Parents and teachers do not help screen principal candidates. Principals, however, have some say in how the resources of the district are distributed. One observer felt leadership is "more able at the elementary schools than in the secondary schools."

Parent organizations' influence on school decision-making is sometimes effective.

Quality of Instruction
Additional learning opportunities for gifted students is rated fair, and additional instruction for low-achieving students is considered fair to poor. The curriculum for students planning on college is rated good, while the curriculum for students not planning on college is considered fair to good.

Quality of School Environment
The level of classroom disruption and student vandalism is low, and the quality of building maintenance and repair is excellent.

MIDWEST CITY

ADDRESS OF CENTRAL OFFICE:
P.O. Box 10630, Midwest City, OK 73110
ESI:52*

STATISTICAL PROFILE	DATA	ESI
Grade organization: K–6/7–9/10–12		
Percentage of schools built before 1955	38%	
Total enrollment	16,000	
Average Daily Attendance (ADA)	94%	7
Current expense per pupil in ADA	$3,733	10
Dropout rate	6%	10
Percentage of eligible students who took the ACT	40%	5
Average combined score on ACT	18	4
Percentage of graduates who enrolled in 2- or 4-year colleges	70%	
Percentage of students who passed the state reading test	NA	
Percentage of students who passed the state math test	NA	
Teacher–student ratio in elementary grades	1:24	6
Teacher–student ratio in secondary grades	1:24	4
Counselor–student ratio in secondary grades	1:400	2
Number of students per music specialist in elementary grades	†	0*
Number of students per art specialist in elementary grades	†	
Number of volumes in senior high school library	16,799	
Beginning teacher's salary	$16,913	
Maximum teacher's salary	$34,014	
Average years of experience among teachers	12	
Number of students suspended and expelled	100	
Subjects in which Advanced Placement courses are offered: Biology, Calculus, Chemistry, Physics	4	4

†The district's statistic is one specialist per school.

FAIR APPRAISAL

Quality of School Leadership

The School Board hires principals because of their educational leadership ability, and the quality of leadership is generally uniform throughout the system. Parents and teachers do not have a say in principal selection, but principals have some say about the allotment of resources to the schools.

Parent organizations are sometimes effective influencing district policy decisions.

Quality of Instruction

Additional learning opportunities for gifted students are rated good. One elementary school is set aside for gifted students. Additional instruction for low-achieving students is considered fair. The curriculum for students bound for college is called excellent, while the curriculum for students not planning on college is rated good.

Quality of School Environment

The level of classroom disruption and student vandalism is very low, and the quality of building maintenance and repair is excellent. District voters have approved 33 out of 34 bond issues in recent years, and construction and renovation are ongoing.

MOORE

ADDRESS OF CENTRAL OFFICE:
400 North Broadway, Oklahoma City, OK 73160
ESI:56

STATISTICAL PROFILE	DATA	ESI
Grade organization: K–6/7–8/9–10/11–12		
Percentage of schools built before 1955	4%	
Total enrollment	15,691	
Average Daily Attendance (ADA)	99%	10
Current expense per pupil in ADA	$2,800	5
Dropout rate	6%	10
Percentage of eligible students who took the ACT	35%	4
Average combined score on ACT	19.3	5
Percentage of graduates who enrolled in 2- or 4-year colleges	62%	
Percentage of students who passed the state reading test	NA	
Percentage of students who passed the state math test	NA	
Teacher–student ratio in elementary grades	1:22	8
Teacher–student ratio in secondary grades	1:30	0
Counselor–student ratio in secondary grades	1:300	6
Number of students per music specialist in elementary grades	400	7
Number of students per art specialist in elementary grades	None	
Number of volumes in senior high school library	16,187	
Beginning teacher's salary	$16,187	
Maximum teacher's salary	$27,470	
Average years of experience among teachers	12	
Number of students suspended and expelled	100	
Subjects in which Advanced Placement courses are offered: English	1	1

FAIR APPRAISAL

Quality of School Leadership
 Principals are selected primarily for their ability as educational leaders, and the quality of leadership is generally uniform throughout the system. Parents and teachers do not have a role in screening principal candidates, but principals are quite influential regarding the allotment of resources to the schools.
   Parent organizations are effective influences on district decision-making.

Quality of Instruction
Additional learning opportunities for gifted students and additional instruction for low-achieving students are both rated fair. The college-preparatory curriculum is considered good, while the curriculum for students not planning on college is termed fair.

Quality of School Environment
The incidence of classroom disruption and student vandalism is low, and the quality of building maintenance and repair is good.

NORMAN

ADDRESS OF CENTRAL OFFICE:
1133 West Main Street, Norman, OK 73069
ESI:69

STATISTICAL PROFILE	DATA	ESI
Grade organization: K–5/6–8/9–10/11–12		
Percentage of schools built before 1955	22%	
Total enrollment	10,027	
Average Daily Attendance (ADA)	95%	8
Current expense per pupil in ADA	$2,667	4
Dropout rate	14%	9
Percentage of eligible students who took the ACT	25%	2
Average combined score on ACT	22.0	10
Percentage of graduates who enrolled in 2- or 4-year colleges	65%	
Percentage of students who passed the state reading test	NA	
Percentage of students who passed the state math test	NA	
Teacher–student ratio in elementary grades	1:23	7
Teacher–student ratio in secondary grades	1:25	3
Counselor–student ratio in secondary grades	1:131	10
Number of students per music specialist in elementary grades	350	8
Number of students per art specialist in elementary grades	None	
Number of volumes in senior high school library	17,000	
Beginning teacher's salary	$15,688	
Maximum teacher's salary	$36,892	
Average years of experience among teachers	11	
Number of students suspended and expelled	281	
Subjects in which Advanced Placement courses are offered: Biology, Calculus, Chemistry, Computer Science, English, French, Music Theory, Spanish	8	8

FAIR APPRAISAL

Quality of School Leadership
The School Board seeks principals who demonstrate educational leadership ability. The quality of leadership does not vary greatly from school to school. Parents and teachers do not screen principal candidates. Principals, however, have some say about the distribution of resources to the schools.
   Parent organizations are generally ineffective influencing school decision-making.

Quality of Instruction
Additional learning opportunities for gifted students and additional instruction for low-achieving students are both considered good. The high school sponsors an annual tour of select eastern colleges for about 20 qualified seniors. Colleges include Harvard, Radcliffe and M.I.T. The curriculum preparing students for college is rated excellent, and the curriculum for students heading directly for the job market is rated good.

Quality of School Environment
Classroom disruption and student vandalism are not problems, and the quality of building maintenance and repair is good.

OKLAHOMA CITY

ADDRESS OF CENTRAL OFFICE:

900 North Klein Avenue, Oklahoma City, OK 73106
ESI:27

STATISTICAL PROFILE	DATA	ESI
Grade organization: K–4/5–6/7–8/9–12		
Percentage of schools built before 1955	69%	
Total enrollment	40,139	
Average Daily Attendance (ADA)	91%	4
Current expense per pupil in ADA	$2,711	5
Dropout rate	46%	0
Percentage of eligible students who took the ACT	26%	3
Average combined score on ACT	15.3	0
Percentage of graduates who enrolled in 2- or 4-year colleges	NK	
Percentage of students who passed the state reading test	NA	
Percentage of students who passed the state math test	NA	
Teacher–student ratio in elementary grades	1:25	5
Teacher–student ratio in secondary grades	1:27	1
Counselor–student ratio in secondary grades	1:450	0
Number of students per music specialist in elementary grades	676	2
Number of students per art specialist in elementary grades	None	
Number of volumes in senior high school library	14,546	
Beginning teacher's salary	$16,250	
Maximum teacher's salary	$35,196	
Average years of experience among teachers	13	
Number of students suspended and expelled	NK	
Subjects in which Advanced Placement courses are offered:	7	7
American History, Art, Calculus, Computer Science, English, Foreign Languages, Science		

FAIR APPRAISAL

Quality of School Leadership

Racial balance is a consideration in principal selection along with educational leadership ability. The quality of leadership is generally uniform throughout the system. Parents and teachers do not screen principal candidates. Principals have some say in how resources of the district are allotted to the schools.

Parent organizations are effective influencing district policies. It is believed that PTAs in Oklahoma City are adding members faster than any other PTA in the country, said observers. The PTA Council is currently evaluating elementary education and setting guidelines for parent participation in school affairs.

Quality of Instruction

Additional learning opportunities for gifted students and additional instruction for low-achieving students are rated fair to good. A big problem with these and many other programs is the decline in school funding caused by the drop in oil prices that wreaked havoc with the state's economy. For example, a special school for gifted students had to be eliminated. The observers report that, starting in 1987–88, improved counseling for children in kindergarten through grade 4 should better identify those with potential learning problems. The curricula for students going to college and those not planning on college are both rated good. The district had seven National Merit Scholarship finalists in 1986–87. Observers report some excellent magnet schools, one devoted to an introduction to health-medical professions.

Minority students are gradually improving their scores on standardized achievement tests, according to observers.

Quality of School Environment

The level of classroom disruption and student vandalism is low (increased security and discipline). The quality of building maintenance and repair, however, is rated fair to poor. Many schools were built before 1940, and some go back to World War I.

METROPOLITAN AREA

Omaha, NE

Three districts in the Omaha area completed Statistical Profiles.
The state of Nebraska does not have competency tests in reading and math;
therefore, *NA* (not applicable) appears on the lines requesting those statistics.
Districts in this area may be compared to those in the Boise, ID Metropolitan Area.

AREA AT A GLANCE

SCHOOL DISTRICT	ENROLLMENT	ESI
Millard	14,800	56
Papillion-Lavista	6,214	48
Westside	4,915	89

SCHOOL DISTRICT

MILLARD

ADDRESS OF CENTRAL OFFICE:
1010 South 144th Street, Omaha, NE 68154
ESI:56

STATISTICAL PROFILE	DATA	ESI
Grade organization: †		
Percentage of schools built before 1955	0%	
Total enrollment	14,800	
Average Daily Attendance (ADA)	96%	9
Current expense per pupil in ADA	$3,000	4
Dropout rate	2%	10
Percentage of eligible students who took the ACT	35%	4
Average combined score on ACT	20.8	10
Percentage of graduates who enrolled in 2- or 4-year colleges	70%	
Percentage of students who passed the state reading test	NA	
Percentage of students who passed the state math test	NA	
Teacher–student ratio in elementary grades	1:23	7
Teacher–student ratio in secondary grades	1:24	4
Counselor–student ratio in secondary grades	1:360	3
Number of students per music specialist in elementary grades	530	5
Number of students per art specialist in elementary grades	None	
Number of volumes in senior high school library (average)	30,000	
Beginning teacher's salary	$16,165	
Maximum teacher's salary	$33,785	
Average years of experience among teachers	10	
Number of students suspended and expelled	2,000	
Subjects in which Advanced Placement courses are offered:	None	0

†The district has two patterns: K–5/6–8/9–12 and K–6/7–8/9–12.

FAIR APPRAISAL

Quality of School Leadership

Internal politics play a small part in principal selection, but principals are hired primarily for their educational leadership ability. Parents and teachers do not screen principal candidates, but principals have some say concerning the allotment of district resources. Some principals have more "political clout" than others, said an observer.

Parent organizations are sometimes effective as an influence in district decision-making.

Quality of Instruction

Additional learning opportunities for gifted students and additional instruction for low-achieving students are both rated good. Many teacher aides help the latter program. The college preparatory curriculum is rated good, while the curriculum for students not planning on college is only fair. Counseling for both kinds of students "needs improvement," said an observer.

Quality of School Environment

Classroom disruption and student vandalism are not problems and the quality of building maintenance and repair is considered good.

PAPILLION-LAVISTA

ADDRESS OF CENTRAL OFFICE:
7552 South 84th Street, Omaha, NE 68128
ESI:48

STATISTICAL PROFILE	DATA	ESI
Grade organization: K–6/7–9/10–12		
Percentage of schools built before 1955	NK	
Total enrollment	6,214	
Average Daily Attendance (ADA)	97%	10
Current expense per pupil in ADA	$2,617	2
Dropout rate	3%	10
Percentage of eligible students who took the ACT	70%	10
Average combined score on ACT	19	5
Percentage of graduates who enrolled in 2- or 4-year colleges	60%	
Percentage of students who passed the state reading test	NA	
Percentage of students who passed the state math test	NA	
Teacher–student ratio in elementary grades	NK	0
Teacher–student ratio in secondary grades	NK	0
Counselor–student ratio in secondary grades	1:375	3
Number of students per music specialist in elementary grades	500	5
Number of students per art specialist in elementary grades	None	
Number of volumes in senior high school library	19,000	
Beginning teacher's salary	$15,585	
Maximum teacher's salary	$33,508	
Average years of experience among teachers	9	
Number of students suspended and expelled	226	
Subjects in which Advanced Placement courses are offered: American History, Calculus, English	3	3

FAIR APPRAISAL

Quality of School Leadership

The School Board seeks principals who demonstrate educational leadership ability, and the quality of leadership is generally uniform throughout the system. Parents and teachers do not screen principal candidates. Principals, on the other hand, have some say about the distribution of resources to the schools.

The School Board and administration are receptive to parents' suggestions and constructive criticisms, but, according to an observer, parents don't have much to say.

Quality of Instruction

Additional learning opportunities for gifted students are rated good, although the program is only a few years old. Gifted students are excused from regular classes for enrichment classes. Additional instruction for low-achieving students is considered excellent. A special staff and parent volunteers help the program. The curriculum for college-bound students and the curriculum for job-bound students are both rated good. The district does "very well with the funds available," said an observer.

Quality of School Environment

The level of classroom disruption and student vandalism is very low, but the quality of building maintenance and repair is only fair. The district has been putting most of its capital funds into new construction, said an observer, and older buildings "have suffered as a result." The population in Douglas County, which surrounds Omaha, has gone from 30,000 in 1960 to more than 100,000 in 1987.

WESTSIDE

ADDRESS OF CENTRAL OFFICE:
909 South 76th Street, Omaha, NE 68114
ESI:89

STATISTICAL PROFILE	DATA	ESI
Grade organization: K–6/7–8/9–12		
Percentage of schools built before 1955	40%	
Total enrollment	4,915	
Average Daily Attendance (ADA)	96%	9
Current expense per pupil in ADA	$4,563	10
Dropout rate	8%	10
Percentage of eligible students who took the ACT	78%	10
Average combined score on ACT	21.0	10
Percentage of graduates who enrolled in 2- or 4-year colleges	75%	
Percentage of students who passed the state reading test	NA	
Percentage of students who passed the state math test	NA	
Teacher–student ratio in elementary grades	1:16	10
Teacher–student ratio in secondary grades	1:15	10
Counselor–student ratio in secondary grades	1:253	7
Number of students per music specialist in elementary grades	433	7
Number of students per art specialist in elementary grades	1,083	
Number of volumes in senior high school library	26,619	
Beginning teacher's salary	$15,900	
Maximum teacher's salary	$42,700	
Average years of experience among teachers	13	
Number of students suspended and expelled	39	
Subjects in which Advanced Placement courses are offered: American History, Calculus, Chemistry, European History, Foreign Language, Physics	6	6

FAIR APPRAISAL

Quality of School Leadership

Principals are hired primarily for their ability as educational leaders, and the quality of leadership does not vary greatly from school to school. Parents and teachers take no part in screening principal candidates. Principals have some role in deciding how resources will be distributed.

Parent organizations are sometimes effective influencing policy decisions. For example, they helped soften the blow when the School Board closed three schools in recent years.

Quality of Instruction

Additional learning opportunities for gifted students and additional instruction for low-achieving students are both rated excellent. Also rated excellent is the college preparatory curriculum. The curriculum for students not planning on college is considered good.

Quality of School Environment

Classroom disruption and student vandalism are not problems, and the quality of building maintenance and repair is considered excellent. The district "compares favorably with the best in the country," said an observer, but unlike other districts in the county, "it won't grow in enrollment because it is surrounded by the city of Omaha."

Philadelphia, PA

Twenty districts in the Philadelphia area, which includes parts of New Jersey and Delaware as well as Pennsylvania, completed Statistical Profiles. Fair Appraisals alone were received for another seven districts. Some districts did not include scores for state competency tests in reading and math; one district said the statistics were not applicable in Pennsylvania. However, the State *does* administer basic skills (compentency) tests, called TELLS, and most districts included their students' scores on these tests. Districts in this area may be compared to districts in the New York City Metropolitan Area.

AREA AT A GLANCE

SCHOOL DISTRICT	ENROLLMENT	ESI
Bensalem	7,730	50
Brandywine, DE	11,132	
Cherry Hill, NJ	10,708	77
Colonial	3,688	83
Chichester	3,447	56*
Council Rock	8,994	47*
Hatboro–Horsham	3,159	
Haverford Township	4,425	
Interboro	3,065	68
Lower Merion	5,550	85
Marple–Newtown	3,100	87
Methacton	3,350	78
North Penn	9,070	
Penn–Delco	3,200	54
Philadelphia	201,000	35
Phoenixville	2,939	
Radnor Township	2,604	
Southeast Delco	3,613	61*
Tredyffrin–Easttown	4,357	71
Upper Merion	3,254	92
Upper Moreland Township	3,034	55
Wallingford–Swarthmore	2,772	83
Washington Township, NJ	6,600	50
West Chester	9,208	65
William Penn	4,790	
Willingboro, NJ	6,982	45
Wissahickon	2,900	69*

Indicates district misinterpretation of one or more statistics in the ESI. For each misinterpreted statistic, a score of 0 was given instead of a possible score of 0 to 10 points.

BENSALEM

ADDRESS OF CENTRAL OFFICE:
3000 Donallen Avenue, Bensalem, PA 19020
ESI:50

STATISTICAL PROFILE	DATA	ESI
Grade organization: †		
Percentage of schools built before 1955	20%	
Total enrollment	7,730††	
Average Daily Attendance (ADA)	95%††	8
Current expense per pupil in ADA	$3,668	2
Dropout rate	31%	0
Percentage of eligible students who took the SAT	13%	0
Average combined score on SAT	866††	2
Percentage of graduates who enrolled in 2- or 4-year colleges	28%	
Percentage of students who passed the state reading test	76%††	
Percentage of students who passed the state math test	72%††	
Teacher–student ratio in elementary grades	1:17	10
Teacher–student ratio in secondary grades	1:15	10
Counselor–student ratio in secondary grades	1:325	5
Number of students per music specialist in elementary grades	287	10
Number of students per art specialist in elementary grades	526	
Number of volumes in senior high school library	30,639	
Beginning teacher's salary	$18,641††	
Maximum teacher's salary	$43,327††	
Average years of experience among teachers	15	
Number of students suspended and expelled	400	
Subjects in which Advanced Placement courses are offered:	3	3
Calculus, English, Science		

† The district misinterpreted this statistic.
††1986–87 statistics.

FAIR APPRAISAL

Quality of School Leadership
Principals are hired primarily because of their educational leadership ability; the quality of leadership is generally uniform throughout the district. Parents and teachers do not screen principal candidates. However, pricipals have some say as to what resources are allotted their school.

Parent organizations are sometimes effective influencing school policy decisions. Recently, parents of handicapped children have been working to improve the program for their children.

Quality of Instruction
Additional learning opportunities for gifted students and additional instruction for low-achieving students are rated good. Also rated good is the curriculum for students planning on college. The curriculum for students not planning on college is considered fair. The latter program has suffered from budget cuts and dropping enrollment, said an observer.

Quality of School Environment
The level of classroom disruption and student vandalism is low, and the quality of building maintenance and repair is good.

BRANDYWINE, DE

ADDRESS OF CENTRAL OFFICE:
Pennsylvania Avenue, Claymont, DE 19703
ESI:None†

STATISTICAL PROFILE	DATA	ESI
Grade organization:		
Percentage of schools built before 1955		
Total enrollment		
Average Daily Attendance (ADA)		
Current expense per pupil in ADA		
Dropout rate		
Percentage of eligible students who took the SAT		
Average combined score on SAT		
Percentage of graduates who enrolled in 2- or 4-year colleges		
Percentage of students who passed the state reading test		
Percentage of students who passed the state math test		
Teacher–student ratio in elementary grades		
Teacher–student ratio in secondary grades		
Counselor–student ratio in secondary grades		
Number of students per music specialist in elementary grades		
Number of students per art specialist in elementary grades		
Number of volumes in senior high school library		
Beginning teacher's salary		
Maximum teacher's salary		
Average years of experience among teachers		
Number of students suspended and expelled		
Subjects in which Advanced Placement courses are offered:		

†A Statistical Profile was not received from this district.

FAIR APPRAISAL

Quality of School Leadership
The School Board hires principals who demonstrate educational leadership ability, and the quality of leadership is generally uniform throughout the district. Parents and teachers serve on committees that screen principal candidates. Principals have some voice on how district resources are distributed.

Parent organizations are sometimes effective influences on district policies. In addition to PTAs, each school has a citizen advisory committee, the result of a desegregation plan involving the city of Wilmington. Eleven northern Delaware districts were combined into four.

Quality of Instruction
Additional learning opportunities for gifted students and additional instruction for low-achieving students are both rated excellent. Also rated excellent are the curricula for students going to college and for those going into the world of work. Brandywine High School was selected as one of 72 outstanding high schools in the country.

As part of the desegregation plan, Brandywine students in grades 4–6 are bused into Wilmington. Minority students are doing better, said an observer, but it's possible the district will never adequately meet the needs of all minority students.

Quality of School Environment
Classroom disruption and student vandalism are not problems; the quality of building maintenance and repair is only fair. However, the district has plans for building improvements.

CHERRY HILL, NJ

ADDRESS OF CENTRAL OFFICE:
P.O. Box 5015, Cherry Hill, NJ 08034
ESI:77

STATISTICAL PROFILE	DATA	ESI
Grade organization: K–6/7–8/9–12		
Percentage of schools built before 1955	0%	
Total enrollment	10,708	
Average Daily Attendance (ADA)	95%	8
Current expense per pupil in ADA	$5,373	5
Dropout rate	4%	10
Percentage of eligible students who took the SAT	90%	10
Average combined score on SAT	990	9
Percentage of graduates who enrolled in 2- or 4-year colleges	78%	
Percentage of students who passed the state reading test	98%	
Percentage of students who passed the state math test	95%	
Teacher–student ratio in elementary grades	1:21	9
Teacher–student ratio in secondary grades	1:22	6
Counselor–student ratio in secondary grades	1:240	8
Number of students per music specialist in elementary grades	392	8
Number of students per art specialist in elementary grades	522	
Number of volumes in senior high school library (average)	33,000	
Beginning teacher's salary	$18,500	
Maximum teacher's salary	$39,644	
Average years of experience among teachers	18	
Number of students suspended and expelled	1,498	
Subjects in which Advanced Placement courses are offered: Biology, Calculus, French, Spanish	4	4

FAIR APPRAISAL

Quality of School Leadership
Principals are hired mostly for their educational leadership ability. There is some variation in the quality of leadership within the district, according to observers. The district is historically divided between east and west sections, said an observer, and the east section has traditionally gotten the "best" principals and teachers. However, observers report the situation is changing. Parents and teachers do not interview principal candidates. Principals have some influence over the allotment of resources to their school.

Parent organizations are sometimes effective influencing school policies. They are invited to sit on various planning committees.

Quality of Instruction
Additional opportunities for gifted students and additional instruction for low-achieving students are rated good. The college preparatory curriculum is considered excellent, while the curriculum for students not planning on college is rated good.

Quality of School Environment
Classroom disruption and student vandalism are not problems, and the quality of building maintenance and repair is good.

COLONIAL

ADDRESS OF CENTRAL OFFICE:
230 Flourtown Road, Plymouth Township, PA 19462
ESI:83

STATISTICAL PROFILE	DATA	ESI
Grade organization: Pre-K–5/6–8/9–12		
Percentage of schools built before 1955	0%	
Total enrollment	3,688	
Average Daily Attendance (ADA)	94%	7
Current expense per pupil in ADA	$4,143	5
Dropout rate	2%	10
Percentage of eligible students who took the SAT	63%	10
Average combined score on SAT	927	6
Percentage of graduates who enrolled in 2- or 4-year colleges	62%	
Percentage of students who passed the state reading test	86%	
Percentage of students who passed the state math test	82%	
Teacher–student ratio in elementary grades	1:19	10
Teacher–student ratio in secondary grades	1:13	10
Counselor–student ratio in secondary grades	1:222	9
Number of students per music specialist in elementary grades	270	10
Number of students per art specialist in elementary grades	521	
Number of volumes in senior high school library	30,000	
Beginning teacher's salary	$15,469	
Maximum teacher's salary	$41,401	
Average years of experience among teachers	21	
Number of students suspended and expelled	939	
Subjects in which Advanced Placement courses are offered: Biology, Calculus, Chemistry, Computer Science, English, European History	6	6

FAIR APPRAISAL

Quality of School Leadership
Longevity in the district helps, but most principals hired from within the ranks are selected because of educational leadership ability, and the quality of leadership does not vary greatly from school to school. Parents and teachers do not interview principal candidates. Principals have some say in determining how resources of the district are used.

"In four years we've made great strides with parent participation," said an observer, and parent organizations are deemed to be effective influences on district decision-making.

Quality of Instruction
Additional learning opportunities for gifted students are rated good, but one observer said the program is not very strong in the elementary schools. Additional instruction for low-achieving students is only rated fair. The curricula for students preparing for college and for students not planning on college are both considered good.

Quality of School Environment
Classroom disruption and student vandalism are not problems; the quality of building maintenance and repair is good.

CHICHESTER

ADDRESS OF CENTRAL OFFICE:
P.O. Box 2100, Marcus Hook, PA 19061
ESI:56*

STATISTICAL PROFILE	DATA	ESI
Grade organization: K–6/7–9/10–12		
Percentage of schools built before 1955	83%	
Total enrollment	3,447	
Average Daily Attendance (ADA)	94%	7
Current expense per pupil in ADA	$3,558	2
Dropout rate	13%	10
Percentage of eligible students who took the SAT	33%	4
Average combined score on SAT	†	0*
Percentage of graduates who enrolled in 2- or 4-year colleges	44%	
Percentage of students who passed the state reading test	80%	
Percentage of students who passed the state math test	82%	
Teacher–student ratio in elementary grades	1:17	10
Teacher–student ratio in secondary grades	1:13	10
Counselor–student ratio in secondary grades	1:282	6
Number of students per music specialist in elementary grades	438	7
Number of students per art specialist in elementary grades	438	
Number of volumes in senior high school library	25,000	
Beginning teacher's salary	$18,879	
Maximum teacher's salary	$38,322	
Average years of experience among teachers	14	
Number of students suspended and expelled	1,971	
Subjects in which Advanced Placement courses are offered:	None	0

†The district misinterpreted this statistic.

FAIR APPRAISAL

Quality of School Leadership
The School Board seeks principals with educational leadership ability; the quality of leadership is generally uniform throughout the system. Parents and teachers do not screen principal candidates. Principals have some influence over the distribution of district resources.

Parent organizations are sometimes effective as an influence in policy decisions.

Quality of Instruction
Additional learning opportunities for gifted students are rated excellent. The "recently enhanced" program was praised in a study by a visiting University of Pennsylvania professor, according to an observer. Additional instruction for low-achieving students is considered good. "Lots of teachers stay after school to help kids," said an observer. There are also special classes. The curriculum for college-bound students is rated excellent ("a growing interest in college among students"), while the curriculum for students not planning on college is rated good.

Quality of School Environment
The level of classroom disruption and student vandalism is low, and the quality of building maintenance and repair is good.

COUNCIL ROCK

ADDRESS OF CENTRAL OFFICE:
Twining Ford Road, Richboro, PA 18954
ESI:47*

STATISTICAL PROFILE	DATA	ESI
Grade organization: K–6/7–9/10–12		
Percentage of schools built before 1955	15%	
Total enrollment	8,994	
Average Daily Attendance (ADA)	95%	8
Current expense per pupil in ADA	$2,894	0
Dropout rate	2%	10
Percentage of eligible students who took the SAT	42%	6
Average combined score on SAT	†	0*
Percentage of graduates who enrolled in 2- or 4-year colleges	71%	
Percentage of students who passed the state reading test	87%	
Percentage of students who passed the state math test	91%	
Teacher–student ratio in elementary grades	1:27	3
Teacher–student ratio in secondary grades	1:24	4
Counselor–student ratio in secondary grades	1:361	3
Number of students per music specialist in elementary grades	303	9
Number of students per art specialist in elementary grades	455	
Number of volumes in senior high school library	47,000††	
Beginning teacher's salary	$18,510	
Maximum teacher's salary	$41,414	
Average years of experience among teachers	15	
Number of students suspended and expelled	315	
Subjects in which Advanced Placement courses are offered: Calculus, English, Foreign Languages, Science	4	4

† The district misinterpreted this statistic.
††This number seems unusually high.

FAIR APPRAISAL

Quality of School Leadership
Principals are selected primarily for their educational leadership ability, and the quality of leadership is generally uniform in the district. Parents and teachers do not help screen principal candidates. Principals have some influence over use of district resources.

Quality of Instruction
Additional learning opportunities for gifted students are considered good, although the program is better in the higher grades than in the elementary schools. Additional instruction for low-achieving students is rated fair. The district is "geared toward the gifted," said an observer. The curriculum for students planning on college is called excellent, but the curriculum for students not planning on college is only rated fair.

Quality of School Environment
Classroom disruption and student vandalism are not problems, and the quality of building maintenance and repair is good. New schools are being built to accommodate enrollment increases.

HATBORO–HORSHAM

ADDRESS OF CENTRAL OFFICE:
229 Meetinghouse Road, Horsham, PA 19044
ESI:None†

STATISTICAL PROFILE	DATA	ESI
Grade organization:		
Percentage of schools built before 1955		
Total enrollment		
Average Daily Attendance (ADA)		
Current expense per pupil in ADA		
Dropout rate		
Percentage of eligible students who took the SAT		
Average combined score on SAT		
Percentage of graduates who enrolled in 2- or 4-year colleges		
Percentage of students who passed the state reading test		
Percentage of students who passed the state math test		
Teacher–student ratio in elementary grades		
Teacher–student ratio in secondary grades		
Counselor–student ratio in secondary grades		
Number of students per music specialist in elementary grades		
Number of students per art specialist in elementary grades		
Number of volumes in senior high school library		
Beginning teacher's salary		
Maximum teacher's salary		
Average years of experience among teachers		
Number of students suspended and expelled		
Subjects in which Advanced Placement courses are offered:		

†A Statistical Profile was not received from this district.

FAIR APPRAISAL

Quality of School Leadership
The School Board hires principals who demonstrate educational leadership ability, and the quality of leadership does not vary greatly from school to school. Committees that screen principal candidates include parents and teachers. Also, principals have a great deal to say about the allotment of resources to their school.

Parents sit on curriculum committees and meet regularly with the superintendent; their influence is considered very effective.

Quality of Instruction
Additional learning opportunities for gifted students and additional instruction for low-achieving students are rated good. So are the curricula for college-bound students and for students heading into the job market after graduation.

Quality of School Environment
The incidence of classroom disruption and student violence is very low, and the quality of building maintenance and repair is excellent.

HAVERFORD TOWNSHIP

ADDRESS OF CENTRAL OFFICE:
1801 Darby Road, Havertown, PA 19083
ESI:None†

STATISTICAL PROFILE	DATA	ESI
Grade organization:		
Percentage of schools built before 1955		
Total enrollment		
Average Daily Attendance (ADA)		
Current expense per pupil in ADA		
Dropout rate		
Percentage of eligible students who took the SAT		
Average combined score on SAT		
Percentage of graduates who enrolled in 2- or 4-year colleges		
Percentage of students who passed the state reading test		
Percentage of students who passed the state math test		
Teacher–student ratio in elementary grades		
Teacher–student ratio in secondary grades		
Counselor–student ratio in secondary grades		
Number of students per music specialist in elementary grades		
Number of students per art specialist in elementary grades		
Number of volumes in senior high school library		
Beginning teacher's salary		
Maximum teacher's salary		
Average years of experience among teachers		
Number of students suspended and expelled		
Subjects in which Advanced Placement courses are offered:		

†A Statistical Profile was not received from this district.

FAIR APPRAISAL

Quality of School Leadership
The School Board hires principals primarily because of their educational leadership ability; the quality of leadership is generally uniform throughout the system. Parents and teachers do not screen principal candidates, but parents can express preferences and opinions. Principals have a great deal to say about the use of district resources.

Parent organizations are effective as an influence on school policies. An active education committee at the middle school makes recommendations for change to the principal.

Quality of Instruction
Additional learning opportunities for gifted students in the elementary schools are excellent, according to an observer, but they are just being developed in the higher grades. Additional instruction for low-achieving students is considered excellent, also. The curricula for students going to college and students preparing for the world of work are both deemed excellent.

Quality of School Environment
Classroom disruption and student vandalism are not problems, and the quality of building maintenance and repair is considered good.

INTERBORO

ADDRESS OF CENTRAL OFFICE:
9th & Washington Avenues, Prospect Park, PA 19076
ESI:68

STATISTICAL PROFILE	DATA	ESI
Grade organization: K–8/9–12		
Percentage of schools built before 1955	60%	
Total enrollment	3,065	
Average Daily Attendance (ADA)	94%	7
Current expense per pupil in ADA	$4,998	9
Dropout rate	9%	10
Percentage of eligible students who took the SAT	44%	6
Average combined score on SAT	859	2
Percentage of graduates who enrolled in 2- or 4-year colleges	64%	
Percentage of students who passed the state reading test	NK	
Percentage of students who passed the state math test	NK	
Teacher–student ratio in elementary grades	1:22	8
Teacher–student ratio in secondary grades	1:19	9
Counselor–student ratio in secondary grades	1:274	7
Number of students per music specialist in elementary grades	254	10
Number of students per art specialist in elementary grades	522	
Number of volumes in senior high school library	14,678	
Beginning teacher's salary	$18,575	
Maximum teacher's salary	$40,824	
Average years of experience among teachers	15	
Number of students suspended and expelled	405	
Subjects in which Advanced Placement courses are offered:	None	0

Quality of School Leadership
Principals are hired because of their ability as educational leaders, and the quality of leadership does not vary greatly from school to school. Parents and teachers do not help screen principal candidates. Principals have some say in how resources will be allotted to the schools.

Parent organizations are sometimes effective influencing school decision-making, although this is mostly at the elementary level.

Quality of Instruction
Additional learning opportunities for gifted students and additional instruction for low-achieving students are rated good, as are the curricula for students preparing for college and students preparing for the world of work.

Quality of School Environment
Classroom disruption and student vandalism are not problems, and the quality of building maintenance and repair is good.

LOWER MERION

ADDRESS OF CENTRAL OFFICE:
301 Montgomery Avenue, Ardmore, PA 19003
ESI:85

STATISTICAL PROFILE	DATA	ESI
Grade organization: K–5/6–8/9–12		
Percentage of schools built before 1955	66%	
Total enrollment	5,550	
Average Daily Attendance (ADA)	93%	6
Current expense per pupil in ADA	$6,500	10
Dropout rate	11%	10
Percentage of eligible students who took the SAT	81%	10
Average combined score on SAT	1,045	10
Percentage of graduates who enrolled in 2- or 4-year colleges	87%	
Percentage of students who passed the state reading test	NK	
Percentage of students who passed the state math test	NK	
Teacher–student ratio in elementary grades	1:16	10
Teacher–student ratio in secondary grades	1:14	10
Counselor–student ratio in secondary grades	1:250	8
Number of students per music specialist in elementary grades	285	10
Number of students per art specialist in elementary grades	380	
Number of volumes in senior high school library	20,000	
Beginning teacher's salary	$20,500	
Maximum teacher's salary	$46,931	
Average years of experience among teachers	24	
Number of students suspended and expelled	741	
Subjects in which Advanced Placement courses are offered: Calculus	1	1

Quality of School Leadership
Principals are selected primarily for their educational leadership ability, and the quality of leadership is generally uniform throughout the system. Parents help screen principal candidates. Principals have some infuence in the way district resources are used.

"Very educated, articulate parents in the community demand an accounting of all decisions," said an observer. Parent organizations are considered very effective influencing school policies.

Quality of Instruction
Observers rate as good additional learning opportunities for gifted students and additional instruction for low-achieving students. Also rated good are the curricula preparing students for college and preparing students for the world of work.

While observers feel the district tries hard to meet the educational needs of minority students, some black families complain the district used test scores to segregate blacks from whites.

Quality of School Environment
The incidence of classroom disruption and student vandalism is low, and the quality of building maintenance and repair is good.

MARPLE–NEWTOWN

ADDRESS OF CENTRAL OFFICE:
120 Media Line Road, Newtown Square, PA 19073
ESI:87

STATISTICAL PROFILE	DATA	ESI
Grade organization: K–6/7–8/9–12		
Percentage of schools built before 1955	0%	
Total enrollment	3,100	
Average Daily Attendance (ADA)	95%	8
Current expense per pupil in ADA	$6,405	10
Dropout rate	2%	10
Percentage of eligible students who took the SAT	81%	10
Average combined score on SAT	982	8
Percentage of graduates who enrolled in 2- or 4-year colleges	78%	
Percentage of students who passed the state reading test	97%	
Percentage of students who passed the state math test	96%	
Teacher–student ratio in elementary grades	1:16	10
Teacher–student ratio in secondary grades	1:14	10
Counselor–student ratio in secondary grades	1:204	9
Number of students per music specialist in elementary grades	490	6
Number of students per art specialist in elementary grades	490	
Number of volumes in senior high school library	19,500	
Beginning teacher's salary	$19,622	
Maximum teacher's salary	$40,550	
Average years of experience among teachers	17	
Number of students suspended and expelled	75	
Subjects in which Advanced Placement courses are offered: American History, Biology, Calculus, Chemistry, English, Physics	6	6

FAIR APPRAISAL

Quality of School Leadership
Principals are hired because of their educational leadership ability; the quality of leadership does not vary greatly from school to school. Parents and teachers do not take part in screening principal candidates. Principals, however, have some say about the allotment of resources to their school.

While parent organizations have some effect on school policy decisions, they are more influential when it comes to getting "things" or buying "things" for the schools.

Quality of Instruction
Additional learning opportunities for gifted students and additional instruction for low-achieving students are both rated excellent. Gifted students learn as a group and are "mainstreamed" only for physical education, music and art. Also considered excellent is the curriculum preparing students for college. The curriculum preparing students for the job market is rated good.

Quality of School Environment
Classroom disruption and student vandalism are not problems; the quality of building maintenance and repair is good, but one observer said the district's preoccupation recently with asbestos removal "has allowed regular upkeep to suffer a little."

METHACTON

ADDRESS OF CENTRAL OFFICE:
Kriebel Mill Road, Norristown, PA 19403
ESI:78

STATISTICAL PROFILE	DATA	ESI
Grade organization: K–5/6–8/9–12		
Percentage of schools built before 1955	0%	
Total enrollment	3,350	
Average Daily Attendance (ADA)	96%	9
Current expense per pupil in ADA	$4,100	5
Dropout rate	4%	10
Percentage of eligible students who took the SAT	69%	10
Average combined score on SAT	944	6
Percentage of graduates who enrolled in 2- or 4-year colleges	65%	
Percentage of students who passed the state reading test	91%	
Percentage of students who passed the state math test	87%	
Teacher–student ratio in elementary grades	1:22	8
Teacher–student ratio in secondary grades	1:18	10
Counselor–student ratio in secondary grades	1:300	6
Number of students per music specialist in elementary grades	200	10
Number of students per art specialist in elementary grades	600	
Number of volumes in senior high school library	40,000†	
Beginning teacher's salary	$17,880	
Maximum teacher's salary	$38,170	
Average years of experience among teachers	17	
Number of students suspended and expelled	75	
Subjects in which Advanced Placement courses are offered: Biology, Calculus, Chemistry, English	4	4

†This number seems unusually high.

FAIR APPRAISAL

Quality of School Leadership
Popularity of candidates from within the district is an important factor, but principals are mostly chosen for their educational leadership ability. The quality of leadership does not vary greatly from school to school. Parents and teachers help screen principal candidates, and principals have a voice in determining how district resources will be allotted.

Parent participation has been declining, according to one observer, but observers still feel parent organizations are sometimes effective influencing school policies. For example, one observer said the PTA "has been instrumental in keeping the district from cutting the hours of the school libraries and the number of librarians."

Quality of Instruction
Additional learning opportunities for gifted students and additional instruction for low-achieving students are rated good. One observer thought the program for low-achievers has slipped a little. The curricula for students going to college and students going on to the world of work are rated good. However, one observer advised parents to "stay on top of counselors."

Quality of School Environment
Classroom disruption and student vandalism are not problems, and building maintenance and repair are good.

NORTH PENN

ADDRESS OF CENTRAL OFFICE:
400 Penn Street, Lansdale, PA 19446
ESI:None†

STATISTICAL PROFILE	DATA	ESI
Grade organization:		
Percentage of schools built before 1955		
Total enrollment		
Average Daily Attendance (ADA)		
Current expense per pupil in ADA		
Dropout rate		
Percentage of eligible students who took the SAT		
Average combined score on SAT		
Percentage of graduates who enrolled in 2- or 4-year colleges		
Percentage of students who passed the state reading test		
Percentage of students who passed the state math test		
Teacher–student ratio in elementary grades		
Teacher–student ratio in secondary grades		
Counselor–student ratio in secondary grades		
Number of students per music specialist in elementary grades		
Number of students per art specialist in elementary grades		
Number of volumes in senior high school library		
Beginning teacher's salary		
Maximum teacher's salary		
Average years of experience among teachers		
Number of students suspended and expelled		
Subjects in which Advanced Placement courses are offered:		

†A Statistical Profile was not received from this district.

FAIR APPRAISAL

Quality of School Leadership

The School Board hires principals who evidence ability as educational leaders. The quality of leadership is generally uniform throughout the system. Parents and teachers do not screen principal candidates. Principals have some say, but not much, as to the distribution of district resources.

Parent organizations are sometimes effective in influencing school policy decisions.

Quality of Instruction

Additional learning opportunities for gifted students are rated fair, while additional instruction for low-achieving students is rated good. The curriculum preparing students for college is considered excellent, and the curriculum for students preparing for the job market is called good.

Quality of School Environment

The level of classroom disruption and student vandalism is low, and the quality of building maintenance and repair is rated excellent.

PENN–DELCO

ADDRESS OF CENTRAL OFFICE:
95 Concord Road, Aston, PA 19014
ESI:54

STATISTICAL PROFILE	DATA	ESI
Grade organization: K–5/6–8/9–12		
Percentage of schools built before 1955	90%	
Total enrollment	3,200	
Average Daily Attendance (ADA)	93%	6
Current expense per pupil in ADA	$3,200	0
Dropout rate	5%	10
Percentage of eligible students who took the SAT	60%	9
Average combined score on SAT	907	5
Percentage of graduates who enrolled in 2- or 4-year colleges	55%	
Percentage of students who passed the state reading test	92%	
Percentage of students who passed the state math test	93%	
Teacher–student ratio in elementary grades	1:22	8
Teacher–student ratio in secondary grades	1:25	3
Counselor–student ratio in secondary grades	1:300	6
Number of students per music specialist in elementary grades	400	7
Number of students per art specialist in elementary grades	400	
Number of volumes in senior high school library	20,000	
Beginning teacher's salary	$18,000	
Maximum teacher's salary	$37,100	
Average years of experience among teachers	15	
Number of students suspended and expelled	NK	
Subjects in which Advanced Placement courses are offered:	None	0

FAIR APPRAISAL

Quality of School Leadership

Although seniority is considered, educational leadership ability is the main criterion used in the selection of principals. Also, the quality of leadership does not vary greatly from school to school. Parents and teachers do not take part in screening principal candidates. Principals, however, have some say in how resources are allotted.

Parent organizations are effective influences on school policy decisions. For example, parents lobbied for an additional third grade class and got it.

Quality of Instruction

Additional learning opportunities for gifted students are rated fair to good. They are better at the elementary level than in the upper grades, said an observer. Resource rooms help students with learning problems, and the observers rate the additional instruction for low-achieving students as good. Also considered good are the curricula for students planning on college and for students not planning on college.

Quality of School Environment

The level of classroom disruption and student vandalism is low, and the quality of building maintenance and repair is fair to good. The district usually waits "until something goes wrong," said an observer; there is a lack of preventive maintenance.

PHILADELPHIA

ADDRESS OF CENTRAL OFFICE:
Parkway at 21st Street, Philadelphia, PA 19103
ESI:35

STATISTICAL PROFILE	DATA	ESI
Grade organization: †		
Percentage of schools built before 1955	80%	
Total enrollment	201,000	
Average Daily Attendance (ADA)	85%	0
Current expense per pupil in ADA	$5,882	10
Dropout rate	NK	0
Percentage of eligible students who took the SAT	NK	0
Average combined score on SAT	772	0
Percentage of graduates who enrolled in 2- or 4-year colleges	NK	
Percentage of students who passed the state reading test	NK	
Percentage of students who passed the state math test	NK	
Teacher–student ratio in elementary grades	1:20	10
Teacher–student ratio in secondary grades	1:17	10
Counselor–student ratio in secondary grades	1:500	0
Number of students per music specialist in elementary grades	NK	0
Number of students per art specialist in elementary grades	NK	
Number of volumes in senior high school library	NK	
Beginning teacher's salary	$16,640	
Maximum teacher's salary	$38,498	
Average years of experience among teachers	18	
Number of students suspended and expelled	NK	
Subjects in which Advanced Placement courses are offered: American History, Calculus, English, Foreign Language, Science	5	5

†There are 19 variations in grade organization.

Quality of School Leadership

Most principals are hired because of their educational leadership ability, although seniority is a consideration. The quality of leadership varies greatly from school to school, but this seems to be due largely to the size of the district and the number of principals hired over many years. Parents and teachers do not screen principal candidates. Principals have some say, but not much, in the distribution of district resources.

Parent organizations are sometimes effective. It takes a major issue to rally parents throughout the city, and parents at particular schools cannot influence change much.

Quality of Instruction

Additional learning opportunities for gifted students and additional instruction for low-achieving students are both rated fair. Generally, the observers rate the curriculum for students preparing for college as good, although they point out that the quality of preparation varies depending on the high school. There are some magnet schools that are very strong in academic subjects and the arts. The curriculum for students preparing for the world of work is considered fair.

The observers think the district is not adequately meeting the educational needs of minority students. However, the district has published data that show scores on standardized achievement tests to be on the rise among black and Hispanic students as well as white students.

Quality of School Environment

The incidence of classroom disruption and student vandalism is high, but not all schools are affected. The quality of building maintenance and repair is rated fair to poor. A budget crunch in the Seventies is blamed for shortcomings by observers.

PHOENIXVILLE

ADDRESS OF CENTRAL OFFICE:
1120 South Day Street, Phoenixville, PA 19460
ESI:None†

STATISTICAL PROFILE	DATA	ESI
Grade organization:		
Percentage of schools built before 1955		
Total enrollment		
Average Daily Attendance (ADA)		
Current expense per pupil in ADA		
Dropout rate		
Percentage of eligible students who took the SAT		
Average combined score on SAT		
Percentage of graduates who enrolled in 2- or 4-year colleges		
Percentage of students who passed the state reading test		
Percentage of students who passed the state math test		
Teacher–student ratio in elementary grades		
Teacher–student ratio in secondary grades		
Counselor–student ratio in secondary grades		
Number of students per music specialist in elementary grades		
Number of students per art specialist in elementary grades		
Number of volumes in senior high school library		
Beginning teacher's salary		
Maximum teacher's salary		
Average years of experience among teachers		
Number of students suspended and expelled		
Subjects in which Advanced Placement courses are offered:		

†A Statistical Profile was not received from this district.

FAIR APPRAISAL

Quality of School Leadership

The School Board seeks principals who have ability as educational leaders, and the quality of leadership does not vary greatly from school to school. Parents and teachers do not screen principal candidates. Principals have a great deal to say about the distribution of district resources to the schools.

Parent organizations are sometimes effective influencing school policy decisions.

Quality of Instruction

Additional learning opportunities for gifted students are rated good. The program is strong at all levels. Additional instruction for low-achieving students is considered excellent. "Much individual attention is offered," said an observer. The curricula for college-bound students and job-bound students are rated excellent.

Quality of School Environment

Classroom disruption and student vandalism are not problems, and the quality of building maintenance and repair is good.

RADNOR TOWNSHIP

ADDRESS OF CENTRAL OFFICE:
135 South Wayne Avenue, Wayne, PA 19087
ESI:None†

STATISTICAL PROFILE	DATA	ESI
Grade organization:		
Percentage of schools built before 1955		
Total enrollment		
Average Daily Attendance (ADA)		
Current expense per pupil in ADA		
Dropout rate		
Percentage of eligible students who took the SAT		
Average combined score on SAT		
Percentage of graduates who enrolled in 2- or 4-year colleges		
Percentage of students who passed the state reading test		
Percentage of students who passed the state math test		
Teacher–student ratio in elementary grades		
Teacher–student ratio in secondary grades		
Counselor–student ratio in secondary grades		
Number of students per music specialist in elementary grades		
Number of students per art specialist in elementary grades		
Number of volumes in senior high school library		
Beginning teacher's salary		
Maximum teacher's salary		
Average years of experience among teachers		
Number of students suspended and expelled		
Subjects in which Advanced Placement courses are offered:		

†A Statistical Profile was not received from this district.

FAIR APPRAISAL

Quality of School Leadership

The School Board looks for principals with educational leadership ability, and the quality of leadership is generally uniform throughout the system. Parents and teachers do not screen principal candidates, although they may make their views known informally. Principals have some influence over the division of district resources among the schools.

Strong parent organizations exist at each school, said an observer, and principals meet with organization leaders frequently.

Quality of Instruction

Additional learning opportunities for gifted students and additional instruction for low-achieving students are rated excellent. Also considered excellent are the college preparatory curriculum and the curriculum designed for students not planning on college. "We recently won an award for being one of the best school districts in the state," said an observer.

Quality of School Environment

The level of classroom disruption and student vandalism is very low, and the quality of building maintenance and repair is very high.

SOUTHEAST DELCO

ADDRESS OF CENTRAL OFFICE:
Delmar Drive & Primos Avenue, Folcroft, PA 19032
ESI:61*

STATISTICAL PROFILE	DATA	ESI
Grade organization: K–6/7–8/9–12		
Percentage of schools built before 1955	0%	
Total enrollment	3,613	
Average Daily Attendance (ADA)	92%	5
Current expense per pupil in ADA	$5,661	10
Dropout rate	15%	8
Percentage of eligible students who took the SAT	80%	10
Average combined score on SAT	800	0
Percentage of graduates who enrolled in 2- or 4-year colleges	44%	
Percentage of students who passed the state reading test	NK	
Percentage of students who passed the state math test	NK	
Teacher–student ratio in elementary grades	1:21	9
Teacher–student ratio in secondary grades	1:19	9
Counselor–student ratio in secondary grades	†	0*
Number of students per music specialist in elementary grades	303	9
Number of students per art specialist in elementary grades	612	
Number of volumes in senior high school library	14,000	
Beginning teacher's salary	$19,500	
Maximum teacher's salary	$39,071	
Average years of experience among teachers	14	
Number of students suspended and expelled	373	
Subjects in which Advanced Placement courses are offered: English	1	1

†The district supplied an inappropriate statistic.

Quality of School Leadership
Internal politics play a part in principal selection, but primarily the district looks for principals with educational leadership ability. The quality of leadership is generally uniform throughout the system. Parents and teachers do not help screen principal candidates, but principals have some say in the allotment of resources to their school.

Parents do very well with bake sales, said one observer, but another observer reported that parents' influence in important matters "really doesn't count."

Quality of Instruction
Additional learning opportunities for gifted students and additional instruction for low-achieving students are rated good. Also rated good are the curricula for college-bound students and for students heading into the world of work. However, an observer noted that although the vocational-technical program is excellent, the district "has trouble getting students to enroll."

Quality of School Environment
The level of classroom disruption and student vandalism is low, and the quality of building maintenance and repair is good.

TREDYFFRIN–EASTTOWN

ADDRESS OF CENTRAL OFFICE:
First Street & Bridge Avenue, Berwyn, PA 19312
ESI:71

STATISTICAL PROFILE	DATA	ESI
Grade organization: K–6/7–9/10–12		
Percentage of schools built before 1955	25%	
Total enrollment	4,357	
Average Daily Attendance (ADA)	94%	7
Current expense per pupil in ADA	$3,893	4
Dropout rate	1%	10
Percentage of eligible students who took the SAT	90%	10
Average combined score on SAT	984	8
Percentage of graduates who enrolled in 2- or 4-year colleges	86%	
Percentage of students who passed the state reading test	94%	
Percentage of students who passed the state math test	95%	
Teacher–student ratio in elementary grades	1:23	7
Teacher–student ratio in secondary grades	1:25	3
Counselor–student ratio in secondary grades	1:188	10
Number of students per music specialist in elementary grades	440	7
Number of students per art specialist in elementary grades	440	
Number of volumes in senior high school library	35,000	
Beginning teacher's salary	$18,449	
Maximum teacher's salary	$49,592	
Average years of experience among teachers	18	
Number of students suspended and expelled	NK	
Subjects in which Advanced Placement courses are offered: American History, Art History, European History, French, Spanish	5	5

Quality of School Leadership
Principals are hired mainly because of their educational leadership ability; the quality of leadership is generally uniform throughout the system. Parents and teachers have hardly any say in the selection of principals. However, principals have some say in how the resources of the district are distributed.

Parent organizations are effective as an influence on district policy-making. Parents have had a voice recently in such matters as sex education, transportation, and girls' sports.

Quality of Instruction
Additional learning opportunities and additional instruction for low-achieving students are rated good. The curriculum preparing students for college is considered excellent, but the curriculum for students not planning on college is only rated fair to good.

Quality of School Environment
Classroom disruption and student vandalism are not problems, and the quality of building maintenance and repair is generally good. However, one observer pointed out that asbestos removal set back other improvement projects.

UPPER MERION

ADDRESS OF CENTRAL OFFICE:
435 Crossfield Road, King of Prussia, PA 19406
ESI:92

STATISTICAL PROFILE	DATA	ESI
Grade organization: K–4/5–8/9–12		
Percentage of schools built before 1955	0%	
Total enrollment	3,254	
Average Daily Attendance (ADA)	96%	9
Current expense per pupil in ADA	$7,111†	10
Dropout rate	6%	10
Percentage of eligible students who took the SAT	82%	10
Average combined score on SAT	986	9
Percentage of graduates who enrolled in 2- or 4-year colleges	77%	
Percentage of students who passed the state reading test	95%	
Percentage of students who passed the state math test	98%	
Teacher–student ratio in elementary grades	1:11	10
Teacher–student ratio in secondary grades	1:11	10
Counselor–student ratio in secondary grades	1:210	9
Number of students per music specialist in elementary grades	120	10
Number of students per art specialist in elementary grades	135	
Number of volumes in senior high school library	25,860	
Beginning teacher's salary	$21,290†	
Maximum teacher's salary	$42,150†	
Average years of experience among teachers	19	
Number of students suspended and expelled	146†	
Subjects in which Advanced Placement courses are offered: American History, Calculus, English, Foreign Languages, Science	5	5

†1986–87 statistics.

FAIR APPRAISAL

Quality of School Leadership

Principals are hired primarily because they have the ability to be educational leaders; the quality of leadership does not vary greatly from school to school. Parents and teachers have hardly any say in the selection of principals, but principals have some say about the use of district resources.

Parent organizations are sometimes effective influencing school decision-making.

Quality of Instruction

Additional learning opportunities for gifted students are considered good, but additional instruction for low-achieving students is rated only fair. The curricula for students going to college and for students going into the work force are both rated good.

Quality of School Environment

Classroom disruption and student vandalism are not problems, and the quality of building maintenance and repair is good.

UPPER MORELAND TOWNSHIP

ADDRESS OF CENTRAL OFFICE:
Terwood Road, Willow Grove, PA 19090
ESI:55

STATISTICAL PROFILE	DATA	ESI
Grade organization: K–5/6–8/9–12		
Percentage of schools built before 1955	0%	
Total enrollment	3,034	
Average Daily Attendance (ADA)	95%	8
Current expense per pupil in ADA	$4,734	8
Dropout rate	NK	0
Percentage of eligible students who took the SAT	72%	10
Average combined score on SAT	953	7
Percentage of graduates who enrolled in 2- or 4-year colleges	59%	
Percentage of students who passed the state reading test	87%	
Percentage of students who passed the state math test	83%	
Teacher–student ratio in elementary grades	1:22	8
Teacher–student ratio in secondary grades	1:24	4
Counselor–student ratio in secondary grades	1:338	4
Number of students per music specialist in elementary grades	384	
Number of students per art specialist in elementary grades	792	
Number of volumes in senior high school library	31,199	
Beginning teacher's salary	$15,020	
Maximum teacher's salary	$36,585	
Average years of experience among teachers	15	
Number of students suspended and expelled	360	
Subjects in which Advanced Placement courses are offered: Biology, Calculus, Chemistry, English, European History, Physics	6	6

FAIR APPRAISAL

Quality of School Leadership

Longevity helps, but principals are selected primarily for their educational leadership ability. The quality of leadership does not vary greatly from school to school. Parents and teachers do not take part in screening principal candidates. Principals, on the other hand, have some say about the allotment of resources to their school.

"The School Board is very responsive to parents," said an observer, and parents organizations are generally effective influencing district decisions.

Quality of Instruction

Additional learning opportunities for gifted students and additional instruction for low-achieving students are rated good. Also considered good are the curricula for college-bound students and for students bound for the world of work.

Quality of School Environment

The incidence of classroom disruption and student vandalism is low, and the quality of building maintenance and repair is good.

WALLINGFORD–SWARTHMORE

ADDRESS OF CENTRAL OFFICE:
200 South Providence Road, Wallingford, PA 19086
ESI:83

STATISTICAL PROFILE	DATA	ESI
Grade organization: K–5/6–8/9–12		
Percentage of schools built before 1955	86%	
Total enrollment	2,772	
Average Daily Attendance (ADA)	95%	8
Current expense per pupil in ADA	$3,790	3
Dropout rate	1%	10
Percentage of eligible students who took the SAT or ACT	90%	10
Average combined score on SAT or ACT	995	9
Percentage of graduates who enrolled in 2- or 4-year colleges	84%	
Percentage of students who passed the state reading test	95%	
Percentage of students who passed the state math test	97%	
Teacher–student ratio in elementary grades	1:18	10
Teacher–student ratio in secondary grades	1:12	10
Counselor–student ratio in secondary grades	1:349	4
Number of students per music specialist in elementary grades	325	9
Number of students per art specialist in elementary grades	432	
Number of volumes in senior high school library	30,000	
Beginning teacher's salary	$17,200	
Maximum teacher's salary	$40,172	
Average years of experience among teachers	17	
Number of students suspended and expelled	184	
Subjects in which Advanced Placement courses are offered:	13	10
American History, Biology, Calculus AB, Calculus BC, Chemistry, Computer Science, English Language and Composition, English Literature and Composition, French Language, Physics (mechanics), Physics (electricity-magnetism), Spanish Language, Spanish Literature		

FAIR APPRAISAL

Quality of School Leadership

The School Board hires principals who evidence ability as educational leaders; the quality of leadership is generally uniform throughout the system. Parents and teachers serve on committees that help screen principal candidates. Also, principals influence the distribution of the district's resources.

Parents and other community residents serve on curriculum evaluation committees, and they were helpful in planning for the closing of some schools.

Quality of Instruction

Additional learning opportunities for gifted students and additional instruction for low-achieving students are rated good. The program for gifted children is being revamped, an observer said, which should make it even better. The college preparatory curriculum is considered excellent. The number of Advanced Placement courses is particularly high for a district of this size. The curriculum for students not planning on college is considered good.

The district does not have a large minority enrollment, and most minority students do well in the system. However, one observer noted that a strict tracking system "prevents some minority students from switching from a lower to a higher track."

Quality of School Environment

The level of classroom disruption and student vandalism is low, and the quality of building maintenance and repair is good.

WASHINGTON TOWNSHIP, NJ

ADDRESS OF CENTRAL OFFICE:
RD 3, Box 286, Sewell, NJ 08080
ESI:50

STATISTICAL PROFILE	DATA	ESI
Grade organization: K–6/7–9/10–12		
Percentage of schools built before 1955	11%	
Total enrollment	6,600	
Average Daily Attendance (ADA)	92%	5
Current expense per pupil in ADA	NK	0
Dropout rate	NK	0
Percentage of eligible students who took the SAT	53%	8
Average combined score on SAT	901	4
Percentage of graduates who enrolled in 2- or 4-year colleges	55%	
Percentage of students who passed the state reading test	92%	
Percentage of students who passed the state math test	80%	
Teacher–student ratio in elementary grades	1:27	3
Teacher–student ratio in secondary grades	1:15	10
Counselor–student ratio in secondary grades	1:280	6
Number of students per music specialist in elementary grades	129	10
Number of students per art specialist in elementary grades	616	
Number of volumes in senior high school library	25,763	
Beginning teacher's salary	$18,500	
Maximum teacher's salary	$35,700	
Average years of experience among teachers	12	
Number of students suspended and expelled	117	
Subjects in which Advanced Placement courses are offered:	4	4
American History, Calculus, Chemistry, English		

FAIR APPRAISAL

Quality of School Leadership

The School Board selects principals primarily for their educational leadership ability, and the quality of leadership does not vary greatly from school to school. Parents and teachers do not help screen principal candidates. Principals, however, have some say in how district resources are allotted to their school.

Parent organizations are not very effective influencing district policy decisions.

Quality of Instruction

Additional learning opportunities for gifted students and additional instruction for low-achieving students are rated fair. Observers complained that both programs are weakest in the elementary grades. The curriculum for students planning on college is considered good, but the curriculum for students not planning on college is only rated fair to poor. One observer said not every student who could profit from vocational-technical training can get into the county vocational school because of "insufficient spaces allotted to the district."

The district generally meets the educational needs of minority students, but one observer complained that district officials "like to ignore the fact that the district has minorities."

Quality of School Environment

Classroom disruption and student vandalism are not problems, and the quality of building maintenance and repair is considered good.

WEST CHESTER

ADDRESS OF CENTRAL OFFICE:
829 Paoli Pike, West Chester, PA 19380
ESI:65

STATISTICAL PROFILE	DATA	ESI
Grade organization: K–5/6–8/9–12		
Percentage of schools built before 1955	14%	
Total enrollment	9,208	
Average Daily Attendance (ADA)	95%	8
Current expense per pupil in ADA	$4,679	8
Dropout rate	4%	10
Percentage of eligible students who took the SAT	70%	10
Average combined score on SAT	948	7
Percentage of graduates who enrolled in 2- or 4-year colleges	NK	
Percentage of students who passed the state reading test	NK	
Percentage of students who passed the state math test	NK	
Teacher–student ratio in elementary grades	1:22	8
Teacher–student ratio in secondary grades	1:23	5
Counselor–student ratio in secondary grades	1:330	9
Number of students per music specialist in elementary grades	302	
Number of students per art specialist in elementary grades	540	
Number of volumes in senior high school libraries (average)	20,250	
Beginning teacher's salary	$18,480	
Maximum teacher's salary	$43,504	
Average years of experience among teachers	15	
Number of students suspended and expelled	NK	
Subjects in which Advanced Placement courses are offered:	None	0

FAIR APPRAISAL

Quality of School Leadership

Principals are hired primarily because of their educational leadership ability; the quality of leadership is generally uniform throughout the system. Parents and teachers do not aid in the screening of principal candidates, but principals have some say in how district resources will be allotted to their school.

Parent organizations are sometimes effective influencing school decision-making. In some schools, an observer said, parent organizations are primarily fund-raisers, but in other schools they influence curriculum and other matters.

Quality of Instruction

Additional learning opportunities for gifted students are considered excellent, although one observer said that some parents are not happy with the selection process. Additional instruction for low-achieving students is only rated fair. The program is good through about grade 2, observers said, but after that "there's very little." The curriculum preparing students for college is rated excellent, while the curriculum for students not planning on college is rated good.

The observers are divided on whether the district is adequately meeting the educational needs of minority students. One observer reported that the NAACP has censored the district for a poor desegregation plan.

Quality of School Environment

The level of classroom disruption and student vandalism is low, and the quality of building maintenance and repair is excellent.

WILLIAM PENN

ADDRESS OF CENTRAL OFFICE:
Bell Avenue and MacDade Boulevard, Yeadon, PA 19050
ESI:None†

STATISTICAL PROFILE	DATA	ESI
Grade organization:		
Percentage of schools built before 1955		
Total enrollment		
Average Daily Attendance (ADA)		
Current expense per pupil in ADA		
Dropout rate		
Percentage of eligible students who took the SAT		
Average combined score on SAT		
Percentage of graduates who enrolled in 2- or 4-year colleges		
Percentage of students who passed the state reading test		
Percentage of students who passed the state math test		
Teacher–student ratio in elementary grades		
Teacher–student ratio in secondary grades		
Counselor–student ratio in secondary grades		
Number of students per music specialist in elementary grades		
Number of students per art specialist in elementary grades		
Number of volumes in senior high school library		
Beginning teacher's salary		
Maximum teacher's salary		
Average years of experience among teachers		
Number of students suspended and expelled		
Subjects in which Advanced Placement courses are offered:		

†A Statistical Profile was not received from this district.

FAIR APPRAISAL

Quality of School Leadership

The School Board hires principals who evidence ability as educational leaders; the quality of leadership does not vary greatly from school to school. Parents and teachers do not screen principal candidates. Principals have some say about the way district resources are used.

Parent organizations are sometimes effective influencing school decision-making.

Quality of Instruction

Additional learning opportunities for gifted students are rated good. At the elementary level, gifted students have enrichment for a half day every six days. Additional instruction for low-achieving students is also rated good. The district's reading remediation program is "highly successful," said one observer. The college preparatory curriculum is considered good, and the curriculum for students not planning on college is rated fair.

Quality of School Environment

Classroom disruption and student vandalism are not problems. The quality of building maintenance and repair is rated fair to good.

WILLINGBORO

ADDRESS OF CENTRAL OFFICE:
Levitt Building, Salem Road, Willingboro, NJ 08046
ESI:45

STATISTICAL PROFILE	DATA	ESI
Grade organization: K–7/8–12		
Percentage of schools built before 1955	0%	
Total enrollment	6,982	
Average Daily Attendance (ADA)	91%	4
Current expense per pupil in ADA	$3,548	2
Dropout rate	23%	0
Percentage of eligible students who took the SAT	35%	4
Average combined score on SAT	900	4
Percentage of graduates who enrolled in 2- or 4-year colleges	60%	
Percentage of students who passed the state reading test	†	
Percentage of students who passed the state math test	†	
Teacher–student ratio in elementary grades	1:19	10
Teacher–student ratio in secondary grades	1:25	3
Counselor–student ratio in secondary grades	1:320	5
Number of students per music specialist in elementary grades	442	7
Number of students per art specialist in elementary grades	500	
Number of volumes in senior high school library	40,000††	
Beginning teacher's salary	$18,500	
Maximum teacher's salary	$35,315	
Average years of experience among teachers	20	
Number of students suspended and expelled	1,200	
Subjects in which Advanced Placement courses are offered: American History, Calculus, Computer Science, English, Foreign Language, Science	6	6

† The district inadvertently left out these statistics.
††This number seems unusually high.

FAIR APPRAISAL

Quality of School Leadership
Longevity and popularity are factors in choosing principals, but principals are hired primarily for their educational leadership ability. Some variation in quality of leadership exists, according to observers. Parents and teachers do not take part in principal selection. Principals, however, have some influence over the distribution of district resources.

Parent organizations are considered sometimes effective.

Quality of Instruction
"Both parents and teachers are happy" with the additional learning opportunities for gifted students, said an observer, and the program is rated excellent. In the upper grades, said another observer, gifted students are grouped for all subjects, and at the elementary level gifted students have special enrichment one day a week. Additional instruction for low-achieving students is considered only fair. The curricula for college-bound students and for those students heading for the world of work are both considered good.

The district meets the educational needs of most minority students, but one observer complained that only 5 percent of teachers are black when approximately 50 percent of the students are.

Quality of School Environment
The level of classroom disruption and student vandalism is on the high side, but the quality of building maintenance and repair is good to excellent.

WISSAHICKON

ADDRESS OF CENTRAL OFFICE:
601 Knight Road, Ambler, PA 19002
ESI:69*

STATISTICAL PROFILE	DATA	ESI
Grade organization: K–3/4–5/6–8/9–12		
Percentage of schools built before 1955	0%	
Total enrollment	2,900	
Average Daily Attendance (ADA)	99%	10
Current expense per pupil in ADA	$4,694	8
Dropout rate	10%	10
Percentage of eligible students who took the SAT	76%	10
Average combined score on SAT	950	7
Percentage of graduates who enrolled in 2- or 4-year colleges	73%	
Percentage of students who passed the state reading test	94%	
Percentage of students who passed the state math test	94%	
Teacher–student ratio in elementary grades	1:24	5
Teacher–student ratio in secondary grades	1:14	10
Counselor–student ratio in secondary grades	1:283	6
Number of students per music specialist in elementary grades	†	0*
Number of students per art specialist in elementary grades	†	
Number of volumes in senior high school library	19,811	
Beginning teacher's salary	$19,971	
Maximum teacher's salary	$40,566	
Average years of experience among teachers	17	
Number of students suspended and expelled	253	
Subjects in which Advanced Placement courses are offered: American History, Calculus, English	3	3

†The district misinterpreted this statistic.

FAIR APPRAISAL

Quality of School Leadership
Principals are hired primarily for their ability as educational leaders, and the quality of leadership does not vary greatly from school to school. Parents and teachers serve on committees screening principal candidates. Principals also have a great deal of influence over the allotment of resources to their school.

Parent organizations are effective influencing school decisions. For example, they have initiated some curricular changes and have lobbied for a full-day kindergarten.

Quality of Instruction
Additional learning opportunities for gifted students are rated good, although one observer said the quality is better in the elementary schools than in the upper grades. Additional instruction for low-achievers is considered good. "It's a dynamic program," said one observer. The curricula for students planning on college and for students planning to enter the job market are rated excellent.

Quality of School Environment
The level of classroom disruption and student vandalism is low, and the quality of building maintenance and repair is excellent.

METROPOLITAN AREA

Phoenix, AZ

Completed Statistical Profiles were received from five districts. Districts in this area may be compared to districts in the San Antonio, TX Metropolitan Area.

AREA AT A GLANCE

SCHOOL DISTRICT	ENROLLMENT	ESI
Chandler	9,587	62
Deer Valley	13,600	35
Gilbert	6,658	58
Mesa	56,000	34
Peoria	16,000	21*

Indicates district misinterpretation of one or more statistics in the ESI. For each misinterpreted statistic, a score of 0 was given instead of a possible score of 0 to 10 points.

SCHOOL DISTRICT

CHANDLER

ADDRESS OF CENTRAL OFFICE:
500 West Galveston Street, Chandler, AZ 85224
ESI:62

STATISTICAL PROFILE	DATA	ESI
Grade organization: K–6/7–9/10–12		
Percentage of schools built before 1955	25%	
Total enrollment	9,587	
Average Daily Attendance (ADA)	97%	10
Current expense per pupil in ADA	$2,630	5
Dropout rate	6%	10
Percentage of eligible students who took the ACT	38%	5
Average combined score on ACT	20.8	10
Percentage of graduates who enrolled in 2- or 4-year colleges	55%	
Percentage of students who passed the state reading test	99%	
Percentage of students who passed the state math test	99%	
Teacher–student ratio in elementary grades	1:22	8
Teacher–student ratio in secondary grades	1:20	8
Counselor–student ratio in secondary grades	1:450	0
Number of students per music specialist in elementary grades	852	0
Number of students per art specialist in elementary grades	5,676	
Number of volumes in senior high school library	17,027	
Beginning teacher's salary	$20,000	
Maximum teacher's salary	$37,000	
Average years of experience among teachers	10	
Number of students suspended and expelled	100	
Subjects in which Advanced Placement courses are offered:	6	6
Calculus, English, French, German, Science, Spanish		

FAIR APPRAISAL

Quality of School Leadership
The School Board hires principals primarily for their educational leadership ability, and the quality of leadership does not vary greatly from school to school. PTO representatives serve on a "paper" screening committee, which examines the applications of principal candidates. Principals have little say in how the district distributes resources to the schools.

Parent organizations are sometimes effective influencing school decision-making.

Quality of Instruction
Additional learning opportunities for gifted students are rated good. Gifted students in the elementary grades are grouped together for instruction. The International Baccalaureate program is available to exceptional students in the high school. Additional instruction for low-achieving students is considered only fair. The curriculum preparing students for college is rated good, while the curriculum preparing students for the world of work is called fair.
Some of the schools have received awards for excellence from the state and federal education departments.

Quality of School Environment
The level of classroom disruption and student vandalism is low. Students have an incentive to prevent acts of vandalism. Each school is given a sum of money at the start of the school year to pay for damage caused by vandalism. Whatever money is left at the end of the year can be used for an activity arranged by students (and approved by school officials). The quality of building maintenance and repair is good.

DEER VALLEY

ADDRESS OF CENTRAL OFFICE:
20402 North 15th Avenue, Phoenix, AZ 85027
ESI:35

STATISTICAL PROFILE	DATA	ESI
Grade organization: †		
Percentage of schools built before 1955	7%	
Total enrollment	13,600	
Average Daily Attendance (ADA)	95%	8
Current expense per pupil in ADA	$2,800	5
Dropout rate	NK	0
Percentage of eligible students who took the SAT or ACT	NK	0
Average combined score on SAT or ACT	NK	0
Percentage of graduates who enrolled in 2- or 4-year colleges	60%	
Percentage of students who passed the state reading test	89%	
Percentage of students who passed the state math test	NK	
Teacher–student ratio in elementary grades	1:18	10
Teacher–student ratio in secondary grades	1:18	10
Counselor–student ratio in secondary grades	1:450	0
Number of students per music specialist in elementary grades	NK	0
Number of students per art specialist in elementary grades	NK	
Number of volumes in senior high school library	NK	
Beginning teacher's salary	$17,425	
Maximum teacher's salary	$36,767	
Average years of experience among teachers	NK	
Number of students suspended and expelled	NK	
Subjects in which Advanced Placement courses are offered: Calculus, Science	2	2

†The district misinterpreted this statistic.

FAIR APPRAISAL

Quality of School Leadership
Principals are hired mostly for their educational leadership ability. An "old boy" system of hiring that prevailed in the past has resulted in some variations in the quality of leadership in the system, said an observer. Parents and teachers have hardly any say in the selection of principals, and principals have little say over resource allotment.

Parent organizations have some influence in school policy, but nothing compared to the teachers' union, said an observer. Parents are more influential in established areas of the district, less so in fairly new housing developments.

Quality of Instruction
Additional learning opportunities for gifted students are rated fair. "They're just getting up to the levels of other districts," said an observer. Also rated fair is additional instruction for low-achieving students. "But it's getting better," said an observer. The curriculum for college-bound students is good, and the curriculum for students not planning on college is rated excellent. The vocational-technical program is one of the best in the state, said one observer. "It's the district's strong suit."

Quality of School Environment
Classroom disruption and student vandalism are not problems. Building maintenance and repair are good.

GILBERT

ADDRESS OF CENTRAL OFFICE:
P.O. Drawer 1, Gilbert, AZ 85234
ESI:58

STATISTICAL PROFILE	DATA	ESI
Grade organization: K–6/7–8/9–12		
Percentage of schools built before 1955	12%	
Total enrollment	6,658	
Average Daily Attendance (ADA)	94%	7
Current expense per pupil in ADA	$3,422	8
Dropout rate	8%	10
Percentage of eligible students who took the ACT	36%	5
Average combined score on ACT	18.9	5
Percentage of graduates who enrolled in 2- or 4-year colleges	62%	
Percentage of students who passed the state reading test	98%	
Percentage of students who passed the state math test	98%	
Teacher–student ratio in elementary grades	1:24	6
Teacher–student ratio in secondary grades	1:26	2
Counselor–student ratio in secondary grades	1:400	2
Number of students per music specialist in elementary grades	320	9
Number of students per art specialist in elementary grades	None	
Number of volumes in senior high school library	13,268	
Beginning teacher's salary	$18,640	
Maximum teacher's salary	$36,292	
Average years of experience among teachers	8	
Number of students suspended and expelled	138	
Subjects in which Advanced Placement courses are offered: American Government, Biology, Chemistry, English	4	4

FAIR APPRAISAL

Quality of School Leadership
Most principals are hired for their educational leadership ability, and the quality of leadership is generally uniform throughout the system. Parents and teachers do not interview principal candidates, but principals have some say in how the district divides resources.

Parent organizations are sometimes effective as an influence on district policy.

Quality of Instruction
Additional learning opportunities for gifted students are rated excellent, while additional instruction for low-achieving students is rated good. The curricula for college-bound students and job-bound students are both considered excellent. The district is growing rapidly, like most districts in the Phoenix area, and, according to an observer, people who move in here are "really pleased about the schools."

Quality of School Environment
The level of classroom disruption and student vandalism is low, and the quality of building maintenance and repair is excellent.

MESA

ADDRESS OF CENTRAL OFFICE:
549 North Stapkey Drive, Mesa, AZ 85203
ESI:34

STATISTICAL PROFILE	DATA	ESI
Grade organization: †		
Percentage of schools built before 1955	6%	
Total enrollment	56,000	
Average Daily Attendance (ADA)	95%	8
Current expense per pupil in ADA	$3,200	7
Dropout rate	24%	0
Percentage of eligible students who took the ACT	14%	0
Average combined score on ACT	20.5	8
Percentage of graduates who enrolled in 2- or 4-year colleges	79%	
Percentage of students who passed the state reading test	82%	
Percentage of students who passed the state math test	78%	
Teacher–student ratio in elementary grades	1:28	2
Teacher–student ratio in secondary grades	1:26	2
Counselor–student ratio in secondary grades	1:450	0
Number of students per music specialist in elementary grades	874	0
Number of students per art specialist in elementary grades	1,050	
Number of volumes in senior high school library	††	
Beginning teacher's salary	$18,317	
Maximum teacher's salary	$38,038	
Average years of experience among teachers	NK	
Number of students suspended and expelled	456	
Subjects in which Advanced Placement courses are offered: American History, Art, Calculus, English, Foreign Language, Music, Science	7	7

† The district misinterpreted this statistic.
††The district uses the statistic of 11 books per student.

FAIR APPRAISAL

Quality of School Leadership
Principals are hired for their leadership ability, and the quality of leadership does not vary greatly from school to school. According to an observer, the district has a strong training program for would-be principals among the district's teachers. Parents and teachers have hardly any say in the selection of principals, and principals have little influence over allotment of district resources.

Parent organizations are considered effective.

Quality of Instruction
Additional learning opportunities for gifted students are rated good. Students in the elementary grades are excused from regular classes to attend enrichment classes one day a week. Additional instruction for low-achieving students is also rated good. The program is particularly strong in kindergarten through grade 3, said an observer. The curriculum for students preparing for college is called good and "getting better." The curriculum for students not planning on college is rated only fair.

The district has a very good program for teaching English as a second language, said an observer.

Quality of School Environment
The level of classroom disruption and student vandalism is low. Building maintenance and repair are good.

PEORIA

ADDRESS OF CENTRAL OFFICE:
P.O. Box 39, Peoria, AZ 85345
ESI:21*

STATISTICAL PROFILE	DATA	ESI
Grade organization: K–8/9–12		
Percentage of schools built before 1955	6%	
Total enrollment	16,000	
Average Daily Attendance (ADA)	96%	9
Current expense per pupil in ADA	NK	0
Dropout rate	22%	1
Percentage of eligible students who took the SAT or ACT	NK	0
Average combined score on SAT or ACT	NK	0
Percentage of graduates who enrolled in 2- or 4-year colleges	70%	
Percentage of students who passed the state reading test	NK	
Percentage of students who passed the state math test	NK	
Teacher–student ratio in elementary grades	1:26	4
Teacher–student ratio in secondary grades	1:24	4
Counselor–student ratio in secondary grades	1:370	3
Number of students per music specialist in elementary grades	††	0*
Number of students per art specialist in elementary grades	†††	
Number of volumes in senior high school library	NK	
Beginning teacher's salary	$20,000	
Maximum teacher's salary	$41,000	
Average years of experience among teachers	9	
Number of students suspended and expelled	NK	
Subjects in which Advanced Placement courses are offered:	None†	0

† See Fair Appraisal.
†† Two per school.
†††Handled by classroom teachers.

FAIR APPRAISAL

Quality of School Leadership
The School Board hires principals who demonstrate ability as educational leaders. The quality of leadership is generally uniform throughout the system. Parents and teachers have hardly any say in the selection of principals, but principals have some influence over the distribution of district resources.

Parent organizations are sometimes effective as an influence on school policy.

Quality of Instruction
Additional learning opportunities for gifted students are rated fair, and so is additional instruction for low-achieving students. However, one observer praised the district's dropout prevention program. The curricula for students going to college and for those not planning on college are both considered good. An adjacent community college offers high-level courses for especially bright high school students.

Quality of School Environment
Classroom disruption and student vandalism are not problems, and the quality of building maintenance and repair is excellent.

Pittsburgh, PA

Seventeen districts completed Statistical Profiles, and a Fair Appraisal alone is provided for one other district. Some districts did not include scores for state competency tests in reading and math; one district said the statistics were not applicable in Pennsylvania. However, the State does administer basic skills (competency) tests, called TELLS, and most districts included their students' scores on these tests. Districts in this area may be compared to districts in the Philadelphia, PA and Cincinnati, OH Metropolitan Areas.

AREA AT A GLANCE

SCHOOL DISTRICT	ENROLLMENT	ESI
Baldwin-Whitehall	4,640	74
Canon-McMillan	4,200	61
Chartiers Valley	2,780	74*
Fox Chapel Area	3,339	92
Hampton Township	2,458	
Hempfield Area	7,835	55
Keystone Oaks	2,943	78
Moon Area	3,384	68
Mount Lebanon	5,031	92
North Allegheny	6,607	63
North Hills	4,651	62
Peters Township	2,475	61
Pittsburgh	40,038	49
Plum Borough	4,361	68
Shaler Area	4,876	66*
Upper St. Clair Township	3,780	79
West Jefferson Hills	2,800	74
West Mifflin Area	3,169	55*

Indicates district misinterpretation of one or more statistics in the ESI. For each misinterpreted statistic, a score of 0 was given instead of a possible score of 0 to 10 points.

BALDWIN–WHITEHALL

ADDRESS OF CENTRAL OFFICE:
4900 Curry Road, Pittsburgh, PA 15236
ESI:74

STATISTICAL PROFILE	DATA	ESI
Grade organization: K–6/7–8/9–12		
Percentage of schools built before 1955	2%	
Total enrollment	4,640	
Average Daily Attendance (ADA)	92%	5
Current expense per pupil in ADA	$5,068	10
Dropout rate	6%	10
Percentage of eligible students who took the SAT	70%	10
Average combined score on SAT	912	5
Percentage of graduates who enrolled in 2- or 4-year colleges	82%	
Percentage of students who passed the state reading test	83%	
Percentage of students who passed the state math test	83%	
Teacher–student ratio in elementary grades	1:22	8
Teacher–student ratio in secondary grades	1:16	10
Counselor–student ratio in secondary grades	1:291	6
Number of students per music specialist in elementary grades	439	7
Number of students per art specialist in elementary grades	390	
Number of volumes in senior high school library	22,346	
Beginning teacher's salary	$19,100	
Maximum teacher's salary	$35,952	
Average years of experience among teachers	18	
Number of students suspended and expelled	185	
Subjects in which Advanced Placement courses are offered: American History, English, European History	3	3

FAIR APPRAISAL

Quality of School Leadership

Principals are hired for their educational leadership ability, but the district hasn't appointed a principal for approximately six years because of declining enrollment and school closings. The quality of leadership is generally uniform throughout the system. Parents and teachers do not help screen principal candidates. Principals, however, have some influence over the distribution of district resources.

Parent organizations are sometimes effective influencing school decisions.

Quality of Instruction

Additional learning opportunities for gifted students are rated good, but the program only goes as far as grade 6, according to the observers. Additional instruction for low-achieving students also is rated good. The curricula for students planning on college and for those not planning on college are both rated good.

Quality of School Environment

The incidence of classroom disruption and student vandalism is low, and the quality of building maintenance and repair is good.

CANON–McMILLAN

ADDRESS OF CENTRAL OFFICE:
1 North Jefferson Avenue, Canonsburg, PA 15317
ESI:61

STATISTICAL PROFILE	DATA	ESI
Grade organization: †		
Percentage of schools built before 1955	NK	
Total enrollment	4,200	
Average Daily Attendance (ADA)	97%	10
Current expense per pupil in ADA	NK	0
Dropout rate	4%	10
Percentage of eligible students who took the SAT	75%	10
Average combined score on SAT	840	1
Percentage of graduates who enrolled in 2- or 4-year colleges	60%	
Percentage of students who passed the state reading test	86%	
Percentage of students who passed the state math test	82%	
Teacher–student ratio in elementary grades	1:19	10
Teacher–student ratio in secondary grades	1:17	10
Counselor–student ratio in secondary grades	1:425	1
Number of students per music specialist in elementary grades	500	5
Number of students per art specialist in elementary grades	700	
Number of volumes in senior high school library	12,000	
Beginning teacher's salary	$13,600	
Maximum teacher's salary	$33,100	
Average years of experience among teachers	15	
Number of students suspended and expelled	100	
Subjects in which Advanced Placement courses are offered: American History, Calculus, English, Science	4	4

†The district misinterpreted this statistic.

FAIR APPRAISAL

Quality of School Leadership

Principals are selected primarily for their ability as educational leaders, and the quality of leadership is generally uniform throughout the system. Parents and teachers have no say in principal selection. Principals, however, have a great deal of influence over the allotment of district resources.

Parent organizations are effective influencing district decision-making. Representatives of parents' groups meet monthly with principals and central administrators.

Quality of Instruction

Additional learning opportunities for gifted students are rated excellent. Two elementary teachers work full time with the gifted program at that level, and a master teacher coordinates the program at the secondary level. The additional instruction for low-achieving students is considered good. Individual help is offered. The curriculum for students preparing for college and the curriculum for job-bound students are considered good.

Quality of School Environment

The level of classroom disruption and student vandalism is very low, and the quality of building maintenance and repair is excellent. In the past six years, most of the schools have been renovated.

CHARTIERS VALLEY

ADDRESS OF CENTRAL OFFICE:
2030 Swallow Hill Road, Pittsburgh, PA 15220
ESI:74*

STATISTICAL PROFILE	DATA	ESI
Grade organization: K–5/6–8/9–12		
Percentage of schools built before 1955	12%	
Total enrollment	2,780	
Average Daily Attendance (ADA)	94%	7
Current expense per pupil in ADA	$3,718	3
Dropout rate	2%	10
Percentage of eligible students who took the SAT	59%	9
Average combined score on SAT	†	0*
Percentage of graduates who enrolled in 2- or 4-year colleges	58%	
Percentage of students who passed the state reading test	87%	
Percentage of students who passed the state math test	87%	
Teacher–student ratio in elementary grades	1:20	10
Teacher–student ratio in secondary grades	1:17	10
Counselor–student ratio in secondary grades	1:292	6
Number of students per music specialist in elementary grades	281	10
Number of students per art specialist in elementary grades	422	
Number of volumes in senior high school library	12,000	
Beginning teacher's salary	$18,500	
Maximum teacher's salary	$40,589	
Average years of experience among teachers	22	
Number of students suspended and expelled	NK	
	9	9
Subjects in which Advanced Placement courses are offered: American History, Biology, Calculus, Chemistry, Computer Science, English Language and Composition, English Literature and Composition, European History, Physics		

†The district misinterpreted this statistic.

Quality of School Leadership
The School Board hires principals who demonstrate educational leadership ability; the quality of leadership does not vary greatly from school to school. Parents and teachers have little say in principal selection, but principals have some influence over the allotment of resources to their school.

Parent organizations are effective influencing school policy decisions.

Quality of Instruction
Additional learning opportunities for gifted students are rated excellent. "Progress reports are done regularly, so children are always challenged," said an observer. Additional instruction for low-achieving students is rated good. The curricula for college-bound students and job-bound students are rated excellent. Nine Advanced Placement courses are a large number for a district of this size.

Quality of School Environment
Classroom disruption and student vandalism are not problems, and the quality of building maintenance and repair is excellent.

FOX CHAPEL AREA

ADDRESS OF CENTRAL OFFICE:
611 Field Club Road, Pittsburgh, PA 15238
ESI:92

STATISTICAL PROFILE	DATA	ESI
Grade organization: K–6/7–8/9–12		
Percentage of schools built before 1955	33%	
Total enrollment	3,339	
Average Daily Attendance (ADA)	98%	10
Current expense per pupil in ADA	$4,333	6
Dropout rate	2%	10
Percentage of eligible students who took the SAT	80%	10
Average combined score on SAT	969	8
Percentage of graduates who enrolled in 2- or 4-year colleges	78%	
Percentage of students who passed the state reading test	NK	
Percentage of students who passed the state math test	NK	
Teacher–student ratio in elementary grades	1:14	10
Teacher–student ratio in secondary grades	1:14	10
Counselor–student ratio in secondary grades	1:226	8
Number of students per music specialist in elementary grades	180	10
Number of students per art specialist in elementary grades	307	
Number of volumes in senior high school library	22,000	
Beginning teacher's salary	$18,500	
Maximum teacher's salary	$38,400	
Average years of experience among teachers	18	
Number of students suspended and expelled	256	
	10	10
Subjects in which Advanced Placement courses are offered: American History, Biology, Calculus AB, Calculus BC, Chemistry, Computer Science, English Language & Literature, Modern European History, Music, Physics		

Quality of School Leadership
Principals are chosen because of their educational leadership ability; the quality of leadership is generally uniform throughout the system. Parents and teachers do not help screen principal candidates. Principals, however, have a say about how district resources are distributed.

Parent organizations are sometimes an effective influence on school policy decisions.

Quality of Instruction
Additional learning opportunities for gifted students are rated excellent. Some gifted high school students attend a nearby university part-time. Additional instruction for low-achieving students is considered good. Some low achievers choose to attend an evening alternative school. The curriculum for students heading for college is excellent, while the curriculum for students heading for the job market is good.

Quality of School Environment
The level of classroom disruption and student vandalism is low, and the quality of building maintenance and repair is good.

HAMPTON TOWNSHIP

ADDRESS OF CENTRAL OFFICE:
4482 Mount Royal Boulevard, Allison Park, PA 15101
ESI:None†

STATISTICAL PROFILE	DATA	ESI
Grade organization:		
Percentage of schools built before 1955		
Total enrollment		
Average Daily Attendance (ADA)		
Current expense per pupil in ADA		
Dropout rate		
Percentage of eligible students who took the SAT		
Average combined score on SAT		
Percentage of graduates who enrolled in 2- or 4-year colleges		
Percentage of students who passed the state reading test		
Percentage of students who passed the state math test		
Teacher–student ratio in elementary grades		
Teacher–student ratio in secondary grades		
Counselor–student ratio in secondary grades		
Number of students per music specialist in elementary grades		
Number of students per art specialist in elementary grades		
Number of volumes in senior high school library		
Beginning teacher's salary		
Maximum teacher's salary		
Average years of experience among teachers		
Number of students suspended and expelled		
Subjects in which Advanced Placement courses are offered:		

†A Statistical Profile was not received from this district.

FAIR APPRAISAL

Quality of School Leadership
The School Board selects principals primarily for their educational leadership ability; the quality of leadership is generally uniform throughout the system. Parents and teachers do not help screen principal candidates. Principals exercise a great deal of influence over the distribution of district resources.

Parent organizations are effective as an influence on district policy.

Quality of Instruction
Additional learning opportunities for gifted students are rated fair, while additional instruction for low-achieving students is considered good. Much individual attention is offered to "slow learners." The curriculum for college-bound students is rated excellent, and the curriculum for students not planning on college is considered good.

Quality of School Environment
The incidence of classroom disruption and student vandalism is low, and the quality of building maintenance and repair is excellent.

HEMPFIELD AREA

ADDRESS OF CENTRAL OFFICE:
RD 6, Box 76, Greensburg, PA 15601
ESI:55

STATISTICAL PROFILE	DATA	ESI
Grade organization: K–6/7–9/10–12		
Percentage of schools built before 1955	NK	
Total enrollment	7,835	
Average Daily Attendance (ADA)	94%	7
Current expense per pupil in ADA	$3,850	4
Dropout rate	11%	10
Percentage of eligible students who took the SAT	50%	7
Average combined score on SAT	913	5
Percentage of graduates who enrolled in 2- or 4-year colleges	48%	
Percentage of students who passed the state reading test	88%	
Percentage of students who passed the state math test	86%	
Teacher–student ratio in elementary grades	1:19	10
Teacher–student ratio in secondary grades	1:19	9
Counselor–student ratio in secondary grades	1:510	0
Number of students per music specialist in elementary grades	752	0
Number of students per art specialist in elementary grades	752	
Number of volumes in senior high school library	23,345	
Beginning teacher's salary	$17,100	
Maximum teacher's salary	$29,550	
Average years of experience among teachers	15	
Number of students suspended and expelled	NK	
Subjects in which Advanced Placement courses are offered:	3	3
Biology, Calculus, Physics		

FAIR APPRAISAL

Quality of School Leadership
Longevity is a factor in selection, but principals are hired primarily for their ability as educational leaders. The quality of leadership is generally uniform throughout the district, but one observer believes principals are stronger at the secondary level than at the elementary level. Parents and teachers have hardly any say in principal selection, but principals have some say in deciding how resources will be divided among the schools.

Parent organizations are sometimes effective influencing district decision-making.

Quality of Instruction
Additional learning opportunities for gifted students and additional instruction for low-achieving students are rated good. Considered excellent is the curriculum for students planning on college. The curriculum for students not planning on college is rated good. One observer thought counselors are not as effective as they should be.

Quality of School Environment
Generally, the level of classroom disruption and student vandalism is low, although one observer reported a "high incidence" at the high school during 1986–87. The quality of building maintenance and repair is good.

KEYSTONE OAKS

ADDRESS OF CENTRAL OFFICE:
1000 Kelton Avenue, Pittsburgh, PA 15216
ESI:78

STATISTICAL PROFILE	DATA	ESI
Grade organization: K–5/6–8/9–12		
Percentage of schools built before 1955	72%	
Total enrollment	2,943	
Average Daily Attendance (ADA)	94%	7
Current expense per pupil in ADA	$3,768	3
Dropout rate	9%	10
Percentage of eligible students who took the SAT	58%	9
Average combined score on SAT	917	5
Percentage of graduates who enrolled in 2- or 4-year colleges	58%	
Percentage of students who passed the state reading test	NK	
Percentage of students who passed the state math test	NK	
Teacher–student ratio in elementary grades	1:18	10
Teacher–student ratio in secondary grades	1:16	10
Counselor–student ratio in secondary grades	1:275	7
Number of students per music specialist in elementary grades	280	10
Number of students per art specialist in elementary grades	375	
Number of volumes in senior high school library	23,000	
Beginning teacher's salary	$20,000	
Maximum teacher's salary	$38,112	
Average years of experience among teachers	16	
Number of students suspended and expelled	140	
Subjects in which Advanced Placement courses are offered: American History, Biology, Calculus, Chemistry, English, European History, German	7	7

FAIR APPRAISAL

Quality of School Leadership
Principals are hired because of their ability as educational leaders, and the quality of leadership does not vary greatly from school to school. Parents and teachers do not help in the screening of principals. However, principals have some say over the distribution of resources to the schools.

Parent organizations are sometimes an effective influence on district decision-making.

Quality of Instruction
Additional learning opportunities for gifted students are rated good. The program is "very good" at the elementary and middle schools, said an observer, where students are excused from regular classes to attend enrichment sessions. Remedial teachers in the elementary schools are responsible for making the additional instruction for low-achieving students excellent, according to one observer. The college preparatory curriculum is considered good, while the curriculum for students not planning on college is rated excellent.

Quality of School Environment
The level of classroom disruption and student vandalism is low, and the quality of building maintenance and repair is good.

MOON AREA

ADDRESS OF CENTRAL OFFICE:
1407 Beers School Road, Coraopolis, PA 15108
ESI:68

STATISTICAL PROFILE	DATA	ESI
Grade organization: K–6/7–9/10–12		
Percentage of schools built before 1955	43%	
Total enrollment	3,384	
Average Daily Attendance (ADA)	95%	8
Current expense per pupil in ADA	$2,837	0
Dropout rate	2%	10
Percentage of eligible students who took the SAT	70%	10
Average combined score on SAT	925	5
Percentage of graduates who enrolled in 2- or 4-year colleges	64%	
Percentage of students who passed the state reading test	95%	
Percentage of students who passed the state math test	95%	
Teacher–student ratio in elementary grades	1:19	10
Teacher–student ratio in secondary grades	1:14	10
Counselor–student ratio in secondary grades	1:249	8
Number of students per music specialist in elementary grades	540	5
Number of students per art specialist in elementary grades	540	
Number of volumes in senior high school library	25,000	
Beginning teacher's salary	$19,700	
Maximum teacher's salary	$38,850	
Average years of experience among teachers	15	
Number of students suspended and expelled	75	
Subjects in which Advanced Placement courses are offered: English, European History	2	2

FAIR APPRAISAL

Quality of School Leadership
Longevity plays a part in principal selection, but the School Board primarily seeks men and women who have educational leadership ability. The quality of leadership is generally uniform throughout the system. Parents and teachers do not help screen principal candidates. On the other hand, principals have considerable influence over the allotment of resources to their school.

Parent organizations are effective influencing school decisions. "Parents kept some schools from closing," said an observer.

Quality of Instruction
Additional learning opportunities for gifted students and additional instruction for low-achieving students are rated only fair. Speaking of the program for gifted students, an observer said, "it's the bare minimum; librarians are handling the gifted program at the elementary schools." Another observer, speaking of the program for low-achieving students, said, "There is nothing definite for them." The curricula for students going on to college and for those not planning on college are both considered good.

Quality of School Environment
Classroom disruption and student vandalism are not problems. Building maintenance and repair are excellent.

MOUNT LEBANON

ADDRESS OF CENTRAL OFFICE:
7 Horsman Drive, Pittsburgh, PA 15228
ESI:92

STATISTICAL PROFILE	DATA	ESI
Grade organization: K–6/7–8/9–12		
Percentage of schools built before 1955	80%	
Total enrollment	5,031	
Average Daily Attendance (ADA)	94%	7
Current expense per pupil in ADA	$5,512	10
Dropout rate	11%	10
Percentage of eligible students who took the SAT	87%	10
Average combined score on SAT	995	9
Percentage of graduates who enrolled in 2- or 4-year colleges	79%	
Percentage of students who passed the state reading test	97%	
Percentage of students who passed the state math test	96%	
Teacher–student ratio in elementary grades	1:19	10
Teacher–student ratio in secondary grades	1:17	10
Counselor–student ratio in secondary grades	1:278	6
Number of students per music specialist in elementary grades	250	10
Number of students per art specialist in elementary grades	563	
Number of volumes in senior high school library	45,000†	
Beginning teacher's salary	$19,715	
Maximum teacher's salary	$40,080	
Average years of experience among teachers	18	
Number of students suspended and expelled	256	
Subjects in which Advanced Placement courses are offered:	10	10
American Hisory, Biology, Calculus, Chemistry, Computer Science, English, European History, French, German, Physics		

†This number seems unusually high.

FAIR APPRAISAL

Quality of School Leadership

Most principals are chosen because of their educational leadership ability, and the quality of leadership does not vary greatly from school to school. Parents and teachers are not part of the committees screening principal candidates. Principals have some say about the way district resources are divided among the schools.

Parent organizations are effective influences on district policies. Parents meet regularly with administrators and faithfully attend School Board meetings.

Quality of Instruction

Additional learning opportunities for gifted students are rated fair to good. They are only fair at the elementary school level, according to observers, but are considered better in the upper grades. Additional instruction for low-achieving students is rated good. The curriculum preparing students for college is called good to excellent, and the curriculum for students preparing for the world of work is rated good.

Quality of School Environment

The incidence of classroom disruption and student vandalism is very low, and the quality of building maintenance and repair is rated excellent.

NORTH ALLEGHENY

ADDRESS OF CENTRAL OFFICE:
200 Hillvue Lane, Pittsburgh, PA 15237
ESI:63

STATISTICAL PROFILE	DATA	ESI
Grade organization: K–5/6–8/9–10/11–12		
Percentage of schools built before 1955	33%	
Total enrollment	6,607†	
Average Daily Attendance (ADA)	95%	8
Current expense per pupil in ADA	$4,539	7
Dropout rate	NK	0
Percentage of eligible students who took the SAT	58%	9
Average combined score on SAT	906	5
Percentage of graduates who enrolled in 2- or 4-year colleges	79%	
Percentage of students who passed the state reading test	95%	
Percentage of students who passed the state math test	95%	
Teacher–student ratio in elementary grades	1:26	4
Teacher–student ratio in secondary grades	1:17	10
Counselor–student ratio in secondary grades	1:282	6
Number of students per music specialist in elementary grades	379	8
Number of students per art specialist in elementary grades	531	
Number of volumes in senior high school library	17,000	
Beginning teacher's salary	$21,080	
Maximum teacher's salary	$39,625	
Average years of experience among teachers	15	
Number of students suspended and expelled	543	
Subjects in which Advanced Placement courses are offered:	6	6
American History, Calculus, Chemistry, English Language and Composition, European History, Latin		

†1986–87 statistic.

FAIR APPRAISAL

Quality of School Leadership

The School Board seeks principals who demonstrate educational leadership ability, and the quality of leadership is uniform throughout the system. Parents and teachers do not help screen principal candidates. Principals have some say in deciding how resources will be allotted to the schools.

Parent organizations are sometimes effective influencing school decisions.

Quality of Instruction

Additional learning opportunities for gifted students and additional instruction for low-achieving students are considered excellent. Also rated excellent is the curriculum for students planning on college. The curriculum for students not planning on college is rated good.

Quality of School Environment

The level of classroom disruption and student vandalism is very low, and the quality of building maintenance and repair is very high.

PETERS TOWNSHIP

ADDRESS OF CENTRAL OFFICE:
616 East McMurray Road, Canonsburg, PA 15317
ESI:61

STATISTICAL PROFILE	DATA	ESI
Grade organization: K–5/6–8/9–12		
Percentage of schools built before 1955	20%	
Total enrollment	2,475	
Average Daily Attendance (ADA)	95%	8
Current expense per pupil in ADA	$3,200	0
Dropout rate	2%	10
Percentage of eligible students who took the SAT	84%	10
Average combined score on SAT	946	7
Percentage of graduates who enrolled in 2- or 4-year colleges	78%	
Percentage of students who passed the state reading test	95%	
Percentage of students who passed the state math test	96%	
Teacher–student ratio in elementary grades	1:24	6
Teacher–student ratio in secondary grades	1:18	10
Counselor–student ratio in secondary grades	1:380	2
Number of students per music specialist in elementary grades	312	5
Number of students per art specialist in elementary grades	500	
Number of volumes in senior high school library	15,576	
Beginning teacher's salary	$16,200	
Maximum teacher's salary	$35,201	
Average years of experience among teachers	14	
Number of students suspended and expelled	13	
Subjects in which Advanced Placement courses are offered: American History, Computer Science, English	3	3

FAIR APPRAISAL

Quality of School Leadership

The School Board hires principals primarily based on their educational leadership ability, and the quality of leadership is generally uniform throughout the system. Parents and teachers do not screen principal candidates. However, principals have a great deal to say about how the district uses its resources.

Parent organizations are sometimes effective influencing school policy decisions. In addition to PTAs, parents have a voice on ad hoc advisory committees.

Quality of Instruction

Additional learning opportunities for gifted students are rated good, and additional instruction for low-achieving students is considered fair to good. The curriculum for students planning on college is termed excellent, while the curriculum for students not planning on college is rated good.

Quality of School Environment

The level of classroom disruption and student vandalism is low, and the quality of building maintenance and repair is excellent.

NORTH HILLS

ADDRESS OF CENTRAL OFFICE:
200 McIntyre Road, Pittsburgh, PA 15237
ESI:62

STATISTICAL PROFILE	DATA	ESI
Grade organization: K–6/7–9/10–12		
Percentage of schools built before 1955	38%	
Total enrollment	4,651	
Average Daily Attendance (ADA)	95%	8
Current expense per pupil in ADA	$4,256	6
Dropout rate	14%	9
Percentage of eligible students who took the SAT	37%	5
Average combined score on SAT	922	5
Percentage of graduates who enrolled in 2- or 4-year colleges	70%	
Percentage of students who passed the state reading test	90%	
Percentage of students who passed the state math test	92%	
Teacher–student ratio in elementary grades	1:26	4
Teacher–student ratio in secondary grades	1:25	3
Counselor–student ratio in secondary grades	1:331	4
Number of students per music specialist in elementary grades	346	9
Number of students per art specialist in elementary grades	346	
Number of volumes in senior high school library	27,625	
Beginning teacher's salary	$16,000	
Maximum teacher's salary	$35,974	
Average years of experience among teachers	17	
Number of students suspended and expelled	467	
Subjects in which Advanced Placement courses are offered: American History, Biology, Calculus, Chemistry, English, European History, French, German, Physics	9	9

FAIR APPRAISAL

Quality of School Leadership

Although seniority is a factor, principals are hired primarily for their educational leadership ability. The quality of leadership does not vary greatly from school to school. Parents and teachers have hardly any say in principal selection, but principals have some say in the allotment of resources to their school.

Parent organizations are mostly ineffective when it comes to influencing school decision-making.

Quality of Instruction

Additional learning opportunities for gifted students are rated good, and additional instruction for low-achieving students is considered fair to good. One observer was highly critical of the district's attitude toward low-achievers: "They don't want to even bother with the problems of underachievers." The curricula for college-bound students and job-bound students are both considered good.

Quality of School Environment

The incidence of classroom disruption and student vandalism is low, and the quality of building maintenance and repair is good.

PITTSBURGH

ADDRESS OF CENTRAL OFFICE:
341 Bellefield Avenue, Pittsburgh, PA 15213
ESI:49

STATISTICAL PROFILE	DATA	ESI
Grade organization: K–5/6–8/9–12		
Percentage of schools built before 1955	80%	
Total enrollment	40,038	
Average Daily Attendance (ADA)	88%	1
Current expense per pupil in ADA	$4,902	9
Dropout rate	29%	0
Percentage of eligible students who took the SAT	35%	4
Average combined score on SAT	839	1
Percentage of graduates who enrolled in 2- or 4-year colleges	42%	
Percentage of students who passed the state reading test	62%	
Percentage of students who passed the state math test	72%	
Teacher–student ratio in elementary grades	1:23	7
Teacher–student ratio in secondary grades	1:18	10
Counselor–student ratio in secondary grades	1:344	4
Number of students per music specialist in elementary grades	390	8
Number of students per art specialist in elementary grades	755	
Number of volumes in senior high school library (average)	11,483	
Beginning teacher's salary	$17,600	
Maximum teacher's salary	$37,790	
Average years of experience among teachers	20	
Number of students suspended and expelled	8,270	
Subjects in which Advanced Placement courses are offered: American History, Biology, Calculus, English, European History	5	5

FAIR APPRAISAL

Quality of School Leadership

Principals are hired mostly because of their educational leadership ability, but the quality of leadership varies greatly from section to section of the district, according to observers. Said one observer, "The east side of the city always gets better administrators; they're sensitive about who they put there because they know they'll have to deal with more assertive parents." Parents and teachers do not take part in principal selection. Principals, though, have quite a lot of influence over what resources they will receive.

Parent organizations are sometimes effective influencing district policies.

Quality of Instruction

Additional learning opportunities for gifted students are rated excellent. "The enrichment program is wonderful!" said one observer. The program is especially good at the secondary level, where gifted students can attend centers for advanced study. On the other hand, observers consider additional instruction for low-achieving students to be fair to poor. "They are the neglected population," said an observer. The curriculum for college-bound students is rated good to excellent, while the curriculum for students not planning on college is considered good.

Quality of School Environment

The incidence of classroom disruption and student vandalism is considered low, a departure from most large city districts. The quality of building maintenance and repair is rated good.

PLUM BOROUGH

ADDRESS OF CENTRAL OFFICE:
200 School Road, Pittsburgh, PA 15239
ESI:68

STATISTICAL PROFILE	DATA	ESI
Grade organization: K–6/7–9/10–12		
Percentage of schools built before 1955	25%	
Total enrollment	4,361	
Average Daily Attendance (ADA)	95%	8
Current expense per pupil in ADA	$3,935	4
Dropout rate	4%	10
Percentage of eligible students who took the SAT	57%	10
Average combined score on SAT	931	6
Percentage of graduates who enrolled in 2- or 4-year colleges	60%	
Percentage of students who passed the state reading test	NK	
Percentage of students who passed the state math test	NK	
Teacher–student ratio in elementary grades	1:20	10
Teacher–student ratio in secondary grades	1:17	10
Counselor–student ratio in secondary grades	NK	0
Number of students per music specialist in elementary grades	430	7
Number of students per art specialist in elementary grades	865	
Number of volumes in senior high school library	13,000	
Beginning teacher's salary	$18,250	
Maximum teacher's salary	$35,350	
Average years of experience among teachers	14	
Number of students suspended and expelled	110	
Subjects in which Advanced Placement courses are offered: American History, Calculus, English	3	3

FAIR APPRAISAL

Quality of School Leadership

Internal politics and seniority are the most important considerations when hiring principals, according to the observers. Consequently, the quality of leadership varies greatly from school to school. The better principals are in the secondary schools, said the observers. Parents and teachers have no say in principal selection, and principals don't have much say in how district resources are allotted to the schools.

Parents are sometimes effective as an influence on school decision-making.

Quality of Instruction

Overall, the program for gifted students is rated good, but observers point out that it is only fair at the elementary level and very good in the secondary grades. Additional instruction for low-achieving students is considered fair. The curricula for college-bound students and job-bound students are both rated good.

Quality of School Environment

The level of classroom disruption and student vandalism is low, but the quality of building maintenance and repair is considered only fair. Some older schools are "not as clean as they should be," said one observer.

SHALER AREA

ADDRESS OF CENTRAL OFFICE:
1800 Mt. Royal Boulevard, Glenshaw, PA 15116
ESI:66*

STATISTICAL PROFILE	DATA	ESI
Grade organization: K–6/7–9/10–12		
Percentage of schools built before 1955	22%	
Total enrollment	4,876	
Average Daily Attendance (ADA)	95%	8
Current expense per pupil in ADA	$3,843	4
Dropout rate	15%	8
Percentage of eligible students who took the SAT	68%	10
Average combined score on SAT	†	0*
Percentage of graduates who enrolled in 2- or 4-year colleges	87%	
Percentage of students who passed the state reading test	NK	
Percentage of students who passed the state math test	NK	
Teacher–student ratio in elementary grades	1:18	10
Teacher–student ratio in secondary grades	1:14	10
Counselor–student ratio in secondary grades	1:317	5
Number of students per music specialist in elementary grades	404	7
Number of students per art specialist in elementary grades	505	
Number of volumes in senior high school library	18,588	
Beginning teacher's salary	$18,040	
Maximum teacher's salary	$36,080	
Average years of experience among teachers	20	
Number of students suspended and expelled	NK	
Subjects in which Advanced Placement courses are offered:	4	4
American History, Calculus, English Literature and Composition, European History		

†The district supplied an inappropriate statistic.

FAIR APPRAISAL

Quality of School Leadership

Principals are selected mainly on the basis of their ability as educational leaders; the quality of leadership is generally uniform throughout the system. Parents and teachers do not screen principal candidates. Principals have some say in the allotment of resources to their school.

Parent organizations are sometimes effective influencing district policy-making.

Quality of Instruction

Additional learning opportunities for gifted students and additional instruction for low-achieving students are both rated good. Also considered good are the curricula for students preparing for college and for students preparing for the job market.

Quality of School Environment

Classroom disruption and student vandalism are not problems; the quality of building maintenance and repair is good.

UPPER ST. CLAIR TOWNSHIP

ADDRESS OF CENTRAL OFFICE:
1820 McLaughlin Run Road, Pittsburgh, PA 15241
ESI:79

STATISTICAL PROFILE	DATA	ESI
Grade organization: K–4/5–6/7–8/9–12		
Percentage of schools built before 1955	17%	
Total enrollment	3,780	
Average Daily Attendance (ADA)	95%	8
Current expense per pupil in ADA	$5,065	10
Dropout rate	1%	10
Percentage of eligible students who took the SAT	92%	10
Average combined score on SAT	989	9
Percentage of graduates who enrolled in 2- or 4-year colleges	91%	
Percentage of students who passed the state reading test	96%	
Percentage of students who passed the state math test	97%	
Teacher–student ratio in elementary grades	1:26	4
Teacher–student ratio in secondary grades	1:22	8
Counselor–student ratio in secondary grades	1:256	7
Number of students per music specialist in elementary grades	290	10
Number of students per art specialist in elementary grades	460	
Number of volumes in senior high school library	15,100	
Beginning teacher's salary	$18,704	
Maximum teacher's salary	$41,385	
Average years of experience among teachers	13	
Number of students suspended and expelled	94	
Subjects in which Advanced Placement courses are offered:	3	3
American History, English, European History		

FAIR APPRAISAL

Quality of School Leadership

Principals are hired primarily because of their ability as educational leaders; the quality of leadership does not vary greatly from school to school. Parents and teachers do not take part in the selection of principals. Principals, on the other hand, have some voice in deciding how resources are distributed.

Parent organizations are sometimes effective influencing district policies. "Parents hold little sway with the superintendent," said one observer, "but parents have a lot of input and influence over other administrators."

Quality of Instruction

Additional learning opportunities for gifted students and additional instruction for low-achieving students are both rated good. The curricula for students preparing for college and for those preparing for jobs are rated excellent. "The curriculum, even in kindergarten, is completely amazing," said an observer. "It's wonderful!"

Quality of School Environment

The level of classroom disruption and student vandalism is very low, and the quality of building maintenance and repair is excellent.

WEST JEFFERSON HILLS

ADDRESS OF CENTRAL OFFICE:
P.O. Box 18019, Pittsburgh, PA 15236
ESI:74

STATISTICAL PROFILE	DATA	ESI
Grade organization: K–5/6–8/9–12		
Percentage of schools built before 1955	100%	
Total enrollment	2,800	
Average Daily Attendance (ADA)	95%	8
Current expense per pupil in ADA	$3,200	0
Dropout rate	5%	10
Percentage of eligible students who took the SAT	60%	9
Average combined score on SAT	911	5
Percentage of graduates who enrolled in 2- or 4-year colleges	75%	
Percentage of students who passed the state reading test	NK	
Percentage of students who passed the state math test	NK	
Teacher–student ratio in elementary grades	1:18	10
Teacher–student ratio in secondary grades	1:15	10
Counselor–student ratio in secondary grades	1:400	2
Number of students per music specialist in elementary grades	180	10
Number of students per art specialist in elementary grades	219	
Number of volumes in senior high school library	10,500	
Beginning teacher's salary	$16,175	
Maximum teacher's salary	$39,148	
Average years of experience among teachers	15	
Number of students suspended and expelled	294	
Subjects in which Advanced Placement courses are offered:	10	10
American History, Biology, Calculus, Chemistry, English Language and Composition, English Literature and Composition, European History, French, Latin, Spanish		

FAIR APPRAISAL

Quality of School Leadership
Most principals are hired because of their educational leadership ability, although longevity in the district is a factor. While the quality of leadership is generally high, an observer believes principals in the elementary schools are not as good on average as those in the secondary schools. Parents and teachers do not help screen principal candidates. However, principals have some say in the allotment of resources to their school.

"PTAs have become stronger in recent years," said an observer, and another observer reported that "parents were instrumental in the improvement of the gifted program."

Quality of Instruction
Additional learning opportunities for gifted students are rated fair to good, with the program showing steady improvement. One observer complained that the program in the elementary grades has consisted mostly of "extra library time." The curriculum for students preparing for college is rated excellent, while the curriculum for students not planning on college is considered good.

Quality of School Environment
Classroom disruption and student vandalism are not problems, and the quality of building maintenance and repair is excellent.

WEST MIFFLIN

ADDRESS OF CENTRAL OFFICE:
515 Camp Hollow Road, West Mifflin, PA 15122
ESI:55*

STATISTICAL PROFILE	DATA	ESI
Grade organization: K–5/6–8/9–12		
Percentage of schools built before 1955	50%	
Total enrollment	3,169	
Average Daily Attendance (ADA)	94%	7
Current expense per pupil in ADA	†	0*
Dropout rate	5%	10
Percentage of eligible students who took the SAT	45%	6
Average combined score on SAT	879	3
Percentage of graduates who enrolled in 2- or 4-year colleges	51%	
Percentage of students who passed the state reading test	NK	
Percentage of students who passed the state math test	NK	
Teacher–student ratio in elementary grades	1:25	5
Teacher–student ratio in secondary grades	1:15	10
Counselor–student ratio in secondary grades	1:320	5
Number of students per music specialist in elementary grades	415	7
Number of students per art specialist in elementary grades	623	
Number of volumes in senior high school library	14,600	
Beginning teacher's salary	$16,475	
Maximum teacher's salary	$39,055	
Average years of experience among teachers	16	
Number of students suspended and expelled	707	
Subjects in which Advanced Placement courses are offered:	2	2
English, Physics		

†The district supplied an inappropriate statistic.

FAIR APPRAISAL

Quality of School Leadership
The School Board hires principals primarily for their ability as educational leaders, and the quality of leadership is generally uniform throughout the system. Teachers have some say in principal selection; parents do not. Principals have some say in the way resources are distributed to the schools.

Parent organizations have some influence over school policy decisions.

Quality of Instruction
Additional learning opportunities for gifted students and additional instruction for low-achieving students are rated good. The college preparatory curriculum is called fair to good, but is improving. The curriculum for students not planning on college is considered good.

Quality of School Environment
Classroom disruption and student vandalism are not problems, and the quality of building maintenance and repair is good.

METROPOLITAN AREA

Portland, OR

Four districts completed Statistical Profiles, and a Fair Appraisal is provided
for one other district. Oregon does not test student competency in reading and mathematics.
Therefore, a *NA* (not applicable) appears on the lines requesting those statistics.
Districts in this area may be compared to districts in the Seattle, WA Metropolitan Area.

AREA AT A GLANCE

SCHOOL DISTRICT	ENROLLMENT	ESI
Beaverton	21,318	74*
Newberg	3,996	38
North Clackamas	11,502	
Portland	51,880	44*
Tigard	6,700	59*

Indicates district misinterpretation of one or more statistics in the ESI. For each misinterpreted statistic, a score of 0 was given instead of a possible score of 0 to 10 points.

SCHOOL DISTRICT

BEAVERTON

ADDRESS OF CENTRAL OFFICE:
P.O. Box 200, Beaverton, OR 97075
ESI:74*

STATISTICAL PROFILE	DATA	ESI
Grade organization: K–6/7–9/10–12		
Percentage of schools built before 1955	29%	
Total enrollment	21,318	
Average Daily Attendance (ADA)	97%	10
Current expense per pupil in ADA	†	0*
Dropout rate	4%	10
Percentage of eligible students who took the SAT	55%	8
Average combined score on SAT	971	8
Percentage of graduates who enrolled in 2- or 4-year colleges	50%	
Percentage of students who passed the state reading test	NA	
Percentage of students who passed the state math test	NA	
Teacher–student ratio in elementary grades	1:24	6
Teacher–student ratio in secondary grades	1:21	7
Counselor–student ratio in secondary grades	1:281	6
Number of students per music specialist in elementary grades	216	10
Number of students per art specialist in elementary grades	None	
Number of volumes in senior high school libraries (average)	27,700	
Beginning teacher's salary	$17,399	
Maximum teacher's salary	$32,791	
Average years of experience among teachers	14	
Number of students suspended and expelled	854	
Subjects in which Advanced Placement courses are offered:	9	9
Biology, Calculus, Computer Science, English, French, German, Music Theory, Physics, Spanish		

†The district supplied an inappropriate statistic.

FAIR APPRAISAL

Quality of School Leadership
Most principals are selected for their educational leadership which is generally uniform throughout the system. Parents and teachers do not screen principal candidates. Principals have some say in resource distribution.

Each school has a three-member parent committee that advises the principal. Fourteen other parents and citizens serve as an advisory committee to the School Board.

Quality of Instruction
The program for gifted students, which is rated good to excellent, begins in grade 4 with special classes held once a week. Additional instruction for low-achieving students is considered fair to good. The district has adopted more stringent graduation standards, and the curriculum for students going to college is considered excellent. "The curriculum is particularly strong in science and math," said an observer. The curriculum for students not planning on college is only rated fair to good. The latter curriculum "would be better," said an observer, "if more students who aren't really interested in college at the moment were counseled into preparing for the job market."

Quality of School Environment
Classroom disruption and student vandalism are low. Building maintenance and repair are excellent.

NEWBERG

ADDRESS OF CENTRAL OFFICE:
1421 Deborah Road, Newberg, OR 97132
ESI:38

STATISTICAL PROFILE	DATA	ESI
Grade organization: †		
Percentage of schools built before 1955	50%	
Total enrollment	3,986	
Average Daily Attendance (ADA)	85%	0
Current expense per pupil in ADA	$3,158	1
Dropout rate	15%	8
Percentage of eligible students who took the SAT	51%	8
Average combined score on SAT	905	4
Percentage of graduates who enrolled in 2- or 4-year colleges	60%	
Percentage of students who passed the state reading test	NA	
Percentage of students who passed the state math test	NA	
Teacher–student ratio in elementary grades	1:24	6
Teacher–student ratio in secondary grades	1:21	7
Counselor–student ratio in secondary grades	1:389	2
Number of students per music specialist in elementary grades	600	
Number of students per art specialist in elementary grades	None	
Number of volumes in senior high school library	17,039	
Beginning teacher's salary	$15,659	
Maximum teacher's salary	$30,031	
Average years of experience among teachers	NK	
Number of students suspended and expelled	777	
Subjects in which Advanced Placement courses are offered: American History, English	2	2

†The district misinterpreted this statistic.

Quality of School Leadership

Most principals are selected for their educational leadership ability, and the district often looks for new principals outside the system. The quality of leadership does not vary greatly from school to school. Parents and teachers have some say in principal selection, but not as much as they once did. They are less likely now to be included on committees screening principal candidates. Principals have little say in how district resources are allocated to the schools.

Parent organizations are only occasionally effective as an influence in district decision-making.

Quality of Instruction

The district has had "a tough time" passing tax levies in recent years, said an observer, and "the decrease in funding has made a difference in the quality of the educational program." For example, additional learning opportunities for gifted students and additional instruction for low-achieving students, which once might have been considered good, are now rated only fair. The curriculum for college-bound students is still thought of as good, but the curriculum for students not planning on college is considered fair. "More attention is always paid to the college preparatory curriculum," said an observer, "because the parents of college-bound students are the ones the School Board most often hears from."

Quality of School Environment

The level of classroom disruption and student vandalism is low, and the quality of building maintenance and repair, while slipping a little because of the failed tax levies, is still rated good.

NORTH CLACKAMAS

ADDRESS OF CENTRAL OFFICE:
4444 South East Lake Road, Milwaukie, OR 97222
ESI:None†

STATISTICAL PROFILE	DATA	ESI
Grade organization:		
Percentage of schools built before 1955		
Total enrollment		
Average Daily Attendance (ADA)		
Current expense per pupil in ADA		
Dropout rate		
Percentage of eligible students who took the SAT		
Average combined score on SAT		
Percentage of graduates who enrolled in 2- or 4-year colleges		
Percentage of students who passed the state reading test		
Percentage of students who passed the state math test		
Teacher–student ratio in elementary grades		
Teacher–student ratio in secondary grades		
Counselor–student ratio in secondary grades		
Number of students per music specialist in elementary grades		
Number of students per art specialist in elementary grades		
Number of volumes in senior high school library		
Beginning teacher's salary		
Maximum teacher's salary		
Average years of experience among teachers		
Number of students suspended and expelled		
Subjects in which Advanced Placement courses are offered:		

†A Statistical Profile was not received from this district.

FAIR APPRAISAL

Quality of School Leadership
The School Board hires principals who demonstrate ability as educational leaders, and the quality of leadership does not vary greatly from school to school. Parents and teachers serve on committees that screen principal candidates. Also, principals have a great deal to say about how district resources are distributed.

Each school has a parent advisory committee that meets monthly with the school principal. The minutes of the meetings are sent to the central administration and School Board for review.

Quality of Instruction
Learning opportunities for gifted students are rated excellent. Five schools each sent a team of gifted students to an international competition several years ago, and they scored better than most other teams present. Additional instruction for low-achieving students also is rated excellent. The curricula for students planning on college and for those planning on the world of work after graduation are both considered excellent.

Quality of School Environment
Classroom disruption and student vandalism are not problems, and the quality of building maintenance and repair is rated good.

PORTLAND

ADDRESS OF CENTRAL OFFICE:
P.O. Box 3107, Portland, OR 97208
ESI:44*

STATISTICAL PROFILE	DATA	ESI
Grade organization: K–5/6–8/9–12		
Percentage of schools built before 1955	75%	
Total enrollment	51,880	
Average Daily Attendance (ADA)	95%	8
Current expense per pupil in ADA	$4,000	5
Dropout rate	NK	0
Percentage of eligible students who took the SAT	43%	6
Average combined score on SAT	938	6
Percentage of graduates who enrolled in 2- or 4-year colleges	65%	
Percentage of students who passed the state reading test	NA	
Percentage of students who passed the state math test	NA	
Teacher–student ratio in elementary grades	1:23	7
Teacher–student ratio in secondary grades	1:22	6
Counselor–student ratio in secondary grades	1:400	2
Number of students per music specialist in elementary grades	†	0*
Number of students per art specialist in elementary grades	†	
Number of volumes in senior high school libraries (average)	40,000	
Beginning teacher's salary	$17,050	
Maximum teacher's salary	$33,748	
Average years of experience among teachers	15	
Number of students suspended and expelled	1,554	
Subjects in which Advanced Placement courses are offered:	4	4
Calculus, English, Foreign Language, Science		

†One specialist per school.

FAIR APPRAISAL

Quality of School Leadership
Principals are hired mostly for their educational leadership ability, but, according to observers, major variations in the quality of leadership exist in the schools. One observer complained that some principals' views on educating minorities "are not very current." Another observer believes some principals lack "sufficient up-to-date training." Parents and teachers do not interview principal candidates, and principals have little say about resource allocation.

Quality of Instruction
Additional learning opportunities for gifted students are rated good, but additional instruction for low-achieving students is considered only fair. The curriculum for college-bound students is rated good, but one observer complained that "not enough minority students are counseled into the college preparatory curriculum." The curriculum for job-bound students is rated fair. "Vocational education has not kept up with changes in technology," said an observer.

While the district generally meets the educational needs of minority students, "more attention has to be paid," said an observer.

Quality of School Environment
Classroom disruption and student vandalism are low. Building maintenance and repair are fair.

TIGARD

ADDRESS OF CENTRAL OFFICE:

13137 Southwest Pacific Highway, Portland, OR 97223
ESI:59*

STATISTICAL PROFILE	DATA	ESI
Grade organization: K–6/7–9/10–12		
Percentage of schools built before 1955	30%	
Total enrollment	6,700	
Average Daily Attendance (ADA)	98%	10
Current expense per pupil in ADA	†	0
Dropout rate	9%	10
Percentage of eligible students who took the SAT	55%	8
Average combined score on SAT	962	7
Percentage of graduates who enrolled in 2- or 4-year colleges	66%	
Percentage of students who passed the state reading test	NA	
Percentage of students who passed the state math test	NA	
Teacher–student ratio in elementary grades	1:24	6
Teacher–student ratio in secondary grades	1:22	6
Counselor–student ratio in secondary grades	1:325	5
Number of students per music specialist in elementary grades	†	0*
Number of students per art specialist in elementary grades	None	
Number of volumes in senior high school library	23,000	
Beginning teacher's salary	$16,854	
Maximum teacher's salary	$33,034	
Average years of experience among teachers	10	
Number of students suspended and expelled	785	
Subjects in which Advanced Placement courses are offered: American History, Art, Calculus, Chemistry, Computer Science, English, Music Theory	7	7

†The district supplied an inappropriate statistic.

Quality of School Leadership

Principals are chosen for their ability as educational leaders; the quality of leadership does not vary greatly from school to school. Parents and teachers have hardly any say in principal selection, but principals have some influence over the distribution of district resources.

School advisory committees are an effective means of influencing school decision-making.

Quality of Instruction

Additional learning opportunities for gifted students and additional instruction for low-achieving students are rated good. Also considered good are the curricula preparing students for college and preparing students for the world of work.

Quality of School Environment

The incidence of classroom disruption and student vandalism is low, and the quality of building maintenance and repair is good.

Providence, RI

Five districts completed Statistical Profiles, and Fair Appraisals alone were received for two other districts. Rhode Island does not administer state competency tests in reading and math; therefore, *NA* (not applicable) appears on the lines requesting those statistics. Districts in this area may be compared to districts in the Boston, MA Metropolitan Area.

AREA AT A GLANCE

SCHOOL DISTRICT	ENROLLMENT	ESI
Attleboro, MA	5,470	57*
Burrillville	2,701	42
Cranston	9,024	
Pawtucket	8,386	64
Providence	19,685	36*
Warwick	12,017	
Woonsocket	6,700	44*

Indicates district misinterpretation of one or more statistics in the ESI. For each misinterpreted statistic, a score of 0 was given instead of a possible score of 0 to 10 points.

SCHOOL DISTRICT

ATTLEBORO

ADDRESS OF CENTRAL OFFICE:
Rathbun Willard Drive, Attleboro, MA 02703
ESI:57*

STATISTICAL PROFILE	DATA	ESI
Grade organization: K–4/5–8/9–12		
Percentage of schools built before 1955	60%	
Total enrollment	5,470	
Average Daily Attendance (ADA)	96%	9
Current expense per pupil in ADA	$3,137	0
Dropout rate	11%	10
Percentage of eligible students who took the SAT	48%	7
Average combined score on SAT	905	4
Percentage of graduates who enrolled in 2- or 4-year colleges	52%	
Percentage of students who passed the state reading test	NA	
Percentage of students who passed the state math test	NA	
Teacher–student ratio in elementary grades	1:23	7
Teacher–student ratio in secondary grades	1:22	6
Counselor–student ratio in secondary grades	1:280	6
Number of students per music specialist in elementary grades	†	0*
Number of students per art specialist in elementary grades	†	
Number of volumes in senior high school library	20,000	
Beginning teacher's salary	$18,000	
Maximum teacher's salary	$30,765	
Average years of experience among teachers	15	
Number of students suspended and expelled	NK	
Subjects in which Advanced Placement courses are offered: Biology, Calculus, Chemistry, English, French, Music, Physics, Spanish	8	8

†The district misinterpreted this statistic.

FAIR APPRAISAL

Quality of School Leadership
Principals are selected primarily for their educational leadership ability, and the quality of leadership does not vary greatly from school to school. Parents and teachers have hardly any say in principal selection, but principals have some say in how resources are allocated to the schools.

Parent organizations are sometimes effective. Recently, for example, after the School Board proposed busing students to relieve overcrowding at an elementray school, parents made a case against the busing and for portable classrooms at the school. The parents won.

Quality of Instruction
Additional learning opportunities for gifted students are rated good. The program has "come a long way" in recent years, said an observer. It starts in grade 4. Additional instruction for low-achieving students is rated only fair. The college preparatory curriculum is considered fair to good, while the job-bound curriculum is termed good.

Quality of School Environment
Classroom disruption and student vandalism are on the high side. A number of burglaries were reported in 1986–87, and a school library was burned. Building maintenance and repair are rated poor. As a result of budget cutbacks, the district is "not able to keep up" with necessary repairs.

BURRILLVILLE

ADDRESS OF CENTRAL OFFICE:
95 East Avenue, Harrisville, RI 02830
ESI:42

STATISTICAL PROFILE	DATA	ESI
Grade organization: K–3/4–6/7–12		
Percentage of schools built before 1955	75%	
Total enrollment	2,701	
Average Daily Attendance (ADA)	94%	7
Current expense per pupil in ADA	$3,110	0
Dropout rate	25%	0
Percentage of eligible students who took the SAT	37%	5
Average combined score on SAT	886	3
Percentage of graduates who enrolled in 2- or 4-year colleges	33%	
Percentage of students who passed the state reading test	NA	
Percentage of students who passed the state math test	NA	
Teacher–student ratio in elementary grades	1:25	5
Teacher–student ratio in secondary grades	1:15	10
Counselor–student ratio in secondary grades	1:300	6
Number of students per music specialist in elementary grades	450	6
Number of students per art specialist in elementary grades	450	
Number of volumes in senior high school library	NK	
Beginning teacher's salary	$16,239	
Maximum teacher's salary	$33,658	
Average years of experience among teachers	10	
Number of students suspended and expelled	NK	
Subjects in which Advanced Placement courses are offered:	None	0

Quality of School Leadership

The School Board hires principals because of their educational leadership ability, and the quality of leadership does not vary greatly from school to school. Parents and teachers serve on committees that interview principal candidates. Principals have some say about the allotment of resources to the schools.

Parent organizations generally are effective as an influence on school decision-making.

Quality of Instruction

Additional learning opportunities for gifted students are rated fair. The district has recently started a program, and a teacher for the gifted was appointed beginning in 1987–88. Additional instruction for low-achieving students is rated good. Also considered good are the curricula for college-bound students and job-bound students. The latter program is currently being strengthened.

Quality of School Environment

The incidence of classroom disruption and student vandalism is very low, and the quality of building maintenance and repair is good.

CRANSTON

ADDRESS OF CENTRAL OFFICE:
845 Park Avenue, Cranston, RI 02910
ESI:None†

STATISTICAL PROFILE	DATA	ESI
Grade organization:		
Percentage of schools built before 1955		
Total enrollment		
Average Daily Attendance (ADA)		
Current expense per pupil in ADA		
Dropout rate		
Percentage of eligible students who took the SAT		
Average combined score on SAT		
Percentage of graduates who enrolled in 2- or 4-year colleges		
Percentage of students who passed the state reading test		
Percentage of students who passed the state math test		
Teacher–student ratio in elementary grades		
Teacher–student ratio in secondary grades		
Counselor–student ratio in secondary grades		
Number of students per music specialist in elementary grades		
Number of students per art specialist in elementary grades		
Number of volumes in senior high school library		
Beginning teacher's salary		
Maximum teacher's salary		
Average years of experience among teachers		
Number of students suspended and expelled		
Subjects in which Advanced Placement courses are offered:		

†A Statistical Profile was not received from this district.

FAIR APPRAISAL

Quality of School Leadership
Most principals are selected based on their educational leadership ability, and the quality of leadership is generally uniform throughout the system. Parents and teachers help screen principal candidates, and principals have some say in how the district's resources are allotted the schools.

Parents are sometimes effective influencing school decision-making.

Quality of Instruction
Additional learning opportunities for gifted students and additional instruction for low-achieving students are rated fair. The college preparatory curriculum is considered good, and the curriculum for students not planning on college is considered fair.

Quality of School Environment
The level of classroom disruption and student vandalism is low, but the quality of building maintenance and repair is called poor. Too little money and too little planning are blamed.

PAWTUCKET

ADDRESS OF CENTRAL OFFICE:
Park Place, Pawtucket, RI 02860
ESI:64

STATISTICAL PROFILE	DATA	ESI
Grade organization: K–6/7–8/9–12		
Percentage of schools built before 1955	46%	
Total enrollment	8,386	
Average Daily Attendance (ADA)	92%	5
Current expense per pupil in ADA	$3,700	1
Dropout rate	6%	10
Percentage of eligible students who took the SAT	47%	7
Average combined score on SAT	799	0
Percentage of graduates who enrolled in 2- or 4-year colleges	51%	
Percentage of students who passed the state reading test	NA	
Percentage of students who passed the state math test	NA	
Teacher–student ratio in elementary grades	1:21	9
Teacher–student ratio in secondary grades	1:12	10
Counselor–student ratio in secondary grades	1:246	8
Number of students per music specialist in elementary grades	325	9
Number of students per art specialist in elementary grades	325	
Number of volumes in senior high school library	9,741	
Beginning teacher's salary	$15,211	
Maximum teacher's salary	$30,669	
Average years of experience among teachers	34	
Number of students suspended and expelled	148	
Subjects in which Advanced Placement courses are offered:	5	5
American History, Calculus, English, French, Science		

FAIR APPRAISAL

Quality of School Leadership
Although seniority is a factor, most principals are selected for their ability as educational leaders. The quality of leadership is generally uniform throughout the district. Parents have little say in the selection of principals, and principals don't have much say concerning the distribution of resources to the schools.

Parent organizations are a "power to be reckoned with," according to an observer.

Quality of Instruction
Additional learning opportunities for gifted students are rated good, and the additional instruction for low-achieving students is called fair to good (the district does well with potential dropouts). The college preparatory curriculum is only rated fair. "It is not their strong suit," said an observer. The curriculum for students not planning on college is considered to be much stronger.

Quality of School Environment
The level of classroom disruption and student vandalism is called "average." The quality of building maintenance and repair is rated fair. "They do the best with what they have," said an observer.

PROVIDENCE

ADDRESS OF CENTRAL OFFICE:
Charles Street, Providence, RI 02904
ESI:36*

STATISTICAL PROFILE	DATA	ESI
Grade organization: †		
Percentage of schools built before 1955	33%	
Total enrollment	19,685	
Average Daily Attendance (ADA)	87%	0
Current expense per pupil in ADA	$4,270	4
Dropout rate	47%	0
Percentage of eligible students who took the SAT	42	6
Average combined score on SAT	†	0*
Percentage of graduates who enrolled in 2- or 4-year colleges	40%	
Percentage of students who passed the state reading test	NA	
Percentage of students who passed the state math test	NA	
Teacher–student ratio in elementary grades	1:26	4
Teacher–student ratio in secondary grades	1:15	10
Counselor–student ratio in secondary grades	1:250	8
Number of students per music specialist in elementary grades	837	0
Number of students per art specialist in elementary grades	802	
Number of volumes in senior high school libraries (average)	36,307	
Beginning teacher's salary	$17,238	
Maximum teacher's salary	$31,794	
Average years of experience among teachers	18	
Number of students suspended and expelled	381	
Subjects in which Advanced Placement courses are offered:	4	4
Biology, Calculus, Chemistry, Foreign Language		

†The district misinterpreted this statistic.

FAIR APPRAISAL

Quality of School Leadership

Internal politics are a factor in principal selection, but principals are hired primarily because of their educational leadership ability. The quality of leadership does not vary greatly from school to school at the elementary level, but there is some wide variation at the secondard level. Parents and teachers do not interview principal candidates. However, principals have some say in how district resources are allotted to the schools.

Parent organizations are more active and more effective on the fringes of the city; parental involvement in the center city is less. However, said an observer, "people are beginning to see that the public schools are vital" to the future of the city.

Quality of Instruction

Additional learning opportunities for gifted students are considered excellent. Gifted students generally attend a magnet elementary school designed for them and the magnet secondary schools designed for students with high academic and creative abilities. Additional instruction for low-achieving students is rated only fair, but "moving toward good." Several pilot programs for low-achieving students in the lower grades were scheduled to begin in 1987–88. The college preparatory curriculum is rated good, particularly at the magnet schools, and the curriculum for students not planning on college is also termed good. Students in business courses, in particular, are usually placed in jobs after graduation.

Quality of School Environment

The level of classroom disruption and student vandalism is low, but the quality of building maintenance and repair is only considered fair to poor. The buildings need "extensive repairs," said an observer.

WARWICK

ADDRESS OF CENTRAL OFFICE:
34 Warwick Lake Avenue, Warwick, RI 02889
ESI:None†

STATISTICAL PROFILE	DATA	ESI
Grade organization:		
Percentage of schools built before 1955		
Total enrollment		
Average Daily Attendance (ADA)		
Current expense per pupil in ADA		
Dropout rate		
Percentage of eligible students who took the SAT		
Average combined score on SAT		
Percentage of graduates who enrolled in 2- or 4-year colleges		
Percentage of students who passed the state reading test		
Percentage of students who passed the state math test		
Teacher–student ratio in elementary grades		
Teacher–student ratio in secondary grades		
Counselor–student ratio in secondary grades		
Number of students per music specialist in elementary grades		
Number of students per art specialist in elementary grades		
Number of volumes in senior high school library		
Beginning teacher's salary		
Maximum teacher's salary		
Average years of experience among teachers		
Number of students suspended and expelled		
Subjects in which Advanced Placement courses are offered:		

†A Statistical Profile was not received from this district.

FAIR APPRAISAL

Quality of School Leadership
Principals are chosen for their educational leadership ability, and the quality of leadership is generally uniform throughout the system. Parents and teachers have some say in principal selection (offering informal opinions), and principals have some say in the distribution of the district's resources.

Parent organizations are effective in their influence over school policy decisions.

Quality of Instruction
Additional learning opportunities for gifted students are rated good to excellent, but the additional instruction for low-achieving students is considered only fair. The curriculum for students planning on college is rated excellent, while the curriculum for students not planning on college is considered good.

Quality of School Environment
The level of classroom disruption and student vandalism tend to be on the high side. The quality of building maintenance and repair is good.

WOONSOCKET

ADDRESS OF CENTRAL OFFICE:
108 High Street, Woonsocket, RI 02895
ESI:44*

STATISTICAL PROFILE	DATA	ESI
Grade organization: K–6/7–9/10–12		
Percentage of schools built before 1955	66%	
Total enrollment	6,700	
Average Daily Attendance (ADA)	89%	2
Current expense per pupil in ADA	$4,073	3
Dropout rate	12%	10
Percentage of eligible students who took the SAT	34%	4
Average combined score on SAT	†	0*
Percentage of graduates who enrolled in 2- or 4-year colleges	45%	
Percentage of students who passed the state reading test	NA	
Percentage of students who passed the state math test	NA	
Teacher–student ratio in elementary grades	1:25	5
Teacher–student ratio in secondary grades	1:19	9
Counselor–student ratio in secondary grades	1:319	5
Number of students per music specialist in elementary grades	†	0*
Number of students per art specialist in elementary grades	†	
Number of volumes in senior high school library	15,735	
Beginning teacher's salary	$15,483	
Maximum teacher's salary	$29,907	
Average years of experience among teachers	18	
Number of students suspended and expelled	318	
Subjects in which Advanced Placement courses are offered:	6	6
American History, Art, Biology, Calculus, English, European History		

†The district supplied an inappropriate statistic.

FAIR APPRAISAL

Quality of School Leadership
The School Board hires principals who demonstrate educational leadership ability, and the quality of leadership is generally uniform throughout the system. Parents and teachers have some say in principal selection, and principals have some say on the allotment of district resources.

Parent groups are considered strong and effective influences in decision-making.

Quality of Instruction
Additional learning opportunities for gifted students are rated excellent. Especially noteworthy is the art program for those students with exceptional talent. Additional instruction for low-achieving students is considered good. The district offers special help to pre-kindergarten and pre-first grade students who have potential learning problems. The curriculum for college-bound students is rated good, while the curriculum for students planning on entering the world of work is considered excellent.

Quality of School Environment
Classroom disruption and student vandalism are not problems, and the quality of building maintenance and repair is rated excellent.

Riverside–San Bernadino, CA

One district supplied a Statistical Profile; Fair Appraisals alone are provided for two other districts. California does not administer a state test of student competency in reading and mathematics. Therefore, *NA* (not applicable) appears on lines requesting those statistics. Districts in this area should be compared to districts in the Los Angeles–Orange County, CA Metropolitan Area.

AREA AT A GLANCE

SCHOOL DISTRICT	ENROLLMENT	ESI
Colton	12,561	
Fontana	17,625	17*
San Bernadino	33,300	

Indicates district misinterpretation of one or more statistics in the ESI. For each misinterpreted statistic, a score of 0 was given instead of a possible score of 0 to 10 points.

SCHOOL DISTRICT

COLTON

ADDRESS OF CENTRAL OFFICE:
1212 Valencia Drive, Colton, CA 92340
ESI:None†

STATISTICAL PROFILE	DATA	ESI
Grade organization:		
Percentage of schools built before 1955		
Total enrollment		
Average Daily Attendance (ADA)		
Current expense per pupil in ADA		
Dropout rate		
Percentage of eligible students who took the SAT		
Average combined score on SAT		
Percentage of graduates who enrolled in 2- or 4-year colleges		
Percentage of students who passed the state reading test		
Percentage of students who passed the state math test		
Teacher–student ratio in elementary grades		
Teacher–student ratio in secondary grades		
Counselor–student ratio in secondary grades		
Number of students per music specialist in elementary grades		
Number of students per art specialist in elementary grades		
Number of volumes in senior high school library		
Beginning teacher's salary		
Maximum teacher's salary		
Average years of experience among teachers		
Number of students suspended and expelled		
Subjects in which Advanced Placement courses are offered:		

†A Statistical Profile was not received from this district.

FAIR APPRAISAL

Quality of School Leadership
Most principals are selected based on their ability as educational leaders. The quality of leadership is generally uniform throughout the system. Parents and teachers do not screen principal candidates. Principals, however, have some say in the distribution of district resources.

Parent organizations are effective influencing school decision-making.

Quality of Instruction
Additional learning opportunities for gifted students are rated fair, but additional instruction for low-achieving students is considered good. The curricula for college-bound students and for job-bound students are rated good.

Quality of School Environment
The incidence of classroom disruption and student vandalism is said to be on the high side, but the quality of building maintenance and repair is good.

FONTANA

ADDRESS OF CENTRAL OFFICE:
9680 Citrus Avenue, Fontana, CA 92335
ESI:17*

STATISTICAL PROFILE	DATA	ESI
Grade organization: K–6/7–9/10–12		
Percentage of schools built before 1955	30%	
Total enrollment	17,625	
Average Daily Attendance (ADA)	93%	6
Current expense per pupil in ADA	$3,180	4
Dropout rate	40%	0
Percentage of eligible students who took the SAT	23%	2
Average combined score on SAT	†	0*
Percentage of graduates who enrolled in 2- or 4-year colleges	36%	
Percentage of students who passed the state reading test	NA	
Percentage of students who passed the state math test	NA	
Teacher–student ratio in elementary grades	1:30	0
Teacher–student ratio in secondary grades	1:33	0
Counselor–student ratio in secondary grades	1:450	0
Number of students per music specialist in elementary grades	1,140	0
Number of students per art specialist in elementary grades	None	
Number of volumes in senior high school libraries (average)	20,000	
Beginning teacher's salary	$21,688	
Maximum teacher's salary	$37,832	
Average years of experience among teachers	11	
Number of students suspended and expelled	4,662	
Subjects in which Advanced Placement courses are offered: American Government, American History, Computer Science, English, Spanish	5	5

†The district supplied an inappropriate statistic.

FAIR APPRAISAL

Quality of School Leadership
Most principals are hired for their educational leadership ability, and the quality of leadership is generally uniform throughout the system. Parents and teachers have no say in principal selection, but principals have some influence over the allocation of district resources.

Parent organizations are sometimes effective influencing school policy decisions.

Quality of Instruction
Additional learning opportunities for gifted students are rated fair to poor. No program exists in the elementary grades. Rated fair to good is additional instruction for low-achieving students. The curriculum preparing students for college is called fair, but the curriculum for students planning on entering the job market is considered good. The district has a "top vocational program," said an observer, funded in part by private money (Kaiser Steel).

Quality of School Environment
The level of classroom disruption and student vandalism is low, but the quality of building maintenance and repair is fair.

SAN BERNADINO

ADDRESS OF CENTRAL OFFICE:
777 North F Street, San Bernardino, CA 92415
ESI:None†

STATISTICAL PROFILE	DATA	ESI
Grade organization:		
Percentage of schools built before 1955		
Total enrollment		
Average Daily Attendance (ADA)		
Current expense per pupil in ADA		
Dropout rate		
Percentage of eligible students who took the SAT		
Average combined score on SAT		
Percentage of graduates who enrolled in 2- or 4-year colleges		
Percentage of students who passed the state reading test		
Percentage of students who passed the state math test		
Teacher–student ratio in elementary grades		
Teacher–student ratio in secondary grades		
Counselor–student ratio in secondary grades		
Number of students per music specialist in elementary grades		
Number of students per art specialist in elementary grades		
Number of volumes in senior high school library		
Beginning teacher's salary		
Maximum teacher's salary		
Average years of experience among teachers		
Number of students suspended and expelled		
Subjects in which Advanced Placement courses are offered:		

†A Statistical Profile was not received from this district.

FAIR APPRAISAL

Quality of School Leadership
Achieving racial balance is a concern in principal selection, but the primary criterion for hiring is educational leadership ability. Although the quality of leadership is generally uniform throughout the system, one observer complained that "skilled principals sometimes are promoted to higher administrative positions and replaced by persons with fewer qualifications." Parents and teachers do not screen principal candidates, and principals do not have much to say about the allotment of district resources to the schools.

Parent organizations are sometimes an effective influence on school decision-making.

Quality of Instruction
Additional learning opportunities for gifted students and additional instruction for low-achieving students are rated fair. Also, the curricula preparing students for college and preparing students for the job market are termed only fair.

Quality of School Environment
The incidence of classroom disruption and student vandalism is high, and the quality of building maintenance and repair is fair.

METROPOLITAN AREA

Rochester, NY

Five districts completed Statistical Profiles. Districts in this area
may be compared to districts in the Albany, NY Metropolitan Area.

AREA AT A GLANCE

SCHOOL DISTRICT	ENROLLMENT	ESI
Brighton	3,062	98
Churchville–Chili	3,440	73
Greece	10,937	63
Rochester	32,348	41
Rush–Henrietta	5,738	71

100 is perfect
58 is median

SCHOOL DISTRICT

BRIGHTON

ADDRESS OF CENTRAL OFFICE:
600 Grosvenor Road, Rochester, NY 14610
ESI:98

STATISTICAL PROFILE	DATA	ESI
Grade organization: K–2/3–5/6–8/9–12		
Percentage of schools built before 1955	50%	
Total enrollment	3,062	
Average Daily Attendance (ADA)	96%	9
Current expense per pupil in ADA	$6,700	10
Dropout rate	3%	10
Percentage of eligible students who took the SAT	90%	10
Average combined score on SAT	1,050	10
Percentage of graduates who enrolled in 2- or 4-year colleges	88%	
Percentage of students who passed the state reading test	97%	
Percentage of students who passed the state math test	100%	
Teacher–student ratio in elementary grades	1:17	10
Teacher–student ratio in secondary grades	1:14	10
Counselor–student ratio in secondary grades	1:217	9
Number of students per music specialist in elementary grades	216	10
Number of students per art specialist in elementary grades	611	
Number of volumes in senior high school library	16,000	
Beginning teacher's salary	$18,738	
Maximum teacher's salary	$44,409	
Average years of experience among teachers	15	
Number of students suspended and expelled	80	
Subjects in which Advanced Placement courses are offered:	11	10
American History, Biology, Calculus, Chemistry, Computer Science, English, European History, French Literature and Language, German Language, Physics, Spanish Literature and Language		

FAIR APPRAISAL

Quality of School Leadership
The School Board looks for principals who evidence ability as
educational leaders, and the quality of leadership is generally
uniform throughout the system. Parents and teachers have
some say in principal selection, and principals have some say in
how resources are allotted to the schools.

Parent organizations are effective influencing district
policies. Recently, parents conducted a survey to see who was
for and against an open campus policy at the high school. The
survey showed most parents, teachers and students favored the
policy.

Quality of Instruction
Additional learning opportunities for gifted students are rated
excellent, with students in the lower grades excused from
regular classes for enrichment. Additional instruction for low-
achieving students is considered good. The college preparatory
curriculum is described as excellent, and the curriculum for
students not planning on college is termed fair to good. The
district's major efforts are concentrated on students going to
college.

Quality of School Environment
The level of classroom disruption and student vandalism is low,
and the quality of building maintenance and repair is considered
good.

CHURCHVILLE–CHILI

ADDRESS OF CENTRAL OFFICE:
139 Fairbanks Road, Churchville, NY 14428
ESI:73

STATISTICAL PROFILE	DATA	ESI
Grade organization: K–5/6–8/9–12		
Percentage of schools built before 1955	20%	
Total enrollment	3,440	
Average Daily Attendance (ADA)	95%	8
Current expense per pupil in ADA	$3,181	0
Dropout rate	4%	10
Percentage of eligible students who took the SAT	40%	5
Average combined score on SAT	1,012	10
Percentage of graduates who enrolled in 2- or 4-year colleges	53%	
Percentage of students who passed the state reading test	96%	
Percentage of students who passed the state math test	76%	
Teacher–student ratio in elementary grades	1:17	10
Teacher–student ratio in secondary grades	1:13	10
Counselor–student ratio in secondary grades	1:289	6
Number of students per music specialist in elementary grades	297	10
Number of students per art specialist in elementary grades	774	
Number of volumes in senior high school library	18,225	
Beginning teacher's salary	$17,036†	
Maximum teacher's salary	$43,064†	
Average years of experience among teachers	21	
Number of students suspended and expelled	156	
Subjects in which Advanced Placement courses are offered: American History, Calculus, Computer Science, English Literature and Composition	4	4

†1986–87 statistics.

Quality of School Leadership

Principals are selected primarily for their educational leadership ability; the quality of leadership does not vary greatly from school to school. Parents and teachers do not take part in screening principal candidates, but principals have some say in the allotment of resources to the schools.

Parents are effective influencing school decision-making. An anti-drug and alcohol program was instituted by parents, and parents have been influential regarding a computer program for elementary schools and the revamping of high school sports. Communication between parents, teachers and administrators is excellent, said an observer. "This is a nice place to live if you're not looking for the fast lane."

Quality of Instruction

Additional learning opportunities for gifted students are rated fair to good. The district is "not noted" for its program for gifted students, said an observer. The quality of additional instruction for low-achieving students is considered good. Rated fair is the college preparatory curriculum, but the curriculum for students not going to college is considered good.

Quality of School Environment

The level of classroom disruption and student vandalism is low. Building maintenance and repair are excellent.

GREECE

ADDRESS OF CENTRAL OFFICE:
P.O. Box 300, North Greece, NY 14515
ESI:63

STATISTICAL PROFILE	DATA	ESI
Grade organization: K–3/4–6/7–8/9–12		
Percentage of schools built before 1955	9%	
Total enrollment	10,937	
Average Daily Attendance (ADA)	95%	8
Current expense per pupil in ADA	$5,339	4
Dropout rate	10%	10
Percentage of eligible students who took the SAT	64%	10
Average combined score on SAT	928	5
Percentage of graduates who enrolled in 2- or 4-year colleges	53%	
Percentage of students who passed the state reading test	96%	
Percentage of students who passed the state math test	86%	
Teacher–student ratio in elementary grades	1:25	5
Teacher–student ratio in secondary grades	1:25	3
Counselor–student ratio in secondary grades	1:314	5
Number of students per music specialist in elementary grades	255	10
Number of students per art specialist in elementary grades	457	
Number of volumes in senior high school libraries (average)	24,251	
Beginning teacher's salary	$17,328	
Maximum teacher's salary	$39,744	
Average years of experience among teachers	13	
Number of students suspended and expelled	845	
Subjects in which Advanced Placement courses are offered: Calculus, English, Science	3	3

Quality of School Leadership

Most principals are hired because of their educational leadership ability, and the quality of leadership is generally uniform throughout the system. Parents and teachers do not interview principal candidates. Principals have some say in how resources are divided among the schools. They exercise this influence not only through budget requests, but, more importantly, through their impact on curriculum. Greece was one of the first districts in the area to give principals a 12-month contract.

Parent organizations are sometimes effective as an influence on decision-making.

Quality of Instruction

Additional learning opportunities for gifted students are rated excellent, with the program being strongest in grades 4–6 (self-contained classrooms). Additional instruction for low-achieving students is rated good. There is an "increased emphasis" on meeting the needs of these students, said an observer. The curricula for college-bound students and job-bound students are both considered good. The district has introduced a latch-key program for students from families where no adult is at home after school.

Quality of School Environment

The incidence of classroom disruption and student vandalism is low. The quality of building maintenance and repair, however, is only fair. "They do well on the major things," said an observer, "but it's the minor stuff that makes some schools look tacky—doors that won't close properly, for example."

ROCHESTER

ADDRESS OF CENTRAL OFFICE:
131 West Broad Street, Rochester, NY 14614
ESI:41

STATISTICAL PROFILE	DATA	ESI
Grade organization: K–6/7–12†		
Percentage of schools built before 1955	58%	
Total enrollment	32,348	
Average Daily Attendance (ADA)	90%	3
Current expense per pupil in ADA	NK	0
Dropout rate	60%	0
Percentage of eligible students who took the SAT	31%	4
Average combined score on SAT	846	1
Percentage of graduates who enrolled in 2- or 4-year colleges	52%	
Percentage of students who passed the state reading test	88%	
Percentage of students who passed the state math test	61%	
Teacher–student ratio in elementary grades	1:23	7
Teacher–student ratio in secondary grades	1:17	10
Counselor–student ratio in secondary grades	1:284	6
Number of students per music specialist in elementary grades	None	0
Number of students per art specialist in elementary grades	None	
Number of volumes in senior high school libraries (average)	13,783	
Beginning teacher's salary	$17,661	
Maximum teacher's salary	$39,331	
Average years of experience among teachers	NK	
Number of students suspended and expelled	4,945	
Subjects in which Advanced Placement courses are offered: American History, Biology, Calculus, Chemistry, Computer Science, English, European History, French, German, Physics, Spanish	11	10

†This is the primary pattern; there are variations.

Quality of School Leadership

For the most part, principals are chosen for their educational leadership ability, but internal politics and the desire to achieve racial balance are also important factors. The quality of leadership varies greatly from school to school, mainly for the reasons mentioned above. Parents and teachers serve on the committees that screen principal candidates. Principals have some say in determining the distribution of district resources, primarily through school-based planning.

Parent organizations are sometimes effective influencing district decisions. Parents and other community residents serve on planning committees that help decide district policies.

Quality of Instruction

Additional learning opportunities for gifted students are rated good; the program begins in grade 4. Additional instruction for low-achieving students is considered fair, but getting better. "Tons of new programs have been started," said one observer, most of them quite recently. The curriculum for college-bound students is rated good, but observers believe more students need to be encouraged to take high-level courses. The curriculum for students not planning on college is termed fair to poor.

The district is "very committed and tries very hard," but it does not adequately meet the needs of minority students, said observers. However, a new contract with teachers holds them "accountable" for the academic progress of students. In return, the average teacher's salary could reach $45,000 by 1990.

Quality of School Environment

The level of classroom disruption and student vandalism tends to be on the high side, and the quality of building maintenance and repair is fair.

RUSH–HENRIETTA

ADDRESS OF CENTRAL OFFICE:
2034 Lehigh Station Road, Henrietta, NY 14467
ESI:71

STATISTICAL PROFILE	DATA	ESI
Grade organization: K–6/7–8/9–12		
Percentage of schools built before 1955	10%	
Total enrollment	5,738	
Average Daily Attendance (ADA)	94%	7
Current expense per pupil in ADA	$4,441	0
Dropout rate	4%	10
Percentage of eligible students who took the SAT	48%	7
Average combined score on SAT	948	7
Percentage of graduates who enrolled in 2- or 4-year colleges	62%	
Percentage of students who passed the state reading test	98%	
Percentage of students who passed the state math test	88%	
Teacher–student ratio in elementary grades	1:23	7
Teacher–student ratio in secondary grades	1:16	10
Counselor–student ratio in secondary grades	1:235	8
Number of students per music specialist in elementary grades	352	8
Number of students per art specialist in elementary grades	572	
Number of volumes in senior high school library	28,636	
Beginning teacher's salary	$17,000	
Maximum teacher's salary	$39,854	
Average years of experience among teachers	18	
Number of students suspended and expelled	NK	
Subjects in which Advanced Placement courses are offered:	7	7
American History, Biology, Calculus, Chemistry,		
English, European History, Physics		

FAIR APPRAISAL

Quality of School Leadership

The School Board primarily hires principals who demonstrate ability as educational leaders, and the quality of leadership is generally uniform throughout the system. Parents and teachers have hardly any say in principal selection, but principals have some say in the allotment of district resources.

Parent organizations are an effective influence on decision-making. A major task force of parents and other community residents recently paved the way for the merger of two high schools.

Quality of Instruction

The gifted program and additional instruction for low-achieving students are rated good. Also considered good are the curricula for students planning on college and for students not planning on college.

Quality of School Environment

The level of classroom disruption and student vandalism tend to be on the high side, but the quality of building maintenance and repair is good.

St. Louis, MO

Fourteen school districts submitted Statistical Profiles, and Fair Appraisals
alone were received from two other districts. Since the state of Illinois does not require
tests of reading and math competency, Illinois districts included in this area show
NA (not applicable) on the lines requesting those statistics. Districts in the St. Louis
Metropolitan Area may be compared to districts in the Kansas City, MO Metropolitan Area.

AREA AT A GLANCE

SCHOOL DISTRICT	ENROLLMENT	ESI
Alton, IL	7,368	51
Bethalto, IL	3,000	64
East St. Louis, IL	18,901	31
Edwardsville, IL	4,507	62
Ferguson–Florissant	11,347	61*
Fort Zumwalt	8,382	
Francis Howell	11,681	34
Kirkwood	4,847	88
Ladue	3,077	76*
Lindbergh	4,980	61
Mascoutah, IL	3,095	
Mehlville	9,839	63*
Normandy	6,313	57
Ritenour	7,000	44*
St. Charles	6,100	76
Webster Groves	3,805	77

Indicates district misinterpretation of one or more statistics in the ESI. For each misinterpreted statistic, a score of 0 was given instead of a possible score of 0 to 10 points.

ALTON

ADDRESS OF CENTRAL OFFICE:
1854 East Broadway, Alton, IL 62002
ESI:51

STATISTICAL PROFILE	DATA	ESI
Grade organization: K–1/2–5/6–8/9–12		
Percentage of schools built before 1955	82%	
Total enrollment	7,368	
Average Daily Attendance (ADA)	92%	5
Current expense per pupil in ADA	$3,328	4
Dropout rate	17%	6
Percentage of eligible students who took the ACT	41%	6
Average combined score on ACT	19.3	5
Percentage of graduates who enrolled in 2- or 4-year colleges	55%	
Percentage of students who passed the state reading test	NA	
Percentage of students who passed the state math test	NA	
Teacher–student ratio in elementary grades	1:21	9
Teacher–student ratio in secondary grades	1:26	2
Counselor–student ratio in secondary grades	1:400	2
Number of students per music specialist in elementary grades	300	9
Number of students per art specialist in elementary grades	None	0
Number of volumes in senior high school library	19,100	
Beginning teacher's salary	$17,455	
Maximum teacher's salary	$35,490	
Average years of experience among teachers	16	
Number of students suspended and expelled	1,245	
Subjects in which Advanced Placement courses are offered: English, Calculus, Physics	3	3

FAIR APPRAISAL

Quality of School Leadership
Popularity and internal politics are important factors in selection of principals. As a consequence, the quality of leadership varies greatly within the system. Parents and teachers have hardly any say in principal selection, but principals have some say in the allotment of district resources.

Parent organizations are sometimes effective influencing district policy.

Quality of Instruction
Additional learning opportunities for gifted students are rated excellent. The top five percent of students in grades 1–8 are involved. Additional instruction for low-achieving students is termed only fair. The curriculum for students planning to attend college is rated excellent, while the curriculum for students not planning on college is termed good.

Quality of School Environment
The level of classroom disruption and student vandalism is very low, and the quality of building maintenance and repair is excellent.

BETHALTO

ADDRESS OF CENTRAL OFFICE:
322 East Central Street, Bethalto, IL 62010
ESI:64

STATISTICAL PROFILE	DATA	ESI
Grade organization: †		
Percentage of schools built before 1955	25%	
Total enrollment	3,000	
Average Daily Attendance (ADA)	95%	8
Current expense per pupil in ADA	$2,750	1
Dropout rate	10%	10
Percentage of eligible students who took the ACT	67%	10
Average combined score on ACT	18.7	4
Percentage of graduates who enrolled in 2- or 4-year colleges	55%	
Percentage of students who passed the state reading test	NA	
Percentage of students who passed the state math test	NA	
Teacher–student ratio in elementary grades	1:22	8
Teacher–student ratio in secondary grades	1:20	8
Counselor–student ratio in secondary grades	1:250	8
Number of students per music specialist in elementary grades	500	5
Number of students per art specialist in elementary grades	None	0
Number of volumes in senior high school library	25,000	
Beginning teacher's salary	$16,000	
Maximum teacher's salary	$30,000	
Average years of experience among teachers	15	
Number of students suspended and expelled	100	
Subjects in which Advanced Placement courses are offered: Calculus, English	2	2

†The district misinterpreted this statistic.

FAIR APPRAISAL

Quality of School Leadership
Longevity and internal politics are factors in the selection of principals, but the candidates' educational leadership ability is still the most important criterion. Therefore, the quality of leadership is generally uniform throughout the system. Parents and teachers do not screen principal candidates. Principals, however, have some say in determining how district resources are spent.

Parents are sometimes effective influencing district decision-making. The School Board is "not always receptive to parents' suggestions and criticism," said an observer.

Quality of Instruction
Additional learning opportunities for gifted students are rated excellent. Also considered excellent is the additional instruction for low-achieving students. Four communities are included in this district, and the quality of instruction for low-achieving students varies in the elementary schools in these communities, said an observer. The curriculum for college-bound students is rated good, while the job-bound curriculum is considered excellent with a strong regional vocational-technical school.

Quality of School Environment
The level of classroom disruption and student vandalism is low, and building maintenance and repair are good.

EAST ST. LOUIS

ADDRESS OF CENTRAL OFFICE:
1005 State Street, East St. Louis, IL 62201
ESI:31

STATISTICAL PROFILE	DATA	ESI
Grade organization: Pre-K–6/7–9/10–12		
Percentage of schools built before 1955	12%	
Total enrollment	18,901	
Average Daily Attendance (ADA)	88%	1
Current expense per pupil in ADA	$1,952	0
Dropout rate	21%	2
Percentage of eligible students who took the ACT	60%	9
Average combined score on ACT	11.4	0
Percentage of graduates who enrolled in 2- or 4-year colleges	42%	
Percentage of students who passed the state reading test	NA	
Percentage of students who passed the state math test	NA	
Teacher–student ratio in elementary grades	1:25	6
Teacher–student ratio in secondary grades	1:29	0
Counselor–student ratio in secondary grades	1:338	4
Number of students per music specialist in elementary grades	300	9
Number of students per art specialist in elementary grades	300	
Number of volumes in senior high school libraries (average)	20,000	
Beginning teacher's salary	$18,500	
Maximum teacher's salary	$35,450	
Average years of experience among teachers	23	
Number of students suspended and expelled	241	
Subjects in which Advanced Placement courses are offered:	None	0

FAIR APPRAISAL

Quality of School Leadership

Until recently, according to an observer, the School Board president was very powerful, and principal candidates had to satisfy him. However, the hiring system has changed, and the quality of leadership is generally uniform throughout the system. Parents and teachers have hardly any say in principal selection, and principals have little say in the allotment of district resources.

Parent organizations are not very influential in district decision-making.

Quality of Instruction

Both gifted students and low-achieving students are identified early in the grades, said an observer, and provided additional help right away. The program for gifted students is considered excellent. Gifted students at the elementary and middle school level go to special schools. Instruction for low-achieving students is rated good. Special administrators are assigned to gifted students and low-achieving students. However, the curriculum for students planning on college is only rated fair to good, while the curriculum for students not planning on college is only considered fair to poor.

The district is "noted for its high school marching bands, and competition for the bands is stiff," according to an observer.

Quality of School Environment

The level of classroom disruption and student vandalism tends to be high. Security guards were hired for the middle and high schools in the spring of 1987.

EDWARDSVILLE

ADDRESS OF CENTRAL OFFICE:
708 St. Louis Street, Edwardsville, IL 62025
ESI:62

STATISTICAL PROFILE	DATA	ESI
Grade organization: †		
Percentage of schools built before 1955	63%	
Total enrollment	4,507	
Average Daily Attendance (ADA)	90%	3
Current expense per pupil in ADA	$2,323	0
Dropout rate	5%	10
Percentage of eligible students who took the ACT	58%	9
Average combined score on ACT	19.9	5
Percentage of graduates who enrolled in 2- or 4-year colleges	60%	
Percentage of students who passed the state reading test	NA	
Percentage of students who passed the state math test	NA	
Teacher–student ratio in elementary grades	1:10	10
Teacher–student ratio in secondary grades	1:18	10
Counselor–student ratio in secondary grades	1:315	5
Number of students per music specialist in elementary grades	361	8
Number of students per art specialist in elementary grades	723	
Number of volumes in senior high school library	13,324	
Beginning teacher's salary	$15,200	
Maximum teacher's salary	$32,528	
Average years of experience among teachers	17	
Number of students suspended and expelled	260	
Subjects in which Advanced Placement courses are offered: American History, English	2	2

†The district misinterpreted this statistic.

FAIR APPRAISAL

Quality of School Leadership

Most principals are selected for their educational leadership ability, and the quality of leadership does not vary greatly from school to school. Parents and teachers helped select the superintendent recently, but they play hardly any role in principal selection. Principals have some say in the disbursement of district resources.

Parent organizations are an effective influence on district policy-making. A citizens advisory council and a host of standing committees involve parents and other citizens in decision-making.

Quality of Instruction

Generally, the program for gifted students is rated good. However, an observer said the program at the junior high consists mostly of extra homework. The additional instruction for low-achieving students is rated excellent. Also rated excellent are the curricula for students planning on college and for those planning on the world of work.

Quality of School Environment

Classroom disruption and student vandalism are not problems. Building maintenance and repair are good.

FERGUSON–FLORISSANT

ADDRESS OF CENTRAL OFFICE:
1005 Waterford Drive, Florissant, MO 63033
ESI:61*

STATISTICAL PROFILE	DATA	ESI
Grade organization: K-6/7–8/9–12		
Percentage of schools built before 1955	50%	
Total enrollment	11,347	
Average Daily Attendance (ADA)	95%	8
Current expense per pupil in ADA	$3,936	9
Dropout rate	33%†	0*
Percentage of eligible students who took the ACT	41%	6
Average combined score on ACT	19.2	5
Percentage of graduates who enrolled in 2- or 4-year colleges	50%	
Percentage of students who passed the state reading test	99%	
Percentage of students who passed the state math test	93%	
Teacher–student ratio in elementary grades	1:22	8
Teacher–student ratio in secondary grades	1:24	4
Counselor–student ratio in secondary grades	1:287	6
Number of students per music specialist in elementary grades	240	10
Number of students per art specialist in elementary grades	490	
Number of volumes in senior high school libraries (average)	35,660	
Beginning teacher's salary	$18,300	
Maximum teacher's salary	$36,789	
Average years of experience among teachers	14	
Number of students suspended and expelled	2,844	
Subjects in which Advanced Placement courses are offered: American History, Calculus, English, Foreign Language, Science	5	5

†This statistic may have been provided by the district in error.

FAIR APPRAISAL

Quality of School Leadership

Most principals are hired for their ability as educational leaders, and the quality of leadership does not vary greatly from school to school. Parents and teachers have little say in the selection of principals, but principals have some say in the allotment of resources to the schools.

Parent organizations are not very effective influencing district decision-making.

Quality of Instruction

Additional learning opportunities for gifted students are rated excellent, and additional instruction for low-achieving students is considered good. Also rated good are the curricula for students planning on college and for those planning on work after graduation.

The district "does not meet the educational needs of minority students as well as it should," said an observer.

Quality of School Environment

The incidence of classroom disruption and student vandalism is low, and the quality of building maintenance and repair is good.

FORT ZUMWALT

ADDRESS OF CENTRAL OFFICE:
110 Virgil Street, O'Fallon, MO 63366
ESI:None†

STATISTICAL PROFILE	DATA	ESI
Grade organization:		
Percentage of schools built before 1955		
Total enrollment		
Average Daily Attendance (ADA)		
Current expense per pupil in ADA		
Dropout rate		
Percentage of eligible students who took the ACT		
Average combined score on ACT		
Percentage of graduates who enrolled in 2- or 4-year colleges		
Percentage of students who passed the state reading test		
Percentage of students who passed the state math test		
Teacher–student ratio in elementary grades		
Teacher–student ratio in secondary grades		
Counselor–student ratio in secondary grades		
Number of students per music specialist in elementary grades		
Number of students per art specialist in elementary grades		
Number of volumes in senior high school library		
Beginning teacher's salary		
Maximum teacher's salary		
Average years of experience among teachers		
Number of students suspended and expelled		
Subjects in which Advanced Placement courses are offered:		

†A Statistical Profile was not received from this district.

FAIR APPRAISAL

Quality of School Leadership
Longevity and popularity are important criteria for principal selection, and the quality of leadership varies from school to school. Parents and teachers have hardly any say in principal selection, but principals have a lot to say about the disbursement of district resources.

Parent organizations are an effective influence in school decision-making.

Quality of Instruction
Additional instruction for gifted students is rated good, while additional instruction for low-achieving students is considered only fair. Rated good are the curricula for college-bound students and job-bound students.

Quality of School Environment
The level of classroom disruption and student vandalism is low, and the quality of building maintenance and repair is good.

FRANCIS HOWELL

ADDRESS OF CENTRAL OFFICE:
7001 Highway 94 South, St. Charles, MO 63303
ESI:34

STATISTICAL PROFILE	DATA	ESI
Grade organization: K–6/7–9/10–12		
Percentage of schools built before 1955	18%	
Total enrollment	11,681	
Average Daily Attendance (ADA)	85%	0
Current expense per pupil in ADA	$2,818	4
Dropout rate	18%	5
Percentage of eligible students who took the ACT	41%	6
Average combined score on ACT	19.5	5
Percentage of graduates who enrolled in 2- or 4-year colleges	60%	
Percentage of students who passed the state reading test	NK	
Percentage of students who passed the state math test	NK	
Teacher–student ratio in elementary grades	1:25	5
Teacher–student ratio in secondary grades	1:25	3
Counselor–student ratio in secondary grades	1:383	2
Number of students per music specialist in elementary grades	575	4
Number of students per art specialist in elementary grades	625	
Number of volumes in senior high school libraries (average)	15,281	
Beginning teacher's salary	$17,470	
Maximum teacher's salary	$31,230	
Average years of experience among teachers	9	
Number of students suspended and expelled	61	
Subjects in which Advanced Placement courses are offered:	None	0

FAIR APPRAISAL

Quality of School Leadership
Longevity and popularity are important considerations when hiring a principal. The quality of leadership, therefore, is not uniform throughout the system. Parents and teachers have hardly any say in principal selection. However, principals have much to say about the use of district resources.

Parent organizations are an effective influence in decision-making by school officials.

Quality of Instruction
Additional learning opportunities for gifted students are rated good to excellent. Students in the program are recommended by their teacher(s) and demonstrate high cognitive skills, according to observers. The additional instruction for low-achieving students also is rated good to excellent. Special classes are restricted to 15 students, said an observer. The curricula for students planning on college and for those planning on the job market are considered good.

Quality of School Environment
The incidence of classroom disruption and student vandalism is low, and the quality of building maintenance and repair is good. However, some buildings are overcrowded.

KIRKWOOD

ADDRESS OF CENTRAL OFFICE:
11289 Manchester Road, St. Louis, MO 63122
ESI:88

STATISTICAL PROFILE	DATA	ESI
Grade organization: K–5/6–8/9–12		
Percentage of schools built before 1955	63%	
Total enrollment	4,847	
Average Daily Attendance (ADA)	95%	8
Current expense per pupil in ADA	$4,016	10
Dropout rate	15%	8
Percentage of eligible students who took the ACT	48%	7
Average combined score on ACT	21.4	10
Percentage of graduates who enrolled in 2- or 4-year colleges	75%	
Percentage of students who passed the state reading test	99%	
Percentage of students who passed the state math test	96%	
Teacher–student ratio in elementary grades	1:19	10
Teacher–student ratio in secondary grades	1:18	10
Counselor–student ratio in secondary grades	1:245	8
Number of students per music specialist in elementary grades	180	10
Number of students per art specialist in elementary grades	718	
Number of volumes in senior high school library	23,156	
Beginning teacher's salary	$19,500	
Maximum teacher's salary	$39,800	
Average years of experience among teachers	16	
Number of students suspended and expelled	1,630	
Subjects in which Advanced Placement courses are offered: American History, Biology, Calculus, Chemistry, English, European History, Physics	7	7

FAIR APPRAISAL

Quality of School Leadership
Most principals are hired based on their educational leadership ability; the quality of leadership is generally uniform throughout the system. Parents and teachers have hardly any say in principal selection, but principals have some influence over the distribution of district resources.

Parent organizations are effective in their influence over school policies. "School leaders are responsive to parents," said an observer.

Quality of Instruction
Additional learning opportunities for gifted students are good to excellent, with strong enrichment in art, music and math. The additional instruction for low-achieving students is rated good. The curriculum for college-bound students is rated excellent, while the curriculum for students planning on the world of work is good.

The district, like many other suburban districts in the area, particpates in a voluntary busing program with St. Louis to relieve racial imbalance in the city schools.

Quality of School Environment
Classroom disruption and student vandalism are not problems. The district has an "excellent program" to encourage harmony between white and black students, said an observer. The quality of building maintenance and repair is excellent.

LADUE

ADDRESS OF CENTRAL OFFICE:
9703 Conway Road, St. Louis, MO 63124
ESI:76*

STATISTICAL PROFILE	DATA	ESI
Grade organization: K–5/6–8/9–12		
Percentage of schools built before 1955	50%	
Total enrollment	3,077	
Average Daily Attendance (ADA)	93%	6
Current expense per pupil in ADA	$5,500	10
Dropout rate	7%	10
Percentage of eligible students who took the ACT	59%	9
Average combined score on ACT	20.5	8
Percentage of graduates who enrolled in 2- or 4-year colleges	84%	
Percentage of students who passed the state reading test	100%	
Percentage of students who passed the state math test	95%	
Teacher–student ratio in elementary grades	1:20	10
Teacher–student ratio in secondary grades	1:21	7
Counselor–student ratio in secondary grades	1:205	9
Number of students per music specialist in elementary grades	†	0*
Number of students per art specialist in elementary grades	†	
Number of volumes in senior high school library	25,968	
Beginning teacher's salary	$19,000	
Maximum teacher's salary	$46,900	
Average years of experience among teachers	18	
Number of students suspended and expelled	164	
Subjects in which Advanced Placement courses are offered: American History, Biology, Calculus, Chemistry, English, French, Spanish	7	7

†The district supplied an inappropriate statistic.

FAIR APPRAISAL

Quality of School Leadership
The School Board chooses principals who demonstrate educational leadership ability. The quality of leadership does not vary greatly from school to school. Parents and teachers have hardly any say in principal selection. Principals, on the other hand, have some influence over resource allotment.

Parent organizations are an effective influence on decision-making at individual schools. They are less influential with the School Board and superintendent.

Quality of Instruction
Additional learning opportunities for gifted students are rated excellent, and additional instruction for low-achieving students is considered good. However, an observer said the instruction for low-achieving students needs some improvement. The curriculum for college-bound students is termed excellent, and the curriculum for job-bound students is rated good.

Quality of School Environment
The level of classroom disruption and student vandalism is very low, and the quality of building maintenance and repair is very high.

LINDBERGH

ADDRESS OF CENTRAL OFFICE:
4900 South Lindbergh Boulevard, St. Louis, MO 63126
ESI:61

STATISTICAL PROFILE	DATA	ESI
Grade organization: K–5/6–8/9–12		
Percentage of schools built before 1955	28%	
Total enrollment	4,980	
Average Daily Attendance (ADA)	92%	5
Current expense per pupil in ADA	$3,200	6
Dropout rate	13%	10
Percentage of eligible students who took the ACT	50%	7
Average combined score on ACT	20.6	9
Percentage of graduates who enrolled in 2- or 4-year colleges	79%	
Percentage of students who passed the state reading test	99%	
Percentage of students who passed the state math test	94%	
Teacher–student ratio in elementary grades	1:24	6
Teacher–student ratio in secondary grades	1:22	6
Counselor–student ratio in secondary grades	1:378	2
Number of students per music specialist in elementary grades	658	2
Number of students per art specialist in elementary grades	658	
Number of volumes in senior high school library	30,000	
Beginning teacher's salary	$18,400	
Maximum teacher's salary	$43,976	
Average years of experience among teachers	NK	
Number of students suspended and expelled	211	
Subjects in which Advanced Placement courses are offered:	8	8
American History, Biology, Chemistry, Calculus, English, French, German, Spanish		

FAIR APPRAISAL

Quality of School Leadership
Principals are generally selected because of their ability as educational leaders. The quality of leadership is generally uniform throughout the system. Parents and teachers do not screen principal candidates. Principals have some say in the distribution of district resources.

Parent organizations are an effective influence on school policy-making.

Quality of Instruction
Additional learning opportunities for gifted students and additional instruction for low-achieving students are rated good. Also considered good are the curricula for students bound for college and for students bound for the world of work.

The district participates in the voluntary busing plan that brings minority students into the district each day.

Quality of School Environment
Classroom disruption and student vandalism are not problems, and the quality of building maintenance and repair is excellent.

MASCOUTAH

ADDRESS OF CENTRAL OFFICE:
720 West Harnett, Mascoutah, IL 62258
ESI:None†

STATISTICAL PROFILE	DATA	ESI
Grade organization:		
Percentage of schools built before 1955		
Total enrollment		
Average Daily Attendance (ADA)		
Current expense per pupil in ADA		
Dropout rate		
Percentage of eligible students who took the SAT		
Average combined score on SAT		
Percentage of graduates who enrolled in 2- or 4-year colleges		
Percentage of students who passed the state reading test		
Percentage of students who passed the state math test		
Teacher–student ratio in elementary grades		
Teacher–student ratio in secondary grades		
Counselor–student ratio in secondary grades		
Number of students per music specialist in elementary grades		
Number of students per art specialist in elementary grades		
Number of volumes in senior high school library		
Beginning teacher's salary		
Maximum teacher's salary		
Average years of experience among teachers		
Number of students suspended and expelled		
Subjects in which Advanced Placement courses are offered:		

†A Statistical Profile was not received from this district.

FAIR APPRAISAL

Quality of School Leadership
Principals are hired primarily for their educational leadership ability, and the quality of leadership is generally uniform throughout the schools. Parents and teachers have hardly any say in the selection of principals, but principals have considerable influence over how district resources are used.

Parent organizations are sometimes effective influencing school policies.

Quality of Instruction
Additional learning opportunities for gifted students and additional instruction for low-achieving students are both rated excellent. The program for gifted students is a full-day enrichment beginning at grade 5. Also rated excellent is the curriculum for students planning on college; the curriculum for students not planning on college is called good.

Quality of School Environment
The level of classroom disruption and student vandalism is very low, and the quality of building maintenance and repair is excellent.

MEHLVILLE

ADDRESS OF CENTRAL OFFICE:
3120 Lemay Ferry Road, St. Louis, MO 63125
ESI:63*

STATISTICAL PROFILE	DATA	ESI
Grade organization: K–6/7–8/9–12		
Percentage of schools built before 1955	23%	
Total enrollment	9,839	
Average Daily Attendance (ADA)	98%	10
Current expense per pupil in ADA	†	0*
Dropout rate	15%	8
Percentage of eligible students who took the ACT	60%	9
Average combined score on ACT	19.7	5
Percentage of graduates who enrolled in 2- or 4-year colleges	59%	
Percentage of students who passed the state reading test	99%	
Percentage of students who passed the state math test	89%	
Teacher–student ratio in elementary grades	1:25	5
Teacher–student ratio in secondary grades	1:18	10
Counselor–student ratio in secondary grades	1:308	5
Number of students per music specialist in elementary grades	486	6
Number of students per art specialist in elementary grades	972	
Number of volumes in senior high school library	35,570	
Beginning teacher's salary	$16,000	
Maximum teacher's salary	$33,880	
Average years of experience among teachers	13	
Number of students suspended and expelled	1,911	
Subjects in which Advanced Placement courses are offered: American History, Calculus, English, Foreign Language, Science	5	5

†The district supplied an inappropriate statistic.

FAIR APPRAISAL

Quality of School Leadership

Principals are selected primarily for their educational leadership ability, and the quality of leadership is generally uniform throughout the system. Parents and teachers play an informal role in principal selection, but do not screen candidates. Principals have some say in the allotment of district resources.

Parent organizations are an effective influence in school decision-making. A citizens advisory council composed of 49 parents and other citizens regularly makes suggestions to district officials.

Quality of Instruction

Additional learning opportunities for gifted students and additional instruction for low-achieving students are both rated good. Also considered good are the curricula for students who are bound for college and for those who are heading into the job market.

Quality of School Environment

The level of classroom disruption and student vandalism, particularly the latter, tends to be on the high side. The quality of building maintenance and repair is good.

NORMANDY

ADDRESS OF CENTRAL OFFICE:
7837 Natural Bridge Road, St. Louis, MO 63121
ESI:57

STATISTICAL PROFILE	DATA	ESI
Grade organization: K–6/7–8/9–12		
Percentage of schools built before 1955	91%	
Total enrollment	6,313	
Average Daily Attendance (ADA)	93%	6
Current expense per pupil in ADA	$3,037	5
Dropout rate	30%	0
Percentage of eligible students who took the SAT	75%	10
Average combined score on SAT	880	3
Percentage of graduates who enrolled in 2- or 4-year colleges	40%	
Percentage of students who passed the state reading test	95%	
Percentage of students who passed the state math test	87%	
Teacher–student ratio in elementary grades	1:24	6
Teacher–student ratio in secondary grades	1:24	4
Counselor–student ratio in secondary grades	1:162	10
Number of students per music specialist in elementary grades	306	9
Number of students per art specialist in elementary grades	673	
Number of volumes in senior high school library	23,474	
Beginning teacher's salary	$14,600	
Maximum teacher's salary	$30,806	
Average years of experience among teachers	18	
Number of students suspended and expelled	220	
Subjects in which Advanced Placement courses are offered: American History, Calculus, English, Science	4	4

FAIR APPRAISAL

Quality of School Leadership

The district may undergo some major changes in leadership and direction in the near future. The person who has been superintendent for approximately 30 years is retiring soon. For the most part, principals are selected for their educational leadership ability, and the quality of leadership does not vary greatly from school to school. Parents and teachers do not screen principal candidates. Principals have some say in how district resources are disbursed.

Parent organizations are sometimes effective influencing school policies.

Quality of Instruction

Additional learning opportunities for gifted students are rated fair to good, while additional instruction for low-achieving students is considered good to excellent. "A major effort is made," said an observer, "to identify and help at-risk children as early as possible." The curriculum for college-bound students is rated good, but the curriculum for students not planning on college is considered to be only fair.

Quality of School Environment

The incidence of classroom disruption and student vandalism is low, but the quality of building maintenance and repair is only fair. According to an observer, the district has had great difficulty in getting a bond issue passed for building improvements. A $5 million issue was finally passed in 1986–87.

RITENOUR

ADDRESS OF CENTRAL OFFICE:
2420 Woodson Road, St. Louis, MO 63114
ESI:44*

STATISTICAL PROFILE	DATA	ESI
Grade organization: K–5/6–8/9–12		
Percentage of schools built before 1955	80%	
Total enrollment	7,000	
Average Daily Attendance (ADA)	†	0*
Current expense per pupil in ADA	$4,000	10
Dropout rate	NK	0
Percentage of eligible students who took the ACT	45%	6
Average combined score on ACT	18.0	4
Percentage of graduates who enrolled in 2- or 4-year colleges	56%	
Percentage of students who passed the state reading test	97%	
Percentage of students who passed the state math test	92%	
Teacher–student ratio in elementary grades	1:24	6
Teacher–student ratio in secondary grades	1:18	10
Counselor–student ratio in secondary grades	1:331	4
Number of students per music specialist in elementary grades	563	4
Number of students per art specialist in elementary grades	563	
Number of volumes in senior high school library	28,145	
Beginning teacher's salary	$18,000	
Maximum teacher's salary	$40,000	
Average years of experience among teachers	18	
Number of students suspended and expelled	NK	
Subjects in which Advanced Placement courses are offered:	None	0

†The district supplied an inappropriate statistic.

FAIR APPRAISAL

Quality of School Leadership
Generally, principals are hired based on their educational leadership ability, and the quality of leadership does not vary greatly from school to school. Parents and teachers have only an informal say in principal selection. Principals, on the other hand, have more say in the allotment of district resources.

Parent organizations are sometimes an effective influence in school policy-making. According to an observer, district officials are "careful to describe in detail all major policies and practices." This helps to prevent major controversy. "They explain something until it comes out of the people's ears, but it works," said an observer.

Quality of Instruction
Additional learning opportunities for gifted students are rated fair, but additional instruction for low-achieving students is considered good. Also rated good are the curricula for students planning on college and for those planning on the world of work.

Like most other suburban school systems, the district participates in the voluntary busing program with St. Louis.

Quality of School Environment
Classroom disruption and student vandalism are not problems. The quality of building maintenance and repair is fair. Limited funding for building improvements has not always been spent wisely, an observer complained.

ST. CHARLES

ADDRESS OF CENTRAL OFFICE:
1916 Elm Street, St. Charles, MO 63301
ESI:76

STATISTICAL PROFILE	DATA	ESI
Grade organization: K–5/6–8/9–12		
Percentage of schools built before 1955	25%	
Total enrollment	6,100	
Average Daily Attendance (ADA)	94%	7
Current expense per pupil in ADA	$3,719	8
Dropout rate	9%	10
Percentage of eligible students who took the SAT	51%	8
Average combined score on SAT	1,056	10
Percentage of graduates who enrolled in 2- or 4-year colleges	55%	
Percentage of students who passed the state reading test	98%	
Percentage of students who passed the state math test	93%	
Teacher–student ratio in elementary grades	1:21	9
Teacher–student ratio in secondary grades	1:20	8
Counselor–student ratio in secondary grades	1:229	8
Number of students per music specialist in elementary grades	510	5
Number of students per art specialist in elementary grades	1,400	
Number of volumes in senior high school library	15,000	
Beginning teacher's salary	$18,073	
Maximum teacher's salary	$33,886	
Average years of experience among teachers	NK	
Number of students suspended and expelled	475	
Subjects in which Advanced Placement courses are offered: American History, Art History, English	3	3

FAIR APPRAISAL

Quality of School Leadership
Longevity and popularity are important criteria for principal selection, and the quality of leadership varies greatly from school to school. Parents and teachers have hardly any say in principal selection, but principals have much influence over the use of district resources.

Parent organizations are generally effective as an influence in district decision-making.

Quality of Instruction
Additional learning opportunities for gifted students are rated excellent, but additional instruction for low-achieving students is considered only fair. The curriculum for students planning on college is thought to be good, while the curriculum for students not planning on college is rated excellent. Observers think very highly of the district's technical school.

Quality of School Environment
The incidence of classroom disruption and student vandalism is low, and the quality of building maintenance and repair is good.

WEBSTER GROVES

ADDRESS OF CENTRAL OFFICE:
16 Selma Avenue, Webster Groves, MO 63119
ESI:77

STATISTICAL PROFILE	DATA	ESI
Grade organization: K–6/7–8/9–12		
Percentage of schools built before 1955	87%	
Total enrollment	3,805	
Average Daily Attendance (ADA)	95%	9
Current expense per pupil in ADA	$3,700	8
Dropout rate	16%	7
Percentage of eligible students who took the SAT	85%	10
Average combined score on SAT	997	9
Percentage of graduates who enrolled in 2- or 4-year colleges	79%	
Percentage of students who passed the state reading test	98%	
Percentage of students who passed the state math test	96%	
Teacher–student ratio in elementary grades	1:21	9
Teacher–student ratio in secondary grades	1:22	6
Counselor–student ratio in secondary grades	1:236	8
Number of students per music specialist in elementary grades	485	6
Number of students per art specialist in elementary grades	605	
Number of volumes in senior high school library	27,500	
Beginning teacher's salary	$19,100	
Maximum teacher's salary	$38,300	
Average years of experience among teachers	16	
Number of students suspended and expelled	145	
Subjects in which Advanced Placement courses are offered: American History, Calculus, English, Foreign Language, Science	5	5

FAIR APPRAISAL

Quality of School Leadership
The School Board seeks principals who demonstrate educational leadership ability, and the quality of leadership generally is uniform throughout the system. Parents and teachers do not screen principal candidates. Principals, however, have some say in how district resources are used.

Parent organizations are sometimes an effective influence over school policies.

Quality of Instruction
Additional learning opportunities for gifted students are considered excellent. Additional instruction for low-achieving students is rated fair to good ("getting better"). The curriculum for students planning on college is rated good, while the curriculum for students not planning on college is termed excellent.

Quality of School Environment
Classroom disruption and student vandalism are not problems, and the quality of building maintenance and repair is excellent.

Salt Lake City, UT

No Statistical Profiles were returned.
However, five Fair Appraisals are provided.

AREA AT A GLANCE

SCHOOL DISTRICT	ENROLLMENT	ESI
Davis County	48,136	
Granite	68,384	
Jordan	60,080	
Murray City	5,328	
Salt Lake City	24,616	

SCHOOL DISTRICT

DAVIS COUNTY

ADDRESS OF CENTRAL OFFICE:
45 East State Street, Farmingtom, UT 84025
ESI:None†

STATISTICAL PROFILE	DATA	ESI
Grade organization:		
Percentage of schools built before 1955		
Total enrollment		
Average Daily Attendance (ADA)		
Current expense per pupil in ADA		
Dropout rate		
Percentage of eligible students who took the SAT		
Average combined score on SAT		
Percentage of graduates who enrolled in 2- or 4-year colleges		
Percentage of students who passed the state reading test		
Percentage of students who passed the state math test		
Teacher–student ratio in elementary grades		
Teacher–student ratio in secondary grades		
Counselor–student ratio in secondary grades		
Number of students per music specialist in elementary grades		
Number of students per art specialist in elementary grades		
Number of volumes in senior high school library		
Beginning teacher's salary		
Maximum teacher's salary		
Average years of experience among teachers		
Number of students suspended and expelled		
Subjects in which Advanced Placement courses are offered:		

†A Statistical Profile was not received from this district.

FAIR APPRAISAL

Quality of School Leadership
The Mormon Church and a "good old boy" system are very
influential in the selection of school principals, and the quality
of leadership varies greatly from school to school as a result.
Parents and teachers have hardly any say in principal selection,
but principals have some say in how district resources are used.
  Parent organizations are not an effective influence on school
policy.

Quality of Instruction
Additional learning opportunities for gifted students are rated
fair to good; so is additional instruction for low-achieving
students. The curriculum for students going to college is
considered excellent, and the curriculum for students not going
to college is rated good.

Quality of School Environment
The level of classroom disruption and student vandalism is low,
and the quality of building maintenance and repair is good. The
system is coping reasonably well with fast-paced growth in
enrollment, said observers.

GRANITE

ADDRESS OF CENTRAL OFFICE:
340 East, 3545 South, Salt Lake City, UT 84115
ESI:None†

STATISTICAL PROFILE	DATA	ESI
Grade organization:		
Percentage of schools built before 1955		
Total enrollment		
Average Daily Attendance (ADA)		
Current expense per pupil in ADA		
Dropout rate		
Percentage of eligible students who took the SAT		
Average combined score on SAT		
Percentage of graduates who enrolled in 2- or 4-year colleges		
Percentage of students who passed the state reading test		
Percentage of students who passed the state math test		
Teacher–student ratio in elementary grades		
Teacher–student ratio in secondary grades		
Counselor–student ratio in secondary grades		
Number of students per music specialist in elementary grades		
Number of students per art specialist in elementary grades		
Number of volumes in senior high school library		
Beginning teacher's salary		
Maximum teacher's salary		
Average years of experience among teachers		
Number of students suspended and expelled		
Subjects in which Advanced Placement courses are offered:		

†A Statistical Profile was not received from this district.

FAIR APPRAISAL

Quality of School Leadership

Most principals are hired for their educational leadership ability which is generally uniform. Candidates for principal positions attend a "principal academy" that helps prepare them for the job. Parents and teachers influence principal selection informally; principals have a great deal to say about the distribution of district resources.

Parent organizations are sometimes effective influencing school decision-making. Administrators and the School Board have a "reputation for listening," said an observer.

Quality of Instruction

Additional learning opportunities for gifted students and additional instruction for low-achieving students are both rated fair. The curricula for college-bound and job-bound students are considered good.

The more affluent west side of the district tends to have "better schools," said an observer, because "parents demand more services from the schools."

Quality of School Environment

Classroom disruption and student vandalism are not problems, and the quality of building maintenance and repair is good. The district does not have the problems associated with rapid growth that affect some other school systems in the area.

JORDAN

ADDRESS OF CENTRAL OFFICE:
9361 South, 300 East, Sandy, UT 84070
ESI:None†

STATISTICAL PROFILE	DATA	ESI
Grade organization:		
Percentage of schools built before 1955		
Total enrollment		
Average Daily Attendance (ADA)		
Current expense per pupil in ADA		
Dropout rate		
Percentage of eligible students who took the SAT		
Average combined score on SAT		
Percentage of graduates who enrolled in 2- or 4-year colleges		
Percentage of students who passed the state reading test		
Percentage of students who passed the state math test		
Teacher–student ratio in elementary grades		
Teacher–student ratio in secondary grades		
Counselor–student ratio in secondary grades		
Number of students per music specialist in elementary grades		
Number of students per art specialist in elementary grades		
Number of volumes in senior high school library		
Beginning teacher's salary		
Maximum teacher's salary		
Average years of experience among teachers		
Number of students suspended and expelled		
Subjects in which Advanced Placement courses are offered:		

†A Statistical Profile was not received from this district.

FAIR APPRAISAL

Quality of School Leadership

Principals are hired primarily for their educational leadership ability, and the quality of leadership does not vary greatly from school to school. Parents and teachers do not help screen principal candidates. Principals have some say in the allotment of district resources.

Parent influence on decision-making is sometimes effective.

Quality of Instruction

Additional learning opportunities for gifted students are rated fair, and additional instruction for low-achieving students also is considered fair. The curriculum for college-bound students is good, but the curriculum for job-bound students is rated only fair.

The district is one of the fastest growing in the state. It is, therefore, "hard-pressed to offer more than the barest of services," said an observer. As one way to cope with the pressure of expansion, the schools are operated on a year-round basis.

Quality of School Environment

The level of classroom disruption and student vandalism is very low, and the quality of building maintenance and repair is good.

MURRAY CITY

ADDRESS OF CENTRAL OFFICE:
147 East, 5065 South, Murray, UT 84107
ESI:None†

STATISTICAL PROFILE	DATA	ESI
Grade organization:		
Percentage of schools built before 1955		
Total enrollment		
Average Daily Attendance (ADA)		
Current expense per pupil in ADA		
Dropout rate		
Percentage of eligible students who took the SAT		
Average combined score on SAT		
Percentage of graduates who enrolled in 2- or 4-year colleges		
Percentage of students who passed the state reading test		
Percentage of students who passed the state math test		
Teacher–student ratio in elementary grades		
Teacher–student ratio in secondary grades		
Counselor–student ratio in secondary grades		
Number of students per music specialist in elementary grades		
Number of students per art specialist in elementary grades		
Number of volumes in senior high school library		
Beginning teacher's salary		
Maximum teacher's salary		
Average years of experience among teachers		
Number of students suspended and expelled		
Subjects in which Advanced Placement courses are offered:		

†A Statistical Profile was not received from this district.

FAIR APPRAISAL

Quality of School Leadership
"It's who you know and how well you conform that are important when it comes to being selected as a principal," said an observer. As a result, the quality of leadership is not uniform throughout the system. This is a "small district in a pocket of the metro area that has retained the small town . . . ways of doing business," said an observer, and the "Mormon culture is ingrained into the system." Parents and teachers do not help in the selection of principals, although principals have some say in the distribution of district resources.

Parent organizations are sometimes effective influencing school policy.

Quality of Instruction
Additional learning opportunities for gifted students are rated fair, while additional instruction for low-achieving students is considered poor. Also rated fair are the curricula for students planning on college and for those not planning on college.

Quality of School Environment
The incidence of classroom disruption and student vandalism is very low, and the quality of building maintenance and repair is good.

SALT LAKE CITY

ADDRESS OF CENTRAL OFFICE:
440 East First, South, Salt Lake City, UT 84111
ESI:None†

STATISTICAL PROFILE	DATA	ESI
Grade organization:		
Percentage of schools built before 1955		
Total enrollment		
Average Daily Attendance (ADA)		
Current expense per pupil in ADA		
Dropout rate		
Percentage of eligible students who took the SAT		
Average combined score on SAT		
Percentage of graduates who enrolled in 2- or 4-year colleges		
Percentage of students who passed the state reading test		
Percentage of students who passed the state math test		
Teacher–student ratio in elementary grades		
Teacher–student ratio in secondary grades		
Counselor–student ratio in secondary grades		
Number of students per music specialist in elementary grades		
Number of students per art specialist in elementary grades		
Number of volumes in senior high school library		
Beginning teacher's salary		
Maximum teacher's salary		
Average years of experience among teachers		
Number of students suspended and expelled		
Subjects in which Advanced Placement courses are offered:		

†A Statistical Profile was not received from this district.

FAIR APPRAISAL

Quality of School Leadership
The School Board seeks principals who demonstrate ability as educational leaders, and the quality of leadership is generally uniform throughout the system. Parents and teachers have some influence in principal selection, but mostly in the informal expression of opinion. Principals, however, have a great deal of influence over the allotment of district resources to the schools. The "better" principals and the "better" schools tend to be on the east side of the district, said an observer, because that is where the more prosperous families live.

Parent organizations are sometimes effective influencing school decision-making.

Quality of Instruction
Additional learning opportunities for gifted students and additional instruction for low-achieving students are rated fair. Considered good is the curriculum for college-bound students. Those students not planning on college have a fair program. An observer said the district is one of the best in the state.

Quality of School Environment
The level of classroom disruption and student vandalism is very low, and the quality of building maintenance and repair is good.

METROPOLITAN AREA

San Antonio, TX

Statistical Profiles were received from five districts, and Fair Appraisals are provided for an additional four districts. Unlike many cities, San Antonio does not have just one city school system. Instead, a number of districts serve various neighborhoods or sections of the city. Districts in this area may be compared to those in the Phoenix, AZ Metropolitan Area.

AREA AT A GLANCE

SCHOOL DISTRICT	ENROLLMENT	ESI
Alamo Heights	3,158	81
East Central	5,548	51
Edgewood	15,557	
New Braunfels	4,709	65
Northeast	36,869	
Northside	44,702	58
San Antonio	57,438	
South San Antonio	11,300	39
Southwest	6,699	

ALAMO HEIGHTS

ADDRESS OF CENTRAL OFFICE:

7101 Broadway, San Antonio, TX 78209

ESI:81

STATISTICAL PROFILE	DATA	ESI
Grade organization: K–5/6–8/9–12		
Percentage of schools built before 1955	60%	
Total enrollment	3,158	
Average Daily Attendance (ADA)	96%	9
Current expense per pupil in ADA	$4,100	9
Dropout rate	23%	0
Percentage of eligible students who took the SAT	85%	10
Average combined score on SAT	969	8
Percentage of graduates who enrolled in 2- or 4-year colleges	77%	
Percentage of students who passed the state reading test	91%	
Percentage of students who passed the state math test	92%	
Teacher–student ratio in elementary grades	1:14	10
Teacher–student ratio in secondary grades	1:13	10
Counselor–student ratio in secondary grades	1:250	8
Number of students per music specialist in elementary grades	300	9
Number of students per art specialist in elementary grades	300	
Number of volumes in senior high school library	17,542	
Beginning teacher's salary	$17,920	
Maximum teacher's salary	$34,720	
Average years of experience among teachers	13	
Number of students suspended and expelled	49	
Subjects in which Advanced Placement courses are offered: Biology, Calculus, Chemistry, English, French, Latin, Physics, Spanish	8	8

Quality of School Leadership

Most principals are selected because of their ability as educational leaders, and the quality of leadership is generally uniform from school to school. Parents and teachers do not help screen principal candidates. Principals have a say about resource distribution.

Parent organizations are very effective influencing school policy decisions.

Quality of Instruction

Additional learning opportunities for gifted students are rated excellent, while additional instruction for low-achieving students is considered good. The curriculum for students planning on college is termed excellent. "This district wants most students to go to college," said an observer. The curriculum for students not planning on college is rated good. Although the district does not pay top salary, said an observer, teachers are attracted to the system because of strong parental support for quality education.

Quality of School Environment

The level of classroom disruption and student vandalism is very low. Building maintenance and repair are good.

EAST CENTRAL

ADDRESS OF CENTRAL OFFICE:

6634 New Sulphur Springs Road, San Antonio, TX 78263

ESI:51

STATISTICAL PROFILE	DATA	ESI
Grade organization: †		
Percentage of schools built before 1955	0%	
Total enrollment	5,548	
Average Daily Attendance (ADA)	95%	8
Current expense per pupil in ADA	$2,793	8
Dropout rate	4%	10
Percentage of eligible students who took the SAT	35%	4
Average combined score on SAT	793	0
Percentage of graduates who enrolled in 2- or 4-year colleges	55%	
Percentage of students who passed the state reading test	93%	
Percentage of students who passed the state math test	91%	
Teacher–student ratio in elementary grades	1:17	10
Teacher–student ratio in secondary grades	1:17	10
Counselor–student ratio in secondary grades	1:440	0
Number of students per music specialist in elementary grades	728	1
Number of students per art specialist in elementary grades	None	
Number of volumes in senior high school library	16,145	
Beginning teacher's salary	$18,300	
Maximum teacher's salary	$31,810	
Average years of experience among teachers	9	
Number of students suspended and expelled	2	
Subjects in which Advanced Placement courses are offered:	None	0

†The district misinterpreted this statistic.

Quality of School Leadership

Principals are hired primarily for their educational leadership ability, and the quality of leadership does not vary greatly from school to school. Parents and teachers do not help screen principal candidates. Principals have some say in the allotment of district resources to the schools.

"The district encourages community input," said an observer, and parent organizations are generally effective influencing school decision-making.

Quality of Instruction

Additional learning opportunities for gifted students and additional instruction for low-achieving students are rated good. Extensive use of computers provides one-to-one remedial instruction for low-achievers, said an observer. The curricula for students going to college and for those planning on the world of work are both considered good.

According to an observer, the district is changing from a "stereotypical rural district into an academically-oriented and innovative suburban district."

Quality of School Environment

Classroom disruption and student vandalism are not problems, and the quality of building maintenance and repair is excellent.

EDGEWOOD

ADDRESS OF CENTRAL OFFICE:
5358 West Commerce Street, San Antonio, TX 78237
ESI:None†

STATISTICAL PROFILE	DATA	ESI
Grade organization:		
Percentage of schools built before 1955		
Total enrollment		
Average Daily Attendance (ADA)		
Current expense per pupil in ADA		
Dropout rate		
Percentage of eligible students who took the SAT		
Average combined score on SAT		
Percentage of graduates who enrolled in 2- or 4-year colleges		
Percentage of students who passed the state reading test		
Percentage of students who passed the state math test		
Teacher–student ratio in elementary grades		
Teacher–student ratio in secondary grades		
Counselor–student ratio in secondary grades		
Number of students per music specialist in elementary grades		
Number of students per art specialist in elementary grade		
Number of volumes in senior high school library		
Beginning teacher's salary		
Maximum teacher's salary		
Average years of experience among teachers		
Number of students suspended and expelled		
Subjects in which Advanced Placement courses are offered:		

†A Statistical Profile was not received from this district.

FAIR APPRAISAL

Quality of School Leadership
The School Board seeks principals who demonstrate educational leadership ability. The quality of leadership does not vary greatly from school to school. Parents and teachers have hardly any say in principal selection, but principals have some say in how district resources are used.

Parent organizations are sometimes effective as an influence over district policy.

Quality of Instruction
Additional learning opportunities for gifted students are considered fair, but additional instruction for low-achieving students is rated good. The curriculum for college-bound students is considered fair, while the curriculum for students not planning on college is rated excellent.

Approximately 90 percent of the student population is Hispanic, and test scores, while improving, are "still quite low," according to an observer. It is felt, therefore, that the district is not yet adequately meeting the educational needs of minority students. However, an observer also pointed out that while this is "one of the poorest" districts in the state, administrators and teachers "make a little go a long way."

Quality of School Environment
The level of classroom disruption and student vandalism is very low, and the quality of building maintenance and repair is excellent. A recent accreditation team "marveled at the care taken with dilapidated facilities," said an observer.

NEW BRAUNFELS

ADDRESS OF CENTRAL OFFICE:
P.O. Box 1061, New Braunfels, TX 78131
ESI:65

STATISTICAL PROFILE	DATA	ESI
Grade organization: K–2/3–5/6–8/9–12		
Percentage of schools built before 1955	43%	
Total enrollment	4,709	
Average Daily Attendance (ADA)	95%	8
Current expense per pupil in ADA	$3,201	5
Dropout rate	8%	10
Percentage of eligible students who took the SAT	50%	7
Average combined score on SAT	950	7
Percentage of graduates who enrolled in 2- or 4-year colleges	30%	
Percentage of students who passed the state reading test	96%	
Percentage of students who passed the state math test	95%	
Teacher–student ratio in elementary grades	1:23	7
Teacher–student ratio in secondary grades	1:22	6
Counselor–student ratio in secondary grades	1:300	6
Number of students per music specialist in elementary grades	450	6
Number of students per art specialist in elementary grades	None	
Number of volumes in senior high school library	22,000	
Beginning teacher's salary	$16,356	
Maximum teacher's salary	$29,497	
Average years of experience among teachers	17	
Number of students suspended and expelled	51	
Subjects in which Advanced Placement courses are offered: Chemistry, Computer Science, English	3	3

Quality of School Leadership

The School Board seeks principals who demonstrate ability as educational leaders. The quality of leadership is generally uniform throughout the system. Parents and teachers have hardly any say in principal selection, but principals have some say on the disbursement of district resources.

Parent organizations are sometimes effective influencing school decision-making.

Quality of Instruction

Additional learning opportunities for gifted students are rated good to excellent, and additional instruction for low-achieving students is considered good. After-school tutoring is one aid available to low-achieving students. The curricula preparing some students for college and others for the world of work are both rated good.

Quality of School Environment

The incidence of classroom disruption and student vandalism is low, and the quality of building maintenance and repair is excellent.

NORTHEAST

ADDRESS OF CENTRAL OFFICE:
10333 Broadway, San Antonio, TX 78217
ESI:None†

STATISTICAL PROFILE	DATA	ESI
Grade organization:		
Percentage of schools built before 1955		
Total enrollment		
Average Daily Attendance (ADA)		
Current expense per pupil in ADA		
Dropout rate		
Percentage of eligible students who took the SAT		
Average combined score on SAT		
Percentage of graduates who enrolled in 2- or 4-year colleges		
Percentage of students who passed the state reading test		
Percentage of students who passed the state math test		
Teacher–student ratio in elementary grades		
Teacher–student ratio in secondary grades		
Counselor–student ratio in secondary grades		
Number of students per music specialist in elementary grades		
Number of students per art specialist in elementary grades		
Number of volumes in senior high school library		
Beginning teacher's salary		
Maximum teacher's salary		
Average years of experience among teachers		
Number of students suspended and expelled		
Subjects in which Advanced Placement courses are offered:		

†A Statistical Profile was not received from this district.

FAIR APPRAISAL

Quality of School Leadership
Most principals are selected for their educational leadership ability, and the quality of leadership does not vary greatly from school to school. Parents and teachers have hardly any say in principal selection, but principals have some say about the allotment of district resources.

Parent organizations are effective as an influence over school decision-making. According to an observer, the PTA council has its own office among the central administrative offices.

Quality of Instruction
Additional learning opportunities for gifted students and additional instruction for low-achieving students are rated excellent. A survey was taken among low-achieving students to determine their characteristics and needs, said an observer, and a program was tailored to address those characteristics and needs. The curricula for students going to college and for those going into the job market are rated excellent.

Quality of School Environment
The level of classroom disruption and student vandalism is low. Students compete to devise projects aimed at combatting vandalism. The quality of building maintenance and repair is excellent, even though many classrooms are overcrowded. Voters defeated a school construction bond issue in 1986–87 because, according to an observer, the School Board did not convince them of the long-term need for new schools.

NORTHSIDE

ADDRESS OF CENTRAL OFFICE:
5900 Evers Road, San Antonio, TX 78238
ESI:58

STATISTICAL PROFILE	DATA	ESI
Grade organization: PreK–5/6–8/9–12		
Percentage of schools built before 1955	1%	
Total enrollment	44,702	
Average Daily Attendance (ADA)	92%	5
Current expense per pupil in ADA	$2,941	3
Dropout rate	4%	10
Percentage of eligible students who took the SAT	49%	7
Average combined score on SAT	893	4
Percentage of graduates who enrolled in 2- or 4-year colleges	62%	
Percentage of students who passed the state reading test	94%	
Percentage of students who passed the state math test	91%	
Teacher–student ratio in elementary grades	1:18	10
Teacher–student ratio in secondary grades	1:18	10
Counselor–student ratio in secondary grades	1:375	3
Number of students per music specialist in elementary grades	700	1
Number of students per art specialist in elementary grades	None	
Number of volumes in senior high school libraries (average)	25,000	
Beginning teacher's salary	$18,200	
Maximum teacher's salary	$34,561	
Average years of experience among teachers	11	
Number of students suspended and expelled	2,165	
Subjects in which Advanced Placement courses are offered: Biology, Calculus, Chemistry, English, Physics	5	5

FAIR APPRAISAL

Quality of School Leadership
Principals are chosen mainly because of their leadership ability, but "political contacts with School Board members help." The quality of leadership is generally uniform throughout the system. Parents and teachers may informally influence principal selection. Principals have some say about how district resources are disbursed to the schools.

Parent organizations are sometimes effective influencing district policy.

Quality of Instruction
Additional learning opportunities for gifted children are rated excellent, but additional instruction for low-achieving students is considered only fair. The curricula for students planning on college and for those not planning on college are both rated excellent.

Quality of School Environment
The level of classroom disruption and student vandalism is low, and the quality of building maintenance and repair is excellent.

SAN ANTONIO

ADDRESS OF CENTRAL OFFICE:
141 Lavaca Street, San Antonio, TX 78210
ESI:None†

STATISTICAL PROFILE	DATA	ESI
Grade organization:		
Percentage of schools built before 1955		
Total enrollment		
Average Daily Attendance (ADA)		
Current expense per pupil in ADA		
Dropout rate		
Percentage of eligible students who took the SAT		
Average combined score on SAT		
Percentage of graduates who enrolled in 2- or 4-year colleges		
Percentage of students who passed the state reading test		
Percentage of students who passed the state math test		
Teacher–student ratio in elementary grades		
Teacher–student ratio in secondary grades		
Counselor–student ratio in secondary grades		
Number of students per music specialist in elementary grades		
Number of students per art specialist in elementary grades		
Number of volumes in senior high school library		
Beginning teacher's salary		
Maximum teacher's salary		
Average years of experience among teachers		
Number of students suspended and expelled		
Subjects in which Advanced Placement courses are offered:		

†A Statistical Profile was not received from this district.

FAIR APPRAISAL

Quality of School Leadership

While educational leadership ability is the primary criterion for selecting most principals, some principals "are firmly entrenched and have political affiliations on the School Board that permit them to remain," said an observer. Consequently, the quality of educational leadership may vary greatly from school to school. Parents and teachers do not serve on principal selection committees, but they can influence selections by expressing their views. Principals have some say about district allotment of resources to the schools.

Parent organizations are very effective as an influence over district decision-making. According to an observer, the School Board uses "parental input to check up on how employees do their jobs."

Quality of Instruction

Additional learning opportunities for gifted students and additional instruction for low-achieving students are rated good. The curriculum for college-bound students is considered only fair, but the curriculum for students not planning on college is considered good.

This is the district for San Antonio's inner city or central section. The enrollment is heavily Hispanic. Even the district's brightest students "rarely rank high when comparing with other districts in Bexar County," said an observer.

Quality of School Environment

The incidence of classroom disruption and student vandalism tends to be high. The quality of building maintenance and repair is good.

SOUTH SAN ANTONIO

ADDRESS OF CENTRAL OFFICE:
2515 Sioux Street, San Antonio, TX 78224
ESI:39

STATISTICAL PROFILE	DATA	ESI
Grade organization: K–5/6–8 and K–6/7–8 and 9–12		
Percentage of schools built before 1955	4%	
Total enrollment	11,300	
Average Daily Attendance (ADA)	92%	5
Current expense per pupil in ADA	$3,002	4
Dropout rate	35%	0
Percentage of eligible students who took the SAT	34%	4
Average combined score on SAT	797	0
Percentage of graduates who enrolled in 2- or 4-year colleges	49%	
Percentage of students who passed the state reading test	82%	
Percentage of students who passed the state math test	77%	
Teacher–student ratio in elementary grades	1:18	10
Teacher–student ratio in secondary grades	1:16	10
Counselor–student ratio in secondary grades	1:450	0
Number of students per music specialist in elementary grades	605	3
Number of students per art specialist in elementary grades	None	
Number of volumes in senior high school libraries (average)	20,264	
Beginning teacher's salary	$18,250	
Maximum teacher's salary	$33,000	
Average years of experience among teachers	10	
Number of students suspended and expelled	2,247	
Subjects in which Advanced Placement courses are offered: Biology, Calculus, English	3	3

FAIR APPRAISAL

Quality of School Leadership
According to observers, the district is very political, with the School Board calling most of the shots. Principals are chosen more for their political support of board members than for their educational leadership ability. As a result, the quality of leadership varies greatly from school to school. Parents and teachers have no say in principal selection; principals have some say (but not much) in how district resources are distributed.

Parent organizations are sometimes effective influencing school decisions. However, the School Board, which is politically split, "ignores some parents and pampers others," said an observer.

Quality of Instruction
Additional learning opportunities for gifted students and additional instruction for low-achieving students are both rated fair. Also considered fair is the curriculum for students planning on college. The curriculum for students planning on the world of work is rated good.

"Teachers are doing a good job under extremely difficult political circumstances," said an observer. State authorities are carefully monitoring the situation, said the observer. "I would not recommend that anyone move into this district," the observer said.

Quality of School Environment
The level of classroom disruption and student vandalism is high, and the quality of building maintenance and repair is poor. "Buildings are falling apart," said an observer, "and Band-aid measures are not alleviating the problem."

SOUTHWEST

ADDRESS OF CENTRAL OFFICE:
11914 Edwards Road, San Antonio, TX 78227
ESI:None†

STATISTICAL PROFILE	DATA	ESI
Grade organization:		
Percentage of schools built before 1955		
Total enrollment		
Average Daily Attendance (ADA)		
Current expense per pupil in ADA		
Dropout rate		
Percentage of eligible students who took the SAT		
Average combined score on SAT		
Percentage of graduates who enrolled in 2- or 4-year colleges		
Percentage of students who passed the state reading test		
Percentage of students who passed the state math test		
Teacher–student ratio in elementary grades		
Teacher–student ratio in secondary grades		
Counselor–student ratio in secondary grades		
Number of students per music specialist in elementary grades		
Number of students per art specialist in elementary grades		
Number of volumes in senior high school library		
Beginning teacher's salary		
Maximum teacher's salary		
Average years of experience among teachers		
Number of students suspended and expelled		
Subjects in which Advanced Placement courses are offered:		

†A Statistical Profile was not received from this district.

FAIR.APPRAISAL

Quality of School Leadership

Popularity is an important criterion in principal selection, and the quality of leadership is not uniform throughout the system. Parents and teachers have little to say about principal selection, and principals have little to say about the allotment of district resources.

Parent organizations are sometimes effective influencing school policy.

Quality of Instruction

Additional learning opportunities for gifted students and additional instruction for low-achieving students are both rated fair. The curriculum for students going to college is good, while the curriculum for students planning on the world of work is excellent. The district is "vocationally-oriented," said an observer.

Quality of School Environment

The level of classroom disruption and student vandalism is high. "Buildings were built cheaply," said an observer, "and kids don't respect or take care of them." The quality of building maintenance and repair is fair. A new superintendent is trying to "catch up with years of neglect."

METROPOLITAN AREA

San Diego, CA

Three districts returned Statistical Profiles. The California Department of Education requires competency tests in reading and math, but allows local districts to develop their own test questions. Because of possible variations in the testing, no scores are listed. Instead, all district profiles show *NA* (not applicable) on the lines requesting the test data. Districts in this area may be compared to those in the San Francisco, CA Metropolitan Area.

AREA AT A GLANCE

SCHOOL DISTRICT	ENROLLMENT	ESI
Poway	18,355	43*
Ramona	4,268	35
San Diego	113,393	37

Indicates district misinterpretation of one or more statistics in the ESI. For each misinterpreted statistic, a score of 0 was given instead of a possible score of 0 to 10 points.

SCHOOL DISTRICT

POWAY

ADDRESS OF CENTRAL OFFICE:
13626 Twin Peaks Road, Poway, CA 92064
ESI:43*

STATISTICAL PROFILE	DATA	ESI
Grade organization: NK		
Percentage of schools built before 1955	1%	
Total enrollment	18,355	
Average Daily Attendance (ADA)	98%	10
Current expense per pupil in ADA	$3,335	4
Dropout rate	5%	10
Percentage of eligible students who took the SAT	48%	7
Average combined score on SAT	942	6
Percentage of graduates who enrolled in 2- or 4-year colleges	50%	
Percentage of students who passed the state reading test	NA	
Percentage of students who passed the state math test	NA	
Teacher–student ratio in elementary grades	1:30	0
Teacher–student ratio in secondary grades	1:26	2
Counselor–student ratio in secondary grades	1:510	0
Number of students per music specialist in elementary grades	†	0*
Number of students per art specialist in elementary grades	None	
Number of volumes in senior high school libraries (average)	20,000	
Beginning teacher's salary	$22,535	
Maximum teacher's salary	$38,681	
Average years of experience among teachers	13	
Number of students suspended and expelled	32	
Subjects in which Advanced Placement courses are offered: Calculus, English, Foreign Language, Science	4	4

†The district supplied an inappropriate statistic.

FAIR APPRAISAL

Quality of School Leadership
Principals are hired mostly for their educational leadership ability, and the quality of leadership is generally uniform throughout the system. Parents and teachers do not screen principal candidates. Principals, however, have some say about the use of district resources.

Parent organizations are effective influencing school policy-making. Parents are "listened to," said an observer.

Quality of Instruction
Additional learning opportunities for gifted students are considered good, while additional instruction for low-achieving students is considered excellent. Also rated excellent is the curriculum for students planning on college. The curriculum for students not planning on college is called good.

Quality of School Environment
Classroom disruption and student vandalism are not problems, but the quality of building maintenance and repair is considered only fair.

RAMONA

ADDRESS OF CENTRAL OFFICE:
720 Ninth Street, Ramona, CA 92065
ESI:35

STATISTICAL PROFILE	DATA	ESI
Grade organization: †		
Percentage of schools built before 1955	17%	
Total enrollment	4,269	
Average Daily Attendance (ADA)	98%	10
Current expense per pupil in ADA	$3,305	4
Dropout rate	15%	8
Percentage of eligible students who took the SAT	28%	3
Average combined score on SAT	898	4
Percentage of graduates who enrolled in 2- or 4-year colleges	60%	
Percentage of students who passed the state reading test	NA	
Percentage of students who passed the state math test	NA	
Teacher–student ratio in elementary grades	1:28	2
Teacher–student ratio in secondary grades	1:28	0
Counselor–student ratio in secondary grades	1:650	0
Number of students per music specialist in elementary grades	1,175	0
Number of students per art specialist in elementary grades	2,350	
Number of volumes in senior high school library	12,000	
Beginning teacher's salary	$20,000	
Maximum teacher's salary	$38,000	
Average years of experience among teachers	13	
Number of students suspended and expelled	201	
Subjects in which Advanced Placement courses are offered:	4	4
American History, Biology, Calculus, English		

†The district misinterpreted this statistic.

FAIR APPRAISAL

Quality of School Leadership
Most principals are hired for their educational leadership ability; the quality of leadership does not vary greatly from school to school. Teachers and parents take part in the screening of principal candidates. Principals also have a lot to say about the allotment of district resources to the schools.
Parent organizations are effective influencing district decision-making.

Quality of Instruction
Additional learning opportunities for gifted students are rated good, but additional instruction for low-achieving students is rated excellent, while the curriculum for students not planning on college is considered fair to poor. One observer said the district is simply "not preparing" students for the world of work.

Quality of School Environment
The level of classroom disruption and student vandalism tends to be on the high side. The quality of building maintenance and repair is poor. "Old schools are falling apart," said an observer.

SAN DIEGO

ADDRESS OF CENTRAL OFFICE:
4100 Normal Street, San Diego, CA 92103
ESI:37

STATISTICAL PROFILE	DATA	ESI
Grade organization: †		
Percentage of schools built before 1955	37%	
Total enrollment	113,393	
Average Daily Attendance (ADA)	98%	10
Current expense per pupil in ADA	$3,419	5
Dropout rate	21%	2
Percentage of eligible students who took the SAT	47%	7
Average combined score on SAT	901	4
Percentage of graduates who enrolled in 2- or 4-year colleges	66%	
Percentage of students who passed the state reading test	NA	
Percentage of students who passed the state math test	NA	
Teacher–student ratio in elementary grades	1:31	0
Teacher–student ratio in secondary grades	1:28	0
Counselor–student ratio in secondary grades	1:415	1
Number of students per music specialist in elementary grades	NK	
Number of students per art specialist in elementary grades	None	
Number of volumes in senior high school libraries (average)	23,200	
Beginning teacher's salary	$20,265	
Maximum teacher's salary	$39,810	
Average years of experience among teachers	NK	
Number of students suspended and expelled	5,383	
Subjects in which Advanced Placement courses are offered:	8	8
American History, Art, Calculus, Computer Science, English, Foreign Language, Music, Science		

†The district misinterpreted this statistic.

FAIR APPRAISAL

Quality of School Leadership
Most principals are hired because of their educational leadership ability. However, a "good old boy" network exists, according to observers, and the quality of leadership varies greatly from school to school. Parents and teachers take part in screening principal candidates. Also, principals have some say in how district resources are allotted.
Parent organizations are effective influencing school decisions.

Quality of Instruction
Additional learning opportunities for gifted students are rated good, but additional instruction for low-achieving students is considered poor. The quality of the program for low-achieving students and the counseling of these students are both poor, said an observer. The curriculum for college-bound students is termed good, while the curriculum for students not planning on college is rated only fair.
The observers do not believe the district is adequately meeting the educational needs of minority students.

Quality of School Environment
The incidence of classroom disruption and student vandalism is low, but the quality of building maintenance and repair is fair to poor.

San Francisco–Oakland, CA

One district supplied a Statistical Profile. Fair Appraisals alone were received for an additional four districts. The California Department of Education requires competency tests in reading and math, but allows local districts to develop their own test questions. Because of possible variations in the testing, no scores are listed. Instead, all district profiles show *NA* (not applicable) on the lines requesting the test data. Districts in this area may be compared to those in the San Diego, CA Metropolitan Area.

AREA AT A GLANCE

SCHOOL DISTRICT	ENROLLMENT	ESI
Alameda	8,242	
Berkeley	8,317	
Oakland	50,548	13
San Leandro	6,000	
San Rafael	4,603	

SCHOOL DISTRICT

ALAMEDA

ADDRESS OF CENTRAL OFFICE:
2200 Central Avenue, Alameda, CA 94501
ESI:None†

STATISTICAL PROFILE	DATA	ESI
Grade organization:		
Percentage of schools built before 1955		
Total enrollment		
Average Daily Attendance (ADA)		
Current expense per pupil in ADA		
Dropout rate		
Percentage of eligible students who took the SAT		
Average combined score on SAT		
Percentage of graduates who enrolled in 2- or 4-year colleges		
Percentage of students who passed the state reading test		
Percentage of students who passed the state math test		
Teacher–student ratio in elementary grades		
Teacher–student ratio in secondary grades		
Counselor–student ratio in secondary grades		
Number of students per music specialist in elementary grades		
Number of students per art specialist in elementary grades		
Number of volumes in senior high school library		
Beginning teacher's salary		
Maximum teacher's salary		
Average years of experience among teachers		
Number of students suspended and expelled		
Subjects in which Advanced Placement courses are offered:		

†A Statistical Profile was not received from this district.

FAIR APPRAISAL

Quality of School Leadership
Most principals are hired for their educational leadership ability, and the quality of leadership is generally uniform throughout the system. Parents and teachers have hardly any say in principal selection, but principals have some influence over the use of district resources.

Parent organizations are sometimes effective influencing district decisions.

Quality of Instruction
Additional learning opportunities for gifted students are rated fair to poor, while additional instruction for low-achieving students is considered good. Also termed good is the curriculum for students bound for college. However, the curriculum for students not planning on college is considered only fair.

Quality of School Environment
The level of classroom disruption and student vandalism leans toward the high side. The quality of building maintenance and repair is fair. Many classrooms are overcrowded, said an observer, and roofs need replacing on some buildings.

BERKELEY

ADDRESS OF CENTRAL OFFICE:
2134 Martin Luther King Way, Berkeley, CA 94704
ESI:None†

STATISTICAL PROFILE	DATA	ESI
Grade organization:		
Percentage of schools built before 1955		
Total enrollment		
Average Daily Attendance (ADA)		
Current expense per pupil in ADA		
Dropout rate		
Percentage of eligible students who took the SAT		
Average combined score on SAT		
Percentage of graduates who enrolled in 2- or 4-year colleges		
Percentage of students who passed the state reading test		
Percentage of students who passed the state math test		
Teacher–student ratio in elementary grades		
Teacher–student ratio in secondary grades		
Counselor–student ratio in secondary grades		
Number of students per music specialist in elementary grades		
Number of students per art specialist in elementary grades		
Number of volumes in senior high school library		
Beginning teacher's salary		
Maximum teacher's salary		
Average years of experience among teachers		
Number of students suspended and expelled		
Subjects in which Advanced Placement courses are offered:		

†A Statistical Profile was not received from this district.

FAIR APPRAISAL

Quality of School Leadership

The School Board seeks principals who demonstrate educational leadership ability and the quality of leadership does not vary greatly throughout the system. Parents and teachers have some informal influence over principal selection; principals have a lot to say about how district resources are distributed.

Parent organizations are very effective influencing school policy. Parents of the most able students are the most effective lobby, said an observer.

Quality of Instruction

Additional learning opportunities for gifted students are rated good to excellent. However, the program in the elementary schools has suffered some because of "budget woes," said an observer. Additional instruction for low-achieving students is considered fair. The curriculum for students planning on college is considered excellent. An observer said the high school is "among the best in the state." However, the curriculum for students not planning on college is rated only fair.

The district does not adequately meet the needs of minority students. Extra help for slow and low-achieving minority students is lacking at the junior and senior high levels, said an observer.

Quality of School Environment

Classroom disruption and student vandalism are not problems, but the quality of building maintenance and repair is considered poor.

OAKLAND

ADDRESS OF CENTRAL OFFICE:
1025 Second Avenue, Oakland, CA 94606
ESI:13

STATISTICAL PROFILE	DATA	ESI
Grade organization: †		
Percentage of schools built before 1955	39%	
Total enrollment	50,548	
Average Daily Attendance (ADA)	NK	0
Current expense per pupil in ADA	$2,411	0
Dropout rate	NK	0
Percentage of eligible students who took the SAT	NK	0
Average combined score on SAT	807	0
Percentage of graduates who enrolled in 2- or 4-year colleges	77%††	
Percentage of students who passed the state reading test	NA	
Percentage of students who passed the state math test	NA	
Teacher–student ratio in elementary grades	1:30	0
Teacher–student ratio in secondary grades	1:28	0
Counselor–student ratio in secondary grades	1:325	5
Number of students per music specialist in elementary grades	350	8
Number of students per art specialist in elementary grades	None	
Number of volumes in senior high school libraries (average)	7,000	
Beginning teacher's salary	$19,159	
Maximum teacher's salary	$31,780	
Average years of experience among teachers	16	
Number of students suspended and expelled	798	
Subjects in which Advanced Placement courses are offered: American Government, American History, English, European History	4	4

† The district misinterpreted this statistic.
††Percentage of students said they *intended* to enroll in a college.

Quality of School Leadership
Internal politics, popularity, and race are all criteria for principal selection, said observers, and often they are given more weight than a candidate's ability as an educational leader. Consequently, the quality of leadership varies greatly from school to school. One observer said principals in some schools are excellent, while others are "extremely incompetent and negligent. Parents and teachers are sometimes involved in principal selection (evidently at the whim of the central administration). Principals have some say in the allotment of district resources to their school.

Parent organizations are occasionally successful as an influence on school policy-making. However, administrators tend to look to the parent groups more for help in fund-raising rather than advice on school policy and practice.

Quality of Instruction
Additional learning opportunities for gifted students and additional instruction for low-achieving students are both rated fair. Also rated fair are the curricula for students planning on college and for those going directly into the job market.

The observers believe the district is not adequately meeting the educational needs of minority students.

Quality of School Environment
The level of classroom disruption and student vandalism is high. One observer blamed the problem partly on large class size. The quality of building maintenance and repair is rated fair to poor. Observers blamed lack of funds and poor use of available funds.

SAN LEANDRO

ADDRESS OF CENTRAL OFFICE:
14735 Juniper Street, San Leandro, CA 94579
ESI:None†

STATISTICAL PROFILE	DATA	ESI
Grade organization:		
Percentage of schools built before 1955		
Total enrollment		
Average Daily Attendance (ADA)		
Current expense per pupil in ADA		
Dropout rate		
Percentage of eligible students who took the SAT		
Average combined score on SAT		
Percentage of graduates who enrolled in 2- or 4-year colleges		
Percentage of students who passed the state reading test		
Percentage of students who passed the state math test		
Teacher–student ratio in elementary grades		
Teacher–student ratio in secondary grades		
Counselor–student ratio in secondary grades		
Number of students per music specialist in elementary grades		
Number of students per art specialist in elementary grades		
Number of volumes in senior high school library		
Beginning teacher's salary		
Maximum teacher's salary		
Average years of experience among teachers		
Number of students suspended and expelled		
Subjects in which Advanced Placement courses are offered:		

†A Statistical Profile was not received from this district.

FAIR APPRAISAL

Quality of School Leadership
Most principals are hired because of their educational leadership ability, and the quality of leadership does not vary greatly throughout the system. Parents and teachers may influence principal selection informally. Principals have some say in how district resources are used.

Parent organizations are not very effective influencing school policy.

Quality of Instruction
The quality of additional learning opportunities for gifted students is rated good, but additional instruction for low-achieving students is considered only fair. The curriculum for college-bound students is termed good, while the curriculum for students heading into the job market is rated only fair.

Quality of School Environment
The incidence of classroom disruption and student vandalism is low, and the quality of building maintenance and repair is good.

SAN RAFAEL

ADDRESS OF CENTRAL OFFICE:
225 Woodland Avenue, San Rafael, CA 94901
ESI:None†

STATISTICAL PROFILE	DATA	ESI
Grade organization:		
Percentage of schools built before 1955		
Total enrollment		
Average Daily Attendance (ADA)		
Current expense per pupil in ADA		
Dropout rate		
Percentage of eligible students who took the SAT		
Average combined score on SAT		
Percentage of graduates who enrolled in 2- or 4-year colleges		
Percentage of students who passed the state reading test		
Percentage of students who passed the state math test		
Teacher–student ratio in elementary grades		
Teacher–student ratio in secondary grades		
Counselor–student ratio in secondary grades		
Number of students per music specialist in elementary grades		
Number of students per art specialist in elementary grades		
Number of volumes in senior high school library		
Beginning teacher's salary		
Maximum teacher's salary		
Average years of experience among teachers		
Number of students suspended and expelled		
Subjects in which Advanced Placement courses are offered:		

†A Statistical Profile was not received from this district.

FAIR APPRAISAL

Quality of School Leadership
Popularity is an important criterion for selection of principals, and the quality of leadership is not uniform throughout the system. Parents and teachers have hardly any say in principal selection, and principals are not very influential over the distribution of district resources. Also, parent organizations are not effective as an influence in school decision-making.

Quality of Instruction
Additional learning opportunities for gifted students are rated fair, but additional instruction for low-achieving students is considered good. According to an observer, the district identifies low-ability students early. The curriculum for college-bound students is rated excellent, while the curriculum for students not planning on college is considered only fair. Everything is "slanted towards college preparation," said an observer.

Quality of School Environment
Classroom disruption and student vandalism are not problems. However, building maintenance and repair are rated poor. Lack of funding is blamed.

METROPOLITAN AREA

San Jose, CA

Two districts supplied Statistical Profiles, and a Fair Appraisal alone was received
for a third district. The California Department of Education requires competency tests
of reading and math, but allows local districts to develop their own test questions.
Because of possible variations in the testing, no scores are listed. Instead, all district
profiles show *NA* (not applicable) on the lines requesting the test data.
Districts in this area may be compared to those in the San Francisco, CA Metropolitan Area.

AREA AT A GLANCE

SCHOOL DISTRICT	ENROLLMENT	ESI
New Haven	11,068	24
Palo Alto	7,957	
San Jose	29,471	55

SCHOOL DISTRICT

NEW HAVEN

ADDRESS OF CENTRAL OFFICE:
34200 Alvarado-Niles Road, Union City, CA 94587
ESI:24

STATISTICAL PROFILE	DATA	ESI
Grade organization: K–4/5–8/9–12		
Percentage of schools built before 1955	57%	
Total enrollment	11,068	
Average Daily Attendance (ADA)	98%	10
Current expense per pupil in ADA	$2,543	0
Dropout rate	24%	0
Percentage of eligible students who took the SAT	24%	2
Average combined score on SAT	942	6
Percentage of graduates who enrolled in 2- or 4-year colleges	41%	
Percentage of students who passed the state reading test	NA	
Percentage of students who passed the state math test	NA	
Teacher–student ratio in elementary grades	1:30	0
Teacher–student ratio in secondary grades	1:30	0
Counselor–student ratio in secondary grades	1:550	0
Number of students per music specialist in elementary grades	709	1
Number of students per art specialist in elementary grades	1,722	
Number of volumes in senior high school library	24,629	
Beginning teacher's salary	$21,489	
Maximum teacher's salary	$41,414	
Average years of experience among teachers	11	
Number of students suspended and expelled	1,595	
Subjects in which Advanced Placement courses are offered: American History, Calculus, English, Foreign Language, Science	5	5

FAIR APPRAISAL

Quality of School Leadership
Most principals are hired because of their educational
leadership ability, and the quality of leadership does not vary
greatly from school to school. Parents and teachers have hardly
any say in principal selection, but principals have some say in
the way district resources are used.

A parent council has increased the influence of parents over
school policy.

Quality of Instruction
Additional learning opportunities for gifted students are rated
excellent, while additional instruction for low-achieving
students is considered fair to good. The curriculum for students
heading for college is called excellent, but the curriculum for
students not planning on college is rated only fair.

The district does a good job of meeting the educational needs
of minority students, even though more than 30 different
languages (mostly Asian) are spoken by students.

Quality of School Environment
The level of classroom disruption and student vandalism is low,
but the quality of building maintenance and repair is only fair.
The district is growing, and a bond issue for building
construction and improvement is needed, said an observer.

PALO ALTO

ADDRESS OF CENTRAL OFFICE:
25 Churchill Avenue, Palo Alto, CA 94306
ESI:None†

STATISTICAL PROFILE	DATA	ESI
Grade organization:		
Percentage of schools built before 1955		
Total enrollment		
Average Daily Attendance (ADA)		
Current expense per pupil in ADA		
Dropout rate		
Percentage of eligible students who took the SAT		
Average combined score on SAT		
Percentage of graduates who enrolled in 2- or 4-year colleges		
Percentage of students who passed the state reading test		
Percentage of students who passed the state math test		
Teacher–student ratio in elementary grades		
Teacher–student ratio in secondary grades		
Counselor–student ratio in secondary grades		
Number of students per music specialist in elementary grades		
Number of students per art specialist in elementary grades		
Number of volumes in senior high school library		
Beginning teacher's salary		
Maximum teacher's salary		
Average years of experience among teachers		
Number of students suspended and expelled		
Subjects in which Advanced Placement courses are offered:		

†A Statistical Profile was not received from this district.

Quality of School Leadership
The School Board chooses principals who demonstrate educational leadership ability, and the quality of leadership does not vary greatly from school to school. Parents and teachers have some say in principal selection, and principals have some say in how district resources are disbursed.

Parent organizations are considered effective. The superintendent and the principals are "responsive" to parent suggestions and criticism, said an observer.

Quality of Instruction
Additional learning opportunities for gifted students are rated excellent. According to an observer, "more than 50 percent of the students are identified as gifted, so the regular classroom experience is enriched." However, additional instruction for low-achieving students is considered only fair. The curriculum for students planning on college is termed excellent, but the curriculum for students heading into the world of work is rated only fair.

Quality of School Environment
Classroom disruption and student vandalism are not problems, and the quality of building maintenance and repair is considered good.

SAN JOSE

ADDRESS OF CENTRAL OFFICE:
1605 Park Avenue, San Jose, CA 95126
ESI:55

STATISTICAL PROFILE	DATA	ESI
Grade organization: †		
Percentage of schools built before 1955	NK	
Total enrollment	29,471	
Average Daily Attendance (ADA)	98%	10
Current expense per pupil in ADA	$2,967	3
Dropout rate	3%	10
Percentage of eligible students who took the SAT	46%	7
Average combined score on SAT	932	6
Percentage of graduates who enrolled in 2- or 4-year colleges	25%	
Percentage of students who passed the state reading test	NA	
Percentage of students who passed the state math test	NA	
Teacher–student ratio in elementary grades	1:30	0
Teacher–student ratio in secondary grades	1:31	0
Counselor–student ratio in secondary grades	1:955	0
Number of students per music specialist in elementary grades	175	10
Number of students per art specialist in elementary grades	None	
Number of volumes in senior high school libraries (average)	24,328	
Beginning teacher's salary	$21,279	
Maximum teacher's salary	$35,978	
Average years of experience among teachers	19	
Number of students suspended and expelled	1,661	
Subjects in which Advanced Placement courses are offered:	9	9
American History, Biology, Calculus, Chemistry, English, French, Music, Physics, Spanish		

†The district misinterpreted this statistic.

Quality of School Leadership
Most principals are hired because of their ability as educational leaders. The quality of leadership is generally uniform throughout the system. Parents and teachers often help screen principal candidates. Principals have some say in the allotment of district resources.

Parent organizations are effective influencing school policy. A new superintendent is more responsive to parents' ideas, said an observer.

Quality of Instruction
Additional learning opportunities for gifted students are rated good to excellent, and additional instruction for low-achieving students is considered good. Also rated good are the curricula for students planning on college and for those going directly into the world of work.

Quality of School Environment
Overall, the level of classroom disruption and student vandalism is low, but one observer pointed out there is more of a problem at the high schools. The quality of building maintenance and repair is considered fair to poor. "The schools are just plain old," said one observer.

Seattle, WA

Four districts completed Statistical Profiles, and a Fair Appraisal was received for one other district. The state does not administer competency tests in reading and math. Therefore, *NA* (not applicable) appears on lines requesting statistics. Districts in this area may be compared to those in the Portland, OR Metropolitan Area.

AREA AT A GLANCE

SCHOOL DISTRICT	ENROLLMENT	ESI
Edmonds	16,689	
Federal Way	15,463	37*
Kent	17,300	31*
Lake Washington	19,700	39
Seattle	43,564	25*

Indicates district misinterpretation of one or more statistics in the ESI. For each misinterpreted statistic, a score of 0 was given instead of a possible score of 0 to 10 points.

SCHOOL DISTRICT

EDMONDS

ADDRESS OF CENTRAL OFFICE:
3800 146th Street, SW, Lynnwood, WA 98036
ESI:None†

STATISTICAL PROFILE	DATA	ESI
Grade organization:		
Percentage of schools built before 1955242		
Total enrollment		
Average Daily Attendance (ADA)		
Current expense per pupil in ADA		
Dropout rate		
Percentage of eligible students who took the SAT		
Average combined score on SAT		
Percentage of graduates who enrolled in 2- or 4-year colleges		
Percentage of students who passed the state reading test		
Percentage of students who passed the state math test		
Teacher–student ratio in elementary grades		
Teacher–student ratio in secondary grades		
Counselor–student ratio in secondary grades		
Number of students per music specialist in elementary grades		
Number of students per art specialist in elementary grades		
Number of volumes in senior high school library		
Beginning teacher's salary		
Maximum teacher's salary		
Average years of experience among teachers		
Number of students suspended and expelled		
Subjects in which Advanced Placement courses are offered:		

†A Statistical Profile was not received from this district.

FAIR APPRAISAL

Quality of School Leadership
Longevity and popularity are key factors in principal selection; therefore, the quality of leadership can vary greatly from school to school. "Seniority sometimes provides a good leader," said an observer, but not always. Parents and teachers have hardly any say in principal selection, but principals have some say about the allotment of district resources to the schools.

Parent organizations are sometimes effective influencing district policy.

Quality of Instruction
Additional learning opportunities for gifted students are rated fair, while additional instruction for low-achieving students is called good. Some of the system's best teachers assist low-achieving students, said an observer. The curriculum for students planning on college is considered excellent. The curriculum for students going directly into the world of work is termed good.

Quality of School Environment
The incidence of classroom disruption and student vandalism is low, and the quality of building maintenance and repair is good.

FEDERAL WAY

ADDRESS OF CENTRAL OFFICE:
31455 28th Avenue South, Auburn, WA 98003
ESI:37*

STATISTICAL PROFILE	DATA	ESI
Grade organization: K–6/7–9/10–12		
Percentage of schools built before 1955	13%	
Total enrollment	15,463	
Average Daily Attendance (ADA)	NK	0
Current expense per pupil in ADA	†	0*
Dropout rate	15%	8
Percentage of eligible students who took the SAT	21%	2
Average combined score on SAT	980	8
Percentage of graduates who enrolled in 2- or 4-year colleges	51%	
Percentage of students who passed the state reading test	NA	
Percentage of students who passed the state math test	NA	
Teacher–student ratio in elementary grades	1:26	4
Teacher–student ratio in secondary grades	1:27	1
Counselor–student ratio in secondary grades	1:387	2
Number of students per music specialist in elementary grades	425	7
Number of students per art specialist in elementary grades	None	
Number of volumes in senior high school libraries (average)	16,500	
Beginning teacher's salary	$16,450	
Maximum teacher's salary	$31,539	
Average years of experience among teachers	12	
Number of students suspended and expelled	1,014	
Subjects in which Advanced Placement courses are offered: American History, Biology, Calculus, English, European History	5	5

†The district supplied an inappropriate statistic.

FAIR APPRAISAL

Quality of School Leadership
Most principals are hired because of their ability as educational leaders, and the quality of leadership does not vary greatly from school to school. Most principals are moved from one school to another every four or five years, said an observer. Parents and teachers have little say in principal selection; principals, on the other hand, have some say in how district resources are used.

Parent organizations are very effective as an influence in school decision-making. A number of standing committees involve parents and other citizens.

Quality of Instruction
Additional learning opportunities for gifted students are rated fair. An observer said there is "more talk than action" concerning the program for gifted students. Additional instruction for low-achieving students, however, is considered good. Also termed good is the curriculum for college-bound students. The curriculum for students heading into the job market is called fair. The trouble with the vocational-technical program, said an observer, is that "too many students who could profit from the program are instead counseled into college preparation."

Quality of School Environment
The level of classroom disruption and student vandalism is low, said and observer, but the problem is growing. The quality of building maintenance and repair is fair, but a major improvement program is underway.

KENT

ADDRESS OF CENTRAL OFFICE:
12033 Southeast 256th Street, Kent, WA 98031
ESI:31*

STATISTICAL PROFILE	DATA	ESI
Grade organization: †		
Percentage of schools built before 1955	41%	
Total enrollment	17,300	
Average Daily Attendance (ADA)	94%	7
Current expense per pupil in ADA	$3,000	2
Dropout rate	††	0*
Percentage of eligible students who took the SAT	31%	4
Average combined score on SAT	960	7
Percentage of graduates who enrolled in 2- or 4-year colleges	54%	
Percentage of students who passed the state reading test	NA	
Percentage of students who passed the state math test	NA	
Teacher–student ratio in elementary grades	1:27	3
Teacher–student ratio in secondary grades	1:31	0
Counselor–student ratio in secondary grades	1:740	0
Number of students per music specialist in elementary grades	562	4
Number of students per art specialist in elementary grades	None	
Number of volumes in senior high school libraries (average)	13,347	
Beginning teacher's salary	$16,500	
Maximum teacher's salary	$29,840	
Average years of experience among teachers	13	
Number of students suspended and expelled	NK	
Subjects in which Advanced Placement courses are offered: American History, Art, Calculus, English	4	4

† The district misinterpreted this statistic.
††The district supplied an inappropriate statistic.

FAIR APPRAISAL

Quality of School Leadership
Most principals are hired because of their educational leadership ability, and the quality of leadership does not vary greatly from school to school. Parents and teachers have little say in principal selection, but principals have some influence over the allotment of district resources.

Parent organizations are sometimes effective influencing school decision-making.

Quality of Instruction
Additional learning opportunities for gifted students are rated good, while additional instruction for low-achieving students is considered only fair. The curriculum for college-bound students is rated fair to good, while the curriculum for students not planning on college is considered fair.

Quality of School Environment
The level of classroom disruption and student vandalism is low, but the quality of building maintenance and repair is fair.

LAKE WASHINGTON

ADDRESS OF CENTRAL OFFICE:
P.O. Box 2909, Kirkland, WA 98083
ESI:39

STATISTICAL PROFILE	DATA	ESI
Grade organization: K–6/7–9/10–12		
Percentage of schools built before 1955	13%	
Total enrollment	19,700	
Average Daily Attendance (ADA)	96%	9
Current expense per pupil in ADA	$2,680	0
Dropout rate	NK	0
Percentage of eligible students who took the SAT	32%	4
Average combined score on SAT	980	8
Percentage of graduates who enrolled in 2- or 4-year colleges	67%	
Percentage of students who passed the state reading test	NA	
Percentage of students who passed the state math test	NA	
Teacher–student ratio in elementary grades	1:25	5
Teacher–student ratio in secondary grades	1:27	1
Counselor–student ratio in secondary grades	1:400	2
Number of students per music specialist in elementary grades	450	6
Number of students per art specialist in elementary grades	None	
Number of volumes in senior high school libraries (average)	13,805	
Beginning teacher's salary	$15,805	
Maximum teacher's salary	$36,352	
Average years of experience among teachers	12	
Number of students suspended and expelled	2,018	
Subjects in which Advanced Placement courses are offered: American History, Calculus, English, Science	4	4

FAIR APPRAISAL

Quality of School Leadership

The School Board seeks principals who demonstrate educational leadership ability, and the quality of leadership is generally uniform throughout the system. Parents and teachers serve on committees that screen principal candidates. Also, principals have a great deal of influence over the disbursement of district resources.

Parent organizations are effective influencing decision-making. A citizens advisory council and the PTA meet regularly with school officials to discuss issues affecting the district.

Quality of Instruction

Additional learning opportunities for gifted students are rated fair to poor. The problem, said an observer, is that the classes for gifted students are "not more exciting, only harder and [give] much more homework." Additional instruction for low-achieving students is considered fair. The curriculum for college-bound students is considered excellent, and the curriculum for students not planning on college is rated good.

Quality of School Environment

The level of classroom disruption and student vandalism is very low, and the quality of building maintenance and repair is good.

SEATTLE

ADDRESS OF CENTRAL OFFICE:
815 4th Avenue, North, Seattle, WA 98109
ESI:25*

STATISTICAL PROFILE	DATA	ESI
Grade organization: K–5/6–8/9–12 and 6/7–8/9–12		
Percentage of schools built before 1955	61%	
Total enrollment	43,564	
Average Daily Attendance (ADA)	NK	0
Current expense per pupil in ADA	NK	0
Dropout rate	37%	0
Percentage of eligible students who took the SAT	35%	4
Average combined score on SAT	944	6
Percentage of graduates who enrolled in 2- or 4-year colleges	NK	
Percentage of students who passed the state reading test	NA	
Percentage of students who passed the state math test	NA	
Teacher–student ratio in elementary grades	1:27	3
Teacher–student ratio in secondary grades	†	0*
Counselor–student ratio in secondary grades	1:400	2
Number of students per music specialist in elementary grades	None	0
Number of students per art specialist in elementary grades	None	
Number of volumes in senior high school libraries (average)	15,973	
Beginning teacher's salary	$16,538	
Maximum teacher's salary	$34,420	
Average years of experience among teachers	NK	
Number of students suspended and expelled	4,400	
Subjects in which Advanced Placement courses are offered: American Government, American History, Art(Studio), Biology, Calculus, English, European History, French, German, Latin, Spanish	11	10

†The district supplied an inappropriate statistic.

FAIR APPRAISAL

Quality of School Leadership

Internal politics play an important part in principal selection, and the quality of leadership varies greatly from school to school. Speaking of principal selection, an observer said, "It's who you know and where." Parents and teachers do not help screen principal candidates. Principals have little say in how district resources are deployed.

Parent organizations are sometimes effective influencing school policy.

Quality of Instruction

Additional learning opportunities for gifted students are rated fair, while additional instruction for low-achieving students (some in highly-rated alternative schools) is considered good. Also termed good is the curriculum for students planning on college, but the curriculum for students planning on the world of work is rated only fair.

The district is working on a reorganization plan that could allow parents more choice on where to send their children to school. A voluntary busing program designed to combat racial segregation has been the target of complaints from many white and black parents.

Quality of School Environment

Classroom disruption and student vandalism are high. Building maintenance and repair are fair to poor.

Tampa–St. Petersburg, FL

Florida has county school systems, and three county districts serve the Tampa–St. Petersburg Metropolitan Area. All three have supplied Statistical Profiles. Districts in this area may be compared to those in the Fort Lauderdale and Miami, FL Metropolitan Areas.

AREA AT A GLANCE

SCHOOL DISTRICT	ENROLLMENT	ESI
Hillsborough County	115,371	14
Manatee County	22,312	51
Pinellas County	85,566	38

SCHOOL DISTRICT

HILLSBOROUGH COUNTY

ADDRESS OF CENTRAL OFFICE:
P.O. Box 3408, Tampa, FL 33601
ESI:14

STATISTICAL PROFILE	DATA	ESI
Grade organization: K–6/7–9/10–12		
Percentage of schools built before 1955	72%	
Total enrollment	115,371	
Average Daily Attendance (ADA)	NK	0
Current expense per pupil in ADA	$1,865	0
Dropout rate	NK	0
Percentage of eligible students who took the SAT	37%	5
Average combined score on SAT	912	5
Percentage of graduates who enrolled in 2- or 4-year colleges	42%	
Percentage of students who passed the state reading test	99%	
Percentage of students who passed the state math test	99%	
Teacher–student ratio in elementary grades	1:26	4
Teacher–student ratio in secondary grades	1:33	0
Counselor–student ratio in secondary grades	1:550	0
Number of students per music specialist in elementary grades	850	0
Number of students per art specialist in elementary grades	None	
Number of volumes in senior high school libraries (average)	20,747	
Beginning teacher's salary	$17,001	
Maximum teacher's salary	$29,744	
Average years of experience among teachers	21	
Number of students suspended and expelled	17,257	
Subjects in which Advanced Placement courses are offered:	15	10
American History, Art (Studio Drawing/General), Biology, Calculus AB/BC, English Language & Composition, English Literature & Composition, European History, French Language, French Literature, Physics B, Physics C (Mechanical), Spanish Language, Spanish Literature		

FAIR APPRAISAL

Quality of School Leadership
Most principals are selected because of their educational leadership ability, and the quality of leadership does not vary greatly from school to school. However, said an observer, principals hired before the current program of leadership workshops for potential principals and stricter screening tend to be weaker educational leaders. Parents and teachers do not take part in the screening process. Principals have some say in the allotment of resources to the schools.

Parent organizations are sometimes an effective influence in school policy-making.

Quality of Instruction
Learning opportunities for gifted students are rated good, and additional instruction for low-achieving students is considered excellent. A dropout prevention program exists in all schools, said an observer. The curricula for college-bound students and job-bound students are both rated good. An observer said the overall quality of education has "improved tremendously" in the last 15 years.

Quality of School Environment
Classroom disruption and student vandalism are not problems. The quality of building maintenance and repair is good.

MANATEE COUNTY

ADDRESS OF CENTRAL OFFICE:
P.O. Box 9069, Bradenton, FL 33506
ESI:51

STATISTICAL PROFILE	DATA	ESI
Grade organization: †		
Percentage of schools built before 1955	37%	
Total enrollment	22,312	
Average Daily Attendance (ADA)	94%	7
Current expense per pupil in ADA	$3,172	3
Dropout rate	33%	0
Percentage of eligible students who took the ACT	39%	5
Average combined score on ACT	18.7	4
Percentage of graduates who enrolled in 2- or 4-year colleges	51%	
Percentage of students who passed the state reading test	100%	
Percentage of students who passed the state math test	99%	
Teacher–student ratio in elementary grades	1:20	10
Teacher–student ratio in secondary grades	1:20	8
Counselor–student ratio in secondary grades	1:504	0
Number of students per music specialist in elementary grades	510	5
Number of students per art specialist in elementary grades	739	
Number of volumes in senior high school libraries (average)	33,815	
Beginning teacher's salary	$15,520	
Maximum teacher's salary	$30,817	
Average years of experience among teachers	13	
Number of students suspended and expelled	NK	
Subjects in which Advanced Placement courses are offered:	9	9
American History, Biology, Calculus AB, Chemistry, Computer Science, English Literature and Composition, French Language, Physics B, Spanish Language		

†The district misinterpreted this statistic.

FAIR APPRAISAL

Quality of School Leadership

Most principals are now selected for their educational leadership ability, but popularity used to be an important consideration. The quality of leadership varies greatly from school to school. "The more affluent sections of the county tend to get the best principals," said an observer. Also, principals hired under the former "old boy" system tend to be less competent leaders, said another observer. An internship program now helps groom potential principals. Parents and teachers have hardly any say in principal selection, but principals have some say about the disbursement of district resources.

Parent organizations are not very effective as an influence in school decision-making.

Quality of Instruction

Additional learning opportunities for gifted students and additional instruction for low-achieving students are rated fair to good. The curriculum for students planning on college is considered good, but the curriculum for students not planning on college is rated fair to poor.

Some schools, particularly in poor, black areas, "seem to be staffed by people who will keep their mouth shut," said an observer. The same observer said minority students continue to score lower on every test than white students.

Quality of School Environment

The level of classroom disruption and student vandalism is low. One observer credited strict discipline, including corporal punishment. The quality of building maintenance and repair is rated good to excellent. "The only problem," said one observer, "is they can't build schools fast enough."

PINELLAS COUNTY

ADDRESS OF CENTRAL OFFICE:
P.O. Box 4688, Clearwater, FL 33518
ESI:38

STATISTICAL PROFILE	DATA	ESI
Grade organization: K–5/6–8/9–12		
Percentage of schools built before 1955	36%	
Total enrollment	85,566	
Average Daily Attendance (ADA)	93%	6
Current expense per pupil in ADA	$2,518	0
Dropout rate	31%	2
Percentage of eligible students who took the SAT	57%	9
Average combined score on SAT	917	5
Percentage of graduates who enrolled in 2- or 4-year colleges	76%	
Percentage of students who passed the state reading test	89%	
Percentage of students who passed the state math test	83%	
Teacher–student ratio in elementary grades	1:24	6
Teacher–student ratio in secondary grades	1:27	1
Counselor–student ratio in secondary grades	1:423	1
Number of students per music specialist in elementary grades	816†	0
Number of students per art specialist in elementary grades	816†	
Number of volumes in senior high school libraries (average)	18,618	
Beginning teacher's salary	$16,750	
Maximum teacher's salary	$29,150	
Average years of experience among teachers	11	
Number of students suspended and expelled	17,276	
Subjects in which Advanced Placement courses are offered:	9	9
American History, Art, Biology, Calculus, Chemistry, Computer Science, English, European History, Spanish		

†Approximate.

FAIR APPRAISAL

Quality of School Leadership
Most principals are hired because of their educational leadership ability, and the quality of leadership is generally uniform throughout the system. Parents and teachers have hardly any say in principal selection; however, principals have some say in determining how district resources are allotted.

Parent organizations are sometimes effective influencing school policy.

Quality of Instruction
Additional learning opportunities for gifted students and additional instruction for low-achieving students are rated good. Also considered good are the curricula for students planning on college and for those planning on the world of work. Magnet high schools exist for students who are talented in the arts or are "academically superior."

Quality of School Environment
The level of classroom disruption and student vandalism is low, and the quality of building maintenance and repair is good.

Washington, DC

Washington is surrounded by mostly county school districts in Maryland and Virginia. Two districts supplied Statistical Profiles, and Fair Appraisals alone are provided for two other districts. Districts in this area may be compared to those in the Baltimore, MD Metropolitan Area.

AREA AT A GLANCE

SCHOOL DISTRICT	ENROLLMENT	ESI
Arlington County, VA	15,000	
District of Columbia	86,893	17*
Fairfax County, VA	136,646	
Montgomery County, MD	92,871	63

Indicates district misinterpretation of one or more statistics in the ESI. For each misinterpreted statistic, a score of 0 was given instead of a possible score of 0 to 10 points.

SCHOOL DISTRICT

ARLINGTON COUNTY

ADDRESS OF CENTRAL OFFICE:
1400 North Quincy Street, Arlington, VA 22201
ESI:None†

STATISTICAL PROFILE	DATA	ESI
Grade organization:		
Percentage of schools built before 1955		
Total enrollment		
Average Daily Attendance (ADA)		
Current expense per pupil in ADA		
Dropout rate		
Percentage of eligible students who took the SAT		
Average combined score on SAT		
Percentage of graduates who enrolled in 2- or 4-year colleges		
Percentage of students who passed the state reading test		
Percentage of students who passed the state math test		
Teacher–student ratio in elementary grades		
Teacher–student ratio in secondary grades		
Counselor–student ratio in secondary grades		
Number of students per music specialist in elementary grades		
Number of students per art specialist in elementary grades		
Number of volumes in senior high school library		
Beginning teacher's salary		
Maximum teacher's salary		
Average years of experience among teachers		
Number of students suspended and expelled		
Subjects in which Advanced Placement courses are offered:		

†A Statistical Profile was not received from this district.

FAIR APPRAISAL

Quality of School Leadership
Principals are hired mainly because of their educational leadership ability, and the quality of leadership is generally uniform throughout the system. Parents and teachers help screen principal candidates. Also, principals have quite a lot to say about the allotment of district resources to the schools.

Parent organizations are effective influencing school decision-making. Parents and other citizens serve on a variety of advisory committees.

Quality of Instruction
Some schools serve exclusively gifted students or only low-achieving students, and both programs are rated excellent. Also considered excellent is the curriculum for students planning on college. For those students not planning on college, the curriculum is rated good.

A number of families from Central America and Asia have settled in the county, but the schools seem to be adequately meeting most children's educational needs.

Quality of School Environment
The incidence of classroom disruption and student vandalism is low, and the quality of building maintenance and repair is good.

DISTRICT OF COLUMBIA

ADDRESS OF CENTRAL OFFICE:
415 12th Street NW, Washington, DC 20004
ESI:17*

STATISTICAL PROFILE	DATA	ESI
Grade organization: †		
Percentage of schools built before 1955	67%	
Total enrollment	86,893	
Average Daily Attendance (ADA)	90%	3
Current expense per pupil in ADA	$4,290	0
Dropout rate	††	0*
Percentage of eligible students who took the SAT	31%	4
Average combined score on SAT	704	0
Percentage of graduates who enrolled in 2- or 4-year colleges	NK	
Percentage of students who passed the state reading test	NA	
Percentage of students who passed the state math test	NA	
Teacher–student ratio in elementary grades	1:25	5
Teacher–student ratio in secondary grades	1:26	2
Counselor–student ratio in secondary grades	1:450	0
Number of students per music specialist in elementary grades	600	3
Number of students per art specialist in elementary grades	500	
Number of volumes in senior high school libraries (average)	††	
Beginning teacher's salary	$17,768	
Maximum teacher's salary	$36,733	
Average years of experience among teachers	12	
Number of students suspended and expelled	NK	
Subjects in which Advanced Placement courses are offered:	None	0

† The district misinterpreted this statistic.
††The district supplied an inappropriate statistic.

Quality of School Leadership

Most principals are selected for their educational leadership ability, although seniority is an important factor. The quality of leadership, however, varies greatly from school to school. One observer pointed out there is "not much performance review" of principals. Parents and teachers have some say in deciding how district resources will be disbursed.

Parent organizations are sometimes effective influencing school decisions but the effectiveness varies greatly from school to school.

Quality of Instruction

Additional learning opportunities for gifted students are rated fair to good, with the program being better at the high school level than in the elementary and junior high schools. Two magnet schools serve gifted students in the arts and academic subjects. Banneker High School for exceptionally bright students in academic subjects has an excellent record for placing graduates in good colleges. Additional instruction for low-achieving students is considered fair, although volunteer tutors help many students. The curriculum for college-bound students is rated good, but the curriculum for students not planning on college is considered fair.

Quality of School Environment

The level of classroom disruption and student vandalism is low, but the quality of building maintenance and repair is fair.

FAIRFAX COUNTY

ADDRESS OF CENTRAL OFFICE:
10700 Page Avenue, Fairfax, VA 22030
ESI:None†

STATISTICAL PROFILE	DATA	ESI
Grade organization:		
Percentage of schools built before 1955		
Total enrollment		
Average Daily Attendance (ADA)		
Current expense per pupil in ADA		
Dropout rate		
Percentage of eligible students who took the SAT		
Average combined score on SAT		
Percentage of graduates who enrolled in 2- or 4-year colleges		
Percentage of students who passed the state reading test		
Percentage of students who passed the state math test		
Teacher–student ratio in elementary grades		
Teacher–student ratio in secondary grades		
Counselor–student ratio in secondary grades		
Number of students per music specialist in elementary grades		
Number of students per art specialist in elementary grades		
Number of volumes in senior high school library		
Beginning teacher's salary		
Maximum teacher's salary		
Average years of experience among teachers		
Number of students suspended and expelled		
Subjects in which Advanced Placement courses are offered:		

†A Statistical Profile was not received from this district.

FAIR APPRAISAL

Quality of School Leadership
The School Board seeks principals who demonstrate educational leadership ability, and the quality of leadership does not vary greatly from school to school. Parents and teachers have hardly any say in principal selection, although principals have some influence over the allotment of district resources.

Parent organizations are sometimes effective influencing school policy.

Quality of Instruction
Additional learning opportunities for gifted students are rated good to excellent. Programs exist in every school, and a few schools serve only gifted students. Additional instruction for low-achieving students is considered fair. The curriculum for students planning on college is rated good to excellent. Among the top academic high schools are Annandale, Langley, McLean and West Springfield. The curriculum for students planning to enter the job market after graduation is fair.

Quality of School Environment
Classroom disruption and student vandalism are not problems, and the quality of building maintenance and repair is good.

MONTGOMERY COUNTY

ADDRESS OF CENTRAL OFFICE:
850 Hungerford Drive, Rockville, MD 20850
ESI:63

STATISTICAL PROFILE	DATA	ESI
Grade organization: †		
Percentage of schools built before 1955	33%	
Total enrollment	92,871	
Average Daily Attendance (ADA)	93%	6
Current expense per pupil in ADA	$4,315	5
Dropout rate	11%	10
Percentage of eligible students who took the SAT	71%	10
Average combined score on SAT	983	8
Percentage of graduates who enrolled in 2- or 4-year colleges	85%	
Percentage of students who passed the state reading test	100%	
Percentage of students who passed the state math test	NA	
Teacher–student ratio in elementary grades	1:25	5
Teacher–student ratio in secondary grades	1:24	4
Counselor–student ratio in secondary grades	1:278	6
Number of students per music specialist in elementary grades	595	4
Number of students per art specialist in elementary grades	594	
Number of volumes in senior high school libraries (average)	14,000	
Beginning teacher's salary	$16,573	
Maximum teacher's salary	$38,151	
Average years of experience among teachers	12	
Number of students suspended and expelled	2,995	
Subjects in which Advanced Placement courses are offered: American History, Calculus, English, Foreign Language, Science	5	5

†The district has a great variety of grade organization patterns.

FAIR APPRAISAL

Quality of School Leadership

Most principals are chosen for their educational leadership ability, and the quality of leadership is generally uniform throughout the system. Parents and teachers have some say in principal selection, and principals have some say in the allotment of district resources to the schools.

Parent organizations are effective as an influence on district policy. The School Board is "very responsive" to parents and other citizens, said an observer.

Quality of Instruction

Additional learning opportunities for gifted students are considered excellent. Enrichment programs are offered: through area colleges as well as in the schools. Additional instruction for low-achieving students is rated fair. The curriculum for college-bound students is called excellent. Among the best high schools are Whitman, Wootton, Churchill, Walter Johnson, Rockville, Seneca Valley and Bethesda-Chevy Chase. One observer advised that the district is often undergoing reorganization, in part to maintain racial balance. This means that locating in a certain section of the county does not automatically mean that a student will attend the high school nearest to his/her home. The curriculum for students not planning on college is improving, but is still rated fair.

Quality of School Environment

Classroom disruption and student vandalism are not problems, and the quality of building maintenance and repair is considered good.

Current Expense Per Pupil In ADA 1985–86

STATE	EXPENSE	STATE	EXPENSE
U.S.	$3,677	MISSOURI	3,155
ALABAMA	2,508	MONTANA	4,337
ALASKA	8,044	NEBRASKA	3,285
ARIZONA	2,829	NEVADA	3,142
ARKANSAS	2,642	NEW HAMPSHIRE	3,115
CALIFORNIA	3,573	NEW JERSEY	5,544
COLORADO	3,740	NEW MEXICO	3,374
CONNECTICUT	4,888	NEW YORK	5,616
DELAWARE	4,517	NORTH CAROLINA	3,366
DISTRICT OF COLUMBIA	5,020	NORTH DAKOTA	3,059
FLORIDA	3,731	OHIO	3,547
GEORGIA	2,980	OKLAHOMA	2,867
HAWAII	3,766	OREGON	4,123
IDAHO	2,390	PENNSYLVANIA	4,235
ILLINOIS	3,621	RHODE ISLAND	4,669
INDIANA	2,973	SOUTH CAROLINA	2,912
IOWA	3,568	SOUTH DAKOTA	2,967
KANSAS	3,914	TENNESSEE	2,533
KENTUCKY	2,853	TEXAS	3,384
LOUISIANA	3,046	UTAH	2,297
MAINE	3,346	VERMONT	3,554
MARYLAND	4,349	VIRGINIA	3,210
MASSACHUSETTS	4,255	WASHINGTON	3,705
MICHIGAN	3,789	WEST VIRGINIA	2,821
MINNESOTA	3,864	WISCONSIN	4,168
MISSISSIPPI	2,305	WYOMING	5,479

Source: Estimates of School Statistics 1985–86, National Education Association, Washington, DC.

State Dropout Rates 1985

STATE	DROPOUT RATE
U.S.	
ALABAMA	33%
ALASKA	22%
ARIZONA	32%
ARKANSAS	24%
CALIFORNIA	25%
COLORADO	21%
CONNECTICUT	22%
DELAWARE	11%
DISTRICT OF COLUMBIA	42%
FLORIDA	35%
GEORGIA	34%
HAWAII	18%
IDAHO	22%
ILLINOIS	23%
INDIANA	22%
IOWA	12%
KANSAS	17%
KENTUCKY	32%
LOUISIANA	43%
MAINE	23%
MARYLAND	19%
MASSACHUSETTS	23%
MICHIGAN	26%
MINNESOTA	9%
MISSISSIPPI	35%

STATE	DROPOUT RATE
MISSOURI	24%
MONTANA	17%
NEBRASKA	16%
NEVADA	25%
NEW HAMPSHIRE	23%
NEW JERSEY	17%
NEW MEXICO	29%
NEW YORK	33%
NORTH CAROLINA	31%
NORTH DAKOTA	5%
OHIO	18%
OKLAHOMA	20%
OREGON	27%
PENNSYLVANIA	20%
RHODE ISLAND	25%
SOUTH CAROLINA	34%
SOUTH DAKOTA	15%
TENNESSEE	35%
TEXAS	31%
UTAH	15%
VERMONT	15%
VIRGINIA	24%
WASHINGTON	25%
WEST VIRGINIA	23%
WISCONSIN	16%
WYOMING	18%

Source: Education Commission of the States, Denver, CO.

Average State Scores on ACT and SAT Tests 1986

STATE	TEST	AVERAGE SCORE		STATE	TEST	AVERAGE SCORE
U.S. (average)	ACT	18.8		U.S. (average)	SAT	906
ALABAMA	ACT	18.2		MISSOURI	ACT	19.2
ALASKA	ACT	18.1		MONTANA	ACT	19.8
ARIZONA	ACT	19.3		NEBRASKA	ACT	20.0
ARKANSAS	ACT	18.1		NEVADA	ACT	19.0
CALIFORNIA	SAT	904		NEW HAMPSHIRE	SAT	935
COLORADO	ACT	19.9		NEW JERSEY	SAT	889
CONNECTICUT	SAT	914		NEW MEXICO	ACT	17.9
DELAWARE	SAT	917		NEW YORK	SAT	898
DC	SAT	852		NORTH CAROLINA	SAT	835
FLORIDA	SAT	895		NORTH DAKOTA	ACT	18.5
GEORGIA	SAT	842		OHIO	ACT	19.3
HAWAII	SAT	880		OKLAHOMA	ACT	17.8
IDAHO	ACT	19.2		OREGON	SAT	930
ILLINOIS	ACT	19.1		PENNSYLVANIA	SAT	894
INDIANA	SAT	874		RHODE ISLAND	SAT	898
IOWA	ACT	20.6		SOUTH CAROLINA	SAT	826
KANSAS	ACT	19.2		SOUTH DAKOTA	ACT	19.9
KENTUCKY	ACT	18.1		TENNESSEE	ACT	18.0
LOUISIANA	ACT	16.9		TEXAS	SAT	877
MAINE	SAT	900		UTAH	ACT	19.1
MARYLAND	SAT	911		VERMONT	SAT	916
MASSACHUSETTS	SAT	909		VIRGINIA	SAT	908
MICHIGAN	ACT	18.9		WEST VIRGINIA	ACT	17.7
MINNESOTA	ACT	20.3		WISCONSIN	ACT	20.5
MISSISSIPPI	ACT	16.3		WYOMING	ACT	19.7

Note: Washington State was omitted because fewer than 35 percent of students took either test.   Source: U.S. Department of Education.

ESI Computations
Possible total ESI (Statistical Profile only) = 100 points

AVERAGE DAILY ATTENDANCE (ADA)	
87% or less	0
88%	1
89%	2
90%	3
91%	4
92%	5
93%	6
94%	7
95%	8
96%	9
97% or more	10

COMBINED SCORE ON SAT (See ACT if applicable)	
80 or more points below	0
60–79 points below	1
40–59 points below	2
20–39 points below	3
0–19 points below	4
0–19 points above	5
20–39 points above	6
40–59 points above	7
60–79 points above	8
80–99 points above	9
100 points or more above	10

TEACHER–STUDENT RATIO IN SECONDARY GRADES	
More than 1:28	0
1:27	1
1:26	2
1:25	3
1:24	4
1:23	5
1:22	6
1:21	7
1:20	8
1:19	9
1:18 or less	10

CURRENT EXPENSE PER PUPIL IN (ADA)	
$1000 or more below	0
$ 800–$999 below	1
$ 600–$799 below	2
$ 400–$599 below	3
$ 200–$399 below	4
$ 000–$199 below	5
$ 000–$199 above	6
$ 200–$399 above	7
$ 400–$599 above	8
$ 600–$799 above	9
$ 800 or more above	10

COMBINED SCORE ON ACT (See SAT if applicable)	
1.8–1.9 points below	0
1.6–1.7 points below	1
1.4–1.5 points below	2
1.2–1.3 points below	3
0.0–1.1 points below	4
0.0–1.1 points above	5
1.2–1.3 points above	6
1.4–1.5 points above	7
1.6–1.7 points above	8
1.8–1.9 points above	9
2 points or more above	10

COUNSELOR–STUDENT RATIO IN SECONDARY GRADES	
1:426 or more	0
1:401–1:425	1
1:376–1:400	2
1:351–1:375	3
1:326–1:350	4
1:301–1:325	5
1:276–1:300	6
1:251–1:275	7
1:226–1:250	8
1:200–1:225	9
Less than 1:200	10

DROUPOUT RATE	
Even or above	0
1% below	1
2% below	2
3% below	3
4% below	4
5% below	5
6% below	6
7% below	7
8% below	8
9% below	9
10% or more below	10

SUBJECTS IN WHICH ADVANCED PLACEMENT COURSES ARE OFFERED	
0 courses	0
1 course	1
2 courses	2
3 courses	3
4 courses	4
5 courses	5
6 courses	6
7 courses	7
8 courses	8
9 courses	9
10 courses or more	10

NUMBER OF STUDENTS PER MUSIC SPECIALIST IN ELEMENTARY GRADES	
750 or more	0
700–749	1
650–699	2
600–649	3
550–599	4
500–549	5
450–499	6
400–449	7
350–399	8
300–349	9
250–299	10

PERCENT OF ELIGIBLE STUDENTS WHO TOOK THE SAT OR ACT	
above 60%	10
56%–60%	9
51%–55%	8
46%–50%	7
41%–45%	6
36%–40%	5
31%–35%	4
26%–30%	3
21%–25%	2
16%–20%	1
below 16%	0

TEACHER–STUDENT RATIO IN ELEMENTARY GRADES	
More than 1:30	0
1:29	1
1:28	2
1:27	3
1:26	4
1:25	5
1:24	6
1:23	7
1:22	8
1:21	9
1:20 or less	10

N

WHAT'S NEXT?
Career Strategies After 35
by Jack Falvey

Falvey explodes myths right and left and sets you on a straight course to a satisfying and successful mid-life career. Bring an open mind to his book and you'll be on your way. A liberating book to help us all get happily back into work.

192 pages, 6×9
Quality paperback, $9.95

INTERNATIONAL CAREERS:
An Insider's Guide
by David Win

If you long for a career that combines the excitement of foreign lifestyles and markets, the opportunity to explore your own potential, the promise of monetary and personal reward, then learn from David Win how to get off the stateside corporate ladder and into the newly emerging areas of international careers. Now's the time!

224 pages, 6×9, charts
Quality paperback, $10.95

THE CAMPER'S COMPANION TO NORTHERN EUROPE:
A Campground & Roadside Travel Guide

THE CAMPER'S COMPANION TO SOUTHERN EUROPE:
A Campground & Roadside Travel Guide
by Dennis & Tina Jaffe

More than just campground directories, these travel guides share the best of each country off-the-beaten path. The Jaffes rate over 700 campgrounds covering all of Northern Europe in one volume, Southern Europe and Northern Africa in the other volume. Country-by-country campgrounds.

300 pages, 6×9, maps, tables
Quality paperback, $13.95 each

TO ORDER

At your bookstore or order directly from Williamson Publishing. We accept Visa or MasterCard (please include number, expiration date and signature), or send check to **Williamson Publishing Co., Church Hill Road, P.O. Box 185, Charlotte, Vermont 05445.** (Toll-free phone orders: 800-356-8791.) Please add $1.50 for postage and handling. Satisfaction guaranteed or full refund without questions or quibbles.